THE CRUCIFIED

To Fathers Vincent J. Dinan, C.S.Sp., Michael F. McCarthy, C.S.Sp., and Michael O'Carroll, C.S.Sp., who ensured that Blackrock College was truly an *alma mater* to Alfred O'Rahilly at the eleventh hour

ALFRED O'RAHILLY

The Crucified

Edited by
J. ANTHONY GAUGHAN

KINGDOM BOOKS

Printed in the Republic of Ireland
at the Leinster Leader, Naas, County Kildare,
for
KINGDOM BOOKS
79 The Rise, Mount Merrion, County Dublin.

First published 1985

BRITISH LIBRARY CATALOGUING IN PUBLICATION DATA

O'Rahilly, Alfred
The Crucified.
1. Holy Shroud.
I. Title   II. Gaughan, J. Anthony
232.9′66   BT587.S4

ISBN 0-9506015-5-1 Kingdom Books

Contents

List of Illustrations

xv

The front of the cover is a detail from Salvador Dali's 'Christ of St John of the Cross', the back is from a photograph of Alfred O'Rahilly, president of University College, Cork, 1943-54.

Foreword

Ever since the Holy Shroud, today known as the Shroud of Turin, made its appearance in France in the middle of the fourteenth century it has been the subject of speculation and controversy. Yet never in its history has it been subjected to such detailed examination and widespread discussion as in the past decade.

Since 1898, when Secondo Pia photographed the Shroud for the first time, and found to his amazement that the imprint on it was a negative image, anyone maintaining that the image was no more than a clever painting by an artist has been confronted with formidable difficulties. Today these difficulties have been multiplied. The application to the Shroud of techniques perfected by the National Aeronautic and Space Administration (NASA) in the U.S.A. in the study of satellite photographs has further underlined its extraordinary character.

Such is the depth and intensity of the pattern on the Shroud that scientists have been able to reconstruct from them a full three-dimensional image of a scourged and crucified man — something that could not be obtained from any painting.

Also, a remarkable series of tests of the traces of pollen found in the Shroud has shown that some of the pollen is from plants not found outside the Holy Land, leading to the conclusion that the Shroud was at some time exposed to the air in Palestine.

The science of numismatics has also made its contribution: ancient coins from Our Lord's time show Jewish prisoners-of-war wearing shoulder-length hair and beards, in contrast to the clean-shaven faces and short hair which are shown on Greek, Roman and Egyptian portraits of the same period; the fact that the image on the Shroud is that of a bearded man with long hair is yet another indication that he was a first-century Jew.

When Alfred O'Rahilly wrote *The Crucified* in the late 'fifties he did not have the above evidence at his disposal. Nevertheless, from the knowledge available at the time, he put together a very telling case in favour of the Shroud's authenticity. At a period when the weight of scholarly opinion was definitely against authenticity — one has only to recall such names as Fr Herbert Thurston, S.J., in England, or Canon Cyr Ulysse Chevalier in France — to defend the opposite view called for exactly the kind of independence of mind and tenacity in research which Alfred O'Rahilly possessed to an exceptional degree. How much easier it is to champion the Shroud today when a scholar of the reputation of the late Bishop John A. T. Robinson has written:

> For me the burden of proof has shifted. I began by assuming its inauthenticity until proved otherwise and then asking how one

xxiii

explained it. On the hypothesis of a medieval forgery, or any other I could think of, this was very difficult. I now find myself assuming its authenticity until proved otherwise.

Dr O'Rahilly's book is still valuable today for his careful history of the Shroud, his description and analysis of the markings upon it, and his forceful arguments to show that the Shroud is not a painting, and in no way conflicts with the evidence of the Gospels. *The Crucified* is much more than a study of the Shroud, however. It is also a detailed analysis of the sufferings of Christ as known not only from the Gospels but from the many ancient sources which throw light on crucifixion and scourging as practised by the Romans.

The author also draws on the history of the crucifixion in art and on modern medical studies of death by crucifixion and the exact nature of the terrible sufferings it entailed. One cannot read this book without coming to appreciate much more fully the atrocious nature of the sufferings inflicted on Jesus by his executioners. Perhaps we speak too glibly at times of the price paid by Christ for the redemption of mankind. This book is a useful antidote against any such tendency.

Initially, one might have expected to find a good deal of material which would at least be questioned by modern biblical scholarship. That such expectations are not borne out is due, no doubt, to the fact that Dr O'Rahilly is concerned almost exclusively with the Passion accounts, the historicity of which scholars are much less inclined to question than some other details of the Gospel narratives. Even though we have learned a good deal in recent times about the aims and methods of the biblical authors and the way in which the Gospels were composed, it is doubtful if Dr O'Rahilly's argumentation is thereby invalidated at any point.

It was a courageous decision by Father J. Anthony Gaughan to publish this work of Dr O'Rahilly so many years after his death. It would have been a pity had such a scholarly and well-argued study never seen the light of day. It deserves a place in libraries and institutions of learning and for anyone interested in the Holy Shroud it provides much valuable material not to be found in the spate of more popular books now available on the subject. The fact that each chapter is clearly sub-divided under a number of headings is a considerable help to the reader.

✠ KEVIN McNAMARA
Bishop's House
Killarney
County Kerry
1 September 1984

Introduction

Alfred O'Rahilly, author of *The Crucified*, was one of the most remarkable persons of his time. He was born in Listowel, Co. Kerry, on 19 September 1884, eighth in a family of fifteen from which eventually came two priests, four nuns, two outstanding Irish scholars, a cartoonist *cum* journalist and a number of teachers. On his father's side he was related to Aodhgán Ó Rathaile, the poet, and on his mother's side with Eoghan O'Curry, the scholar. He received his early education at the local convent and national schools and his secondary education at St Michael's College, Listowel, and Blackrock College, Dublin.

In November 1901 he entered the novitiate of the Society of Jesus at St Stanislaus College, Tullabeg, County Offaly. Here he completed two years' novitiate, a year's pre-university course and First Arts under the aegis of the Royal University of Ireland before transferring to 86 St Stephen's Green, Dublin, in September 1905. In this establishment, then known as University College, Dublin, and presided over by the distinguished educationalist, Father William Delaney, S.J., he spent the next three years, taking his B.A. and M.A. in mathematical and experimental physics in 1907 and 1908 respectively. He gave ample evidence of his brilliant mind from his first year at school, and entries in the *Royal University calendar* for 1909 concerning O'Rahilly's M.A. indicate that he had won First Place, First Class Honours and was awarded a gold medal for highly distinguished answering, as well as a University Studentship.

O'Rahilly spent the next three years at St Mary's Hall, Stonyhurst, in England, where, besides obtaining a diploma in pedagogics and lecturing in mathematics, he prepared for, and was later awarded, a doctorate in philosophy. In September 1911 he was back in Dublin at 35 Lower Leeson Street, a recently opened house of studies for Jesuit professors and students associated with University College, Dublin, a constituent college of the National University of Ireland. At nearby University Hall, O'Rahilly tutored resident students in mathematics and acted as librarian. In addition, with Father Thomas Finlay, S.J., professor of economics, and Father Timothy Corcoran, S.J., professor of education, he was co-founder and co-editor of the highly-regarded quarterly *Studies*. For its first few years under his own name and pseudonyms he wrote a considerable part of each issue, and was eventually its most prolific contributor.

In September 1913 he began his theological studies at Milltown Park. The following May he was informed by the authorities that it had been decided he would not be a suitable candidate for the priesthood. His fiercely independent mind, his extraordinary self-righteousness and what was then regarded in the Society as eccentric behaviour did not advance his cause. However, the most important and immediate factor leading to this apparently harsh decision seems to have been that O'Rahilly was under great mental strain at this time, due to years of intensive study, reflection, writing and tutoring, and, as he refused to take a holiday, his superiors feared for his health.

After an extended holiday in Jesuit houses of studies in Belgium and elsewhere on the Continent, O'Rahilly began a pre-medicine course in London University. However, in October he was appointed an assistant lecturer in mathematics in the department of mathematical physics, University College, Cork, and thus began his forty year association with the college during which he was sub-warden of the Honan Hostel from 1915 to 1916, professor of mathematical physics from 1917 to 1943, registrar from 1920 to 1943 and president from 1943 to 1954.

Within two years of his arrival at U.C.C. O'Rahilly married Agnes O'Donoghue, his first cousin, in the church of Our Immaculate Lady of Refuge, Rathmines, Dublin.

In controversy with H. G. Wells, O'Rahilly wrote in January 1940: 'I come from Catholic forbears whose consolation amid the persecution of Mr Wells' fellow-countrymen was — after Mass in a bleak field — the recital of the Rosary . . .' Not surprisingly he was greatly affected by the Rising of 1916 in which his first cousin, The O'Rahilly (Michael O'Rahilly), was one of the leaders. He was soon generally regarded as the spokesman of those in U.C.C. who supported, or were sympathetic to, Sinn Féin. By mid-1917 there was a great deal of tension between this group and the college establishment which consisted of a carefully selected Anglo-Irish ascendancy majority in the governing body presided over by Sir Bertram C. A. Windle, a committed English imperialist. Windle discouraged everything in the college which smacked of nationalism, and during world war one he enthusiastically promoted recruitment to the British Army and was indefatigable in urging conscription. O'Rahilly and his Sinn Féin colleagues opposed Windle on these issues and thwarted his plan to hand over some of the college buildings for use as a British Army hospital. This opposition, together with the prospect of a Sinn Féin administration in Ireland, caused Windle to resign and take up an appointment in St Michael's College, Toronto. Before he left he ensured that he was succeeded by a 'Home-Ruler' (Patrick J. Merriman) rather than the Sinn Féin candidate (Professor William Magennis of U.C.D.).

In the meantime O'Rahilly placed his spare time, extraordinary energy and remarkable talent at the service of the Sinn Féin movement. He contributed anonymously to the more vigorous nationalist periodicals, nearly all of which were suppressed by Dublin Castle, and in 1918, under the pseudonym *Lector*, he published two pamphlets *The German plot: German or English?* and *The issues: the case for Sinn Féin*. Over his own name he disputed allegations in the press that Sinn Féin was Marxist or anti-Catholic. He was asked to go forward in the Sinn Féin interest for Cork City constituency in the general election of 1918, but declined, owing to his wife's indifferent health, and his place was taken by Professor William F. Stockley.

In January 1920 O'Rahilly was elected as a Sinn Féin member of Cork City Corporation. Subsequently he was closely associated with the short-lived administrations of Tomás MacCurtain and Terence MacSwiney. He proposed both for the office of lord mayor and later helped to organise their political funerals. Throughout the war of independence he was the most influential apologist for the Irish Republican Army's campaign of resistance against the British forces. From September 1916 onwards he wrote at length in the *Catholic Bulletin* and *Studies* about the Church's teaching on government, democracy and national determination. He argued in a subtle and convincing manner for a restatement of the morality of revolution for the purpose of ending domination by a foreign power which had been merely acquiesced in by a nation. The application to Ireland was obvious, especially in 'Some theology about tyranny' which had been published in Maynooth's *Irish Theological Quarterly* of October 1920. Realising how damaging this article could be to their cause, the British establishment, lay and clerical, expressed outrage as much at its source as at its content. In Ireland this article and a number of widely publicised contributions by O'Rahilly in the City Council Chamber seriously undermined the unequivocal condemnation of the activities of the I.R.A. by Cork's Bishop Daniel Cohalan and the Irish Hierarchy's definite pro-establishment attitude to the worsening conflict.

Appalled by the atrocities being committed by the British forces and the I.R.A., O'Rahilly advocated, in letters to the press towards the end of 1920, the ending of the military campaign and its replacement by civil disobedience. In December he prepared and had published anonymously under the aegis of the Irish Labour Party the booklet *Who burnt Cork City?* which, notwithstanding official denials, established that the British forces had destroyed much of the centre of the city as a reprisal. From early 1920 he was aware that he was being sought by the British and took refuge with the University chaplain, Reverend Dr Daniel Cohalan, the bishop's nephew. He narrowly escaped an attempt to assassinate him, but was eventually arrested at the end of April 1921 during a night raid on the chaplain's residence. No formal charges were brought against him, but he was interned in Victoria (now Collins) barracks for a week, thereafter in Spike Island prison, Cork harbour, for three weeks and on Bere Island from 24 May to 17 October, when he was released on parole.

Soon after his formal release O'Rahilly went to London at the request of Éamonn de Valera to act as constitutional adviser to the Irish leaders who were negotiating the Anglo-Irish treaty. He subsequently supported the treaty and with characteristic honesty and courage immediately defended it in *The case for the treaty*. At the beginning of the civil war and towards its end he was involved in attempts to bring the two sides together. In the general election of 27 August 1923 he was elected to Dáil Éireann for Cork City. He neither sought the candidacy nor campaigned for election beyond stating that his sole purpose in going forward was 'to end anarchy and force de Valera and his followers to accept majority rule'. He was generally regarded as one of the most influential members of the committee charged with drafting the first constitution of the Irish Free State in 1922. He subsequently served on the Second Banking Commission (1934-8), the Senate Commission (1936) and the Commission on Vocational Organisation (1940-3).

O'Rahilly resigned his seat in Dáil Éireann on 1 August 1924, but remained a strong supporter and champion of the Cumann na nGaedheal government. Before his resignation he was the government delegate at the International Labour Organisation's conference in Geneva in 1924, and he acted again in this capacity in 1925 (and again in 1932 under the Fianna Fáil administration). He was frequently consulted by ministers and, even when not consulted, attempted to influence government policy. However, by 1931 he had become disillusioned with the government. He was especially critical of their preference for free trade over tariff protection, arguing that this prevented them from honouring earlier promises to promote widespread industrial development. Other reasons for his disenchantment were: their failure to initiate a significant afforestation programme, their refusal to establish a central bank which would effectively limit the British government's control of Irish fiscal affairs, and the 'infiltration' of Cumann na nGaedheal by Anglophiles. Earlier than most prominent Cumann na nGaedheal supporters he realised that de Valera's suggestions for constitutional change, including the abolition of the oath of allegiance to the British king, were nothing more than attempts to implement the 'stepping-stone' policy of Michael Collins. He also found himself more in tune with the Fianna Fáil attitude to the land annuities issue. Consequently, the general election of February 1932 saw him firmly and publicly committed to supporting Fianna Fáil, and helping de Valera with his policy statements and campaign literature.

During the rest of the 1930s and the early 1940s O'Rahilly

remained a strong supporter of de Valera. He staunchly defended his upholding of the democratic rights of the majority against the I.R.A.-Sinn Féin movement. And he applauded de Valera's policy of neutrality during world war two.

By the mid-1940s, however, he had become a trenchant critic of the Fianna Fáil administration, charging that, in spite of twelve years of rhetoric to the contrary, little progress had been made in afforestation, the development and protection of Irish industry, monetary reform or the national control of fiscal policy. Such was the influence of his lecturing, writing and pamphleteering on these subjects that he was regarded as one of the main inspirations behind the rise of Clann na Poblachta and even by some political pundits as the architect of the Inter-party government of 1948-51.

O'Rahilly in the meantime was not neglecting his main responsibilities and he had a remarkable influence on the development of University College, Cork. As unsalaried director of the library from 1931 to 1954, he added 350,000 volumes to its stock of 50,000, making it the third largest in the country. He founded the Cork University Press in 1925 and continued as editorial director until 1954. During 1926-7 he studied sociology at Harvard and on his return to U.C.C. lectured on the subject in a voluntary capacity from 1937 to 1943. With Professor Timothy A. Smiddy he had organised the University and Labour series of extension lectures as early as 1915 and from these developed adult education courses in 1946 and the establishment of the department of adult education. In 1942, with Father James P. Bastible, D.D., dean of residence, he organised general lectures on Catholic apologetics and earlier, at the instigation of Dr Bastible, had facilitated the introduction of obligatory courses in ethics for medical students. Just before he retired, in order to provide theology within the university, he set up a statutory lectureship in general philosophy and provided for the establishment of a chair in theology, both to be held by the same person.

As registrar, O'Rahilly was mainly responsible for obtaining the faculty of dairy science for U.C.C. and, as president, he established the department of electrical engineering. During his presidency, to promote a corporate spirit, he had general facilities for students greatly improved, gave considerable status to the students' council and encouraged social activities. To this end also, in 1944, he launched the Cork University Record in lieu of the sessional lists.

O'Rahilly held that value judgements could not be excluded in the teaching of many subjects. He saw no conflict between this and the charter of the National University of Ireland which, in his opinion, provided for multi-denominational rather than undenominational education. In confessional matters he was scrupulously fair and, besides the course in Catholic apologetics, he provided a three-year

xxix

course of religious instruction for Church of Ireland students. And when, as president, he instituted new ceremonial, including a formal procession and Red Mass, for conferring day, he also provided facilities for Church of Ireland and Presbyterian religious ceremonies.

Apart from his exceptional skills as lecturer, educationalist and administrator, O'Rahilly brought enormous prestige to the college by virtue of his extra-mural activities. Moreover, throughout his tenure a never-ending flow of papers, articles, pamphlets and books came from his pen on an exceptionally wide range of subjects and his scholarship in a number of fields won him international acclaim as well as doctorates in science and literature. In addition, he had few, if any, peers as a polemicist and in every major controversy, as one Cork admirer noted, 'he advanced on all fronts with his quill drawn'.

O'Rahilly was an indefatigable battler for the rights of working people. From 1923 to 1924 he was chairman of the Cork Arbitration Board and in 1924 he was chairman of the I.L.O.'s international commission for the abolition of night work in bakeries. During his time in U.C.C. he was frequently consulted by the leaders of the Labour and trade union movement in the city. Many of these leaders, at his urging, attended the extension lectures and the adult education courses of the university and thereby imbibed, among other things, the social teaching of the papal encyclicals. Throughout his time in Cork he acted successfully as arbitrator in many industrial disputes in the city. His passion for justice, strong inclination to identify with the less-fortunate members of society, prodigal generosity to the poor, total lack of affectation and admiration for the integrity of local trade union officials were appreciated by Cork Labour leaders who attempted, on many occasions, to persuade him to stand for public office in the Labour interest.

Even after his departure from the Society of Jesus, O'Rahilly by virtue of his Ignatian training regarded himself as continuing as a private, albeit a rather important one, in the army of Christ. He frequently described Catholic Action as Catholic Inaction or the interference of the laity in the affairs of the clergy. For him the principal obligation of the educated lay Catholic was to use his or her professional competence to support and defend the role of the Church in society. He himself never evaded an opportunity to do so in private or in public, no matter how unfashionable or unpopular such interventions might be. He enjoyed intellectual jousts immensely and, although agressive and uncompromising, harboured no bitterness whatsoever towards opponents. His role as 'defender of the Church' did not go unrewarded. When he retired as president of U.C.C. in 1954 Pope Pius XII conferred on him the Order of St Gregory and in 1960 he was made a domestic prelate by Pope John XXIII.

From his earliest years in U.C.C. he fostered a magnificent obsession, that of writing a comprehensive, multi-volume life of Jesus Christ. He informed friends, colleagues, acquaintances and even complete strangers of this intention and throughout his academic life accumulated voluminous notes and research material for this purpose. His puckish sense of humour and mildly eccentric behaviour gave rise to considerable merriment among his colleagues, as did their occasional references to his lifelong project. When, at a meeting of the N.U.I. senate Professor Henry St J. Atkins, registrar of U.C.C., told Monsignor Pádraig de Brún, president of University College, Galway, that 'Alfred' was making progress with his life of Christ and that it should be interesting, de Brún replied that it would not be half as interesting as Christ's life of Alfred.

Most of O'Rahilly's research material for the life of Christ was lost in a fire in the archives of Blackrock College in February 1984. Fortunately he had used some of his notes for *Christ, the brother of the worker* (pamphlet, Dublin 1935), *By the lakeside* (pamphlet, Dublin 1939), *The woman of Samaria* (pamphlet, Dublin 1939), *On the road to Emmaus* (pamphlet, Dublin 1942) and *The burial of Christ* (pamphlet, Cork 1942). These he regarded as mere interim reports on his, by that time, projected twelve-volume life of Christ. For him, *The family at Bethany* (Cork and Oxford 1949), a commentary on all Scripture passages connected with the story of Mary, Martha and Lazarus, was the first volume to appear of his *magnum opus*. In 1949, heartened by encouraging reviews, he began to prepare two volumes on the Passion and Death of Christ, under the title 'The Crucified: on the Shroud and in Art'.

In October 1954 O'Rahilly retired from the presidency of U.C.C. and went to reside in Blackrock College. His wife had died in Sept. 1953, his son, Ronan, was married and on the medical faculty of Wayne State University, Detroit, Michigan, as an associate professor of anatomy, and O'Rahilly had provided for his unmarried daughter, Sybil. He expressed his intention to spend his remaining years completing a sixteen-volume life of Christ. He informed Browne and Nolan Ltd. of this and that a volume on the Passion and Death of Christ was near completion. Accordingly, they listed *The Crucified* in their catalogue for 1956.

In the meantime O'Rahilly decided to fulfil a lifelong ambition and was ordained for the archdiocese of Nairobi in December 1955. He was most generous in responding to requests to give public lectures. For the most part he lectured on the Shroud of Turin, that is, the relic preserved in Turin's Cathedral of St John the Baptist and traditionally believed to be the linen cloth in which Jesus Christ was wrapped in the tomb. However, he also lectured on the Holy Land, which he visited in August 1954, and on the stigmata of Thérèse

Neumann, whom he met soon after world war two and again in June 1956. He continued to contribute articles to periodicals and newspapers, a series of thirty-eight articles on the Passion in the *Irish Press* and other material being published as *Gospel Meditations* in 1958. In addition, he was advising the archbishop of Dublin, Dr John C. McQuaid, on adult education and educational matters in general. At this time he was clearly over-estimating his capacity to do all the things he wished to do and in 1955 even signed a contract to prepare a documentary on the 'Holy Shroud'. Despite periodic requests from Browne and Nolan Ltd., he could not bring himself to complete *The Crucified*. It seems he always wished to do further research and add more chapters to his proposed book.

Eventually he was persuaded to have *The Crucified* published in 1959. This scholarly treatment of the Passion and Death of Christ had as its main theme an extensively documented account of the Shroud of Turin. An index, now lost, was prepared by Father Seán Corkery, librarian in St Patrick's College, Maynooth. The final page proofs were given the *Nihil Obstat* of the archdiocese of Dublin, on the recommendation of Father Joseph A. Carroll, L.S.S., of Holy Cross College, Clonliffe. Monsignor John M. T. Barton, Consultor of the Pontifical Biblical Commission, was asked to prepare an introduction for the work. However, O'Rahilly continued to have reservations some of which he expressed to the representative of the publisher as follows: 'the book is out of date and to publish it as it stands, without apology and without promising further treatment, would lead to severe criticisms'. Towards the end of July 1960 Browne and Nolan Ltd. made a further unsuccessful request to be allowed to publish the work. Although O'Rahilly continued to tell his friends and others that he intended to publish *The Crucified* and another book *Passio Christi* (meditations on the Passion), which he had also undertaken to write for Browne and Nolan Ltd., there were no further developments before he died on 5 August 1969.

Fortunately, two sets of the final page proofs survived, one in the possession of Father Michael F. McCarthy, C.S.Sp., O'Rahilly's executor, and the other in the possession of Professor Ronan O'Rahilly. I have corrected the proofs and added a list of illustrations, introduction, list of sources and index. My determination to produce a book selling at a reasonable price has prevented me from improving the quality and presentation of the illustrations which are a remarkable survey of the iconography of Christ from the frescoes in the catacombs to the elaborations of modern art.

I am indebted to Father James McPolin, S.J., D.S.S., for a report on the book. While acknowledging the value of its content as well as O'Rahilly's thoroughness and clarity of presentation, he advises me that the work's main limitation from a modern scriptural point of view is the author's failure to distinguish between the factual and symbolic meaning of texts. He also points out that O'Rahilly's Christology would nowadays be regarded as incomplete. In addition to such understandable limitations in a book which was to be published in 1959, the author's poelmical style would not be appropriate in the more eirenic climate of today's literary and scholarly world.

Most of the developments in the historical and scientific investigation of the Shroud of Turin since 1959 complement rather than date *The Crucified*. In *The Turin Shroud* (London 1978) Dr Ian Wilson shed some fascinating new light on the possible whereabouts of the Shroud prior to the middle of the fourteenth century. The developments in the scientific field have been quite remarkable. In October 1978 scientists made a full-scale study of the Shroud, using the most modern equipment to perform physical, chemical and biological tests. Such has been the corroborative effect of the results of these and of a series of scientific investigations in 1969, 1973 and 1976, that few would disagree with the Anglican bishop of Woolwich, the late Dr John A. T. (*Honest to God*) Robinson, who, in March 1977 at a conference on the scientific investigations, stated that now the burden of proof is on those who believe that the Shroud is a fake.

More positive claims have emerged from the current intensive scientific investigation of the Shroud, as is clear from K. E. Stevenson's and G. R. Habermas' *Verdict on the Shroud* (London 1982). Stevenson edited the *Proceedings of the 1977 United States Conference of Research on the Shroud of Turin* (New York 1977) which considered the work of previous researchers in the field. Both he and Habermas were members of the Shroud of Turin Research Project which conducted the scientific investigations in 1978 and thereafter. In their book, subtitled *Evidence for the Death and Resurrection of Jesus Christ*, as a result of the most scientific investigation of the Shroud, they conclude:

> ... the historical arguments and the scientific arguments are very probable empirical indicators that Jesus did rise from the dead. When combined they provide a strong twofold argument for this event. The converging evidence is not proof, but it does show that the literal, physical resurrection of Jesus of Nazareth is by far the best explanation for the physical, medical and historical facts.

The most important recent publication on the Shroud is J. H. Heller's *Report on the Shroud of Turin* (Boston 1983), which was summarised in the *Reader's Digest* of April 1984. Heller was also a member of the Shroud of Turin Research Project. In his conclusions he does not leave the domain of empirical science, stating that there was nothing on the Shroud that would negate the actual presence of a scourged, crucified man lying in that linen. But exactly whose body was it? Science has no way of determining the answer. We just do not know.

In March 1983 in accordance with the will of Umberto II, the deposed king of Italy, ownership of the Shroud passed from the House of Savoy to the papacy. A year later Pope John Paul II, who had been honoured with a private showing of the Shroud in April 1980, decreed that it should continue to be kept in Turin with the serving archbishop as its custodian. On a visit to Turin in September 1984 I learned from informed sources that there are no plans for a public exhibition or a further scientific investigation of the Shroud in the immediate future. However, I was informed that it was probable that such an exhibition and scientific investigation would be arranged for 1988, with Rome as the most likely venue. With regard to the carbon-14 dating test, the authorities in Turin are extremely cautious about applying it to the Shroud, mainly because of the widely varying opinions of scientists on its accuracy. However, this dating technique is constantly being improved and will almost certainly be part of the next scientific investigation.

For help and encouragement in preparing Alfred O'Rahilly's *The Crucified* for publication I wish to thank Father Michael F. MacCarthy, C.S.Sp. (provincial superior), Cornelius Murphy (rights commissioner), Dr Michael O'Carroll, C.S.Sp., Maurice O'Connell (assistant-secretary, department of finance) and Professor Ronan O'Rahilly (University of California, Davis). For helpful criticism I am indebted to Dr Henry St J. Atkins, Canon James P. Bastible, Fiona Biggs, Walter McGrath (*Cork Examiner*), Professor Kathleen O'Flaherty, Patrick O'Kelly and Dr Christopher J. Woods. Thanks are due to Helen Murray for typing the extra material and to Liam Miller who is responsible for the design and layout of the book. I am particularly grateful to Bishop Kevin McNamara for providing the foreword and to Cardinal Tomás Ó Fiaich for consenting to launch the book.

In this century the increase in interest in the Shroud of Turin has been such that now there is a new discipline, sindonology or the study of the Shroud. To promote this new discipline the International Centre of Sindonology was established in Turin in December 1959. It fulfils its main function by publishing *Sindon* which specialises in articles dealing with the artistic, exegetical, historical and medical aspects of the Shroud. With a few exceptions, *Sindon* has been published annually since 1959, with two or three issues appearing in some years. Besides publishing scholarly articles, it is a digest of general information on the Shroud.

O'Rahilly's fascination with the Shroud for over sixty years arose from the fact that he considered that for Christians it could throw light on the smallest details of the Passion and Death of Christ, that central drama of Redemption which dominates our brief earthly existence and settles the course of our eternal destiny. He invariably began a talk on the Shroud of Turin by announcing to his audience: 'This is not intended as a lecture on the Shroud, but as a meditation on the Passion.' It is in this spirit that *The Crucified* is here presented to the public.

As an *envoi* to the reader, I suggest that such are the theme and concise style of this book that it deserves and requires to be read carefully.

J. ANTHONY GAUGHAN
University Church
87 St Stephen's Green
Dublin 2
1 October 1984

CHAPTER I

A TEXTILE DOCUMENT

(1) The Relic

THERE is in Turin a piece of ancient unbleached linen, which is at least now 14 feet long by 3½ ft. wide. Besides two parallel lines due to an accidental fire in 1532, the sheet contains the double imprint, back and front, of a human figure. For the last fifty years this imprint has excited world-wide interest and controversy. There is a strong case for regarding this impression as made by the Dead Christ. But even if this claim is not admitted, the cloth is still worth examination. For it contains at least some hitherto unexplained method of representing the Crucified with a realistic accuracy unequalled in art. We can study the scourge-marks, the nail-wounds, the post-mortem side-wound ; and we can deduce the mode of suspension on the cross. Moreover, by means of a photographic negative (first made in 1898), we can now gaze on the real features of the Man in the Shroud. No one disputes the value of supplement-ing and vivifying our study of the Gospels by calling to our aid historical texts, archaeological data and artistic representation. There can, similarly, be no question concerning the advantage of studying this Turin cloth in connection with the Crucifixion of Our Lord. (See fig. i. 1.)

Since 1452 it has been in possession of the House of Savoy, which then resided in Chambéry. After various vicissitudes, it was in 1578 transferred to Turin to facilitate St. Charles Borromeo. It was seen there in 1613 by St. Francis de Sales and in 1639 by St. Jane Frances de Chantal. The present chapel in which the relic is kept was erected by Guarini in 1694. It used to be solemnly exhibited on 4th May every year. But, lest is should become injured by unrolling and exposure, Victor Amadeus suppressed the ceremony in 1720. There were however, expositions on special occasions in the years 1814, 1815, 1842, 1868, 1898, 1931 and 1933. The first photographs were taken in 1898 ; but these have now been super-seded by those officially taken by Giuseppe Enrie in 1931. During the war it was removed for safety to the Convent of Montevergine. It is now back in Turin in the custody of the Archbishop.

(2) The Story of the Shroud

In 1353 Geoffrey I, of Charny, founded a collegiate church in the village of Lirey near Troyes. Next year this was approved and granted special privileges by Innocent VI. Though no actual record or deed now exists, it is admitted that Charny made this foundation for enshrining this relic which had mysteriously come into his possession. Charny took part in the war against the English. On the last day of 1349 he organised an attempt to capture Calais ; he was taken prisoner and released for a high ransom in August 1351. He was made captain-general in Picardy, but in October 1352 he resigned and retired to Champagne. He was killed at Poitiers on 19th September 1356, as porte-oriflamme of France, shielding King Jean with his body.[1] The shroud had for safety been removed from Lirey, and remained in the keeping of the Charney family at Saint-Hippolyte on the banks of the Doubs until 1389, when the son Geoffrey II restored it to Lirey.[2]

Thus we can trace the identity of the shroud from the middle of the fourteenth century until to-day. But where did it come from? Unless we essay a séance with the deceased Count de Charny, we cannot tell.[3] Conjectures are of course possible. There are many vague floating traditions.[4] A Byzantine historian[5] tells us that the Empress Eudocia " found the sepulchral cloths " in Jerusalem in

---

[1] Charny also wrote prose and verse: see A. Piaget, Le livre messire Geoffroy de Charny, *Romania* 26 (1897) 394-411. He accompanied the Dauphin on the Crusade of 1336.

[2] The subsequent history may be summarised. In 1418, owing to civil war and invasion, the Lirey canons confided the relic to Humbert, Count de la Roche, son-in-law of Geoffrey II de Charny. It remained at Saint-Hippolyte until 1449, when it was removed by Marguerite de Charny, widow of Count Humbert. A few months later we find it at Chimay, a village in the diocese of Liége, where the authorities made a demand for its authentication. After further wanderings, Marguerite brought it to Chambéry, and in 1452 she ceded it to Anne de Lusignan, wife of Louis I Duke of Savoy, who retained it in spite of the protests of the canons of Lirey. It was first kept in the church of the Franciscans ; in 1456 it was removed to a specially built chapel ; in 1502 it was placed in a new reliquary, and that same year it narrowly escaped destruction by fire. Barring a temporary removal to Bourg-en-Bresse in 1503 to be shown to Archduke Philip of Austria, the shroud remained in Chambéry from 1452 to 1578, when it was transferred to Turin to spare St. Charles Borromeo the fatigue of crossing the Alps.

[3] There seems to have been a deliberate vagueness about the provenance of the shroud. Geoffrey's son said his father had received it as a present, his grand-daughter said it had been acquired in war.—Chevalier ii. 13, 31.

[4] See my *Burial of Christ*, 1942, p.58.

[5] Nicephorus Callistes († 1350), *Hist. Eccl.* 14[2]: P.G. 146. 1061. It is doubtful if this expression is really to be taken as plural. Even in classical Greek the names of materials—cloth, sand, barley, milk, salt, blood, etc.—were used in the plural. So St. John's *othonia*.

438 and sent them to Constantinople. Long afterwards (in 1171), William of Tyre,[6] accompanying Amaury I, King of Jerusalem, to Constantinople, was by a very special privilege shown the secret chamber where the Emperor (Michael Comnenus) kept precious relics, among them the sindon (presumably in a case). A Greek writer[7] describes the sindon in Constantinople in 1201 made of ordinary linen and still smelling of myrrh. There is no reference to any impression on the cloth ; it may have been rolled up in a reliquary. And would a Byzantine writer, used to hieratic ikons, have admitted crude and faint tracings (such as are found in the Turin shroud) as a pictorial representation or " image " of Christ? The only reference thereto is made by a French writer, Robert de Clari, who in 1203 saw the shroud exhibited out of its case :

> There was a monastery called St. Mary of Blachernae where the sindon in which Our Lord had been enveloped was exposed every Friday, stretched upright,[8] so that one could easily see the figure of our Saviour. But no one, neither Greek nor Frank, knows what became of this sindon when the town was taken.— Riant ii. 232 ; Lauer, *La conquête de Constantinople*, 1924, p.90.

I. 1.—The Shroud exhibited outside the Cathedral of Turin (1933)

There was then an imaged shroud in Constantinople when it was sacked by the Crusaders in 1204. Was the Lirey shroud among the booty brought to France? We do not know. Nor if we did,

---

[6] Riant, *Exuviae sacrae constant.*, 1878, ii. 216.
[7] Nicholas Mesarites, in A. Heisenberg, *Die Palastrevolution des Johannes Komnenos*, 1907, p.30.
[8] Vignon (i. 55) and Beecher (p.140) incorrectly translate : " on which, when one stood straight up, could plainly be seen the figure."

would it avail us to bridge the gap between 1204—or even 438—and the year 30.

There is a rather interesting miniature[9] which is worth reproducing (fig. i. 2). It is taken from a manuscript (St. Elizabeth's Prayerbook) now in Cividale Museum. It was made for Hermann, Landgraf of Thuringia (✝1217) and his wife Sophia. Their son Louis (✝1227) married Elizabeth (1207–1231) daughter of Andrew II of Hungary. The manuscript came into the saint's possession and she gave it to her uncle Berthold, Patriarch of Aquileia. Thus the miniature is certainly prior to the year 1217. And yet it portrays the shroud being shown, with a rough human figure on it, by the angel to the three women. Thus the evidence for the belief in an imprinted shroud is definitely attested for the twelfth century.

(3) The Dispute of 1389

We must now consider a document which has been much quoted and discussed since it was published by Chevalier[1] in 1900. It is an unsigned and undated draft of an appeal sent by Pierre d'Arcis, Bishop of Troyes, to Robert of Geneva, the Antipope and originator of the great Western Schism, who was at that time reigning at Avignon under the title of Clement VII, accepted as true Pope by the whole of France. The draft is couched in rather violent language and accuses the Lirey canons of the basest motives of personal gain. Some critics have denied its authenticity. Some such appeal, perhaps toned down, must have been sent, for we have the Antipope's answer.[2] Let us accept the document and also the date (1389) which Chevalier assigned to it. The relevant portions are as follows:

[9] Haseloff, *Eine thüringisch-sächsische Malerschule des 13 Jahrh.*, 1897, fig. 42. The lettering on the left appears to be: Mulieres sedentes ad mon. lam. fl. d. In fig. 50 of my *Family at Bethany* (1949) there is an illustration from a St. Gall MS. of the 11th century. This also appears to have marked on the sudarium a rough indication of an imprint.

[1] Chevalier i. (document G) pp. vii-xii. An English translation is in Beecher, pp.190-197. Its content was however known long before 1900. In 1870, in his *Mémoire sur les instruments de la Passion* (p.241f), Rohault gives the arguments of d'Arcis and refers to Chifflet (1624)—who in ch. 23 protests against the " iniquitous sentence " of the Antipope Clement—as well as to Dom Lanzellé and to Baillet. There is no copy of the memoir in the Avignon archives in the Vatican.—Chevalier iii. 10.

[2] Chevalier says (iii. 10) that there is a double copy on parchment in vol. 154 of the Champagne Collection. At the head of one of them is the note: " Truth about the Lirey cloth, which had long been exhibited and now once again, concerning which I intend to write to our lord the Pope in the following form and as soon as possible."

Some time since in this diocese of Troyes the Dean of a certain collegiate church, to wit that of Lirey, falsely and deceitfully—being consumed with the passion of avarice and not from any motive of devotion but only of gain—procured for his church a certain cloth cunningly painted, upon which by a clever sleight of hand was depicted the twofold image of one man, that is to say, the back and front : he falsely declaring and pretending that this was the actual shroud in which our Saviour Jesus Christ was enfolded in the tomb and upon which the whole likeness of the Saviour had remained thus impressed together with the wounds which He bore.

This story was put about not only in the kingdom of France but so-to-speak throughout the world, so that from all parts people came together to view it. And further to attract the multitude so that money might cunningly be wrung from them, pretended miracles were worked ; certain men being hired to represent themselves as healed at the moment of the exhibition of the shroud, which all believed to be the shroud of our Lord.

The Lord Henry of Poitiers, of pious memory, then Bishop of Troyes—becoming aware of this and urged by many prudent persons to take action, as was indeed his duty in the exercise of his ordinary jurisdiction—set himself earnestly to work to fathom the truth of the matter.

For many theologians and other wise persons declared that this could not be the real shroud of our Lord, having the Saviour's likeness thus imprinted upon it, since the holy Gospel made no mention of any such imprint ; while, if it had been true, it was quite unlikely that the holy Evangelists would have omitted to record it, or that the fact should have remained hidden until the present time.

Eventually, after diligent inquiry and examination, he discovered the fraud and how the said cloth had been cunningly painted : the truth being attested by the artist who had painted it, to wit, that it was a work of human skill and not miraculously wrought or bestowed . . .

He began to institute formal proceedings against the said Dean and his accomplices, in order to root out this false persuasion. They, seeing their wickedness discovered, hid away the said cloth, so that the Ordinary could not find it. And they kept it hidden afterwards for thirty-four years or thereabouts down to the present year.

And now the present Dean of the said church—with fraudulent intent and for the purpose of gain—suggested, as it is reported, to the Lord Geoffrey de Charney . . . to have the said cloth replaced in the said church . . . The Knight went to the Cardinal de Thury, your Holiness's Nuncio and Legate in French territory . . . The said Lord Cardinal . . . granted to the petitioner by apostolic authority that—without asking leave of the Ordinary or of any other person—he might set up this picture or figure of the shroud of our Lord in the said church or in any other decent place . . .

I prohibited the said Dean under pain of excommunication . . . from exhibiting this cloth to the people until otherwise might be determined. He however, refusing obedience and lodging an appeal, in defiance of the prohibition went on with the exhibition as before . . .

The Knight above-mentioned has been beforehand with me and . . . has obtained from your Holiness a Brief, in which the said Lord Cardinal's letters are substantially confirmed *ex certa scientia* and permission is granted that—in spite of all prohibitions and appeals—the said cloth may be shown and exposed for the veneration of the faithful. While—as I hear, for I have not been able to procure a copy of the said Brief—perpetual silence is enjoined upon myself.

This document begins with a partisan attack on the canons of Lirey, who are accused of covetousness and fraud. No proofs are produced and the answer of the canons is not extant. We know however that the Antipope did not accept these accusations ; so neither can we of to-day. This unjustified diatribe must therefore count against the fairness and the veracity of the writer.

He next alleges, without proof, that his predecessor, Henry of Poitiers, made a judicial inquiry into the matter thirty-four years before (i.e. in 1355). In the archives of Troyes or elsewhere there is no trace of any relevant official document or of any canonical investigation. A year after he is supposed to have unmasked the trickery of the Lirey canons, Bishop Henry " confirmed with eulogies their pious establishment," and a few months before Geoffrey's death (1356) the Bishop lauded his " devotion and affection to divine worship."[3] All of which makes us sceptical of the statement of Pierre d'Arcis.

The first advice alleged to have been given to Henry of Poitiers was theological or rather exegetical : the Gospels do not mention any such imprint. There are so many other things which they do not mention ! For instance, they do not tell us that the cross was buried ; yet d'Arcis believed that it had been unearthed after three centuries. Moreover this objection, that both Gospels and tradition are completely silent concerning an image-imprinted shroud, can be

---

[3] Camuzat, *Promptuarium sacrarum antiquitatum*, p.422 (which I have not seen) ; Chevalier, p.23 ; Beecher, p.49f. The successor of d'Arcis (Louis Raguier) knew as much of the archives as he did. Yet he took part in the negotiations between the Duke of Savoy and the Canons of Lirey and in three official documents admitted the authenticity.

retorted against the writer. For if this be so, then why, in the absence of any tradition or any pious demand, should a painter invent this peculiar type of mortuary cloth?[4] Even a fraudulent relic does not arise in a void ; it presupposes an expectant clientèle.

It is next asserted that Henry discovered the fraud and how the cloth had been cunningly painted (*artificialiter depictus*). There is no record of this discovery ; we have merely, in a very partisan document, the bald assertion that this discovery had been made thirty-four years previously. In other words, A in 1389 writes that B in 1355 proved it was a painting. Now it may be true that, in the absence of the technical means which are nowadays available for coming to a decision, the church authorities of the fourteenth century came to the conclusion that the figure was painted on the cloth. But we certainly should not accept this on the bare assertion of a biased writer writing a generation later, a man who admittedly had himself no first-hand knowledge whatever of the cloth. It is distressing to observe the ready gullibility of modern church-historians who accept the belated *ipse dixit* of Pierre d'Arcis as if it were the outcome of credit-worthy research.[5]

It is furthermore asserted that in 1355 a man had come forward and claimed to have painted the image. We don't know if this be true ; the alleged confession of this nameless artist is not availables Nowadays the police are familiar with neurotic people who confes. to crimes they have read about. This man may have been such ; or he may have wished to ingratiate himself with the bishop and his " many theologians." Those who, on the strength of an *ex parte* document filed in a litigation, are so ready to believe that the Lirey priests were deliberately obtaining money on false pretences, can hardly object to the suggestion that this man was suborned by their rivals.

There is another simple solution which has not occurred to these historical experts. Let us suppose that Henry of Poitiers really found an artist who had been paid to paint a shroud, say, for the de Charney family, or for Lirey or for Besançon. There is still no

---

[4] It is no answer to this to urge the existence of Eastern *epitaphioi* (textiles with the painted or embroidered image of the buried Christ). For they contain only the frontal image, in the form of a drawing and not crude tracery, and they have been made only since the 15th century. See Vignon ii. 186.

[5] For example, Dom Baudot, in *Dict. prat. des connaissances rel.* 6 (1928) 474f : " The painter who had made it confessed that this image was his work," Canon Chevalier " established that the Holy Shroud of Turin is nothing but a simple representation made in the 14th century."

proof that this was the particular shroud now in Turin. In fact, if this latter is proved *not* to be a painting, then the cloth referred to by Pierre d'Arcis *must* have been a different one.

But we have really no proof whatever that this man ever existed. We merely have a brief reference to him in a document submitted, or intended to be submitted, in judicial proceedings a generation later. The man's name is not given, no deposition from him is quoted, no record of his alleged intervention exists, no explanation is given as to how he made the painting and succeeded in imposing upon Geoffrey de Charny. If such an assertion were submitted by the defendant in a legal case to-day, it would be at once countered by a request for proof. On what grounds are we asked to be less exigent concerning a document six centuries old?

What is really ludicrous is to find serious critics of to-day trotting out this unnamed and perhaps non-existent person, of unspecified competence and unknown veracity, as an authority on the shroud ! Now even if the shroud had since been lost or destroyed, it would be childish credulity to accept the written rumour of this verdict. But the shroud exists and is available for investigation to-day. Surely a proof or a disproof can *now* be had as to whether it is a fourteenth century French painting on contemporary cloth. This simple expedient seems to be repugnant to certain historians who have become so absorbed in deciphering old written documents that they lose cognisance of present-day realities. Listen, for instance, to Chevalier (iii.16) :

> The documents exhumed in my *Etude* and partly reproduced here have established, with evidence clear to anyone with a critical sense, that we are in presence of a painting whose date they determine with all the exactness that could be desired.

Practically all his documents are entirely irrelevant ; one of them is Calvin's attack on relics ! The only relevant document is this draft of a letter of Pierre d'Arcis. In other words, the unsupported rumour concerning the alleged confession of an anonymous artist, contained in the unsigned memoir of a biased disputant, is to be accepted by everyone " with a critical sense," simply because it exists in a centuries-old manuscript ! It is like quoting the Mechanics of Pseudo-Aristotle or the experiments of Paracelsus to settle a scientific problem. " We are in presence of a painting," says Chevalier with unconscious irony. We are in presence of the shroud ; and we have to determine scientifically to-day whether or

not it is a painting. It is futile for the men of 1950 to try to place the
onus on an anonymous artist of 1355. It is putting the cart before
the horse. The first task is to investigate the cloth, and *then* to
examine this document. For the cloth carries its own story, it is
not a *tabula rasa*. It is not something which lacks any impression
of the event in which it is asserted to have been involved, like, say,
the pen with which Napoleon signed his abdication at Fontaine-
bleau. If the cloth were just a piece of linen, nothing short of an
authentication affixed by Nicodemus and Joseph of Arimathea
would convince us that it was Christ's winding-sheet. But the
shroud is asserted to bear its own self-authenticating characteristics
which can be investigated with all the technique at our disposal
to-day. Instead of facing this contemporary task, these historians
take refuge in a palæographic alibi.

Let us now glance briefly at the Bishop's grievance and its outcome. When the Antipope's Legate was passing through Champagne, he granted—without consulting the Bishop—an indult to
Geoffrey II and the Dean of Lirey to exhibit the shroud. The
Bishop prohibited exposition. But an appeal from the Dean to the
Antipope resulted in a confirmation of the privilege and the imposition of silence on the Bishop, without even informing him.[6]
Hence the present memoir which the Bishop planned to send to
the Antipope, Robert of Geneva. Some pressure was evidently
brought to bear upon him to modify his high-handed action ; perhaps the influence of the King (Charles VI) was invoked. So Robert
was in a difficult position. But he extricated himself diplomatically.
He did not hold any inquiry whatever ; the shroud was not examined, the custodians were not cited. He did not even consider
any accusations against the Lirey chapter, he renewed their privileges, he confirmed once more their right to exhibit the relic, he did
not remove the silence imposed on the Bishop. On the other hand,
" to remove all occasion for error or idolatry " [*sic*], he prohibited
the use of vestments or lights during the exposition of the relic and
he ordered the exhibitor to " preach publicly to the people and
declare in a loud intelligible voice, all deception ceasing, that the
said figure or representation is not the true Shroud of Our Lord
Jesus Christ but a painting or picture made into a figure or represen-

[6] Text of Brief (28 July–3 August 1389) in Chevalier iii. 31. The Antipope uses
the expression " a figure or representation of the Shroud of Our Lord." The same
expression occurs in the next document (1390), *ibid.* p.33.

tation of the Shroud."[7] It was a neat solution, pacifying all sides. But it was not a judicial decision arrived at after canonical investigation ; it was a disciplinary ukase issued from Avignon.[8]

Upon these proceedings the late Father Thurston built an argument (v. 63) :

> Upon three facts we have unchallengeable documentary evidence : (1) The Canons did not venture to maintain to the [Anti-] Pope that the cloth was the true shroud of Christ. (2) The [Anti-] Pope was not prejudiced in favour of the bishop, who wished to suppress the exposition of the sudarium altogether. But (3) Clement nevertheless decided that it was never to be shown without the people being told that this was not the shroud itself but only a devotional representation of it.

Fr. Thurston characterised (i. 28) his first point as " the most damning piece of evidence," namely, that the canons did not maintain the authenticity " to the Pope." We really do not know whether they did or not ; we certainly do not know what they held in their own minds.[9] There seems to have been, on the part of the original donor and of the custodians, a deliberate silence concerning the provenance of the relic ; there may have been prudential reasons for this reticence. Anyway, they were hardly given a chance, for they were never cited to answer before the Antipope. That they really believed in the authenticity of the shroud, is accepted by Fr. Thurston on the strength of the assertion of Pierre d'Arcis. So whether they could but did not make this claim at Avignon, seems quite irrelevant. And if they had, would Chevalier and Thurston have been convinced? If so, they would have been strangely credulous. For the opinion of the canons, one way or the other, is of no scientific validity to-day for us who can much more competently examine the relic.[10]

---

[7] Date 6 Jan.—6 Feb. 1390 : Chevalier iii. 35. Is there not an implication that there existed a true Shroud which could be copied?

[8] On the Anti-Pope (Clement VII) L. Salembier writes : " One day he tries to gain the upper hand by policy, the next by force . . . For sixteen years he lives by expedients . . . He always behaves as a clever but egotistical ruler, who lives for himself and his ambition rather than for his people and his duty."—*The Great Schism of the West*, 1907, p.138.

[9] Apart from the offensive accusation of Pierre d'Arcis, there is no written record that the canons maintained the authenticity *to anyone*. If this be so, it is an unusual tribute to these men in an age which was fantastically credulous about relics. But then why all the pother?

[10] Chevalier (i. p.lix, document GG) publishes the plaint of one of the canons deploring the loss of " the most holy Shroud of the Lord." In the petition of the Lirey chapter (1472/82) against Marguerite de Charney, they speak of the " precious Shroud of Our Lord."—Chevalier iii. 40.

As to the Antipope's decision, it has no value whatever. He never saw the shroud, never had it investigated, had no qualifications to settle the question.[11] What curious perversity it is to prefer the *ipse dixit* of Robert of Geneva, to the views of Vignon of Paris !

(4) The Dispute To-day

In 1930 Fr. Thurston (v.52) summed up the position as follows :

Roughly speaking, we are confronted by a situation in which all the recognised authorities on Church history and archaeology have pronounced against the genuineness of the alleged Holy Shroud. On the other hand, the traditional belief, accepted unquestioningly for the last five centuries, is upheld by a number of devout and earnest people, who seem to regard any expression of doubt on the subject as a disloyalty to the Holy See . . . For the present I am content to abide by the decision of so many historical experts.

The position of Thurston was quite intelligible. He had debunked so many false claims that his instinct was to add another scalp to his belt. But it is not quite fair to insinuate that the upholders of the authenticity rely on considerations of piety. The provocation and the appeal to authority were mostly on the other side.[2] Typical of the unfair tactics of Chevalier (iii. 24) was his assertion that in 1902 Leo XIII requested the Congregation of Indulgences and Relics to inquire into the shroud, that he received an explicit verdict against its authenticity, but that he refrained from publishing this

---

[11] He declared : " I offer myself as ready to supply all information sufficient to remove any doubt concerning the facts alleged both from public report and otherwise."—Beecher, p. 197. The Antipope did not think it worth while to call for this information. The reference to " public report " makes us suspicious that rumours were a large ingredient. In the surviving archives there is no record of this information.

[1] " The laity nearly everywhere were convinced, but the clergy were sceptical and held aloof."—Beecher, p.117. Nowadays the clergy are very wary lest they be caught out ! An exception to Fr. Thurston's generalisation was Père A. d'Alès, who in a review of Terquem's book wrote : " The unprejudiced reader will appreciate the objectivity of his method and the solidity of his conclusions."—*Etudes* 228 (1936) 133. But Chevalier's pamphlets were approved in the *Analecta Bollandiana* 19 (1900) 215, 350. It is pleasant however to note that individual members of the various Religious Orders—Benedictines, Dominicans, Jesuits—are at variance among themselves.

[2] Elsewhere Thurston (ii. 763) admitted that " the violence of many of its assailants prejudiced their own cause." Chevalier was full of sneers for his opponents : " Certain Catholics do not know how to avoid all passion to glorify their pious beliefs " (iii. 6).

owing to his delicate relations with the House of Savoy. Needless to say, there was not a word of truth in this attempt to browbeat defenders of the shroud.[3]

Apart however from manners and motives, the fundamental issue is science versus alleged history :

> A historical truth, established according to critical rules, cannot be contradicted by a fact in the scientific order ; this latter must have been badly observed.—Chevalier, *L'art et l'autel*, June 1902, p.238, cited with approval by Père Pègues, p.355.

The converse proposition seems much more reasonable : A scientific truth, established according to critical rules, cannot be contradicted by historical testimony concerning the same object ; it must have been badly observed in the past. Nobody would credit a claim found in a manuscript of the fourteenth century that the writer had sculptured the Venus of Milo or the Belvedere Apollo. Yet, in spite of all the investigative processes at our disposal to-day, the ' historical ' criterion is paraded as alone decisive :

> It is this historical thesis [of Chevalier] which to my thinking is the point of supreme importance ; for a vivid imagination cannot so easily play tricks with documentary evidence as it can with the interpretation of the photograph of a half-defaced picture. —H. Thurston, S.J. (iii. 623).
> The problem is above all historical, and from this viewpoint it is far from being decided.—G. de Jerphanion, S.J., *Nouvelle revue théol.*, March 1938, p.265.

There is ambiguity here. What is this so-called historical thesis? It is certainly not a proof that the relic was manufactured in France in the fourteenth century, it is merely the unsupported assertion of a litigant who had himself neither directly nor indirectly examined the shroud. Even if we admit the truth of his statements about an alleged artist's confession, it does not follow that the artist's claim was true, even though the vivid imagination of some contemporary historians may portray this anonymous artist as infallible. And even if the artist's claim were true, it does not follow that he was referring to the particular cloth now in Turin. All these difficulties occur

---

[3] Noguier de Malijay, p.93 ; Renié, p.155 ; *Les dossiers du S.S. de Turin*, May 1939, p.6. On the contrary in 1903 Chevalier was asked to abandon his attacks, and the Jesuit General was asked to intervene with the Bollandists. On the attitude of Pius XI see p.55.

apart from a well-founded suspicion that no such artist ever existed. To attempt to sweep away all these doubts in the name of critical history is a piece of academic bullying which should be strenuously resisted.

Or perhaps it may be meant that we can never accept the authenticity of an archaeological monument until it has attached to it documentary evidence of its origin. Surely such a contention is absurd. It would play havoc with all prehistoric objects, with ruins, sculptures, coins. External criteria are lacking in most of these cases ; even when available, they are not always certain, for they may not be referring to this particular monument. Internal criteria—style, technique, iconography—are often decisive in a negative sense. Even here care is required. The Arch of Constantine is an important historical document in stone ; yet its sculptures consist partly of pieces from the times of Trajan and Marcus Aurelius and partly of 19th century restorations. But sweeping scepticism is quite unjustified.[4] We have learnt much from monuments which were not historically certified. Those of Asia Minor showed that in the third century certain towns in Phrygia were almost entirely Christian ; the numerous graffiti in the triclia of St. Sebastian revealed a widespread third century cult of SS. Peter and Paul ; the buried churches and monasteries of Cappadocia gave us information about the tenth century not otherwise available.

Now the Lirey-Turin shroud is a textile monument which has to be critically examined. It is certainly a pity that so far we have been unable to unearth historical evidence about it prior to 1353. " It is for history to make the necessary discoveries," says Vignon (ii.105). " But suppose it cannot. Why make the shroud responsible for this historical deficiency? This does not prevent it from being what it is." The shroud exists here and now in its own right, just as a flint, an effigy or a coin that had been dug up yesterday. We don't fling such finds into the dustbin because they have not a sealed authentication attached to them. Nor do we reject them because we know nothing about their origin. Then why urge[5] as a decisive argument against the shroud that " no intelligible account, beyond wild conjecture, can be given of the previous history of the shroud or of

[4] The first Roman catacomb was rediscovered in 1578 through ground-subsidence. Bishop Burnet (1685) and Misson (1714), unwilling to admit the inconvenient evidence about the Early Church, maintained that the catacombs were pagan cemeteries to which superstitious monks later added paintings, etc., to deceive the people !

[5] Thurston ii. 763.

its coming to Lirey "? Let us concede that we have no account of how the cloth reached Lirey. Is not this very lacuna a favourable argument? We are familiar with romantic legends woven *post factum* to provide a pedigree for a doubtful relic. We are equally ignorant of the provenance of many archaeological objects, unless they happen to be scientifically investigated *in situ*. And cannot we retort that neither Thurston nor anyone else has succeeded in giving an intelligible account of how the imprints could have been faked?

Moreover, Fr. Thurston has made himself liable to the criticism which he himself made against Duchesne :

> For him the transition is so easy from the proposition " these things are not proved " to the proposition " these things are untrue," that he sometimes seems to treat the two as identical.— *Month* 93 (1899) 75f.

The absence of written proof can never amount to actual disproof. Most of what happens in the world is not recorded in writing at all. So, even if its previous history is a blank, the shroud presents a problem which can be decided only by examining the object itself.

(5) Some Similar Cases

It will not be irrelevant to discuss briefly some instances in which, owing to the absence of sufficient historical evidence, the authenticity of a relic has had to be decided by an investigation of the object itself. Let us begin with two small pieces of parchment which are alleged to contain the handwriting of St. Francis (✝1226).

There is in Assisi a small document containing the Praises of God (mostly illegible) on one side and on the reverse the Biblical blessing dictated to Brother Leo with, at the bottom, a personal blessing purporting to be written by St. Francis himself. What are the historical data?[1]

(1) Thomas of Celano in his *Vita Secunda*, written probably in 1247, tells us that when the Saint was in La Verna, " one of his companions," beset by a spiritual temptation, desired some writing of Francis as a keepsake and help. Knowing this unspoken wish, the Saint " wrote with his own hand the *Laudes Dei*, . . . and finally a Blessing for the Brother. Take this paper, he said, and carefully

---

[1] To avoid cumbrous and unnecessary source-references, I refer to R. Balfour, *The Seraphic Keepsake*, 1905, pp.107-119, also 51-106 ; Paschal Robinson, O.F.M., *The Writings of St. Francis of Assisi*, 1906. pp.146-149.

keep it until the day of your death. At once all temptation was dispelled. The writing was preserved and subsequently effected miracles." The statement was repeated by St. Bonaventure in 1260.

(2) We next find it mentioned in an inventory of relics in Assisi dated 1338 : " a wooden frame with glass on both sides, in which is the Blessing which the Holy Father Francis gave to his companion Brother Leo, written with his own hand, and also his Praises." The Brother's name is now given as Leo, 67 years after his death. We do not know how or when the document reached the Conventual Friars in Assisi.

(3) According to an inventory made in 1350 the sheet was still in its wooden frame ; an appendix quotes the text of the Praises and Leo's authenticating note.

(4) An inventory of 1473 mentions " a silver tabernacle in which there is a document in the writing of St. Francis."

(5) " The Histories of the Seraphic Order " by Friar Peter Ridolfo of Tossignano, published in 1586, quotes the autograph Blessing which with the Praises was preserved in Assisi.

(6) Wadding saw the relic there in 1619.

(7) The relic used to be borne in procession on the 1st August. In 1720 a great controversy arose about the authenticity of the relic and the propriety of the cult paid to it. Both were defended by Prosper Lambertini (afterwards Benedict XIV) in 1721.

(8) In 1895 the German Catholic archaeologist-historian F. X. Kraus, after examining a poor facsimile, declared that the relic was a fraud. The handwriting he pronounced to be of the late 14th or early 15th century. Having been answered by experts in palaeography, Kraus boldly said that the unexposed side of the parchment did not contain the Praises. The reliquary was opened and the Praises (largely obliterated) were found on the back.

History cannot decide the genuineness of this document, which is first mentioned as being in Assisi 114 years after it purports to have been written, and without any explanation as to how it reached this place. A captious critic might even query whether the present relic is that first mentioned in 1338. The examination of the writing has now convinced everyone of its genuineness. It contains an authentication by Leo, whose handwriting is available also in a breviary at San Damiano.

The second document[2] is much more deficient in any historical

---

[2] Balfour, pp. 7-31 ; Robinson, pp. 130-133.

pedigree. It is a small piece of parchment containing an autograph letter of St. Francis to Brother Leo (about 1220).

(1) But we first hear of its existence in the Conventual Friary at Spoleto in 1604—just 333 years after Leo's death (✝1271). Presumably Leo kept it on his person for 51 years. After his death the most likely depository was the Convent of the Poor Clares in Assisi. If so, how and when did they part with it? And how did it reach Spoleto and remain hidden there for centuries? To use Fr. Thurston's language, no intelligible account, beyond wild conjecture, can be given of its previous history—484 years !—or of its coming to Spoleto.

(2) It was still there in 1623 when Fr. Luke Wadding published his *Opuscula S. Francisci*. But after that it disappeared. It is not mentioned in Jacobilli's catalogue of all the relics in the churches of Umbria, published in 1661.

(3) In 1895 it turned up again, after another 270 years of complete oblivion. It was discovered—no one knows how or where—by a priest in Spoleto. It was first given to Leo XIII, who gave it to the Cathedral of Spoleto where it now is.

Can its authenticity be decided? Apparently it can, for it is now universally admitted. The handwriting can be compared with that in the Blessing and the Praises. There are some discrepancies, which are probably due to the fact that someone later tried to refresh the original strokes of the writing. There is an apparent grammatical difficulty in one phrase, and the occasion for writing the letter is disputed. The main point is that this parchment, lacking all " historical " proof, is, on internal grounds, acknowledged to be genuine.

The third example is even more interesting, for it is the case of a shroud whose authenticity has been definitely disproved by actual examination. Says the Jesuit author[3] of the disproof:

> The critical study of the written documents had made me suspicious of this relic. But this personal opinion was opposed by a widespread contrary persuasion, supported by a tradition of eight centuries, by the repeated declarations of ecclesiastical authorities, by a long series, of miracles.—J. Francez S.J., *Un pseudo-linceul du Christ*, 1935, p.9.

This cloth is known to have been in Cadouin in 1117 ; a church

---

[3] It is worth noting that Père Francez, in a review of Vignon, has accepted the authenticity of the Turin Shroud.

was built to honour it in 1150–54. The first public exposition of it (in Paris) took place in 1392. It has no image upon it ; it is about 3 yards long and 1 yard wide, with ornamental bands at the ends. It was honoured by popes and kings. Its authenticity was strongly defended. After an inquiry in 1644, the bishop of Sarlat declared : " We do not think that in all Christendom there is a better attested relic."[4] Yet it has now been shown to be a Muhammadan shawl, made in Upper Egypt in the time of the Fatimids (969–1171), dating from the end of the eleventh century, probably taken at the capture of Antioch. For the ornamental band has been shown to contain Sufic[5] prayers of the time when Musta-Ali ruled in Egypt (1094–1101). Hundreds of thousands of eyes had seen this pattern without suspecting its significance. Needless to say, the cloth was at once withdrawn (in accordance with canon 1284 of Canon Law). To obviate theological difficulties, it may be well to quote Père Francez (pp.51, 53) :

> When the heads of the Church authorise and encourage the cult of a relic, they do so only after investigating the historical tradition on which it relies . . . But they do not claim to declare that the authenticity of the object is part of the deposit of revelation . . . Belief in the value of a relic is an act of purely human faith, which is worth only as much as the arguments supporting this mental adhesion . . . Relics have always a relative, not an absolute, value . . . The relic may be apocryphal, like the false portrait of a saint ; the cult given to these materially false objects is directed to the person who is honoured ; and the acts of piety, accomplished in good faith by the faithful believing in their authenticity, are good and meritorious.

Our interest however lies in the analogy with the Turin shroud. The historical lineage of the Cadouin cloth was longer by well over two centuries ; yet it has been shown to be fraudulent. Not how-

---

[4] Rohault de Fleury, *Mém. sur les instr. de la Passion*, 1870, p.237. Even as late as 1929, Noguier de Malijay (p.x) wrote : " At first glance the Oriental character of this magnificent work strikes one ; and a pious tradition has it that it was the Blessed Virgin herself who wove and embroidered this cloth in view of the burial of Jesus, the *sudarium capitis* of which St. John speaks." Père Gaffre was ill-advised when he wrote (p.139) : " The Suaire of Cadouin has a history of which that of Turin has reason to be jealous."

[5] Sufic is a form of writing Arabic which was used only for a few centuries from the beginning of the Hegira (622). Similarly a white cloth, with coloured bands decorated with animals, which was venerated in the Cathedral of Apt as the veil of St. Anne, has been shown to be a muslim cloth taken by the Crusaders in 1099. All through the twelfth century Oriental tissues reached France and had an appreciable influence on art.

ever through any historical procedure, but by means of an examination of the markings on the cloth, made with more competence than was formerly possible. It is by exactly the same kind of investigation that the credit of the Turin cloth must stand or fall. In view of the Cadouin affair,[6] and of the known medieval credulity concerning relics, it is even advisable to approach this investigation with a healthy dose of scepticism.[7]

(6) The Title of the Cross[1]

An examination of the existing relic which is claimed to be a fragment of the Title has a twofold relevance. It interests us as a contribution to the archaeology of the Passion. And it also throws light upon this issue of intrinsic versus extrinsic criteria of authenticity.

While we have satisfactory accounts of the discovery of the Holy Sepulchre in Jerusalem (A.D. 326), the finding of the Cross is involved in historical difficulties ; so much so that by some critics it is dated *after* the dedication of the basilicas in Jerusalem (A.D. 335).[2] Constantine in his letter to Macarius, Eusebius in his *Life of Constantine* (337) and *The Bordeaux Pilgrim* (333) mention the Holy Sepulchre, but say nothing of the Cross. The first to ascribe the discovery to Helena's active intervention seems to be St. Ambrose in a sermon (*De obitu Theodosii*, 45) preached in A.D. 395. Besides

---

[6] On the other hand, some curious results have emerged concerning the woollen Tunic preserved in Argenteuil. In 1892 some traces, almost invisible to the eye, were chemically shown to be bloodstains. Subsequently infra-red photography revealed the stains clearly, the most important being on the shoulder-blade.— L. Parcot, *La sainte tunique d'Argenteuil*, 1934[2]. (The first positive document about this tunic is dated 1156).

[7] A rather interesting case of a relic is discussed by Dr. Louis Vervaeck in the *Analecta Bollandiana* 40 (1922) 155-170. A. What was, on the strength of good historical documents, assumed to be the skeleton of St. Albert of Louvain (†1192) was exhumed at Rheims in 1612 and transferred to Brussels. B. On 26 Sept. 1919 another tomb was uncovered at Rheims. Examination of the bones, the wounds inflicted, the colour of the hair, etc., led to the conclusion that this was really St. Albert's body. So it is now held that A is the skeleton of Odalric (†971) Archbishop of Rheims, though there is no record of his death through injury (accidental fall?). This incident shows the importance of an intrinsic examination of a relic.

[1] This reproduces (with some additions) an article which was published in the *Irish Eccles. Record*, May 1945.

[2] This seems quite impossible. The pilgrim Etheria (about 385) tells us that the dedication of the Constantinian churches at the Holy Sepulchre was annually celebrated on " the day when the Cross of the Lord had been found."—*Pilgrimage*, trans. McClure and Feltoe, p.95. There was a definite discovery, and it was prior to these buildings.

a number of legends apparently originating in Edessa, there were discrepant versions of the recovery in which St. Helena (†330) was represented as taking the chief part. (1) Three crosses were found, our Lord's was distinguished by being in the middle and by having a title.—St. Ambrose, St. John Chrysostom. (2) Three indistinguishable crosses and one title were found ; our Lord's was identified by the Bishop of Jerusalem who used it to heal a dying woman.—Rufinus, Socrates. (3) It was St. Helena who adopted the test, the restoration of a corpse to life.—St. Paulinus, Sulpicius Severus.

Though we cannot now reconstruct the details, nevertheless we know that the Cross, or at least what contemporaries held to be the Cross, was found. In A.D. 347 St. Cyril, Bishop of Jerusalem, said (*Cat.* x. 19) : " The holy wood of the Cross bears witness, which is seen among us to this day ; and from this place now almost filling the whole world by means of those who in faith take portions from it." In 1890 a dated inscription was found at Tixter in Algeria, which showed that already in 359 fragments of the Cross were enclosed in altar-slabs. In 363 the Emperor Julian accused the Christians of adoring the Cross. We find that in 379 St. Macrina, sister of St. Gregory of Nyssa, possessed a fragment in a reliquary. About 380 St. Mary of Egypt was converted at the exposition of the Cross in Jerusalem. About 385 the pilgrim Etheria described this ceremony which she witnessed. In 386 *The Letter of Paula and Eustochium* (§ 7) speaks of kissing the wood of the Cross. About 392 Porphyry (afterwards Bishop of Gaza) was appointed custodian of the relic in Jerusalem.

These general remarks are merely preliminary to a consideration of the Title on the Cross.[3] The exact wording is not clear from the Gospels :[4]

Matt. 27[37] This is Jesus the King of the Jews.
Mark 15[26] The King of the Jews.
Luke 23[38] This is the King of the Jews.
John 19[19] Jesus the Nazarene the King of the Jews.

[3] Here is a brief bibliography : Leander de Corrieris, *De Sessorianis praecipuis Passionis reliquiis commentarius*, Rome, 1830 (really 1831). Ch. Rohault de Fleury. *Mémoire sur les instruments de la Passion*, 1870, pp.183-198, 367f. J. H. Friedlieb, *Archéologie de la Passion*, French trans. Abbé F. Martin, 1897, pp.332-338. L. de Combes, *The Finding of the Cross*, English trans. L. Cappadelta, 1907, pp.170-197. H. Thurston, S.J., " Relics, Authentic and Spurious," *The Month* 155 (1930) 420-429. H. M. Gillett, *The Story of the Relics of the Passion*, 1935, pp.56-62.
[4] The apocryphal Gospel of Peter (A.D. 110-130), gives the Title in the form (n. 11) : " This is the King of Israel."

According to St. John, it " was written in Hebrew, Latin and Greek." By Hebrew—as elsewhere in the Gospels and Acts—it is certain that Aramaic, the current language of Palestine, was meant. All the Evangelists agree that over our Lord's head it was proclaimed that He was King of the Jews. The Jewish leaders objected that it ought to read that He merely claimed to be King. But Pilate, whose hand they had already forced, was in no mood to make this concession. He probably meant it not merely to insult the Sanhedrin, but also to pay tribute to the Prisoner whose attitude to Kingship and Truth impressed him. We might almost call this inscription the first agnostic tribute to Christ as a King among men. So not only from the practical point of view in a country which was then—as it is to-day with Arabic, Neo-Hebrew and English—trilingual, but also prophetically and providentially, this three-lined Title was appropriate; for it proclaimed His cause in the three great languages of the Mediterranean world. Some important Greek manuscripts of St. Luke, followed by the Latin Vulgate, say that the inscription was " written in Greek, Roman and Hebrew letters." From which—and from the fragment preserved in Rome—some have inferred that the three inscriptions were in the Latin language, though written in Hebrew, Greek and Latin *letters*.[5]

We have already seen the lacunae in the accounts of the finding of the Cross. This lack of knowledge is even more evident as regards the Title. According to later writers—St. Ambrose (✝397), St. John Chrysostom (✝407), Rufinus (✝410), Socrates, Sozomen— the Title was found with the Cross. The pilgrim Etheria about A.D. 385 thus describes the Good Friday ceremony in Jerusalem :

> A chair is placed for the Bishop in Golgotha behind the Cross which is now standing. The Bishop duly takes his seat in the chair, and a table covered with a linen cloth is placed before him. The deacons stand round the table, and a silver-gilt casket is brought in which is the holy wood of the Cross. The casket is opened and [the wood] is taken out, and both the wood of the Cross and the Title are placed on the table. Now when it has been put upon the table, the Bishop as he sits holds the extremities of the sacred wood firmly in his hands, while the deacons who stand around guard it. It is guarded thus because the custom

---

[5] Fleury, p.196, following Abbé Sionnet (1845). Friedlieb (p.337) rejects the contention. Rufinus (H. E. i. 7) says : " Near by was the title itself on which Pilate had written in Greek, Latin and Hebrew letters." Sozomen (H. E. ii. 1) says that the inscription was written " in white letters in Hebrew, in Greek and in Latin."

is that the people, both faithful and catechumens, come one by one, and bowing down at the table, kiss the sacred wood and pass through. And because—I know not when—someone is said to have bitten off and stolen a portion of the sacred wood, it is thus guarded by the deacons who stand around, lest anyone approaching should venture to do so again. And as all the people pass by one by one, all bowing themselves, they touch the Cross and the Title first with their foreheads and then with their eyes ; then they kiss the Cross and pass through, but none lays his hand upon it to touch it.—*The Pilgrimage of Etheria*, trans. McClure and Feltoe, p.74f.

At a first reading this seems to imply that the Title remained in Jerusalem. But this inference is not necessary. She calls " the Cross " a portion small enough for the bishop to hold with its extremities in his hands ; and we know that in fact only a fragment was retained in Jerusalem. The Title was just as likely to be distributed in parts as the Cross ; indeed more likely, as it may have already been split by the nails. And if a portion was retained in Jerusalem, the Aramaic inscription was the most natural portion to keep there.

About two centuries later (A.D. 570) a Piacenza pilgrim tells us that the Title was still in Jerusalem :

In Constantine's Basilica which is adjacent to the tomb, or Golgotha, in the atrium of the Basilica itself, is a chamber (*cubiculum*) where is placed the wood of the Holy Cross which we adored and kissed. For I also saw the Title which was placed above the head of Jesus, and on which was written : Jesus of Nazareth, King of the Jews. This I held in my hands and kissed.—*Of the Holy Places visited by Antoninus Martyr*, n. 20, trans. A. Stewart, 1885, p.17.

Once more we must interpret this as referring only to a portion of the Title. And if the Roman fragment is genuine, we must reject the statement that the Jerusalem portion contained (in Latin?) the words ' *Jesus Nazarenus Rex Judaeorum.*'

There is no reason to doubt the statement—though it is given by late authorities[6]—that Constantine established a basilica in the Sessorian Palace in Rome and that he " called it Jerusalem." He is also said to have presented to it a fragment of the Cross enclosed in a golden reliquary—there is no mention of the Title. There is an inscription later than 1492—given in Fleury, p.367—which

[6] *Liber Pontificalis* : *The Book of the Popes*, trans. L. R. Loomis, 1916, p.58. Anastasius (ninth-century Vatican librarian), *S. Silvester* : Migne P. L. 127, 1521.

asserts that St. Helena, after her return from Jerusalem, erected in Rome the basilica Santa-Croce-in-Gerusalemme, so called because founded on earth brought from Calvary, and that she presented the Title to it. But historians now generally reject the alleged return to Rome of the octogenarian Empress ; she probably died in Nicomedia in 330. Nor is it likely that Constantine presented the Title ; for there is no mention of the gold or silver reliquary in which he would have enshrined it.

> Who then presented it? An unknown person? This is hardly likely, for the Eastern emperors were too jealous of their treasure to part with it without good reasons. The history of the Title from 327 to the reign of Valentinian III [425-455] is an utter blank. Hence it is the Title itself we must examine for proof of its authenticity.—Combes, p.171.

The subsequent discovery of the relic lends verisimilitude to the late statement that Placidius Valentinian III (425-455) embellished Santa Croce and had the Title blocked up in a small high-up cavity in the apse. This concealment of the relic was probably not so much to guard it against enemies (Visigoths and Vandals) as to protect it against the ill-advised piety of the faithful. Relics were often thus concealed—e.g., the body of St. Peter in Rome, that of St. Francis in Assisi, that of St. Paulinus in Trier ; sometimes with the effect that their very existence was forgotten for centuries. So in course of time, the inscription being no longer visible from the nave, the Title in Santa Croce was largely ignored in favour of the visible relic of the Cross. It unexpectedly came to light again on 1st February, 1492, when some workmen were effecting repairs. On the reliquary was found a seal of Cardinal Caccianemici (afterwards Pope Lucius II) of the year 1143, when we know that the Basilica was restored. Meanwhile its existence was not altogether forgotten, for we find a pilgrim (William Brewyn) writing about 1470 :

> The title of the Lord's cross, on which is written *Hic est IHS Nazarenus Rex Iudeorum* has been hidden away in the sham window which is painted over the arch in the middle of the church in its outer face.—*A Fifteenth Century Guide-Book to the Principal Churches of Rome*, trans. C. E. Woodruff, 1933, p.53f.

The wording here given is quite wrong; it is also incorrectly assumed that the whole Title was in Rome. Even three supposedly accurate contemporary witnesses of the re-discovery in 1492 give a totally erroneous account : their measurements are wrong, their

I.3.—Fragment of the Title in Rome

reading of the tablet (brick, not marble) and of the Title is wrong :

The workmen found a small cavity in which lay a leaden box two hands [2 Roman " palms "=17½ inches] in length and hermetically sealed. Above it a rectangular marble slab bore the words : Here is the Title of the True Cross (*Hic est titulus verae crucis*). In the box was a small tablet a hand and a half in length [about 13 inches], one side of which had been gnawed by time. On one side had been engraved, and then coloured red, these words : Jesus of Nazareth, King of the Jews (*Jesus Nazarenus Rex Judaeorum*). The inscription was incomplete ; two letters (UM) were wanting in the last syllable (RUM), because this side of the tablet had perished. The first line was in Latin, the second in Greek, and the third in Hebrew characters.—Combes, p.186. Cf. Fleury, p.185.

The first accurate sketch of the fragment seems to have been published in 1831 by de Corrieris, reproduced by Rohault de Fleury in 1870. It is reproduced in fig. i.3.

The following conclusions are now established.

(1) The niche or cavity was covered by a tablet of baked clay (*terra cotta*) still existing, which bears the inscription " Titulus Crucis." The dimensions of the tablet or brick are 12.6 by 8.3 inches. The engraved lettering is Roman, certainly pre-medieval. See fig. i.4.

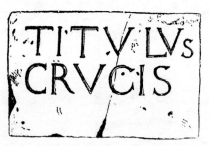

I. 4—Tablet covering the cavity containing the Title.

(2) The relic was enclosed in a leaden box whose face, measuring 10.2 by 5.9 inches, just fitted inside the cavity.

(3) The existing fragment measures 9.5 by 5.1 inches. Hence the box was made for this fragment and could never have contained the whole Title. Even the letters *Jesus Nazarenus Rex Judaeor* would, on the same scale, require a length of over 16½ inches. Hence

the assertion[7] that the whole Title was brought to Rome must be rejected ; already in 1617 Bosio had shown that only about a third of the Title was in Rome.

(4) The inscription runs from right to left, as do Hebrew and Aramaic. But we know from coins and vases that Greek and Latin were sometimes so written ; and such right-to-left writing would be natural to a Semitic workman. The last line of the fragment is clearly Latin. Written from left to right, it reads " Nazarinus Re " (*Nazarinus* is for *Nazarenus*, *e* being often replaced by *i* in inscriptions). Thus it is portion of the Latin inscription :

[*Iesus*] *Nazarinus Re*[*x Iudeorum*]

(5) The wood, now very fragile, is apparently some hardwood such as oak or poplar. The letters are lightly incised with a chisel ; they were once coloured red, which is no longer visible to the naked eye. The background was once white, but is now dark.

(6) The upper line of the fragment, also printed from right to left, is in Greek letters. Reversing it and using Roman letters, we have Nazarenousi. This is a really surprising result. It is not really Greek at all, but the Latin *Nazarenus*.[8] Moreover the E is short (*epsilon* instead of *ēta*), the ending OS is represented by OUS, and in this the diphthong OU is written in an abbreviated combined form. Long ago J. Gretser, S.J. (*De Cruce Christi*, 1600-05) and Père Nicquet (*Titulus S. Crucis*, 1648) showed that these orthographical peculiarities could be paralleled from early inscriptions, coins and vases ; and since then the contraction for the Greek *ou* has been shown to be compatible with a date in the first century :

Ausonius in a celebrated distich regarded the *ou* (obviously contracted as in fig. i. 3) as one letter, not a diphthong.—Ed. H. White (Loeb Library), 1 (1919) 304, 2 (1921) 116. I have consulted an expert paleographer, Dr. Ludwig Bieler of Dublin. He informs me as follows. The *ou*-ligature does not become frequent on Greek monuments before the fifth century A.D. There are, however, occasional instances of it in inscriptions of an informal type as early as the first century. There are instances in the

---

[7] Still repeated, e.g., by H. Lesêtre, *Dict. de la Bible* 5 (1922) 2255. " Calvin had maliciously twitted Catholics with their many churches which claimed to possess the Title of the Cross . . . Some good Catholics, with more faith than common sense, had repeated the evasions of St. Paulinus of Nola and St. Cyril, and maintained that the Title was animated with a recuperative power which could replace anew every fragment torn from it."—Combes, p.189.

[8] The only complete word on the fragment (" Nazarene ") is that recorded by St. John alone.

Greek inscriptions from Pompeii and Herculaneum (destroyed A.D. 79) : C.I.L., (vol. iv), nos. 2725, 2851, 6275, 6436. Thus it is certain that the ligature of *o* and *u* was known as early as the first century of our era, and was used mainly in inscriptions of an informal or occasional character.

These peculiarities have been urged by Gosselin as an argument against the relic being a forgery :

> We can show that the title of the Cross as it exists to-day carries intrinsic proofs of its authenticity. How could we suppose that a forger would have been so stupid as to manufacture the title as we have it to-day : epsilon for eta against the current custom, *ou* for *o*, *Nazarenous* for *Nazoraios* employed by St. John? The improbability of these suppositions eliminates, it seems to us, all suspicions against the authenticity, which moreover is established by respectable testimonies and monuments.—Cited by Rohault de Fleury, p.195.

But the question of language remains. The inscription given by St. John is as follows, with the Greek in Roman letters and with the three definite articles in brackets :

Iēsous [hŏ] Nazōraios [hŏ] Basileus [tōn] Ioudaiōn.

If the inscription was in the Greek language—in spite of using *nazarenous* for *nazoraios*—the final stroke (on the extreme left of the upper line) is the beginning of the letter B, the first letter of *basileus* ; if it is Latin written in Greek letters, it is portion of R, the first letter of *rex*. The first solution—three different languages— seems much more probable.

(7) On top of the fragment we observe five (four large and one small) curved strokes, which look very like the tail-ends of Semitic letters. Our Lord's name in full was *Yĕhōshūa*, commonly abbreviated into *Yēshūa* or *Yēshū*. This abbreviated form is found on an ossuary from Jerusalem of the early imperial period—a namesake and probably a contemporary of Jesus.[9] (Fig. i.5).

In Hebrew " Jesus of Nazareth King of the Jews " would be

Yēshūa' ha-nōtsrī melek yĕhūdīm.

In Aramaic

Yēshūā' nātserāyā malekhōn dī hūdāyē.

[9] Macalister, *A Century of Excavation in Palestine*, 1925, p.252 ; Deissmann in *Mysterium Christi*, ed. Bell and Deissmann, 1930, p.8. The letters from right to left are : yodh (*y*), shin (*sh*), shureq (*ū*), ayin (representing a breathing). The vowels *e* and *a* (written as flat lines underneath) are not inserted.

The five strokes may represent the lower parts of these letters : the two first extremities of *h* or *n*, the third the end of the letter *ts*, the fourth that of *r*, the fifth that of *y* or *i* which was very elongated in ancient writing.

I. 5.—The Name ' Jesus ' in Hebrew or
Aramaic.

These conclusions lend great probability to the inference that this Roman relic of the Title is authentic. Even such a critic as the late Father Thurston writes (p.428) as follows—observe that he invokes no " historical reason " against the genuineness :

> There is absolutely no sound palaeographic or archaeological reason for pronouncing it to be impossible or even unlikely that the fragmentary title now at Santa Croce was written in Jerusalem at the time of the Crucifixion of our Lord.

Father Thurston goes on to say (p.429) :

> It is only the right-hand portion which is now preserved in the basilica of Santa Croce . . . On the other hand the left-hand portion, bearing the words *Rex Judaeorum*, was that which Etheria and the Piacenza pilgrim saw at Jerusalem. We have no evidence that later on it had been taken to Constantinople ; but as we learn from Durandus at the close of the thirteenth century, it was to be seen in the Sainte Chapelle at Paris, whither it had been brought with the Crown of Thorns by St. Louis.

It is a pleasant task, which rarely occurs, to have to accuse Father Thurston of credulity ! There is no evidence as to what words (if any) Etheria read in the title-fragment in Jerusalem. The Piacenza pilgrim, taken literally, says he read the words ' *Jesus Nazarenus Rex Judaeorum* '—which contradicts the evidence of the Roman relic. Neither could Durandus have read the word " Rex," since the letters " Re " are still on the piece in Rome. Here is what Durandus says (*circa* A.D. 1280) :

> I saw in Paris in the Chapel of the illustrious King of the Franks : the tablet or written chart in which Pilate wrote ' *Jesus*

Nazarenus Rex Judaeorum,' together with the crown of thorns, the blade and handle of the lance, the purple robe in which they clad Christ, the shroud in which His body was wrapped, the sponge, the wood of the Cross, one of the nails, and many other relics.— Durand of Mende († 1296), *Rationale divinorum officiorum,* vi. 80 ; cited in Riant, *Exuviae sacrae const.* 2 (1878) 250.

This account must be received with considerable scepticism, especially as he speaks of the Title as a parchment (*charta scripta*) ! The historian Ch. Riant does not admit that any fragment of the Title reached Paris from Jerusalem or from Constantinople :

> Riant attaches little importance to this isolated testimony. Had the Title been given by Baldwin to St. Louis, it would certainly have been mentioned in the chart then drawn up ; or had it been already in Louis's possession, we should have otherwise heard of it. The Title unearthed in 327 was made of wood, for according to Sozomen it was painted white. Evidently the document seen by Durand was simply one of those forgeries, once so frequent, similar to Christ's Letter to Abgar.—Combes, p.197.

A similar judgment must be passed on " the title " once possessed by the church of La Daurade at Toulouse ; it was either a fragment (perhaps completed), or a facsimile.

Apart from its intrinsic interest, this investigation of the Title of the Cross is very apposite to the present-day discussion concerning the Shroud. So let us sum up our results :

(1) The Gospel texts do not decide the exact wording ; they do not even make it certain that three languages were used. They are of course completely silent as to what happened to the Title.

(2) The subsequent three centuries are a complete blank. The Title appears to have been discovered, perhaps in 326 with the Cross, perhaps some time between 335 and 347. The earliest reference to its finding dates from 390. The earliest reference to the Title being in Jerusalem is dated 386 ; and we *infer* that only portion of the Title was there. Any *historical* proof of its authenticity is completely lacking.

(3) The only surviving portion is in Rome. There is no acceptable account of how it reached its present location. There is absolute silence as regards the first hundred years, then one brief reference ; the next date being A.D. 1143.

(4) There are rival claimants—e.g., Paris and Toulouse—to possession of the Title.

(5) The only course left is direct investigation of the Roman relic. This was first reliably made about 1830. The lettering on the enclosing brick is certainly pre-medieval, that on the Title-fragment itself has peculiar characteristics which are archaeologically compatible with genuineness and are improbable as the work of a forger.[10]

[Further Note:—It is difficult to assess the date and the accuracy of the sketch of the Title given on p.23. A practically identical illustration (with *Nazarenus*) is given in Bosio's *Crux Triumphans*, 1617, p.63. The inscription *Yeshua* given on p.27 is taken from Clermont-Ganneau, *Arch. Researches in Pal.* 1 (1899) 437. It is curious that several, besides Fr. Thurston, who reject the Shroud accept the Title. For instance, H. Leclercq: "The original Title is preserved in Rome"—DACL. 7 (1926) 1154.]

---

[10] There are some other embroidered (not painted) cloths similar to that of Cadouin (p.16 above). For example, there is in the treasury of the Church of Apt (France) a relic known as the Veil of St. Anne. It is really a Muhammadan flag containing the name of the Khalif El-Mostali from whom the Crusaders captured Jerusalem in 1099.— Mâle, *L'art religieux du xii. siècle en France*, 1924², p.343.

CHAPTER II

THE MARKS ON THE CLOTH

(1) Folds and Fires

THE MATERIAL of the Turin shroud (4.38 metres long and 1.10 wide) is handwoven unbleached linen.[1] The construction is that of a three-and-one twill,[2] the warp (longitudinal threads) concealing three transverse or weft threads and showing the fourth. The weaving of such a cloth required four pedals. Ancient tissues just as complicated have been found in Pòmpei, Martes-de-Veyre, Mainz, Palmyra ; excavations at Antinoe have revealed cloths of the same breadth but greater in length. There does not appear to be any archaeological objection to a first-century date.[3]

Figure ii. 1 allows us a first glimpse of the marks on the shroud. Those that first strike the eye—two longitudinal dark lines, with enlargements and triangular patches—are entirely irrelevant, being due to an accidental burning. On the night of 3 December 1532 a fire consumed the chapel at Chambéry. The door was broken open, the silver casket containing the shroud was doused with water and carried to safety, but not before damage was done. Figure ii. 2 shows how the shroud was folded : four times along the width and twelve times along the length, so as to form a bundle of 48 thicknesses. A drop of molten silver fell on a corner of the folded shroud and thus caused the symmetrically placed burns which are seen when the shroud is straightened out flat (fig. ii. 3).[4] The intense heat at one edge produced the two carbonised lines (like linen under an overheated iron). This accounts for the two charred lines each with four holes. The white triangular spaces are patches of altar linen sewn on by the Poor Clares in 1534.

[1] See Timossi's book and Vignon ii. 77-83.
[2] The twill does not run straight through, but is formed into a herringbone (chevron) pattern on each 40 threads of warp.
[3] Timossi (p.55) gives a piece of reconstructed cloth. Mr. J. P. Twohig, President of the Woollen and Worsted Manufacturers of Ireland, kindly made for me some rough measurements from this specimen. He estimates the weight as 234 grams per sq. metre (Timossi says 240). The linen count (length/weight) in the English system is estimated to be 50s for the warp yarn and 30s for the weft yarn.
[4] This can be practically illustrated by taking a long slip of paper, folding it a number of times longitudinally and transversely, and snipping off one corner of the bundle. When opened out, the paper will have a number of symmetrically placed holes.

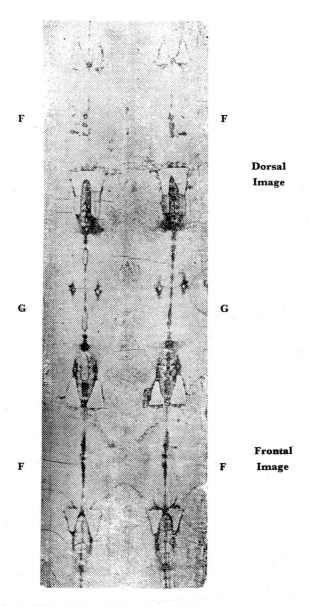

II. 1.—The marks on the Shroud

There is also a row of six relatively paler lozenges with serrated edges, with half-lozenges along the sides. These are shown by dotted lines in the diagram of fig. ii. 3 ; they can be clearly seen in fig. ii. 5.

These are stains made by the water used in extinguishing the fire, the rest of the cloth remaining dry. Hynek (iii. 3) seems to be incorrect in taking them to be the dry spots in a saturated cloth.

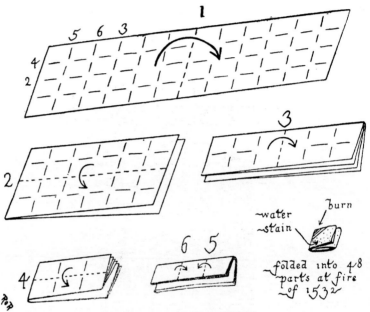

II. 2.—How the Shroud was folded in 1532

These considerations dispense us from being further distracted by the most obvious marks on the shroud, which also happen to be purely accidental and irrelevant. It is in the image between these lines of charring that we are interested. Providentially this image is practically intact inside these parallel burns which form a kind of frame for it.

There are also some fainter marks caused by an earlier fire when the cloth was folded differently. These are fortunately shown in a copy made in 1516 by Dürer, now in Lierre (Belgium). This was reproduced by Canon Thiéry in 1905, and is exhibited in fig. ii. 4. In the frontal portion can be seen two sets of four dots which are mirror-images ; there is a similar phenomenon on the dorsal half of the shroud. These can be discerned in the shroud to-day ; see the portion marked F on fig. ii. 1 (or better on fig. ii.5). The black dots on the dorsal portion are still clearly visible ; those on the frontal part can also be seen on the carbonised lines of 1532. The 1516 painter (Dürer), thinking they were bloodstains, made them red. In this case the fire was sudden and localised, for the burns are sharp and without a brown halo. From their grouping we infer **that on that** occasion the cloth was folded into only 12 parts.

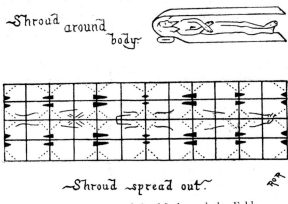

II. 3.—Diagram of the Marks and the Folds

(2) The Double Human Figure

The real interest of the shroud lies in the double human figure, front and back, which can be clearly seen in fig. ii. 5. As the impression must have been made—so we shall see later—partly by direct contact and partly by some influence from the body immediately on to the cloth, the right and left sides of the body are the opposite of what we find in a painting or in a photograph. This is easily understood by the reader imagining himself facing the paper ; or in the case of the dorsal image, with his back to it.

Let us begin with the frontal image (the lower half of the illustration). It is generally held that the head was slightly elevated on a cushion or block (as represented in fig. ii. 3).[1] Below the beard

[1] There is a space (G in fig. ii. 1 or D in fig. ii. 5) between the front and back impressions of the head : " A chin-cloth must have been tied at the top of the head for the image and the blood-imprint vanish here, the facial and dorsal silhouette, being clearly separated. There is there only one of the large stains left by the water used in putting out the fire."—Cordonnier, p.22.

there is no mark of the neck; the cloth resumes contact only at the breast ; the sternum and the navel can be discerned. The trace of the arms has disappeared in the fire, but the forearms are visible, with the left hand over the right.[2]

The wound on the right side can be seen as a dark stain at the side of the white triangular patch. The right side of the breast seems broader than the left and the right arm too long. Here is the explanation given by Legrand (p.23). The side-wound so far from the body-axis would not appear at all if the cloth had remained stretched taut, supported by the forearms. A hand however applied the shroud gently against the wound. The breast was thus more enveloped on this side ; and small folds still visible were formed on the right forearm. When the part of the shroud between breast and biceps was straightened out (as it is now), it displaced the image of the forearm outwards and downwards (as shown in fig. ii. 6).

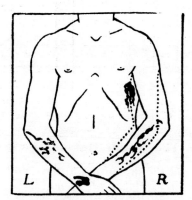

II. 6.—Explanation of the Displacement of the Image of the Right Arm. (The dotted line shows the correct position).   *Legrand.*

The frontal image lacks any impression of the ends of the legs and of the feet.[3] This is apparently due to the fact that the dorsal end of the cloth was turned up over the front of the feet. But this portion is now missing (i.e. from the top of fig. ii. 5). Presumably

---

[2] In the region of the right forearm, and also on the abdomen, there are transverse stripes, alternately dark and pale. (These can be seen more clearly in fig. x.i). These are due to small folds which were on the shroud.

[3] There is a large dark bloodstain which seems situated nowhere ; at the left extremity there is a small mark, surrounded by a paler circle, which seems to indicate the entry-wound of the nail on the left foot.

it was distributed as relics. Also it can be seen from the illustration that a longitudinal strip (nearly 3 inches wide) had once been cut from the left side (along AB) and sewn on again, after two pieces— $14\frac{1}{2}$ inches long at A, 6 inches long at B—had been cut off and replaced by a different cloth.

Turning to the dorsal image, we observe that the back of the neck and the shoulders are clearly indicated ; this was probably due to the cushion already referred to. The numerous marks of the scourging merge at the top, at the shoulders, into a large bruise ; it would seem that lymph has oozed from the compression of fresh wounds. The right shoulder is slightly lower than the left.[4] The thighs seem narrower on the dorsal than on the frontal image ; this is due to the fact that the cloth in its upper portion enveloped the members, while it was flat underneath. The left leg has had less contact with the cloth than the right ; only the right sole has left a complete impression.

Let us now, following Gedda, see how the height of the Man in the Shroud has been estimated. The only life-size photo taken by Enrie in 1931 was of the face. The axial distance of the two transverse lines caused by folds (see fig. vii. 70) was measured 23.4 cm.). From this the scale of the photographs of the full figure can be determined. The dorsal image,[5] on which the axial line is quite visible, was selected for estimation of the height, which was found (from the top of the head to the heel) to be 188 cm. (6.17 feet).[6] Two corrections must be applied to this : (1) Textile experts estimate that in course of time there was an extension of the material of about 2 cm. (2) Owing to the undulation of the spine for the purpose of support, the stature of a person standing is about 3 cm. less than when he is lying down. Subtracting 5 from 188 cm., we obtain

[4] One explanation is that the right foot was flat against the cross, hence the right knee is slightly higher than the left. This flexion caused a lowering of the right hip which cannot be verified as the cloth was kept at a distance by the forearms. Another explanation is that the right shoulder bore the weight of the cross. But Dr. Gedda (p.16) points out that, as is well known to tailors, this relative lowering of the right shoulder exists in all right-handed people owing to the laterally diverse development of the muscles. See pp.135, 200.

[5] On the posterior image the cloth was not modelled over the body, and it was sufficiently stretched to avoid folds. The traction was from above, as is shown by the distances between the two images of the head, probably there was a chin-cloth passing over the head ; similarly at the feet, the shroud was folded up over the legs.

[6] Gedda was able to make a direct measurement (though without precise instruments) on the shroud when it was at Montevergine in 1946. He obtained 187/8 cm., thus confirming his previous result.

183 cm. (6.00 feet) as approximately the man's height.[7] Other anthropometric indices have also been estimated.[8] The various proportions have been found to be normal; the anatomical conformation is perfect.[9]

(3) The Poor Clares (1534)

In 1534 the shroud was officially examined and the damages made by the fire two years previously were repaired with patches by the Poor Clares of Chambéry. From a nun who was an eyewitness we have an account of the precautions taken and of the repairs effected, together with some interesting observations on the relic.[1] A brief was issued from Rome on 23 April 1533, instructing the Cardinal Legate to investigate the cloth and if necessary to make repairs, to reassure those " who perhaps think that the cloth was entirely destroyed in the fire."[2] Rabelais in fact had asserted that not a scrap had remained ; and Geneva was delighted at the rumour.[3] The Legate asked the counts and barons if the shroud was the same as the one they had seen before the fire. " These, after having carefully examined it on one side and on the other,

[7] It is interesting to observe that the same result (6 ft.) is obtained (1) from a curious monument in the cloister of the Basilica of St. John (Lateran), four columns supporting a platform to indicate Christ's height ; and (2) from an eighteenth century ribbon made to record the height from the Shroud.—Gedda, p.13. Some other estimates of the man's height (in cm.) are : Barbet (i. 26) 178 ; Vignon (ii. 85) 175 to 180 ; Judica-Cordiglia (i. 74) 181, he obtained 184 on the Shroud. Previous estimates were Chifflet (in 1624) 187 and Paleotti (in 1606) 180 : Quaresmius, p.402 ; Rohault de Fleury, p.249. About the year 670 Arculf made a careful measurement of the sepulchral slab of the Holy Sepulchre ; his result expressed in cm. is 207 (7 feet).—Francez, p.46. This is precisely what it is to-day.—Vincent-Abel, Jérusalem Nouvelle, p.221. It may be relevant to observe that the height of Pius XII is 182 cm.

[8] Gedda (p.15) estimates : ratio of trunk-length to transverse diameter of thorax 1.9, ratio of length of limbs to that of trunk 2.5. Judica Cordiglia, taking the stature in the vertical position to be 181 cm., says (i.73f) that this is 8 times the length of the head. By means of certain empirical rules, he estimates the cranial index to be 80, and the cranial capacity at 1571 c.c. (pp.77, 79).

[9] Père Gaffre (p.33) reproduces from a manuscript (Pluteo xxv.3) in the Laurentian Library, Florence (written 1300–1350) a figure of Christ with a line 15 cm. long. It has (in Latin) the following inscription : " This line multiplied twelve times gives the height of the Lord's body. It was taken from Constantinople from the holy gold cross with Christ's figure." This gives 180 cm. Was this the figure of Christ erected by Constantine and destroyed by Leo Isaurian in 727?

[1] This was published by Canon L. Bouchage, Le saint-suaire de Chambéry, 1891 ; then by Chevalier iii. 46-52. I quote this latter.

[2] Chevalier, iii. 45. Rabelais, Hist. de Gargantua, i. 27.

[3] A. C. Coppier, in Mercure de France, 1 June 1938 ; summary in Revue apol. 67 (1938) 439. According to Coppier, Duke Charles faked a new relic to replace the allegedly destroyed shroud, Sodoma reconstituted the figure, and the Papal Legate authenticated it! See refutation by Viale in SS, p.167.

testified that it was the same." A number of prelates and ecclesias-
tics gave similar testimony. It was left a fortnight in a frame to be
repaired by a selected sworn group of nuns. It was they who
affixed the white patches[4] which we see in fig. ii. 5. During the
repairs which lasted fifteen days, four guards held lighted tapers
before the relic, and the grill was frequently opened to allow people
to view it. The nuns had a unique opportunity of viewing the
shroud, and their description is worth quoting.

We gazed repeatedly on all the bloody wounds of His sacred
body, of which vestiges appeared on this holy shroud... We saw
on it still the traces of a face ravaged and bruised by blows, His
divine head pierced with large thorns whence came blood-
trickles which flowed over His forehead and divided into branches,
decking Him in the most precious purple in the world. We
remarked on the left side of the forehead one drop larger and
longer than the others, undulating like a wave. The eyebrows
seemed well formed, the eyes somewhat less. The nose, being the
most prominent part of the face, is well imprinted. The mouth is
well formed, it is rather small. The swollen and disfigured cheeks
show that they were cruelly struck, especially the right. The beard
is neither too long nor too short, in the manner of the Nazareans.
In one place it is sparse, because it had been partly plucked in
derision, and the blood had glued the rest.

Then we saw a long trace descending on the neck. This led us
to believe that He was bound with an iron chain when He was
taken in the Garden of Olives ; for it is seen to be swollen in
several places as if it had been pulled and shaken. The furrows
and whip-blows are so frequent on the stomach and the breast
that one can scarcely find a place as big as a pinpoint free from
blows. They are interlaced and extend all along the body as far
as the soles of the feet. A great heap of blood marks the openings
in the feet.

The left hand is well marked and is crossed upon the right whose
wound it covers. The openings of the nails are in the middle of
the hands,[4a] long and beautiful, whence there meanders a blood-
trickle from the sides to the shoulders. The arms, which are
rather long and beautiful, are in such a position that they allow
a full view of the abdomen cruelly torn by whip-blows. The
wound of the divine side appears to have a breadth sufficient to
admit three fingers. It is surrounded with a blood-trace four
fingers broad, narrowing below, and about half a foot long.

[4] If we look at the second group of patches (C) from the top of the illustrations (ii.5) we
can see below them the remains of apparently older patches, slightly darker and sewn
rather differently. There must have been some previous damage. Note, in addition to
the earlier fire already mentioned, the two pairs of marks (at D) between the front and
back images of the head.
[4a] The nail-mark is really shown in the left wrist.

On the second face of the holy shroud, representing the back of our Saviour's body, one sees the back of the head pierced by big long thorns. These are so numerous that one sees from them that the Crown was made like a hat and not in circlets as are those of princes and as painters represent it. On attentively considering the back of the head, one sees that it is more wounded than the rest and that the thorns penetrated more deeply there where there are large drops of blood glued to the hair . . . The shoulders are quite torn and bruised with the whip-blows which extend everywhere . . . On the middle of the body one observes the vestiges of the iron chain which bound Him so tightly to the column that it appears all bloody. The diversity of the blows shows that there were employed different kinds of whips, such as rods bound with osiers, and iron wires. These tore Him so cruelly that on looking beneath the shroud, when it was stretched on the cambric sheet, we see the wounds as if we had looked through a glass.

There are a few false inferences in this account, such as the reference to the alleged chain (see p.342). But on the whole it is accurate. With our modern photographs we can appreciate in the description the large undulating trickle on the left side of the forehead, the bruised cheeks (especially the right), the position of the hands with only the left nail-wound visible, the flow from the side-wound, the probable shape of the crown of thorns. It will be noticed that the nuns used the terms right and left to designate these respective sides of the body. This was natural to those who were closely observing the shroud for a fortnight and who thought that all the marks were due to direct bloodstains from the enclosed body. Obviously they could not have considered it as the painted portrait of a man facing the observer.

After the operation the shroud was " folded on a roller with a veil of red silk." The shroud itself appears to have been tacked or sewn on to cambric tissue (*toille d'Holande*).[5] The curious assertion has been made that the nuns made a mistake: they described the back of the shroud and then they lined it with the wrong side out. This allegation was invented as one of the numerous subterfuges adopted to escape the implications of the 1898 photograph (which will be presently considered). Chevalier, who like many historians

[5] This was done at the beginning (Chevalier, p.47. Apparently this cloth was then removed and the shroud covered with violet taffeta. In 1694 Bl. Sebastian Valfré relined the Shroud; in 1868 Princess Clotilda of Savoy renovated the lining. At present the back of the shroud is covered with a fine white cloth, sewn on all along the length, with a blue border containing metal plates (probably to obtain extension when the shroud is held by the upper edge) ; the red silk is not sewn on.—Tonelli, p.61.

was very credulous in scientific matters, was misled by an amateur photographer,[6] who, in addition to vague hints at the faking of the photo, suggested that the nuns exposed the wrong side of the " painting."

Now the nuns certainly left exposed the same side as is represented in Dürer's painting (fig. ii. 4), which in a Latin and German inscription is dated 1516. In this the side-wound is on the right of the body, also the left hand is crossed over the right as the nuns declared. The sisters must have had some definite reason for taking this to be the correct surface of the cloth, especially as it was examined on both sides. Probably the imprints are much fainter on the reverse surface. It is incorrect to interpret their statements to mean that the cloth, or rather the figure on it, is transparent. What they said (as quoted above) is that the wounds (the bloodstains) are visible on both sides. A phenomenon which one can verify by examining a drop of blood on a handkerchief. What the inventors of this alleged mistake really meant was not that the same image is to be seen on both sides of the cloth, but that on the lined underside there is what in modern photographic parlance is called the negative of the visible impression (at least in so far as this does not contain direct bloodstains). There are very strong arguments against this gratuitous supposition. For we are asked to believe that striking portrait of the face now discernible in the photographic negative is plainly visible on the underside of the cloth. This assumption involves two rather incredible consequences. A French artist of the 14th century directly produced this portrait so utterly beyond the iconography of the time. And all those who in 1534 inspected both sides of the shroud, including the Poor Clare who wrote the account, having once glimpsed this wonderful portrait, hastily hid in with lining, told us not a word about their vision, and exposed for subsequent veneration the rather crude face-tracing now visible. These reasons seem to me decisive against any expectation that the problem of the shroud will be elucidated by inspecting its reverse side. Nevertheless, it is most desirable that, without injuring the fabric, the underside should be investigated.

[6] H. Chopin, *Le saint suaire de Turin photographié à l'envers*, 1902 ; Chevalier i. 50-55, Opponents used formerly to rely on the egregious Chopin, e.g. Donnadieu (p.26). Gaffre (p.118). One is surprised to find this hypothesis revived by Père Braun (p.65f), although he concedes that the image is not a painting. Chopin also invented the different hypothesis that the positive image on the upper side turned into a negative.

(4) **Descriptions and Copies**

In 1502 the Duke of Savoy (Philibert II) took the shroud to
Bourg-en-Bresse to show it to his brother-in-law Philip Archduke of
Austria. The chronicler Antoine Lalaing who was present, has left
us the following description :[1]

> It is the precious sindon and noble shroud bought by Joseph
> of Arimathea, 16 to 17 feet long, about 7 feet broad . . . One
> sees it clearly stained by the most precious blood of Jesus our
> Redeemer, as if the thing had been done to-day. One sees on it
> the impression of all His holy body : head, face, mouth, eyes,
> nose, body, hands, feet, and His five wounds, especially that of
> the side, about a good half-foot long and strongly stained. And
> on the other side—as He was covered over and under by the
> shroud—one sees the imprint of His back, head, hair, crown and
> shoulders.

There is a similar description of the appearance of the shroud in
1449.[2] Concerning these Fr. Thurston wrote (v.55) : " While the
witnesses of the 15th or early 16th centuries speak of the image as
being then so vivid that the blood seemed freshly shed, it is now
darkened and hardly recognisable without minute attention." I
confess to having grave doubts concerning any such degeneration
of the image. Certain historians are inclined to give too ready
credence to people who, while not exactly liars, may be misled by
bias or imagination and are often incapable of scientific observation
—simply because they happened to have written down their views
a few centuries ago. Lalaing was certainly wrong about the dimensions of the shroud, he did not see the *five* wounds and the feet on it.
Why should we believe him when he says that the wounds might
have been imprinted that very day ?[3]

I am still more sceptical concerning the following statement of
Lalaing :

---

[1] *Collection de voyages des souverains des Pays-Bas*, ed. Gachard, 1 (1876) 285 ;
Chevalier, i. p. xlvi (document DD) ; Loth, pp.15, 21.
[2] By the chronicler Cornelius Zantfliet on the occasion of its being exhibited at
Chimay (Chev. i. 10) : " A certain cloth in which, excellently and with wonderful
artifice, there had been pictured the form of the body of our Lord Jesus Christ
with all the lineaments of each member; as if from recent wounds and stigmata
of Christ, feet, hands and side were seen stained blood-red."
[3] Says Pére Noguier de Malijay (p.50) : " There have always been people who
see much more with their imagination than with their eyes." In 1898 he heard a
preacher in Turin using the same exaggerated language as Lalaing in 1503 !

To prove whether it is the same, it was boiled in oil, put into [or on?] the fire (*bouté en feu*),[4] washed and rinsed (*buet*) several times. But the aforesaid impression and figure could not be effaced or removed.

Lalaing may have been told this tall story by some enthusiastic devotee ; it is hard to believe that he was writing as an eye-witness. But people like Fr. Thurston cannot have it both ways. If they accept the chronicler's evidence on one point, they must also welcome his testimony on the other, i.e. that the shroud has survived with its imprints intact after being several times boiled in oil, scorched with fire and vigorously washed as in a laundry. If that be so, then there can be no question of a painting. In fact, the experiment looks like a miracle. But can we really believe that a venerated relic was actually treated so drastically and ignominiously?

At any rate, the 1516 painting (fig. ii. 4) shows us the image as it is to-day. But through faulty observation and interpretation the artist has made many mistakes. The eyes are open, the face is a crude positive drawing, the neck is shown, the hair falls in plaits down the back. Both hand-wounds are visible, also the front of both feet with all the toes. There are no scourge-marks. And so on.

Figure ii. 7 shows portion of a brown monochrome water-colour on cloth, probably of the 16th century, in Notre-Dame de Chambéry. Observe the sharp contours of the body, the fine lines all over the body (made under the idea that the image was formed by liquid blood), the loincloth,[5] the right hand crossed over the left, the complete frontal representation of the feet. Figure ii. 8 gives Chifflet's reproduction of the frontal image on the Turin shroud.[6] This has the same defects in a more exaggerated form.

Figure ii. 9 reproduces a picture in the Pinacoteca, Turin, which has been attributed to Giulio Clovio (1498-1578) a pupil of Raphael.[7] The image on the shroud is like those just given. Below this is a representation of the dead Christ in the shroud at the foot of the Cross. In the image above the left hand is correctly over the right ; whereas underneath Our Lord has His right hand over the left, also He wears a loin cloth. (Note that the wound is located in the wrist).

[4] Beecher (p.153) says that *bouté en feu* means " boiled after the manner of soiled linen that is being washed." *Bouter = pousser, heurter. Buet* from *buer = laver, nettoyer.*
[5] Chifflet (Ugolino p.930), with Salmeron, saw traces of a loin-cloth in the Turin shroud (but not in that of Besançon). Others denied this (Quaresmius, p.406).
[6] Chifflet, p.198 (in Ugolino, p.931) ; Quaresmius, p.404 ; Vignon, i.65.
[7] It is probably by the 17th century artist G. B. della Rovere.

Finally let us read the description written by Mgr. Jeancart, bishop of Cérame, who saw the shroud when it was exhibited in Turin in 1842 :

> It is a piece of cloth about four metres long, made of linen, somewhat yellowed by age and streaked like dimity. Large spots, some of which certainly indicate the place of the head, can be attributed only to the divine blood with which this holy shroud was stained. Age has made in the tissue imperceptible holes of which some have been repaired by the princesses.— Rohault de Fleury, p.243.

Obviously the good prelate discerned only a series of crude stains on the cloth.[8]

(5) The Besançon Cloth

In 1204 the Crusaders sacked Constantinople. The shrine of St. Mary of Blachernae was officially guarded to prevent indiscriminate looting. Garnier de Trained, bishop of Troyes, who accompanied the expedition, had the authority and the duty of preserving the relics. He sent a number to Europe, but the shroud was not included. He died in Constantinople in 1205. His subordinates were chiefly from Champagne ; at least one of them, Otho de la Roche, was related to Geoffrey de Charny. Though there is no proof, it is likely that the Lirey shroud came in some unofficial way from looted Constantinople.

It has been suggested that Otho stole the shroud and about 1208 entrusted it to the Bishop of Besançon, where it remained till the Cathedral was burnt in 1349. About four years later a crudely painted image was given to Besançon, while the true shroud— rescued from the fire—passed to Lirey. There are, however, serious difficulties in this story. There is no trace of any protest or claim on behalf of the Besançon clergy. The Lirey shroud was much larger, containing both frontal and dorsal images ; the Besançon

---

[8] In the volume *L'ostensione della S. Sindone* (Turin 1931) a large number of reproductions are illustrated. Practically all of them have a loin-cloth, a large number exhibit the right hand over the left, in several both wrist-wounds are shown. Plate 73, from the prayerbook of Marguerite of Valois, reproduces a miniature of Christopher Duch. The date 1559 is given and it is called " the oldest picture of an exposition of the Shroud, made probably in the Chapel of Chambéry." There is a loin-cloth and the right hand is over the left. But—like fig. ii. 4 but less correctly—it contains only the few marks of the previous fire. Was it made, or based on a picture made, before 1532?

copy, containing only the frontal image, could hardly be mistaken for the original. Above all, there is no record that there was any shroud at all in Besançon prior to the fire of 1349. All the old inventories are silent ; the first assertion of its presence is dated 1523.

Besides the Lirey-Turin shroud, there are only three others with figures on the cloth. Two of them are still extant at Silos (Spain) and at Xabregas (Portugal) ; both are now admitted to be copies of that in Turin. The same was almost certainly true also of the Besançon shroud which was burnt in 1794 by the Committee of Public Safety.[1]

II. 10.—Woodcut of the Besançon Shroud (17th cent.)

So we have to rely for our knowledge on woodcuts and impressions on silk. Figure ii. 10 (from Vignon i. 70) reproduces a 17th century engraving. Fig. ii. 11 is from a sepia drawing on linen preserved in the library at Besançon ; it was made in the 16th century by Pierre Dargent. Fig. ii. 12 is another copy. We cannot of course be sure how far these rather hideous and disproportioned Gothic figures reproduce the image which was on the Besançon shroud. Such as they are they indicate that the image was a crude painting of the figure on the Lirey-Turin shroud.[2]

[1] Fr. Thurston (v. 62) regretted that a similar fate did not overtake the Turin shroud : " If the Turin shroud had been before them, they would have arrived at the same conclusion and—so far as any evidence is known to me—they would have been equally justified in so deciding." Gaffre (p.118) quotes from the *Moniteur* (xx. 557) Vau's report to the Convention : " You are being sent not only this figured cloth of modern workmanship, but also the transfer-design or moulded model (*le poncis ou le moule découpé*) which was used every year to renew the imprint whose miraculous preservation caused wonder." Well, no such renovating process has been applied to the Turin Shroud !
[2] According to Chifflet (in Ugolino, p.924) the height of the figure was the same (5¾ ft.) as that in Turin. Another authority (Dunot in Rohault de Fleury, p.308) says that the body was painted in pale yellow and was equally visible on both sides ; the hands were crossed so that both hand-wounds were plainly visible.

CHAPTER III

NOT A PAINTING

(1) **The Stains**

THE STAINS marking the figure on the shroud can be divided into two classes, which it is proposed to distinguish by names which provisionally imply that they have been made by a wounded dead man. (a) Transfers: hematic rose-coloured stains caused by wounds. (b) Imprints: somatic sepia-coloured stains produced by the skin and hair. Only those who have had the opportunity of closely studying the original shroud have been able to distinguish the colours.[1]

As regards the transfer-stains, there is no means of discriminating between venous and arterial blood; but we can distinguish between living and dead. On the shroud (fig. ii. 5) we can see blood which, through heart-action in life, flowed from wounds, e.g., on the forehead and back of the head, on the left wrist and on the forearms, on the sole of the right foot. These stains have definite contours and result from blood which clotted on the living body.[2] Post-mortem bloodstains also occur, especially in the sidewound where we see blood, dark and thick, which dripped and spread merely through gravity. The margins of these stains are indistinct and surrounded by a serous halo. This blood, already dry, was subsequently

---

[1] Dr. Barbet (i. 36) was able, at less than a yard to examine the shroud (without glass) in daylight: " I saw, without expecting it, that all the images of the wounds had a colour clearly different from that of the rest of the body ; and this colour was that of dried blood which had impregnated the material. There was then no question (as for the remainder) of emanations which had darkened the aloes of the shroud and reproduced the relief of the cadaver. The blood itself had tinted the cloth by direct contact ; that is why the images of the wounds are positive while all the rest is negative." Dr. Gedda had a still better opportunity on 28 Oct. 1946 at Montevergine and confirmed the difference in colour. See his article in the periodical *Tabor*, January 1947.

[2] Coagulation or clotting is not yet fully understood ; its object is to stop bleeding and so to prevent fatal haemorrhage. It is greatly accelerated by contact with tissues (e.g. on wounded surfaces) or with foreign bodies ; it is not due to contact with air or to stoppage of circulation. The clot separates into two portions : (1) serum which is a clear liquid slightly straw-coloured, and (2) a solid contracted clot consisting of the corpuscles plus some serum plus an insoluble protein called fibrin. (The term *plasma* should be kept for the blood minus the corpuscles, i.e. the liquid part *before* coagulation).

redissolved, but it did not take a new direction when the body was placed in a horizontal position.[3]

If this explanation be correct, then we are faced with the mysterious result that the solid deposits on the shroud are still intact, whereas we should expect that the dry blood would easily scale off, especially from a cloth handled so much. Vignon (ii. 22) effected the transfer of dried bloodstains from bristol board on to linen compresses soaked in a solution of ammonium carbonate. Great care had to be taken to await the correct amount of redissolution of the blood (caused by the ammoniacal vapours) and to detach the cloth slowly. The cloth was then turned and spread out to allow the blood to dry ; yet in less than three years the stains showed scaling and cracking. We cannot see how a human hand could have removed the long sheet about the body without disturbing these transfers ; nor can we explain their continued survival.

The body itself, apart from these special wounds, is figured on the shroud by what we have called imprints. The prominent parts of the body are imprinted in a rusty-brown colour: hair, nose, moustache and beard, lips, shoulders, forearms and hands, thighs and knees. The imprint of the back is differentiated so as to reveal the scourge-marks.[4] The appearance of relief is based on a gradation of the imprints, which decrease in intensity as the distance from the shroud increases. The parts of the body distant a few millimetres from the cloth are without any trace. There are no imprints of the sunken parts of the body: eyesockets, furrows between nose and cheeks, opening between the lips, neck, clavicle, upper part of the chest, sides of the abdomen, on the dorsal figure the popliteal fossae and the lower part of the left leg.

When viewed in diffuse light so that the threads do not cast shadows, the browning is observed not to lie on the surface but to impregnate each thread. In a magnified photo, the general flow is accentuated and the contours disappear. The brightest (yellowish white) portions of the cloth merely show the natural colour of the linen. That they have no trace of colouring matter is clearly shown on photographic enlargements.[5]

[3] When bleeding occurs during life it saturates clothes, etc., with a homogeneous colour, pale rose to red and subsequently dark brown. Postmortal blood coagulates on the cloth, with a dark clot surrounded by a larger lighter stain with serrated edges.—Hynek i. 110, ii. 144. This serous condition can be observed on the shroud, especially on the right sole and on the small of the back. These are not transfer-stains but are due to blood flowing on the cloth after death.
[4] These are presumably due to small transfers from the numerous ecchymoses.
[5] " Aniline pigments, dissolved in a volatile essence, are an invention of the last century. In the Middle Ages they used only the tempera : a mixture of albumen or glue and pigments."—Hynek i. 119.

(2) The Photographic Negative

Fifty years ago an amateur photographer took the most famous picture ever taken. After much diplomacy, Secondo Pia secured permission to photograph the shroud which had not been exhibited for thirty years. The shroud was under glass and it was exposed at six yards' height, so a scaffolding was erected. In spite of these difficulties the result was surprising. When Pia was developing the plate,[1] he suddenly saw realistic features of a face emerging on the negative, which he almost let fall in his excitement. Until then the markings on the shroud had been taken as a crude drawing of a human figure. The only detailed inspection undertaken had been that made by the Poor Clares of Chambéry in 1534 ; but even they misinterpreted the mode of reproduction and failed to see the full implications. But after 1898 a photographic facsimile replaced the inaccurate sketches hitherto prevalent and allowed a leisurely scientific examination of the imprinted figure. And from 1931 the splendid official photographs of Giuseppe Enrie have been available.[2] So for the first time in centuries the shroud can be subjected to accurate investigation.

But it was Pia's negative of the face which excited world-wide interest. Until then no one had—or could have had—the slightest suspicion that the real features of the Man in the Shroud were hidden in the apparently ugly face depicted and could be extracted therefrom were there available a physical process for reversing light and shade. We are nowadays so accustomed to photography that we may fail to grasp the extraordinary nature of this discovery.

It was only in the nineteenth century that the very idea of a " negative " came into existence.[3] The physical method of obtaining

---

[1] He used ferrous oxalate, which makes the image come out almost at once. Pia's plate was 60 cm. (slightly less than 2 ft.) long, i.e. his photo was about one-sixth natural size. Here is a contemporary notice : " As the plate was developed, something quite unexpected was observed to appear. It was the perfect and complete portrait of the holy face, hands and members which came to light . . . So the shroud was itself an exact negative, apparently undecipherable, of the blood-stained body which had been placed in it."—*Oss. Rom.* 14 June 1898 ; Loth, p.27.

[2] For a really scientific investigation, there would be necessary further procedures which have hitherto not been allowed lest the fabric should be damaged : Examination of both sides of the shroud, life-size photographs section by section, the use of infra-red light (which has revealed stains in the Tunic at Argenteuil). But as Vignon suggested, even this would not be decisive ; for a ' faker ' might have worked with real blood and with aloes and myrrh !—M. de Iriarte i. 7, ii. 209.

[3] The earliest quotation of the use of the word " negative " (in the photographic sense) which the Oxford English Dictionary gives is dated 1853.

a negative, and then a positive therefrom, is of quite recent origin.[4] The blackening effect of light on silver salts was known to the alchemists and further studied in the 18th century by Schulze and Scheele. By contact with paintings on glass, Wedgwood (✝1805) made shadow-negatives on paper or leather impregnated with a silver salt. Herschel (✝1871), inventor of the word ' photograph,' discovered the fixing properties of sodium thiosulphate, commonly but incorrectly called hyposulphite ; this was in 1819 but he did not utilise the result until twenty years later. If permanency is taken as the criterion, the first photographs were produced in 1827 by Niépce (✝1833) ; they depended on the action of light in reducing the oil solubility of a preparation of asphalt and lavender oil spread upon a plate of silver or glass. Daguerre (✝1851), who entered into partnership with Niépce and the latter's son, used a different process (daguerrotype) in which the silver-coated plate was polished, fumed with iodine, exposed, developed and fixed in hot brine ; his formula was released to the public in 1839. W. H. Fox Talbot (✝1877) published his process in 1835 : a crude method of preservation by bathing the paper in common salt or potassium iodide. By contact with the wax-treated paper negative, Talbot was able to make any number of positives ; he also made the first lens-photograph. In 1851 F. Scott Archer invented or perfected the wet plate (a glass plate coated with collodion holding silver nitrate). The wet plate, which had to be prepared immediately before use, was in 1871 replaced by the gelatine dry plate introduced by R. L. Maddox (✝1902). In 1888 George Eastman first put cheap box cameras (with a roll of sensitised film) into mass production.[5]

Figure iii. 1 reproduces a signed photograph of Pius X, and fig. iii. 2 shows the negative. The relations of light and shade, and the lateral inversion, can be seen at once by comparing the two illustrations. Figure iii. 5 is Enrie's photographic negative of the shroud. (This should be compared with fig. ii. 1, the positive which represents the shroud as it appears to the eye). It will be noticed that the lines of carbonisation now appear white and the linen patches are black, as is also the cloth background. All the transfer-

[4] See J. E. Mack and M. J. Martin, *The Photographic Process*, New York, 1939.
[5] How are negatives (such as fig. iii. 5) reproduced? (1) First a negative is obtained in the ordinary way. (2) From this a positive proof is obtained on a sensitised glass plate instead of on paper. (3) This diapositive is next employed (as if it were an ordinary negative) to obtain copies on paper with the chiaroscuro reversed, i.e. so as to give a negative of the original.

stains of the wounds also appear white. The chief interest of the negative lies in the face, which is shown separately in fig. iii. 7 (and better in fig. vii. 71). Here we can distinguish the two types of stains. First there are direct bloodstains : a few deep incisions made by the crown of thorns are seen on the forehead, there are also blood-trickles on the hair which frames the face. On the shroud these are rose-coloured, in the negative they are white. The remaining impressions, which we have called imprints, are due to some chemical action of the dead body on the cloth. On the shroud they are brown, the colour being the more intense the closer the contact. This gradation of chiaroscuro is reversed in the negative ; and from this reversal there results a realistic portrait of the Man in the Shroud. This portrait was taken, not by photography but by what we can call chemography, just as a zinc-coated object is found to affect a sensitive plate in the dark.[6] Thus—apart from transfer-stains—the face as seen on the shroud (our photographic positive) is really a *chemographic negative*. From this, by the modern process called photography, we can construct an image with light and shade reversed. This image (which we call a photographic negative) is really a *chemograph* of the face, a real portrait though not a photo-graph. It is only by means of this comparatively new technique that we have succeeded in extracting or resurrecting the man's real features from the shroud.

Not until this inversion was effected (first in 1898) was it possible to interpret the markings properly, or indeed to locate the mouth or the eyebrows correctly. Looking at figure iii. 6, we naturally take the dark line beneath the nose as the mouth ; but we see from fig. iii. 7 that it is really the moustache. Similarly a shadow be-neath this " mouth " turns out to be the lower lip. The real mouth is indeed admirably marked in the chemograph ; we infer with some astonishment that its impression is due to a lack of contact with the cloth between the moustache and the lower lip. The chemograph—which can best be studied by holding figure vii. 71 at a little distance—is not unlike a photograph obtained with light coming from the right (the reader's left).[7] There is no deformation

[6] Terquem (p.21) describes a simple experiment for obtaining an impression by chemical means without the action of light. A hard-boiled egg, freshly shelled, is placed on—or with a knitting needle held close to—a silver plate, lightly heated so as to avoid condensation of water-vapour. After some time there is a graded image, darkest where the egg is closest and fading gradually. The plate serves as a sensitive surface for the feeble sulphurous emanations emitted by the egg.

[7] This seems to be due to the relatively greater swelling of the right cheek caused by injuries.

such as would ordinarily result from a cloth placed over an oval-shaped surface and then straightened out flat. We have the effect of an orthogonal projection on a plane surface. This is due to the fact that providentially the cloth was supported at each side of the head—on the matted hair and probably on rolls of cloth—so that it was stretched like a screen above the face. Only the end of the nose was lightly enveloped and this appears enlarged. It is marvellous how the eyes, nose and lips are marked. Instead of the graded discoloration obeying the laws of distance—such as characterises these chemical imprints—we observe " gaps " under the eyes and at the sides of the nose. It may be suggested that this is caused by the path of tears which have flown down along the nose into the moustache. Let us remember that this wonderful portrait has been made by a series of stains without contour on a piece of coarse linen.

It is not every configuration of light and shade which, on being reversed or made negative, gives us a real portrait. This can be done without artistic change for a line-drawing ; it is what we do when we reproduce a drawing or a graph on paper by means of white chalk on a blackboard. But for works of art a reversal usually produces a hideous caricature. Figures iii. 3 and 4 show the negatives of two pictures included later in this book. From a comparison between the negatives and the originals we can deduce that no artist would dream of making an unnatural negative for the purpose of subsequently having even a monochrome positive. Before photography was invented, the very idea could not occur to him. And even to-day it is almost impossible to copy any graded negative without spoiling the resultant positive. This is shown by making a chemographic positive (i.e. a photographic negative) of the sketches which artists have made of the visible face on the shroud. Not one of these can compare with the chemograph obtained directly from the shroud.[8]

It must be understood that the illustrations of the face in figs. iii. 7 and vii. 71 are devoid of all " touching-up " or manipulation of the photograph. Hence certain extraneous elements have been allowed to remain. The dark colour-value of the blood-trickles (on forehead and hair) has not been restored ; they are left white.

[8] See the reproductions (in Enrie, p.130) of the negatives of copies of the shroud made by Reffo (1868) and by Cussetti (1898). Neither of these can compare with fig. vii. 71. Nor can the sketch by Villé in Gaffre, p.104.

Across the top of the head and across the beard there are two white lines (slightly inclined to the horizontal). These (which of course are darkish on the shroud) are slight folds or crinkles of the material which cannot now be eliminated. In fig. vii. 71 there is a semicircular mark above the head ; this is merely a water-stain.

(3) Some Objections

Needless to say, objections were made against Pia's photograph. Chevalier showed himself far more sceptical as regards Pia's document than he was towards the statement of Pierre d'Arcis. And he foolishly entered the scientific arena. He invoked a now forgotten pamphlet by an amateur photographer called Chopin. This he characterised as a " peremptory reply " and as an " apodictic dissertation."[1] These vague suggestions that the 1898 photograph was untrustworthy or faked never deserved any consideration. Pia's photo—taken with a time-exposure of 20 minutes in artificial light—was at the time confirmed by an instantaneous photograph taken by Padre Sanno Solaro and a photo of the shroud in its frame on the altar taken by Fino.[2] But the outcry has been completely silenced by Enrie's photographs of 1931. Father Thurston took no part in this affair, but had recourse to a more ingenious explanation which he published in the *Catholic Encyclopedia* in 1912 (v.55) :

> The suggestions made of blundering or bad faith on the part of those who photographed the shroud were quite without excuse. From the scientific point of view, however, the difficulty of the negative impression on the cloth is not so serious as it seems. This shroud, like the others, was probably painted without fraudulent intent to aid the dramatic setting of the Easter Sequence . . . It was painted to represent the impression made by the sweat of Christ, i.e. probably in a yellowish tint upon unbleached linen, the marks of wounds being added in brilliant red. This yellow stain would turn brown in the course of centuries, the darkening process being aided by the effects of fire and sun. Thus the lights of the original picture would become the shadows of the image as we now see it.

The blackening of paintings is not an unknown phenomenon.

[1] Chevalier, i. 50, 55 ; he still refers to Chopin in 1903 (iii. 6). Chopin is cited 35 years later by Dom Baudot (p.475) ! On the objections to Pia see Vignon, i. 108, Enrie, p.123. On subsequent reflection both Lippmann and F. de Mély withdrew their objections. But Chevalier to the end rejected the camera.
[2] Noguier de Malijay, pp.26, 30.

In St. Alban's Cathedral, England, there is a Crucifixion (of about 1220) in which the faces are now black.

Owing possibly to the use of lead in the pigment, the colours have gone very black, producing an effect — not unknown in early Italian work and due there to similar causes—akin to that of a photographic negative ; unless—as indeed appears more probable—this result in the present case has been brought about by wilful repainting.—Borenius and Tristram, *English Medieval Painting*, 1927, p.7 (and plate 12).

There is another example in the frescos of Cimabue in the upper Church of Assisi.[3] This blackening of frescoes—noted long ago by Vasari—can be called negative only in a very loose sense. There is no inversion of the original colours at all, there is only a blackening of colours subsequently applied to retouch and improve the original fresco which was painted at once when the lime was fresh. The darkening of faces is probably due to the reaction of white of lead and cinnabar.

Let us now see if this phenomenon could have happened to the shroud. (1) According to Fr. Thurston, the lights of the alleged original painting have become the shadows of the image as we now see it. That is, what we have called the chemograph (photographic negative) of the face is really the portrait as executed by a French artist in the 14th century. The acceptance of this would, as will be pointed out in the next section, revolutionise the whole history of art. To avoid the implications of Pia's photograph, we are asked to believe in an artistic miracle. (2) Furthermore, it has to be admitted that all the marks of the wounds were exempt from the process of inversion, for they have retained their dark colour. (3) The darker places now in the shroud correspond to the parts of the body more in relief, i.e. the parts which the artist is said to have left unpainted or in lighter tones. The hollow regions, on the contrary, he must have painted as shadowed and hence in darker hues. But in these portions, which now appear yellowish-white, the closest examination has not revealed any trace of pigment or colouring matter, we see only the original intact surface of the cloth. Hence the painter must have omitted all paint from the shadowed and darker parts. In other words, he must have deliberately constructed a " negative."

---

[3] See Vignon, i. 117-125, Enrie, pp.135-152. The repainting of the Assisi frescoes is evidenced by irregularities and errors, e.g. a bald head showing through the eye of a person behind.

This last conclusion is rather incredible. A 14th century painter could not possibly have had the faintest idea of a negative. Even if he had, he lacked the technical means of verifying it. Now why should a forger go to the trouble of concocting impressions which were not discernible for five centuries? Even forgery, being a business, must supply in accordance with demand, it must give customers what they want—not a negative whose existence could not even be suspected for centuries. Meanwhile their devotion had to be content with what was really a caricature.

(4) Paint and Painter

For a long time it was maintained that " the simplest, the most obvious and the only straightforward answer to the question how the image was produced is that it is a time-worn painting." Thus wrote a chemist relying on church-historians.[1] But, we must ask, where is the paint? There is not a trace of pencil or brush, of pigment or colouring matter. The figure has resulted from an intimate tincture of the material, not from superposed colouring. A number of the longitudinal threads are specially dark ; in some places these are grouped and form bands, e.g. under the loins and another lower down ; these have received no imprint. But the aspect of the imprinted parts is identical with these zones whose ochre tint results merely from a darkening of the material. In both cases the threads are tinted throughout their thickness, they are as-it-were dyed.[2] One of Enrie's photographs[3] was taken with tangential lighting so as to bring the tissue into relief. Had there been traces of painting, this would have revealed them. On an area of about four square yards, it is inevitable that a painter's hand should display some irregularities of colouring matter and technique; none such is here discoverable.

We know from old reproductions of the shroud—as also from the so-called Veronica pictures—that the lineaments were taken to have been impressed on the shroud exactly as an artist might work, i.e. as we now say, positively ; though some more careful observers (such as the Poor Clares) correctly gave right and left oppositely

---

[1] R. Meldola, *Nature* 67 (1903) 242, reviewing Vignon's work. He accepted Fr. Thurston's thesis.
[2] Timossi, p.80.
[3] Enrie, p.80. In the absence of a photomicrograph, Enrie's photo of the Face in natural size gives a clearer image than an enlargement (cf. his fig. 52).

to what occurs in a portrait. Furthermore, the figure was always represented with definite contours as in human handiwork. But an examination of the natural-sized photograph of the face disproves this view. The imprints fade gradually into the surrounding cloth, there is a general *estompage* characteristic of physico-chemical processes. Not a trace of human instrumentality.

Our difficulties continue when we come to consider the alleged anonymous painter of about 1350. Previously to 1898, a shroud more impressive to the eye, more in accordance with contemporary and previous portrait painting, would have been far more popular. What could have induced an artist to give us these obscure smudges whose details have been unravelled only in our own time? He chose a most inconvenient size ; the two full body-lengths would make exposition very difficult. Five visible wounds would have better satisfied the devotional requirements of the time ; yet on the shroud the wound in one hand is completely covered by the other hand, and only in our day has the wound in the right sole been located. He broke with traditional iconography ; Our Lord's body was depicted nude, so copyists hastened to add a loin-cloth ; the wound in the right hand is located in the wrist ; the sufferings were depicted with brutal realism. Moreover, there was a waste of incredible subtlety ; for all the various physiological and anatomical details, presumably inserted in defiance of current artistic procedure, remained entirely unnoticed and unknown for about 550 years.

No true school of painting existed in France about 1350. Apart from miniatures in manuscripts there are but few authenticated documents of French painting in the fourteenth century. Any pictures executed on a larger scale were mainly carried out by foreign artists, at first from Italy and later from Flanders. Gothic churches left no large plane surfaces, hence ecclesiastical art was chiefly confined to sculptures and glass. In none of the products of the time, or indeed much later, can we find anything approaching the Face of Christ on the shroud-chemography. But even if we assume that this masterpiece was only by some mysterious accident potentially inscribed on the cloth, and confine our attention to the actual shroud (and the positive photograph of it), the artistic improbability remains overwhelming. Here we have the frontal and dorsal figures of a crucified man. The scourge-marks are depicted in a realistic way totally unknown to art of any period. The right side is shown pierced after death but while the body was still suspended

on the cross ; the flow of blood and water is also represented
differently from the artistic tradition. In an age when art was
dominated by the rigid lanky figures of Gothic, the body of this man
is depicted in perfect anatomical proportions. Various types of
wounds are shown on the living flesh—perforations, punctures, cuts,
bruises, abrasions ; they are all physiologically correct ; even the
very coagulation of the blood-drops—central nucleus and pale
penumbra—is accurately shown. Could a man of the 14th century
have painted all this? Turn to the greatest painter, Giotto (✝1337)
Here are some criticisms of his work :

> His style does not transcend the limits of his age. The heads
> and bodies are typical rather than individual . . . In Giotto's
> work the heads are stronger, with a greater squareness and
> prominence of jaw, without the graceful oval of his predecessors.
> His mouths, like theirs, are small, and his eyes narrow and often
> not set quite on the same level. The faces are alike, except for the
> differences of sex and age, each age being represented by its
> established type . . . The bodies still show a want of independent
> study of nature ; the proportion of the several members, as we
> know by the Handbook of Cennino, were regulated by a fixed
> system of measurements. The hands are still long and their
> structure imperfectly understood ; the feet are weak and gener-
> ally disappear under the drapery. The drawing is still on the
> whole conventional, and the modelling not carried far.—Wolt-
> mann and Woermann, *History of Painting*, 1 (1880) 438.
> Giotto generally contrived to make the greatest possible use of
> his draperies to help out his dramatic telling of the story ; but
> in the drawing of his nude figures he was not so successful.—J.
> Ward, *History and Methods of Ancient and Modern Painting*, 2
> (1917) 36.

No art-historian, after studying the figure on the shroud regarded
as a painting, would dream of attributing it to Giotto or to any
known artist of the period. Its realism and its anatomical accuracy
are completely at variance with the proposed chronology.[1]

It must be remembered, however, that there is no direct scientific
proof of the absence of pigment or of the presence of blood, for no

---

[1] A century or so later we find some accurate sculptures of the dead Christ. There
is a Sepulchre of painted limestone in the church of Neufchâteau in Lorraine, prior
to 1497 : " The extended Christ is a scrupulous corpse-study . . . The body is of
irreproachable anatomy : the elevation of the thoracic cage, the epigastric
depression, the rigidity of the members, the folding of the fingers." There is of
course a loincloth, and the arms lie along the body.—A. Philippe and P. Marot,
Revue d'hist. franciscaine 1 (1924) 160, with illustration on p.151.

chemical or spectroscopic tests have been applied to the shroud.[5]
But even without this confirmation, we have quite sufficient evidence to maintain that the markings are not due to human handwork. On 5th September, 1936, Pius XI distributed images of the shroud to French pilgrims. He is quoted as having made the following statement to them :

> They are the most suggestive, beautiful and precious images that one can imagine. They come directly from this object which is still mysterious but which is surely not made by human hands—one can already hold this as proved—I mean the Shroud of Turin . . . One can now assert that it is definitely established in the most positive way—even if we prescind from every idea of faith or Christian piety—that it is certainly not a human work.—*Oss. Rom.* 7/8 Sept. 1936; *Dossiers du Saint-Suaire de Turin*, no. 1, May 1939.

Now Pius XI was a critical scholar. As Mgr. Ratti he was Prefect of the Ambrosian Library (Milan) ; he was personally acquainted with Duchesne, Delehaye, Chevalier. He attended the 1898 Exposition and saw Pia's photograph. In 1931 he studied Enrie's photographs and he had a long discussion with Dr. Barbet. He cannot therefore be accused of pious credulity when, after studying the evidence, he declared : *Certo non è opera umana.*

---

[5] In the case of the Tunic of Argenteuil, chemical analysis proved the presence of bloodstains, this was confirmed by infra-red photography. See Parcot, *La sainte tunique d'Argenteuil* (1934²) and Hynek i.122. Dr. Barbet (ii. 57) was greatly moved when he saw the Turin Shroud quite close and without the interposition of glass : " Without expecting it, I saw that all the wound-images had a colour distinctly different from the rest of the body ; and this colour was that of blood which had dried after impregnating the material."

The coincidence of the shroud-markings with some art-forms prevalent in the 14th century (but not, say, in the 11th or earlier) is *pro tanto* an argument for questioning the authenticity. I refer to the briar-crown on the Crucified and one nail through both feet. These points will be discussed after we have seen the case for holding that the shroud contained a dead body.

CHAPTER IV

A DEAD BODY

(1) Explanations

IT IS a principle accepted among Catholic theologians that natural causes must always be explored before invoking supernatural ones. This is logical on the view which Christian philosophers have always held, namely, that creation is continued by conservation, that God though transcendent acts immanently in the world. Hence it is a false concept which regards secondary causes as somehow having replaced God whose task was finished with an initial act of creation. Much of the present-day hostility of scientists to religion is due to their being imbued with this false deistic idea so prevalent since the shallow eighteenth century. If in former times philosophers and theologians have often been too ready to abandon hope of a natural explanation of certain phenomena,[1] this attitude was not adopted in principle, recourse was not had to a miracle under the impression that ordinary causes implied an absentee deity. It was due to the undeveloped state of science whose possibilities were discovered only in recent times; and also to the delusion—still current—that contemporary science had said the last word. Even Newton was guilty of this shortsightedness when he invoked divine intervention to eke out the lacunae in his mathematical analysis of celestial motions: a point on which he was corrected by Laplace.

While thus agreeing that natural explanations must be pushed as far as they will go, while in many cases leaving unexplained facts as an unresolved problem with a view to further exploration of natural possibilities, Catholic theologians and historians do not start out with an a priori rejection of miracles. They have not fettered themselves with a closed philosophy which would oblige

---

[1] Two examples selected at random. In his *De cursu stellarum ratio*, Gregory of Tours enumerates seven perpetual miracles : tides, growth from seed, the phoenix, Mt. Etna, the hot springs at Grenoble, sun and moon.—*M. G. H. Script. rer. merov.* i. 2 (1885) 860. In his *Enarrationes in Genesim*, Luther mentions as phenomena worked by God's direct intervention : incorruptibility of the heavens, the path of sun and planets, the fact that the sea does not pour over the earth.—*Opera*, 6 (Witeb. 1556) 6a, 7a, 8b, 106a.

them to distort texts and to reject otherwise acceptable evidence.

It is not the task of a historian to make amateur excursions into chemistry or to dabble in medicine for the purpose of evacuating all evidence which is not reconcilable with what he fancies is contemporary orthodox science. Here is an example. Stones which fell from heaven were worshipped by the Greeks. Such falls have been frequently recorded in history. " In most cases, however, the witnesses of such an event have been treated with the disrespect usually shown to reporters of the extraordinary, and have been laughed at for their supposed delusions."[2] Concerning a fall which occurred near Agram in 1751, a Viennese professor (Stuetz) wrote in 1790 :

> This fall from heaven could be believed in 1751 even by educated people in Germany, owing to the ignorance which then prevailed concerning natural history and physics. But in our own time it would be unforgivable to regard such legends even as probable.—Cited in C. Braun, *Ueber Kosmogonie*, 1895[2], p.337.

In 1790 the municipality of Juillac in Gascony submitted to the Paris Academy a report, signed by over 300 eyewitnesses, on a fall of stones which had taken place there. The report was received with ridicule. " Is it not sad," said the referee Bertholon, " to see a whole municipality confirm by a formal inquiry popular legends which call only for pity? " In 1803 a similar fall occurred near Paris, and Biot was commissioned by the Minister of the Interior to investigate it. Biot had to admit the fact and ended his report thus :

> I leave to the sagacity of physicists the numerous consequences that can be deduced, and I shall esteem myself happy if they find that I have succeeded in placing beyond doubt one of the most astonishing phenomena that men have observed.—Biot, *Mélanges* 1 (1858) 46.

On this disedifying story of scientific dogmatism, a great physicist has thus commented :

> I commend this history to the notice of those scientific men who are so sure that they understand the character of Nature's operations as to feel justified in rejecting without examination reports of occurrences which seem to conflict with ordinary experience. Every tiro now knows that the stones to be seen in most museums had an origin thought impossible by some of the leading and most instructed men of about a century ago.—Lord Rayleigh, *Life*, 1924, p.387.

[2] Sir L. Fletcher, *Introd. to the Study of Meteorites*, 1908[10], p.17.

It may also be commended to historians. The scientists rejected
the stories of stones coming from the sky because the historians told
them it was a superstitious legend. The historians rejected the
stories because they thought they were opposed to science. To-day
the schoolboy who inspects meteorites in a museum can have a
laugh at both sets of pundits. This particular phenomenon has
been selected as a typical example. There are numerous parallels :
dowsing, telepathy, and so on.

The proper attitude of a historian is to accept authenticated facts,
even though he or his scientific colleague cannot " explain " them.
This is the duty even of those who on a priori grounds do not believe
in miracles. Here are two examples. Renan and Coulton, in spite
of the evidence, rejected the reality of the stigmata of St. Francis of
Assisi.[3] The attitude of Sabatier is fairer :

> I have come to conclude the reality of the stigmata. They may
> have been a unique fact without being more miraculous than
> other phenomena . . . The testimony appears to me to be at once
> too abundant and too precise not to command conviction.—
> *Life of St. Francis*, Eng. trans. 1904, p.434.

Similarly Voltaire and Anatole France pontifically rejected the
supernormal occurrences in the life of St. Joan of Arc. But the
freethinking Quicherat felt compelled by the evidence to write as
follows :

> For each of these three kinds of clairvoyance—knowledge
> of the most secret thoughts of certain persons, perception of things
> beyond the range of the senses, discernment and prediction of the
> future—the documents prove at least one instance, based on
> foundations so solid that one cannot reject them without rejecting
> the very foundations of history.—*Aperçus nouveaux sur l'histoire
> de Jeanne d'Arc*, 1850, p.61.

(2) **Theories of the Shroud**

The foregoing general considerations have perhaps travelled far
afield. But they will serve as a preliminary to considering theories
of the shroud.

It is doubtful if a single believer in the authenticity of the shroud

---

[3] This rejection is the more unjustified as there are numerous other cases of
stigmata, including more than one which can be studied to-day.

has suggested that the image has originated miraculously.[1] One and all, they have conscientiously striven to obtain a scientific explanation ; and their efforts, though not fully satisfying, have met with increasing success. The nearest approach to invoking a miracle has occurred in the case of those who hold it to be a 14th century painting. For an event, while not *per se* miraculous, may be so in a given historical context. Examples would be : Caesar smoking a cigar while crossing the Rubicon, the use of machine-guns at Crecy, Nelson telegraphing the news from Trafalgar. The particular techniques did not then exist. In exactly the same way, the painting-advocates may fairly be accused of asserting an aesthetic and artistic miracle.

It must be maintained that the question of authenticity is entirely independent of any attempt to account for the image. The shroud itself is a fact, a historical document. It does not cease to exist just because we may find it inexplicable. Several explanations have been proposed. The problem remains even if all of them are definitely proved to be false. Nor do differences of opinion among upholders militate against the authenticity. The late Dr. Vignon supported what he called the vaporographic theory, which was once widely held but is now generally rejected. Yet he wrote (iii. 13) : " I will never make my faith in the authenticity and the value of the shroud depend on the success of this or of any other hypothesis." From the start the late Dr. Beecher found Vignon's theory " unconvincing " and he wrote as follows :

> We wish to make it perfectly clear that we are dealing with facts and that theory does not matter ; indeed we are rather unwilling to touch on theory at all, lest it may obscure the main issue.—Beecher, p.21.

The attitude of the eminent church-historians who rejected the claims for the shroud has been quite different. In 1902 Chevalier wrote :

> It is not enough to eliminate the possibility of a negative being painted ; it must be established how the negative became fixed on the sheet.—Cited by Vignon i. 126.

[1] According to the visions of Anne Catherine Emmerich, the body of Our Lord was washed and anointed, packed with aromatics and bandages. After the Resurrection the outer sheet was found to contain an impression of the body with all its wounds, while all the bands underneath remained as white as before, i.e. the image was miraculous.—*The Dolorous Passion*, Eng. tr. 1926[25], p.299. (According to Therese Neumann (in Hynek ii. 257), the body was wrapped in a long linen sheet and thus borne for burial ; but the sheet was *not* left on it in the tomb).

This is an extraordinary assertion. That a photographic negative gives the features is a fact. What right has a historian to declare that before we admit this fact " it must be established how " it came to be? There are many facts whose " how " we do not know and may never know.

Thurston was equally irrelevant when he wrote in 1903 (i. 170) :

> It is no injustice to insist that M. Vignon's main conclusion that the shroud is not a painting must stand or fall with the rival explanation which he himself propounds of the origin of the figures.

Not at all. The refutation of the hypothesis that the image is a painting stands on its own arguments. If we are satisfied that it is not an artefact, then—unless we have recourse to a miracle—we have to assume that it is a natural product due to physico-chemical factors.[2] This general conclusion is the only alternative ; and it holds good whether or not we can specify the factors or reproduce the conditions.

These historians not only confuse facts with theories about the facts, but they also misunderstand the tentative and progressive nature of scientific hypotheses. Padre Solaro maintained against Vignon that the image was the result of direct contact of the cloth with the dead body. An Italian doctor (Caviglia) hurriedly and unsuccessfully tried to secure a comparable impression on a cloth from a head smeared with coloured grease. Criticising these results Chevalier[3] wrote in 1902 : " They are contemptible ; yet in this way they claim to have demonstrated the authenticity of the shroud of Turin." This was a grossly unfair criticism, besides being a completely erroneous view of the status of these and similar experiments. They are not in the least designed to prove the authenticity ; they are merely intended to give us the further mental satisfaction of knowing how the image might have originated. They could of themselves neither prove that the image, as a matter of historical fact, did so arise, nor demonstrate that the body was that of Christ.

Chevalier failed to realise that, like other scientific procedures, these first groping experiments were capable of increasing improvement. Neither did Fr. Thurston when he complained (i. 171) that

---

[2] Like, say, the perspiration-stains which gradually appear on unwashed linen. We might of course maintain that in the case of the shroud the effect is not intrinsically miraculous but that it is so *quoad modum*.
[3] Cited in Vignon i. 127.

·" nothing has been done to show that impressions can be obtained
of such delicacy as to rival those of the shroud." One might almost
think that he was hoping that they would be forthcoming, in further
disproof of his painting-hypothesis ! Now it is true that Vignon's
first attempt to obtain impressions by contact were not a success,[4]
so that he was driven to his emanation theory. But, as will be
presently seen, later experiments with dead bodies have been much
more successful.

(3) Vignon's Theory

The late Dr. Paul Vignon of Paris deserves the credit for pioneer
work on the chemical formation of an image on cloth by an object
representing a corpse. Having failed in his attempts to reproduce a
face mechanically—he made the mistake of moulding the cloth
closely over the face, thus producing a distorted caricature—he
proposed what he called a vaporographic theory. This means that
the image is produced on the cloth by emanations or vapours
arising from the body. Either the cloth is steeped in a solution of
powdered aloes in oil or water,[1] or else the aloes is put on the body
itself and the shroud is impregnated with oil and myrrh-resin.[2]
On a corpse, especially after wounds and agony, there are nitro-
genous waste products such as sweat, serum, wounds, etc., which
give rise to ammoniacal vapours. It is not the urea in blood and
sweat which evaporates, but the ammonium carbonate resulting
from its decomposition (with the help of a micro-organism).
Alkaline substances (such as ammonia) react with aloes, forming a
reddish-brown colouring matter.

To this theory there are, however, many objections.[3] In order
to obtain an undistorted image, the cloth must be stretched in a
plane ; it is not then easy to see how an orthogonal projection can be
obtained, since vapour does not diffuse in parallel lines. To obtain

[4] See the illustrations, in Vignon i. 132, of impressions obtained on cloth from a
living head smeared with red chalk, and the photographic negatives. The results
were hideous and distorted.
[1] It is very difficult to secure uniform distribution of a powder over the cloth, so it
is steeped in a tincture. If the aloes is in olive oil, it is difficult to dry the cloth
afterwards, as liquid droplets remain ; it is easier to work with aloes in water or
alcohol.
[2] A shroud impregnated with myrrh in a liquid form would have considerable
consistency and even rigidity.
[3] Dezani in Judica Cordiglia, i. 109.

the detailed accurate impressions such as are found on the Turin shroud, a regular or regulated emanation would be necessary. But the distribution of sweat-glands is not uniform, and sweat has a variable reaction according to its location, conditions, etc. As regards a crucified person, much of the sweat must have been absorbed beforehand on the clothes ; on the cross the time-interval would hardly be sufficient and no drink was supplied. On a body exposed to sun and air, sweat would rapidly evaporate ; the urea would be crystallised or solidified on the body and this would not be vaporised at ordinary temperatures. Thus it would seem difficult to admit the amount of ammoniacal vapour required to produce the reaction assumed by Vignon. Direct development of ammonia could not occur on the skin of a fresh cadaver. It might be developed in the buccal cavity if there were putrefactive processes in the intestines ; but in the shroud there is no sign of intensity in the imprint of the mouth.

While thus the details of Vignon's theory are not now generally accepted, he helped to initiate investigations into the chemical development of coloration in cloth. In particular, it has been shown[4] that aloes decomposes on cloth with the help of water or alkaline substances (such as sweat). Two fundamental colours are identifiable : bistre due to aloetin and rose-carmine due to aloin. Cloths immersed for a few minutes in an aqueous solution of aloin are at first clear-yellow. After being exposed to the atmosphere for a few months, the colour becomes red-carmine ; this coloration is acquired more intensely and more rapidly by exposure to sunshine (ultra-violet light). This result seems to exclude the idea that the aloes was in solution over the whole shroud. Aloes of course is only one possible substance.[5] There is also myrrh, a resin which, when treated with alkalis, gives a reaction producing a red colour ; but it does not seem to have been thoroughly investigated. There are many other relevant colouring matters not yet isolated or examined. For example, plant-tissues are easily dehydrated and can be kept without decomposition. From examples of old herbariums[6] it is known that plant-specimens may make on paper imprints which sometimes have great precision ; a photographic negative can reveal many details of structure.

[4] Padre Pietro Scotti in *Oss. Rom.* 16 June 1939 and in Judica i. 114.
[5] The presence of aloes in the shroud would be proved directly if in ultra-violet light the stains were seen to fluoresce ; but some chemical change may have occurred.
[6] Volckringer, p.24.

(4) **Contact with a Statue**

It has been suggested that the image on the shroud was deliberately produced with the help of a stone statue or a wooden bas-relief. As an exponent of this view Père F. M. Braun, O.P., of Fribourg may be selected.[1] " There exist," he says (p.66), " reasons for thinking that the shroud is not a painted cloth. Agreed. But an impression, direct and retouched (as the memoir of Pierre d'Arcis suggests), on a mould with feeble relief? " So he puts forward the theory that in the 14th century an unknown person procured a statue of Christ and smeared it with a layer of, say, tincture of aloes. While this layer was fresh, he spread the cloth successively over the back and the front of the statue, pressing it lightly with his hands. The salient parts were browned ; half-tones were produced by the unequal absorption in the rough-meshed tissue. Finally he added the wound-marks artificially with a colouring tincture.

To illustrate this theory, Père Braun published an impression and its photographic negative which a correspondent sent to him. These are due to Clément (†1939), a specialist in restoring paintings. He selected a bust of the painter Géricault ; to this he added hair falling along the sides of the face, also a beard and a moustache of cotton ; and over the open eyes he placed small wads of cotton. The bust was then soaked in an aqueous solution of aloes. While this was fresh, a cloth was applied ; over the reliefs it was lightly pressed with the hands, while contact with the receding portions was avoided. The new cloth proved to be too white in the untouched portions ; so it was dipped for a few seconds in a very dilute solution of aloes. The result is given in figures iv. 1 and 2.

Father Wuenschel, an American Redemptorist, declares that " M. Clément's imprint is a crude caricature, coarse, unsightly."[2]

---

[1] Le linceul de Turin : note complémentaire, *Nouv. revue théol.* 67 (1940) 322-324. This is inserted under the heading " *Complément* " at the end of his brochure : *Le linceul de Turin et l'évangile de S. Jean,* 1939. Dom Germain Morin hailed Père Braun's pamphlet as the final refutation of the shroud : " Among the numerous symptoms of a want of critical spirit in our time, one of the most striking is the attitude of the masses as well as of scholars towards the question of the shroud exhibited at Turin."—Art. in *La Cité Chrétienne,* 5 May 1940, p.349. Evidently a critical faculty concerning patristics is quite compatible with credulous dogmatism in other domains.

[2] *Catholic Biblical Quarterly* 7 (1945) 416. Père Aubert, a fellow-religious of Père Braun, also criticises (p.26) Clément, who did not choose a 14th century statue but a modern beardless bust to which he attached a beard. R. P. Aubert experienced " a certain feeling of astonishment " at those who were so exacting as regards Barbet's experiments and so credulous as regards Clément.

This is not quite fair ; for such an experiment is in itself quite legitimate as illustrating in principle how the shroud-image might have been obtained, even though the result is aesthetically very much inferior. What is much more serious is the statement that Père Braun was led "to become unwittingly a party to a fraud" (p.415), inasmuch as "it had been extensively retouched, clearly for the purpose of aping the shroud " (p.417). It certainly makes one suspicious at the start to learn that in 1939 Clément refused to submit his photos to Vignon for investigation. The suspicion is confirmed by Fr. Wuenschel's analysis. Let us compare figures iii. 6 and iv. 1 (and similarly the negatives iii. 7 and iv. 2). On the shroud there is on the right side of the face (to the reader's left in fig. iii. 6) a light-coloured straight band from the forehead to the end of the beard ; this is a pure accident, probably due to a local insensitiveness of the cloth. This was imitated by Clément (fig. iv. 1). Again on fig. iii. 6 careful inspection will show a thin dark line[3] running from top to bottom of the image, through the light areas of the eye and of the depression beside the nose (where there was certainly no contact) ; this is obviously due to a flaw in the weave of the cloth. Once more we find it faked in Clément's photo ! There are also blood-trickles in the hair and punctures on the brow in imitation of the shroud. And the sharply defined halfmoons representing the closed eyes do not look like the impressions which would have been produced by wads of soft yielding cotton. This much-advertised photograph is therefore open to the gravest suspicion.

Let us argue however as if some kind of tolerable face-image had been honestly obtained. This would be no argument whatever in favour of a statue against a corpse, for which we shall presently reproduce similar images. But we shall have to ask some questions concerning this alleged 14th century manoeuvre. Why should it have been undertaken at all? How was this curious unrecorded technique hit upon? Especially as, until we could take a negative photograph, it led to a very crude result which could have been reached more expeditiously and efficiently by some form of direct painting or dyeing. And where did the manipulator secure the statue which, on Père Braun's admission, must have been rather wonderful?

[3] This is more clearly discernible in larger photos of the face. In the negative (fig. vii. 71) it can be seen as a narrow white line to the right of the nose.

Certainly the striking impression left upon the cloth venerated at Turin, its astonishing realism, its impersonal and almost sculptural character, assuredly alien to medieval painting, remain a mystery.—Braun, p.64.

What is the use of a theory which involves the employment of a statue which is a chronological mystery? But it is when we leave the face that the most serious difficulties begin. In the remainder of the body-impression on the shroud, we encounter an astonishing accuracy of anatomy and physiology, witness the realistic exactitude of the wound-marks and blood-flows. If these were not on the hypothetical masterpiece of statuary, they were added by this unknown predecessor of Leonardo da Vinci. Certainly this over-taxes our credulity. Would it not be much simpler to assume[4] that this ingenious medieval worked with the corpse of a crucified? For after all it is much less of a strain on us to believe that this highly original Frenchman of six centuries ago hit upon this simple expedient of securing a *corpus vile*, than to assume that he unearthed an anatomically perfect statue of the Dead Christ (now lost), thought of replacing it by unartistic contact-stains on a long strip of cloth, to which he then added woundmarks of a startling realism never recorded by artists before or since. *Pace* Père Braun, this last is a much greater " mystery."

The positive evidence for assuming that the shroud contained a corpse and not a statue will be considered in detail later on. Meanwhile Dr. Barbet,[5] who has done so much to elucidate these details, may be quoted :

> In a question concerning a human cadaver, the intervention of an anatomist seemed indispensable for verifying and clarifying many points. It was necessary to experiment, to radiograph and to dissect the fresh cadaver, as well as to explore and to radiograph the living. This I have done for a year and a half in a spirit of independence as for any scientific research . . . I began my researches on the images of the shroud with a certain scepticism, ready to query the authenticity if they did not agree with anatomical truth.—Barbet, i. 8, 37.

---

[4] As for example with M. de Meurville, *Correspondant*, 10 May 1902, p.560.
[5] This is all that Père Braun has to say (p.67) : " The experiments of Dr. Barbet have been contested by Dr. Eskenazy." He refers to the medical thesis : *Le saint suaire de Turin devant l'histoire, la science et la médicine*, 1938. But he omits to tell us that the author is a Turkish Jew who believes that Christ never existed. See also p133.

(5) **Contact with a Corpse**

Experiments on cloth-impressions of corpses have in fact been performed ; they have mostly been confined to the face, as this is not only most convenient but also the best test. Prof. Maurizio Masera of Genoa, admitting elimination of urea through the sweat-glands as the primary cause of the reaction, painted a corpse with a solution of urea ; after this evaporated, he sprinkled the body with aloes and myrrh. But he was unable to obtain appreciable images on cloth.[1] Prof. Romanese of Turin[2] was more successful. His best results were obtained by sprinkling the face of the cadaver with droplets of salt solution (physiological standard) and using a cloth on which there was powdered aloes ; though he also obtained good results when the aloes was strewn on the corpse. Care had to be taken in lightly pressing the cloth ; and to avoid deformation, the face was packed with cotton at the sides and at the top. It was thus shown that the humidity of the corpse sufficed, without Vignon's assumption of ammoniacal exhalations. Powdered aloes and myrrh with nothing else but water can give permanent browning to the cloth where it is in contact ; presumably the aloes is oxidised by the oxygen dissolved in the water. Dr. Giovanni Judica Cordiglia, Professor of Legal Medicine in Milan University, made numerous experiments which gradually became more successful. On the face he sprinkled powdered aloes and myrrh in almost equal parts. The cloth he soaked in a solution of turpentine and olive oil.[3] On perceiving in transparency that the image was fixed on the cloth, he removed it for drying ; the residual powder adhering to the dried cloth was then brushed off. The resultant image was more intensely coloured and more contrasting with the white cloth than the shroud-image ; also it had much sharper contours. He made many efforts to obtain greater *sfumatura* or gradation and softness. He eventually obtained the effect by placing the cloth in water vapour. Thus the *flou* of the shroud-image could have been pro-duced by subsequent exposure to a humid atmosphere. Figure iv. 3 shows one of his results and fig. iv. 4 is the corresponding negative.

[1] Judica, i. 121.
[2] Judica, i. 115 ; Trossarelli, p.525 ; *Oss. Rom.* 5 May and 16 June 1939.
[3] Distillation was not known in the time of Christ. Products rich in essential oils were used with olive oil. He interprets the *aromata* used at Our Lord's burial as drugs infused in olive oil (i. 24, 118).

Dr. Judica Cordiglia interposed a fine linen veil (sudarium) between the face of the cadaver and the outer cloth (sindon). Figures iv. 5 to 8 are of the same face. Figure iv. 5 reproduces the impression made on the inner veil ; this is a much cruder picture than that on fig. iv. 2. The image is still impressed through the veil on to the cloth, as is shown in fig. iv. 7. It will be observed that the negative of fig. iv. 8 is much better than that of fig. iv. 6.

Having thus obtained light-sepia imprints with the help of aloes, he next tried to imitate the rusty-red colour found on the shroud. For this purpose he impregnated the cloth with turpentine mixed with olive-oil ; he chose turpentine because one component of this oleo-resin, namely colophony, has been found in Egyptian embalming substances ; and he chose infusion in olive-oil because in ancient times neither distillation nor alcohol was known.

In his experiments on corpses, he also tried blood-stains artificially placed on certain parts. The blood was found to form with the mixture—aloes, myrrh, turpentine, olive-oil—a paste which came off in close adherence to the cloth. After exposure to water-vapour, this transfer " dissolved, forming a soft halo around a central nucleus." This halo (resembling serum) assumed a tint sometimes red and sometimes violet ; this is due to a chromatic reaction of the aromatic substances in presence of blood.

It is not claimed that these and similar experiments have produced a replica of the shroud. In any case, the conditions prevailing when a freshly crucified man was wrapped in the shroud cannot now be reproduced ; neither do we know all the concurrent circumstances which then occurred. But the results so far obtained, though relatively crude, have considerable probative value in strengthening the thesis that the image on the shroud is the physico-chemical effect of an enclosed dead body plus certain aromatics.

CHAPTER V

DELAGE ON THE SHROUD

Introduction

THIS chapter contains the complete translation of a letter-article by Yves Delage, which appeared in the *Revue scientifique*, 31 May 1902, pp.683-687. The occasion which gave rise to the publication of this protest is worth recalling. In the Proceedings of the Paris Academy of Sciences[1] for 21 April 1902 the following appeared: "On the formation of negative images by the action of certain vapours: Note of M. P. Vignon, presented by M. Yves Delage, (Extract)." This is only an "extract," and thereby hangs a tale.

The paper summarised investigations on the chemical (non-photic) formation of images on textile or paper, carried out by Vignon in conjunction with Herovard and Colson in Delage's laboratory. It was the 1898 photograph of the shroud which led to this research; and as a result all four became convinced that they had found a natural explanation of the image on the shroud.

The paper was read by Yves Delage (1859-1920), Professor of Zoology at the Sorbonne, who as a scientist was rigorously agnostic and excluded even the possibility of miracle[2], and who as a man openly professed atheism. The Secretary of the Academy was the chemist Marcelin Berthelot (1827-1927), who was much more virulently antireligious than Delage. It may not be irrelevant to say something about him. In 1845 when Renan (aged 23) left the seminary, he became friends with Berthelot (aged 18) whom he seems to have turned into an agnostic.

> When we entered into relation, there remained in me a tender attachment towards Christianity; Berthelot also held from his father the remains of Christian beliefs. A few months were enough to relegate these vestiges of faith into the part of our souls consecrated to remembrance . . . The clear scientific view of a universe in which no will superior to man's has any appreciable

[1] *Comptes Rendus* 134 (1902) 902-904.
[2] "Even in its boldest hypotheses, natural science must appeal only to natural forces; and everything referring to soul or divinity is outside science."—Delage, *L'hérédité et les grands problèmes de la biologie générale*, 1903[2], p.438.

influence became, since the first months of 1846, the immovable anchor from which we have never moved.—Renan, *Souvenirs d'enfance et de jeunesse* (1883), Nelson edition, p.242f.

Two or three words which we discretely exchanged soon showed us that we had what creates the closest bond between men, I mean the same religion. This religion was the cult of truth . . . What we understood by truth was science.—Discourse of Renan, 27 Nov. 1885 : Berthelot, *Science et morale*, 1897, p.51.

How well we did, my dear friend, to fix, when we were young and whole, our philosophy of life.—Renan's last letter to Berthelot 20 July 1892 : *Correspondance*, 1898, p.537.

So these two young men adopted deterministic agnosticism, not owing to researches in chemistry or Christianity, but at the outset of their career. As undergraduates they had finally decided what was truth ! So Berthelot was displeased when Delage presumed even to mention Christ at this meeting of the Academy of Sciences. Loth[3] who was present tells us that " while M. Delage was speaking, M. Berthelot, alone, seated on the left of the President, pretended not to hear and affected to write all the time." Having failed to stop the paper or to silence Delage, Berthelot as Secretary only allowed portion of the paper to be published in the *Comptes Rendus*. Truth[4] !

Delage's article is worth reproducing as, while showing up the intolerant bigotry of certain scientists, it also demonstrates that the question of the authenticity of the shroud is not one of faith but of human evidence and may be answered affirmatively by even an agnostic.[5]

---

[3] *Le Figaro* 22 June 1902, cited by Beecher, p.107. Canon Chevalier who was *not* present erroneously declared that " the Academy refused to ratify the communication of M. Delage."—Beecher, p.108.
[4] In the *Lancet* for 26 April 1902 (p.1216), the Paris correspondent gave a laudatory account of Vignon's paper. It was translated in *Nature* 66 (1902) 13, followed by a condemnatory letter Fr. Thurston had written to the *Times*. In *Nature* 67 (1903) 241 there is a dogmatically ignorant review of Vignon's work by the English chemist R. Meldola : " Dr. Vignon is either the victim of credulity or he has overdone his evidence to such an extent as to have damaged his own reputation as an expert scientific witness." As I have recalled the tergiversations of Catholic historians when faced with an inconvenient photograph, it is only fair to record the intolerance of some anti-Catholic scientists.
[5] I have inserted some headings (in square brackets) but have added no notes or corrections. It will be noticed that Delage accepted Vignon's vaporographic theory. Père Aubert (p.11) gives an interesting quotation from *Je Sais Tout*, November 1934 : " One need not have the faith. But this confirmation coming nineteen centuries after a legendary fact is rather disturbing. Let us without reserve admire this prodigious masterpiece of chance which is the image of Christ received on the Shroud. It is the first photograph taken on earth, and it reproduces the features of the most famous man in the world."

Delage's Article

Letter to M. Charles Richet

My dear Director :

[Reply to Criticisms by Fellow-Rationalists]

When some months ago I went to see you in your laboratory to introduce to you M. Vignon and the curious documents concerning the Turin shroud which we were investigating, did you anticipate the passionate disputes which would be excited in the press by this question which we discussed so coldly, as if we were dealing with some problem in physiology? No ; you did not. And later when, with the aid of M. Colson, M. Vignon had found the scientific explanation of the formation of the image on the shroud, do you remember the deep joy we felt at having at length discovered the key to the enigma? For weeks and months our minds were obsessed with this disconcerting contradiction between a material fact which had to be accepted and the apparent impossibility of finding a natural explanation for it, thus playing into the hands of those who accept miracles which my philosophical opinions do not admit at any price. And then suddenly there arose the natural explanation, luminous in its simplicity, ousting miracle. Naïvely we thought that it was believers—at least those whose minds were enslaved by a too narrow religion—who would be in opposition to us. That of course would not have stopped us. As for myself, I deserved no credit, as I have no religious belief. But M. Vignon, who is a believer, was in a different position. It redounds to the honour of his character and of his intelligence that, no more than myself, did he draw back. Let me add that it is also to the honour of my laboratory that men of the most diverse and the most opposed opinions were able to engage there in studying the same subject which closely touched their dearest philosophical opinions, in discussing it with ardour, without any change in the cordiality of their relations ; and that they arrived at the same conclusion which they proclaimed because they believed it to be true, without allowing themselves to be influenced by any consequences it might have. Yes, it is a spectacle of which we have the right to be proud, especially when we compare it with that presented by a section of the press, in which personal attacks have been made upon us by people who have never given twelve hours' reflection to the problem, who have hardly if at all understood the documents, who by their objections show that they have completely misunderstood most of the arguments.

You rightly consider that these attacks leave me quite cold ; time is too valuable to me to waste it in replying. But there is another class of persons, to whose opinion I am less indifferent and who in good faith have been able to believe—so disfigured have the facts become—all or part of what is said in certain journals : namely that, unconsciously or unscrupulously, I have betrayed science and been unfaithful to my opinions as a freethinker. For them I wish to re-establish the facts and for this I ask the hospitality of your journal.

[*Protest against Berthelot's Action*]

I should have no need to do this if the Bureau of the Academy had agreed to publish the explanations which I gave when presenting M. Vignon's work. But since the permanent secretary who was acting that day refused my note, it so happens that I spoke and officially took part in the debate on the shroud, without there being any written record to which I might refer in order to show for what I do or do not accept responsibility. In these circumstances it has been easy to confuse the issues. I wish then to give a rapid summary of what I said at the Academy and to add some remarks clarifying my position and my attitude in the debate, remarks I could not have made at the Academy because they would not have been relevant there.

I omit a short exordium in which I explained that certain historical, artistic and archaeological considerations by which I began my account, however out of place they might seem at the Academy of Sciences, were nevertheless necessary and would eventually lead to scientific facts concerning physics, chemistry and physiology. I also omit the description of the shroud as understood in 1898. I now go on to reproduce the very note which I destined for the Proceedings (*Comptes rendus*).

[*The Suppressed Note*]

Hitherto there was question only of a relic which from the scientific standpoint had no interest for us. But in 1898, on the occasion of the centennial exhibition of sacred art at Turin, the shroud was photographed, with serious guarantees. Then two curious facts were verified, and these raised the scientific problem here discussed. (1) The image on the shroud is a negative, i.e. the parts in relief are dark, and inversely. (2) The negative of this image, becoming positive relatively to the object represented, assumes an unexpected clearness and displays an anatomical perfection and an aesthetic character hitherto unsuspected. The body becomes accurately modelled ; and the head, rather repellent in the real reproduction of the shroud, becomes, after this reversal of light and shade, so admirable and expressive that, in the opinion of competent painters, not a single head of Christ by artists of the Renaissance is superior to it. The reproductions which I submit to you allow you to form a judgement.

The question then arises : How has this image been formed?

At first sight it would seem that the image on the shroud is not, as has been admitted, an imprint ; for this could give only a rough representation of the general form. It would seem then to be a painting made for the purpose of a pious fraud. But when this hypothesis is examined with care, we see that it must be rejected for the following reasons :

(1) As the shroud is authenticated since the fourteenth century, if the image is a faked painting, there must at this epoch have existed an artist—who has remained unknown—capable of executing a work hardly within the power of the greatest Renaissance painters. While this is already very difficult to admit for an image painted as a positive, it becomes quite incredible in the case of a negative image, which lacks all aesthetic character in this form and assumes its value only when lights and shades are reversed, while strictly respecting their contours and values. Such an operation would be almost impossible except by photography, an art unknown in the 14th century. The forger, while painting a negative, must have known how to distribute light and shade so that after reversal they would give the figure which he attributed to Christ, and that with a perfect precision ; for we know how little is required to change a beautiful head into a caricature, especially when its beauty is due to the expression.

I add this argument whose force will be felt on reflection : *Why should this forger have taken the trouble to realise a beauty not visible in his work and discernible only after a reversal which only later was made possible?*

He was working for his contemporaries and not for the twentieth century and the Academy of Sciences.

The idea that the image could have been painted in positive and changed to negative, as has happened to certain paintings on cloth and certain frescos, is contradicted *inter alia* by the fact that the image is in monochrome and consequently could not have undergone two inverse modifications from clear to shadow and from shadow to clear.

(2) The image results from the juxtaposition of graded tints, without definite delineation or sketching, like a badly focussed photograph: a procedure quite alien to the artistic conceptions of the fourteenth century.

(3) The image is strongly realist, impeccable, without defect or omission ; only imperfectly does it take account of tradition, it is neither schematic nor conventional: characteristics not to be found in any of the artistic productions of this epoch nor to such an extent in those of any epoch.

[*Summary of Some Arguments*]

I now summarise my note without reproducing the exact text :

(*a*) The blood-drops—which are not in the form of Prince Rupert's drops—flowing immediately from the wounds ; in particular that of the forehead so strikingly realistic, those of the forearm separated by an interval from the wound in the wrist.

(*b*) The marks of the flagellation in the form of a dumb-bell, such as might be made by a *flagrum* with thongs ending in hard heavy masses of the same form, analogous to those in certain archaeological museums. It would be interesting to know if people of the 14th century knew this construction of the *flagrum* ; if they did not, this is a further proof. And the convergence of these marks, downward on the back, crosswise on the thighs, upward on the calves, towards a point where the executioner's hand could be ! A forger does not think of all that. To be convinced, one need only examine the pictures of the epoch ; and yet these artists had an equal desire to represent the truth.

(*c*) The loins, perhaps the genital region, naked : which would have been considered most irreverent. The bishop or the prior who might have ordered the shroud from a monastic or lay artist, would not have failed to require the addition of a loin-cloth. For we must place ourselves in the epoch in which the fraud might have been carried out ; the shroud destined to enflame the zeal of the faithful should not at the same time shock their feelings or scandalise them. This is so true that the loin-cloth has been added to certain copies.

(d) The hands pierced through the wrist and not through the palm, in conformity with the anatomical requirements and against tradition.

(e) The wound in the left side and not at the right, owing to the inversion of the image.

(f) The character of continuous gradation [without sharp contours], in exact accordance with what would result from the mode of formation to be presently described, and quite different from what an artist would have devised, etc., etc.

[Continuation of the Text of the Note]

For these and many other reasons which need not be specified, there results the conviction that the image on the shroud is not a painting made by the hand of man, but that it has been obtained through some physico-chemical phenomenon. And the scientific question which arises is this : How can a corpse produce on its enveloping shroud an image which reproduces its outlines and the details of the face?

We must reject the idea of an imprint obtained by contact with the body soiled with sweat and blood or with an artificial colouring matter. Such a procedure gives only a rough image, devoid of aesthetic value and deformed when the cloth is spread flat after having contacted the contours of the body in order to receive the imprint of the hollow parts. Here are some images obtained by M. Vignon by means of this procedure ; we see the effects of the deformation : the face is broadened, the eyes are lowered, etc.

A careful examination of the image on the shroud allows us to recognise the law of its formation. Here it is : The image is an almost orthogonal projection, slightly diffuse ; and the intensity of the tint at each point varies inversely as the distance of this point from the corresponding point of the body ; this intensity decreases very rapidly as the distance increases, it vanishes when the distance reaches a few centimetres.

So the problem becomes this : What radiations or image-producing substances can emanate from a corpse, following the conditions of this law? How can the shroud, or the substances with which it might be impregnated, receive and fix the impression?

M. Vignon was put on the track of the solution of the problem by an experiment of M. Colson which the latter communicated to him. A polished plate of zinc, placed in the dark on a photographic plate, makes an impression ; the zinc emits vapour which is fixed on the plate ; under the influence of the developer, the zinc oxidises and liberates hydrogen which reduces the silver. A zinc plate not polished but roughened gives an image of these rugosities. M. Vignon extended the experiment and found that a medal dusted with powdered zinc gives a negative image having the principal characteristics of that of the shroud.

But on the corpse there is no zinc ; and the shroud is not a photographic plate. What is it that, in the possible conditions of the buried body, has been able to replace the zinc and the photographic plate?

Comparison of the physiological, chemical and archaeological data has given rise to the following hypothesis. A cloth impregnated with an emulsion of aloes in olive oil contains a thin layer of aloetin, which becomes brown under the action of alkaline vapours such as might come from the formation of ammonium carbonate from the urea abundant in the febrile sweat of the body during execution. The hypothesis has been corroborated by the following experiment. A plaster hand was covered with a glove of suède kid which was immersed in a weak solution of ammonium carbonate or simply in urine ; above this was stretched a cloth satured with an emulsion of aloes in oil. Next day there appeared on the cloth an image of the hand showing all the principal characteristics of that on the shroud.

I consider as highly suggestive, and as evidence of the scientific character of this research, the fact that the problem of the shroud has led to the discovery of two new processes for forming images, one hardly glimpsed previously and the other entirely unknown.

Thus M. Vignon's idea, to which I completely subscribe, is that the body of the victim was laid on the shroud half of which was folded over the body ; that this body was covered with a febrile sweat rich in urea ; that the urea formed ammonium carbonate which, in a calm atmosphere, emitted vapours more and more diluted as they were farther from the emitting surface ; that the shroud was soaked in an emulsion of aloes which became brown under the influence of these alkaline vapours and formed a tint the more intense the nearer was this surface; whence the negative image whose characteristics I described above.

[*The Identity of the Corpse*]

Should I speak of the identity of the person who left his image on the shroud?

(Here I declared that I knew I was altogether going outside those questions with which it is the task of the Academy to occupy itself: I did this only because of the interest which the Academy seemed to give to my exposition and which was proved by the continued attention I aroused. And I did so while expressly admitting that this was by way of complement, independent of the communication strictly so called, rather in the manner of the chats which occur in other societies after the sitting when the secretary ceases to take notes for the minutes).

On the one hand we have the shroud, probably impregnated with aloes—which brings us to the East outside Egypt—and a crucified man who had been scourged, pierced on the right side and crowned with thorns. On the other hand we have an account—pertaining to history, legend and tradition—showing us Christ as having undergone in Judea the same treatment as we decipher on the body whose image is on the shroud.

Is it not natural to bring together these two parallel series and to refer them to the same object?

Let us add that, in order that the image should be produced and not later destroyed, it is necessary that the body should remain in presence of the shroud at least twenty-four hours, the time necessary for the formation of the image, and at most a few days, after which there supervenes putrefaction which destroys the image and finally the shroud. Now this is precisely what tradition—more or less apocryphal, I admit—asserts to have happened to Christ who died on Friday and disappeared on Sunday.

And if it is not Christ, it must be some criminal under the common law. But how is this to be reconciled with the admirably noble expression which you read on this figure?

[*Comments on the Note*]

I now add that there is here a collection of five circumstances, to mention only the principal, which are rather exceptional : the East outside Egypt, the wound in the right side, the crown of thorns, the duration of the burial, the character of the physiognomy. Suppose that for each there should be one chance in a hundred that it should occur in the case of another person. There would then be only one chance in ten thousand million that they should be found together. Of course I do not give these numbers as having any claim to exacness, tbut only to show the improbability of all these conditions occurring together in the case of another person.

Anyway, those who wish to attribute the shroud to another person are in the same condition as ourselves with respect to the other difficulties, with this difference that their person is a pure invention without any mention in history, tradition or legend. Their hypothesis, being without any such basis, is more gratuitous than ours.

I freely recognise that an irrefutable demonstration is not to be found in any of the arguments advanced to prove that the image is not a painting made by a forger, to show how it could have been produced, and especially to identify the person. But it must be admitted that taken in conjunction they constitute a striking bundle of probabilities, some of them very close to proofs, corroborated as regards one point by positive experiments and everywhere by rigid criticism. Hence it is not scientific to shrug one's shoulders and, in order to shirk discussion, to say that these are gratuitous hypotheses. They are hypotheses corroborated to the extent that they could be corroborated. We have adduced reasons which are at least the beginnings of proofs ; it is up to our adversaries to refute them. If they have not received from certain people the welcome they deserved, the sole reason is that there has been unfairly grafted on to this scientific question a religious issue which has excited men's minds and misled right reason. If not Christ but Sargon or Achilles or one of the Pharaohs had been involved, no one would have any objection.

In refusing to insert my note in the Proceedings (*Comptes rendus*), it has been forgotten that this publication contains matters which are much more hypothetical, theories—I can quote them—corroborated by no experiment, and many others based upon arguments far more fragile than those brought forward here. But then there was no question of matters touching religion. There lies all the difference.

[Defence of Reliance on Photographs]

We have been reproached with not having seen the shroud but only photographs, which however were taken under conditions that made their authenticity extremely probable. But we have never concealed this, and we made every attempt to examine the shroud itself. A tentative effort made through Baron Manno failed. At the conclusion of my communication to the Academy, I explicitly declared that we had not seen the shroud and that it was a serious lacuna involving certain reserves as regards the conclusions to be drawn from the reasoning. I asked the Academy to appoint a committee with the object of obtaining permission to see the shroud and to examine it scientifically. It is not my fault if this request was refused, not indeed by the Academy which was not consulted and which perhaps might have decided otherwise.

Will it be said that we should have abstained from all research based on photographs alone? How many pieces of work have been performed on reproductions of documents? And what harm is there in using these reproductions when we have good reasons for regarding them as accurate, when we are unable to procure the original document, when we honestly declare what we have done and on what materials we have worked? Suppose that there were a unique fossil held by the Emperor of China and that a replica of it had been made ; nobody would blame a palaeontologist for describing this fossil, especially if he had found upon the replica traces of histological structure which the Chinese were incapable of producing since they had not the required knowledge. This is a striking comparison with what has happened in the case of the shroud.

It has not been my intention to give here a complete discussion of the question of the shroud. I know the objections which have been urged : the forger's avowal, photography by transparence, the thirty-nine shrouds to be found in the world, the facsimile in the National Library (Paris), positives giving direct negatives because they are very red (!!), the interval of two centimetres between the two images and the necessity for an interval of a metre, etc. I knew most of these before making my communication to the Academy, and I know what they are worth. M. Vignon has the right and the pleasure of demolishing this precarious scaffolding.

My object has merely been to establish as regards what has been printed over my name that for which I am willing to be responsible, so that I may not be judged by tales which confuse persons and things.

In this affair of the shroud nothing has been proved in the manner of a mathematical truth or of a fact of observation ; but there are a number of considerations for and against which one has the right to weigh. Now, all things considered, I remain convinced that the image on the shroud is not a painting, the work of a forger ; that it is not an imprint ; that it is a natural reproduction of the buried body, by means of a physico-chemical phenomenon similar in its general lines, if not identical in detail, to that invoked by M. Vignon. Has there been the intervention of a forger, not to make the image but perhaps to retouch, at an epoch more or less recent, either the shroud or the photographs? As a man I say no ; as a scientist bound to prescind from considerations of a moral order, I make reserves and demand the examination of the shroud before affirming. As to the identification of the person with Christ, I also believe, after weighing the evidence, that there are stronger reasons for admitting it than for rejecting it ; and until the contrary is proved, I admit it as well founded. But I willingly recognise that a question of appreciation is here involved, that the value attached to the different arguments has something rather arbitrary, and that others can judge differently. Unfortunately I can hardly see what will ever be able to settle the question one way or the other.

[*Science, not Clericalism*]

In any case, I claim in this matter to have performed a task which is truly scientific—and in no way clerical. For using this word for which I find no short and suitable equivalent, I ask pardon from those convictions—which I respect without sharing—that may be thereby wounded.

I have been faithful to the true scientific spirit by treating this question solely with an eye to the truth, without bothering myself whether it would or would not be in the interests of such and such a religious party. It is by those who have been thus influenced that the method of science has been betrayed.

I have not done a piece of clerical work, because neither clericalism nor anticlericalism has anything to do with the matter. I consider Christ as a historical person, and I see no reason why people should be scandalised if there exists a material trace of his existence.

As to the question whether he was God and son of God, whether he rose on Easter day to ascend to heaven, etc., etc., I have said nothing because I had nothing to say. Those who wish to know what I think of such questions need only refer to my work on Heredity (pp.184, 813), where a certain characteristic phrase will be found. This phrase did me enough harm in certain quarters when I was a candidate for the Academy to justify me in recalling it when it is necessary to show what are my philosophical opinions.

Yves Delage, Member of the Institute.

CHAPTER VI

THE MAN'S IDENTITY

(1) **Whose Body?**

EVEN if we assume that the evidence is preponderantly in favour of there having been a corpse enwrapped in the shroud, there remains the further question : Whose body? In his first book (i. 12), Vignon declared : " In order to approach the subject with the calmness of academic discussion, we shall avoid as long as possible all mention of the historic personage to whom these pages refer." His final opinion was this (iv. 163) : " Was this man really Christ? In the present state of the question, this is the only problem to be solved." It has of course been all along in the mind of both reader and writer, but the issue must now be faced. It is worth reiterating, however, that the value of the shroud is not *totally* dependent on its authenticity. For the weight of the internal evidence is decisively in favour of the shroud containing the impressions of a crucified man. So, apart from further considerations, it is likely—and it will later be verified—that the cloth is a document from which we can learn details of scourging, crucifixion and piercing, not otherwise obtainable.

Now it is just possible to suppose that somebody in the Middle Ages did actually subject someone else to these cruel sufferings, death and post-mortem outrage in order to secure these imprints on the shroud. But one cannot believe that such a blasphemous murder really took place ; or that any medieval, relying only on the Gospels, would know how to carry out the operation as the shroud indicates. The more one examines the noble features of the victim and the scientifically plausible version given of gaps in the Gospel accounts (e.g. the wrist-wounds), the more physically improbable this horrible supposition seems. There is also the moral case, already argued, against such a purposeless forgery ; the idea is put altogether out of court if we have to accept murder as an ingredient. A chance readymade corpse would not do ; for this would not give the *ante mortem* scourge-marks and blood-flows ; the man must have died on a cross.

At any rate, no one has ever put forward this supposition. Upholders and defenders alike admit that, if a dead body was originally contained in the shroud, that body was Our Lord's. We have heard Delage. Here is Father Thurston's admission (i. 19) :

> As to the identity of the body whose image is seen upon the shroud, no question is possible. The five [*sic*] wounds, the marks of a cruel flagellation, the punctures encircling the head, can still be clearly distinguished . . . If this is not the impression of the Body of Christ, it was designed as a counterfeit of that impression. In no other personage since the world began could these details be verified.

By counterfeit he means a painting. His reluctance to admit the inclusion of a dead body was due to his perception of the inescapable consequence that the relic was the Shroud of Christ.

(2) The Gospels

The question whether the cloth contained a dead body is one to be settled, if at all, by an internal examination of the shroud itself. But to decide the identity of the Man in the Shroud requires testimony outside this textile document itself. Subject to certain limitations—e.g. as regards possible dates for the weaving of the cloth—specification of the person involved necessitates an appeal to history, in the present case, to the Gospels. If the details graphically displayed on the shroud can be shown to contradict clear statements of the Evangelists' accounts of the Passion, then for us Catholics the question is closed ; however the shroud be explained, it is not Christ's winding-sheet.

On this issue there has been heated controversy which, on at least one side, has been more gratuitously vehement than convincing. As the present writer has dealt with the question elsewhere, it is not proposed to enter here into exegetical details.[1] Typical of

---

[1] Here is a brief bibliography : P. Bouvier, Le suaire de Turin et l'évangile, *Quinzaine* 47 (1902) 20-32. U. Chevalier, Le saint suaire de Turin et le Nouveau Testament, *Revue biblique* 11 (1902) 565-573. Lévesque, Le suaire de Turin et l'évangile, *Nouv. revue apol.* 1 (1939) 228-237. F. M. Braun, *Le linceul de Turin et l'év. de s. Jean*, 1940. A. O'Rahilly, *The Burial of Christ*, 1942. E. A. Wuenschel, The Shroud of Turin and the Burial of Christ, *Catholic Biblical Quarterly* 7 (1945) 405-437, 8 (1946) 135-178. The exegetical question is also dealt with in several of the publications listed in the bibliography at the end of this book (e.g. Renié). Also in a brochure by Père Aubert, O.P., *Ensevelissement de N.S.J.C. d'après les saintes Ecritures, à l'occasion du S. Suaire de Turin*, Paris 1947.

Chevalier's heavy dogmatism is the following statement (iii. 6) :

It is superfluous to recall the hypotheses by which it was desired to authenticate a shroud as that used in the burial of Christ; they belong to an order of ideas to which historical science is a stranger. Nothing remains of them to-day; in order to destroy their demonstrative force, it has been enough to establish, with the help of the Gospels confirmed by Jewish tradition, in what conditions Jesus was laid in the tomb, the nature of the spices used, the very state of the shroud photographed in 1898.

Chevalier was so sure of so many negations ! But one gets the impression that his scriptural interpretations (at which he was not very expert) were a mere afterthought to bolster up his championship of Pierre d'Arcis. Another Catholic writer Belser[2] makes two unproved assumptions : (1) St. John says or necessarily implies that Our Lord's sindon was cut into strips, and (2) if this be true, the cloth in Turin cannot be genuine. Like others, he seems quite unconscious that both these assumptions are highly debateable, and concludes that " in view of the sacred text "—i.e. his own opinions—the shroud is not authentic. On the next page he dismisses the relic as " a forgery, an ordinary painting " and declares : " It is not worth while to pay any attention to the claims made for the winding-sheet of Turin." How conveniently simple !

Père Braun makes various assumptions including these : (1) St. John definitely says, or clearly implies, that Our Lord's body received a ritually complete washing and anointing ; and (2) this disproves the authenticity of the shroud. He makes no attempt to deal with (2). As to (1) he presses his interpretation with quite unjustified and onesided emphasis, as if *prima facie* this view were not belied by St. Mark and as if numerous commentators did not legitimately disagree with it. Any fair-minded exegete must admit that as regards details of the Crucifixion and Burial of Christ the Gospel testimony is lacking on some points and variously interpretable on others. This being so, the proper procedure is to investigate with care anything purporting to be an archeological datu mlikely to throw light on points left obscure or unnoticed in our written records. I do not think that Père Braun has adopted this method. He has, without leaving room for a different view, a particular interpretation of some phrases in the Gospels, which (so he thinks) compels him to reject *a priori* the case for the shroud. He has

[2] J. E. Belser, *History of the Passion*, 1929, p.561.

certainly shown no sign of having properly investigated this case, which he professes to reject by a few casual disjointed remarks:

> The fact of the Resurrection of Jesus [he says[3]] is too important to be tied to the fate of a relic whose authenticity does not appear to me to be tenable from any point of view. The reasons for this assertion have been sufficiently given elsewhere.

No one known to the present writer has been so stupidly misled as to tie the Resurrection to the genuineness of the shroud ; nor is it easy to understand how it could be " tied." And the sweeping statement that the authenticity is untenable from any point of view is not excused by a reference to his 1940 brochure where he brings forward Clément's fake, asserts that the Poor Clares turned the wrong side out, and casually mentions Pierre d'Arcis. It is too late in the day to play the part of Chevalier Redivivus.

What many exegetical opponents have overlooked is that, in connection with Our Lord's burial, there are two different possibilities concerning the use of the Turin cloth (assumed genuine), which we call a shroud.

(1) It is the sheet or sindon in which His body was temporarily enfolded at the foot of the Cross, and perhaps—with less probability —in which it was transported to the tomb. This is not a new view.[4] It was held by Pingonio (1581), Paleotti (†1610), Malloni (1616), Chifflet (1624). Malloni thinks that the image was impressed on the Turin cloth when the body was taken down from the Cross ; not after washing, unction and limb-binding (which like Père Braun he assumes) ; for, unless a miracle occurred, he says, the spices and bandages would have prevented the formation of an image. This is also the view held by the late Mgr. Barnes (p.40) : " The record imprinted on the shroud must have been completed before the body was ever prepared for the tomb . . . As to what happened during the hours of the entombment, the shroud has for us no message to give."[5] To this it has been objected—e.g. by Père Renié ii. 150—that such an image could not be formed in the short interval between deposition and entombment. But this objection

---

[3] *Jésus : histoire et critique*, 1947, p.182.
[4] Malloni in Paleotti, p.20 ; Chifflet, p.902. Chifflet (pp.838, 845) suggested that the Besançon cloth was the shroud used in the sepulchre. Quaresmius (ii. 405) discusses the question and leaves it open.
[5] On p.38 he refers to the flow from the foot-wound down towards the heel, and infers that the nail had only just been withdrawn. Mgr. Barnes also (like Père Braun) assumed the use of aromatics and bandages and the binding of the limbs.

is based on the acceptance of Vignon's hypothesis (oxidation of aloetin by ammoniacal emanations). The more recent experiments on cadavers show that only a very brief period of contact is required. A more serious objection is that if the body were placed immediately on the shroud, the dorsal portion would have been flooded with blood from the vena cava inferior through the side-wound (see p.342). If this be correct, some interval must be allowed before the body was placed in the shroud.

(2) The commoner view of upholders of the shroud is that it was used only in the tomb.

> The blood in a case of violent death does not necessarily coagulate altogether, but may flow out from deep wounds especially of the blood vessels. This would also increase when rigor mortis passed off. Hence it is not necessary to believe, as some have held, that the body must have been placed on the shroud at the foot of the cross. Had this occurred, that sheet would have been badly and irregularly smudged with bloodstains ; but there is certainly no indication of this.—Dr. P. W. O'Gorman, *Eccles. Review* 102 (1940) 216.
>
> In spite of art-tradition, I do not hold that the shroud served to receive Christ's body when taken down from the Cross, nor for its transport from Golgotha to the sepulchre ; but only inside the tomb for arranging the body on the funeral bed. For otherwise the impressions could not have the great regularity which they possess.—Dr. Gedda, in *Tabor*, January 1947.

Against this view three main objections have been raised. (*a*) It seems impossible to explain naturally the stains on the shroud if Our Lord's body had been washed and anointed.[6] But it is an uncertain inference from the Gospels that the body was so treated. (*b*) St. John speaks of grave-clothes (*othonia*), from which it is inferred that the *sindon* had been cut up into strips or bandages to bind the body. This, however, is a most precarious inference and can be justly denied. It is even very uncertain whether *othonia* has really a plural meaning at all (cf. p.2 above). (*c*) In addition St. John speaks of " the sudarium that was over His head." Some have interpreted this to be the sindon or winding sheet itself ; which

---

[6] " It seems impossible to explain the shroud naturally if Our Lord's body were completely and ritually washed and prepared for the final burial."—C. McNaspy, S.J., p.155. Père Braun who, without the smallest support from the Gospels, maintains washing of the body, etc., feels logically bound to reject the shroud. This attitude is not really exegetical, nor does it involve any serious investigation of the shroud. The washing of Our Lord's body is denied by Brucker, Lévesque, Vaccari, Wuenschel and many others. I have myself argued elsewhere against it.

is very doubtful. Some have said it was *outside* the sheet ; which would be a peculiar position. Others have interpreted it as a chin-strap passing over the head. But even if we suppose that it was a veil over the face but *inside* the sheet, it can no longer be said with Vignon (ii. 69) that, according to the Turin shroud " no veil was interposed between the face of Jesus and the cloth." This is now refuted by the experiments of Dr. Judica Cordiglia recorded above. He interprets the sudarium (i. 29) as " a kind of finely woven handkerchief, like a veil of linen or silk, which covered the face of the corpse before it was enclosed in the sindon."

(3) Theology

In connection with the bloodstains on the shroud—on the assumption that there are such—a theological point may arise. Whatever be the view held as to whether human blood is or is not " informed " by the soul, it would seem to be theologically certain that Christ's Blood was hypostatically united to the Word. As to His dead Body, most of the Western Fathers[1] implied a separation of the Word and the Body of Christ ; this was not a theological teaching properly so called, as the point had not come up for investigation or controversy. The hypostatic union of the Divinity and the dead Body, asserted in the East by St. Gregory of Nyssa and in the West by St. Leo, is now accepted doctrine.

What about the blood shed during the Passion and until the Resurrection? In the 15th century a violent controversy broke out on the subject between the Dominicans and the Franciscans ; the former holding that such blood was an essential, the latter a concomitant, part of the Humanity. After a debate in the presence of Pius II, he imposed silence[2] on both parties in 1464. It is now held that during the period from Death to Resurrection " the

---

[1] " In none of them have we found an explicit affirmation of the hypostatic union of the Word with the dead Body of Christ."—R. Favre, S.J., *Revue d'hist. ecclés.* 33 (1937) 722. Says St. Augustine (*In Ioan.* tr. 78, 2) : " The Man Christ is also Son of God, as even His sole flesh in the sepulchre deserved to be called . . . When we believe in the Son of God who was buried, then assuredly we also call Son of God the flesh which alone was buried." Some references may be given : J. Lebon, Une ancienne opinion sur la condition du corps du Christ dans la mort.—*Rev. d'hist. ecclés.* 23 (1927) 5-43, 209-241. R. Favre, S.J., Credo in Filium Dei mortuum et sepultum.—*Ibid.* 33 (1937) 587-624. A. d'Alès, S.J., La condition du corps du Christ dans la mort.—*Recherches de sc. rel.* 21 (1931) 200f.
[2] Denzinger-Bannwart, *Enchiridion,* n. 718 (1908[10], p.251).

Logos remained hypostatically united at least with that portion of His Precious Blood which He re-assumed after the Resurrection."[3]

Various places[4] claimed relics of the Precious Blood. St. Thomas took a severe view :

> All the blood which flowed from Christ's body, belonging as it does to the integrity of human nature, rose again with His body . . . But the blood preserved as relics in some churches did not flow from Christ's side, but is said to have flowed from some maltreated image of Christ.—3, *q.* 54, *a.* 3, *ad* 3.

But no theologian would to-day deny on purely theological grounds the possibility of such relics[5] ; if they are genuine, the blood was not re-assumed but permanently eliminated from the Divinity.

Cardinal de la Rovere[6] (later Sixtus IV), in his *De sanguine Christi* (1474) spoke of " the shroud in which Christ's body was wrapped when it was taken down from the Cross, which is guarded with great devotion by the Dukes of Savoy and which is reddened with Christ's blood." Julius II made these words his own when in 1506 he approved of Mass and Office for Chambéry, extended to all Savoy by Leo X.

Some writers, thinking that signs of decomposition are to be noticed on the shroud, consider that this does not constitute a theological objection :

> These observations are in conformity with theological data ; until the Resurrection the body of Christ was subject to the general law which governs the human organism, including death and corruption.—J. Francez, S.J., p.241.
> Our Lord's human body would continue to react like a human body after death (as in life) until the moment appointed for its resurrection and glorification.—C. McNaspy, S.J., p.159f.

It is, however, extremely doubtful whether there is on the shroud any evidence whatever of decomposition in the strict sense.[7]

---

[3] Pohle-Preuss, *Christology*, 1916[2], p. 172. Cf. p. 174: "The Blood which Christ shed at the circumcision, and when He was scourged, and during His agony on Mount Olivet, unquestionably left the union with His Godhead for ever."
[4] Particularly Bruges : Mgr. Malou, *Du culte du Saint Sang et de la relique de ce Sang conservé à Bruges,* 1851.
[5] St. Jerome had no difficulty in speaking of " a column, supporting the porch of the Church (of Sion), stained with the Lord's blood."—Ep. 108 : PL. 22. 884.
[6] Chevalier i. p. xlv ; Beecher, p.83 ; Vignon, ii. 102.
[7] Dr. Caselli of Fano and Dr. Masera of Genoa deny any signs of decomposition.—Trossarelli, p.532. But see Vignon, ii. 37.

CHAPTER VII

THE FACE OF CHRIST

(1) The Good Shepherd

IN THE Roman Catacombs close on a hundred representations of Christ as the Good Shepherd have been discovered. The art-influence is Greek ; a himation, not a Roman toga, is represented. Just as Orpheus charming the beasts with his lyre was chosen to figure Christ, so Hermes Criophoros may have been pressed into Christian service.[1] But in addition to the Old Testament and to contemporary agricultural life, the Gospels themselves were sufficient to inspire this imagery. He went to find the strayed sheep (Matt 18^{12}), He even brought it back on His own shoulders (Luc 15^{5}). In St. John (10$^{11.14}$) Our Lord explicitly declares: " I am the Good Shepherd." That the Shepherd in the Catacombs represented Christ amid His flock is made quite clear by the frequent use of the symbol in funerary inscriptions. Figure vii. 1 is the epitaph of Gerontius in the Cemetery of Domitilla (3rd century).

VII. 1.—" Gerontius may you live in God "
Epitaph in the Cemetery of Domitilla

Some illustrations from the Catacombs and elsewhere are given. Figure vii. 2 is from the fresco in the vault of the oldest chamber of the Catacomb of Domitilla (before A.D. 100). Clad in a tunic, He with His two hands supports a lamb on His shoulders. He is standing in a meadow with two sheep near Him. Figure vii. 3

---

[1] But representations of Hermes Criophoros seem not to occur in monumental art after the end of the fourth century B.C.

gives a similar figure from a fresco in the same Catacomb (A.D. 300–350). Behind the two lambs in the meadow are two orantes, on a scale disproportionately small. The Shepherd is Christ ; and it is made clear that the two lambs represent two deceased faithful. Figure vii. 4 gives the central portion of a sarcophagus in the Lateran Museum (about A.D. 350), in which three statues of the Good Shepherd divide crowded vintage scenes full of *putti*. In this case it will be noticed that the Shepherd is bearded. Figure vii. 5 gives a detail from a mosaic filling the arch over the entrance of the Mausoleum erected by the Empress-Regent Galla Placidia (†450) in Ravenna. Clad in a golden tunic and a purple mantle, He sits amid a rocky landscape, surrounded by His sheep. His left hand is raised to hold the golden cross-surmounted staff, His right hand is held out to caress a lamb. Here the symbolism becomes evidenced by the cross and the nimbus. Except in fig. vii. 4 the Shepherd is beardless and youthful. It is obvious that there is no attempt at giving a likeness.

(2) Early Representations

Let us now look at some of the earliest surviving pictures and statues of Christ. Figure vii. 6 gives a detail of a fresco in the Catacomb of Domitilla (about 300 A.D.), the full picture represents Christ as seated.[1] The figure is very youthful ; notice the abundant hair. Figure vii. 7 is the bust[2] from a statuette of Christ seated, now in the Museo Nazionale, Rome (also about 300). When first discovered, the figure was taken to be that of a poetess. Figure vii. 8 gives the central panel of the sarcophagus of Junius Bassus who died in 359. The youthful Christ is seated between Peter and Paul, He is handing the roll of the New Law to Peter ; underneath Him is the world personified by a human figure. The bearded faces of the two Apostles seem meant to be lifelike ; but Our Lord is reverently portrayed with divine youth. The next illustration[3] (fig. vii. 9) is a high-relief of Christ and two Apostles ; the fragment is now in Berlin, it is a marble panel forming part of a sarcophagus, and probably came from Asia Minor. It is usually dated 300–350, but may be more recent. The central tallest figure is Christ, with a

---

[1] Wilpert's *Malereien*, plate 76 (1) ; the full illustration is given on plate 124.
[2] Vignon, ii. 118.
[3] Cabrol, *Dict. d'arch.* 2 (1925) fig. 1537, from Strzygowski, *Orient oder Rom*, plate 2.

crucifer-nimbus, in toga and sandals, taking an attitude adopted
by classical orators. The face is unfortunately damaged, but clearly
it was beardless.

VII. 10.—Fresco in the Catacomb of
Domitilla (sketch by Heaphy)

Let us now turn to some early representations of Christ as bearded
Figure vii. 10 is a sketch made by Heaphy[4] from a life-size fresco
medallion in the Catacomb of St. Callistus, which has now been
destroyed by damp and torch-smoke. Heaphy, who was prone to
early dates, assigned it to " the beginning or middle of the second
century " ; the third century is much more probable. Heaphy's
sketch gives a strikingly " traditional " likeness. Figure vii. 11 is a
fresco from the Catacomb of Domitilla,[5] dated about 250. Here
Christ has a short beard.

In fig. vii. 12 we have a seated figure of Christ (with crucifer
nimbus), between the medallions of Constantine and Fausta. He
is clothed in a rich embroidered tunic, with a mantle thrown over
the left shoulder ; He probably holds a roll in the left hand. The
imaged object is an earthenware bowl or plate which probably
came from Egypt ; it is now in the British Museum. As it has an
inscription mentioning Fausta, wife of Constantine, it must be
prior to her death (A.D. 329).

---

[4] T. Heaphy, *The Likeness of Christ*, 1886[2], p.46 ; C. C. Dobson, *The Face of Christ*,
1933, p.76. Heaphy says : " Unfortunately the smoke from the tapers of visitors
and the damp from the rock have so operated to obscure it that the tints of
colour, beyond light and shade, are indistinguishable."
[5] Wilpert's *Malereien*, plate 40 (2).

Figure vii. 13 shows the bust of Christ as portrayed in the time of Constantine in the mosaic of the apse of the Lateran Basilica. " In the eleventh and twelfth centuries it was believed to be the earliest portrait of our Saviour publicly exhibited in Rome."[6] This heavily-bearded long-haired figure has none of the severe rigidity usual in later Byzantine paintings. This fine majestic bust shows that the " traditional " representation dates from the Constantinian epoch of freedom.

VII. 12.—Earthenware Bowl (prior to 329) now in the British Museum

Figure vii. 14 shows a figure of Christ which occurs in the Catacomb of SS. Peter and Marcellinus (about 400)[7] He has a short beard ; His long hair is parted in the middle and falls on the shoulders ; He has large eyes fixed on the beholder. There is a large nimbus with the XP monogram, alpha and omega.

Figure vii. 15 reproduces a portion of the mosaic in the apse of the Church of St. Pudentiana, Rome, which was enlarged and decorated under Pope Siricius about 395. Christ is seated on purple cushions on a jewelled throne, with His right hand He is blessing, with His left he holds a book with the inscription *Dominus Conservator Ecclesiae Pudentianae.* Around Him but lower are seated the twelve Apostles. Behind them two blue-robed women with brown pallium

[6] H. Grisar, S.J., *History of Rome and the Popes in the Middle Ages*, 3 (1912) 302f. This is the only known photo (by Parker) of this famous figure of Christ taken before its " restoration." (The negative has been destroyed by fire). There was a medieval legend that the likeness miraculously appeared at the dedication of the Basilica by Pope Silvester.
[7] Wilpert's *Malereien*, plates 252-3.

hold crowns ; presumably they are the Church of the Jews and the Church of the Gentiles. On a hill behind, amid towers and churches, there is a huge golden cross ornamented with jewels ; this probably represents Jerusalem of the fourth century. The four animal-symbols of the Evangelists float in the clouds. We have here the forerunner of the Christ of Majesty, though not holding the Last Judgement, but with the Apostles as a celestial senate. The bust of Christ in fig. vii. 16 is from the Catacomb of St. Pontianus[8] ; its date is uncertain, it may be as late as the ninth century.

From these illustrations we can see that the type, familiar to us in later art, was only gradually reached. It is not proved that at the beginning only the beardless type prevailed. It was Hadrian (117–138) who introduced the Roman fashion of wearing beards, which hitherto were regarded as distinctive of the philosopher or the mourner. But even in the first century a beard was probably common among foreigners and perhaps among natives of the lower class ; in the second century the custom became general. Our Lord as a Jew was bearded ; but even when He is so represented in early monuments, there is no indication that an individual likeness was being aimed at. Two artistic modes came into existence. On the one hand, there is the Hellenistic ideal of a beardless adolescent, soon to be accompanied by the nimbus which was given to divinities and is found in the first statues of the Buddha. On the other hand, there is the Oriental type of bearded Christ, of majestic mien and supernormal stature. From the sixth century this latter type prevailed exclusively in the East, while both types persisted in the West even as late as the eleventh century. That both types were symbolic is shown by their simultaneous occurrence. In a third century sarcophagus of Arles (reproduced by Le Blant), Christ is represented as beardless when washing Peter's feet and when appearing before Pilate ; but in the centre of the composition, standing on the mystical mountain whence flow the four rivers of Paradise, He is bearded. In the nave of Sant' Apollinare Nuovo in Ravenna (500–525) there are two series of mosaics : (1) scenes of miracles, where Christ is beardless and youthful ; (2) the Passion and the Resurrection, where He is depicted as bearded and mature.

In the Vatican there is a statue of Augustus of the hellenised and generalised beardless type ; whereas more individual and lifelike

---

[8] Wilpert, plate 257 ; Vignon, ii. 150, who compares it with the face on the shroud.

busts have survived of Vespasian and Caracalla. But in the East, at least in Egypt, real portraiture existed and continued.[9] Orthodox Christians, however, at first seemed reluctant to essay a likeness of Christ, which was probably due to reverence, fear of idolatry and Jewish prejudice.[10] According to Irenaeus, Epiphanius and Hippolytus, the Gnostics had images of Christ and said that His portrait had been painted by Pilate.[11] The literary descriptions of Our Lord are very late : St. John Damascene in the 8th century, Pseudo-Lentulus in the 14th.[12] And we must reluctantly conclude that neither is there any artistic basis for a real likeness.[13]

(3) Christ in Later Art

We can now resume our survey with figure vii. 17, which is part of a seventh century fresco in the Crypt of St. Cecilia in the Catacomb of St. Callistus, Rome. The next example (fig. vii. 18) is from the East ; it gives the head of Christ which occurs in a miniature depicting the cure of the bent woman, in a manuscript of the works of St. Gregory of Nazianzus,[1] written about 880. Figure vii. 19 is a detail from a mosaic in the apse of the Basilica of St. Ambrose, Milan.[2] It is attributed to the Abbot Gaudentius (about 835) ;

[9] There is in Berlin a painted limestone statue of the wife of Ichnaton (c. 1360 B.C.) —Helen Gardner, *Art through the Ages*, 1936[2], p.40. In Graeco-Roman Egypt there prevailed the custom of placing a bust-portrait, painted on wood or cloth, over the face of the mummy. Illustrations are given by A. Reinach, *Revue arch.* 24 (1914) 32-53, 25 (1915) 1-36. In connection with our Shroud, it is interesting to note (p.50) that paintings on cloth were very rare ; but especially in the case of mummies of infants, the shroud might directly receive the portrait. The cloth, mounted on a square frame, was covered with a thin layer of stucco ; the colours were applied with water plus egg-yolk, fig-juice or gummy liquid ; no oil was used.
[10] There is the well-known story of St. Epiphanius destroying a tapestry with an image of Christ, which he found in a village church near Jerusalem. As late as the year 600, Serenus, bishop of Marseilles, destroyed all the images in his diocese, and was reprehended by St. Gregory the Great.
[11] The assertion that St. Luke painted images of Christ and of Our Lady is found in a fragment formerly attributed to St. John Damascene, but probably by St. Andrew of Crete : P.G. 97. 1304. The statue at Paneas mentioned by Eusebius (H. E. vii. 18, 4) was probably a profane work misinterpreted.
[12] It is well known that the Fathers differed, but their views were based, not on tradition, but on passages of the Old Testament. That He was ugly is maintained (on the strength of Isaiah 53[2]) by Justin, Irenaeus, Tertullian, Cyprian, Clement of Alexandria. That He was beautiful is held (on the strength of Psalm 44[3]) by Jerome, Basil, Augustine, Chrysostom.
[13] It is not intended by this remark to reduce the function of art to historical portraiture.
[1] Bibliothèque Nationale, Paris, MS. gr. 510 ; Vignon ii. 156 after Omont.
[2] Vignon, ii. 160 ; he compares it with the face on the shroud.

but it may be more recent. The next illustration (fig. vii. 20) is from the East.[3] It is from the mosaic over the royal door leading from the narthex into the church of St. Sophia, Constantinople, recently uncovered by the Byzantine Institute of America.

Figure vii. 21 gives portion of the mosaic in the central cupola of the church of Daphni in Greece (about 1100) ; it is the typical Pantocrator of Greek artists. There is gain as well as loss in the disappearance of the Good Shepherd behind the stern features of the Majestic King of the Byzantine apse ; fear and law become more prominent than love and grace. By way of contrast, fig. vii. 22 presents a specimen of Gothic art. It is the head of the statue (Le Beau Dieu) at the central door of the west façade of Amiens Cathedral (1200–50). Observe the regular features, the straight nose, the forked beard : almost a classical Grecian type.

With fig. vii. 23 we reach the thirteenth century. It is from the fresco of the Last Judgement in Saint Cecilia, Trastevere, Rome, by Pietro Cavallini (about 1293)[4]. It expresses the classic impassiveness of justice. Figure vii. 24 is a Flemish type, a painting by Jan Van Eyck, dated 1438, now in Berlin. A deviation from the accepted type is given in fig. vii. 25, which is the finished study by Leonardo da Vinci (1452-1519) for his Last Supper. The face is beardless, the eyes are half-closed, the expression is calm but grief-laden ; but there is no religious feeling in the picture. In spite of the current admiration lavished on this representation, the following criticism of Leonardo is fully justified :

> The famous Christ of his Last Supper is simply the handsome and, to our thinking, somewhat effeminate young hero who was the artistic ideal of Renaissance humanism. He bears no relation to the Incarnate God of history and Catholic belief.—E. I. Watkin, *Catholic Art and Culture*, 1944, p.71.

Figure vii. 26 gives us a fresco by Sodoma (1479-1554) in the Convent of St. Anne, Camprena.

The next group of illustrations shows us the conceptions held by four great artists from different countries. Figure vii. 27 is a detail from " The Tribute Money " by Titian (1477-1576), now in Dresden Gallery. Christ is looking intently at the dark-faced Pharisee and

---

[3] J. Pijoan, *Art in the Middle Ages*, 1938, p.97. The full picture is given in Lowrie, *Art in the Early Church*, 1947, plate 77A.
[4] " Cavallini is the creator of sacred Roman painting of the 13th century."— Venturi, *Short History of Italian Art*, 1926, p.117.

points to the coin which is being thrust towards Him. In fig. vii. 28 we have a characteristic picture by El Greco, dated 1604-09, now in the sacristy of Toledo Cathedral. The next (fig. vii. 29) is the bust of Christ from " The Tribute Money " by A. Van Dyck (†1641), now in the Palazzo Bianco, Genoa. Then in fig. vii. 30 we have a representation of Christ by Rembrandt (1606-1669), now in Berlin.

Finally four practically contemporary presentations may be given. Figure vii. 31 is a detail from Munkacsy's famous " Christ before Pilate." Figure vii. 32 is a Russian picture by Vasnetsof (1905)[5]. Figure vii. 33 is the head of the large polychrome statue in stone of the Sacred Heart, by Henri Charlier, erected at Saint-Julien des Landes. In fig. vii. 34 we have one of the deliberately crude imitation-glass paintings by Georges Rouault.

(4) The Suffering Christ

Some illustrations are given of the face depicted in the pathetic thorn-crowned Christ of Pity. Figure vii. 35 is from a life-sized statue, carved in oak, in the Monastery of Fischbeck in Lower Saxony ; it is attributed to the twelfth century and so is an early specimen. The enormous crown of thorns here shown became typical of German art. Figure vii. 36 is the famous representation by Bartolomé Bermejo (*floruit* 1474-95), now in the Museum of Vich, Catalonia. A softer more appealing portrait is that of Cima da Conegliano (about 1500) in the National Gallery, London (fig. vii. 37). There is a lack of feeling in the picture (fig. vii. 38) by Fra Bartolommeo (1475-1517) in the Pinacoteca, Florence.

A detail from the Ecce Homo by Murillo (†1682), now in the Madrid Gallery, is given in fig. vii. 39. The inferior Ecce Homo of Carlo Dolci (1616-1686) is given in fig. vii. 40.

Two representations of the Face of Christ while carrying His Cross are given in figures vii. 41 and 42. The first is by Perugino (1446-1524), the second by El Greco (painted about 1590).

Two views of the Face of Christ suffering on the Cross are given in figures vii. 43 and 44. The first is from a Crucifixion by Guido Reni (1575-1642). The second is from the famous carved-wood Crucifix of Limpias in North Spain, which appears to have been carved by Pedro de Mena (1628-1688).

[5] Stephen Graham, *The Quest of the Face*, 1918.

Finally two specimens are given of the mystical figure of the Man of Sorrows who, though pierced in the side *post mortem*, is represented as alive and appealing to us. Figure vii. 45 is a picture by Meister Francke, which is now in Leipzig. Supported by an angel, He shows His sidewound with His right hand and holds the scourge in the left. The drawing is much better in the other picture (vii. 46), now in Strasbourg Museum ; it is by a pupil of Roger van der Weyden (who died in 1464).

(5) The Dead Christ

We shall now give some illustrations of how artists depicted the face of the Dead Christ. First on the Cross. Figure vii. 47 is a detail from the bronze crucifix in Werden, Germany, which is probably of the late eleventh century. It is cast in simple broad surfaces. Note the closed swollen eyes, and also the hair on the head delineated as if it were a tight-fitting cap. (See the same feature in the crucifix of fig. xii. 61). Figure vii. 48 shows the remains of a crucifix by Claus Sluter (about 1398), now in Dijon Museum. Figure vii. 49 shows a 15th century fragment now in Beauvais museum. Figure vii. 50 introduces a greater element of pain and suffering ; it is the head of the crucifix carved in lime-wood by Wit Stwosz for the altarpiece of Our Lady in Cracow (15th century). In fig. vii. 51 we have a detail from a fresco of the Crucifixion by Giotto (✝1336) in the Chapel of the Scrovegni, Padua. Even calmer and gentler is the face of the Dead Saviour (fig. vii. 52) in the painting by Fra Angelico (1387-1455) in the first cloister of St. Mark's, Florence.

The next two illustrations display an almost brutal realism. In fig. vii. 53 we can see portion of El Santo Cristo of Burgos Cathedral (dating probably from the last years of the fourteenth century). Human hair (as in other Spanish statues) has been added to the head. While the face does not lack nobility, the body is covered with festering wounds. But much more revolting is the face of the Dead Christ as depicted by Correggio (1494-1534), in a painting in Palermo Museum (fig. vii. 54). All traces of divinity have been eliminated from this cadaveric visage.

The next group is from paintings of the Dead Christ at the foot of the Cross. Figure vii. 55 is a detail from the altarpiece of Grüne-

wald (✝1528), now in Colmar Museum. The face of the Crucified
Christ in the central panel (*Family at Bethany*, fig. 40) is even more
ghastly and revolting. Figure vii. 56 is a detail from the well-known
Antwerp diptych by Quentin Matsys (✝1530). Figure vii. 57
reproduces the touching and realistic painting by Luis de Morales
(✝1586) in Madrid. Figure vii. 58 gives a detail from the Descent
from the Cross by Rubens (✝1640) in Lille Museum. Art has an
almost impossible task in depicting God dying the death of a
criminal ; realism carried to excess eliminates the divine element.
But artists have even more signally failed in trying to depict the
Dead Christ. The few examples given show how easy it is to portray
a merely human corpse without dignity or hope.

(6) Veronica

There is a well-known legend[1] that Abgar of Edessa sent a
deputation to ask Our Lord to come and heal him ; after the
Ascension, Thaddeus, at the request of Thomas, went to Edessa
and cured Abgar. This is the account given by Eusebius about
325. About a century later, a document (The Doctrine of Addai)
tells us that one of Abgar's messengers called Hannan, before
quitting Christ, had a portrait of Him made. The image certainly
existed with an established reputation in Edessa in 544, for it was
produced at the siege by the Persians, and at that time it was
regarded as having been miraculously executed. In 944 the Byzantines got hold of the portrait, with Christ's alleged autograph letter
to Abgar, and stored it in the palace of Bucoleon. This image,
which must have exerted great influence on Byzantine art, unfortunately disappeared at the sack of Constantinople in 1204. Copies
more or less exact—the holy *mantĕlion*, a towel with Christ's likeness—circulated in the East. And several places in the West claimed
to possess the original. (1) It was said to have been ceded by
Baldwin II to St. Louis ; this image was still in the Sainte Chapelle,
Paris, in 1790, when it was destroyed by the revolutionaries.[2] (2) An

[1] L. J. Tixeront, *Les origines de l'église d'Edesse et la légende d'Abgar*, 1888 ; Vignon,
ii. 124ff.
[2] About 1150 a pilgrim saw in the Emperor's chapel (Constantinople) the
" mantile " which when applied to the Lord's visage retained the image of His
face."—Riant, *Exuviae sacrae constant.* 1878, ii. 211. About 1200 another pilgrim
saw in the Bucoleon " a cloth representing Christ's face " (p.218). All the relics
in the Bucoleon were ceded by Baldwin to St. Louis (p.132) ; among these was
" a holy towel inserted in a frame " (p.135).

image exists in San Bartolommeo degli Armeni, Genoa. Only a small part of the original is visible, all except the face being covered with a silver plate ; and it is said to be shown only on Ascension Day. Thomas Heaphy succeeded in making a copy, now in the British Museum. The face is of a severe Byzantine type ; there is a Greek inscription (*to hagion mandelion*). (3) A third claimant is an image in Rome, formerly in San Silvestro in Capite, since 1870 in the Vatican. The original does not appear to be very accessible ; figure vii. 59 is the copy made by Heaphy. The eyes are open, the brows are narrow, the forehead is broad, the nose is long and straight ; notice the three curls on the forehead. The head is surrounded by a halo containing the XP monogram. The expression is much more natural and human than in the usual Byzantine paintings.

VII. 60.—Woodcut (1450) :
The Living Christ on a
Veronica veil

In an early apocryphal work[3] we are told that Bernike (in Latin Veronica), the woman cured of an issue of blood, joined with others in giving evidence in Christ's favour before Pilate. A later addition[4]

[3] Acts of Pilate : M. R. James, *Apocryphal New Testament*, 1924, p.102. *Beroniké*= *Pherenike* (bringer of victory) ; hence *Veronica* is not from *vera icon*. On the Veronica legends : Friedlieb-Martin, *Archéologie de la Passion*, 1897, pp.381-392 ; Hoepfl, *Die Stationen des heiligen Kreuzwegs*, 1913, pp.49-55 ; K. Pearson, *Die Fronica*, Strasburg, 1887 ; and the enormous compilation of documents in E. von Dobschütz, *Christusbilder*, 1899.
[4] James, p.157 ; other versions, pp.158, 160.

—subsequently incorporated in the Golden Legend—tells us that Veronica, wishing to have a picture of Christ, took a linen cloth to a painter ; Christ met her on the way and impressed His image on it ; the cloth served to cure the Emperor Tiberius. So until about 1400 we find in art the passion-free face of Our Lord represented on a cloth held by angels or by Veronica. Figure vii. 60 shows a Flemish woodcut of about 1450. On the other hand, fig. vii. 61 shows a German woodcut[5] of about 1476, on which the head is thorn-crowned. The face is certainly not the Byzantine type. Henceforth many artists reproduced the thorn-crowned head of the suffering Christ, with or without Veronica holding the cloth. Figure vii. 62 reproduces a woodcut by Dürer, and vii. 63 a painting by Matsys.

These reproductions show that a later legend connected Veronica with the Passion, making her one of the women who met Our Lord on the way to Calvary, as shown in the engraving by Martin Schongauer (1420-1488) in fig. vii. 64. This version was certainly known in France before 1300, and was connected with the Graal legend ; it reached Germany later.[6] Fifteenth century pilgrims to the Holy Land mention Veronica's house in Jerusalem and identify her cloth with the sudarium in Rome.[7]

[5] Figs. vii. 60 and 61 from Pearson (plates 9 and 11).
[6] It is found in *Le Petit Saint Graal* of Robert de Borron (manuscript dated 1301) : Hucher, *Le Saint Graal*, 1877, ii. 296-305 ; Pearson, p.48. Also, according to Dobschütz (pp.251, 304 *) about 1300 in the Bible of Roger of Argenteuil. It occurs in the mystery-plays : Arnoul Greban's *Le mystère de la Passion* (1452), in the English *Ludus Coventriae* (about 1450). In the *Passion de Roman*, a woman (unnamed) gives the cloth to her daughter to sell it ; but she hands it to the executioner to wipe Christ's face ; there is no mention of an image.—Grace Frank, *La Passion d'Autun*, 1934, p.199. Similarly in Wynkyn de Worde's English version (1509) of an unknown original we read that Syndonia, who supported herself and her mother by silk-weaving, sold a wonderful scarf to Joseph in the market-place of Capernaum (!), and he said : " Now after you I shall name this cloth, for this cloth shall be named Syndonia." There is no mention of an image and no direct connection with the Passion.—W. H. Hulme, *The Middle-English Harrowing of Hell*, (EETS), 1907, p.lix.
[7] Thus Felix Fabri in 1483 : Baldi, *Enchiridion locorum sanctorum*, n.939. Extravagant legendary details are found in Anne C. Emmerich's *Dolorous Passion* (Eng. trans. 1926, p.241), perhaps due to her editor Brentano. Also according to the contemporary visionary Therese Neumann, " St. Veronica who wiped the face of Christ on the way to Calvary was she who had been miraculously cured when, prevented by the Apostles from talking to Him, she had succeeded in touching the hem of His garment."—Roy and Joyce, *Theresa Neumann*, 1940², p.98. According to A. Kneller, S.J., the Veronica station was first mentioned in a MS. (dated 1420) of the Pilgrimage of James of Verona.—*Geschichte der Kreuzandacht*, 1908, p.161. The 16th century breviaries of Milan contained the feast of St. Veronica with a special office (4th Feb.) ; it was expunged by St. Charles Borromeo. In the 17th century the Congregation of Rites refused to allow the veneration of St. Veronica. —Kneller, p.192f.

In addition to the image illustrated in fig. vii. 59, there was another of a different type also in Rome, the Santo Volto. Apparently[8] it existed there at least since 705, in St. Peter's, in the chapel consecrated for it by Pope John VII. When the relic was exhibited, it was adorned with an umbella (baldachino) which no longer exists. On this various scenes were embroidered, including one of the Dead Christ, with sponge and lance, surmounted by three angels with flabella. Grimaldi made a drawing[9] of this, which is **given in fig. vii. 65.**

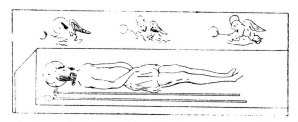

VII. 65.—Grimaldi's Drawing of an image embroidered on the Baldachion for the Santo Volto, Rome

This image was often carried in procession in Rome. Thus[10] in 752, when the city was threatened by the Lombards under Aistulf, Pope Stephen II himself carried " the most sacred portrait of the Lord God and Saviour Jesus Christ." There was a similar procession headed by the image under Leo IV (847–855), and on other occasions. In a work composed before 1143, we are told[11] that the Pope used to go and incense the sudarium of Christ called Veronica. Matthew Paris[12] tells us that in 1216 Innocent III bore

[8] " Since the year 705 there has been preserved at Rome, in St. Peter's, in the chapel *Sancta Maria in Beronica* consecrated for it by Pope John VII, an image of the Saviour called the Veronica."—*Dict. d'arch. chrét.* 7 (1927) 2458. In the *Liber Pontificalis* (ed. Duchesne 1886, i. 385) it is merely said that John VII (705–707) " made an oratory of the Holy Mother of God inside the Church of St. Peter, and decorated its walls with mosaics." In the *Acta Sanctorum* xxvii (Junii vii), 1867, p.76, it is said that besides the main altar dedicated to Our Lady, there was in the oratory another altar, covered with a ciborium or baldachino, where the Sudarium was kept.

[9] The oratory was partly ruined by the opening of the ' holy door ' at the Jubilee of 1300. It was demolished in 1606, and Grimaldi made sketches of some of the mosaics.—E. Muentz, *Revue arch.*, Sept. 1877 ; *Dict. d'arch. chr.* 7 (1927) 2214, fig. 6167.

[10] *Liber Pontificalis*, ed. Duchesne.

[11] Benedicti beati Petri canonici Liber pollicitus, in Mabillon, *Musaeum italicum*, ii. 118 ; quoted by Friedlieb-Martin, p.390.

[12] *Chronica majora*, ed. Luard, 3 (1876) 7.

the Veronica from St. Peter's to the Hospital of the Holy Ghost. Matthew Paris then adds : " The Veronica has this name from a certain woman who was so called, at whose petition Christ made the impression." While we have here the later version that the image was made by Christ Himself, there is as yet no connection with the legend that the image was imprinted on the way to Calvary.

In 1350 there was a great concourse of pilgrims to Rome for the jubilee instituted by Clement VI, and the Sudarium or Veronica was exhibited several times. Chevalier (iii. 17) suggests that it was this event which led to the concoction of the sudarium at Lirey in 1353, " to attract the faithful in crowds and to benefit by their largesse". The Canon had a very poor opinion of his predecessors of the 14th century ; and we need not argue further that the shroud is not a painting. There was a similar jubilee in 1300 when the Veronica was also exhibited ; apparently no one then thought of imitating it. But how could anyone in 1350 think of faking what was universally admitted to be in Rome? And why devise a long winding-sheet with two complete imprints when it was only the Santo Volto that was famous? Furthermore, there is no evidence that at this date the Romans connected their image with the Passion, most certainly not with the Dead Christ. There was a popular guide for pilgrims to Rome called *Mirabilia Urbis Romae*. After the invention of printing there were many editions. That printed in Rome in 1515 contains an illustration (fig. vii. 66). This shows the Pope exhibiting the image which contains no traces of the Passion.

It is curiously difficult to obtain any idea of this image. It is in a silver and gilt frame allowing only the face to be seen, and the painting is covered by glass. It is apparently now almost effaced. Close inspection is not allowed. But the indefatigable Thomas Heaphy (1813-1873) claimed to have, by devious methods, obtained access to it. He made a copy which is reproduced in fig. vii. 67. This is his description :

> It is much obscured and in many parts nearly obliterated by the decay of the cloth on which it is executed. But the very rags and stains, by dimming its execution and taking away the appearance of the hand of man, seem to add to its singular impressiveness. The wet matted hair, the tears, the blood-drops from the crown of thorns, are expressive of the stern reality of death ; while the calm nearly-closed eyes, the gently-parted lips, speak not of corruption but of the spirit at that moment in Paradise

and of the shortly to be accomplished Resurrection . . . Like other
of the greatest triumphs of art, this effort has been accomplished
with the meanest instruments : a piece of cloth without anything
in the shape of preparation, a little transparent pigment, apparently nothing more than a mere stain without colour. Nevertheless this dimly-figured head on a tattered rag—for its inspiration,
its conception and its power of execution—is certainly unsur-
passed, perhaps hardly equalled, in the whole range of art. —*The
Likeness of Christ*, 1886², p.51f.

VII. 66.—The Veronica Image : Illustration from *Mirabilia Urbis Romae*.
1515

Here (unlike fig. vii. 59) the eyes are closed ; to express the superhuman, the face and the nose are made relatively long. (Presumably the white marks are due to injuries in the cloth). It lacks the
crown of thorns which came into vogue in such pictures only about
1425–50. It is not quite clear whether the picture is meant to have
any connection with the Passion, though the face conveys suffering.
It has been in fact denied that it depicts the Dead Christ.[13]

Alleged facsimiles on cloth, taken from a plate of the 18th (or

[13] " There is no proof that the picture in St. Peter's represents the Dead Christ ;
when approached by an object, the eyes close through an instinctive movement."
—Friedlieb-Martin, p.388. In fact the Roman Veronica seems to have been first
connected with Gethsemani (to wipe the blood-sweat) rather than with the Via
Dolorosa.—Romanus Canonicus cited in the *Acta Sanctorum*, Junii vii. 68.

perhaps 17th) century, have long been in circulation. Fig. vii. 68 reproduces one such, widely propagated by Léon Dupont (1797-1876), " the holy man of Tours." Artistically it is certainly unprepossessing ; it is much cruder than Heaphy's copy, though it has a general resemblance. Nevertheless, it has inspired thousands with devotion.

It is very doubtful whether Heaphy's reproduction of the Santo Volto can be accepted as accurate. We do not know how far he obtained access to it.

> It is impossible to make a copy. Only once a year, on Holy Thursday, is the venerable relic exposed, from the top of a tribune at St. Peter's, to the veneration of the faithful. The distance is such that nobody in the crowd could distinguish any trait of the image. Only officials of the Basilica can approach it ; and I learn from an eminent prelate that it is impossible for the most careful observer to trace any line on the cloth or to find in it the least form of a human face.—Gaffre, p.156.

Heaphy admitted that the picture was " much obscured and in many parts nearly obliterated." This is tantamount to an admission that his reproduction was not an accurate rendering of what he claimed to have seen. He could not have really seen all these features in a picture which was admittedly illegible. He was, however, familiar with alleged copies which were in circulation. It seems certain that he drew upon one of these for his inspiration ; in Père Gaffre's book (p.155) there is reproduced an engraving (of the seventeenth century) which closely resemble's Heaphy's picture. There is no proof that these ' copies ' were accurate reproductions of the Veronica ;[14] in fact they differ completely from the older versions which were of the type of fig. vii. 66. So we really know nothing of the image (now effaced) on the cloth. From the art-historical standpoint it is very difficult to believe that such a picture as Heaphy's originated as early as the eighth century. And of course his statement (p.51) that " the ascertained history of the work reaches back directly to the second century " is quite untenable.

[14] According to Père Gaffre (p.157), in 1248 Jacques de Troyes (afterwards Urban IV) charged a painter with the task of copying the Veronica in Rome. This was sent to his sister and is now in the Cathedral of Laon. It is " a Graeco-oriental interpretation of the Veronica, made by a Slav painter." See the reproduction in Gaffre (p.156) or Vignon (ii. 185). In reality, the Holy Face of Laon is a Russian icon. On p.152 Père Gaffre has an illustration of a copy of the Veronica made in the 16th century for the Escorial. This is an unrecognisably idealised version—eyes open, no trace of suffering, etc.—closely resembling the Flemish Christs.

(7) **The Face on the Shroud**

St. Thérèse of Lisieux (†1897) had great devotion to the Holy Face in the reproduction circulated by Dupont. When Pia's photograph of the shroud was published in 1898, her sister Céline spent six months in making an excellent copy, which is reproduced in fig. vii. 69. This was equivalent to " touching up " the photo and removing extraneous accidentals such as the transverse folds of the cloth. She interpreted too literally some features which were due to defects in Pia's photograph (e.g. the tearing of the right eyelid) ; and the pronounced fracture of the nose was really caused by the cloth not being carefully stretched ; the white line across the left eyelid (and the upper part of the nose) is really due to a small defect in the weave of the cloth.

Though the visage on the shroud has already been briefly described some further remarks are now in order at the end of our iconographic survey. Figure vii. 70 shows us the face as it actually appears on the cloth. Let us see how the details were interpreted in the absence of the negative photograph shown in fig. vii. 71. The real interpretation thus discovered is added in brackets. The eyebrows and the nose are heavily marked in the form of a T. (The crossline is really the forehead, not the eyebrows which have made no special mark and are distinguished from the forehead only by progressive shading). The eyes are faintly marked with the centres vaguely resembling the pupils. (The light spots beneath the T correspond to the lower edge of the eyebrows and the eye-cavities). The moustache seems drawn to the left side. (The right side of the moustache is missing owing to a vertical defect in the cloth). The dark mouth is very close to the nose. (This is really the moustache which appears white in fig. vii. 71). A pale band just beneath appears to be a lit-up lower lip. (This is really the mouth or rather the lower end of the moustache.) Next there comes a dark line in fig. vii. 70 like a shadow beneath the lower lip. (This is actually the lower lip itself). Then comes a lighter space like a chin whose lit-up prominence was beardless. (This is portion of the beard). From these corrections it is clear that the lineaments of the face became properly deciphered only with the aid of the photographic negatives of 1898 and 1931.

Vignon (ii. 123ff.) has propounded and elaborated the thesis that the presence of the shroud can be traced by its iconographic influence back to an early date. The Edessa image, painted in the fifth century, was based on the shroud ; so was the " mandilion " dear to Byzantines since the tenth century. The Byzantine-Slav Holy Faces since the twelfth century show striking resemblances to the face visible on the shroud : absence of neck and shoulders, the long hair framing the sides of the face, and many other minutiae. Such is the thesis, difficult to assess objectively and not generally accepted.

We are on surer ground when we compare the chemograph on the shroud with art-representations of the living or dead Christ. According to Chevalier indeed (i.56), " it is a 14th century type such as one admires in the Beau Dieu of Amiens Cathedral." One has only to refer to fig. vii. 22 to see the absurdity of this judgement. It has actually been suggested[1] that the painter was Sodoma : compare fig. vii. 26. One good history of Christian art[2] tells us that " old and new copies show frontal and dorsal images of a corpse, which to an expert immediately evoke the impression of being representations of the late Middle Ages." But the problem concerns photos of the Shroud, not painted copies. The difficulty of attributing the human figure, with its anatomy and wounds, to a medieval painter has already been pointed out. A similar difficulty applies to the face which is not painted but chemographically impressed. Since 1898 we have been able to study the features of the " model " which imprinted itself on the cloth. Can we fit this into the art of the 14th century or indeed of any epoch? Perhaps Vignon was over-enthusiastic when he wrote (i.107) :

> Among all the works of art which the world has ever known— sculpture or painting—the portrait on the Holy Shroud has never been equalled, much less surpassed. It stands alone.

There is certainly something unique about this image which is not an artefact at all. All works of art reveal a school, an epoch, a particular technique. But this document is out of line, it cannot be classed or dated or given a signature. This portrait, formed by contour-lacking stains on a sheet of coarse linen, has a striking realism. Still more wonderful is the reproduction of the expression

---

[1] Coppier in *Mercure de France*, 1 January 1938, p.335.
[2] Künstle, *Ikonographie der christlichen Kunst* 2 (1928) 589. He did not trouble to inspect the 1898 photograph, he tells us that there are 42 cloths claiming the imprint, he says that " several bishops of Troyes were obliged already in the 14th century to denounce the superstitious veneration of the cloth and to declare the relic not genuine."—*Voilà tout* !

itself with such power and delicacy. No vulgarity of the culpable condemned, no impatience of the rebellious victim. In this noble face there is extraordinary peace, gentle calm, without a trace of human passion ; it shows outraged and merciful dignity. It is the visage of one who though dead is living ; the inner life shows through the features. In vain do we seek for such an effect among the greatest paintings of the Dead Christ. Look, for example, at fig. vii. 56 one of the masterpieces of the Flemish school. The grief-stricken tenderness in the faces of the living actors is well portrayed by Matsys ; but he failed in the detail here reproduced. The face of Christ is simply that of a corpse irretrievably dead—it is the end ! Or turn to fig. vii. 53 where Correggio has depicted a dead face with despairing finality. It is with relief that we come back to the image on the shroud. Are we at last in presence of the real features of Our Lord?

CHAPTER VIII

THE SCOURGING

(1) Roman Flagellation

THE JEWISH punishment of flogging was comparatively mild. The strokes were limited to 39 in order to keep within the maximum of 40 allowed by the Law (Deut 25[2]). Instructions are contained in the Mishnah Tractate *Makkoth* (3[12]). " They bind his two hands to a pillar on either side, and the minister of the synagogue lays hold of his garments . . . so that he bares his chest." While one of the judges recited passages of Scripture, the synagogue-attendant stood on a stone set behind the man, and with a triple strap of cowhide administered 13 strokes on the chest and 13 on each shoulder. Besides being thrice beaten with rods and once stoned, St. Paul " five times received 39 stripes from the Jews " II Cor 11[24]. Hence he could say : " On my body I bear the marks of the Lord Jesus " Gal 6[17]. This is St. Paul's only reference—but how pathetically personal—to the scourging of Our Lord. Peter and John were also flogged by order of the Sanhedrin (Acts 5[43]).

The Roman flagellation, sometimes a separate punishment and sometimes a preliminary to execution, was much more horrible and cruel than the bastinado of the Mosaic law. A lighter penalty was the flogging (*castigatio*) which the lictors inflicted on criminals with the rods of birch or hazel of which their fasces were composed. According to Roman Law[1] in cases involving flogging " a free man is struck with rods but a slave is ordered to be struck with scourges." This scourge was like the Russian knout or the English cat-o'-nine-tails. Leaden balls, sheep-bones or sharp pieces of metal were fixed on the ends of the cords of the *flagrum*.[2] Such an instrument would lacerate the flesh and might injure the internal organs ; with the number of blows unlimited, it often caused death.

At Philippi the magistrates stripped Paul and Silas and ordered them to be beaten with rods (Acts 16[22]). St. Paul declared : " They have beaten us in public without trial, though we are Roman citizens " (16[37]). Later when Paul was in danger of being lynched in the Temple, the Commandant of the Citadel sent soldiers down

---

[1] *Digest*, 48. 19, 10.
[2] Sheep-bones : Apuleius, *Metam* 8[30]; Plutarch, *Adv. Coloten* 33. *Brevis aculeus* : *Codex Theodos.* 8, 5, 2. By an edict of 375 the use of lead-loaded scourges was restricted to *poena ignobilium.*—*Ibid.* 9. 35, 2.

to rescue him. The officer ordered that, in order to elicit information " he should be examined by flogging "—on the very spot where Our Lord had been scourged a few years before. When they had fastened him up[3] with straps, Paul said to the Centurion standing by : " Have you authority to flog one who is a Roman citizen and has not been tried ? " From this we learn that a Centurion was in charge of the punishment, and that the victim's hands were stretched out and bound to a column or columns.[4]

Josephus tells us a story of a Jew, Jesus son of Ananias, who was disturbing the people with his cries of woe about the year 62. " Some of the leading citizens . . . arrested the fellow and inflicted many blows on him." As he continued his warnings, " the rulers [magistrates] brought him before the Roman Governor " Albinus, who ordered him to be scourged :

> Though flayed to the bone with scourges, he neither sued for mercy nor shed a tear. But merely introducing the most mournful variations into his ejaculation, he responded to each stroke with " Woe to Jerusalem." When Albinus the Governor asked him who and whence he was and why he uttered these cries, he answered him never a word but unceasingly reiterated his dirge over the City, until Albinus pronounced him a maniac and let him go.—Josephus, *JewishWar*, vi. 5, 3 (304).

Philo complained of the cruel treatment meted out by the Governor of Egypt to the Jews of Alexandria :

> He ordered them all to be stripped and lacerated with scourges which are commonly used for the degradation of the vilest malefactors. In consequence of the flogging some had to be carried out on stretchers and died at once, while others lay sick for a long time despairing of recovery.—Philo, *In Flaccum* 10[75].

Philo declared that hitherto a distinction had been made according to the status of the culprit. Alexandrian citizens were beaten with rods by lictors, while Egyptians from the country were scourged. He protested against prominent Jewish citizens being " cruelly whipped as if they were Egyptian criminals of the lowest class." But there was no protest in the case of Our Lord.

---

[3] *Proeteinan.* The verb *proteinō* is always used of stretching out the hands.
[4] We read elsewhere of a *columna* (Plautus, *Bacch.* iv. 6, 24) or a *palus* (Aulus Gellius 10[3]). Slaves, like the Christians later, were often hung up while being flogged : " When it was wished to make the punishment more severe, the culprit was manacled and drawn up to a beam, from which he was suspended by the wrists, while a heavy weight was attached to his feet."—W. Ramsay, *The Mostellaria of Plautus*, 1869, p.254.

(2) **The Scourging of Christ**

Many mystics have given us rather gruesome details of the Scourging. According to John Tauler O.P. (†1361)[1], Our Lord was completely stripped, He was tied first facing the pillar and then with His back to it. His body was " all covered with blood and with gaping wounds," His blood " flowed down in large streams upon the earth." St. Bridget of Sweden († 1373) tells us that " when bidden by the lictor, He took off His clothes and embraced the column to which He was bound. His whole body was lacerated and ploughed up by scourges in which sharp points were inserted."[2] And here is an account by a contemporary visionary :

> The column to which the Saviour is bound is rather high. He is drawn up by His hands, yet in such a way that the feet still touch the ground ; and so the body is rigidly stretched out. Two men lash Him mercilessly at the same time ; and twice the torturers change off ; thus they are six. The dear Saviour is being scourged to the extreme over the whole body, first on the back and then on the front. To be deprived of clothes is His greatest suffering. The skin swells up from continued blows ; then it is torn, and the blood streams. The whole body is mangled and seems red from blood and wounds.—E. de Hovre, *The Riddle of Konnersreuth*, 1933, p.118.

The Gospels are much more sober ; each of them merely use one word to indicate the scene. St. Luke (23[16.22]) tells us that Pilate, to induce the crowd to ask for the release of Jesus instead of Barabbas, twice proposed : " I am going to punish Him and then let Him go." The word here used[3] strictly means to educate or to instruct and hence came to be used for to correct or to punish. Pilate offered to release Our Lord after punishment, obviously flogging. St. Luke says no more; he does not even assert that the punishment was carried out. It has been objected that Pilate could

[1] *Meditations on the Life and Passion of Our Lord Jesus Christ*, Eng. trans. 1925, ch. 24, p.143f. Mystics have given various high estimates of the number of blows, e.g. Maria de Agreda : 5115. St. Bridget gives no number for the strokes, though generally credited with the estimate 5,000. Ludolph of Saxony († 1378) quotes a " holy matron " for the number 5490.—*Vita J.C.* ii. 58, 4. " The number of blows inflicted cannot be known for certain except by revelation."—*ibid.* ii. 62, 9.
[2] *Revelationes*, iv. 70, Moguntiae 1680, p.289. Compare the letter from the Christians of Smyrna : " The bystanders were filled with horror when they saw the flesh of the martyrs torn off, their veins and arteries laid bare, even their entrails exposed to view."—Eusebius, HE iv. 23.
[3] Aorist participle in a future sense : *paideusas*. The verb is used in Greek O.T. especially for punishment by God. In Deut 22[18] Hebrew *yissar*, Greek *paideuein*, Latin *verberare*. In Prov 3[12] cited in Hebr 12[6] the verb is made parallel with " scourge."

not publicly offer to scourge a man whom he had pronounced innocent. But Pilate never said that He was innocent from the *Jewish* standpoint. While not criminal or seditious, He was regarded as a misguided fanatic. After being scourged, He would be discredited and lose influence. This was the compromise proposed by the Governor to placate the Jews and to save the Prisoner from a worse fate. That neither Jews nor Romans would have felt any scruple about an admonitory whipping is shown by the quotations already given.

Both Matthew (27^{26}) and Mark (15^{15}) use a stronger word and tell us laconically that, while Barabbas was released, " he had Jesus scourged [*phragellōsas*][4] and handed over to be crucified." We cannot infer from this summary sentence that the scourging was part of, and immediately followed by, the punishment of crucifixion. For both Evangelists proceed to tell us of the mockery-scene and then add $(M27^{31} Mk15^{21})$ that He was led out to be crucified. So the preceding brief reference to crucifixion is by way of an anticipated summary of what befell Christ in contrast to Barabbas. It does not follow that a final sentence of crucifixion had been pronounced before the scourging.

St. John (19^{1-16}) throws light on the situation by telling us of the events which happened between the release of Barabbas and the verdict on Christ. He begins with the simple stark statement: " Then Pilate had Jesus taken and scourged [*emastigōsen*]." There is no attempt to harrow the reader's feelings or even to excite compassion. Then John describes the mockery by the soldiers and the Ecce Homo scene in which Pilate made a last futile effort to soften the Oriental crowd. Thus John agrees with Luke in regarding this cruel punishment which to-day revolts us—or did until we learned worse contemporary horrors—as a well-meant device of Pilate to save his Prisoner from the cross.

A Note on the Column[5]

The first pilgrims who have left accounts—the Bordeaux pilgrim (A.D. 333), Etheria (385), St. Jerome, Theodosius (530), the

---

[4] The Gospels, by a well-known idiom, speak of Pilate scourging Jesus $(J19^1)$, just as Pilate " wrote " the title $(J19^{22})$, in the sense of ordering these things to be done. Bede misinterprets, holding that Pilate himself flogged Christ: *In Marcum*: PL. 92. 284.

[5] E. von Dobschütz, *Christusbilder*, 1899, pp.71f, 138*-142*. H. Thurston, The Praetorium of Pilate and the Pillar of the Scourging: *Dublin Review*, January 1906, pp.120-142. Vincent-Abel, *Jérusalem nouvelle*, 1914, 454ff, 578ff. E. Power, Colonnes de la Flagellation: *Dict. Bibl. Suppl.* 2 (1934) 60-67. Baldi, *Enchiridion locorum sanctorum*, 1935, nn.729ff.

Breviarius (570), the Piacenza pilgrim (570)[6]—describe the column of the Scourging as built into a portico of the Church of the Cenacle, in the Christian Sion. They mention some curious facts: it was stained with the Lord's blood (St. Jerome), it had imprints of arms and hands. Something in the column suggested these observations: red streaks due to iron oxide, ridges and holes due to friability. As already in the fourth century the Christians of Jerusalem believed that Christ had also been attached to a pillar in the house of Caiaphas and scourged by the Jews, it is more likely that this pillar was brought, not from the distant Antonia (the Roman barracks north of the Temple) but from the much nearer palace of Caiaphas, which is most probably to be located on the Assumptionist site of St. Peter in Gallicantu, where recent excavations have revealed a Jewish prison. In fact Theodosius (Baldi 739) explicitly asserts this transfer.

After the sixth century there is no further reference to this column on Sion. (Jerusalem was pillaged by the Persians in 614.) In 670 (Baldi 745) Arculf saw only "a stone on which it is said that the Lord was scourged." When the city was recaptured by the Franks in 1099, after four and a half centuries of Arab domination, memory remained only of the most important sites and monuments. After the Crusades, several fragments of columns emerged. There is one under the altar of the Chapel of the Improperia in the Church of the Holy Sepulchre. Another was brought from Jerusalem to Rome (Church of St. Praxedis) in 1223 by Cardinal John Colonna. It is of black marble with white veins, only 2.3 ft. high (with base of diameter 1.5 ft.). It is illustrated on fig. viii. 9. It seems certain that these relics have no connection with the column formerly on Sion, and still less with any pillar to which Our Lord was tied in the Antonia.

(3) The Evidence of the Shroud

According to the Poor Clares (p.38), different sorts of whips were used ; the blows were so numerous that hardly a pinpoint of the skin was exempt. But the marks cannot be explained by the punctures of thorns. The numerous contusions on the back are shown on fig. viii. 1. The only wounds recorded on the cloth are those which burst the skin ; and there is no trace of the blood issuing from the wounds ; perhaps it was absorbed by the clothes when restored to the Victim. The marks occur all over the body[1] (see

[6] It is also mentioned by Prudentius († 424) as " bearing up the church " of Sion : *Dittochaeum* 40 : PL. 60. 108.
[1] The body was completely nude and the blows were distributed everywhere. It is utterly improbable that any medieval artist would have depicted these two features. By turning fig. ii. 5 upside down, the reader can discern on the dorsal image the marks on the calves, thighs, etc.

fig. ii. 5) and form a terrible pattern of injury and pain. The successive blows ploughed up the skin, exposing the nerve endings. This resulted in the absorption of histamine from the devitalised tissue. It seems likely also that there were severe internal injuries to thorax and abdomen.

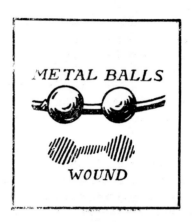

VIII. 2.—The Shape of the Wounds

A curious and unexpected feature of these wounds will be observed on closer inspection: they are practically all double, shaped like a dumb-bell (fig. viii. 2). This is explained by the fact that the scourge[2] was somewhat like that depicted in fig. viii. 3. This is a whip consisting of a small stick with two or more thongs, each loaded at the end with double knobs of metal or bone with two protuberances about 3 cm. apart. Sometimes one ball has struck harder than the other ; sometimes the cord or thong joining them has cut the skin.

It looks as if the Victim stood upright with hands tied high above the head. Otherwise it is hard to understand how He could have been beaten all down the front and the back. The scourge appears to have been worked with a circling motion, not to cut or lash, but to flick the weights with powerful jerks ; generally the thongs made little or no contact.

On the back the marks cross one another ; sometimes drawing blood, sometimes making a welt ; serum surrounds the severer

---

[2] This is rather a *flagrum* than the even more terrible *flagellum* of knotted lashes which cut the skin in ribbons.

wounds. On the upper part of the back and on the shoulders the
blows seem to be oblique and upward ; they are horizontal on the
small of the back ; oblique and downward on the calves. Especially
on the left thigh the cords rolled round the leg and cut the flesh.

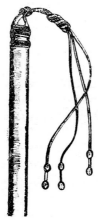

VIII. 3.—The Scourge
(Flagrum)

This complicated system of scars is unique ; there is nothing like
it in art. It tells us with poignant eloquence how brutal and cruel,
though not mortal, was the Scourging.

(4) The Scourging in Art

The Scourging seems to have been first depicted in the tenth
century, e.g. in a miniature in the Codex Egberti (Trier). At first
Our Lord was represented as fully clothed, with His hands bound
round a tall slender pillar. This is illustrated in fig. viii. 4, one of the
first wall-paintings to picture the scene. (On the beholder's left is
Pilate washing his hands and turning his head to look at Christ).
There is a considerable development in realism in fig. viii. 5, which
is an illustration from a twelfth century English Psalter in the British
Museum (Cotton MS. Nero c. iv). Pilate sits as a king on a throne,
Our Lord (bearded) is blindfolded and clothed with a long loin-
cloth. One executioner is holding Christ's hands tied, the other is
ferociously using the scourge.
A painting by Duccio (1260-1320) shows the Scourging also in

presence of Pilate but with a crowd looking on (fig. viii. 6). Our
Lord's body shows deep wound marks, which certainly could not
have been produced by the instruments shown. Fig. viii. 7 shows
a detail from a painting in Cologne by an able Flemish artist of the
fifteenth century. The bystanders are realistically depicted ; there
is a haughty Pharisee in the background, another is gazing at Christ
with concentrated hatred. In the foreground note the stance of the
executioner with his back to us ; with legs apart and arms raised
he is about to inflict a violent blow. The instrument is a birch-rod,
and the ground is strewn with broken twigs. The body of Christ
should be striped with the strokes. But the artist has erroneously
covered the body with small separate stabs or punctures, each with
a trickle of blood. Less harrowing is the scene as depicted (fig. viii. 8)
by Fra Angelico (1387-1455). It takes place in a room without onlookers. Two almost gentle soldiers with one hand hold a string with
which Our Lord is tied to the pillar, and with the other hand they
brandish fragile rods, while the Victim looks on them with compassion.

VIII. 10.—The Christ of Pity : Woodcut
(15th century)

A fresco (fig. viii. 9) in the Church of Santa Prassede in Rome is
unusual in that it tries to utilise the small column which was brought
there from Jerusalem in 1223.

Figure vii. 10 reproduces a devotional woodcut of the fifteenth century. It depicts the Christ of Pity. It is included here to illustrate the erroneous scourge-wounds which were assumed. On the other hand, in the picture of Sodoma (G. A. Bazzi, 1474-1554), the only wounds are a few trickles from the crown of thorns, though the flesh of the arm is livid where the cords bind it (fig. viii. 11). In spite of the calm dignity of the face, one feels that the picture is too much the accurate study of a torso. In some instances—e.g. the statue in the Church of Saint-Nicolas in Troyes (c.1540)—we have merely a muscular hero bound unscathed to a pillar. By way of contrast, fig. viii. 12 shows us the Ecce Homo carved in 1679 by Pedro de Mena (1628-1688). Here the scourging has left gruesome marks: long continuous streams of blood over chest and shoulders.

The next two illustrations also show Christ at the column, without other figures. Figure viii. 13 shows a painting in Avila by Hernandez (1566-1636). Our Lord's hands are bound to the top of a low column. There are isolated gashes on the body, and for some reason wounds on the knees. Figure viii. 14 reproduces a painting made in 1910 by Georges Desvallières.

Next come two illustrations of Christ after the Scourging. In the picture by Velazquez (1599-1660), Our Lord is seated on the floor with His arms still tied to the column, and the scourges flung down beside Him (fig. viii. 15). There are long slender streams of blood on His body, His back appears to be lacerated. On His face is an expression of pain and resignation. The pathos of the scene is enhanced by the kneeling compassionate child, accompanied by its angel guardian. From the faint aureole encircling Christ's head a light-ray proceeds towards the clasped hands of the child. In the picture by Murillo (1618-1682), Christ, with no trace of wounds on His body, is struggling to gather up His clothes, watched by two angels (fig. viii. 16).

CHAPTER IX

THE BRIAR-CROWN

(1) **The Thorns**

WE HAVE to guess at the material and the form of the crown which the Roman mercenaries placed in mockery on Our Lord's head. It is commonly assumed that they used the plant now known as *zizyphus spina Christi* ; but, at least to-day, this is very rare near Jerusalem. More probably[1] they used what Linnaeus called *poterium spinosum*, so called from its flowers resembling little pots. This is one of the commonest bushes in Palestine, extensively used for fuel ; it is still plentiful round Jerusalem. Coal being non-existent and wood scarce, there probably were piles of these shrubs stored for fuel in the courtyard of the Antonia. So the garrison had the material at hand. Felix Fabri, O.P., who made a pilgrimage in 1480–83, pertinently writes :

> Round about Jerusalem there grow exceeding sharp thorns, whereof I wove a crown and carried it to Ulm with me. We ought not to believe that it was sea-thorns which were used to crown Christ, but the common thorns which grow in the neighbourhood of Jerusalem, on the Mount Sion and on the Mount of Olives and in the valleys. For the crowning of Christ was not a premeditated act of either Jews or Gentiles ; but when He was brought before the judge and accused of having said that He, Christ, was a King, then of a sudden it came into their minds that He ought to be crowned in mockery and with torment. And they brought thorns from the nearest bushes, or perhaps found them in the kitchen of the house [of Pilate] among the faggots of wood for the fire. For I have seen with my own eyes that even at the present day they have no firewood save thorns, and their kitchens are full of exceeding sharp thorns for burning in the fire.—Fabri, *Book of the Wanderings*, trans. A. Stewart, 1 (1892) 356.

The relics of the crown have no early history ; it is not recorded among the discoveries of St. Helena.[2] Quite incidentally the crown is mentioned in 409 by St. Paulinus of Nola,[3] later by St.

---

[1] E. Ha-Reubeni, L'épine de la couronne de Jésus: *Revue biblique* 42 (1933) 230-234. Hebrew : *sirāh* or *sirīm* ; Arabic : *nefesh* (or is it *billān*?).
[2] Rohault de Fleury, *Les instruments de la Passion*, 1870, pp.199-224. Friedlieb-Martin, *Archéologie de la Passion*, 1897, pp.338-346. F. de Mély, *Exuviae sacrae constant.* 3 (1904) 165-440. H. Thurston, Crown of Thorns : *Cath. Enc.* 4 (1908) 540f.
[3] Ep. 49 : PL. 61. 407.

Germanus of Autun (†576), by Cassiodorus (†575), and by Gregory of Tours. Also various pilgrims[4] tell us that the crown was in the Basilica of Mount Sion : the Breviarius of 530, the Piacenza pilgrim of 570, an Armenian description (7th century), Bernard the monk in 870. About 1063 the relic was transferred to Constantinople (Mély, p.172)[5]. After the capture of this city by the Crusaders in 1204, it was carried off by Baldwin to Venice. It was sold to St. Louis by Baldwin II in 1239, and was kept in Villeneuve near Sens until 1248, when the beautiful Sainte Chapelle in Paris was built. Since 1806 it has been in Notre-Dame, Paris. (It appears to be now back again in the Sainte Chapelle).

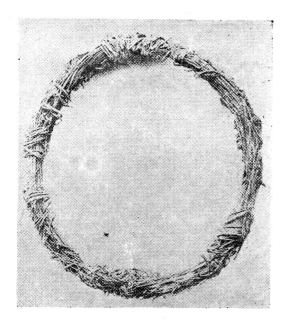

IX. 1.—The Paris Relic

About 800 the Empress Irene sent to Charlemagne several thorns which he donated to Aachen. St. Louis continued this procedure of

---

[4] Baldi, *Ench. loc. sanct.*, 1935, nn. 740, 741, 747, 753.
[5] Among other relics shown, as a special favour, in 1171 by the Emperor to Amaury I, King of Jerusalem was the crown of thorns : William of Tyre, *Recueil des hist. des Croisades. Hist. occid.* 1 (1844) 985.

distributing thorns (e.g. to Solesmes).[6]   To-day there is no
thorn on the Paris relic (fig. ix. 1). It is merely a circlet
of reeds or rushes twisted together, kept in an annular crystal
case. It is now a plaited fillet, not unlike the band still used in
Syria to retain the flowing head-dress. The internal diameter is
210 mm. (about 8½ inches) ; hence it is much too big to fit directly
on the head. So it looks as if this circlet was used as a support
to prevent the thorny branches from separating. In that
case the so-called crown must really have taken the form of
a bonnet or helmet covering the entire head.[7] This was certainly
not the view held in the Middle Ages. But it is confirmed by the
Shroud.

   According to Dalman,[8] the object was not to give physical pain
but to mark a contrast with the royal crown of gold. So he suggests
" insignificant thistles which grow everywhere and could easily
be fetched " or else the thorny knapweed. So also Klausner[9] says
that the crown was woven from *akkabith* (Arabic *akkub*, *Gundelia
Tournelii*, Jewish thorn) ; " it was not a crown of thorns, since the
intention was not to pierce his head with thorns but to scoff at him
in his character of king." But this distinction between painless
mockery and brutal horseplay is wasted on these Roman mercenaries,
probably anti-Jewish Syrians and Samaritans. They had just cruelly
flogged Christ. And now they " kept striking Him on the head "
(M27[30] Mk15[19] J19[3]) with their hands and with a stick. Briars
with sharp thorns were readily accessible in fuel-dumps in
the barracks of a country without coal or turf and short of trees ;
much more so than thistles or soft plants. There is no justification for rejecting the emphasis which the Gospels place on the
thorns.

---

[6] There are many isolated thorns or short branches in various places, e.g. Autun,
Milan, Rome, Andrea, Pisa. There are two in England : one in the British
Museum (!), the other (which once belonged to Mary Queen of Scots) in Stonyhurst. Some of these were detached from the crown, others merely touched it ;
others are probably facsimiles or pious mementos.
[7] Dr. E. Ha Reubeni says in the article cited in note 1 : " The crown did not have
the form of a ring . . . but rather of a bonnet . . . It was enough to take three or
four of these thorny bushes, to twine them together round the head. And, in order
to fit them together on the head, they struck with a reed this skull-cap enveloping
the head." He arrives at this view of the ' crown ' by examining the nature of the
' thorns.'
[8] *Sacred Sites and Ways*, 1935, p.247f.
[9] *Jesus of Nazareth*, reprint 1947, p.350.

(2) **Did Christ Wear the Crown on the Cross ?**

Two Evangelists tell us that, after the mockery, the soldiers took the purple cloak off Our Lord and put His own clothes on Him (M27[31] Mk15[23]). But this cannot have taken place immediately, for St. John (19[5]) says that Pilate had Him brought out " wearing the crown of briars and the purple cloak." Christ went to Calvary, wearing His own garments : a seamless inner tunic and an outer cloak. Whether en route or on the Cross He wore the crown, the Gospels do not tell us.

As regards Calvary, in L23[37] the Sinaitic-Syriac version omits " offering Him vinegar " and adds " placing on Him a crown of briars." The Curetonian Syriac has " and they placed a crown of briars on His head." The Greek-Latin Codex D reads : " saying ' Hail, King of the Jews,' placing on Him a briar-crown."

In the tenth chapter of the apocryphal Acts of Pilate,[1] we read according to recension B :

> Pilate sat down upon his throne to pass sentence. And they brought a crown of thorns and put it on His head, and a reed into His right hand. And he passed sentence.

Further, during the procession to Calvary, St. John is represented as asking Our Lady : " Do you see Him wearing the crown of thorns and having His hands bound ? "

But in recension A we read :[2]

> Jesus went forth out of the praetorium, and the two malefactors with Him. And when they came to the place, they stripped Him of His clothes, girded Him with a towel, and put a crown of thorns on Him round His head. And they crucified Him.

In one account He wore the crown on the way to Calvary ; according to the other it was placed on Him just before crucifixion.

According to Tertullian,[3] " Christ bore the Cross on His shoulders

---

[1] A. Walker, *Apocryphal Gospels, Acts and Revelations*, 1873, p.157f. The earlier Gospel of Peter (n.8) seems to place the mockery and the crowning on Calvary : James, *Apocr. N.T.*, 1924, p.91. St. Bridget of Sweden, after describing the affixing to the cross, says : " They again placed and fitted to His most sacred head the crown of thorns which they had removed from His head while He was being crucified."—*Revelationes* 7[15], 1680, p.597. Anne C. Emmerich (or her editor Brentano) is confused. A boy carried the crown to Calvary.—*Dolorous Passion*, Eng. tr. p.234. Yet on arrival it was torn off and again put on Christ's head (p.251f).
[2] Walker, p.135 ; James, *Apoc. N.T.*, 1924, p.104 ; Tischendorf, *Ev. apoc.*, p.246. An Irish version of the Acts of Pilate also says the crown was imposed on Calvary : R. Atkinson, *Passions and Homilies from Leabhar Breac*, 1887, p.367.
[3] *Adv. Iud.* 13.

. . . with a briar-crown encircling His head." And Origen[4] speaks of " the briar-crown once placed and never removed."

There is also a passage of Clement of Alexandria (†c.215) which depicts Christ as wearing the crown after being raised aloft on the Cross :

> Jesus having been lifted up (*hypsōmenon*), they crowned Him, thus testifying to their own ignorance. For this is just what these hard-hearted ones do not understand : what they call an outrage done to the Lord is really a prophecy fulfilled. The erring people did not recognise the Lord . . . Him whom they crucified as a malefactor they crowned as king . . . Though they refused to show the Lord [as such], they have testified this to Him by lifting Him up, when they set the diadem of justice upon Him, who has been uplifted above every name, by means of the ever-blooming thorn.[5]—*Paedagogus* ii. 8 (p.214 Potter).

In spite of this early tradition, most modern commentators hold that after the mockery the crown was removed and never replaced. There is, however, no positive evidence whatever for this contention ; any early statements extant are against it.[6] The retention of the crown—or its imposition on the cross—is quite in consonance with what we read in the Gospels.

After the Scourging, presumably Our Lord again put on His tunic and cloak. Then, as there was an interval, some of these anti-Jewish mercenaries thought of a bit of horseplay which would express their hatred of this royal pretender. So Christ was taken into some room off the courtyard. A mantle—St. Matthew says a red military cape—was flung over His shoulders in substitution for His outer garment ; there was no point in removing His tunic. A crown was put on His head, a stick into His hand. Mock court was paid to Him ; He was struck and even spat upon. It is not clear whether Pilate connived at the scene or even gave orders to have the Prisoner attired as a mock King of the Jews. At any rate he utilised the scene and had Jesus brought out to be displayed as a harmless and powerless claimant who deserved no further punish-

---

[4] In M27[31] : PG.13.1775. In the *Sibylline Oracles* (i.372) Christ is also depicted with the thorn-crown on the cross.

[5] This last phrase appears to be a reference to *Or. Sib.* viii. 294 : " From thorns will be made the eternal crown of the holy elect." Cf. Lactantius, *Div. inst.* iv. 26 : " The thorny crown placed on His head declared that He would gather a divine people from the guilty."

[6] In the 10th century Euthymius (on M27[31] : PG. 129. 719) asserted that the crown was removed and not replaced. Is there any earlier instance?

ment. *Ecce Homo.* There is the Man, he said, pointing to the briar-crowned Figure with a red or purple cloak flung over His shoulders. The appeal was in vain.

Before setting out for Calvary, they took off what St. Matthew calls the chlamys (a short military cape) and what St. Mark calls " the purple." It is not said that they bothered to remove the crown which, unlike the cloak, was of no value to anyone and would not be claimed by an owner. What is really surprising is to be told that " they put on His own clothes (*himatia*) on Him,"[7] i.e. His outer garment. There are in Our Lord's case many exceptional features not recorded for ordinary executions. One is that He retained His clothes while carrying the Cross. But why did they restore His outer mantle or cloak? Perhaps because it was to be a perquisite of the executioners ; they cut it into four pieces, one for each, at the foot of the Cross. Or it may have been to give more mock-dignity to this King about to be crucified. Is it not likely enough that, for the same reason or because it was valueless, they left the crown on His head? It seems rather unlikely that one of the soldiers brought the briar-crown as well as the Title to Calvary. If He wore it on the Cross, He probably wore it along the Via Dolorosa.

On the Cross the crown would be peculiarly appropriate. By Pilate's express order, He was preceded by a placard proclaiming that He was King of the Jews ; and this was nailed over His head on the Cross. Pilate knew about the crown and publicly exhibited his Prisoner as crowned. Might he not have said : Let Him wear it to the end? In any case would not the crown be a further aggravation of, a graphic commentary upon, the royal Title?

There is, therefore, nothing in the Gospel accounts incompatible with the early tradition and with the evidence furnished by the Shroud.

(3) On the Shroud

The Turin shroud appears to be rather unique in that it shows not a crown but the wounds that the crown had caused. Also it displays, with an accuracy unknown to art, the effects of sharp points pricking a living person.

---

[7] The plural form of the word need cause no difficulty. See p.2.

Turning to fig. vii. 70, we observe numerous sharp wounds with sinuous flows on the forehead, and also bloodstains on the hair framing the face. One of these deserves particular attention ; it is near the centre over the left eyebrow, and it is shaped like a reversed 3. It springs from a definite point and has two horizontal divagations in its course. Is this meandering due to wrinkles or to sweat? Dr. Judica says (i. 92) : " Through contraction of the frontal muscle in a supreme spasm of pain, it descended sinuously along the forehead, following the corrugations of the skin." Père d'Armailhacq suggested that the interruptions were due to the woven reeds in the circlet (now in Paris). After overcoming the final obstacle, it formed a final drop on the left eyebrow. This last drop has a pale centre, which is simply explained. The blood had already dried (this would take about an hour). The border (formed by fibrin) is thicker ; the centre, formed by serum, becomes depressed when the liquid part evaporates. When pressed against cloth the thicker part is more fully transferred.[1]

From fig. viii. 1 we can see that the lesions are more pronounced at the back of the head. A dense liquid has traversed the obstacle of the hair and then coagulated. In photos of the natural size one can observe numerous little clear circles of separated serum. According to Prof. Caselli (in Judica i. 92), " a rather interesting discovery is that the blood-stains are more evident higher up from the occiput to the vertex of the head."

From these stains we conclude as follows :

(1) The crown was worn when the Man was being affixed to, and when on, the cross. Had the crown been removed before cruci-fixion, " there would have been no serpentoid streams of blood at the back of the head, but the blood, sweat, dust and hair would have been matted in one dark mass " (Hynek i. 49). The deeper wounds at the back of the head are due to the pressure of the cross.

(2) Between the two head-impressions on the shroud there is an interval of 9½ inches, probably due to chin-band or cloth-packets. So we have no impression of the top of the head. Hence it is not so easy to determine whether the crown took the form of a helmet or that of a ring. But careful observers, beginning with the Poor

---

[1] According to Hynek (ii. 119), a number of single drops on the temple and those at the nape of the neck are formed by sharp punctures of arteries, while that over the left eyebrow is of venous origin. But I do not know how he deduces this.

Clares[2] in 1534, have concluded, especially from the rear wounds, that the crown covered the whole head. This is illustrated by Dr. Villandre's crucifix (figs. ix. 2 and 3).

The Crown of Thorns in Dr. Villandre's Crucifix

IX. 2.—Front View   IX. 3.—Side View

(3) The stains are a natural effect, not a human contrivance. No painter ever aimed at such minute exactness as is displayed in the flow over the left eyebrow. In fact painters have usually depicted straight vertical streams ; for instance, Francke (vii. 45) and Dolci (vii. 40). And what artist would, while leaving the contours of the back of the head ill-defined, invent the deep wounds with obscure details (e.g. numerous whitish circles)?

(4) Mystics and Stigmatics

The nun who wrote the account of 1534 says that " the sticks with which they struck the crown made the thorns enter as far as the brain, so that, having received mortal wounds, it was a miracle

[2] See. p.38. So Paleotti (p.208) : " With the crown they not only circumscribed the Lord's head, but covered it all up to the top."

that He did not die under the blows."[1] In using this exaggerated language she was merely repeating what many mystical writers had said.

> They plaited them [the thorns] together into the form of a cap or helmet so that the thorns were in great part fastened to the head. And with such great force and cruelty did they press down this fearful crown upon Christ's sacred head, that, as St. Bernard saith, the thorns pierced into the brain and penetrated through the veins and nerves and bones of the head, so that His blood became mixed up with His sacred brain and flowed down in streams over His face and neck and hair.—John Tauler, O.P. (†1361), *Meditations on the Life and Passion of O.L.J.C.*, Eng. tr. 1925, p.161. [Probably not by Tauler]

It will be observed that, according to Tauler, the crown was in the form of a cap or helmet. His contemporary St. Bridget of Sweden (†1373), after describing the nailing (apparently on the ground), represents Our Lady as saying:

> Then they fitted a crown of thorns on His head. This so strongly pierced the revered head of my Son that from the blood-flow His eyes were filled, His ears stopped and His whole beard stained.—*Revelationes*, i. 10, ed. 1680, p.17.

The editor (Durantus) of the 1680 edition of her Revelations says:

> In these books of the revelations of Blessed Bridget I found no definite number for the thorns. I only found that the Blessed Virgin revealed to her that this most sacred crown was not small like a garland, as the painters of our time depict it, but in the form of a cap which reached and wounded the whole head and even the forehead.—*Ibid.*, p.600.

A similar view was expressed by the stigmatised Belgian visionary Louise Lateau (1850-1883)[2]:

> Outside the ecstasy Louise was interrogated as to the manner in which the crown of thorns had been made; she replied that the thorns were much longer and more thickly set than those growing in our hedges . . . The crown she sees is not a circumference or ring; it covers the summit of the head, forming a definite skull-cap the centre of which has been badly and clumsily made.— Didry and Wallemacq, *Louise Lateau of Bois d'Haine*, 1930, p.31.

---

[1] Chevalier, iii. 50. "They smote Him grievously oftimes upon the head, full of sharp thorns the which pierced grievously in to the brain-pan and made it all full of blood."—Nicholas Love, *The Mirrour of the Blessed Lyfe of Jesu Christ* (before 1410), ed. L. F. Powell, 1908, p.231.
[2] So also Gemma Galgani (1878-1903): "It was not in the shape of a crown but of a cap."—Father Germanus, C.P., *Life of Gemma Galgani*, 1914, p.72.

Similarly our contemporary Therese Neumann :

They make Him sit down on a hewn stone bench against the wall.
The crown of thorns is prepared. It is not a wreath of thorns, as
usually represented, but rather a hat of thorns which is put on
His head and pressed down with long sticks by one of the torturers.
Blood streams over His face, upon which can be seen signs of
the most cruel pain. Then the ruffians place something into His
hands which looks like a staff and has a naturally grown ear on
the end. Now they taunt the Saviour ; they mockingly bow
before Him . . . The Saviour is spat upon, and they jeer at Him
as He sits bound and harmless.—De Hovre, *The Riddle of
Konnersreuth*, 1933, p.118.

These testimonies regarding the form of the crown are rather
extraordinary. That they are based on the shroud, or that they are
copied from one another, is extremely unlikely.[3]

Furthermore, there is the similarity of the head-wounds of the
stigmatics themselves. According to her biographer (p.72), Gemma
Galgani's " head was seen at the time to be encircled with punctures
from which fresh blood flowed, and not only was this around her
head but all over it." As to Therese Neumann,[4] Dr. Hynek says
(i. 94) :

I have always noticed the remarkable similarity between the
eight or nine stigmata of the thorny crown on the head of Theresa
and the bloodstains from the same on the imprints of the Holy
Shroud . . . More blood appears on the back of Theresa's head.

(5) In Art

The Ecce Homo scene and the Mockery are probably the most
recent of all the Passion incidents to be depicted in art.[1] Two
illustrations are here given. Figure ix. 4 shows a painting on wood

---

[3] It must also be observed that Therese Neumann (who knows only a German
dialect) correctly gave in Aramaic what the soldiers said (Hail King of the Jews) :
Shālōm malkā dī-hūdayē.—De Hovre, p.149 ; F. von Lama, *Further Chronicles of
Konnersreuth*, 1932, p.155.
[4] " We saw a white square handkerchief such as the Bavarian women wear over
their heads. On this were many blood-stains which ran together. It was possible
to trace out nine spots in the pattern of a circle with an open space about four inches
wide not stained. This was at the forehead."—Bernard Sailly, in *Catholic Digest*,
Sept. 1945, p.65.
[1] There is a fresco (100/150 A.D.) in the Catacomb of Praetextatus (Wilpert,
Malereien, plate 18). But it is extremely doubtful that this represents the Mockery.

by Albrecht Dürer (1471-1528)[2] and fig. ix. 5 shows one by Titian (1477-1526) in the Louvre. The latter is marred by the over-muscularity of Christ and the anachronism of a bust of Tiberius. Both painters, as was customary, represent the soldiers as deliberately using sticks to drive the thorns into Our Lord's head.[3]

The representation of Christ as thorn-crowned while on the way to Calvary is very rare before the late thirteenth century (compare Schongauer, fig. vii. 64). Figure ix. 6 shows a fresco of the eleventh century in St. Mark's, Venice.[4] It is a combination of the Mockery and the Via Crucis. Pilate pointing to Christ asks: Shall I crucify your King? Our Lord is clad in a white robe with a brown mantle and a large gold breast-plate. In His right hand He carries a reed, and He bears a scroll: I am crowned with thorns. Round His head is a narrow wreath—not very cruel, it looks almost like a laurel garland—surmounted by a crucifer nimbus. Two men are insulting Him, two others adore in derision. Simon is carrying the Cross—of unnaturally small dimensions—with the title already fixed.[5] Figure ix. 7 shows a painting[6] of the twelfth century in one of the rediscovered churches of Cappadocia. Though His hands are free, Our Lord is being led with a halter round His neck. The Cross is not represented, except in so far as it is symbolised by the crucifer nimbus; or more probably it is assumed to be borne by Simon. On His head is the crown which, as in all early representations, resembles an ornamental garland.

In earlier representations of the Crucifixion the head of Our Lord was represented as bare, at most with a nimbus. Later art gave Him a royal crown on the Cross. Three twelfth-century examples are reproduced. In fig. ix. 8 we see an enamelled copper crucifix, now in the Vatican Museum.[7] A wooden crucifix[8] in the Church of San Pietro, Bologna, is shown in fig. ix. 9. The next figure (ix. 10) shows the surviving fragment of the stone cross of Tuam (Ireland); here the crown has become the headgear of a priest. The underlying idea is graphically displayed in a fresco (dated 1248) of the Church

---

[2] P. Lacroix, Les arts au moyen âge, 1873[4], p.315.
[3] Incidentally—what is very rare in art—the crown in Dürer's picture approximates to a helmet or woven bonnet.
[4] Rohault de Fleury, Les évangiles, ii. 254 (plate 85).
[5] Compare the Lateran sarcophagus, fig. xii.i.
[6] Jerphanion, La voix des monuments, 1930, plate 48; Millet, Icon. de l'év., 1916, fig. 391.
[7] Ann. archéol. 27 (1870) 12.
[8] Geza de Francovich, Scultura medioevale in legno, 1943, plate 48.

of the Quattro Incoronati, Rome. This, as sketched by d'Agincourt[9], is shown in fig. ix. 11. An angel is exchanging the briar-crown for a royal crown. But already in the twelfth century the Crucified is represented with a crown of thorns.[10] The idea of suffering for sinners begins to be more emphasised in art than the victory over death.

IX. 11.—Fresco in the Church of the Quattro Incoronati, Rome (1248)

There are variations in the type of briar-crown depicted by artists. Sometimes it is massive and formidable, especially in German art: thus the Fischbeck Christ of Pity (fig. vii. 35), El Greco (vii. 42). Stwosz (vii. 50), Dürer (vii. 62). Sometimes it is a narrow circlet of thorns, especially in Italian art: thus Cima (vii. 37), Bartolommeo (vii. 38), Perugino (vii. 41), Angelico (vii. 52). There is no crown at all in the Werden crucifix (vii. 47) nor in Giotto's (vii. 51).

---

[9] Jameson, *History of Our Lord as exemplified in Works of Art*, 1864, ii. 175.
[10] F. de Mély—*Exuviae* 3 (1904) 168—does not appear to be correct when he says that Christ was not depicted on the cross with the crown of thorns prior to the reception of the crown by St. Louis (1239) and that the earliest example is on the cover of the Evangelary of the Sainte-Chapelle (c.1248), now in the Bibliothèque Nationale.

CHAPTER X

ON THE CROSS

(1) The Wrist-Wound

LET US now examine the shroud to see what information we can obtain concerning the nailing of the hands and feet. The forearms and hands can be studied in fig. x. 1. Some artists, making the arms horizontal on the Cross, show the blood dropping from the palm-wounds. Others (e.g. fig. vii. 46) show long narrow rivulets of blood flowing along the forearms. In no case except here do we find irregular meanders on the forearms, with no apparent connexion with the wounds. The cloth did not touch the forearms for some little distance, hence the gap ; or perhaps there was a narrow band keeping the arms in position. On the Cross the blood on the forearms flowed from the wrists, sometimes escaping for a while in the vertical direction, also perhaps made irregular by the roughness of the wood.

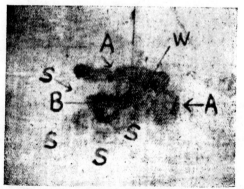

X. 2.—The Wrist-Wound

The left hand is over the right so that only one wound is visible. No artist would have foregone showing us both nail-marks, so much so that most copyists have shown both.[1] Moreover, against all the

---

[1] It is almost incredible that Père de Jerphanion, S.J., could have reversed this argument : " A friend recently remarked to me with great penetration that, on the hypothesis of a painting, the greater length of one arm is explained by the naive desire to show the nail-wound which, if the two arms had been equal, would have been covered by the other hand."—*Orient. Christ. period.*, 1938, p.566. Did he reject the Shroud without even looking at the photographs?

canons of artistic tradition, the one visible wound is not in the palm but in the wrist.

Figure x.2 shows the wrist-marks with some letters indicating the analysis of Vignon (ii. 3). The wound itself—the hole made by the nail—is shown by W. A is " the blood which having first flowed vertically dried on the hand shortly afterwards." B is " the last blood which escaped from the wound flowing along the same vertical." The serum stains (after the drying of the blood) are shown by S. I confess that I do not find this explanation very lucid. There are two flows, A and B, from the wound. Barbet plausibly takes B as marking the vertical direction when the left wrist was nailed to the Cross. Then how can we account for the flow marked A? The body would have to sink—perhaps during the process of unnailing after death—to make the direction A vertical. Or there may have been some obstacle causing the flow A ($5°$ or $10°$ from the vertical).[2] The point has not been cleared up.[3]

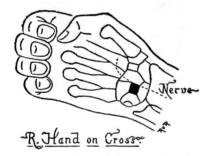

X. 3.—Position of the Nail through the Wrist

To locate the position of the wound in the wrist, and to find a reason for it, Dr. Barbet (i. 18) experimented about a dozen times on cadavers and on freshly amputated arms. Using a square nail (about 8 mm. a side), he found that one blow of a hammer drove it through the wrist without breaking any of the small bones composing it. The hand was laid flat on a plank, the nail was held vertical

[2] In his 1937 edition (i. 10) Dr. Barbet gives the angle between the two flows as $10°$, but in the 1948 edition (ii. 16) he makes the angle $5°$. There is obviously some uncertainty as the nail-wound is not a geometrical point.
[3] Dr. Barbet has later (ii. 16) given a plausible explanation, namely, the changes in position of the body on the Cross. See further on, p.277. The victim can empty his lungs (by expiration) only by raising his body on his nailed feet ; consequently the forearm rises and the vertical flow makes an increased angle with the axis of the forearm.

with its point on the middle of the wrist. After penetrations of the soft parts, the point slides between the small bones so that the nail becomes inclined towards the elbow and it emerges at the back about 1 cm. above the point of entry. The nail always comes out at the same point of the back of the wrist, in a normal man about 8 cm. (3 ins.) from the head of the third metacarpal (knuckle-bone), corresponding to the wound-mark on the shroud.[4] Thus there exists " a preformed normal anatomical path, a natural path" through what French anatomists call " Destot's space." The position of the nail is shown diagramatically in fig. x.3. Dr. Tribout made for Dr. Barbet a radiograph shown in fig. x.4 ; this shows the nail pushing the small wrist-bones aside without breaking any of them.

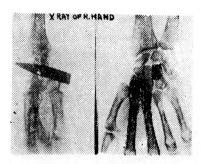

X. 4—Posterior and Lateral Radiographs of Nailed Wrist

A variable interval is found between the lunate, triquetral, capitate and hamate bones of the carpus. This was described by the French anatomist Etienne A. J. Destot (1864-1918), though there is no reference to it in his *Injuries of the Wrist, a Radiological Study*, Eng. trans. 1925. Apparently Destot pointed out that in dislocation of the lunate, part of that bone projects between the triquetrum and capitate and so obliterates the space. This can be verified in X-radiographs of dislocations. The interval called Destot's space was observed by T. H. Bryce in a skiagram of his own hand taken some months after the discovery of X-rays— *J. Anat.* 31 (1896) 59-79. Alterations in the space in wrist-movements were described by Johnston, *ibid* 41 (1907) 109, 280, also by Wright, *ibid.* 70 (1935) 137. According to Wood Jones, *Principles of Anatomy as seen in the Hand*, 1941,[2] p.198, " very often the unciform [hamate] and semilunar [lunate] are widely separate in all positions that the carpus can assume," thus forming Destot's space.—Note by Dr. Ronan O'Rahilly.

[4] Dr. Barbet (ii. 21, 29) verified this distance (8 cm. = 3.2 ins.) both on natural-sized photos of the shroud and on amputated arms.

In its course the nail meets no important artery and causes no great haemorrhage. But it meets the median nerve and wounds it without destroying it.[5] The wounded nerve remains in contact with the nail. This must have caused excruciating agony to the victim.

Dr. Barbet brought to light another unexpected phenomenon owing to the fact that the median nerve is motor as well as sensory. When he drove the nail through the wrist of a freshly amputated arm—i.e. one possessing living nerves and muscles—he found that the thumb always suddenly became flexed against the palm.

> The nail stimulates the median nerve. Below the wrist this nerve gives a branch to the ball of the thumb, i.e., to the thenar muscles, which react by flexing the thumb against the palm. The long muscles of the fingers are not affected, as they are supplied above the wrist. The other branches of the median nerve below the wrist are all sensory—thus causing pain but not motion— with the exception of two small motor branches going to very small muscles of the two fingers nearest to the thumb. Any effect produced on these would probably be overshadowed by the fact that the nail would injure the long flexor tendons, which are bunched somewhat together at the wrist and then spread out fanwise to the four fingers (exclusive of the thumb), two for each finger. The nail might well produce mechanical deformation of these tendons, resulting in shortening—some of them perhaps tending to be driven through the back of the wrist with the nail— and consequently producing flexion of the fingers.—Note by Dr. Ronan O'Rahilly.

Now it is a very striking fact that on the shroud no thumbs are visible, they must be closely flexed against the palms. It certainly looks as if this were due to the wounding of the median nerve; by the nails, the position of the thumbs being retained by cadaveric rigidity. But on the shroud the fingers other than the thumbs are perfectly straight.[6] In fig. x. 3 (as on Villandre's crucifix, fig. x. 13), the fingers are represented as slightly flexed, on the assumption of a mechanical injury to the flexor tendons.[7]

---

[5] Dissection of amputated arms which had been nailed through the wrist showed grave injury to the median nerve.—Barbet ii. 31.

[6] According to Dr. Judica Cordiglia (i. 95f), the nail cut the flexor tendons to the fingers but not the extensor tendons. Hence there would be an abnormal traction of the extensor muscles deprived of their antagonistic muscles. He thus explains the extension of the four fingers shown on the shroud. Obviously the matter requires further investigation.

[7] Vignon (ii. 71) illustrates the flexed thumbs by reference to a late Jewish custom of arranging the fingers of a corpse.

(2) **The Angle of the Arms**

Taking the outer flow (B in fig x. 2). as having been vertical on the cross, Dr. Barbet measured (on the shroud) the angle which this makes with the axis of the forearm ; this he found to be about 65°. Instead of using the positive photograph (fig. x. 1), I have taken the corresponding negative and marked the angles on it (fig. x. 5). According to this the arms on the cross made 65° with the vertical or 25° with the horizontal as indicated on fig. x. 6. A rear view is provided in fig x. 7.

X. 7.—View of the Crucified from the back

Let us now, ignoring any support by the feet[1] or by cords, find what would be the pull on each wrist for a man weighing 10 stone. His arms, making angles of 25 degrees with the horizontal, are not only being pulled up (to support the weight) but also being pulled out with considerable force. A simple calculation shows that the tension along each arm is 167 lb. (fig. x. 8). If we assume these conditions, we have a further argument in favour of nails through the wrists. If the nails were through the palms—say, between the third and fourth metacarpals—the suspended body would tear the flesh. Experimenting with freshly amputated arms, Dr. Barbet found that the palm was torn through when the arm supported a weight of 88 lb.

Other experiments on *corpses* do not refute Dr. Barbet's results. Thomas Bartholinus[2] crucified an executed robber and found that the nailed palms gave a firm grip. Similarly, Donnadieu (p.144) suspended by one nailed palm a corpse obtained from the Lyons Medical School. This was a light emaciated body whose fingers

---

[1] If the knees are flexed (as in fig. x.12), the foot-nail supports only a negligible portion of the body-weight.
[2] *De cruce Christi*, 1651, i. 13.

were so flexed against the palm that they could not be completely straightened. The corpse was considerably dried, it had been prepared for dissection by injection of the arteries. Eskenazy[3] also suspended two corpses by the nailed palms ; these were the bodies of men seven and eight days after drowning. All these cases are irrelevant for they refer to the resistance of the tissues of a corpse and so do not correspond to the case of a living crucified. Dr. Barbet dealt with palms in which the tissues were still living.

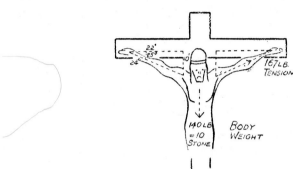

X. 8.—The Pull on the Wrists
for a man weighing 10 stone.

(3) The Feet-Marks

Turning to the frontal image on fig ii. 5, we see that there are no feet, the lower parts of the legs are not marked, there is only a vague tone for the shins. Looking at the dorsal image, we see that the right sole is very clearly marked ; obviously the cloth was in close contact all over it. The explanation is that the lower portion of the shroud was turned up from below over the feet (contacting the right sole) and was interposed between the feet (and shins) and the upper or frontal portion of the cloth. The portion of the dorsal half of the shroud (at the top of fig. ii. 5), which was drawn up over the feet, is now missing ; it must have been cut off and distributed as relics. (Note at A a patch of lighter-coloured cloth which has replaced a cut-out rectangle).[1] Incidentally it may be

[3] See p.65, note 5. Eskenazy was a disciple of the ' mythomaniac ' Couchoud who holds that Our Lord never existed. Dr. Barbet (ii. 24) describes his work as " a poisonous pamphlet rather than a doctoral thesis in medicine."
[1] On the frontal image at the position of the right instep, there is a bloodstain (at the bottom of fig. ii. 5) ; this must be due to blood which has percolated through from the upturned lower cloth.

remarked that a forger would have clearly marked the nail-prints on both feet, both front and back—as in fact all the copyists have done.[2]

Let us now study the right sole in fig. x. 9. This can be seen from heel to toes. The impression seems to be cut off before the end of the heel, probably due to the fact that the heel pressed on the ground. (It has also been suggested that the hands of one of the bearers covered the heel.) According to Dr. Barbet (i. 23), on a large photograph, one can distinguish the five toes, which are slightly separated, as would occur in the case of a person accustomed to walking barefoot or with sandals. About the middle of the sole there is a rectangular stain which seems to be the origin of the blood-flows. This is the place of the wound ; it is not near the ankle as most artists depict it, but lower down between the second and third metatarsals (fig. x. 10). From this there were two blood-streams. (1) The first, in two thin curved columns, is towards the toes. This took place when the Man was on the cross, with feet inclined towards the ground. This stream had dried, but on the shroud it softened and left a transfer. (2) The second was towards the heel ; this was a post-mortem flow which occurred after the nail was extracted and the Man lay horizontally with heels downward. Half-coagulated the blood came from the re-opened wound ; a clot still fluid contained serum which it expelled as it moved ; before reaching the heel, this clot formed a transverse flaque bordered by serous liquid. (According to Vignon, it also pushed a powder, such as aloes, out to the edges). This half-clotted blood could have come only from a corpse. Moreover this blood directly wetted the cloth ; in fact it is the only case where it is certain that liquid blood has left its trace. The blood has indeed flowed quite outside the foot on to the linen, as is seen in the stain outside the sole in fig. x. 9. There was here a fold in the cloth, the two sides of which were moistened together while the stain did not reach the top of the fold.[3]

In the 1898 photograph, owing to the fact that the frame was too short and the full shroud was not exhibited, the feet were not visible. They were investigated for the first time in 1931. The

[2] Numerous examples are given in the volume *L'Ostensione della Santa Sindone*, Turin 1931.

[3] There are traces of other folds outside the impressions. " Why these folds? Because presumably the cloth was here pressed against the feet to fix the heels which tended to separate from one another."—Vignon ii. 15.

result seemed rather confusing. The left foot made little impression and the left leg appeared shorter than the right. In fig. x. 9, a vague confused impression of the left sole can be discerned, chiefly a sinuous blood-trickle towards the heel. It had no contact with the cloth ; when carefully examined, the left sole is found to be turned obliquely behind the right, the front portion (toes) not being visible at all. The explanation of this difference between the two feet seems clear : the left foot was nailed over the right (fig. x. 10). This conclusion was not only difficult of decipherment, but it is opposed to the general artistic tradition which represented the two feet separately nailed or the right foot nailed over the left.[4] The left leg, slightly bent and therefore shortened in cadaveric rigor, was not straightened out after removal from the cross[5] ; it was simply taken off the right foot and pushed over to the left, thus deviating from the axial line of the body. This axis passes through head, neck, vertebral column, the centre of the right sole (at nail-mark) ; this results in a slight curvature of the body to the left.[6]

(4) Verification on a Corpse

Having secured from the shroud indications as to how crucifixion was performed, Dr. Pierre Barbet, a Paris surgeon, used the procedure on a fresh corpse (i. 41). A light cross was fixed on a platform which could be tilted up from a horizontal to a vertical position. Three nails of square section (about three-tenths of an inch in side) were used. The body was placed horizontally on the cross with the arms stretched out at right angles to the body. One blow of the

[4] On the artistic tradition consult p.258. The case of Louise Lateau may be quoted : " As to the feet one is placed over the other, and there is only one nail. It is to be noted that on Friday after midday, Louise's feet are always placed in the same manner : one upon the other, the left foot always placed upon the right." —Didry and Wallemacq, *Louise Lateau*, Eng. tr. by Dom Izard, 1930, p.70. So Gemma Galgani : the wound on her instep was larger than that on the sole, the instep-wound of the right foot was as large as that on the sole of the left, i.e., as if the left foot had been nailed on top of the right.—Germanus, *Life of Gemma Galgani*, 1914, p.62. There are other cases, however, of stigmatics with right foot over left in their Passion-mimesis, e.g. Rosalie Put, cited in Joergensen, *Autobiography* 2 (1929) 347.
[5] St. Bridget cites Our Lady as saying : " I could not bend the rigid arms to arrange them over the breast, but only over the abdomen. Also I could not straighten out the knees, they were bent as they became rigid on the cross."— *Revelationes* iv. 70, ed. 1680, p.290.
[6] This would account for the slight lowering of the right shoulder, easily verified on the dorsal image.

hammer sufficed to nail each wrist. One blow also was sufficient to pierce the left foot kept flat against the ground ; this left foot was then placed over the right ; a second blow pierced the right foot and fixed the nail in the wood. The anatomical time involved was only a few seconds. The only difficulty was to pierce holes in the wood at the marked places.

The cross was then raised to the vertical position. The body descended until the arms made with the horizontal an angle of 25°, as was already measured on the shroud. As shown on fig. x. 8, the average distance (for a man) between shoulder and wrist is about 22 inches, on the cross the head sinks about 10 inches, and the arm-length increases to 25 inches. (This gives the angle of 25 degrees). Any further extension would cause dislocation at the shoulder-joint.

The entire body-weight was now supported by the nails through the wrists. The suspension is extremely strong and stable ; one could pull strongly on the corpse without dislodging the hands in the slightest. The nails are wedged in between the bones of the wrists ; and connecting these bones in front of the flexor tendons there is a strong transverse ligament (flexor retinaculum) which, unlike the palm of the hand, can support a very considerable weight.

Front and side views of the crucified corpse are given in figures x. 11 and 12. This poor body has been used to provide valuable information.[1] R.I.P.

A colleague of Dr. Barbet's, Dr. Villandre (✝1943) was not only a surgeon but a sculptor. He made a crucifix embodying the results deduced from the shroud (figs. x. 13 and 14). Dr. Barbet (i. 42) tells us that this crucifix was modelled before the experiment on the corpse. Dr. Villandre's crucifix is not only a scientific achievement, embodying all the relevant data ascertainable from the shroud, but also a notable artistic result, one which excites our devotional reverence at least as much as any product of painter or sculptor.

Let us not forget that this crucifix is the three-dimensional version of the shroud, without addition or modification. This artistically satisfying and anatomically accurate crucifix was so-to-speak lying latent and plan-printed on this piece of smudged cloth, waiting for a surgeon-sculptor to decipher and to execute the

---

[1] The muscles were dead, so the thumbs did not flex. The head of itself fell slightly forward, not to one side. This is contrary to what is asserted on the authority of an anatomist by Costantini, *Il crocifisso nell' arte*, 1911, p.47.

directions which remained unread all through the centuries.

The painful position of the body is evident from the illustrations. The victim does not stand up against the cross, he is literally suspended from it. The knees are thrust out at a sharp angle, practically all the weight being put upon the wrists. The chest muscles appear corrugated, the thorax is enlarged and the epigastrium drawn in. (These details were not invented, they were deduced from a careful investigation of the shroud). The head is bent forward; the feet are crossed. With all its poignant realism, the figure retains supreme dignity.

(5) **Palms or Wrists ?**

Practically all artists[1] have placed Our Lord's hand-wounds in the palms ; so have many copyists of the shroud (including Paleotti, p.277). The hand-imprint on the cloth is itself an argument in favour of authenticity. In a forged relic such a parade of independence would not have occurred. Not only would the traditional location (in the palm) have been respected, but care would have been taken to have both hand-wounds clearly exhibited. Moreover, the intrinsic suitableness of the wrist has already been shown. The expert executioners under the Roman régime must have empirically discovered that in the wrist there was an easily found path among the small bones, quickly penetrable inasmuch as no bone had to be fractured, and that—owing to the presence of a strong transverse ligament—a nail thus driven provided a rigid and stable suspension capable of supporting the body-weight and rendering the use of ropes or cords superfluous.

[1] Also practically all commentators. Ollivier (*Passion* 1901, p.350) leaves it an open question : " The nails for the hands were driven through the wrist or the palm." The only artists who depicted wrist-wounds were those few who had, probably or certainly, known about the Shroud. Most writers speak of Our Lord's " hands" being nailed. But Gregory of Tours (quoted on p.152) speaks of the palms, meaning these literally, though in Virgil and others *palma* is used for *manus*. In one of the *Passions and Homilies from the Leabhar Breac*, tr. Atkinson, 1887, p.381, it is said that the soldiers drove "iron nails through His palms (*dernandaib*) and feet."

In Greek the word *cheir* usually means not hand but arm. So Homer, *Iliad* xi.252 ; Hesiod, *Theog.* 150 ; Euripides, *Iph.* 1404 ; etc. In Xenophon, *Anab.* i. 5, 8, it means wrist (bracelets on their wrists). Hippocrates uses *akrē cheir* for forearm. Arm is probably the meaning in Heb 12[12], and *cheiragōgeō* in Acts 9[8] 22[11] probably means to lead by the arm. When the Fathers speak of Christ stretching out His ' hands ' on the Cross, they really mean arms.

To the location of the hand-wounds in the wrists two objections will now be considered. The first is based on the fact that all stigmatics have the wounds in the palms. To this it may be answered[2] that " the stigmata have a symbolic character and may not be considered as the historically exact reproductions of the wounds of Christ." The subject is so interesting that it is worth while going into details. Let us begin with the first known stigmatic, St. Francis of Assisi,[3] who received the stigmata in 1224. The available descriptions are as follows:

I announce to you great joy, even a new miracle. From the beginning of ages there has not been heard so great a wonder, save only in the Son of God, who is Christ our Lord. For, a long while before his death, our Father and Brother appeared crucified, bearing in his body the five wounds which are verily the Stigmata of the Christ. For his hands and feet had as it were piercings made by nails fixed in from above and below, which laid open the scars and had the black appearance of nails ; while his side appeared to have been lanced, and blood often trickled therefrom. —Official Letter[4] of the Franciscan General (Brother Elias) immediately after the death of St. Francis (3 Oct. 1226), translated in R. Balfour, *The Seraphic Keepsake* 1905, p.38.

There began to appear in his hands and feet the marks of nails, such as a while before he had seen in the Crucified Man above him. His hands and his feet seemed to have been pierced at their middle by nails : the heads of the nails appearing on the inner side of his hands and on the upper side of his feet, and the points of the nails being on the opposite sides. For these marks were round on the inner side of the hands, but on the outer side long and pointed, and there appeared a kind of carbuncle, which rose above the rest of the flesh, like the end of nails bent and driven back. So also in his feet the marks of the nails had been printed, and were raised above the rest of the flesh.

Moreover his right side had been pierced through as it were with a lance ; and the wound was open and often let drop blood, so that his tunic and his drawers were often sprinkled with his sacred blood . . .

[Of Francis's dead body]. It was wonderful to see in the middle of his hands and feet, not merely the punctures of the nails but the nails themselves made of his flesh and retaining the blackness of iron ; and also his right side reddened with blood.—Thomas of Celano, *Vita Prima* (1228), nn.94-95, 113. (Re-edited Quaracchi 1926, translated in Balfour, p.43f.)

[2] E. de Hovre, *The Riddle of Konnersreuth*, Eng. tr. Chicago 1933, p.63.
[3] I have already discussed the historical evidence in " The Stigmata of St. Francis," *Studies*, June 1938, pp.176-198. I am here concerned only with the description.
[4] Two points in this text are discussed in my article (p.183).

They beheld the blessed body [of the dead Francis] adorned with Christ's wound-marks. That is to say, they saw in the hands and feet not [merely] the punctures of the nails but the nails themselves marvellously wrought by the power of God, indeed implanted in the flesh itself, so that if they were pressed in on either side they immediately projected on the other, as if they were one piece of sinew. They also saw his side reddened with blood.—Thomas of Celano, *Tractatus de miraculis S. Franc. Assiensis* (1247/57), n.5, ed. Quaracchi 1928, p.9.

His hands and his feet appeared pierced through in the midst with nails : the heads of the nails being seen in the insides of the hands and the upper part of the feet, and the points on the reverse side. The heads of the nails in the hands and feet were round and black, and the points somewhat long and bent, as if they had been turned back. On the right side, as if it had been pierced by a lance, was the mark of a red wound, from which the sacred blood often flowed and stained his tunic.—St. Bonaventure (1260), *Legenda Major*: in *Legendae duae de vita S.F.* §.13, ed. 1923 ; Eng. tr. in his *Life of St. Francis*, 1929[10], p.123f.

These descriptions—which also include references to the wound in the right side—have been given at length, not only because this is the first recorded instance of a wonderful phenomenon, but because it has a direct bearing on the case of Our Lord. In the palms of St. Francis the fleshy nail-heads were on the inside, as if the hands had been crucified with their backs to the wood. On the reverse (back of the hand) the emergent extremities were turned back and clinched. St. Bonaventure says the same occurred on the soles of the feet.[5]

This phenomenon of the stigmata has occurred many times since. But except in the case of St. Francis the nail-heads appear to have rarely been in the palms, usually on the back of the hand.[6] The case of a contemporary stigmatic, Therese Neumann, is illustrated in fig. x. 15. The following is a first-hand description by a medical man :

[5] No attempt was made to portray this in art. The wounds were marked by a red spot, as in pictures of Our Lord.—V. Facchinetti, O.F.M., *Le stimmate di s. Francesco d'Assisi*, 1924, figs, 1 and 2 (early enamels), 5 (Margaritone), 6-9 (Giotto), etc.

[6] Also in the case of Gemma Galgani (1878-1903). " The wounds in the palms of her hands were covered by a swelling that at first looked like clotted blood, whereas it was found to be fleshy, hard and like the head of a nail, raised and detached and about an inch in diameter."—Father Germanus, *Life of G.G.*, 1914, p.62. " In the inside—that is, in the palms—there was seen a raised piece of flesh like the head of a nail about as large as a halfpenny ; at the back of each hand there was a somewhat deep laceration that seemed to have been caused by a blunt nail forced through the hand from the opposite side."—Signed statement of Father Cajetan, *ibid.* p.81. This raised nail-head " was only observed a few times, and only in the palms of the hands, never on the feet."—*Ibid.*, p.416.

At the back of the left hand . . . I see a nail-head, rectangular in shape, slightly more long than broad in the same direction as the hand. The rectangle is admirably regular . . . about 15 by 10 millimetres. The edges are attenuated and almost sharp like those of an iron nail forged with a hammer. They adhere to the skin along their whole extent. The mass of the nail-head is regularly convex, curved like a dome. The top of the dome is about two or three mm. in thickness. It presents numerous but not remarkable unevenness, as if produced by blows of a black-smith's hammer on a piece of iron.

The colour is brownish red, like a seal of old wax. The skin of the hand is as a whole white ; but at the periphery of the nail-head it forms a margin, a small border distinctly paler than the skin. This border is slightly wrinkled like that of an ordinary cicatrix of not too long standing. Two days before I had already seen this nail-head at close quarters, but not for so long. Besides, it was then suffused with the blood which was oozing from its edges and coagulating on them. I had distinguished only the rounded dome rising above the layer of blood. On the palm of the left hand I now examined the nail-point. It is slanting over the skin, as if beaten down obliquely by a hammer, in the middle of the hollow of the hand, the point being directed towards the ' outer ' edge of the hand. Thus beaten down, it emerges for a length of about 15 mm. It adheres completely to the skin. It is roughly rounded in its breadth, which is about 4 mm. ; and the pointed extremity is not very sharp. It is of the same brownish colour as the nail-head.—Dr. E. Louis, *La Semaine Sainte à Konnersreuth*, Mulhouse 1931, p.34f. Cf. R. Hynek, M.D., i.55.

X. 15.—Hand-Wounds of Therese Neumann

Hence there are discrepancies among stigmatics. The nail-head in the case of St. Francis was on the palm ; in the hand of Therese Neumann[7] it is on the back (fig. x. 15), which cannot be taken literally (hands crucified with palms towards the wood). Further the side-wound when present is sometimes on the right side (St. Francis), sometimes on the left (Therese Neumann). It is therefore impossible to draw any historical conclusions concerning the case of Our Lord.[8]

---

[7] Also in the case of Domenica Lazzari—see a description by a doctor in 1834, in Thurston *Month* 134 (1919) 149—and of many more.
[8] St. Bridget says that " they pierced the hand through the part where the bone was more solid," i.e. apparently through the wrist.—*Revelationes* i[10] 7[15], ed. 1680, pp.17, 597.

The second objection to wounds in the wrists is taken from Psalm 21 (Hebrew 22), verse 17 : They dug (pierced) my hands and my feet.[9] Before examining this difficulty, we can at once demonstrate its irrelevancy by the simple observation that the hand (*manus*) consists of three parts : fingers, palm and wrist, i.e. the parts distal to the forearm.[10]

This is the Psalm whose opening verse (My God, My God, why have You forsaken Me?) is quoted on the Cross by Our Lord Himself, and of which there are echoes in the mocking cries of the bystanders. It is most appropriate to Calvary, whether it be directly or indirectly messianic. Though verse 19 is quoted by St. John in connection with the division of Christ's garments, there is no quotation of verse 17 in the Gospels. The first to apply the verse to the Passion was Justin Martyr (✝163-7) writing in Greek.[11] The Septuagint Greek (*ōryxan*) and the Vulgate Latin (*foderunt*) translate the verb as ' dug ' in the sense of ' pierced '. The corresponding Hebrew reading must have been *kaaru* (ending in the letter waw). The Hebrew text of the modern Bible—based on a Jewish (Massoretic) revision, of which the manuscripts do not date back further than the ninth or tenth century—reads *ka-ari* (ending in the letter yod). There is some evidence that this reading crept from the margin into the text of later Hebrew codices ; the letters waw and yod are frequently confused in MSS. This reading *ka-ari* is usually translated " like a lion." But in the Psalter the word for lion (e.g. in verse 14) is *arieh*, not *ari*. Moreover, this phrase makes no sense.[12] Indeed it is grammatically impossible, for a verb is required and has to be supplied in translation : Like a lion [they are at] my hands

---

[9] Also " Look at My hands and My feet " (L24[39]) " the nail-marks in His hands " (J20[25]) " Place your finger here and see (investigate) My hands " (J20[26]). Cf. Zach 13[6] : " What are those wounds in the midst of your hands? "

[10] " In the human hand, the bones of the wrist (*carpus*) are eight in number ; and they are so closely connected that they form a sort of ball which moves on the end of the radius."—Sir Charles Bell, *The Hand*. 1837, p.94. For the non-anatomist there is certainly a tendency to confine the term ' hand ' to the palm. Cf. Irish *lamh* (hand) from the Latin *palma*. See note on p.143.

[11] *Apol.* i. 35 and *Dial.* 97. Had there been a discrepancy with the existing Hebrew text, Justin's Jewish opponent (Trypho) would surely have pointed it out. The earlier *Epistle of Barnabas* (perhaps written even in the reign of Vespasian) may refer to this when it quotes (5[13]) : " Nail my flesh." Tertullian (✝ c. 225) too applies the verse.—*Adv. Iud.* 10 and 11. Also the Syrian Aphraates (c. 350).—*Dem.* 16 : Graffin, *P. Syr.* i. 809.

[12] Here is a specimen of later Jewish exegesis : " They have encircled me like a lion which makes a circuit with his tail in the forest, and no creature which sees that circle moves out thence for fear of the lion and the terror he inspires."—*The Longer Commentary of R. David Kimchi on the First Book of Psalms*, tr. R. G. Finch, 1919, p.102.

and my feet. All the ancient interpreters except Symmachus—but including Aquila and the Midrashim—read a verbal preterite form ending in waw, which therefore can be taken as critically certain.[13] Not one of them has any reference to a lion.

Moreover, it is difficult to see how the details of this Psalm could apply to David or how his deliverance brought such blessings on the world. The obvious interpretation is that the writer had before him a picture—Oriental, not necessarily Hebrew[14]—of some kind of crucifixion, public suffering and mockery, bones laid bare, clothes divided, piercing (or fettering) of hands and feet, and finally death.

> There can be little doubt that there is some reference here to crucifixion ... We know practically nothing of Hebrew methods of 'hanging on the tree,' so that the possibility of a reference to a nailing of a criminal to a cross in ancient Hebrew literature cannot be denied.—Mgr. P. Boylan, *The Psalms* 1 (1921) 82.

It has not been dogmatically defined that this verse describes the literal nailing of hands and feet (as practised by the Romans and others). It is most natural to take it as doing so. But it is sufficient to maintain that the Psalmist had before him a picture of some contemporary punishment corresponding to the nailing on a cross.[15]

Rt. Rev. Mgr. Edward J. Kissane, President of St. Patrick's College, Maynooth, takes a different view. He proposes a new emendation—based on the confusion (frequent in manuscripts) between the two Hebrew letters lamedh (*l*) and resh (*r*)—in a forthcoming work, from which he kindly allows me to use the following quotation:

---

[13] Septuagint *ōryxan* (= *etrēsan*) pierced. Aquila (in Origen's *Hexapla*, ed. Field, p.199), who was polemically anti-Christian, has *ĕschynan*, literally 'shamed'; but according to Hesychius (*Lexicon* 2157) the verb *aischynō* also means "ill-treat." In his second recension Aquila had *epēdesan*, bound or fettered. St. Jerome, translating directly from the Hebrew, has *fixerunt*; but the famous Codex Amatianus has *vinxerunt*. Other translators (Theodotion, Symmachus) and versions (Latin Syriac, Arabic, Ethiopian) have a verb approximating to that of the Septuagint.

It is true that the root *ka'ar* in later Hebrew and in Syriac means to shame, to deform. But if we take the aleph to denote long *a*—as in the Massoretic text of Ex 28[24] Hos 10[14] Prov10[14] Neh13[16]—we have the root *kūra*, to dig. And this verb means not only to dig the ground but to perforate. So in Ps 39 (40)[7]: You have pierced my ears (*karita-lli*), Vulgate *perfecisti*, but Jerome *fodisti* (cf. Ex 21[6]).

[14] See later on the references to Assyrian fettering and flaying, p.173.

[15] Cornelius a Lapide (on M27) makes an unnecessary effort to reconcile this psalm-verse with the wrist-wound on the Shroud (which he accepts from Malloni) by saying that the nail went obliquely through the wrist and came out on the palm. —*Commentarii*, 15 (1866) 617. Paleotti made a similar suggestion, which Barbet (ii. 65) showed to be impossible.

As regards the reading of the second group (the LXX, Vulg. Syr.) one can understand that it is acceptable to those who maintain that the psalm is Messianic in the direct sense, because it so accurately prophesies the Crucifixion. But the reading is open to two serious difficulties : (a) it presupposes an unusual form and an unusual meaning for the verb ; and (b) like the Hebrew reading, it seems to be excluded by 18b-19. The main point of the strophe is not that these ' dogs ' already mangle him, but that it is vain to look to them for aid. They look on his misery with indifference. There has been no lack of suggested emendations—' they have bound ' (Graetz), ' they encompass ' (Gunkel), ' they have torn ' (Schmidt). But all these are open to the same objections.

In seeking a solution we may assume that 17c is to be combined with 18a to form a couplet :

> . . . . my hands and my feet,
> I can number all my bones.

Now in a very similar context in Job we find the following :
' My flesh is *consumed* from sight,
And my bones which were invisible are laid bare ' (Job 33 :22).

In each case the description is that of a man emaciated by disease. The verb ' consumed ' (*kālû*) in Job is very like that presupposed by the Greek here (*'kāarû*), and the latter might be a corruption of the former. The letter *aleph* is often inserted to represent long *ā*. Hence read : My hands and my feet are consumed.

Artists have almost universally marked the nails through the palms. But I have added two illustrations which depict the nails through the wrists. The first (fig. x. 20) is a painting by Anthony Van Dyck (1599-1641), now in Naples. (Observe the right foot nailed over the left). There are two other pictures by Van Dyck— in Venice and in Genoa—which have wrist-wounds. He may have seen the Shroud in Turin or at least illustrations of it. Figure x. 21 shows a crucifix by François Duquesnoy (1594-1646), now in the Episcopal Palace, Ghent. Here the wounds are clearly in the wrists ; also the left foot is nailed over the right. The angle of the arms, which are almost vertical, has no doctrinal significance ; it is due to the requirements of the material, for the crucifix is carved from a single piece of ivory.[16]

[16] Gazier, Les Christs prétendus jansénistes, *Revue de l'art chrétien* 60 (1910) 77-94.
I observe that in the Basle Nomina Anatomica (1895) and in its Birmingham *Revision* (1933), while the tarsus is classified as part of the foot, the carpus (wrist), is classified neither under hand nor under forearm, but is given a separate status. Note that what is called a " wristlet watch " is really worn on the forearm !

(6) Stand or Seat?

It has already been argued that the general term ' crucifixion ' covered many variations of detail. These different methods must have affected the interval during which the victim survived on the cross. There does not appear to be any reliable evidence as to how long a man supported *only* by nails could live on the gibbet ; medical evidence, to be given later, suggests that the period could hardly exceed a few hours. There is a story in Herodotus :

> Sandoces had once before been taken and crucified by Darius, because he had for a bribe given an unjust decision. But when Sandoces was hanging on the cross, Darius . . . set him free. Thus he escaped from being put to death by King Darius.—Herodotus vii. 194.

It is doubtful whether in this case the man had been nailed ; probably he had been merely bound and for a short time. Josephus (*Vita* 75) tells us that, at his intercession, three Jews crucified by the Romans were taken down ; and one recovered after treatment. There is no indication as to how long they had been hanging. Eusebius speaks as follows concerning the Christian martyrs in Egypt under Diocletian.

> Others were crucified (*anaskolopisthentes*), some as malefactors usually are, while others even more brutally were nailed (*proselō-thentes*) in an inverted position with head downwards, and they were kept alive until they should perish of hunger on the gibbet (*ikriōn*)[1]—*H.E.*, viii.8.

It is doubtful whether we should take ' nailed ' literally or merely as an inadvertently chosen literary variant of ' crucified.' Were those crucified upside-down nailed or merely bound? The victims to whom he refers seem to have survived a considerable time ; we certainly need not accept as exact the diagnosis that their death was caused by starvation. According to Origen,[2] those crucified " live

---

[1] For gibbet Eusebius uses the plural word *ikria*. The singular (post-classical) occurs in Hesychius (*Lexicon* 502) who thus defines *ikrion* : " planking (*sanidōma*) or a post on (or at) which criminals are scraped (*xeontai*)." Perhaps we should read *deontai* (bound). Cf. what Eustathius (on *Iliad* x. 583) says of a plank (*sanis*) : " on which they bind criminals." It would seem that *ikrion* was used when the victim was bound. But Suidas (*sub voce*) says : " The Jews nailed the Saviour to an *ikrion*."

[2] *In Matth.* 140 : P.G. 13. 1793. This would certainly be true for impalement (see p.184).

in great torment, sometimes during the whole night and the whole of the following day." From the medical point of view, if the victim were attached solely by nails, this would be difficult to credit. Yet the interval is supported by an Arabic account of the crucifixion of a Turk near Damascus in A.D. 1247. As authentic narratives of crucifixion are rare, and as the account contains interesting details, it is worth quoting:[3]

> It is said that he had killed his master for some cause or other ; and he was crucified on the banks of the Barada, under the castle of Damascus, with his face turned towards the east. His hands, arms and feet were nailed ; and he remained so from midday on Friday to the same hour on Sunday, when he died. He was remarkable for his strength and prowess ; he had been engaged with his master in sacred war at Askalon, where he slew great numbers of Franks ; and when very young he had killed a lion. Several extraordinary things occurred at his being nailed, as that he gave himself up without resistance to the cross, and without complaint stretched out his hands, which were nailed, and after them his feet. He in the meantime looked on and did not utter a groan or change his countenance or move his limbs.
> I have heard this from one who witnessed it. And he thus remained till he died, patient and silent, without wailing, but looking around him to the right and to the left upon the people. But he begged for water, and none was given him. And the hearts of the people were melted with compassion for him, and with pity on one of God's creatures, who, yet a boy, was suffering under so grievous a trial. In the meantime the water was flowing around him, and he gazed upon it and longed for one drop of it . . . And he complained of thirst all the first day, after which he was silent, for God gave him strength.—Kosegarten, *Chrestomathia Arabica*, 1828, p.63f: cited by Wiseman, *The Connexion between Science and Revealed Religion*, 1842[2], p.178f.

Anyway, apart from the victim's physique, it seems clear that the period of survival was greatly affected by accessory details of the mode of crucifixion. It would be greatly prolonged by using ropes instead of nails, provided the ropes also supported the body. The time of death would also be retarded by providing a peg on which the victim was astride or a block on which the feet could rest.[4]

There is such a dearth of detailed descriptions of affixing to a cross that the case of one of the Jansenist *convulsionnaires* may be

---

[3] Does the account imply that he was affixed while recumbent on the ground? Observe that both feet and hands were nailed. Note also the extreme thirst.
[4] With a foot-rest or a seat-peg the victim would indeed be nailed *to* the Cross, but he would not be hung (by his muscles) *from* the Cross.

quoted. De la Condamine was present at one such incident on Good Friday 13 April 1759 and gave a first-hand account which is contained in Grimm-Diderot, *Corresp. litt., philos. et critique*, 3 (1829) 18-29. The cross, about 6½ feet high, was placed flat on the ground. At 7 a.m. Françoise " is attached to the cross with cords round her waist, below the knees and towards the ankles." Then " with four or five blows of the hammer a square iron nail (2½ ins. long) is driven into the middle of the palm " of the left hand. After an interval of two minutes the right palm is similarly nailed. " A long time is spent in unnailing the foot-rest of the cross in order to bring it nearer so that the feet can reach it and rest flat on it. At 7.30 the two feet were nailed on the foot-rest with square nails more than 3 inches long. " No blood flows from the wounds on the hands, only from one of the feet and in a small quantity, as the nails close up the wounds." At 7.45 the top of the cross was raised up and supported on a chair ; at 7.55 it was raised higher and placed against the wall. At 8.15 the cross was reversed, the foot resting at a height of 3 feet against the wall. At 8.30 the cross was laid on the ground, the cords were removed, her head and her back were supported with books, an iron chain with spikes was placed round her forehead. At 8.45 the cross was raised with its top against the wall ; at 9.20 on the ground, at 9.40 it was again raised against the wall. At 10 a.m. it was placed on the ground, the nails were removed from the hands by pincers. " The hands, especially the right, bleed much ; they are washed with pure water. At 10.12 the cross was raised almost vertically against the wall. A dagger mounted on a stick was inserted " nearly three lines " in her left side near the fourth rib ; a little blood exuded. At 10.35 the cross was placed on the ground, and the nails removed from the feet.

In this superstitious, indeed blasphemous, performance it will be observed that care was taken to avoid making the cross vertical at least until the hands were freed ; cords were used and there was a foot-rest.

It is nowadays practically the unanimous opinion of commentators (including Catholics) that the crucified victims (including Our Lord) sat astride a bar or peg projecting from the front of the cross. This is so much at variance with the view of the older writers that the evidence deserves critical examination.

(*a*) The first argument is the occurrence of expressions such as to sit on the cross, etc. This reference to sitting on the *crux* (not on a projection from it) appears to occur only in Seneca ; and it will be argued later (p.185) that the allusion is really to impalement. The expression *inequitare cruci* (to ride on the cross) is often quoted ; but I have been unable to trace it ; the verb is not included in classical dictionaries.[4a] The expression *sedile*, nowadays accepted, occurs in connection with the cross only in Tertullian's phrase *sedilis excessus* ; this variant for *sella* or *scamnum*—apart from the plural *sedilia*, seats of a theatre—means seat, bench, stool, chair, and occurs in poetry and post-Augustan prose. Its unanimous adoption by present-day writers should not make us forget its very slender connection with crucifixion. As to the Greek word *pegma* accepted also in Latin, used nowadays as if it were a technical term for the alleged cross-peg, there appears to be no ancient authority at all for associating it with crucifixion. It means anything fastened or joined together, a stage or scaffolding for a stage, anything congealed ; Cicero uses the word to designate a bookcase. As to *eculeus*, it has nothing to do with a cross (see p.186).

Accordingly at least one modern scholar has altogether rejected the *sedile* :

> One can hardly avoid the conclusion that the alleged existence of the *sedile*—a special sitting-block on the stake—has arisen from a confusion between execution beside and upon the stake. We must not of course reject the possibility that the introduction of the *sedile* into antiquarian investigations has been due to the special slave-torture of the Roman *eculeus* . . . We must regard the *sedile* as a product of the imagination, due to the confusion of indefinite expressions applicable either to crucifixion or to impalement.—R. von Mansberg, *Z.f. Kulturgesch.* 7 (1900) 61, 65.

This however involves the rejection of certain texts which must now be considered.

(*b*) The sole textual argument is drawn from three early Christian writers, or rather from St. Justin (✝166/7), followed by St. Irenaeus (✝202) and Tertullian (✝after 222). The first of these references occurs in a highly artificial and allegorical interpretation of a few expressions of the Old Testament which are paradoxical only in the Greek Septuagint and the old Latin versions. In the Vulgate translation of the blessing of Joseph this verse occurs (Deut 33[17]) : " His beauty is that of a first-born bull, his horns are the horns of

---

[4a] *Inequito* is post-classical. Some (e.g. Hynek ii. 163) quote *equitabant in cruce*, which I cannot verify. Cicero uses *equitare* with *in eculeis* (to ride on the rack).—*Verr.* ii. 4, 20.

the rhinoceros ; with them he will push the Gentiles to the ends of the earth." The Septuagint has " the horns of the unicorn," which sounds contradictory. So in Psalm 21[22] (Hebr. 22) the Latin has : " Save me out of the mouth of the lion and from the horns of the unicorn my humility." The Hebrew word for the animal is *reem*, nowadays generally interpreted to mean the buffalo or wild-ox.

But this does not explain why the early Greek translators, apparently landing themselves in an immediate contradiction, used the word *unicorn*. It may well be that they were right and that the rhinoceros was meant. There is a picture of a rhinoceros, between an Indian bull and an antelope, on the black obelisk of Shalmaneser II (now in the British Museum) : Layard, *Nineveh*, 1854[6] ii. 435 ; Maspero, *The Struggle of the Nations*, 1896, p.661. The semi-lunar shape of the horn is exactly like that of the Assyrian wicker shield which " most usually curved inwards from a certain height, gradually narrowing at the same time and finally ending in a point."—Rawlinson, *The Five Great Monarchies* 2 (1854) 48, with illustrations. The Assyrian bowman had a companion directing him and protecting him with a large shield, commonly in the form of a horn with the broader end resting on the ground and the pointed end upward. See an example in fig. xi.2. where however the shield is rectangular with a horizontal inner projection on top.

It has therefore been plausibly suggested —e.g. by L. de Feis, *Bessarione* 7 (1900) 473—that the Hebrew *qeren*, translated *keras* in Greek and *cornu* in Latin, really means such a shield. The usual explanation of the horn-metaphor is unsatisfactory ; a man may be compared to a bull in strength, it would be unnatural to regard him as horned. The texts in which ' horn ' occurs thus receive a much easier interpretation. My horn is exalted (my protecting shield is raised up)—I Sam 2[1]. In anger He has cut off all the horns of Israel [He has destroyed their bucklers of defence], He has drawn back His right hand from before the enemy.—Lam 2[3]. Cornua in manibus eius, ita abscondita est virtus eius.—Habacuc 3[4]. The modern Jewish-American translation has : Rays hath He at His side, there is the hiding of his power. How much simpler is the picture of shields in His hands, behind which is hidden His armed might. My shield of defence You have raised up like the horn of the rhinoceros.— Ps 91 (92)[11]. My buckler and my horn of salvation (shield of defence)—II Sam 22[3]. And in Zachary's Benedictus (Luke 1[69]) : He has raised a horn of salvation for us [a shield ensuring our safety] in the house of His servant David.

St. Justin, taking ' horns ' in the literal sense, was puzzled by the apparent contradiction of a unicorn having several horns, which he found in the Greek text before him. He was not interested in the historical reality of the picture or in its application to Joseph. He sought to find the typical sense and a prophetic application to Christ.

> No one could say or prove that the horns of a unicorn represent any fact or figure except the type which portrays the cross.
> For the single horn is the vertical wooden beam from which the upper part rises like a horn when the other beam is fitted to it. And from each side the extremities appear like horns joined to a single horn. What is fixed to the middle, on which those crucified are supported, is also like a projecting horn ; furthermore it appears like a horn fashioned and fixed like the other horns.—Justin, *Dialogus*, 91. 2.

Irenaeus makes a similar remark in connection with the sacred mystery of the number five :

> The very form of the cross has five ends or extremities : two in the length, two in the breadth, and one in the middle where he who is nailed rests.—*Contra Haer*. ii. 24, 4. (This passage survives only in a Latin translation).

Next Tertullian, following Justin, takes up the problem of *cornua unicornis* in Deuteronomy :

> He [Joseph] was not of course designated as a one-horned rhinoceros or a two-horned minotaur. It was Christ who was signified in him : a bull as regards both characteristics, that of being fierce as a judge to some, that of being gentle as a saviour to others. His horns were the extremities of the cross. For the extremites of the transverse arm (*antenna*)[5] are called horns ; and the stake of the central frame (*mediae stipitis palus*) is the unicorn.—*Adv. Marcionem* iii. 18.

It is in another passage that Tertullian refers to the *sedile* :

> Every piece of timber (*robur*) fixed in a vertical position is part—indeed the greater part—of a cross. But there is attributed to us the entire cross, with its transverse arm (*antenna*) and its projecting seat (*cum illo sedilis excessu*).—*Apologeticus* 16.

The older writers interpreted these passages as designating a foot-rest.[6] This still remains a possible, but not a probable, interpre-

---

[5] *Antenna* means a sail-yard, not (as modern usage might suggest) the mast or a vertical post. In Latin *cornu* was used to designate the end or top of any object. Cf. Vergil, *Aeneid* iii. 549 : *cornua velatarum antennarum* (the ends of the sailyards covered with the sails).

[6] For example, Bellarmine : " The ancient Fathers of the Church agree in this opinion, as St. Justin and St. Irenaeus. These authors moreover clearly indicate that each foot rested on the foot-board, and that one foot was not placed over the other."—*The Seven Words*, Eng. tr. 1933, p. vii (preface).

tation. Tertullian managed to allegorise (or typify) the horns of the unicorn without referring to this projection. So it seems exegetically unnecessary when Justin adds a remark about " what is fixed to the middle." He must be alluding to something he had seen or heard about. That this was a 'seat' seems to be indicated by Tertullian.

Thus it can plausibly be assumed that, in the second century, there were instances of a cross being provided with a crotch-projection. But if the custom were early and general we should expect to find other references in ancient writers; yet we find none such.

(c) The third argument is that this ' seat ' was necessary for the support of the victim's body on the cross. Here are a few quotations to this effect :

> This support was needed to hold up the body of the crucified person ; otherwise the hands would soon tear loose and the crucified body would fall to the ground.——Fillion, *Life of Christ*, 3 (1929) 532.
> From the centre of the upright a peg projected upon which the fork or perineum of the victim rested, not indeed to afford ease but to prevent the nailed hands giving way and being torn from their attachments.—Dr. J. Ryland Whittaker, S.J., *Catholic Medical Guardian*, 13 (1935) 86.
> It was presumably to avoid rupture of the hands and to prolong the suffering.—Daniel-Rops, *Jésus*, 1946, p.548.
> Some such support was absolutely necessary. It would have been impossible for the body of the condemned man to be held on the cross by four nails alone, for his weight would soon have torn his hands away.
> This is so evident that the earliest Christian artists pictured Jesus' cross with a *suppedaneum* to which His feet are nailed. This *suppedaneum*, which is not even vaguely attested in the early documents is an archaeological error ; for it would not have been sufficient to support the weight of the body either. But even the error proves the necessity of having the *sedile*.—Ricciotti, *Life of Christ*, 1947, p.628.

This argument would obviously not hold if the body were roped (in addition to being nailed) to the cross. It would also be invalid if the body were fixed only by three or four nails. For if the nails were through the palms, the living victim could tear his hands and fall forward, even if he were astride a peg ; and the dead victim would be in danger of doing so. And if the nails were through the wrists, he could not stir, even if there were no such peg ; nor would there be the slightest danger of detachment from the cross. Hence this third argument must be rejected.

Having examined the arguments in favour of a seat or crotch-support on the cross, I now propose to express serious doubts about its use in the case of Our Lord.

(1) The evidence for a seat at all is curiously confined: three Christian writers (who may not be independent), none before and apparently none subsequently until the seventeenth century. And even these three do not explicitly assert that Christ's cross had such a seat [7]

(2) Even admitting this evidence, we cannot accept the implied assumption that what may have been true somewhere at one period (say in the second century) must also be true everywhere, and specifically in Jerusalem in the first century, where standing crosses cannot be admitted.

(3) If a support were attached to the cross, it was a deliberate contrivance added at some inconvenience. It must have had a definite purpose: certainly not to lighten the culprit's sufferings but to prolong his agony, so that he survived for a long time and had to be despatched otherwise (by birds, beasts or smoke). It is extremely unlikely that a cross with such a contrivance would be used in Judea where the corpse was not allowed to remain on the gibbet at nightfall.[8] This is confirmed by the quick death of Our Lord and by the presumed effect of breaking the bandits' shins (and so depriving them of support).

(4) The evidence of the Shroud must be taken into account. This has been already given.[9]

We now come to the question of a foot-rest.[10] Very few commentators nowadays admit this for the case of Our Lord,[11] in spite of a long artistic tradition. In fact it is generally held that the foot-rest is " obviously a substitute, invented in the Middle Ages, for

[7] Many who accept this *sedile* from Justin and Tertullian do not accept their view that the cross was a T. See p.224.
[8] So Sepp, *Vie de JC*, 1861, iii. 23.
[9] It is accepted by Dr. Hynek (ii. 138) as against a *sedile*: the angle of suspension of the arms, the rigidity of the muscles, the absence of marks from the gluteal region, etc. Daniel-Rops (*Jésus*, 1946, pp.543, 619) accepts the seat and uses it as an argument against the authenticity of the Shroud. Yet Vignon (ii. 47) accepts a *sedile* for Christ ; and Mgr. Barnes accepts a *suppedaneum* (p.38). Barbet (ii. 25, 40) rejects both seat and foot-rest.
[10] The very word *suppedaneum* (translating the Greek *hypopodion*) is ecclesiastical Latin for footstool (*scabellum*). I cannot find any authority for the word *pedale*.
[11] Among rationalists, P. W. Schmidt, *Gesch. Jesu*, 1904, ii. 393. Among Catholics, Père Lebreton : " The feet were fixed by two nails, probably on a sort of support resting on a stake."—*Life and Teaching of JC.*, 1935. ii. 390.

the *sedile* whose representation was rejected on aesthetic grounds."[12]
This seems very unlikely ; there is not a shred of proof that—except
in the rather casual references of the three writers quoted—there
was any consciousness whatever of the use of a seat on a cross, still
less on that of Our Lord. There is no evidence, beyond a modern
guess, that there was any idea whatever of a deliberate aesthetic
substitution. Nor are we really entitled to say that the foot-rest
never existed in reality but was merely added to artistic representations of the Crucifixion. It is true that the first explicit mention
(without the word *suppedaneum*) was made by Gregory of Tours
(✝595). Here are his words :

> The beautiful nails of the Lord's Cross—most precious of
> metals—which held His blessed members, were discovered by
> Queen Helena after the finding of His holy Cross . . . This is the
> reason why the nails were four in number. Two were fixed in
> the palms and two in the soles of the feet. It may be asked why
> the soles were nailed, for they seem to have been attached to the
> holy Cross rather than to have been standing. But it is clear that
> a hole was made in the upright beam, the foot of a small plank
> was inserted in this hole, and on this plank the sacred feet were
> nailed (*adfixae*) as if He were standing.—*Liber in gloria martyrum*
> 5 : P.L. . 71 711; ed. Arndt-Krusch (M.G.H.), 1885, p.491.

This is the description not of an artistic invention, but of a real
mechanical arrangement. Gregory had access to many historical
documents now lost ; he may have taken the description from some
mode of punishment known to him, though not actually crucifixion.[13]
We know so little of the variable details that it would be temerarious
to assert that a footrest was never used in crucifixion. Given that it
was the intention to prolong the culprit's suffering, a foot-rest was a
natural and simple expedient, more easy of manipulation and more
effective than a seat-peg.[14] In most cases, e.g. of the execution of
slaves in Rome, the victim was so slightly elevated that it is likely
that he could practically reach the ground with his feet, and thus

[12] F. X. Kraus, *Gesch. der christl. Kunst*, 2 (1897) 336.
[13] Gregory gives this explanation to account not for a pictorial representation but
for (as he alleges) the discovery of four nails by St. Helena. In reality, " as to
how many nails there were, nobody has the slightest idea."—Gillet, *The Story of
the Relics of the Passion*, 1935, p.47. St. Ambrose is often incorrectly quoted as
maintaining the discovery of four nails. He merely says that she ordered a horse's
bit to be made of one nail and a diadem (crown) of the other : " one for ornament
and one for devotion."—*De obitu Theodosii*, 47 : P.L. 16. 1401.
[14] This is also suggested by texts which speak of the man mounting the cross and
stepping down from it. See p.209.

could be devoured by dogs, wolves etc. It may have been that in some cases his feet actually rested on the ground or were nailed to a block on the ground. There is no proof of the sweeping negation so prevalent among contemporary exegetes.

On the other hand, there is no evidence that a foot-rest was used in Our Lord's case.[15] Some of the arguments adduced against the assumption of a seat hold also against an added foot-board. And against either form of support being attached to the cross would be the carrying of the whole cross, which I shall later maintain to be most probable.

X. 16—Figure on a Roman
Lamp (probably 2nd century).

Figure x. 16 is a representation found on a lamp.[16] It shows a naked man standing on a platform up against a vertical post ; a lion is mounting the inclined plane in order to attack him. Note that the man is standing on the ground ; we know that in other cases of exposure to beasts (see p.182), the victim was nailed to the post.

In fig. x. 17 we see a crucifix by C. Costantini which shows a sitting block. " This crucifix was carved with the simple purpose of

[15] Anne C. Emmerich may be quoted : " The executioners had fastened a piece of wood at the lower part of the cross under where the feet of Jesus would be nailed, that thus the weight of His body might not rest upon the wounds of His hands, as also to prevent the bones of His feet from being broken when nailed to the cross. A hole had been pierced in this wood to receive the nail when driven through His feet."—*Dolorous Passion*, ch. 38, Eng. trs. p.253.
[16] Daremberg-Saglio, *Dict. des ant.* 1 (1887) 1574 ; Leclercq, *Dict. d'arch. chrét.* 1 (1924) 428.

offering a realistic representation on while taking into account two historical elements, the *sedile* and the rope which are almost always neglected in Christian iconography."[17] Figure x. 18 (also from Costantini, p.53) shows a living man reproducing the position of a crucified standing on a foot-block.

(7) Nails or Ropes?

It seems curious that—unlike the Greek *proséloun*—there is no unambiguous word in Latin for the verb *to nail*. The English verb *crucify* is in Latin two words *cruci figere* (or *suffigere* or *affigere*). Yet unless *clavis* (with nails) is added, *figere* (or its compounds) does not unambiguously denote nailing.[1] But nails, in connection with the cross, are mentioned by Latin writers, and Greek writers often use the verb 'to nail.'[2]

It is often stated that the criminal was bound to the cross with ropes or cords in addition to being nailed. (This is illustrated in Costantini's crucifix, fig. x. 17.) But the alleged texts, when examined, are not convincing. Phrases cited from Cicero clearly refer to the fastening of the culprit to a post for the preliminary scourging.[3] Two lines from Lucan's *Pharsalia* (vi. 543f) seem to

[17] C. Costantini, *Il Crocifisso nell' arte*, 1911, p.169. I do not admit that these two 'historical elements' have been proved either in general or for the case of Our Lord.

[1] *Figere* : fix, fasten, drive (e.g. nail), transfix, nail (to cross). *Suffigere* : to affix, to fasten beneath or below, to nail (to cross). *Suffigere* with *cruci* is used in Cicero, Velleius Paterculus, Suetonius ; with *patibulo* in Justin ; with *in cruce* in Catullus and Horace. Lucan (ix. 328) has : *Antennae suffixit lintea summae* (furled the sails tight to the yards). There is a judicial sentence cited by Tertullian (*Ad nationes* i. 3) : *Illum duci, suffigi, ad bestias dari placet* : Let him be led out, fixed (or nailed) i.e. to a post, and exposed to the beasts. There is a phrase of Firmicus Maternus (quoted later on p.194) : *patibulo subfixus*. This does not necessarily mean *nailed*. The Clementine Latin version of Acts 2[23] has *affligentes* which is a corruption of *affigentes*, fastening i.e. nailing (Greek *prospēxantes*) to the cross.

[2] Horace (*Carm.* i. 35, 18) and Cicero (*Verr.* v. 21) speak of beam-nails or spikes (*clavi trabales*). Seneca (*De vita beata* xix. 3) also speaks of nails. A sixth-century Greek writer (cited in Liddell and Scott s.v. *stauros*) speaks of a nail from a cross as an amulet. Josephus several times speaks of Jews being nailed to the cross by the Romans : B.J.ii. 14, 9 and v. 11, 1. Nail from a cross as magical protection : also Apuleius (*Metam.* 3[17]), Pliny (*HN* 28[28]), and the Talmudic treatise *Shabbath* (6[10], trans. Oesterley, 1927, p.26), where it is not regarded as a forbidden 'burden' on the sabbath.

[3] For example, *Verr.* v. 5, 11 : *ad supplicium traditi, ad palum alligati*. In v. 6, 12 the phrase *et ad palum alligatos* must be rejected as an interpolation. Words like *alligare* (to bind) are never used in classical Latin in connection with crucifixion. Hence the text of Licinius (cited on p.194) must not be misinterpreted. Late texts concerning Christian martyrs (e.g. St. Andrew, St. Anastasia) speak of ropes ; if genuine, this late custom must have been for the purpose of prolonging suffering. Martyrs about to be burnt were usually nailed to a post (e.g. St. Pionius † 250). But Polycarp (*Mart.* xiii. 3) said that this was unnecessary as he would not stir ; so they merely bound him.

have been misinterpreted. The enchantress "with her teeth tore asunder the ropes and knots " ; then it is said that "she gathered the hanging bodies and cut down the crosses." There seem here to be two different classes : those hanging by a rope, and those crucified.[4] There remains a text of Pliny the Elder :

> In cases of quartan fever they take a fragment of a nail from a cross, or a rope from [*lit.* out of] a cross ; after wrapping it in wool they attach it to the patient's neck.—H.N. 28. 4, 11.

Nothing is said here as to how or when the rope was used. There is no proof that it was employed (in addition to nails) to bind the criminal's body to the cross. It may have been used for tying the crossbeam to the upright, for raising the cross, or for hoisting up the criminal.[5] This solitary text is a very slender foundation on which to base the assumption that ropes were used in crucifixion. This is attenuated still further by a passage in an early Greek romance.

> They bring him him to where there was a rock overhanging the Nile ; they bind him with ropes to the upright cross, fettering his hands and his feet, as is their method of crucifixion.—Xenophon, *Ephesiaca* iv. 2 : *Erotici Scriptores*, 1856, p.208.

" No stronger proof," it has been said[6], " could be given that ropes were not used elsewhere in the Graeco-Roman world at the time, and so presumably never before." It is doubtful, however, whether a remark occurring in a work of fiction can be taken so seriously. But it remains true that there is exceedingly little evidence—at least,

---

[4] So the scholiast : *sic ubi aut laqueo aliquis obiit aut cruce.* In line 547 there is a reference to nails through the hands : insertum manibus chalybem.

[5] Vignon (ii. 47) assumes ropes for affixing : " Why cords when there were nails? They secured the condemned man while he was being nailed. In any case it was necessary to extend and stretch his hands on the crosspiece." All this is pure supposition. But many mystics have spoken of ropes being thus used during the affixing : Pseudo-Anselm, *Dialogus de Passione* 10 (P.L. 159. 283) ; A. C. Emmerich, *Dol. Passion*, ch. 38, p.253 ; Therese Neumann (E. de Hovre, *Riddle of Konnersreuth*, 1933, p.124). See the quotation from St. Bridget on p.208. Ropes were used in Passion Plays as they were required to affix the actor. A text of Artemidorus (*Oneirocrita* ii. 53) is also quoted. For a bachelor, who dreams of a cross, marriage is presaged " owing to the attachment (*desis*)." This word does not necessarily mean to bind. The author proceeds to compare a ship and a cross, " for a cross consists of timbers and nails." He does not mention ropes which would have helped his comparison.

[6] Oldfather, *Trans. Amer. Philol. Assn.* 39 (1908) 59. Nevertheless I am doubtful of the reliance to be placed on this piece of fiction. The author continues by telling us that a wind arose, the cross and its earth-foundation were thrown down, Habrocomos fell into the river and was saved " without perishing in the water or being impeded by his bonds." Nails simply had to be avoided to secure this magical rescue without injury to the hero. Can we really take seriously the details of the mise-en-scène the romancer adopted?

early—for the use of ropes or cords at all. The expression ' hanging ' certainly does not imply it.[7] Nevertheless, owing to our lack of information concerning the details of crucifixion, we cannot positively exclude the use of ropes in individual cases.[8]

It is often difficult to decide whether nailing or roping is meant. For example in Lucian's *Prometheus on Caucasus*. The Titan has to be nailed up (*prosēlōsthai*). " We have now to select a suitable crag, free from snow, on which the chains (*desma*) will have a good hold and the prisoner will hang (*kremamenos*) in all publicity."—Fowler, *Works of Lucian*, 1905, i. 53. Harmon translates : " so that the irons may be riveted in more firmly."— *Lucian* 2 (1915) 243. " This rock will make a handy cross (*stauros*) . . . Climb up and let yourself be riveted to the mountain . . . Hold out your right hand. Secure it, Hephaestus, and nail it up, and bring your hammer down with a will." But it is uncertain whether Prometheus is merely to be pegged out—the very word *prospattaleuthentas* is used—as in the Assyrian picture (fig. xi. 1.), i.e. with cords attached by nails to the rock as to a plank, or with nails directly through hands and feet. In Lucian's *Dialogue of the Gods* (n.1), Prometheus asks Zeus to release him, and this Zeus is depicted as doing ; which suggests that he was merely bound. But how far can we take seriously the details of this satire?

There is, however, practically no justification for assuming that ropes as well as nails were used in the case of Our Lord. In spite of Tertullian[9], the saying—You will stretch out your hands and another will gird you—interpreted in John 21[18] as a prophecy of Peter's crucifixion, does not prove anything. It is an obscure saying, uttered when Peter was actually putting on his girdle over his clothes just dried at the fire. And this particular phrase may refer to the binding at arrest. Practically the only Father who seems explicitly to assert ropes for Christ is St. Hilary of Poitiers (†366) who speaks of " the suffering of the body hanging on the cross,

[7] The Greek verb *kremannymi* applied to crucifixion is considered later (p.176). The Latin *suspendere* is twice so used by Seneca : *Ep.* vii. 4 and *Consol ad Marc.* xx. 3. Nevertheless the term was not regularly used of crucifixion before Tertullian. Suspension could of course be by nails as well as by ropes. " The hands and feet are pierced (*exterminantur*) only in the case of a man suspended on a gibbet (*in ligno suspenditur*)".—Tertullian, *Adv. Iud.* 11.

[8] The third-century *Acts of Andrew* assume binding instead of nailing as a deliberate and exceptional measure to ensure more prolonged suffering : " He commanded him to be scourged by seven men and afterwards to be crucified ; and charged the executioners that his legs should be left unpierced and so he should be hanged up ; thinking by this means to torment him the more."—M. R. James, *Apocryphal N.T.*, 1924, p.358.

[9] Petrus ab altero vincitur, cum cruci adstringitur.—Tertullian, *Scorpiace* 15.

the strong fetters of the binding ropes, the harsh wounds of the driven-in nails," and he says that " pain invaded the suspended, bound (*nodatam*) and transfixed flesh."[10] But this single late statement is not authoritative. In any case, there is no definite assertion that the ropes were used while Christ was on the cross. He was bound at arrest and while being scourged.

Of course, ropes may have been used temporarily in affixing Him to the cross. But there is no textual evidence and the argument from mechanics is very hypothetical.

> So great was the drag on the hands and feet when they swung forwards as the cross was being manœuvred into position, that a rope had to be fastened round the chest to bind it to the cross, lest the hands might tear through. But as soon as the upright was fixed in position, the rope was withdrawn so that the victim was supported only by the hands and feet and the central peg on which the perineum rested.—Dr. J. Ryland Whitaker, S.J., *Catholic Medical Guardian* 13 (1935) 87, following Dr. Le Bec, *ibid.* 3 (1925) 129.

This assumes that the hands were nailed through the palms ; if this were the case, they would be just as liable to tear on the cross after the ropes were withdrawn. On the other hand, if the hands were nailed through the wrists, no rope would be required even for raising the loaded cross.

With wonderful self-restraint and concision the Gospels merely say : They crucified Him. There is no denunciation, no embellishment, no dwelling on details. The mode of affixing is not described. Only after the Resurrection is there occasion to mention the nail-wounds (John 20[25]). The invitation " See My hands and My feet " (Luke 24[39]) seems clearly to refer to the nail-marks, though this has been denied. In a passage which dates from the early second century there is an explicit reference to the wounds on the feet :

> Then the Lord will appear first to His own, in the flesh as He was before ; and to His own He will show on hands and feet the four wounds (*tessera ichné*).—*Sibylline Oracles* viii. 318.

St. Justin also definitely refers to the piercing of the feet.[11] Neverthe-

---

[10] *De Trinitate* x. 13 : P.L. 10. 352.
[11] *Dial.* 97, referring to Ps. 21. So Tertullian (*Adv. Jud.* 10), who adds that this nailing of both hands and feet " is the real atrocity of the cross." It should be noted that the earliest references to the mode of attachment to the cross are exclusively to nailing. Thus Acts 2[23], also Ignatius, *Smyrn.* i.2 : " really nailed for us in the flesh."

less a number of rationalists have denied that Christ's feet were nailed. Here is a recent example of this assertion :

There is astonishingly little evidence that the feet of a crucified person were ever pierced by nails. The strength of the tradition to that effect is due chiefly to the attempt to fulfil in detail a supposed messianic prophecy, assisted by the need of blood which theology felt.—J. W. Hewitt, *Harvard Theol. Review*, 25 (1932) 45.

The following are some arguments in reply.

(1) There is astonishingly little evidence about all the details of crucifixion. In most accounts we merely have the verb to affix or to nail. There is, apart from the case of Christ, as much evidence for nailing the feet as for nailing the hands. There may have been cases in which the feet were merely tied ; but we have no information.

(2) This writer belongs to the usual armchair type of critic when he says (p.43) : " It is difficult to see what could be gained by nailing the feet except the infliction of a modicum of immediate pain." Could not the same be said about the nailing of the hands? It has been experimentally proved that the nailing of the feet— even with one nail—is an expeditious and effective way of fixing the lower limbs on the cross.

(3) The difficulty is really not to prove the use of nails but to adduce any evidence that ropes or cords were ever used in crucifixion.

(4) Apart from one reference in St. John, the Gospels do not explicitly assert the use of nails at all. They glossed over the gruesome details of crucifixion, which were presumably known to their readers. It is utterly unreasonable to expect them to have anticipated modern academic doubts concerning the feet.

(5) The ' supposed ' messianic prophecy of Psalm 21 (22) has been already considered (p.141). There is no proof whatever that the facts of crucifixion were tampered with to suit the text ; on the contrary, there is reason to believe that the text itself already presupposed some sort of crucifixion.[11a] The argument really should proceed inversely. The reality of the crucifixion with nails led to the selection of this text and its literal interpretation. It was accepted as a notorious fact that Our Lord had been nailed, hand and feet— " the real atrocity of crucifixion," as Tertullian remarks. The text

---

[11a] The fact that the Gospels do not refer to this text has been used as an argument in favour of some reading other than ' pierced ' in the current Hebrew text.

was then quoted to prove that, as it had been prophesied, this infamous punishment did not derogate from His Messiaship. " The Scriptures announce a suffering Messiah," conceded Justin's interlocutor, the Jew Trypho (*Dial.* 89, 2), " but I would like to know if you can show that His suffering was one cursed in the Law."

(7) It is true that some early writers refer only to the hands, without thereby excluding the feet.[12] We might retort the author's argument and say that this concentration on the hands is due to the influence of Isaiah 65^2: " I have stretched out My hands all the day to a rebellious people." This was actually quoted by St. Paul (Rom. 10^{21}), and by 'Barnabas' (13^4) it is applied to the Crucifixion.

(7) The gibe about theology's " need of blood " is unworthy of a serious writer. Did the piercing of the feet add anything appreciable to the blood-flow from the scourging, the thorn-crown, the hand-wounds, the transfixed side? Did not even Cicero—without any theological preoccupation—talk of " the cross which even now is dripping with the blood of a Roman citizen? "[13]

The question of the two bandits crucified with Christ deserves a brief notice. As we shall see, it became a regular artistic tradition to represent these two as merely tied to their crosses.[14] This may possibly have been done to differentiate them from Our Lord ; but some more tangible cause or occasion seems required. Was this in some way connected with the discovery of the buried Cross in Jerusalem? The accounts tell us that the other two crosses were also found (see p.19). If so, could they have been distinguished, apart from a miracle? It has been suggested that two of the crosses had no holes made by body-nails.[15] Certain nails appear to have been discovered ; but it is not clear how it was concluded that they

---

[12] So the Gospel of Pseudo-Peter, 21 : The Jews (!) " tore away the nails from the Lord's hands."

[13] Cicero, *Verr.* iv. 11, 26.

[14] " They tied ropes round their arms and by the help of small ladders dragged them up to their places on the cross. The executioners then bound the arms of the thieves to the cross with cords made of the bark of trees, and fastened their wrists, elbows, knees and feet in like manner, drawing the cords so tight that their joints cracked and the blood burst out."—Anne C. Emmerich, *Dolorous Passion*, ch. 40, p.257.

[15] According to Rohault de Fleury, *Mémoire sur les instruments de la Passion*, 1870, p.74, there is preserved in Santa Croce (Rome) a large piece of wood (7 ft. 3 in. by 6 in.), which he identifies with the transverse of a cross. It is enclosed in a case with a paper marked : *Pars crucis Sancti Dixmae boni latronis.* In the middle where this transverse met the vertical beam there is a small round hole (now much deformed) apparently for receiving a peg. There are no marks of hand-nails.

pertained to Christ's Cross, no miracle is recorded for the purpose. The number of these nails is uncertain ; and the various relics are of doubtful authenticity.[16] One most likely to be genuine, that now in Santa Croce, is illustrated in fig. x. 19 (de Corrieris, p.69). It is 120 mm. (4.7 ins.) long and 8 5 mm. (one-third of an inch) wide at its broadest. (There is a similar nail at Trier). It is likely enough that in addition to nails for crucifying there were nails for fastening the parts of the cross together ; this may account for the number of the nails. The whole subject is purely conjectural. But it is worth mentioning this idea that something connected with the finding of the crosses gave rise to the view that the two bandits were not nailed.[17] There is, however, no positive evidence that the Romans crucified by tying the victim to the gibbet.

X. 19—Nail-relic in Santa Croce, Rome

Returning to Our Lord's case, we may inquire whether His feet were nailed with one nail or with two. It is to-day generally held that each foot was separately nailed. Four chief arguments have been urged in favour of this view.

(1) Iconography : almost until the thirteenth century artistic representations had two nails. But it is very doubtful whether these pictures (relatively late) can be accepted as historical evidence for such a detail.[18] Some of the earliest representations do not show the feet as nailed at all ; others show the nails through the ankles. Most of them exhibit a foot-board which the upholders of two nails do not accept.

(2) The use of a crotch-support :

> His feet were nailed. Naturally this required two nails and not one as Christian art has so often imagined ; for since the prisoner was straddling the *sedile*, his feet hung almost at the sides of the vertical beam and could not be crossed.—Ricciotti, *Life of Christ*, 1947, p.629.

[16] On these nail-relics see the works cited on p.19.
[17] The sixth-century Nonnus (*Paraphrasis* 19, 103) cannot be quoted for this view : " They attached (*dethentes*, not necessarily bound) them to a cross with hard rivets (*kentrois*)." Anything with a sharp point (e.g. a nail) could be called *kentron*.
[18] In my *Family at Bethany* I showed that even the earliest representations (in the Catacombs) of the tomb of Lazarus are historically inaccurate.

It is not clear that a body nailed as in figs. x. 11 and 12 could not also be supported by a seat-peg. In any case, this argument assumes as proven the use of the so-called *sedile*.

(3) Argument from anatomy : if only one nail were used on the feet, the bones would have been broken.

> The doctors I have consulted think that with this procedure it would have been impossible not to break the bones.—Rohault de Fleury, *Mém. sur les instr. de la Passion*, 1870, p.167.
> We can easily understand that one foot could not be placed over the other without extreme difficulty, and it would require a nail of extraordinary length such as would have infallibly broken the bones.—Ollivier, *The Passion*, 1901, p.349.
> It would be almost impossible to fix a living man's two feet with one nail without breaking some bone.—Prat, *Jésus-Christ*, 1933⁴, ii. 393.

The invalidity of this argument can be demonstrated *ad oculos* by looking at the record of Dr. Barbet's experiment in figs. x. 11 and 12. As a result of this experiment with a cadaver, Dr. Barbet thus describes the nailing of Christ's feet (iv. 127). One executioner places His left foot flat on the cross, and with one blow of the hammer the nail is lodged in the middle of the foot. The other executioner bends the other knee and holds the right foot flat on the wood, the left foot is then placed over the right, and with a second blow of the hammer both feet are transfixed with the nail to the cross. Only two minutes' work for two men.

(4) The use of two nails for the feet was " the Roman custom " (Prat ii. 520), as is proved by a sentence in a play of Plautus :

> Ego dabo ei talentum prius qui in crucem excucurrerit :
> Sed ea lege ut offigantur bis pedes, bis brachia.
> I will give a talent to him who will first mount the cross ;
> But on this condition that his feet and his arms are twice nailed.
> *Mostellaria* ii. 1. 12f.

The speaker humorously wishes that for greater security twice the usual number of nails should be used. It may possibly mean that two nails should be driven through each hand and each foot.[19]

> This passage rightly interpreted renders it at the same time preponderantly probable that the nailing of the feet as a rule took place by means of a single iron nail or spike of great strength

---

[19] "In this instance the extraordinary circumstance is that each member is pierced by two nails."—Fillion, *Life of Christ* 3 (1929) 534.

driven in common through the two feet placed the one above the other.—O. Zoeckler, *The Cross of Christ*, 1877, p.416.

With some probability we can deduce from this passage : (1) The feet (as well as the hands) were usually nailed, but (2) only with one nail, so that the demand for two nails was exceptional. But whatever be the interpretation, it would be an unjustified generalisation of the jocose statement to erect it into a general rule compulsorily applicable to Calvary.

Hence, in spite of the view held by most contemporary exegetes, the question of one or two nails through the feet must be regarded as quite open. There is really no evidence one way or the other, except in so far as we admit the Shroud.

Among the older writers, Gregory of Tours has already been quoted (p.152) in favour of two nails. But there are others who hold the theory of one nail. In the sixth century we have the Cave of Treasures (ed. Bezold, p.66) and the Egyptian Nonnus, *Paraphrasis in Joannem* (PG. 43. 901B). The latter's phrases are rather obscure, but he seems to speak of " transfixing both feet with a single nail " and of " an indestructible bond holding both feet superposed." For one nail also are Pseudo-Anselm, *Dialogus de Passione* 10 (P.L. 159. 283) ; and Pseudo-Bonaventure, *Life of Christ*, ch. 78 : " Those three nails bear the whole weight of His body." Durandus in his *Rationale* (vi. 77, n. 24f) says there were four nails, " but others say that Christ was affixed with only three nails." St. Bridget speaks of four sharp nails.— *Revelationes* iv. 70, ed. 1680, p.289. But Anne C. Emmerich (*Dolorous Passion*, ch. 38, p.253) and Therese Neumann (Hynek, *Konnersreuth*, 1932, p.44, and E. de Hovre, *Riddle of Konnersreuth*, 1933, p.124) speak of one nail through the feet. In the later Middle Ages there was a legend, incorporated in Passion Plays and reproduced in art, e.g. by Jean Fouquet, that the Jews (regarded as the executioners) went to a smith to secure three nails ; he excused himself with the plea of an injured hand ; whereupon his wife forged the nails. See R. Morris, *Legends of the Holy Rood* (EETS), 1871, p.84 ; also *La Passion du Palatinus*, ed. Grace Frank, 1922, p.31.

Two illustrations of the use of ropes or cords have already been given. In Costantini's crucifix (fig. x. 17) the hands are tied as well as nailed, there is also a rope round the body. In fig. x. 18 a living man, standing on a foot-block, is tied to the cross.[20]

In figs. x. 20 and 21 Christ is depicted with nails through his wrists.

[20] J. J. Tissot pictured Our Lord as both tied and nailed to the cross (the right foot being nailed over the left on a foot-block).—*Life of Our Saviour Jesus Christ*, 1897, ii. 192f, 196. The thieves are merely tied (p.186). Our Lord wears a domed crown, not a wreath, on the cross (p.140).

CHAPTER XI

THE WAY OF THE CROSS

(1) The Jews and Crucifixion

ACCORDING to later rabbinical interpretation of Old Testament passages, the Jews did not crucify living malefactors, but merely hung up on a gibbet until evening the dead body of one already executed.[1] This interpretation does not appear to be as certain as it is usually taken to be. So the relevant passages will be briefly considered and an alternative view will be suggested as possible.[2]

The " Tree "

In the English versions of the New Testament (and of subsequent Christian literature) we read that Our Lord was crucified on " a tree."[3] Except in a few abberrant artistic representations, this is not usually taken literally. But the peculiarity of the term passes unnoticed through familiarity. The Greek word is *xylon*, which means a literal tree only in Luke 22[31] and four times in the Apocalypse is used to denote the tree of life. It means stocks (in A 16[24]) and also a rod (M xxvi. 47, 55 ; Mk xiv. 43, 48 ; L xxii. 52). Though not in the Gospels, the word *xylon* (translated *lignum* by St. Jerome) is also used to designate Christ's Cross : Acts 5[30] 10[39] 13[29] I Pet 2[24]. The best translation would be *gibbet*, for these passages clearly refer to the Old Testament *ez*, a form of gallows whose construction is not specified.[4] It was certainly not a tree, for

---

[1] Babylonian *Sanhedrin* 46b and other texts in Strack-Billerbeck, *Kommentar* i. 1034.

[2] These observations are made with extreme diffidence, as I have little competence on the subject. In addition to the commentators, the usual view is defended in an article by Pater U. Holzmeister S.J., " De Christi crucifixione quid e Deut 21[22] et Gal 3[13] consequatur," *Biblica* 27 (1946) 18-29. The view suggested in my text is advocated by E. M. Clos, *Kreuz and Grab Christi*, 1895. (This author has, however, peculiar and improbable views : the crucifying of Christ by the Jews, the form of the cross, the location of the sepulchre.)

[3] The medieval Maimonides may be echoing tradition when he writes (*Sanhedrin* 15) : " No one is hanged from a growing tree but from one uprooted, lest its being cut down be inconvenient. For the tree is to be buried with the person hanged, lest he leave a shameful memory in the world or lest it be said : So-and-so hung from this tree."

[4] The original Hebrew lettering is given on the next page, also that of the cognate Aramaic word (*ah*) which occurs in Ezra 6[11]. These approximate transliterations are sufficient for our purpose.

it had to be ' made ' (Esther 5[14]). The Latin version of the Old
Testament usually has *patibulum*, occasionally *lignum* or *crux*.

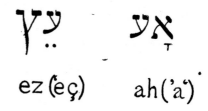

Foreign Executions

Three passages concerning non-Jewish proceedings are first
worth considering, especially on account of some of the expressions
employed.

(1) The first text (Genesis ch. 40) refers to Egyptian proceedings.[5]
Joseph said to the butler (13) : " Within three days shall Pharaoh
lift up thy head (*recordabitur ministerii tui*) and restore thee to thine
office." To the baker he said (19) : " Within three days shall
Pharaoh lift up thy head from off thee (*auferet caput tuum*) and shall
hang thee on a tree (*in cruce*), and the birds shall eat thy flesh from
off thee." On his birthday Pharaoh (20) " made a feast unto all
his servants and he lifted up the head (*recordatus est*) of the chief
butler and the head of the chief baker among his servants." Then
(21) " he restored the chief butler " (21), but (22) " he hanged the
chief baker " (*suspendit in patibulo*).[6] The usual interpretation is that
the baker was beheaded and his headless corpse was hung up.
But this does not at all follow from the text. The phrase " lift up
the head " (*nasa eth rōsh*) is applied to the butler as well as to the
baker, and twice St. Jerome translates it by " remembered." It
seems to mean to take somebody, for restoration in the butler's
case, for execution as regards the baker.[7] It is quite tenable that
this was a case of crucifixion or impalement, with the body left to
be devoured by vultures (Cf. Prov 30[17]).

[5] I give the American Jewish translation from the Hebrew, with some phrases
from the Vulgate.
[6] Josephus uses the verb *anastauroun*.—B.J. ii. 5, 3 (73).
[7] This meaning is not necessarily altered by the addition of the pleonastic *mealekā*
in verse 19. Cf II Kings 25[27]: He " lifted up the head of (i.e. he took) Joachim
out of the prison."

(2)   Persian execution is mentioned in the book of Esther[8], in connection with the hanging of Haman and his sons. It is admitted that this is crucifixion of a living person.

Our present interest lies in the phraseology of the Hebrew and of the Greek and Latin versions. The Hebrew phrase is *tālāh al ez* (to hang on the gibbet). The Greek is to hang (*kremmanumi*) on the gibbet (*xylon*). But once (7[9]) the Greek for " hang him " is *staurē-thēto*, crucify. The Latin usually calls the gibbet *patibulum* ; but in 5[14] it has *trabes* (beam) and in 7[9] *lignum* (wood or tree). The verb in Latin is *appendere* or *suspendere*, but twice *affigere* (8[7] *affigi cruci*, 6[4] *affigi patibulo*).

(3)   The third passage also refers to the Persians. In Ezra 6[11] there is a decree of Darius : " Whosoever shall alter this word, let a beam (*lignum*) be pulled out from his house, and let him be lifted up and fastened thereon (*erigatur et configatur in eo*) ; and let his house be made a dunghill for this."[9] It is admitted that in this case also there is reference to crucifixion (of the living). It is doubtful whether the gibbet (*ah*) is to consist of a roof-beam, it may be a Y-shaped supporting truss. It is also uncertain whether the person was to be nailed[10] or tied. The verb *zĕqaph* translated ' lifted up ' is suggestive in connection with Our Lord's references to His being lifted up, i.e. crucified (John 3[14] 12[32.34]). Evidently in Aramaic this verb was used both of being lifted up and of being crucified.[11]

Jewish Executions

Let us now turn to Jewish proceedings. The leaders of the Jews guilty of idolatry to Baal-Peor were condemned (Num 25[4]) : " Take all the chiefs of the people and hang them up unto the Lord in face

---

[8] Esther ii. 23 ; v.14 ; vi. 4 ; vii. 9, 10 ; viii. 7 ; ix. 4, 13.
[9] This is the American Jewish translation. The next verse reads : " And may the God that hath caused His name to dwell there overthrow all kings and peoples that shall put forth their hand to alter the same, to destroy this house of God which is at Jerusalem." This threat of crucifixion against anyone seeking to destroy the house of God in Jerusalem inevitably reminds us of what happened in Our Lord's case ; and it may have been in the mind of the perpetrators : " You who would destroy the temple . . . come down from the cross ! " (M 27[40]).
[10] Septuagint : *kremasthēnai*, but another Greek version has *plēgēsetai*. Latin : *configatur*. A reference here to impalement seems unlikely.
[11] M. Black, *The Aramaic Approach to the Gospels and Acts*, 1946, p.103. Cf. C. Lattey *J. Theol. Studies* 20 (1919) 335 ; Burkitt, *ibid.* 336 ; Lattey, 21 (1920) 175. In Hebrew the verb also means to raise up : Ps 144 (145)[14] and 145 (146)[8], the Lord raises up (*Adonai zoqeph*). In the Targum on Esther *zĕqaph* and *sĕlabh* (crucify) are used without distinction. In the Targum of Onkelos on Deut 21[23] ' on the gibbet ' is translated by *al selība* (on a cross). In the Syriac NT *zĕqiphā* is used for cross.

of the sun." The obvious interpretation is that this was the punishment to be meted out to the living, not something to be done to the
dead bodies after an execution which is neither commanded nor
specified. The verb used (*hōqīa* from *yaqa*) does not mean hang but
stretch.[12] The phrase ' against the sun ' (*neged ha-shamesh*) means
that the victims were to face the west.

In Joshua 8[29] we are told : " The king of Ai he hanged on a
tree (*suspendit in patibulo*) until the eventide. And at the going
down of the sun Joshua commanded and they took down his
carcass from the tree (*de cruce*)." The Hebrew is *thala al ha-ez*, he
hanged on the gibbet. The Greek is *ekremasen epi xylou didymou*, he
hanged on a fork. The natural interpretation is that the king was
placed alive on the gibbet, and that by sunset he was dead (perhaps
his death was hastened). The next passage however concerning the
execution of the five kings (cf. fig. xi. 6), seems to imply that only the
dead bodies were suspended (10[26]) : " Joshua smote them and put
them to death and hanged them on five trees (*atque suspendit super
quinque stipites*) ; and they were hanging upon the trees until the
evening . . . They took them down off the trees (*de patibulis*) and
cast them into the cave." But even here the Hebrew *waw* translated
' and ' may be merely explicative : He put them to death, namely,
he hanged them on five gibbets, as he did to the king of Ai.

In II Sam 4[12] we are told of the punishment of the murderers
of Ish-bosheth : " David commanded his young men and they
slew them and cut off their hands and their feet and hanged them
up beside the pool in Hebron." It is uncertain whether the men
were first slain and their bodies then mutilated and suspended.
But a much more likely meaning is that David commanded his
warriors to slay them ; so they cut off their hands and feet and then
either hung up the men or impaled them on the walls round the
pond. Compare the Assyrian pictures figs. xi. 2 and 3. In the next
case there is no doubt that the men were hanged alive. The Gibeonites asked David for seven sons of Saul (II Sam 21[6]) : " Let seven
men of his sons be delivered to us, and we will hang them up (*ut cruci-
figamus eos*) to the Lord in Gibeah of Saul . . . They hanged (*cruci-*

---

[12] Fürst gives the radical meaning of this verb (*yaqa*) : to fix firmly, to fasten to a
stake, to impale. The Greek here curiously has *paradeigmatison*, make an example
or exhibition of them. The Latin is : suspende eos contra solem in patibulis.
The next verse (5) refers to a different order given to ' the judges of Israel ' to
execute subordinates : " Slay ye everyone his own men that have joined themselves
to Baal-Peor."

fixerunt) them in the mountain before the Lord." Their dead bodies were guarded from vultures by Rizpah. It would seem that the Gibeonites were proselytes ; in any case their action was done with David's sanction.[13]

We now come to the decisive passage of Deuteronomy 21. After (in verse 21) ordering the rebellious son to be stoned, the text proceeds :

> [22]If a man have committed a sin worthy of death and he be put to death and thou hang him on a tree (*et adiudicatus morti appensus fuerit in patibulo*),[23] his body shall not remain all night upon the tree (*in ligno*). But thou shalt surely bury him the same day—for he that is hanged is a reproach unto God—that thou defile not thy land which the Lord thy God giveth thee for an inheritance.

All of the first part (verse 22) is the protasis (condition), and the three clauses are governed by *ki* (' if ') : If . . . you hang him . . . his body is not to remain all night. Moses is therefore assuming the penalty of hanging, without prescribing it ; but he orders the burial of the body on the same day. Then what about the phrase translated " be put to death " (in Hebrew *hūmath*, the hophal form of *mūth*)? According to the accepted view, this means, says Pater Holzmeister (p.22), " that the culprit's death has preceded suspension, but not that death has been inflicted by suspension." With all due respect, I do not think that this is certain. St. Jerome translates : ' if he is to be put to death,' or ' having been sentenced to death ' (*adiudicatus morti*).[14] So we may translate the text in this way :

> If a man has committed a death-deserving offence and is to be put to death, and if you hang him on a gibbet, his body is not to remain all night on the gibbet. But you are to bury him the same day—for the hanged one is under God's curse—so that you may not defile your land which the Lord your God will give to you for possession.

Hence the following seems to be a tenable interpretation. The written law (Torah) does not contain a complete criminal code ;

---

[13] The Septuagint here uses a curious verb *exēliazein*, to hang up in (or against) the sun.

[14] Nor is it clear that the hophal form of the verb has (necessarily) the meaning of the passive (instead of the gerundive). In II Kings 11[2] and II Chron 22[11] it is said that Jehosheba removed Joash " and stole him away from among the king's sons that were slain "—*ha-mūmathim*, i.e. who were to be slain. He was not taken from among the dead, but from those who were to die.

and in the other books we are told chiefly of the deeds of kings and generals, not the procedure of judges. Crucifixion is certainly not one of the prescribed penalties, like stoning ; neither was David's treatment of the slayers of Ish-bosheth, still less his cruelties in time of war (II Sam 12[31] I Chron 20[3]). There is no prescription that after stoning the dead body is to be hung up. Other penalties are assumed to exist and to be operated, in particular, crucifixion. For we must not say *hanging* in the sense either of strangulation or of neck-breaking. It is ordered that the corpse must be taken down and buried before nightfall ; there is no command to hang up a corpse. The .dead body is not to be left to rot or to be the prey of beasts and birds. As Josephus[15] puts it : " The Jews are so careful about burial that even those crucified by judicial sentence (*tous ek katadikēs anestaurōmenous*) are taken down and buried before sunset."

The later rabbis enumerated, in addition to the stoning specified by the Law, three other forms of legal execution : beheading, strangulation and burning (by pouring molten metal down the mouth).[16] This is an admission that not all penalties were specified in the Mosaic code. The last time we hear of a Jewish crucifixion is when the Maccabean King Alexander Jannai (†B.C. 79) crucified at Jerusalem 800 Jews captured in Bethoma.[17] Later, of course, apart from the Roman monopoly of capital punishment, crucifixion became the specifically Roman punishment of Jewish rebels. Varus once crucified 2,000 Jews.[18] There were many mass-crucifixions of Jews by the Roman Procurators during their rule, as well as at the siege of Jerusalem in A.D. 70.

---

[15] *B.J.* iv. 5, 2 (317).

[16] *Tractate Sanhedrin* vii. 1 : trans Danby, 1919, p.93. Our Lord refers to drowning (with an attached millstone)M18[6] Mk 9[41] L17[2].

[17] Josephus, *Ant.* xiii. 14, 2 (380) ; *B.J.* i. 4, 6 (97). He uses the verb *anastaurein*. Klausner, *Jesus of Nazareth*, 1947, p.349, casts doubt on this. (1) Josephus may be exaggerating the numbers. Probably. (2) " It is also possible that the punishment was not crucifixion but hanging." There is not a vestige of evidence that the Jews (or the Romans) practised hanging by strangulation. (3) " He points out that this was an act of barbarous cruelty in which Alexander was imitating Gentile usage." Josephus does not contrast Jewish mildness and Gentile barbarity. He condemns not the crucifixion but the accompanying circumstances : " He did something inexpressibly cruel. While feasting publicly with his concubines, he ordered some 800 of the Jews to be crucified, and he slaughtered their children and wives in the sight of the still living wretches."

[18] Josephus, *Ant.* xvii. 10, 10. The Talmud once says that Our Lord was stoned and several times that He was ' hanged.'—Dalman and Laible, *Jesus Christ in the Talmud,* trans. Streane, 1893, pp.80, 85. " The Talmud knows nothing of an execution of Jesus by the Romans, but makes it solely the act of the Jews."—R. T. Herford, *Christianity in Talmud and Midrash,* p.83.

I do not press some of the above interpretations. It is very likely that they do not hold. My friend Father Kevin Smyth S.J., does not agree with me and has argued as follows :

(1) That crucifixion of living men was something strange and even shocking to the Jews appears from the remark of Josephus that the victims of Antiochus Epiphanes " were crucified while still alive and breathing." [This text is not very decisive, for it contains the torture of mutilation. Personally I am inclined to think it refers to the impalement of mutilated victims as in fig. xi. 3. " They were scourged, their bodies were mutilated ; and while still alive and breathing, they were impaled (or crucified? *anestaurounto*) ; while their wives and sons . . . were strangled, the children being hung from the necks of their impaled (crucified?) parents."—*Ant.* xii. 5, 4 (256).—A.O'R.]

(2) The primary sense of the passage Jos 10²⁶ (and the *waw*) is that they were put to death and then hanged. This should be retained unless there is positive evidence that it has to be taken otherwise.

(3) I cannot agree that the sense given for II Sam 4¹² is ' much more likely.' The grammar again demands the notion of succession for the three verbs following ' commanded.'

(4) In Deut 21²² I cannot agree that " is to be put to death " is a tenable translation. The *wĕ* seems to me to be consecutive (conversive), reducing the perfect tense to a present, so that the grammar demands the translation : If a man commits a capital crime, and in consequence is put to death and then hanged, his body is to remain, etc.¹⁸ᵃ

The " Curse "

In the text quoted from Deuteronomy there is a significant phrase : *kilĕlath Elōhīm tāluy*, a curse of God [is] a hanged one. This is literally rendered by Aquila and Symmachus. St. Jerome, following the Septuagint, has : *Maledictus a Deo est qui pendet in ligno*, cursed by God is he who hangs on a gibbet. This is also St. Paul's version in Gal iii. 13 : cursed is everyone who hangs on a gibbet.¹⁹ That is, he is accursed, excluded from God's protection, banned from Israel.

There is no doubt that this view was applied to crucifixion. The Sanhedrists chose this death of dishonour and excommunication for Our Lord. It was in virtue of this text of Deuteronomy that they asked to have the bodies taken down from the three crosses

---

¹⁸ᵃ As to II Kings 11² Fr. Smyth admits that the participle in Hebrew often has a future sense, but he doubts if this is true of the passive participle. He thinks the translation " rescued him from among the children who were killed " is enough.
¹⁹ The Septuagint and St. Paul have *pas* (everyone). Cursed : *kekatēramenos* LXX, *epikaratos* Paul. He also omits *hypo Theou* (by God), but it is clearly understood.

(but see p.284). To the Jew the cross was infinitely more than an earthly punishment of suffering and shame ; it connoted also a divine condemnation, rejection by God. There was no deliverance on Calvary, and so the conclusion was drawn : Anathema Jesus (I Cor 12³). Says Rabbi Tarphon in Justin's *Dialogue* (32, 1) : " Your so-called Messiah was so without honour or glory that he fell under the severest curse of God's Law—he was crucified ! " Some might even be prepared to concede the idea of a suffering Messiah—but not one crucified :

> Be assured that our whole nation is waiting for the Messiah, and we admit that all the passages of the Scriptures cited by you refer to him . . . But we doubt whether the Messiah was to be so dishonoured as to be crucified. For a man crucified is in the Law saïd to be cursed. Hence I am very incredulous on the point. Clearly the Scriptures declare that the Messiah is to suffer ; but we wish to know if you can prove to us that it is by the suffering cursed in the Law.—Trypho (Tarphon) in Justin, *Dial.* 89.

Such has since been the attitude towards Him whom later Jews called *ha-Taluy*, the Hanged.

> The very form of his punishment would disprove those claims in Jewish eyes. No Messiah that Jews could recognise could suffer such a death ; for he that is hanged is accursed of God (Deut 21²³), an insult to God (Targum, Rashi).—*Jewish Encycl.* vii. 166.

No wonder that the tragedy of Calvary plunged His followers into utter despondency and hopelessness : " We were hoping that it was He who would redeem Israel." Only the tremendous experience of the Resurrection could re-animate their faith and re-orientate their shattered religious conceptions. " God has raised Him from the dead," proclaimed St. Peter (A3¹⁵), " and of this we are witnesses." It was the curse of the cross—to the Jews a scandal—which was the leading objection made by the Jews to the early Christians. St. Justin retorted by saying that the curse was the anathema which the Jews and the Pagans pronounced against Jesus :

> The text of the Law ' accursed everyone who hangs on a gibbet ' strengthens our hope which hangs from the crucified Christ, not because God curses this Crucified but because He predicts what all you and your fellows were to do, in your ignorance that He is before all things, God's eternal Priest, King and Messiah. With your own eyes you can see this come to pass. For you yourselves in your synagogues curse all those who have after Him become

Christians, while the other nations carry out the curse and put to death those who merely confess that they are Christians.—Justin, *Dial.* 96.

St. Paul replies that Christ has indeed become a ' curse ' in order to free both Jews and Gentiles from the curse pronounced by the Law against those who do not observe its precepts (Deut 27[26]) : " Cursed be he that confirmeth not the words of this Law to do them" :

> Christ has ransomed us from the curse of [pronounced by] the Law by becoming a curse on our behalf—for it is written, Accursed is every man who hangs on a gibbet—so that the blessing of Abraham may reach to the Gentiles in Jesus Christ, that in virtue of faith we may receive the promised Spirit.—Gal. 3[13].

" The Father of the universe," says St. Justin (*Dial.* 95, 2), " wished His Christ, on behalf of men of every race, to take on Himself the curses due to all, knowing that He would raise Him after crucifixion and death." Thus this malediction was taken seriously, incorporated into the idea of Redemption, and used to proclaim that the Law had ceased to be valid.

From Josephus we learn that the Jews introduced a supplementary suspension as a special punishment for blasphemers, or at least so interpreted Deuteronomy in his time : " Let him that has blasphemed God be stoned and hung up for a whole day, and let him be buried in dishonour and darkness."[20] The idea was to bring opprobrium on the corpse of one who was repudiated by God. Later the rabbis discussed whether hanging should always follow stoning : " Everyone stoned is to be hanged, so R. Eleazar ; but the majority hold that only blasphemers and idolators are to be hanged."[21] Certainly the body of St. Stephen was not so treated (Acts 7). There is no known instance of this corpse-hanging after stoning. So it is doubtful whether it is not an ideal or fanciful rule. While Josephus says that the corpse was to be thus exposed all day,

---

[20] *Josephus*, Ant. iv. 8, 6. But he also applies it to those crucified (see p. 168 above).
[21] *Sanhedrin* vi. 4b, trans. Danby, p. 90. The text proceeds : " How was a man hanged? A beam was fixed in the ground with a cross-piece ; the corpse's hands were fastened together, and it was so hanged. According to R. Jose the beam leaned against a wall, the corpse being suspended on it after the manner adopted by butchers. It was then taken down immediately." But we cannot from this draw any reliable conclusions as to how the body was hung up. The ' beam ' (*ha korah*) seems to mean the middle or vertical post. The ' cross-piece ' (*ha ez*) may designate a fork. The meaning would appear to be that the corpse's hands were tied to the structure, not ' fastened together.'

the rabbis said that the hanging was to be only for an instant.[22]

The idea behind this is the rabbinic interpretation of ' a curse of God,' not as cursed by God, but cursing or insulting God : " Why is this one hanged? Because he cursed the Name and the Name of Heaven was found defiled."[23] But while this might account for the hanging, it does not explain the only injunction found in Deuteronomy : the burial before nightfall. If we take ' of God ' as an objective genitive, we can account for the quick burial only by regarding the corpse as prolonging the offence, as if still cursing God. This would be an argument for taking down the corpse quickly, but it fails completely to explain why the corpse should be hung up at all.

This new interpretation is quite intelligible in the light of later historical conditions. The original idea seems to have been that the hanging up of a human being, alive or dead, was, though a necessary evil in certain cases, a degradation of God's handiwork and a profanation of the holy land ; so it had to be ended as soon as possible, certainly before nightfall. But it became inconvenient when so many Jews, regarded as patriots, were crucified by the Romans. So the theory arose that the curse applied only to one who had cursed God, and that the penalty of ' hanging ' was legitimately deserved only by a blasphemer. At the same time, with meticulous literalness, some rabbis held that, to comply with the Law, even one killed by stoning should receive a ' token ' hanging by momentary suspension of his corpse. But this view was expressed centuries after it had any relevance to realities.

These late academic subtleties cannot be relied upon as applying to the first century or earlier. Even if we accept the hanging up of a dead body in certain cases as a fact apart from its explanation, there is no doubt that the passage in Deuteronomy—both as regards the curse and the burial before sunset—was applied, also if not exclusively, to the hanging of a living body in crucifixion. The opprobrium which the Sanhedrin contrived, and which continued to be urged against Christ's Crucifixion, was not based solely on the brief *post mortem* hanging of His dead body on the cross. Crucifixion, already regarded by the Romans as a dishonourable and servile

---

[22] *Sanhedrin*, tosephta ix. 6b, p.92 Danby : " When a man is hanged, at the moment when one is tying him up, another is loosening the knot, in order to carry out what the law of hanging demands." This text goes on to explain that the ' curse of God ' means a cause of cursing God by onlookers.
[23] *Sanhedrin*, p.91 Danby. Rabbinic texts in Strack-Billerbeck, *Kommentar* i. 1012, iii. 544.

punishment, was viewed by the Jews with special horror as involving divine repudiation and malediction, at least when carried out (in some form of hanging) by the Jews themselves or procured by them. Above all, such a fate was, in their view, utterly incompatible with the claim to be the promised Messiah.[24]

(2) Had the Greeks Crucifixion?

The cruel punishments of impalement and crucifixion were in vogue among Scythians, Medes, Persians, Phoenicians and Carthaginians. The Assyrians were one of the most cruel and brutal peoples of antiquity. They had no hesitation in depicting on their monuments, as well as commemorating in their inscriptions, their barbarous treatment of enemies vanquished in war. Among the many horrible tortures represented on surviving monuments, there are scenes of mutilation and impalement ; but there does not appear to be a single case of what we nowadays understand by crucifixion. A near approach is shown in fig. xi. 1, which commemorates the victory of Asurbanipal at the battle of Tulliz (665–660 B.C.) over the Elamite king Tiuman.[1] Two captured

XI. 1.—Assyrians flaying their prisoners alive and carrying away the heads of the slain : Bas-relief at Kouyunjik

---

[24] Loisy objects to St. Paul's use of Deut 21²³ which applied only to a dead body.— *Ep. aux Galates*, 1916, p.149. I have argued against this view of Deut., but even if we admit it, the Jews certainly applied it to crucifixion. After all Our Lord's dead body did hang for a while on the cross. It was not St. Paul and the Christians who first brought forward this inconvenient text about the curse ; it was their Jewish opponents. The word *tālah* in the O.T. and later is used for hanging before or after death.
[1] Layard, *Discoveries in the Ruins of Nineveh and Babylon*, 1853, p.457 ; Maspero, *The Passing of the Empires*, 1900, p.415 (cf. p.235).

leaders are stretched naked at full length on the ground or more probably on planks ; their limbs are held by cords attached to pegs ; and they are being flayed alive.

In classical Athens three different methods of inflicting the death-penalty appear to have been practised : precipitation from an eminence into a rocky chasm (*barathron*), poisoning by hemlock, and a method called *apotympanismos* which merits discussion. Until recently this was interpreted as " beating to death with a club." But in the new edition of the Lexicon of Liddell and Scott it is translated " crucifixion." This change of view is due largely to a book published in 1923 by Keramopoullos, based on excavations at Phalerum. In one grave there were found seventeen skeletons with iron collars round their necks and cramp-irons (to which bits of wood still adhered) about their ankles and their wrists. Keramopoullos holds that they were executed criminals, subjected to savage treatment which came from ancient usage. Accordingly this method of execution could be described thus :

> The criminal was stripped and fastened to a wide upright plank by means of five iron bands encircling his ankles, wrists and neck. From the conditions of the skeletons it would seem that the neck-band was the tightest and supported most of the weight of the body.—Bonner and Smith, *The Administration of Justice from Homer to Aristotle*, Chicago 1938, ii. 280.

Our uncertainty concerning *apotympanismos* shows how difficult it is to discover the details of ancient punishments, at least in the absence of monumental representation. It seems to be now accepted that the verb *apotympanisai* denotes some aberrant form of cruci-fixion by clamping (or nailing?) to a plank. *Tympanon* means not only a kettledrum but the instrument (a plank) for this mode of execution.

> The verb is used by Demosthenes viii. 61 and ix. 61. Vince's translation of the two passages (in the Loeb Classical Library 1930) gives " cudgelled to death " and " knocking on the head." Lysias xiii. 67 : he was executed on the plank. Lucian (*Cataplus* 6) describes the dead criminals as " those executed on the *tympanon* and those impaled (*aneskolopismenous*)." Aristophanes in his *Thesmophoriazusae* has a skit on the punishment. Mnesilochus, fastened to an upright wooden contrivance called both *sanis* and *tympanon*, asks the guard to loosen the nail or the peg and then objects that it has been tightened ; later he complains that he is dying with throat-cutting agonies. The verb hang (*kremazō*) is

used to denote the man's position on the plank. There is another reference in Aristophanes' *Plutus* (476), where (following the scholiast) an editor incorrectly says: " *tympana* are cudgels with which criminals are beaten."—B. B. Rogers, *The Comedies of Aristophanes*, 6 (1907) 52.

Herodotus (vii. 33) tells us that the Athenians crucified (stretched out and nailed) to a plank a Persian enemy who had polluted a temple: *zōnta pros sanida diepassaleusan*. According to Bonner and Smith (ii. 280), this means " to crucify in the oriental manner by driving spikes through the hands and feet." But, they add, " there is no evidence that the Athenians ever crucified their own criminals in this manner." The meaning of the verb *diapassaleuō* is clear from Aristophanes' *Knights* (369/71), where it is applied to a hide pegged out on the ground; *passalos* (attic, *pattalos*) means a peg, a pin, a stake. In another passage (ix. 120), Herodotus describes the punishment of another Persian temple-polluter by the Athenians: " Having nailed (or fastened, *prospassaleusantes*) him to a plank, they hung him up (*anekremasan*), and before his eyes they stoned his son."

Crucifixion (nailing to a cross), as a normal form of punishment, seems to have been brought from the East to the Hellenic world by Alexander the Great.[2] The Greek terms used for crucifixion (by Greeks or non-Greeks) require consideration, especially as the same terms often refer to impalement.

The word for cross (apart from the Hebraic *xylon*) in the New Testament and in subsequent Greek Christian writers is *stauros*. But the earlier meaning is an upright pale or stake, in the plural piles driven to serve as a foundation (and *staurōma* is a palisade). Only later (A.D.) did it come to mean a cross. Another word for stake is *skolops* (Latin *stipes*), which it seems impossible to distinguish from *stauros* until the latter became appropriated to what we know as a cross.[3]

There are two corresponding verbs, either of which may mean impale or crucify: *anaskolopizō* and *anastauroō*, both of which are used interchangeably in Herodotus (ix. 78) for impaling. Only

---

[2] At the capture of Tyre: " The King's anger provided a sad spectacle for the victors. Two thousand, spared from the mad slaughter, affixed to crosses (*crucibus affixi*) were hung up (*pependerunt*) along an immense stretch of the shore."— Curtius Rufus iv. 19. He ordered some surrendered Scythians to be scourged and crucified (*crucibus affigi*).—*Ibid.* vii. 43 Demosthenes speaks of being "in imminent danger of being crucified " (nailed, *proselōsthai*).—*Against Midias* 105.

[3] Eustathius (on *Od.* xiv. 11 and *Il.* xii. 63) identifies them. In his lexicon Hesychius defines *skolops* (1071) as " a sharpened piece of wood " and *stauroi* (1664) as " firmly planted *skolopes*, *charakes* (pointed stakes) and all upright pieces of wood." Yet Festus (ed. C. Mueller 1839, p.315) says: *Stipes fustis terrae defixus.*

later did the latter verb become the technical term for crucifying :

Anaskolopizō : Hector longed to set upon a stake the head of Patroclus.—Homer, *Iliad* xviii. 176. Astyages impaled the Magi. —Herodotus i. 128. The Egyptian physicians were about to be impaled by Darius (iii. 132). At the capture of Babylon, Darius impaled about 3000 of the principal citizens (iii. 159). Similarly it is used for impaling by Persians in iii. 132 and iv. 43. The Queen of Barce (Cyrenaica) had the murderers of her son impaled along the wall.—*ibid.* iv. 202. Thus this appears to have been used practically exclusively to denote impaling (*anaskolopisis*). In medieval Greek *anaskolopisma* appears to have denoted hanging by the neck.

Anastauroō :[4] This also means to impale, only in Roman times did it come to denote crucifixion. The Persians impaled his body on the spot and sent his embalmed head to Darius.—Herodotus vi. 30. Xerxes cut off the head of the dead Leonidas and set it on a pole (ix. 78). The king of Lybia was betrayed and impaled by the Persians.—Thucydides i. 110. The would-be despot is finally impaled or burnt in a coat of pitch.—Plato, *Gorgias* 473C. Hannibal was crucified at Carthage.—Polybius i. 24, 26. The King of the Medes was impaled (or crucified) by the Assyrians.—Diodorus Siculus ii. 1. In Sicily Dionysius crucified the Greeks who had joined the Carthaginians.—*ibid.* xiv. 53.

There is a third much rarer verb which Hesychius (4583 and 4585) declares to be synonymous with the two preceding : *askindyleuō* (from *skindalamos*, a splinter). It occurs in an oft-quoted passage of Plato : " They will say that our just man will be scourged, racked, fettered, have his eyes burnt out, and at last after all kinds of suffering will be impaled."[5]

The Greek verb *kremannymi* (to hang) seems to have been practically exclusively used for crucifixion. The Persian Oroites crucified (*anestaurōse*, impaled?) Polycrates, who having been hung up (*anakremamenos*) was washed by Jupiter when it rained and was anointed by the sun.—Herodotus iii. 125. Diodorus Siculus (xvii. 46) says of the captives crucified by Alexander at Tyre that ' he hanged them.' The verb is used of crucifixion by Josephus, Plutarch and Eusebius. (The Greek of the Old Testament has been considered above). It is used of the bandits in Luke 23[39]. In *Mart. S. Carpi* we read (37) that he was " nailed to the gibbet " and then (40) that he was hanging.

---

[4] In the New Testament[6] the verb for crucify is *stauroō*. The compound *anastauroō* occurs only in Heb 6[6], where the Greek Fathers took it to mean crucify again.
[5] Jowett correctly translates ' impaled,' while A. D. Lindsay has ' crucified.' It is quoted by Clement of Alexandria, *Stromata* v. 14 (p.713 Potter), who in two other places uses the verb of the execution of Christians (ii. 22 and iv. 9). When the passage is quoted in the *Acta S. Apollonii* (40), the verb is changed into *anaskolopisthēsetai.*

(3) Crucifixion among the Romans

Execution by crucifixion was frequent in the Roman world in later republican and imperial times. Though used for traitors and deserters, in special cases for Roman citizens deprived of their rights, it was pre-eminently the punishment for slaves : *servile supplicium*. Yet even for them it was of comparatively recent introduction. The Twelve Tables specify several modes of the death penalty, but there is not a word about crucifixion. For a slave-robber they prescribe " scourging and being thrown from a rock."[1] Under the date B.C. 294, Livy (iii. 18, 10) assumes a distinction between the execution of freemen and that of slaves ; but we do not know how at this period the latter were punished. All the reliable evidence leads us to hold that the Romans learnt crucifixion from the Carthaginians and that they were unfamiliar with it until the beginning of the third century B.C.

With the exception of two utterly discredited statements, there is no recorded case of crucifixion before 217 [B.C. by Romans], when some twenty-five slaves were so punished for a conspiracy at Rome [Livy xxii. 23]. This was only a few weeks after Hannibal had crucified an Italian guide, and most probably to retaliate against his severity.—Oldfather[2], p.62.

The two statements about earlier crucifixion in Rome may be briefly considered. (1) Cassius Hemina says : " Tarquinius Superbus had forced the people to construct sewers ; owing to this affront many hanged themselves ; and he ordered their bodies to be crucified."—Fragment 15 : Peter, *Hist. Rom. fragmenta*, 1883, p.106. Oldfather (p.64) says that the story " improbable and ridiculous in itself," was invented as an aetiological explanation of the religious taboo on self-strangling. " In the pontifical books it was prescribed that he who took his life with a halter was to be thrown out unburied."—Servius on *Aeneid* xii. 603. (2) The second instance is the assertion of Dionysius of Halicarnassus (v. 51) that after a servile insurrection (which he dates 501 B.C.) the captured slaves were crucified or impaled (*anĕskilopisthēsan*). Livy knows nothing of this insurrection ; and Dio Cassius (vii. 13, 11) knows nothing of the mode of punishment. Impalement is possible ; but it is unlikely that an ancient annalist would have bothered to recount details concerning the execution of a handful of mutinous slaves.

[1] Aulus Gellius xi. 18, 8.
[2] I shall several times refer to an excellent but neglected article by W. A. Oldfather, " Livy i. 26 and the Supplicium de More Maiorum," *Trans. Amer. Philol. Assn.* 39 (1908) 49-72.

There is a famous case which is still erroneously quoted as if it were concerned with crucifixion. About 650 B.C. Horatius, after his victory over the three Curatii, met and slew his sister who had been engaged to one of them. Here is the account of Livy:

> The dread formula of the law ran thus : " Let the duumvirs pronounce him guilty of treason ; if he shall appeal from the duumvirs, let the appeal be tried. If the duumvirs win, let the lictor veil his head, let him bind him with a rope to a barren tree, let him scourge him either within or without the pomerium." By the terms of this law duumvirs were appointed. They considered that they might not acquit, under that act, even one who was innocent, and having given a verdict of guilty, one of them pronounced the words : " Publius Horatius, I adjudge you a traitor. Go, lictor, bind his hands."
>
> The lictor had approached and was about to fit the noose.[3] Then Horatius—at the prompting of [King] Tullus who put a merciful construction upon the law—cried " I appeal ! " And so the appeal was tried before the people. What influenced men most of all in that trial was the assertion of Publius Horatius, the father, that his daughter had been justly slain . . . The old man embraced the youth and . . . exclaimed : " This man you saw but lately advancing decked with spoils and triumphing in his victory, can you bear, Quirites, to see him bound beneath a fork and scourged and tortured ? "
>
> The people acquitted him, more in admiration of his valour than from the justice of his cause. And so that the flagrant murder might yet be cleansed away by some kind of expiatory rite, the father was commanded to make atonement for his son at the public cost. He therefore offered certain piacular sacrifices which were thenceforward handed down in the Horatian family ; and erecting a beam across the street to typify a yoke, he made his son pass under it, with covered head.[4] It remains to this day, being restored from time to time at the State's expense, and is known as The Sister's Beam.—Livy i. 26 : trans. B. O. Foster, *Livy* i (1919) 93f.

The punishment prescribed by this old law, with which Horatius was threatened, has been interpreted as crucifixion by historians such as Mommsen and by many writers on crucifixion since Lipsius.

---

[3] This is not a good translation of *iniciebatque laqueum*, especially as Foster agrees with Oldfather in rejecting both hanging and crucifixion. The soldier was about to carry out the order *Colliga manus*, to tie his hands not to put a rope round his neck. *Laqueus* (like the Greek *brochos*) means not only noose or halter, but snare or trap, fetters or hindrance. Here it corresponds to our handcuffs.

[4] The beam (*tigillum*), erected across the street as a symbolic yoke (*iugum*) by the father, is described by Festus as " two beams with a third placed on top."—*De verb. signif.* (s.v. sororium tigillum), ed. C. Mueller 1839, p.297.

Indeed Cicero seems to have been the first to do so in his speech *Pro C. Rabirio perduellionis reo*, in which he tries to discredit his opponent Labienus by accusing him of intending to crucify a Roman citizen. He attributes (iv. 13) the law to " the most proud and cruel king Tarquinius" and quotes the law in a garbled form, omitting the bracketed words: *Caput obnubito, infelici arbori [reste] suspendito, [verberato]*. That is, he omitted the reference to a rope and to scourging as the culmination of the punishment. There is so much chicanery in the speech that no reliance whatever can be placed on the contention of this biased advocate that this old law implied crucifixion.

The arguments against this view are overwhelming :

(1) The details are incompatible with what we know of the crucifixion-procedure, particularly the covering of the head.[5] In numerous accounts of crucifixion we are told that the culprit looked, talked, prayed or cursed.

(2) The last clause of the formula, the final phase of the punishment, was scourging (*verberato*). In all known cases of crucifixion, scourging preceded attachment to the cross—an order which could be inferred from commonsense. Here the victim was to be scourged to death.[5a]

(3) It is utterly improbable that crucifixion was specifically prescribed against citizens for a crime relatively as common as *perduellio* (treason).[6] It is attested, from every period of Roman history in which crucifixion was in usage, that this was the punishment specially applied to slaves.

(4) All the evidence is entirely against the Romans practising crucifixion at this early date.

The speech which Livy puts into the mouth of the father contains

---

[5] By retaining this clause Cicero allowed his misinterpretation to appear. Cf. v, 16 : " Let not the executioner, the covering of the head, the very name of cross, have anything to do not merely with the body of a Roman citizen but with his thoughts, eyes, ears."

[5a] As a specimen of confusion between different punishments, here is the description of Roman crucifixion by a competent German jurist: " The condemned was stripped, his head was covered, the crossbeam or the *furca* was laid on him naked, his hands were usually bound to both ends of this, or more rarely nailed. With the body it was then drawn up on a post erected on the place of execution, the feet were then bound or nailed to the post. Finally the man thus crucified was scourged."—F. Doerr, *Der Prozess Jesu in rechtsgeschichtlicher Beleuchtung*, 1920, p.74.

[6] Strictly Horatius was guilty of *parricidium* (homicide). The ' clemency ' of Tullus consisted in treating it as usurping the function of the State, i.e. as treason, in which the condemned had the right of appeal.

a phrase—sometimes wrongly quoted in connection with crucifixion —which confirms the view given above : " bound beneath a fork, scourged and tortured " (*sub furca vinctum inter verbera et cruciatus*). The expression ' under a fork ' is probably an anachronism taken from another milder punishment inflicted on slaves, which will be presently considered. There seems to be no reference to ' running the gauntlet ' or to a procession during which the culprit, in a fork, was urged on and scourged.[7] He was tied to a fixed stake[8] which is called *arbor infelix*, evidently more primitive than a forked stick.

There is some reason for believing that the arbor infelix of the carmen was a dead tree, possibly a fruit tree. As practically all fruit trees fork close to the ground, the criminal's hands were probably bound to the branching arms, his neck coming naturally into the crotch, where it might have been fastened by a crossbar. The transition from this to an ordinary *furca* would have been an easy one.—Oldfather, p.70.

The punishment here envisaged was being scourged to death while fastened to the ' tree.' It does not mean hanging from a tree ; it would be absurd to begin scourging a criminal only when he was dangling from a noose. The culprit was to be tied up to a tree, perhaps with his feet off the ground.[9]

There is not a particle of evidence that the Romans ever hanged criminals from a gallows. To be sure they were frequently enough strangled in prison ; but this seems to have been done in their cells, and the phrases used distinctly imply suffocation by throttling and not by hanging. But even this practice is comparatively late, the first certain case being the strangling of Aristonikos in 129/8, then that of the followers of G. Gracchus in 121 — Oldfather, p.54.

The Romans had a phrase ' traditional punishment ' (*supplicium*

---

[7] Vignon (ii. 50) seems to think that Horatius was to bear the fork to the place of execution and there to be hanged from it or with it attached to him.

[8] So Livy speaking of traitors punished in B.C. 509 says : " They were standing bound to a stake (*deligati ad palum*) . . . They were stripped, scourged with rods, and beheaded " (after death?).—Livy, ii. 5, 6 and 8.

[9] The phrase is : *infelici arbori reste suspendito*. Notice the rare use of the locative *arbori* instead of *arbore* or *in arbore* : Hang or fasten with a rope on to a tree, not *from* a tree. *Suspendere* does not necessarily mean hanging by the neck. Marcus ordered a mutinous soldier to be fastened (*suspendi*) to a post with his hands tied behind his back ; and he survived.—Ammianus xv. 7, 4. Referring to this law as quoted by Cicero, Nonius says : *Suspensum dicitur alte ligatum*.—Ed. L. Mueller, 1888, i. 631. That is, with feet off the ground. Similar expressions with the adjective *infelix* are applied to crucifixion only in Seneca, *Ep.* 101, 14 (*illud infelix lignum*), and in Minucius Felix, *Oct.* 23, 11 (*infelicis stipitis portio*).

more maiorum), which seems, as in the case of Horatius, to mean beating a man to death while he was tied to a dead tree or a post.[10] This penalty seems to have lapsed in the milder period from the second to the first century B.C. ; it was revived in the early empire,[11] and instances are recorded in Constantinople as late as the eighth century A.D. Perhaps the best description occurs in connection with the decree of the Senate declaring Nero an enemy to be punished *more maiorum*. When he asked what was this punishment, he was told that " the neck of the naked man was inserted in a fork and he was beaten to death with rods."[12]

Before investigating crucifixion, it was necessary to distinguish it from beating to death and hanging ; impalement will be presently considered ; also fork-bearing will be differentiated from cross-carrying. In this way a number of irrelevant texts can be excluded. Those that are left, especially those of early date, are not as informative as we could wish.

Some general considerations may first be given. The punishment of crucifixion has ceased in Europe for sixteen centuries.[13] So we have to rely on the many literary references, which however are exceedingly meagre in details.[14] There is really no description of the actual procedure, no handbook for executioners. Moreover, there is no evidence for the intrinsically improbable assumption, usually made, that there was one ritually prescribed method for affixing the victim to the gibbet. On the contrary, there is evidence that the actual process varied considerably according to the circum-

[10] Pater Holzmeister is wrong in taking this to mean crucifixion.—*Crux Domini*, 1934, p.15. This beating to death was probably the punishment decreed by the Twelve Tables for the harvest-thief : *suspensum Cereri necari*.—Pliny 18[12]. " It was laid down that a slanderer was to be clubbed to death (*fustibus feriretur*) "— Cornutus on Persius i. 137.

[11] Cato proposed that the Catiline conspirators should undergo the traditional punishment. Yet "Lentulus was let down" into the Tullianum and " with a rope they broke his neck."—Sallust, *Cat.* 52, 36 and 55, 5. According to Suetonius, Claudius (n. 34) went to Tibur to see this punishment, but we are merely told that the culprits were *deligati ad palum*. Domitian (n. 11) imposed the punishment on some who were guilty of *maiestas*, but " frightened at the atrocity of the punishment, he intervened."

[12] Suetonius, *Nero* 49 : nudi hominis cervicem inseri furcae, corpus virgis ad necem caedi. So Aurelius Victor, *Ep.* v. 7. Eutropius (vii. 15, 1) inaccurately adds a procession with the fork and (more curiously) being thrown from a rock : " he was to be led naked through the streets, with his head in a fork, beaten to death with rods, and thus thrown from a rock."

[13] It was abolished by Constantine.—Sozomen, H.E. i. 8, 24. There is a story that the Russians recently crucified three priests in Lithuania.

[14] These have been conveniently collected in a pamphlet by U. Holzmeister, S.J., *Crux Domini atque crucifixio*, Rome, 1934. But I am querying several of his interpretations and conclusions.

stances, the status of the victim and his crime, and the country.[15]
Concerning the starving Jews seeking escape from besieged
Jerusalem, Josephus tells us :

> They were scourged and subjected to every kind of torture
> before being killed and crucified in front of the walls. Titus
> indeed pitied their fate, five hundred or sometimes more being
> captured in a day . . . The soldiers out of rage and hatred
> amused themselves by nailing their prisoners in different postures.
> And so great was their number that there was neither room for the
> crosses nor crosses for the bodies.—*Bellum Jud.* v. 11, 1.

Says Seneca :

> There I see crosses, not indeed of one kind but fashioned
> differently by different people. Some are suspended head down-
> wards, some impaled, some have their arms extended on the
> gibbet.—*De consolatione ad Marcellam* 20[3].

Thus the available texts do little to clarify the procedure. It is
likely enough that many of the classical writers were as ill-informed
concerning details as are educated writers of any period concerning
the exact modes of execution. At any rate they displayed no human
or juristic interest in the whole business. A person condemned to
crucifixion thereby lost all civic rights—there was then no real
conception of natural rights, least of all as regards slaves. The law
disdained to specify details ; the condemned was abandoned to the
convenience or the whim of the executioners. It is thus practically
certain that there was considerable latitude as to accidentals

> Some variations in the details of other modes of execution will
> help to strengthen our argument. In Sicily under Verres the
> executioner took money to behead prisoners without unnecessary
> blows or pain.—Cicero, *Verr.* v. 45, 118. The Martyr Phileas
> of Thmuis says of the Egyptian Christians : " When all who
> wished were given a free hand to insult them, some struck them
> with cudgels, others with rods, others with scourges, others again
> with straps and others with ropes."—Eusebius, H. E. viii. 19, 4.
> Those condemned to the beasts were often tied to a stake on top
> of a platform. Yet Eusebius, an eyewitness, says (viii. 7, 4) :
> " You might have seen a youth not twenty years old standing un-

---

[15] Hamilcar deprived Indortes of sight, ill-treated and crucified him.—Diodorus
Siculus xxv. 5, 2. According to Suetonius (*Caesar* 74), Julius Caesar was ' mild '
to bandits : " he ordered that first they should have their throats cut and then be
crucified." There are many other recorded instances of such variations. It is
unnecessary to refer to the inverted crucifixion (head downward) of St. Peter and
of Egyptian Christians.—Eusebius H.E. 3[1] 8[8].

bound, his hands outspread in the form of a cross . . . calmly
engaged in earnest prayer." Without giving references, we may
enumerate some recorded variations in punishment by fire.
Usually the victim was attached to a stake, with hands nailed
(e.g. Pionius). Sometimes on request the executioner used rope
instead of nails (e.g. Polycarp). St. Fructuosus and his deacons
were only bound ; when the bonds burnt, they fell on their knees,
awaiting asphyxiation. Sometimes the victim was on the ground-
level, surrounded by burning faggots ; sometimes he was buried
to the knees. Sometimes he was despatched with a dagger
(e.g. Polycarp). Sometimes he was slowly burnt on a grill (e.g.
Laurence). All these variations occurred under the general term
of punishment *ad ignem*. There is no reason for assuming that the
penalty *ad crucem* was more stereotyped.

Of recent years there has been an increasing tendency to interpret
the few surviving texts as rigidly prescribing one single mode for
crucifixion, and then to apply the result to the case of Our Lord.
Thus, relying on Holzmeister, Vignon (ii. 49) rather dogmatically
declares that " the archaeological [i.e. literary] texts say formally
that the condemned man did not carry a complete cross." I am
convinced neither of this interpretation nor—even if it be admitted
—of its applicability to Christ.

(4) Impalement

The literal meaning of the Greek *stauros* (and the Latin *crux*)
was a stake ; hence the verb which we translate ' crucify ' was also
used to mean ' impale.'[1] Sometimes it was only the victim's head
which was impaled—a custom which lasted in Europe until the
nineteenth century.[2] But the cruel punishment of impaling (or
' spitting ') a living person also long continued not only among
Arabs and Turks but also in Eastern Europe. There were cases
even in the seventeenth century ; in 1632 Gustavus Adolphus at
Nurnberg ordered the impalement of a Swedish corporal. A German
who travelled in the East in 1571 described a Turkish execution
in Constantinople :[3]

[1] The Greek expressions involved have already been investigated, p.176.
[2] Xerxes' treatment of the dead Leonidas : "He ordered his head to be cut off and
impaled (*anastaurōsai*)."—Herodotus vii. 238. Cf. vi. 30 : "They impaled (*anĕstau-
rōsan*) his body and sent his head embalmed to king Darius."
[3] Another traveller writing in 1698 tells us that these unfortunates often lived more
than two days : " Some of them have been known to have lived on the stake until
the third day and to have smoked tobacco if it was given to them.".—Thevenot,
cited by Mansberg, p.60. Impalement was practised by the Turks in the 19th
century.—Zoeckler, *The Cross of Christ*, 1877, p.63.

The other malefactor was also impaled, but, like the other, without touching the heart. The oaken stake, with a sharp iron point, was driven between his legs so that it emerged above at the neck. Then the stake with the man was raised up and fixed on the ground. These two men lived a long time and made gruesome cries in their suffering.—Breuning von Buochenbach, *Reisen*, Strasb. 1612, p.86 : cited by R. von Mansberg, *Z. f. Kulturgesch.* 7 (1900) 60.

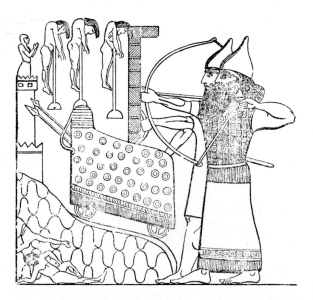

XI. 2.—Tiglath-Pileser III besieging a city: Bas-relief in Nimroud

A century later an Anglican clergyman witnessed similar executions by the Turks. The victim himself had to carry the post, about " eight or nine feet long, very sharp at one end."

They erect the stake, and fasten it in a hole dug in the ground. The criminal, sitting in this manner upon it, remains not only still alive, but also drinks, smokes and talks as one perfectly sensible, and thus some have continued for twenty-four hours. But generally, after the tortured wretch has remained in this deplorable and ignominious posture an hour or two, some one of the standers-by is permitted to give him a gracious stab to the heart, so putting an end to his inexpressible misery.—Rev. Henry Maundrell, *A Journey from Aleppo to Jerusalem at Easter A.D.* 1697 : in T. Wright, *Early Travels in Palestine*, 1848, p.501.

In 1800 the French in Egypt publicly executed Soleyman, the assassin of Kléber. His hands were burnt in a brasier, the pole spitting the body was then raised and dropped into a prepared hole. The victim bore his tortures without flinching. He recited verses of the Koran and then asked for a drink.

A French soldier on guard near the stake, appearing to suffer as much as the victim, was going to satisfy him when the chief of the mamelukes stopped him, saying : Beware of doing that, you will cause this criminal to die at once. Soleyman remained alive on the stake for four hours. And perhaps this horrible existence would have been further prolonged were it not that, after the departure of Bartolomeo and the other assistants, another French official, yielding to the same sentiment of humanity felt by the first soldier, took it on himself, with the aid of a vessel placed on the end of his gun, to give a drink to the unfortunate Syrian who expired as soon as he had swallowed the liquid.—
Victoires, conquêtes . . . des Français de 1792 à 1815, 12 (1819) 269.

XI. 3.—Tortures on Prisoners : Assyrian bas-relief from the bronze gates of Balawât

These horrible scenes are quoted here only to enable us to distinguish clearly between this punishment and that of crucifixion properly so called. For there has been confusion. For example Seneca's remark about the *acuta crux* :

' You may nail[4] me up and set my seat upon the piercing cross.'
Is it worth while to weigh down upon one's own wound and hang impaled upon a gibbet?—Seneca, *Ep.* 101, 12 : Eng. trans. M. Gummere (Loeb Library) 3 (1925) 165.

This has often been quoted (e.g. by Holzmeister, p.9) to prove that there was a ' seat ' on the cross (a point which has been considered p.147). It seems clear, however, that Seneca (as well as Maecenas

[4] It is not certain that *suffigas* here means *nail*. It may merely mean *fasten* or even *impale*—Suetonius has the phrase *caput hasta suffixum*.

whom he quotes) is referring to impalement ; the sole punishment
emphasised is the wound of the ' sitting.'[5]   " Save my life," says
Maecenas quoted by Seneca, " though I sit on the piercing cross,"
i.e. sharpened stake.

XI.   4.—Figure from a
Greek Vase

Figure xi. 2 reproduces an Assyrian bas-relief depicting the siege
of a city.[6] Several different incidents are sketched without perspective.   There is a battering-ram or ' tortoise ' from inside which
soldiers are undermining the walls.   Beside the archer there stands
a shield-bearer to protect him ; the shield, usually horn-shaped,
is here rectangular with an overhang on top.   Three prisoners are
represented as impaled through the chest.   Figure xi. 3 is another
Assyrian picture of prisoners being tortured by the troops of Shal-
manasar II (859/826 B.C.) outside the gate of the city hung with
heads.[7]   The soldiers are cutting off hands and legs ; one of the

[5] There was another instrument of torture which the Romans called *equuleus* or
eculeus (literally a young horse). This was a kind of rack. It is referred to by Cicero,
Seneca, Prudentius, etc. It was often used on the martyrs, who were raised and
stretched on it and then torn with *ungulae*, e.g. Ruinart, *Acta Martyrum*, ed. 1859,
pp.313, 416. Sometimes it is called *lignum* (*ibid.*, pp.382f). The idea of a seat on
a cross may be partly due to confusion with the rack ; as also the use of the post-
classical verb *inequitare (crucem)*. There is a quite incorrect statement (applied to
Christ's Crucifixion) in Daremberg-Saglio, *Dict. des ant.* 1 (1887) 1575 : " In
several passages of the Fathers there is mentioned a ' wooden horse ' (*equuleus*)
on which he was seated, so that his body could not sink when the executioners
attached it to the cross."
[6] Layard, *Nineveh*, 1854[6], ii. 369 ; Maspero, *The Passing of the Empires*, 1900, p.203.
[7] Maspero, *The Struggle of the Nations*, 1896, p.639.

poor mutilated wretches is impailed. Figure xi. 4, from a Greek vase, represents Prometheus impailed, hands outstretched to ward off the attacking eagle.[8]

(5) **The Fork**

In looking for texts concerning crucifixion we must put aside those which refer to impalement and also those which describe a slave *sub furca* being scourged and perhaps led to his death. This ' fork ' was apparently some form of yoke or pillory—what the French call *carcan*—into which the victim's head was inserted and to the arms or prolongations of which his hands were fastened.

The shape of this ' fork ' is uncertain ; probably it varied. It is unlikely that it was specially constructed ; any kind of a Y-shaped tool would suffice.[1] Probably the prongs were thrust forward, with the head in between them and the hands fastened to the two ends ; if there were a shaft pointing backwards, it could be used for controlling the culprit and shoving him onwards. It is curious that there should be such uncertainty concerning the exact shape and use of this fork. The best description seems to occur in the Greek writer Plutarch. To show the uncertainty as to details, I give the second passage as translated by a well-known scholar :

> It was a great punishment for a slave who had committed a fault to have to take (*aramenos*) round through the neighbourhood the wooden piece of a waggon (*xylon hamaxēs*) by which the pole (shaft) is strengthened (or underpropped, *hypereidousin*). A slave who had once undergone this shame in the view of the household and the neighbours, no longer had any trust or credit among them. He was called *furcifer*, since *furca* is the Latin for what the Greeks call *hypostatēs* or *stērigma*.—Plutarch, *Gaius Marcus* (*Coriolanus*), 24.
>
> Anyone who caught one of his own household in any rascality used to make him lift up the forked stick with which they prop up carts, and go about the village [?] or the neighbourhood with it for all to see, that they might mistrust him for the future and be on their guard against him. This stick we call a prop (*stērinx*),

---

[8] Daremberg-Saglio, *Dict. des ant.* 1(1887) 1574. Here it is said " Prometheus appears bound through the middle of the body to a post." But impalement is a much more obvious interpretation. Cf. Hesiod, *Theognis*, 521.
[1] The Latin Dictionary of Lewis and Short defines *furca* : " an instrument of punishment in the shape of a fork (V or U) which was placed on the culprit's neck while his hands were fastened to the two ends, a yoke." But O. Zoeckler says that the *furca* was an X-shaped piece " borne upon the back, the hands being all the while firmly bound to the two lower ends of the beams."—*The Cross of Christ*, 1877, p.63.

the Romans *furca* ; hence the bearer of it is called *furcifer*, prop-
bearer.[2]—Plutarch, *Roman Questions* n. 70, tr. H. J. Rose, 1924.

The latter quotation is in answer to the question : Why is the
term *furciferi* applied to those convicted of theft or any other slavish
offences? Obviously the punishment is envisaged as comparatively
light, not accompanied by physical pain ; and most certainly not
followed by death.[2a]   The description of the fork itself seems to
imply that it is the Y-shaped ending of the single shaft or pole of a
four-wheeled cart ; the two branches or prongs were attached to
the underside of the chassis.[3] This, which was required for ' prop-
ping ' the waggon, could easily be detached when the cart was not
being used. It was a ready-made instrument for constraining the
slave and driving him around in derision or with accompanying
punishment.

That a slave, enmeshed in the fork, could also be flogged while
driven along the streets, is shown by the famous case at the Latin
Games of B.C. 489.   The oldest accounts say nothing whatever
about the subsequent execution of the slave. The whole point of
the story is that the squirming of the culprit under the lash dis-
honoured the Games which were just beginning.   The earlier
accounts are as follows :[4]

> This is what is recounted by all historians, Fabius [Pictor],
> Gellius, Coelius : . . . A slave, bearing a fork (*furcam ferens*) and
> beaten with rods, was led through the Circus.—Cicero, *De divin.*
> i. 26, 55.
> Early on the morning of the Games, before the show had begun,
> a certain householder had driven his slave, while he was under
> the yoke and being beaten (*sub furca caesum*), through the middle
> of the Circus.—Livy ii. 36.

[3] I have doubts about this translation. *Xylon* is probably a piece of wood more
substantial than a *stick*. Instead of *prop up* I think *hyphistasin* means *support*. I
prefer *carry around* as the translation of *aramenon* instead of *lift up*. Cf. Luke 9[23] :
Let him carry (*aratō*) his cross daily.
[2a] Donatus (on Terence, *Andr*. iii. 5, 12) definitely says that the *furca* was used on
slaves " more as a disgrace than as a punishment."
[3] So Hesychius (*Lexicon* 1830) defines *steringes* : " props ; others say the forked
support (*dikroun*) which they place under the yoke of the waggon ; others say a
cudgel."   See the illustration of a single shaft (between the two horses), attached
(by some forked bracing) to the underside of a two-wheeled carriage, in M. C.
Quennell, *Everyday Things in Archaic Greece*, 1931, p.126 (also frontispiece). See also
Daremberg—Saglio, *Dict. des ant.* 1 (1887) 1637, s.v. *currus*, and figs. 2210 and
2216.
[4] So also Macrobius, *Saturnalia* i. 11, 3 : "Through the Circus he drove his slave
while being beaten and enclosed (*constrictum*) in the *patibulum*." Here this word
must mean *furca*. A little later (n.5), Macrobius equates it with the Greek *stauros*.

But later and more imaginative writers embellish the story by adding that the slave was put to death :

A householder drove through the Circus Flaminius his slave, under the yoke and beaten with blows, to execution (*verberibus mulcatum sub furca ad supplicium*).—Valerius Maximus, i. 7, 4.

Some citizen had for some heinous offence given up a servant of his to the other servants, with an order to scourge him first through the market and then to kill him . . . He was scourged along the streets and afterwards put to death.—Plutarch, *Coriolanus*, 24f.

A Roman citizen of no obscure station, having ordered one of his slaves to be put to death, delivered him to his fellow-slaves to be led away. And in order that his punishment might be witnessed by all, he directed them to drag him through the Forum and every other conspicuous part of the city as they whipped him. . . . The men ordered to lead the slave to his punishment, having stretched out both his arms and fastened them to a piece of wood which extended across his breast and shoulders as far as his wrists,[5] followed him, tearing his naked body with whips. The culprit, overcome by such cruelty, not only uttered ill-omened cries forced from him by the pain, but also made indecent movements under the blows.—Dionysius of Halicarnassus, *Antiq. Rom.* vii. 69 : trans. E. Cary (in the Loeb Classical Library), 4 (1943) 355.

XI. 5.—Convoy of Prisoners: Bas-relief of Balawât.

Thus these later writers add the detail of the slave's death,

---

[5] It is hard to know whether we can trust this rhetorically puffed-up account so far as to accept that the ' fork ' enclosed the man in front and behind (like ' stocks ' or the *carcan*). There seems to be no confirmatory evidence whatever.

without definitely saying it was crucifixion.[6] " No better case of the growth of a story in the telling could be found," says Oldfather (p.63). " The simple fact was that a slave had been scourged in the streets of Rome under a *furca*, no more and no less. There is utterly no evidence for crucifixion." The whole evidence points to the introduction of crucifixion into Rome only 250 years or so after this incident. Yet Pater Holzmeister (p.17) assumes that this slave was bearing the cross-arm on the way to crucifixion. Vignon at least sees that a ' fork ' is not a crossbeam ; nevertheless he says (ii. 51) : " This man, whose open hands were bound to the *carcan*, was hoisted on to the post to which cords or nails attached him." The plain fact that the *furca*—a simple agricultural instrument used by the Romans for punishment or at least ignominy centuries before they saw a cross—has no connection whatever with crucifixion ; it is certainly not the transverse portion of a cross. Fork-bearing need not end in death at all, though when crucifixion of slaves became common, confinement in the fork *en route* probably became the regular procedure.

XI.6.—Execution by the Fork: from a
miniature in the Roll of Joshua

---

[3] Lactantius (*Div. inst.* iv. 8) and St. Augustine (*De civ. Dei* iv. 26) simply say : *ad supplicium.* Arnobius (*Adv. gentes* vii. 39) : He had led the slave, while being beaten with rods, through the middle of the Circus and afterwards according to custom punished him with the penalty of the gallows (*multasse post patibuli poena*).

Except for a few Assyrian bas-reliefs, I do not know any ancient representation of anything we can identify as a yoke or a fork on a prisoner. Figure xi. 5 shows a convoy of prisoners with yokes on their necks and with their arms tied behind their backs.[7]

Later indeed we find the *furca* designating a special mode of execution different from crucifixion, namely, strangulation by suspension. We do not know whether it existed in the classical period ; but, after the abolition of crucifixion, the word *furca* was substituted for *crux* in the Digest of Roman Law.[8] This form of capital punishment is illustrated in fig. xi. 6, taken from a miniature in the Roll of Joshua, a Vatican manuscript of the fifth century based on earlier material.[9]

A few remarks may be added concerning ordinary ' hanging,' i.e. death by strangulation, which in most places was during the last century replaced by the ' drop,' i.e. death by fracture of the cervical vertebrae—a quick painless method. "Tyburn Tree," where so many martyrs perished, was really a gibbet or gallows. It was situated a few yards north-west of where London's Marble Arch now stands. The sketch (fig. xi. 6a) is taken from an illustration[10] published in Rome in 1555. It shows Blessed John Houghton and companions being executed (1535). The gibbet (at least until 1571) consisted of a horizontal pole supported on two forked uprights. The victim stood on a cart while the noose was fixed, the cart was then drawn away. Sometimes he was allowed to die by slow strangulation ; the bodies of chained highwaymen were left to rot on the gallows. But in the case of traitors (including those who denied the spiritual but not the temporal supremacy of the totalitarian Tudors), the execution was much more hideously

---

[7] Maspero, *The Passing of the Empires*, 1900, p.63. A similar bas-relief is depicted in Maspero's *Struggle of the Nations*, 1896, p.641. This makes it perfectly clear that the yoke was symbolical, probably imposed with an exorcising purpose. To " subjugate " is literally to place under the yoke.

[8] Thus *Digest* 48 : in furca suspendere (13, 6) ; latrones furca figendos (19. 28, 15) ; in furcam tolluntur (19, 38, 2).

[9] The condemned had his hands tied behind his back: Ammianus Marcellinus, *Hist. rom.* xv. 7, 4 ; Gregory of Tours, *De virt. s. Martini*, i. 21. St. Isidore of Seville († 636) says : "The *patibulum* is commonly called *furca* as supporting the head ; for it thus kills the man who is hanged and strangled. But the punishment of the *patibulum* is less than that of the *crux*, for it immediately kills those suspended while the cross keeps in long torments those fixed to it."—*Origines* v. 27, 34. Festus, *De verb. signif.* ed. C. Mueller 1839, p.88, says : Furcilles sive furcilla quibus homines suspendebant. Holzmeister cites this (p.10) as one of the instruments for affixing to the cross !

[10] Dom Maurice Chauncy, *The Passion and Martyrdom of the Holy English Carthusian Fathers* (1570), ed. Curtis, 1935, p.38.

brutal. In the illustration an executioner mounted on a ladder is depicted cutting down one of the victims. But the gruesome incidents of butchery on the ground have been omitted from our illustration. The martyr was cut down while alive, and usually recovered consciousness on the ground. He was then mutilated and ripped open, his heart was plucked out as well as his entrails. When dead his head and four ' quarters ' were boiled in tar and set up in various public places.[11]

XI.   6a.—Carthusians martyred at Tyburn (1535)

(6) Was only the Crossbeam carried ?

We have already met the word *patibulum*, probably a vague term like our 'gallows' and connected with *pati* (to suffer). It is often used for *furca*.[1] Both classical and post-classical authors employ

---

[11] The *via crucis* was over three miles long, from the Tower to Tyburn. The victims were on their backs on hurdles—sleighs of lathes—drawn over the cobbles and mud by horses. At one point a halt was made and a bowl of ale offered to the condemned. On this occasion a woman wiped the begrimed faces of the Carthusians.

[1] So Macrobius quoted in note 4 above ; a little later (§5) he uses it to translate the Greek *stauros* (which originally meant a stake) ; also Isidore cited in note 9. In the Latin Dictionary of Lewis and Short the meaning is given as " a fork-shaped yoke placed on the necks of criminals and to which their hands were tied, also a fork-shaped gibbet."

the word to mean a gibbet or gallows, even a cross.[2] Agricultural writers use the word to denote a forked prop for supporting vines.[3] There is one doubtful and solitary assertion that *patibulum* was also used to mean the wooden bar for fastening double doors.[4] It is chiefly on the strength of this highly dubious and unsupported statement that the word has been interpreted to mean the transverse beam of a cross.

In the plays of Plautus there are several allusions to the carrying of the *patibulum* by slaves. Thus in the *Mostellaria* (i. 1, 53) : " They will be prodding you with goads as you carry your yoke along the streets."[5] This is interpreted by an editor as follows :

> A heavy log of wood was employed, forked at the extremity (*furca*) or with a crosspiece like a gibbet (*patibulum*). The hands of the slave were attached to the limbs of the log which he dragged about, and [he] was flogged or goaded as he staggered painfully under the load.—W. Ramsay, *The Mostellaria of Plautus*, 1869, p.355.

There is here no reference to a cross-beam or to crucifixion. In another play[6] we read : " You will soon have to trudge out beyond

---

[2] Nonius Marcellus p.366M, *Compendiosa doctrina*, ed. L. Mueller, 1888, i. 595 : Patibulum est crux. He quotes from a lost book of Sallust : In patibulo eminens adfigebatur. Apuleius, *Metamorphoses* x. 12 : Servus patibulo suffigitur. Tacitus, *Ann.* iv. 72 : patibulo adfixi (punishment inflicted by the Frisians). Similarly (xiv. 33, 6) of British executions of Romans : caedes, patibula, ignes, cruces. But (xv. 44) of the Christians under Nero : crucibus adfixi. Vulgate of Num 25[4] : in patibulis. Seneca, *De vita beata*, 19, 3 : quidam ex patibulo suos spectatores conspuerent. Prudentius, *Peristeph.* x. 641 : patibulum ascendere. In the Passion of St. Victor († 290-303), Ruinart, *Acta Martyrum*, 1859, p.337f : The judges ordered him to be fastened up (*affigi*, which cannot here mean nailed) ; he was tortured and raked. Then he was taken down from the *patibulum* (which here means *eculeus*) and put back in prison. Again he was *appensus patibulo* and when *suspensus* beaten with rods and straps.

[3] Pliny, H.N. xvii. 23 (212) ; Cato, *De re rustica* 26.

[4] Nonius cited in note 2. Against this assertion it may be urged : (1) He has just said : Patibulum est crux. (2) He gives the reason " because on its removal the door-leaves open (*pateant*)." This derivation from *patere* (when we should expect *occludere*) seems far-fetched ; the same author derives *vafer* from *valde Afer* ! (But see note 5 for a possible derivation from *pateo* in a different sense.) (3) He has to quote an obscure poet (Titinius) to prove the point. Even so the quotation does not prove that the meaning is a door-bar : " If anyone else to-day knocks on the back-door, I will break his head with this *patibulum*." (4) There appears to be not a single instance in which the word means a bar for fastening a door.

[5] Ita te forabunt patibulatum per vias stimulis. Holzmeister (p.17) interprets this as carrying the transom of a cross. So E. A. Sonnenschein in his edition of the *Mostellaria* (1907, p.69) : " The *patibulum*—literally ' stretcher,' from *pateo*— was a piece of wood fixed, like a milkman's yoke, over the shoulders of the slave to be punished ; to this his arms were fastened . . . To be fastened to the *patibulum* was to undergo the first stage of crucifixion . . . The *patibulum* thus formed the cross-beam of the *crux*."

[6] *Miles gloriosus* ii. 4 (359): dispessis manibus, partibulum quod habebis.

the gate in that attitude, I take it : arms outstretched, bearing the yoke." Here Ramsay (p.258) sees " an allusion to the practice of making the criminal carry the cross or gibbet (to which he was to be nailed) through the streets to the spot outside the walls where the execution took place." But there is no reason for interpreting this passage differently from the former. A better argument for carrying the cross-beam is contained in a sentence from a lost play : " Let him carry the *patibulum* through the city and then let him be nailed to the *crux*."[7] Yet even here there is no suggestion that the *patibulum* was the horizontal arm of the cross. In accordance with the other passages of Plautus, the most natural interpretation is that the slave, with hands and neck enmeshed in the yoke, was driven through the streets ; but his fate was not to be beaten to death but to be nailed to a cross already *in situ*. The same comment may be made on the remaining proof-text :

> A person apprehended in those crimes is, by a severe sentence of the judge, fastened to a patibulum and raised on a cross (*patibulo subfixus in crucem tollitur*).—Julius Firmicus Maternus (A.D. 337), *Mathesis* vi. 31, 58 : ed. Kroll-Skutsch 2 (1913) 164.

There is no proof here that the *patibulum* was a component part of the *crux*. On the contrary, the probability is entirely against this assumption.[7a] The malefactor was rendered helpless by having his hands tied to a yoke or fork so that he could be scourged en route ; on reaching his destination he was nailed to a cross already erected.

Thus the alleged evidence for the carrying of the crossbeam by a *cruciarius* breaks down on examination. The carrying of the cross

---

[7] Plautus, *Carbonaria*, cited in Nonius Marcellus (p.321M), *Compendiosa doctrina*‘ ed. L. Mueller, 1888, i. 331 : Patibulum ferat per urbem, deinde adfigatur cruci. H. Furneaux, *Annals of Tacitus* 1 (1896²) 262, says that *patibulum* here " appears to be the same as the *furca* or yoke, in which the head and hands were held as in a pillory." Nonius also cites Licinius : ad patibulos deligantur et circumferuntur, cruci defiguntur.

[7a] Fr. Smyth objects : " Surely the text must mean that while attached to the beam he is raised on to the cross." This is certainly *prima facie* true. But I have become so sceptical that *patibulum* ever meant a cross-beam and so doubtful about the whole proceeding (even from the mechanical viewpoint), that I am querying even this *pièce de résistance*. I have therefore suggested the meaning : Attached to the *patibulum* (= *furca*), he is harried off to the cross. Alternatively it might mean : Attached to the *patibulum* (= gibbet), he was raised up into a standing cross. See note 6 p.210.

itself is mentioned by Greek writers,[8] also in rabbinical writings and in the New Testament ; in Latin it seems to occur first in the translation (Itala) of the Gospels. The carrying of the whole cross to the place of execution is quite intelligible, especially in Judea where standing crosses would be so religiously offensive ; so also is the system of having standing crosses ready, as at Rome for slaves, while the culprits, with manacles or yoke, were driven to execution. But when one comes to think of it, there is something quite artificial about this alleged custom of carrying the crossbeam to be fixed to a vertical standing post. The mechanical difficulties involved are very great ; it is not easy to see how a rigid structure, capable of bearing a living body, could be thus hastily constructed from two separate pieces, one of which (for no particular reason) was fetched from a distance. The texts usually quoted are quite insufficient to prove the prevalence of such a curious practice.[9]

(7) Our Lord's Case

Yet most contemporary exegetes[1] hold that Our Lord carried only the transverse beam, probably with His hands tied to it, and that the vertical post was already (permanently) erected on Calvary. There are however serious arguments against this view.

(1) The texts which speak of a slave at Rome carrying a *patibulum* —not necessarily to execution—need not be interpreted to mean that a *cruciarius* carried the transom of his cross. There is little evidence,

[8] "The cross is like death and the man who is to be nailed to it carries it (*bastazei*) first."—Artemidorus, *Onirocrit.* ii. 56. "In the body, every criminal who is punished carries forth (*ekpherei*) his own cross."—Plutarch, *De sera numinis vindicta*, 554B. In Chariton's Greek novel (probably of the 2nd century A.D.) *De Chaerea et Callirhoe* iv. 2 (ed. W. Blake, 1926, p.57), we read of sixteen men "chained together by necks and feet, each bearing his cross." This has been quoted to show that each bore only the cross-arm. But (1) we do not know how far this romance can be utilised for historical usages ; (2) the scene is laid in Egypt ; (3) the *stauros* was some structure which the criminal " ascended " (see p.211); (4) there seems nothing impossible in a group of cross-bearers walking in single file, with loose chains from (say) right foot to right foot and neck to neck ; (5) but it is much more likely that the writer meant that each man's feet were manacled with a loose chain while a continuous rope or chain joined their necks. This last is depicted on the rock of Behistun : Maspero, *The Passing of the Empires*, 1900, p.681.
[9] In a review of the new edition of Cardinal Innitzer's book on the Passion, wherein he now holds that Christ carried only the crossbeam, Pater Holzmeister says : " In the last decennium all Catholic and Protestant commentators on the Crucifixion have thus expressed themselves."—*Biblica* 29 (1948) 290. It therefore requires some courage on my part to be so out of tune with this modern harmony.
[1] Christ carried only the crosspiece : Holzmeister, Huby, Lagrange, Ricciotti. Sickenberger, Vosté. He bore the whole cross : Belser, Durand, Lépicier, Pickl.

none pre-Christian, that the word *patibulum* had such a meaning at all.[2] It is quite certain that at least some of the texts refer to the *furca* ; others mean the rack (*eculeus*) or some unspecified form of gallows. Much more decisive evidence would be required to prove that this apparently meaningless procedure ever prevailed. In order to bear securely a living victim the cross would have to be a stable structure ; this would not be easily constructed by bringing one piece from a distance and fixing it for each case to a standing post.

(2) Even if it be admitted that some culprits, at least slaves in Rome, brought the crossbeam, it does not follow that this was always done, that there was a single procedure stabilised in space and time. It is *a priori* most improbable that the execution of those regarded as the lowest criminals was regularised by some code of rigid ritual. We know that the crucified were finally despatched in different ways : death followed by rotting on the gibbet, death with burial by relatives, devouring by wild beasts or birds of prey, suffocation by smoke, stabbing. Why should we assume that there was less variety in the preliminaries?[3]

(3) Near Jerusalem there was no regular execution-place with permanently fixed uprights ; nor indeed is such a place proved except for a spot outside the Esquiline gate of Rome (for slaves). It is utterly improbable that permanent vertical posts, soiled by contact with the dead, would be tolerated just outside the walls of Jerusalem. Jewish law (Deut 21[23]) prescribed that the body should not remain on the gibbet overnight but was to be buried the same day. Though this was a Roman execution, the Jews intervened to honour Passover (see p.284). There is some evidence that the crosses were also buried,[4] and of course this is assumed in the story of the

---

[2] The other terms often quoted—*palus* (stake) *stipes* (trunk or branch), *staticulum* (a statuette), *antenna* (a sail-yard), etc.—are all of late (post-Christian) application to the cross. The terms *crux commissa*, *immissa*, etc., seem to have been invented by Lipsius at the end of the sixteenth century.

[3] Speaking of the treatment of Jews by the Roman Governor in Alexandria, only a few years after Christ's death, Philo says : " Before crucifying them, he did not forget to have them scourged in the middle of the arena, and put through the torture of iron and fire."—*In Flaccum*, x. 78, 299. We know that these tortures were not applied to Our Lord.

[4] " The wood is to be buried with the hanged one."—Maimonides, *Sanhedrin* 15. Sepp (*Vie de J.C.* iii. 67) says that the custom of throwing away the instruments of execution was until recently observed in Germany. Cf. Quintilian, *Declam.* vi. 9 : Cruces succiduntur. Also Cicero, *In Verrem* iv. 11, 26 : " You did not pull down or bury in a pit that cross which, planted before your harbour and city, even now is sprinkled with the blood of a Roman citizen." It is incredible that the Jews would have tolerated such a bloodstained gibbet permanently erected just outside the wall of the Holy City.

finding of the True Cross. But if the upright post were not previously and permanently *in situ*, Christ must have brought the whole cross with Him to Calvary.

(4) While the Gospels soberly record the gruesome act of affixing by the short phrase " they crucified Him," they record a number of accessory incidents not found elsewhere. In fact the story of the Passion is the only account of a politico-religious execution in the Jewish capital in peacetime ; and no other account of a crucifixion has such details. Let us enumerate some of the facts not recorded elsewhere :

    i.   Scourging as an *independent* non-mortal punishment inflicted prior to the condemnation to crucifixion.

    ii.   Mockery of an allegedly accused criminal by the troops.[5]

    iii.   Restoration of clothes to the condemned before cross-bearing.

    iv.   The forcing of a passer-by to carry the cross instead of the condemned.

    v.   The offering of a soporific drink[6] before crucifixion.

    vi.   The affixing of a placard (title) to the top of the cross.

    vii.   The sentries tossing up for a tunic and tearing the mantle into four parts.

    viii.   The giving of vinegar (posca) to a thirsty crucified, whether in mercy or in cruelty.

    ix.   Shin-breaking to accelerate death.

    x.   A spear-thrust to make sure of death.

In view of such an accumulation of otherwise unrecorded incidents, in addition to our general ignorance of the details and the variations of crucifixion in other cases, the recent unqualified

---

[5] The alleged analogies of the *Sacaea*, etc., will in a subsequent volume be shown to be quite irrelevant.

[6] This, according to the Mishnah, appears to have been a Jewish custom. I have met two post-Christian parallels. Tertullian (*De ieiuniis* 12) reproaches the " psychics " for doping their " martyr " Pristinus with spiced wine (*condito mero*), making him so drunk that he did not feel the tortures and died belching. In the Acts of St. Fructuosus 3 († A.D. 259), we are told that Christians " with fraternal charity " offered him and his companions *conditi permixti poculum* ; but it was refused.—Ruinart, *Acta Mart.*, 1859, p.266. In a Syriac document (Acts of Sharbil) there occurs the phrase : " They offered him some wine to drink, according to the custom of murderers to drink " ; but he refused.—*Syriac Documents* trans. B. Pratten, 1871, p.77 (Ante-Nicene Ch. Lib.).

pronouncements concerning Our Lord's case must be regarded as rashly overconfident.[6a]

(5) The question of clothes and of the transfer of the cross is worth further consideration. While the criminal (slave) bore the *patibulum* or *furca*, he was flogged or goaded. So it seems clear that he was naked. But Our Lord was not so treated, and He had His clothes on (M27[31] Mk15[20]). It is therefore certain that the conclusions drawn from the texts already discussed are not applicable to His case. But, says Vignon (ii. 49), " what is apparently difficult to find is the archaeological confirmation of what is thus certain." This is the more difficult for Vignon, since—unlike even Lagrange and Holzmeister—he has seen that most, if not all, of the texts refer to bearing a yoke, not a simple beam. " The condemned man," he says (ii. 51), "in the *carcan* was quite naked and he was pushed with blows to the place where he was to be hanged. But let us see if there was not a less cruel custom." In other words, he has to admit that the preliminaries of crucifixion were not the same in all places and at all periods. He has to abandon all the texts about carrying the *patibulum*. He merely appeals to the descriptions of the solid four-armed cross in SS. Justin, Irenæus, etc. It is curious that Vignon failed to see that he was thus abandoning all the alleged proofs that a *cruciarius* bore the cross-beam, not the fork. Pater Holzmeister, who tries to interpret all the texts as proving the carrying of the cross-beam, has in the end to admit that they are not relevant to the case of Christ (p.26) :

> The ordinary Roman method, according to which the victim deprived of clothes bore the *patibulum*, was not employed. For Christ was led to crucifixion in His own garments. Whether the Lord's arms were or were not bound to the *patibulum* we can hardly determine.

But surely we can say that, once the clothes were left and there was no scourging *en route*, such binding was very improbable, even on the supposition that He bore only the transversal of the cross. It

---

[6a] I may refer, for example, to some statements of that excellent scholar, the late J. M. Vosté, O.P., " Scourging used to precede crucifixion, this was inflicted on the condemned man who was either *bound sub furca* or tied to a column."—*Studia Ioannea*, 1930, p.324. "The vertical beam or rather many of them *always remained planted* and ready in the place of execution. The horizontal beam *called patibulum* was brought there by him who was to be crucified. Sometimes the patibulum *consisted of two beams* inside which the head and hands of the cruciarius were held tied."—*Ibid.* p.322. (Italics are mine).

has already been argued that He carried the whole cross,[7] and this is confirmed by the transfer to Simon of Cyrene. The only plausible reason for this shifting of the burden is that Our Lord was too weak to continue and probably fell. The weight was evidently too much for Him ; this would hardly be the case if He bore only the crossbar. A substitute or a collaborator was easily commandeered; there is no reference to the unbinding of Christ's arms. The prevalent interpretation is that Simon took over the whole cross, leaving Jesus free.[8] Says Père Prat :[9] Simon " not only helped the Saviour to carry His cross, as painters imagine ; he bore it entirely by himself behind Him ; the Gospel is formal on the point." To which with Père Joüon,[10] we can reply : " If Simon had carried the cross by himself, the detail ' behind Jesus ' would be without interest." It is more likely that Christ was not completely relieved of the burden or allowed to walk in front of Simon who would be an attendant carrying the load for Him. But on this view, we must not imagine (as do all modern artists) that Christ bore the heavy top-end and that Simon in the rear held up the lower lighter end (which would be little or no relief). More probably, Christ first carried the cross with the foot-end pointing forward and the cross-piece behind His shoulder, which is the more natural way to carry the cross ; and then the heavier end was loaded on to Simon, while Our Lord bore the foot-end on His shoulders.[11] But whether the transfer

---

[7] On His shoulders: Justin, *Apol.* i. 35, 2 ; Tertullian, *Adv. Marc.* iii. 19. St. John (19[17]) says that Our Lord " went out carrying the cross for Himself (*heautō*)." Following Van Bebber, Belser (*Hist. of the Passion*, 1929, p.477) thinks that there is implied a contrast with the two bandits, i.e. that they did not carry their crosses. This is very doubtful and the reasons alleged are precarious. " Since the condemnation of Jesus could not be foreseen on the previous day, only two men had been engaged." But very probably Christ took the place of Barabbas. It is improbable that the crosses of the two bandits " were carried by pagan porters " to avoid loading them on a sabbatic day. And finally it is more likely that Good Friday was the Eve of Passover (14th Nisan), not the feast-day.

[8] So. SS. Athanasius, Ambrose, Augustine, Jerome. Also *Acta Pilati*, recension B, 10[1] (p.302 Tischendorf) : " They took the cross from Him and gave it to a man that met them, Simon by name."

[9] *Jésus Christ*, 1933[4], ii. 388.

[10] *L'évangile*, 1930, p.446. St. Luke (23[26]) does not employ the usual word (*ŏpisō*), *behind*, but *ŏpisthĕn, from behind.* According to the vision of Therese Neumann, Simon was at first reluctant and angry. " He took hold of the cross at the bottom so that Jesus had the full burden to drag. Simon scolded and yelled. Then the Saviour turned and looked upon him so woefully that Simon drew nearer and began to carry the cross at the other end with Christ."—F. von Lama, *Further Chronicles of T.N.*, Eng. trans. 1932, p.158. This translation is inaccurate. The German says: Simon " carried the cross at the other (heavier) end."—*Konnersr. Jahrb.* 1929, p.145. But how is this to be reconciled with her view of the cross-timbers being carried in a bundle (p.201)?

[11] J. Pickl, *The Messias*, 1946, p.247.

was complete or partial, the incident is against the assumption that only the simple crosspiece was involved or that either Christ or Simon had his hands tied to it.

Having shown that the textual references to crucifixion are incomplete and inconclusive, and that there were in Our Lord's case special features not covered by the general evidence, we are now entitled to consider the indications on the Shroud, which seem to show, though not decisively, that Our Lord bore the whole cross.[12] Figure viii. 1 shows that there were special contusions on the shoulders. Here the scourge-marks have lost their dumb-bell imprints ; while still fresh these wounds must have been compressed or rubbed. There are long heavy marks quite unlike the short double impressions of the scourge-loads. Perhaps the weight of the cross creased the tunic and pressed the folds into the flesh. The shoulder-wounds certainly look as if they had been made by a movable body. Perhaps we may conjecture as follows : The right shoulder, lower and more bruised, seems to have borne the greater weight. It may be, as Hynek suggests, that the stains on the right shoulder and at the back of the neck were caused chiefly by the angle of the two beams of the cross as the long end dragged and bumped along the rough road ; and that the stains on the left shoulder (and on the ridge of the left hipbone?) were caused by the vertical beam striking diagonally across the body as He fell. The left shoulder-blade is considerably bruised ; this could be explained by a fall when the cross would strike across the back. All this is of course conjectural ; we can only be sure of special contusions across the shoulders, made after the scourging.[13]

It hath been observed by some that He was again grievously hurt and wounded in His shoulder. For upon it pressed the great beam of the Cross, which inflicted on it a great wound, making all the wounds one wound ; and the pain thereof pierced His tender Heart. And as some devout doctors teach, this was one of the most grievous of Christ's pains.—John Tauler, O.P. († 1361), *Meditations on the Life and Passion of O.L.J.C.*, ch. 29, Eng. trans. 1925, p.187. [Probably not by Tauler.]

[12] So Hynek i. 123, ii. 125 ; Judica Cordiglia i. 113.
[13] According to Ollivier (*Passion*, 1901, p.317), " St. Bernard had great devotion to the sacred wound of Our Lord's *left* shoulder." Louise Lateau (Didry and Wallemacq, p.169) had a wound on the *right* shoulder. Also Therese Neumann : F. von Lama, *Further Chronicles of Th. N.*, 1932, p.129. But Gemma Galgani (Germanus, p.73) had a " very large and deep " wound on the *left* shoulder.

A few words may be added on the views expressed by some visionaries :

> The archers led Jesus into the middle of the court, the slaves threw down the cross at His feet, and the two arms were forthwith tied on to the centre piece . . . [The soldiers make Christ kneel down, and] place the heavy cross on His right shoulder, supporting its great weight with His right hand . . .
> Whilst He was on His knees and still praying, the executioners put the arms of the crosses—which were a little curved and not as yet fastened to the centre-pieces—on the backs of the two thieves, and tied their hands tightly to them. The middle parts of the crosses were carried by slaves, as the transverse pieces were not to be fastened to them until just before the time of execution . . .
> They pulled Him roughly up, for He was totally unable to rise without assistance ; and He then felt upon His shoulders the weight of that cross which we must carry after Him . . . By means of ropes which the executioners had fastened to the foot of the cross, two archers supported it to prevent its getting entangled in anything ; and four other soldiers took hold of the ropes which they had fastened to Jesus beneath His clothes . . . He supported the cross on His shoulder with His right hand . . .
> And after Jesus came the two thieves, who were likewise led, the arms of their crosses (separate from the middle) being placed upon their backs, and their hands tied lightly to the two ends.— Anne Catherine Emmerich, *The Dolorous Passion*, ch. 30, Eng. trans. p.233f.

According to this, the two bandits carried the two transverse pieces of each cross (supposed to be Y-shaped) with their arms tied thereto, as moderns suppose the so-called *patibulum* to be carried. But the central beams were also carried by attendants ; they were not *in situ*. Apparently Our Lord is depicted as carrying on His right shoulder a bundle formed by the two transverse portions and the central beam (or beams) tied together.

It is curious to find practically the same view expressed by the contemporary stigmatic Therese Neumann :

> The cross that Jesus carries has not the form that we imagine. It is not a cross at all but only the wood for it. It consists of two[14]

---

[14] Elsewhere she speaks of three pieces for she assumes two crosspieces (for the Y cross) which " have been tied one next to the other on the entire length of the upright wood."—E. de Hovre, *The Riddle of Konnersreuth*, 1933, p.123. " She said that Christ's cross was made up of three rafters and the upright one was split in two ; hence there were four pieces."—*Ibid.*, p.103. It is said that she never read Anna Emmerich.—F. von Lama, *Therese Neumann*, 1936, pp.144, 147.

beams, the shorter of which is tied to the longer.—Archbishop J. Teodorowicz, *Mystical Phenomena in the Life of Theresa Neumann*, 1940, p.449.

Not only did these two visionaries—like St. Bridget long before them—hold that Our Lord's cross was shaped like a Y (see p.223), but they both depict Him as carrying the constituent timbers on His shoulder ; the cross being put together on Calvary.   This seems also to be supposed by the medieval representations of the " Waiting Christ " and the widespread idea that Christ was kept in a " prison " near Calvary while the cross was being put together.[15]

A few art-representations of the *Via Crucis* will now be given. Figure xi. 7 reproduces a panel from an ivory casket in the British Museum (A.D. 400/425). The scene is composite. On the left is Pilate, wearing a mantle fastened at the right shoulder, seated on a throne and washing his hands.   Christ, young and beardless, without a nimbus, is carrying a slender cross on His left shoulder.[16] Our Lord is clad in tunic and pallium and wears sandals. The figure beside Him is probably not Simon but an executioner ; his dress is that commonly assigned to Jews in early Christian art. To the right we see St. Peter seated on the ground before a small brazier; above him on a bracket is a cock, and a maidservant is pointing at Peter with her right hand. In fig. xi. 8 the slender— almost purely symbolic—cross is being carried by Simon with one hand. Behind Our Lord, who is bearded and dignified, are a soldier and several priests.   This figure is from a mosaic (6th century) in Sant' Apollinare Nuovo, Ravenna. In the next two figures Simon is also carrying a light cross which has no relation to reality. In fig. xi. 9 we see a fresco from S. Maria Antiqua, Rome, probably dating from the time of John VII (705/707). Christ, with a cruciform nimbus has His right hand stretched in blessing. In fig. xi. 10 —a miniature made by monks of Reichenau for Egbert Archbishop of Trier (977/993)—Simon is stepping out in front.

In this early art there is no trace of realism, there is a reverent

---

[15] There is still in the Church of the Holy Sepulchre in Jerusalem a Greek chapel called the Prison of Christ (already mentioned in the 9th century Greek *Typicon*) which has been repudiated by the Latin Church.—Meistermann, *Guide to the Holy Land*, 1923, p.129. It is curious to observe how these visions of mystics contain not only (1) plausible visualisations filling gaps in the Gospels (but not always consistent) and (2) self-verifying facts (e.g. the Aramaic words given by Therese Neumann and some of the topography of A. C. Emmerich), but also (3) longstanding legends which are nowadays not accepted by historians.

[16] See the Lateran sarcophagus in fig. xii. 1.

reluctance to depict the suffering of the Son of God. We have to wait for the 'pathetic' art of the later Middle Ages to see the *Via Crucis* represented realistically. Only one instance[17] will be included : fig. xi. 11, a partly defaced fresco in Norwich Cathedral. The figure of Christ is emaciated (perhaps merely owing to defective drawing) and is nude except for a purple loin-cloth[18]—which is contrary to the Gospel statement that He wore his own clothes. He carries the cross on His right shoulder and supports the transverse beam with His left hand. Behind Him is a group issuing from the gate of Jerusalem, led by three mounted men. Leading Christ by a cord round His waist, is the sergeant-at-arms with a mace in his left hand.

Two further examples are given of Simon helping Christ to carry the cross. The first (fig. xi. 12) is a group in stone, now in the Louvre (16th century)[19]. The second (fig. xi. 13) is one of Eric Gill's Stations of the Cross in Westminster Cathedral. We see only the spears of the soldiers in front, and the rope round Christ's waist with which one of them is leading Him. In both these cases it is obvious that Simon is doing little to lighten Our Lord's burden.

Since the foregoing was written, I have come across one instance in which Simon is portrayed as carrying the heavier end of the cross. It is given in *Le Christ de la Légende Dorée* by Abbé, J.C.

XI.   13a.—Simon supporting the heavier
end of the Cross

[17] *Norfolk Arch.* 13 (1898) 303. See figures 30 to 33 in my *Family at Bethany*.
[18] This may have come from a Passion Play. In one at York, Our Lord is stripped before carrying the cross though His clothes are not divided until later.—L. T. Smith, *York Plays*, 1885, p.347.
[19] P. Doncoeur, *Le Christ dans l'art français* 1 (1939) 146.

Broussolle, 1904, p.180. He has taken it from an unspecified Cambridge Evangelary. It is reproduced in fig. xi. 13a.

Figure xi. 14 has been added to show a contemporary painting, full of vigour yet penetrated with reverence. It is one of the Stations of the Cross (Christ meets His Mother) by Seán Keating, in Clongowes Wood College, Ireland.

Finally there are some ' mystic ' representations of the *Via Crucis*, which depict Our Lady and the other women helping Christ to carry His cross. This beautiful idea was first portrayed in the twelfth century. Figure xi. 15 is an illustration from St. Elizabeth's Prayer-Book (prior to 1217), from which fig. i. 2 has already been taken (Haseloff, fig. 30). Christ with the cross on His right shoulder is being helped by two women supporting the ends of the cross— an appropriate picture for the prayer-book of a woman-saint! In fig. xi. 16 we see a group in carved and painted wood (15th century), now in the Musée de Cluny (Doncoeur, p.141). Here not only Simon but several women are helping to bear the cross.[20] The lesson is even more graphically conveyed by a fresco (about 1500) in Notre-Dame de Chauvigny (Vienne): fig. xi. 17. Here Our Lord's cross has a prolongation which is being supported by a crowd of kings, prelates, religious and laity, even a child. We are all, in various ways, called to the task: *Crucem portare post Iesum*.

(8) Nude or Clothed?

On the way to Calvary Our Lord wore an inner tunic (for which the squad of four executioners afterwards diced) and an outer mantle (which they cut up into four pieces). The removal of the tunic from the lacerated body must have been painful ; the only mitigation of the rough treatment may have come from the desire not to injure the garment which was a perquisite of these ill-paid Syrian mercenaries. The Romans had no consideration for decency and modesty at executions.[1]   It seems certain that slaves were

---

[20] There is in Nantes Museum an alabaster carving, in which Christ, clad in loin-cloth and with a rope round His waist is led by one executioner, while three others carry ropes, nails and a hammer. They seem to be pressing on the cross to make it harder to support, while Our Lady and St. John try by lifting it to help Our Lord.—W. L. Hildburgh, *Archaeologia*, 93 (1949) 83 and plate xivd.

[1] For example : *Dict. d'arch. chr.* 1 (1924) 455, fig. 89 ; fragment of a vase found in Tours (woman exposed naked). But in fig. 88 (portion of vase found in Bavaria) there appear to be traces of a loincloth.

paraded and crucified quite naked.[2] It is true that the Latin *nudus*, or even the Greek *gymnos*, is not always to be taken literally.[3] Still less the Hebrew *arom* (1 Sam 19[34] 2 Sam 7[20]). We know that Asiatics, and non-Greeks in general, were against nudity at games. The Jews in particular had some regard for modesty.[4] But as regards Roman crucifixions, there is nowhere the smallest hint that a shred of the victim's clothes was left.

Accordingly, many of the Fathers,[5] guided by this custom but without any tradition concerning Calvary, held that Christ was quite naked on the cross. So also many later writers down to to-day:

Although our Lord Jesus both at His birth and His whole life long was poor indeed, yet on the Cross He desired to offer us a perfect example and form of true poverty, by thus suffering Himself to be stripped naked, so as not even to have a thread left Him by which He might cover His pure and modest members.— John Tauler, O.P. († 1361), *Meditations on the Life and Passion of O.L.J.C.*, trans. 1925, p.203.

The Victim was completely stripped of His clothes. However painful this statement may be to Christians desirous of safeguarding the respect due to the Most Holy Humanity of our Saviour, we must indeed accept it as justified by the most authentic testimony.—Ollivier, *The Passion*, trans. 1901, p.348.

Our Lord was dying when He came to crucifixion, swollen all over with wounds, beaten out of human shape. The brutality of His executioners was little likely to have left Him any loin-cloth. Some think His Mother was allowed to supply the want. Or was there any such want? For He was by this time " a worm and no man " (Ps 21[7]), " wound and bruises and swollen weal " (Is 1[6]). When we consider the prevalence of that class of sins in expiation for which, pious writers say, Christ bore the scourges, we no longer wonder.—Joseph Rickaby, S.J., *Waters That Go Softly*, 1919[3], p.131.

Nevertheless, this argument once more sins by applying our meagre general information, assumed to be monolithic, to the case

---

[2] Arrian, *Epictetus* iv. 26 ; Artemidorus, *Oneirocr.* ii. 58. In the Acts of the Martyrs we read of Christian women being stripped and beaten to death, e.g. Eusebius H. E. viii. 9 ; Acts of SS. Claudius, Asterius and Companions (in Cilicia in 285) : Ruinart, *Acta Martyrum*, ed. 1859, p.310f. By way of exception we read of the Carthaginian Cartalo being crucified on a very high cross, clad in full priestly attire.—Justin, *Hist.* xviii. 7.

[3] So Vergil, *Georgics* i. 299 : " Naked plough, naked sow."

[4] " Four cubits from the stoning-place the criminal is stripped. A man should be covered in front, and a woman in front and behind : so R. Meir. But the majority hold that a man should be stoned naked but not a woman."—*Mishnah, Sanhedrin* vi. 3 : trans. Danby, 1919, p.88.

[5] Cyprian, Ambrose, Augustine, Chrysostom, Pseudo-Athanasius, etc.

of Our Lord. Even if we speak only humanly, no one ever inspired such devotion and reverence. Some of His followers, at least the women, were on Calvary. Can we not rely upon them to have intervened, by supplication or bribe? Both recensions of the early *Acts of Pilate* deny complete nudity.

> When they were come to the place, they stripped Him of His garments and girt Him with a linen cloth and put a crown of thorns about His head.—*Acta Pilati* (A) 10¹ : James, *Apocr. N.T.*, 1924, p.134.
> They arrived at the place called Skull which was paved with stones ; and there the Jews erected the cross. Then they stripped Jesus and the soldiers took His clothes and distributed them among themselves. And they put a purple robe on Him and made Him ascend and nailed Him on the cross.[6]—*Acta Pilati* (B) 10³ : Tischendorf, *Ev. apocr.*, 1876², p.283.

In fact a later legend tells us definitely that a bystander or one of the women provided a loin-cloth as a mark of respect.[7]

> Afterwards He was suspended quite naked on the cross. But one of the women who were there threw her head-cloth (*capitegium*) over Him.—St. Bonaventure, *De S. Marci ev.*, sermo ii. 4 : *Opera* ix. 527.
> While my Son was standing there as naked as He was born, a man approached and brought Him a veil (*velum*) which He joyfully put around His loins.—St. Bridget, *Revelationes* i. 10, ed. 1680, p.17.
> When ordered He laid aside His clothes and clothed His loins with a small cloth (*parvum linteum*).—*Ibid.* iv. 70 (p.290).
> His Mother seeth how He is so taken and ordained to the death. Wherefore she, sorrowful out of measure and having shame to see Him so standing all naked—for they left Him naught so much as His privy clothes—she went in haste to her dear Son and clipped [embraced] Him and girt Him about the loins with the kerchief of her head.—*The Mirrour of the Blessed Lyfe of Jesu Christ*, Eng. trans. of Pseudo-Bonaventure (prior to 1410), ed. L. F. Powell, 1908, p.237 (spelling modernised).

---

[6] Purple robe (*rhason kokkinon*). Walker (*Apocr. Gospels*, 1873, p.159) translates " a tattered robe of scarlet." But *rhason* (a post-classical word) means a napless woollen cloth or a garment (especially a monk's) made out of it. Walker also translates : " they raised Him and drew Him up on the cross." The verb *anebibasan* may certainly mean ' they raised ' Him to the cross ; but more usually *anabibazein* is the causal form of *anabainein*: to cause to ascend, to make to mount. And *ēkarphōsan*—in classical Greek occurring doubtfully only once, in a scholion to Aristophanes—means ' they nailed.' In later Greek, *karphoō* is used for *hēloō*, I nail ; and *karphion* means a nail.

[7] This is accepted by Père Prat, *Jésus-Christ*, 1933⁴, ii. 392f ; also by Pater Holzmeister (p.29) in spite of his general principle already combated above.

This touching legend—let us hope that it is true—is illustrated in fig. xi. 18, which is taken from a picture in Cologne Museum.[8]

XI. 18.—Our Lady clothing Our Lord (Cologne Museum)

(9) The Affixing to the Cross

There is no fixed tradition as to how Our Lord was nailed, whether to the cross on the ground or to the already erected cross. On this point the Gospels are silent, so are the earliest Christian writers. The first reference to the matter, in the so-called *Gospel of Peter* (about A.D. 125), assumes that Our Lord was crucified before the cross was erected: " They led the two malefactors and crucified the Lord between them . . . When they had raised (*ōphthōsan*) the cross, they inscribed on it : This is the King of Israel."[1] Some other

---

[8] Mrs. Jameson, *History of Our Lord as exemplified in Works of Art*, 1864, ii. 126. She says that there is a similar picture by Holbein (Senior) in Berlin Museum. Cf. Ludolph, *Vita I.C.* ii. 63, 4 : " His Mother hurries up and approaches her Son, she girds and covers Him with the veil from her head."

[1] *Gospel of Peter* 10-11. Holzmeister (p.30) quotes Vaganay (*Ev. de Pierre*, 1930, p.237) as " rightly " saying " in opposition to the Roman custom." But Vaganay continues : " according to which the victim *ordinarily* was hoisted on to the cross previously fixed in the ground." And he adds : " Is he [the author] simply reproducing the custom of his environment? It is possible."

writers[2] imply that He was nailed to a pre-erected cross. But by this
they did not mean a cross permanently *in situ*, or even its vertical
post ; they meant that the actual whole cross brought to Calvary
by Our Lord was set up first before He was affixed to it. This
procedure was described in detail in one of the visions of St. Bridget
of Sweden :

> When the cross was firmly planted, boards were set around the
> post of the cross like steps, as high up as where the feet of the
> Crucified would be, so that both He and the crucifiers might
> ascend by these steps and stand more conveniently on those
> boards to crucify Him . . . When He was on those boards, He
> extended His arm, not under compulsion but voluntarily ; and
> opening His right hand, he laid it on the cross, which His cruel
> torturers barbarously pierced, driving the nail through the part
> where the bone was more solid. Then violently drawing His
> left hand with a rope, they similarly affixed it to the cross. Next
> stretching His body beyond measure, they placed one shin over
> the other and fastened the two feet together with two nails . . .
> They then re-imposed the crown of thorns which they had
> removed from His head while He was being crucified.—*Revela-
> tiones*, vii. 15, ed. 1680, p.597.

A similar view, but with the use of ladders, is contained in the
Meditations on the Life of Christ attributed to St. Bonaventure but
really by another thirteenth century Franciscan (Johannes de
Caulibus) :[3]

> Behold with your mind's eye some fixing the cross into the
> ground, others preparing the nails and hammers, others getting
> the ladder . . . Two ladders are accustomed to be placed, one on
> one side, the other on the other. Upon these wicked men go up
> with nails and hammers, while another ladder is placed in front,
> reaching to that part of the cross where the feet are to be nailed.
> Our Lord may have been compelled by means of this small
> ladder to ascend the cross . . . He who was behind the cross took
> His right hand and nailed it firmly to the cross. [Similarly the

---

[2] Nonnus (c. 530 A.D.), *Paraphrasis*: P.G. 43, 901B. Holzmeister (p.30) refers
to this poetical cento to prove affixing to a pre-erected cross. But (1) he rejects
the testimony of Nonnus to only one nail being used for the feet (see above, p.162) :
and (2) he holds that Christ was nailed on the ground to the crosspiece, of which
Nonnus has not the smallest suggestion. Pater Holzmeister also quotes Pseudo-
Gregory of Nazianzus, *Christus Patiens*, 660 : P.G. 68, 189A. But this is a medieval
work (probably of the twelfth century). An obscure phrase from IV Esdras in
Barnabas (xii. 1) has been cited to prove affixing on the ground : " When the
tree will lie (or fall, *klithĕ*) and rise, and when the blood will flow from the tree."
[3] St. Bonaventure himself appears to hold that Our Lord was crucified on the
ground.—*Lignum vitae* 26 : *Opera* 8 (1898) 77. So also Ludolph the Carthusian
(† 1378) : *Vita I.C.* ii. 63, 5.

left hand]. After this they descend from the ladders and remove them. The Lord hangs down by the weight of His body, supported only by the nails through His hands. Nevertheless another comes up and draws down His body by His feet with all his might and holds them whilst another drives a nail most cruelly through them.—St. Bonaventure, *Life of Christ* ch. 78, Eng. trans. 1881, pp.266f.

" Bonaventure " adds however (p.268) : " Some think that another method was employed in crucifying Our Lord : that they laid the cross on the ground and there nailed Him to it, and then raised it and fixed it on the ground."[4] In several medieval Passion-plays we find the curious combination of Christ being nailed on the ground but being taken down from the cross by means of two ladders.[5] See fig. xi. 16.

Some irrelevant Patristic texts are often cited (e.g. by Holzmeister p.30). Thus St. Ambrose says : " About to ascend the cross He laid aside His royal garments."—*In Lucam* x. 110 : P.L. 15. 1830. No argument one way or the other should be based on this sentence when studied in its context. The main interest of Ambrose is in the highly allegorical exposition which he develops ; he makes no real assertion about the historical details. Our Lord did not just lay aside His garments, nor were they regal vestments ; He was brutally stripped of His ordinary clothes. Furthermore, Ambrose had no good historical tradition, for (n. 107) he says that Simon—almost certainly a Jew from Cyrene—was a gentile.

Then there is a work of uncertain date, wrongly attributed to Athanasius (*De Passione* 10, P.G. 28. 221A.), where the author speaks of ascending (*anabainein*) the cross. This work is of very doubtful historical value ; Pseudo-Athanasius is interested in homiletics, not in archaeology.

Another work, also of uncertain date, is wrongly attributed to St. John Chrysostom (*In parabolam de ficu* : P.G. 59. 590), where there occurs the phrase " the Lord having ascended

[4] So Pseudo-Anselm, *Dialogus de Passione* 10 : P.L. 159. 282 ; Richard Rolle, in R. H. Benson, *A Book of the Love of Jesus*, 1923, p.56 ; Tauler, *Meditations*, 1925, p.224. Among moderns : Sepp, *Vie de J.C.*, 1861, iii. 23 ; Ollivier, *Passion*, 1901, p.347 ; Le Camus, *Life of Christ* 3 (1923) 368.
[5] Thus J. O. Halliwell, *Ludus Coventriae*, 1841, pp.318, 335. In her visions Therese Neumann pictures Christ as nailed on the ground but describes a ladder consisting of " a vertical pole with the steps alternately placed on each side of the pole."— E. de Hovre, *The Riddle of Konnersreuth*, 1933, p.134. Presumably this ladder was for the deposition. The ancient form of ladder (still used in remote places) had a central post with foot-rests on either side. It was this which suggested the name *Christi scala* (Cristes laddre) for the red-flowered blood-wort centaury, with regular leafage on either side of the stem.

(*anabas*) the gibbet (*ikrion*) of the cross and stretched out His hands." The author (like several early Fathers) cites a text " Let us place wood in his bread," attributed to Jeremiah. Referring to the Eucharist, he says Christ is the bread, and the wood he takes as the cross (he seems to interpret *ikrion* as a plank or a table) and he says it is for us a ladder from earth to heaven. The author's argument would hold provided Christ was lifted up " into the air," whether before or after being nailed. Pseudo-Chrysostom had no interest in the issue, nor could he be accepted as having any competence in the matter.

The Gospels being silent and commentators divided, we have to fall back on general considerations in order to assess the probability of the way in which Our Lord was nailed to the cross. Once more it is proposed to investigate critically what appears to be the view generally accepted to-day, namely that Our Lord was nailed to an already upright cross (or at least its vertical post).

(1) First there are texts. Certain phrases—in particular *in crucem tollere* (*tolli*)[6] found frequently in Cicero, Firmicus Maternus and others—seem clearly to suggest that the victim was in some way hoisted up on the already erected cross. Josephus[7] tells us that Eleazar, one of the leaders of the Jews besieged in Machaerus, was captured by the Romans. Bassus had him stripped and scourged in sight of the fortress. Then " he ordered a cross to be erected (*katapēgnunai*) as though he intended to have Eleazar instantly suspended (*krĕmōn*)." Eleazar besought his fellow-Jews " not to leave him to undergo the most miserable of deaths." So they surrendered. In this instance it is not specified whether the Jew was to be nailed, bound or hanged ; and as Bassus was merely threatening, he had to erect the cross first.

It is significant that in the few instances in which nailing is specifically mentioned, it is said that the victim was nailed before being raised on the cross. Thus we are told of a 2nd or 3rd century martyr : " Papylus, nailed to the gibbet (*xylon*), was raised up ;

---

[6] It is just possible that *tollere* here means, not lift up, but carry off or bear away i.e. to the cross already *in situ*. This is not fanciful. Compare the alternative verb *agere* (drive or force). Cicero, *Verr.* v. 63, 163: in crucem tu agere ausus es quemquam. Valerius Maximus (viii. 3, 2): in crucem actus est. Seneca, *De vita beata* 19, 3: Ad supplicium tamen acti, stipitibus singulis pendent (Driven to execution, they hang each from a cross). Lucian, *Peregrinus* 45: harried off (*apagesthai*) to the cross. Alternatively, *crux* might mean the body-loaded vertical figure †, and *in crucem tolli* might mean to be lifted up to form such a figure. These interpretations are in no way necessary for my main thesis as regards crucifixions near Jerusalem, and in particular that of Our Lord.

[7] *Bellum Iud.*, vii. 6, 4 (200).

and when the fire was brought he peacefully prayed and gave up his soul."[8] And we read in the Acts of St. Pionius († 250) :

> He himself bared his body . . . Placed on the pyre constructed by the ravening pagans, he composed his members for being nailed with beam-spikes . . . Then they raised up Pionius and Metrodorus the priest with the posts on which they were nailed.— Th. Ruinart, *Acta Martyrum*, Ratisb. 1859, p.197.

Once more we must resist the attempt to force the meagre texts— especially phrases applying to the crucifixion of slaves in Rome— to give us a unified world-wide procedure, which without further ado we can apply to the tragedy of Calvary.

(2) A Greek romance is also brought forward in this connection :

> Chaereas is now seen to mount the cross, the remainder of the criminals being dead. They call out various cries : Spare him, Come down, Do not wound him, Let him be. So the executioner refrained from the blow, and Chaereas came down from the cross.—Chariton, *De Chaerea et Callirrhoe* iv. 3 : ed. W. Blake, 1926, p.60.

It is uncertain how far such a novel (of uncertain date) can be used as a proof of historical usage. It is also uncertain whether the reference is to crucifixion at all ; the word *stauros* may merely mean a stake to which the condemned man was bound before being punished and executed. Certainly there is no reference in the text to nailing or to nails.[9] Chaereas is quoted as saying : " I carried a cross " (*stauron ebastata*), not part of a cross. Yet he is also said to mount the cross and to descend from it. Was there a platform? It would be natural to think that there was a foot-block ; yet those who exploit this text hold that such was never used. This stepping up on the cross, as well as getting down from it, at a word, is hard to reconcile with *any* accepted view of crucifixion among the Romans.

(3) Next some considerations about the mechanics of the business.

---

[8] Acts of Carpus, Papylus, Agathonice (n. 37), martyred at Pergamus under Marcus Aurelius (161/180) or Decius (249/251) : Kirch, *Enchir. font. hist. eccles. ant.*, 1910, p.51. Holzmeister (p.20) objects that these cases refer only to punishment by burning. This objection is irrelevant, for the victims were first crucified. If they could be nailed on the ground and then raised up when it was the intention to finish off the victims by fire or smoke, why could not the same procedure have been adopted when the victims were allowed to die more slowly or to be devoured by beasts?
[9] " Chaereas, who has already mounted the cross and is about to be *nailed* to it, suddenly receives a pardon."—Zoeckler, *The Cross of Christ*, 1877, p.413.

" It would be extremely difficult," says Père Buzy,[10] " to raise a heavy cross already supporting its crucified." So according to Père Lebreton,[11] " the cross was set up and the doomed man raised upon it with the aid of straps and cords, then fixed to it with long nails driven through the hands and feet." A German priest has described the procedure more in detail :

> We shall not be wrong if we infer that, especially on Golgotha, the bare cross was fastened in the hole that had been dug, so that it would stand firm for the nailing yet to be done . . . The condemned person is placed with his back to the erected cross, a rope is placed over his breast and drawn under each armpit and then thrown over the respective arm of the cross. Then the criminal was easily raised to the proper position by soldiers standing behind the cross . . . Another soldier then at once can bind the lower limbs of the hanging culprit to the upright of the cross with a rope, winding the rope around, always fastening the feet, as far as the ankles, firmly to the beam, with a few coils holding them in position for the nails.—Rev. Josef Pickl, *The Messias*, Eng. tr. 1946, p.248f.

In writing this account—seemingly as of an eye-witness—there is a danger of forgetting that it is entirely lacking in textual support. It is quite admissible as a piece of imaginative reconstruction. But we must be wary when the author argues that " it could be more easily done " this way than by nailing the victim to the cross on the ground and then raising the loaded gibbet. For this contention is exceedingly doubtful. The cross was not very heavy compared to a man's body ; the stem was probably not so long as to allow much of it to be buried in the ground ; even if a deep hole were dug, it would have to be filled and tamped very thoroughly to give immobility under lateral blows. Ordinary experience tells us that the driving of big nails through obstacles—such as wrists and feet—and then through the wood would be exceedingly difficult in the case of such a comparatively light structure with a single shallow fixture in the ground. In fact, it seems to the present writer that the argument from mechanical convenience is altogether in favour of nailing the man while he was completely under control on the solid ground. The subsequent operation — raising the cross (now loaded with an immobile victim) and dropping the end into a hole in the

---

[10] Pirot, *Sainte Bible*, 9 (1935) 372.
[11] *Life and Teaching of Jesus Christ*, 1935, ii. 390.

ground—would easily be performed by a small squad of executioners.[12]

According to Anne Catherine Emmerich, Our Lord was nailed to the cross while it was on the ground.[13]

When the executioners had finished the crucifixion of our Lord, they tied ropes to the trunk of the cross, and fastened the ends of those ropes round a long beam which was fixed firmly in the ground at a little distance ; and by means of these ropes they raised the cross. Some of their number supported it while others shoved its foot towards the hole prepared for its reception. The heavy cross fell into this hole with a frightful shock . . . The archers pushed the cross to get it thoroughly into the hole, and caused it to vibrate still more by planting five stakes around to support it.—*The Dolorous Passion*, Eng. tr. 1926[25], p.255.

(4) There is a mediating view which appears to be held by most modern commentators. As already indicated, this opinion is that Our Lord, until superseded by Simon, carried only the crossbeam, the vertical post being already erected on Calvary.

Attached first to the patibulum, the condemned man was hoisted on to the pole (already fixed on the ground) by means of ropes or straps. Then he was fixed on the cross by long nails through feet and hands.—Père F. M. Braun, in Pirot, *La sainte Bible*, 10 (1935) 467.

This is a most improbable account. How could a man be hoisted up on a solitary vertical pole by ropes? How could his hands be

[12] Here is a description of a crucifixion in Madagascar in 1825 : " The wooden frame used in place of a cross resembles a gallows. To this the malefactor is nailed whilst it remains flat upon the earth, after which it is lifted up with its miserable burden and fixed in two holes made in the ground for the purpose."—W. Ellis, *History of Madagascar*, 1838, i. 371 : quoted by Stroud, *Treatise on the Physical Cause of the Death of Christ*, 1847, p.21. In the Acts of St. Hitztibouzit we are told that he " stretched himself out upon the tree," to which he was nailed naked, and then it was " set up."—Conybeare, *The Armenian Apology and Acts of Apollonius*, etc., 1896[2], p.269.

[13] The English translation (from a French version) is not very reliable. More accurately according to the original German of the Visions (p. 1013) the first sentence runs : " After the nailing of the Lord, they, with ropes fastened to rings at the back of the cross, drew the upper part of the cross up on the raised platform ; then they threw these ropes over a support erected at a little distance ; and by means of these ropes many executioners raised up the cross." The artist Tissot, in his *Life of Our Saviour* (1897), follows A. C. Emmerich in many of his paintings. Christ was crucified on the ground on a cross with a foot-block (ii. 180f). A horizontal bar temporarily connected the tops of the already erected uprights for the two bandits, and this was used for raising Christ on the cross (p.184f). The bandits were merely tied (p.186), Our Lord both bound and nailed (p.192f), with the right foot nailed over the left (p.196). Thus this elaborate ' historical ' portraiture of the Passion not only lacks religious appeal but factual probability.

nailed to a crosspiece which has only just been hauled up? With greater plausibility others have pictured Our Lord's hands as first nailed to the crosspiece on the ground.[14]

> The prisoner was made to lie on his back on the ground so that his shoulders and outstretched arms lay on the crosspiece he had been carrying, and then his hands were nailed to it. Next, probably by means of a rope fastened about his chest and thrown over the top of the vertical beam, he was hoisted up the latter until he was able to straddle the *sedile* . . . After the prisoner had been lifted up in this manner, the crosspiece was nailed or tied to the vertical beam, and then his feet were nailed.—Ricciotti, *Life of Christ*, 1947, p.629.

This imaginative picture[15] is based on two assumptions which have already been questioned : (*a*) Christ bore only the crossbeam, (*b*) there was a permanently erected execution-post on Calvary. But, even if we prescind from the doubtfulness of these assumptions, we can see at once that the mechanical difficulties of the operation are enormously increased—quite gratuitously and for no apparent purpose whatever. There is no difficulty in nailing the man's hands to the crosspiece on the ground ; but to secure a firm attachment, the probability that the wrists (not the palms) were nailed is greatly increased. The real difficulty is then to haul the man up on the post ; for it is not an easy or a workable method to throw ropes " over the top of the vertical beam " to secure a fulcrum ! Then the crosspiece, bearing the squirming victim, has to be nailed or tied to the upright post. Finally his feet have to be nailed to the comparatively light and not very firmly fixed post.[16] The assumption that the man was hoisted up over a permanently fixed projecting seat-block adds to the difficulties.[17]

On the whole, it seems to the present writer much more likely that Our Lord was nailed to the cross on the ground, and that the loaded cross was then raised to the vertical position. A permanent

[14] So Barbet ii. 26; Daniel-Rops, *Jésus en son temps*, 1946, p.545 ; Holzmeister, p.21. There is no textual proof whatever of such an operation. Barbet is therefore under a misapprehension when he declares his adhesion to Holzmeister's view " based on a considerable number of ancient texts."

[15] Père Lagrange admits that there is no textual authority for this operation, but he thinks it is easier (which I doubt) : " The texts are silent ; but the operation appears easier thus."—*Marc*, 1929[5], p.427.

[16] If this method was used, it is much more likely that the slave's feet were merely tied, not nailed at all.

[17] Moreover, it is quite unnecessary even for the upholders of a *sedile*. If there were a hole or socket in the vertical beam, a peg could be inserted when the victim was in position.

post just outside Jerusalem being entirely improbable, there is no reason to assume that Christ did not bear the whole ready-made cross. The affixing was then carried out in the most convenient way. In spite of current views, which when examined prove to be quite unpractical, it would appear that the operation presenting fewest mechanical difficulties was to affix the Victim on the ground and then to raise the cross. Much of the objection to this view is due to imagining the cross to have been much higher than it really was—a mode of representation first popularised at the Renascence. Our Lord's mouth was reached by a sponge on a short stick or javelin ; His side was pierced with a spear held by a foot-soldier.

XI. 19.—Affixing to the Cross, from the Bologna Casket

A few of the different art-types will now be illustrated. Figure xi. 19 shows a relatively primitive representation, from a casket in Bologna.[18] Here Christ steps on to a little platform or foot-rest. Two men on step-ladders are proceeding to nail His hands to the cross-arm. In fig. xi. 20 we see the representation by Fra Angelico

[18] Millet, *Recherches sur l'iconographie de l'évangile au xiv, xv et xvi siècles,* 1916, fig. 422.

(† 1455) in San Marco, Florence. The cross is now notably higher, so three ladders are employed. Our Lord is depicted as a willing victim, uttering the words: *Pater dimitte illis quia nesciunt quod faciunt.* On His right stand Our Lady and Magdalen, on the left the Centurion and two Jews.[19]

Figure xi. 21 is an illustration for the Passion-Play performed at Valenciennes[20] in 1547. Here we see Our Lord, helped by Simon, carrying the cross and meeting Veronica with her cloth. Next we see Him being nailed to the cross on the ground. Then we see the three rather high crosses, the holy women, the dicing soldiers. The next scene is the deposition from the cross, with the aid of two ladders, and Our Lady swooning underneath. At the extreme right the burial is shown. As already remarked, in the Passion Plays Christ was generally represented as nailed on the ground, but as taken down, with the help of ladders, from the cross still standing.[21] This was already contained in the Byzantine Guide to Painting (which contains early material) :

> *Christ nailed to the Cross* : A crowd of Jews and soldiers seen upon a mountain. A cross laid upon the ground in their midst. The body of Christ upon it. Three soldiers hold it by ropes at the arms and foot. Other soldiers bring nails and drive them with a hammer through His feet and hands.
>
> *Descent from the Cross* : The cross fixed in the ground with a ladder placed against it. Joseph mounts to the top of the ladder, clasps Christ round the waist, and lets Him down. Below is the Holy Virgin standing. She receives the body in her arms and kisses the face. Behind her, women may be seen carrying perfumes ; Mary Magdalen takes the left hand of Christ and kisses it. Behind Joseph stands John Theologos, and kisses the right hand of Christ. Nicodemus is bending down, extracting the nails from the feet of Christ with the help of pincers ; a basket at his side.
> —Trans. in Didron, *Christian Iconography*, 2 (1891) 317f.

The nailing of Christ while recumbent was not an innovation of

---

[19] Note that there is a foot-rest attached to the cross. Holzmeister (p.29) is quite wrong in stating : " It is said that the pre-erected cross is only once depicted in Christian art, by Blessed Angelico." Even the two ladders with a smaller central one for Christ to mount do not constitute a new feature. This is shown in a fresco of the Church of the Peribleptos, Mistra (about 1350).—L. Bréhier, *L'art chrétien*, 1928², p.336. The three ladders are mentioned by "Bonaventure" (p.208 above).
[20] G. Cohen, *Le théâtre en France au Moyen Age* : I, Le th. religieux, 1928, plate 54 (from Ms. fr. 12536 of the Bibl. Nat.). In some ' Mysteries,' Christ was nailed to the erected cross : *Passion du Palatinus*, ed. Frank 1922, p.35.
[21] Were these operations really mimed or acted? If the cross were high, the performance must have been difficult.

the fifteenth century. It occurs already in Greek Psalters of the eleventh century, and these copied from older originals.[22] Later it became popular in the West. Figure xi. 22 shows an alabaster carving in the Church at Afferden, Holland.[23] Three men pull on knotted ropes attached to Our Lord's hands and feet, while three others, each with a hammer, are about to nail them. Figure xi. 23 shows an illustration from the widely read *Speculum Humanae Salvationis*.[24] There is a similar scene in Dürer's *Little Passion* (1511). Figure xi. 24 shows a picture by Philippe de Champagne (✝ 1674), now in Toulouse Museum. In fig. xi. 25 we see how Rubens (✝ 1640) represented the erection of the cross after Our Lord had been nailed to it. There is an unnecessary display of muscularity ; and the cross is probably made higher than it really was.

XI. 23.—Nailing on the Ground (*Speculum Humanae Salvationis*)

The taking down from the cross seems to have been represented in art before the affixing was pictured. Examples of a few of the earliest surviving specimens are given. Figure xi. 26 shows a miniature (about 880) in a Greek manuscript of the works of St.

[22] Mâle, *L'art religieux de la fin du moyen âge en France*, 1922², p.25.
[23] W. L. Hildburgh, *Archaeologia* 93 (1949) plate xvii. d.
[24] Mrs. Anna Jameson, *History of Our Lord*, 1864, ii. 134.

Gregory of Nazianus.[25] Christ, clad in a long violet robe, is standing on a foot-board close to the ground. His left hand has already been detached, He is being supported by Joseph, while Nicodemus is about to unnail the right hand. No ladder is used. At His left side stand Our Lady and St. John. To the right of the illustration the burial is depicted. An even simpler picture is contained in fig. xi. 27, a miniature in the Codex of Archbishop Egbert (950-1000) now in Trier.[26] In fig. xi. 28 is shown what is probably the oldest example of the Byzantine type, from a Greek manuscript in Florence.[27] Again we have the footboard close to the ground ; Christ's clothing has become a skirt. Joseph is holding up the body while Nicodemus extracts the nail from the left hand. John expresses his grief by holding his hand to his face. There is a new and touching feature : Our Lady holds in her veiled hands the unnailed right hand of her Son.

XI. 29.—Bas-Relief near Horn, Germany (1115)

[25] Bib. Nat., Ms. grec 510 : Rohault de Fleury, *Evangile* ii. 271 (plate 91). Observe the sun and the moon, the absence of a crown, the long robe (*colobium*), with no nail-marks on the feet.
[26] F. X. Krauss, *Die Miniaturen in der Stadtbibliothek zu Trier*, 1884, plate 51. Note : Christ's robe has sleeves, there is no foot-board, BVM and John are not represented.
[27] Millet, fig. 495. Mâle (p.101) seems to say that the MS. is of the tenth century.

Figure xi. 29 reproduces a colossal bas-relief on rock (the so-called Externstein), near Horn in the district of Lippe (Germany), on which the date 1115 can be read. Christ, with long hair in tresses, is being received by Nicodemus, while Joseph (mounted on a branch of a tree?) with one of his arms (missing) helps to support the body and leans on the cross with the other. Our Lady's figure is unfortunately mutilated ; she caresses Christ with her hands and has her face close to her Son's head. On the other side stands John (bearded). A remarkable feature of this sculpture is God the Father, holding a cross-banner, and receiving the soul of the dead Christ in the form of a child.[28]

(10) The Form of the Cross

It has already been emphasised that there is a lack of early information, literary or pictorial, concerning the details of crucifying, and that we have no reason to believe that there was any one stereotyped mode. It is therefore possible that in some cases a single stake or post was used. Figure xi. 30 depicts a corpse tied to a vertical post[1]. There is however no actual evidence of such a method, nor have we the slightest ground for applying it to Our Lord's case. On the contrary, there are constant references to His arms being stretched out laterally on the cross.

Moses stretching out his hands during the battle against the Amalekites was constantly cited as prefiguring Christ on the cross.—Justin (Dial. 90) ; Barnabas (12, 2) ; Tertullian, Cyprian, etc. Justin (Dial. 40, 3) aptly compares the Crucified to the paschal lamb[1a] : " When the lamb is roasted, it is arranged in the form of a cross : one of the spits pierces it from below to the head, the other goes through the back, and to it are attached the forefeet of the lamb." Tertullian says : " Since the head rises upwards, the back is vertical and the shoulders project

[28] Notice the sun and the moon represented by busts. Christ's feet are practically standing on the ground. Below this Deposition (more than 3 metres high) there is another scene (not reproduced) : Adam and Eve, enclosed in the folds of the serpent's tail, are embracing the trunk of a tree which is confounded with the tree of the cross.
[1] P. W. Schmidt, Die Geschichte Jesu, 1904 (at the end of vol. ii).
[1a] " It is a striking circumstance that the body of the paschal lamb was literally crucified on two transverse spits. I witnessed the Samaritan Passover on the summit of Mt. Gerizim in 1870 ; and the bodies of the seven lambs as they were prepared for roasting looked exactly as though they were laid on seven crosses."— F. W. Farrar, Life of Christ, new ed. 1894, p.634.

laterally, if you simply place a man with his arms and hands
outstretched, you will make the general outline of a cross."—
Ad. nat. i. 12. In the Sibylline Oracles (viii. 302) we read: "He
will stretch out His hands and measure the whole world." On
which Lactantius (iv. 25) beautifully comments: "In His
Passion He stretched out His hands and measured the world,
to show that from east and west a great crowd of all tongues and
nations would come to be gathered under His wings." Says St.
Athanasius: "It is only on the cross that a man dies with his
hands (arms) spread out. So it was fitting for the Lord to endure
even this and to spread out His hands, that with one He might
draw the ancient people and with the other those from the
Gentiles, and thus unite both in Himself."—*De Incarnatione* 25.

XI. 30.—Corpse tied to
a single Post

Indeed the early Christians saw everywhere the form of Christ's
cross: in a ship with its mast and yardarm, in a plough, an adze,
a banner, as well as in a man praying with extended arms.[2] In

_____
[2] E.g. Justin, *Apol.* i. 55 ; Minucius Felix, *Octavius* 29, 8.

prayer they adopted the attitude we know as " orante." " We not only raise but stretch out our hands," says Tertullian,[3] " thus taking our model from the Lord's Passion, we confess Christ even in prayer." At the martyrdom of Christians in Lyons in A.D. 177, when Blandina's fellow-victims saw her praying with outstretched hands on the gibbet, they at once thought of their Master on the Cross :

> Blandina, hung on a gibbet (*epi xylou kremastheisa*), was exposed as a prey to the wild beasts which were let loose. Seeing her hanging there in the form of a cross (*staurou schēmati kremamenē*) and engaged in earnest prayer, the combatants were inspired with fervour. For in their combat they saw with their bodily eyes in their sister Him who was crucified for them, that He might convince those who believe in Him that all who suffer for the glory of Christ have fellowship for ever with the living God.—Eusebius, *HE* v. 1, 41.

In early times Christians made the sign of the cross much more frequently than we do to-day :[4]

> Let us not be ashamed to confess the Crucified. Let the Cross be our seal made boldly by our fingers on our forehead and on everything : over the bread we eat and the cups we drink, in our coming in and going out, before our sleep when we lie down and when we rise up, when we are travelling and when we are still. It is a great preservative, without cost to the poor or toil for the sick, for it brings grace from God.—St. Cyril of Jerusalem, *Catech.* xiii. 26.

To this custom Julian the Apostate bears witness when he writes : " These two things are the acme of their religion : to hiss at idols and to trace the sign of the cross on their foreheads."[5] Thus

---

[3] *De oratione* 14. The hands were not lifted high but stretched out and moderately raised (*ibid.* 17). The pagan figures on ancient monuments have their hands raised vertically with the elbow forming a right angle. See Dom L. Gougaud, Attitudes of Prayer, *Devotional and Ascetic Practices in the Middle Ages*, 1927, pp.1-43 ; especially for the Irish *cros-figil* (*crucis vigilia*).
See also Tertullian, *De corona* 3 ; St. Ephraem, *Hymni et sermones*, ed. Lamy, 1 (1882) 302. On the sign of the cross : H. Thurston, S.J., The Sign of the Cross, *Month* 118 (1911) 586-602 ; Dom Leclercq, Croix, signe de la, *Dict. d'arch. chrét.* 3 (1914) 3139-3144.
[5] Letter 19 : *Works*, ed. W. C. Wright 3 (1923) 52. It was said that when in peril Julian used instinctively to cross himself !—Theodoret, *HE* iii. 3. The catechumen was taught the sign of the cross before being admitted to the Eucharist : " If we say to a catechumen 'Do you believe in Christ?,' he replies ' I believe,' and he signs himself. He already bears the cross of Christ on his forehead and he is not ashamed of his Lord's cross . . . If we ask him ' Do you eat the flesh and drink the blood of the Son of Man? ' he does not know what we are saying."—St. Augustine, *In Ioann.* tr. 11, 3. Thus the sign of the cross was the recognition-mark and ' password ' among Christians, a compendious profession of faith.

this devotional habit is found to be well established in the second century, and in all probability it goes back to apostolic times. While thus we are quite certain concerning the practice, we are curiously uncertain of the details of the gesture. The earliest writers speak of tracing the cross on the forehead ; later it is expressly mentioned that the sign was made with the finger ; and there are early references to signing the eyes and the breast.[6] Thus it would seem that originally a number of small crosses were traced, just as to-day we sign forehead, lips and heart at the Mass-Gospel. The large sign of the cross, with the hand moving to the shoulders, cannot be shown to have been a common practice in the East before the eighth century ; the earliest clear evidence for the West is not prior to the thirteenth century.

From an incidental reference in Tertullian[7] we learn that the sign was also made over objects. And from an early date it was employed in sacramental rites :[8]

> What is water without the Cross of Christ? An ordinary element without sacramental effect . . . Even a catechumen believes in the Cross of the Lord Jesus, with which he is signed.— St. Ambrose, *De mysteriis* 4, 20.
> It is by the sign of the cross that the Lord's Body is consecrated, the baptismal fonts are sanctified, the priests and the other clerics are initiated ; and everything which is to be sanctified is dedicated by this sign of the cross with the invocation of the name of Christ.—St. Augustine, *Sermo* 181 *De tempore.*
> What is the sign of Christ but the Cross of Christ, as all know? If this sign is not employed on the foreheads of believers, or on the water from which they are regenerated, or on the oil of chrism wherewith they are anointed, or on the sacrifice by which they are

---

[6] The *Apostolic Tradition* of Hippolytus (Latin text) speaks of " sealing the forehead and the eyes with the hand "—p.70 Dix (1937). Prudentius mentions crossing " the forehead and the place of the heart."—*Cathemerinon* vi. 129 : PL 54. 889. Those condemned to the mines (*ad metalla*) had their heads half-shaved and their foreheads branded.—*Dict. d'arch. chr.* 1 (1924) 427. A deacon, thus condemned, himself marked his forehead with the sign of the cross.—Theodoret, *H.E.* iv. 19. Note the cross-mark on the Beauvais fragment (fig. vii. 49).

[7] " When you sign your bed."—*Ad uxorem* ii. 5.

[8] Even our separated brethren have retained the sign of the cross in baptism (though not in the other sacraments). Thus no. 30 of the Canons of 1604 of the Church of England, in spite of subsequent Puritan opposition at the Savoy Conference of 1662. In Canon 30 it is said that " this use of the sign of the cross was held by the primitive Church, as well by the Greeks as the Latins, with great applause " ; hence it is to be retained " purged from all popish superstition and error " (unspecified).—Cardwell, *Synodalia* 1 (1842) 262f. The Church of Ireland forbids the liturgical use of a cross but retains the sign of the cross at baptism.— *The Constitution of the Church of Ireland,* ed. 1934. pp. 138. 149.

fed, none of these is properly carried out.—St. Augustine, *In Ioann.* tr. 118, 5.

From all this it is clear that in the early Church the form of the cross, assumed to be universally admitted and known, was in constant employment both in private life and in the liturgy. It also follows that the cross was not taken as a simple post but had transverse or lateral portions. This does not settle the exact configuration. We may eliminate a framework with two vertical supports.[9] An X-cross, such as is shown in fig. xi. 31 is very improbable.[10] There is no proof that it was ever used by the Romans ; only in a late medieval legend is it specified for St. Andrew. There is more to be said for a Y-shaped cross, of which there are occasional examples in art. One has already been given in fig. ix. 11. Another (Millet fig. 438) is presented in fig. xi. 32. In fig. xi. 33 is shown the Crucifix over the altar of the church at Puenta La Reina, Navarre.[11] We meet this Y-cross in art first about the eleventh century ; the earlier examples appear to show unhewn wood. Perhaps this representation originated in the legend of the 'tree' of the cross growing out of Adam's grave. At any rate such a Y-structure made out of planks or posts could hardly be used for crucifixion unless there were a tie-rod connecting the extremities of the divergent arms. If such a forked form were used, it must have consisted of a tree-trunk with two branches.[12] In spite of certain visionaries,[13] it is most improbable that Christ's cross had this shape.

[9] See fig. 2082 in Daremberg—Saglio, *Dict. des ant.* 1 (1887) 1574 : Andromeda fastened to a gibbet (engraved gem from Praeneste). Cf. the reference to Madagascar, p.213 above, also the Santa Sabina carving (fig. xii. 8).
[10] Costantini, *Il Crocifisso nell' arte,* 1911, p.53. There is an inscription in Palmyra with the date (A.D. 134) between X and X. According to Dom Leclercq, this is the oldest dated representation of the Cross.—*Dict. d'arch.* 3 (1914) 3048. It is exceedingly doubtful if these symbols denote a cross. Sulzberger thinks that they are signs of punctuation.—*Byzantion* 2 (1925) 366. It is said that crucifixion on an X-cross was seen in India in 1874.—Zoeckler, *The Cross of Christ,* 1877, p.66. St. Justin denies that Our Lord's cross was X-shaped.—*Apol.* i. 60, 5.
[11] *Konnersreuther Chronik,* 1928, p.176. The origin and the date are uncertain.
[12] The Greek ('forked tree') of Joshua 8²⁹ has already been referred to (p.166). Cf. fig. xi. 6.
[13] St. Bridget says that the cross was Y-shaped : "The arms of the cross were raised, and the junction was between the shoulder-blades, the cross affording no support to the head ; and the inscription-board was fixed to the two arms which rose above His head."—*Revelationes* iv. 70. The visions of A. C. Emmerich also specify a Y-cross.—*Dolorous Passion,* Eng. tr., p.253. Father Thurston pointed out that in St. Lambert's church at Coesfeld there was a Y-shaped crucifix to which she had great devotion.—*Month* 138 (1921) 243. According to Therese Neumann the bandits were on T-crosses, whereas that of Our Lord was shaped like Y or the Greek letter psi (with the vertical stem prolonged upwards between the divergent arms).—F. von Lama, *Therese Neumann,* 1936, p.195.

We are familiar with the hymn *Vexilla Regis* of Venantius Fortunatus (c. 600 A.D.) : *Impleta sunt quae cecinit . . . Regnavit a ligno Deus*, which we translate : God has reigned from the tree. But see above (p.163) concerning *lignum* as a translation for gibbet. The origin of the phrase is in an interpolation in the Greek and in the Latin versions of Psalm 96 (95)[10] : " Tell the nations, The Lord has reigned *from the tree (apo tou xylou).*" Justin (*Dial.* 73) incorrectly thought that the Jews had deleted the italicised phrase. It is also quoted as authentic by many Latin writers : Tertullian (*c. Marc.* 3[18]), Ambrose, Augustine, Isidore, Gregory. It is obviously impossible to argue from the phrase that Our Lord was crucified on a literal tree.

The choice lies between T and ✝. It is difficult to know how far the early Christian writers meant to make historical assertions when they chose between these two forms, for their statements are generally made in connection with allegorical interpretations of Scripture. But there seems no doubt that T-crosses were used in the first century A.D. The pagan writer Lucian[14] says that the cross (*stauros*) was in the shape of the letter T. And the early Christian apologists[15] are practically unanimous for the T-form, which is also found in second-century inscriptions. It is quite a practical form for a cross without a title.[16] The existence of this in Our Lord's case suggests the four-armed form ✝, which gradually became almost universally accepted.[17]

---

[14] Lucian, *Dike Phonéenton* (*Trial in the Court of Vowels*), 12, where Sigma accuses Tau of bringing misfortune on men, " for in this shape they set up gibbets (*xyla*) to crucify (*anaskolopizein*) men . . . It is called *stauros* by men."

[15] St. Justin (cited above, p.149) implies that the upper part (title) is placed upon the cross (he uses the verb *hyperairō*) after fixing the cross-beam " from which " it emerges. Barnabas (ix. 8) allegorically interpreted the 318 men of Gen 14[14], namely, I (=10) plus H (=8) plus T (=300). " So he indicates Jesus in the two letters and the cross in the other." Tertullian comments on " a mark upon the foreheads " (Latin : signum Thau in frontibus) of Ezek 9[4] : " The Greek letter Tau and our own letter T is the very form of the cross prophesied to be on our foreheads."—*Adv. Marc.* iii. 22. It is curious to observe that in old Hebrew and in Macabean coins the letter Tau was written X.—F. W. Madden, *History of Jewish Coinage*, 1864, table at beginning and p.47. The T form was used for a crozier down to the twelfth century, our ' crutch ' (i.e. cross). St. Francis used T for signature ; it occurs (arising from a head) in his blessing to Brother Leo (referred to, p.14 above) ; see R. Balfour, *The Seraphic Keepsake*, 1905, pp.76-106.

[16] The title might have been pegged on, as it is apparently in fig. xii. 6. The T-arrangement would be greatly facilitated if the vertical post were pointed at the top and the cross-bar had a central hole to fit over it. Ludolph (*Vita I.C.* ii. 63, 13) says : " The cross had nothing above the transverse bar, it had three arms like the letter T," the title (1½ ft.) being affixed above the upright (16 feet).

[17] The Fathers spoke of a four-armed cross in connection with Eph 3[18]. " He denotes by a special word each prolongation of the cross : the upper part he calls height, the lower part depth, the two lateral arms breadth and length."——St. Gregory of Nyssa, *Catech. Discourse* 32, 8.

This shape is shown (fig. xi. 34) in the Cross of Herculaneum,[18] a town which was destroyed in the eruption of Vesuvius A.D. 79. Originally there was a wooden cross fixed to the wall with two nails ; this was forcibly removed, so that what remains is a depression, 45 cm. long with a transverse 36 cm. That it was an object of cult seems certain, but it is disputed whether it was a Christian symbol. Yet there is nothing impossible in this last contention. Consider the language of St. Paul and St. Ignatius about the Cross, and the devotion of the sign of the cross (which must have been much earlier than its literary attestation).[19] Why should there not have been a cross as a reminder or symbol in a private house? The absence of surviving specimens is not an argument against this supposition, for such objects would naturally perish or be destroyed in times of persecution.

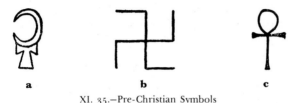

a   b   c

XI. 35.—Pre-Christian Symbols

The use of the cross in public or semi-public inscriptions is, of course, a different matter. Great reserve and prudence had to be observed. Even pre-Christian symbols (fig. xi. 35) were employed. Cruciform ornaments are found on the representations of Assyrian kings ; the cross as an ornament is found in Mexico and Central America ; the figure denoted *a* is a so-called Maltese cross from a Punic tomb at Carthage. In *b* we have the *crux gammata* or swastika (a Sanskrit word). This symbol is prehistoric, it is a sacred sign in India and widespread in the East. Its interpretation is doubtful ; it may mean fire (the apparatus for kindling) or flame (the rotating sun). It was seldom or never used by Christians until nearly 250 A.D., and was then deliberately

---

[18] Its Christian nature is accepted by M. Zerwick S.J., De Cruce Herculanensi, *Verbum Domini* 20 (1940) 65-71. It is rejected by G. de Jerphanion S.J., La croix d'H., *Orient. Christ. Period.* 7 (1941) 5-35.
[19] Later, Christians were accused of being cross-adorers.—Minucius Felix, *Octavius* 29[8] ; Tertullian, *Apol.* 16. Julian the Apostate († 363) upbraids Christians as follows : " Ye worship the wood of the Cross, making images of it on the forehead and engraving it in front of your dwellings."—St. Cyril of Alexandria, *Contra Ivlianum* 6 : P.G. 76. 796,

chosen to portray and also to conceal the Cross of Christ. The remaining figure (*c*) is the so-called *crux ansata*, or T surmounted by a handle. It was especially figured in Ancient Egypt, where it is often portrayed in the hands of the goddess Sekhet. It may denote the sun as the source of life. Later it was adopted by Egyptian Christians.

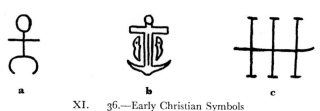

XI.   36.—Early Christian Symbols

The cross, if we exclude the letter T, is rarely depicted in the Roman catacombs ; there appear to be only about twenty instances surviving from the period when the catacombs were used for burial (until 410). But the cross is frequent in a disguised form. Three examples are given in fig. xi. 36 : *a* is from the Cemetery of Domitilla (100/125), *b* from that of Priscilla (c. 250), *c* (I H with cross-bar) also from that of Priscilla (second century). It is poignantly touching for us of to-day to view these concealed expressions of devotion to the Crucified, which were once inscribed in pagan Rome.

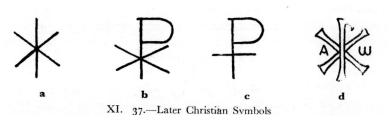

XI.   37.—Later Christian Symbols

The four symbols in fig. xi. 37 are monograms of Christ rather than covert designations of the cross. They are interesting as adaptations of pre-Christian signs. The first (a) is found as an ornament, for the Greek letter psi, on Roman coins (probably for xvi), on Greek coins (as an abbreviation for Chios). As a Christian mark (prior to Constantine) it was not common ; it stood for I (Iesous) X (Christos). The next (b) is the famous Constantinian Chi-Rho monogram (i.e. Ch plus R, the first two

Greek letters of Christos). This is seen in a more developed form in *d*, with Alpha and Omega ; this is taken from the fifth-century funeral slab of Leontia and companion. The combination of X and P intertwined is found in a Roman inscription of 269, but it became common only after Constantine, and at the beginning of the fourth century it became an official symbol (instead of an abbreviation) on mosaics and sarcophagi. A fine reproduction of Constantine's " labarum "[20]—X and P inside a laurel crown, surmounting a cross—can be seen in fig. xii. 1. It is thus described by Lactantius :

> Constantine was directed in a dream to have the heavenly sign delineated on his soldiers' shields and so to proceed to battle. Doing as he had been commanded, he marked on their shields the letter X with a perpendicular line drawn through it and turned round at the top [P, the Greek capital R], this being the cipher of Christ.—*De mort. persec.* 44.

On inscriptions the monogram was usually combined with the cross.[21] In fact, in the fourth century we often find the monogram-cross depicted as in *c* of fig. xi. 37. It is interesting to observe that the XP sign was already used in pagan antiquity, without any religious significance. It is found in Greek coins as an abbreviation of *chrysos* (gold) or of some word indicating the value or the coiner's name. By a singular historic irony the form depicted in fig. xi. 37 (*c*) is found in coins of King Herod.[22] Already on his coinage was the crest of the ' King of the Jews ' whom he sought to destroy in childhood !

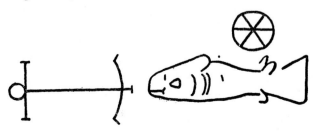

XI. 38.—Anchor, Fish, Eucharistic Bread (on funeral slab of 2nd cent.)

[20] See *Dict. d'arch. chrét.* 8 (1928) 927.
[21] St. Paulinus of Nola (*Poema* xxvii. 608-627) regards the monogram (chrismon) as representing the cross. The cross, he says, is depicted in two forms. (1) A single post with a transverse bar like a sailyard, the Greek sign for 300, i.e. T. (2) With six ends (*cornua*) formed by three rods (i.e. X and P) surrounded by O. The P, he says, has on top a small horizontal projection to the left and thus contains T. So he fancifully reads XPICTOC into the monogram.
[22] Madden, p.83 ; G. F. Hill, *Catalogue of the Greek Coins of Palestine*, 1914, plate 23 (14). There is no satisfactory explanation of this sign ; it is not a mark of value TR (ichalkon), for it is found on coins of four different denominations.

Among the veiled symbols of the cross we find (from the end of the first century) the anchor. This is often combined with one or two fish as in fig. xi. 36 (*b*). Another example is fig. xi. 38, showing the figures —anchor, fish, eucharistic bread—depicted on a funeral slab (of the second century) in the Via Appia (now in the Lateran Museum). The fish-symbol is probably another example of a symbol adapted from paganism.[23] Near the temples of the goddess Atargatis—e.g. in Hierapolis and in Askalon—there were fish-ponds. The fish (a symbol of fertility) was eaten at a sacred meal by the priests and under certain conditions by the lay adherents. It would seem that Christian missionaries triumphantly annexed this symbol: It was the Christians who, especially in the Eucharist, had the true Fish, a heavenly food available to all. Hence the Fish became the symbol for Christ, especially in representations of the eucharistic banquet, where its presence was further suggested by the miracle of the Multiplication.[24] It was then observed that the Greek letters of *ichthys*—see fig. xi. 39—were the initials of *Iēsous Christos Theou Yios Sōter* (Jesus Christ God's Son Saviour), and this confirmed the Christian appropriation of the symbol.[25] This history of the adoption of pagan signs is interesting. It shows how Christianity could take pre-existing modes—words, symbols, customs— and infuse into them a new religious content.

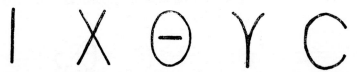

XI. 39.—Christian Inscription : the Greek Letters I—Ch—Th—Y—S, (fish)

Nowadays we are more familiar with the combination IHS, either by itself or in conjunction with pictures of the Passion. It

[23] Dölger, *Ichthys* : *Das Fischsymbol in frühchristlicher Zeit*, Rome, 1910.
[24] " We little fish, according to our Ichthys Jesus Christ, are born in water."— Tertullian (200 /206), *De bapt.* 1. He assumes that the imagery is well known to readers and adversaries. In the famous inscription (180 /216) of Abercius, Bishop of Hierapolis in Phrygia, we read : "Faith led me everywhere and everywhere she gave me for food a Fish from the fountain, mighty and pure, which a holy Virgin had grasped. And this she gave to her friends to eat forever, having excellent wine and giving it mixed with water, together with bread." So in the inscription (200 /220) of Pectorius in Autun : " Lord and Saviour, feed me, I pray You, with the Fish."
[25] The alternative explanation is that the Fish-symbol was used to express the previously employed abbreviation i-ch-th-y-s. Cf. St. Optatus (3²), St. Augustine (*De civ. Dei* 18²³). In *Or. Sib.* viii. 217ff there is an acrostic : Iesous Chreistos Theou Yios Soter Stauros.

probably originated as the first three letters of Jesus in Greek (the H being a capital *ē*), just as XPC (i.e. ch-r-s) was written for Christos. Later when the Greek origin was forgotten, the letters were taken as Latin ; hence the medieval " jhesus." (Subsequently " Iesus Hominum Salvator " was invented to explain IHS.) The letters IHS were on the crucifix of San Damiano (fig. xii. 62) which spoke to St. Francis and decided his vocation. This helped to spread this symbol of devotion among the Franciscans ; it attained great intensity with St. Bernardine (1383-1446). In 1427 he was accused of heresy in using a banner or tablet with the Holy Name (I H S) ; he went to Rome where Martin V acquitted and encouraged him.[26] Subsequently the Society of Jesus adopted the symbol in its official seal (fig. xi. 40).[27]

XI. 40.—Seal of the Jesuit General

On IHS see Hilaire de Barenton, O.F.M.Cap., *La dévotion au Sacré-Coeur*, 1914, pp.110-119 ; Dom Leclercq, *Dict. d'arch. chr.* 1 (1924) 177-180 (abréviations). Garrucci is in favour of the Latin origin of the symbol.—*Storia dell' arte cristiana* 1 (1872) 104. Dom Leclercq thinks that this is not proved, and leaves the question open. Père Hilaire with most scholars favours the Greek derivation.

In inscriptions we find Ih ESU CHRISTO in Spain (627) and IHS in Ravenna (c. 550). IHS occurs in the Rambona ivory

---

[26] Pastor, *Hist. of the Popes* 1 (1906³) 233 ; Thureau-Dangin, *St. Bernardine of Siena*, 1906, p.95.
[27] Notice the cross on top of the *h*. This barred *h* seems to have appeared first about 1450. What is the significance of the two stars and the moon-crescent? (I notice that the University of Geneva has IHS on its seal, like the Jesuits !).

(889), see fig. xii. 32. It is found on coins of Justinian II :
    dN IhS ChS (685/695),
      IhS CRIST D F (705/711),
in each case followed by REX REGNANTIUM. Dom Leclercq
thinks that in the second case *h* cannot stand for *ē*(the Greek *eta*),
and hence neither in the first. But he admits it represents *eta*
in coins of Constantine VI (780/791) :
      IhSUS XRISTUS NICA.
The Greek origin seems however to be vastly more probable.
This is true even in Latin inscriptions ; a 6th century grammarian, Dynamius, says that in Christian inscriptions the Greek
eta (of which H is the capital form) was adopted into the Latin
alphabet. Unless H is a vowel, IHS does not convey the pro-
nunciation ; later, when it was misunderstood, the vowel *e*
had to be added (Jhesus). The obviously Greek form IHC often
occurs, e.g. in an iron mould for altar-breads used by St. Francis.
—Hilaire, p.115.

CHAPTER XII

THE CRUCIFIXION IN ART[1]

(1) The Earliest Christian Art

THE earliest extant specimens of Christian inscriptions and paintings are to be found in the Catacombs round Rome, which were excavated solely for burial and served as temporary refuges in times of persecution ; they were scarcely used for cult before the time of S. Damasus (†384). In these underground crypts lit only by terra cotta lamps one could not expect artistic masterpieces. The paintings are expressed in the contemporary technique which we know from Pompeii. Christianity did not create a new art-form, no more than it invented a new language. Hellenistic-Roman art, varied in motives and abstract in style, was capable of being accommodated to all beliefs. Eliminating the idolatrous and the indecent, Christians adopted the themes, the ornaments and the imagery of their own time. But, though the models were not new, the inspiration was original and religious. The art of the day was made the vehicle of new ideas. Eros awakening Psyche from sleep, Orpheus playing the lyre, the celestial banquet, all these acquired a new meaning even before Old Testament themes began to be portrayed : the sacrifice of Abraham, Moses striking the rock, Daniel in the lion's den, the three youths in the fiery furnace, Jonah. Gradually Gospel scenes emerged : the Baptism, the paralytic with his stretcher, Cana, the Multiplication, but not Calvary.

Even simple crosses were very rare in inscriptions, except in discreet veiled forms such as the swastika, the fish on a trident. Yet at this very time the sign of the cross was continually made in private. There was no shrinking from the idea of salvation through the Cross, witness St. Paul. There was, however, an obvious reluctance to give a plastic representation of the idea. This attitude, aesthetic rather than dogmatic, expressed for the time that complicated largely unanalysed complex which is a collective phenomenon in every age. There was a scruple against material cult in a world still permeated with idolatry and polytheism, there was an inherited

---

[1] This chapter is intended to be a short historical inquiry into the modes and forms by which Christian piety pictorially expressed faith in the Crucified. It is not a history of art nor is it concerned with technique, for both of which there are many works available. Hence bibliographical references have not been included. A further study of ' symbolism ' in Christian art is included in the next chapter, p.308.

Jewish prejudice against pictorial art, there was concession to the classical dislike of portraying suffering, there was a prudent avoidance of what would excite mockery and disgust in pagans, there was a respectful shrinking from any imaginative representation of God dying on the gallows.

Until Constantine the penalty of crucifixion was in constant usage against the lowest criminals. Those who saw corpses on crosses along the roads would naturally refrain from conjuring up the picture of such horrors. But when Christianity received public recognition in the Edict of Milan (313) and the True Cross was discovered in Jerusalem, the sign became the symbol of triumph instead of the badge of shame. We see the great jewelled cross of the Basilica of the Holy Sepulchre portrayed in the apse-mosaic of St. Pudentiana (fig. vii. 15). The artistic ostracism of this erstwhile gibbet ceased.

A sarcophagus in the Lateran Museum, probably from the Cemetery of Domitilla, is an excellent example of the art of the Constantinian epoch (fig. xii. 1).[2] There are five panels which, from the beholder's left to right, depict the following scenes: (1) Simon carrying the cross which is merely indicated on a small scale; he is accompanied by a soldier. (2) Christ (youthful) is being crowned with a laurel-wreath, not with a briar-crown. (3) The central panel will be presently considered. (4) Christ, accompanied by a soldier, appears before Pilate. (5) Pilate washes his hands. At the centre, instead of the Crucifixion, there is a strange scene: a cross surmounted by a laurel-crown containing the Chi-Rho monogram —the emblem of victory. On the arms of the cross are two doves. At the foot are two soldiers, one asleep, the other seated. Above in the angles of the arch are two small heads representing sun and moon.[3] Thus the cross recalls Calvary, the sleeping guards recall the Sepulchre; and the complex image symbolises both the Death and the Resurrection.

There was no dogmatic significance in this exclusion of the Figure

[2] There are numerous minor restorations: the upper part of cross and crown, part of the Tau, the left hand of Christ before Pilate, the left hand of Pilate, the upper part of the soldier's helmet.
[3] This is an early instance of what became for centuries the constant accompaniment of representations of the Crucifixion. In Byzantine art the sun is usually a disc, and the moon a sickle; in the West they were generally personified by busts. Presumably they refer to the darkness at Christ's death and to the sympathy of nature. Later they were given allegorical meaning, e.g. by Bruno of Segni: The New and the Old Testament, the Church and the Synagogue, Gentiles and Jews.—*Expos. in Gen.*, PL. 164. 154.

from the cross, whose whole relevance was that Christ died on it.
Nor was imagination restrained. St. Jerome (A.D. 404) says of
Paula that " she threw herself down in veneration before the Cross
[on Golgotha] as though she beheld the Lord hanging upon it."[4]
This of course also applied to crosses, which persisted long after
the introduction of the crucifix. " For this reason ben Crosses by the
way," says *Dives et Pauper*,[5] " that when folk passing see the Cross,
they should think on Him that died on the Cross and worship Him
above all things." But this aesthetic reluctance to externate in stone
or paint what was left to the imagination became later on an occasion
for favouring heretical doctrine. For example, this Lateran sarcophagus—with Simon bearing the cross and with Christ absent from
the erected cross—was compatible with the heresy of Basilides,
which is thus described by St. Epiphanius :

> He says that Jesus did not suffer but Simon the Cyrenian . . .
> He says that Simon bearing the cross was transformed into Christ's
> appearance and Christ Himself into Simon's ; and that instead
> of Himself He delivered up Simon to be crucified. While he was
> being crucified Jesus stood in front invisibly, laughing at those who
> crucified Simon. But He Himself went up to heaven without
> suffering.—*Adv. haer.* i. 2 (haer. 24).

There was in fact a prolific growth of heretical (gnostic or docetic)
sects which denied the reality of Christ's humanity or of His
sufferings.[6] This stress on the incompatibility of divinity with a
felon's death inevitably produced even among the orthodox a
tendency to draw a veil over the physical side of the Passion. Thus
the artistic difficulty of expressing a Divine Sufferer became a
dangerous concession to dogmatic error. And it was dogmatic
belief which slowly forced art to picture the Crucified.[7]

---

[4] *Ep.* 108, g (to Eustochium).
[5] Written about 1406 and printed by Wynken de Worde in 1496. According to
St. Willibald († 785) it was " the custom of the Saxon race " to erect by the way-
side " the standard of the Holy Cross, dedicated to Our Lord and reverenced with
great honour, lifted up on high so as to be convenient for the frequency of daily
prayer."—*Hodoeporicon*, ch. 3, trans. Brownlow, p.4.
[6] These lasted for centuries. Thus Muhammad knew Christianity only through
heretical sects and apocryphal writings : " They slew him not, neither crucified
him ; but he was represented by one in his likeness . . . They did not really kill
him, but 'God took him up unto himself."—*Koran* 4, tr. Sale, 1795, i. 124.
[7] We in these latter days fail to make allowance for the genuine repugnance of
even orthodox Christians to portray the Crucified. For us, the brutal procedure
of crucifixion, abolished for ordinary human criminals, has become hallowed by
exclusively sacred associations and consecrated by image and devotion. But just
imagine our horror at the idea of Our Lord being hanged in chains, beheaded, or
treated like the Carthusian martyrs (see pp. 191-2). This will help us to realise how
the early Christians felt as regards describing or picturing details of the Passion.

(2) **Substitute Figures**

But at first the problem of portraying a dying Deity was not faced. Substitute figures long continued to be used. So we find the Lamb in the centre of several stone crosses in Ravenna. Another example (fig. xii. 2) is to be found in one of the surviving columns of the ciborium in St. Mark's, Venice (500/550). Though in the other scenes we find Christ displayed realistically, in the Crucifixion the cross merely bears in its centre a medallion with the Lamb in relief.[1] Above the cross-arm are the two busts of sun and moon ; beneath are two guards standing. At the sides are the two crucified bandits on foot-rests.

XII. 2.—Portion of one of the Columns in St. Mark's. Venice (500/550)

Garrucci

Another substitute for the Crucified was the bust or medallion of Christ on or over the cross. There are several examples of this on the silver vessels (ampullae) used by pilgrims to bring back oil from the sanctuary-lamps of Palestine. A number of these are preserved in Monza and in Bobbio. One of these sent to Queen Theodolinda at Monza about 600 A.D. is shown in fig. xii. 3. The lower register shows two women being addressed by the angel at the tomb. Above is a representation of Calvary which includes : the sun and the moon (busts), Our Lady and St. John, two kneeling figures (probably pilgrims), the two bandits tied to their crosses, and the central cross surmounted by a large bust of Our Lord.

One of the flasks at Bobbio, unfortunately injured, contains a

---

[1] St. Paulinus (*Ep.* 32 *ad Severum*) thus explains the symbolism : " Beneath the blood-red cross Christ stands, in the form of a snow-white lamb, as the innocent victim given up to an unjust death."

rather unique combination (fig. xii. 4).[2] Underneath we can see the angel and the tomb, but the women are missing. Above we can discern, in addition to one of the bandits (rather colossal), Our Lord's empty cross with a title, surmounted by a bust. One of the kneeling figures still survives. But though the cross has no Crucified, both the lance-bearer and the sponge-bearer were represented. The surviving figure, on the left of the cross, appears to be presenting the sponge. It is extraordinary that all the realities of Calvary are portrayed except the Victim.

XII.   3.—Figures on a Flask from Palestine, now in Monza (c.600)

Garrucci

Another example, shown in fig. xii. 5, is in the mosaic of the apse at Santo Stefano Rotondo, Rome, constructed under Pope Theodore I (642/649). The cross is no longer isolated as in Santa Pudenziana (fig. vii. 15), it is surmounted by a medallion containing the bust of Christ (bearded). Above this (but not shown in the illustration) is the divine hand holding a crown.

Now this artistic attenuation of the horror of crucifixion began to have deleterious repercussions on the great christological issue which interested men in the fifth and sixth centuries. The Nestorians, condemned at Ephesus in 431, separated the divine from the human in Our Lord, as indeed do many moderns who never heard of this ancient heresiarch. According to Nestorius, it is absurd to speak of

[2] Bobbio no. 11 : Celi, *Civiltà Cattolica* no. 1754 (1923), p.184.

God as an infant in the stable, and therefore of Our Lady as Mother of God ; and the idea of a crucified God was a heathen fable. But the Nestorians agreed with Catholics in asserting the reality of Christ's humanity and suffering : an ambiguous association which persists to-day. By way of reaction, the Monophysites denied the reality of Christ's humanity ; even after the Incarnation there was in Him only one nature, the divine. The heresy that the Passion was only apparent (docetism) was condemned at Chalcedon in 451. On this view the physical sufferings of the Passion are either unreal or else irrelevant inasmuch as they did not happen to a divine Person. And the mental sufferings—the struggle in Gethsemani, the disappointment, the loneliness, the pain of men's ingratitude and sin—have to be denied *in toto*.[2a] The scene of Calvary becomes degraded to a common execution if the chief participant is not the God-Man, uniting two natures in one person. Against this perverted view the crucifix, instead of the cross, becomes a vivid affirmation of the Christian message.

The realisation that art and faith must be brought into harmony found expression in a resolution of a council[3] of Greek bishops held in Constantinople in 692 :

> In some venerable pictures there is depicted a lamb, to which the Forerunner is pointing with his finger, prefiguring for us through the law the true Lamb, Christ our God . . . We order that henceforth instead of the lamb there should be portrayed the human form of Christ our God, so that, thereby contemplating the great humiliation of God the Word, we may be led to remember His human existence, His Passion, His saving Death and His Redemption of the world.—*Conc. Quinisext.* canon 82 : Mansi, *Concilia* xi. 977 ; Kirch, *Enchiridion*, 1910, n. 999, p.610.

(3) Some Exceptional Early Representations

Before considering the gradual growth in the use of the figured cross, it is necessary to consider some exceptional representations which, by anticipation or otherwise, are out of the general line of development. They are artistic ' sports.'

The earliest surviving representation of the crucifixion is a

---

[2a] This is *a fortiori* true of Apollinarism which denied a human soul to Christ.
[3] It is called Quinisext, because it was supplementary to the 5th and 6th Councils of Constantinople. And it is called *in trullo* because it was held in the domed chapel (*trulluo*) of the imperial palace. Soon after this council the iconoclastic controversy drove many monks to the West, where they greatly influenced religious art.

blasphemous caricature (fig. xii. 6). One of the young pagan pages at the Palatine in Rome scratched on a wall an insulting joke against a Christian companion. It is a strange destiny that this graffito—as ephemeral as the scratchings on a modern school-desk —has come down to us as the oldest crucifix. Its date is in the region of 200 A.D. About this time, as we learn from Tertullian,[1] Christians were accused of onolatry, adoration of a donkey-headed divinity, not only in writing but by images. A Carthaginian gladiator exhibited in the streets an ass-headed figure with the inscription " The God of the Christians." A Jew made a figure with ass's ears bearing the same inscription. So this pagan youngster had a gibe ready to hand. The crucified donkey faces a human figure, and there is the Greek inscription : *Alexamenos sebete* (sic) *theon* : Alexamenos worships [his] God. The Christian boy is depicted as raising his left hand in the antique gesture of adoration.[2] This graffito was discovered in 1856, and in 1870 another was found in the same house, namely, the words : *Alexamenos Fidelis,* Alex. a Christian ! One cannot help connecting the two. The young Christian did not give way to the bullying and the scoffing. He boldly scratched his profession of faith on a near-by wall. How precious to us has become this trivial youthful incident of so long ago !

In such rough scribbling it is hard to draw any conclusions about the cross. It is apparently T-shaped, with a title stuck on. The line under the feet appears to be meant for a foot-rest rather than the ground.[3] It is a pity that this young pagan was not better at drawing ![4]

[1] *Apol.* 16 ; *Ad nationes* 14. A pagan caricature of Christ with ass's ears is reproduced in *Dict. d'arch. chr.* 7 (1927) 2448. In Rome there is a street called *Via Affogalasino* (the street Drown-the-Donkey). One wonders whether it is linked with the persecution of the early Church. Was this where the young bloods of Imperial Rome used to beat up or duck those whom they mocked as worshippers of a crucified ass?

[2] " In adoring we convey the *right* hand to the mouth."—Pliny *HN* 18[5]. Minucius says of a worshipper of the image of Serapis: "Moving his hand to his mouth, he kissed it."—*Octavius* 2.

[3] Costantini regards this as a strong argument in favour of the use of a foot-rest : " Certainly the *suppedaneum* cannot here be an invention or an incongruous novelty ; following the most spontaneous and natural design provided for him by memory, the caricaturist has traced the commonest form of cross."—*Il Crocifisso nell' arte,* 1911, p.9.

[4] It has been asserted that the graffito is a representation of the Egyptian god Seth of whom the ass was a symbol. This does not explain the crucifixion ; and it is generally rejected. The letter Y will be noticed above the cross. This may be a cabalistic sign not belonging to the graffito at all. More likely it stands for Yakinthos (i.e. Hyacinth), a name which occurs several times on neighbouring walls. Marucchi writes : " The Palatine graffito is also important as showing that the Christians used the crucifix in their private devotions at least as early as the third century."—*Cath. Encycl.* iv. 527. This may be true, but it hardly follows from this caricature.

The first Christian representation to be considered is a carved panel on an ivory casket in the British Museum (fig. xii. 7). Its provenance is uncertain (probably Roman), and its most likely date is 400/450. The cross appears to be T-shaped ; the title *Rex Iud* (*aeorum*) is inscribed on the border of the panel ; the ends of the cross are splayed. There is no foot-rest, there are indeed no traces of nails on the feet. The arms are quite horizontal, with nails in the palms. Christ is young and beardless, with long hair ; He is nude save for a meagre cincture ; the nimbus round the head may have been incised subsequently. He is alive, with open eyes, and shows no trace of suffering.

XII. 6.—Caricature (c. 200 A.D.)

The grouping of the other figures is quite exceptional. On the beholder's left is Judas hanging from an oak-tree, on a branch of which a bird is feeding her two young in a nest (probably to denote the season of spring) ; on the ground is the spilled bag of money. The next figure is Our Lady with her hands folded inside her cloak. Between her and the cross stands St. John. At Christ's left, on the other side of the cross, is a man whose right hand is raised threateningly. This figure has been generally interpreted as Longinus piercing Christ's side, the lance having been broken off. But there are fatal objections to this view. (1) The man is meant to be a Jew ; this is shown by his bonnet, a Jewish headgear known from sarcophagi. (2) It is difficult to see how the lance could have fitted on the carving, and there does not appear to be any sign of fracture. (3) The piercing of Christ's *left* side is not only very unusual but is contradicted by another panel of the casket.[5]

Another exceptional carving (in cedar wood) is shown in fig. xii. 8. It is one of 28 panels (of which 10 have disappeared), showing the concordance of the Old and New Testaments, on the door of Santa Sabina on the Aventine, Rome.   This was built under Celestine II (422/432), and there is no reason for making the door more recent.   The former opposition to an early date was due to a reluctance to admit pre-medieval representations of the Crucifixion ; its interpretation as the three Hebrews in the fiery furnace was due to the same prejudice.   This panel is artistically inferior to the others, and it is placed high up so as not to be noticeable ; perhaps the artist realised that he was daring.

The crosses are merely implied by the bars of the architectural background, representing the walls or buildings of Jerusalem.   The three figures are living, with open eyes ; they are deliberately portrayed in the orante-posture.   Broad nail-heads are seen in the palms ; there are no traces of nails in the feet, which rest on a *suppedaneum*, if not on the ground.   No fourth limb of the cross is indicated at the back of the heads ; so probably a T-shape is implied. Christ is pictured as of larger stature than the bandits ;   He has a beard and long hair, and is nude except for a very narrow cincture.

XII.   9.—Carnelian Intaglio in the British Museum (enlarged)

[5] There are four panels. (1) Pilate washing his hands and Christ carrying His cross. This is reproduced in fig. xi. 7. (2) The Crucifixion (fig. xii. 6). (3) The Women and the guards at the Sepulchre. This is fig. 52 of my *Family at Bethany*. (4) The incredulity of St. Thomas who is extending his forefinger towards Christ's *right* side.

There are a few intaglios, destined to ornament rings, which contain crude representations of the Crucifixion. It is almost impossible to date them ; they have been assigned to the second century and to the fifth. At any rate they are early ; it is probable that the scene appeared on these small private objects before being exhibited in churches, and even before figuring in the miniatures of manuscripts. Some of them seem to be of heretical (gnostic) origin.

Figure xii. 9 shows a carnelian found at Constanza and now in the British Museum. In the centre, upon an exergual line, is a nude figure of Christ facing the spectator but with head and feet turned towards His left. Behind the figure is a T-shaped cross, beneath whose transverse the arms are extended without any apparent means of support ; perhaps the arms are depicted below the crossbeam so that it can be seen. On either side, on a much smaller scale, are six figures (three are missing through breakage) ; these are the twelve apostles. On top there is l-ch-th-y-s in Greek (as in fig. xi. 39) : owing to chipping the first letter is imperfect. In the figure (made from an impression) these letters are in reverse, though in direct order on the actual stone.

XII. 10.—Carnelian Intaglio (enlarged)
Garrucci

The next figure (xii. 10) shows another carnelian intaglio, published by Garrucci in 1880 as in possession of a collector in Rome. Here the central figure (apparently nude) is not represented as superhuman in size ; but it is raised high up on a definitely marked foot-rest attached to a real T-cross. Below the arms and retrograde in the impression, are the Greek letters : *Iesous Christos*, with *e* (epsilon) twice written for *i* (iota). The last two letters (OC)

are continued underneath in the exergue, separated by a lamb.
There is a nimbus round Christ's head.

XII. 11.—Red Jasper from Gaza (enlarged)

Most peculiar of all is a red jasper from Gaza in Syria, published
by Le Blant in 1883 (fig. xii. 11). The central figure, naked and
twisted, is seen in profile ; there is no trace of a cross, but there is a
crucifer nimbus. The figure is flanked by two others, who seem to be
a man and a woman worshipping. Above, and also on the back of
the gem, is an inscription which has not been deciphered. It has
been suggested that a Christian used the reverse of a heretical
talisman for engraving a crude picture of the Crucifixion.

XII. 12.—Green Jasper in Corpus Christi College, Cambridge

More in accord with orthodox art, and therefore later in date, is a green jasper in the Lewis Collection (of gems and rings) of Corpus Christi College, Cambridge (fig. xii. 12). The central figure wears a skirt and has a nimbus. There is a trace of the cross below, but the cross-arms are not visible. Apparently it is indicated that the hands were tied. The feet are on a foot-rest (or on the ground). Above are two curious bugle-like symbols, which may stand for sun and moon. There are two smaller figures, obviously the lance and sponge bearers.

(4) The Living Robed Christ

Apart from the premature and anticipatory items just considered, it seems clear that the first experiments in representing the Crucifixion pictured Our Lord on the cross as alive and clothed in a long robe (*colobium*). This is shown by the surviving specimens which we can date at least approximately.

In fig. xii. 13 we see one of the scenes[1] depicted on a silver plate of Syrian origin, found at Perm (Russia). Its date is between 450 and 550 A.D. Except for the lower portions and the foot-rests, the three crosses are merely indicated. The nails are not shown. Christ, with a halo, is beardless and has wide-open eyes. On His right is the sponge-bearer; the sponge is in cup form (as on Irish high crosses). There are two unusual features about Longinus: he is at Our Lord's left side and his lance is resting on the ground. Beneath are two men, dicing for the tunic or guarding the cross.

Figure xii. 14 reproduces a miniature from the Syriac Gospels of Rabula, written in 586 in the Monastery of St. John of Zagba in Mesopotamia, now in the Laurentian Library, Florence.[2] Though this is the first definitely dated ' historical ' representation

---

[1] J. Reil, *Die frühchristlichen Darstellungen der Kreuzigung Christi*, 1904, fig. 3. In addition to the soldiers watching the tomb, Peter and the Cock, Daniel and the lions, the plate contains three circular scenes : (1) the Crucifixion here reproduced; (2) the women at the tomb, reproduced in my *Family at Bethany*, fig. 53 ; (3) the Ascension.

[2] There is also a reproduction in my *Family at Bethany*, fig. 34. The interpolation in St. Matthew (to be considered later p.312) though it already existed in older MSS., is not contained in Rabula's text. Hence the illustrations may be based on older—perhaps Cappadocian—models ; notice that *Longinos* is written in Greek. Reil (pp.66, 69) thinks that the illustration has been subjected to alterations more recent than the manuscript ; e.g. that in the original picture the feet were fastened by ropes and that nails were inserted, the grief of the women and the expression of pain in Christ are also asserted to be later modifications. There is no proof of all this. See Morey in *Festschrift Clemen*, 1926, p.163f.

of Calvary, it must have been preceded by a long development. The fact that Lo(n)ginos is written in Greek suggests a Cappadocian model. Anyway we have here a frankness and a completeness of treatment not adopted for publicly exhibited pictures until much later.

Above a background of two hills we see a red sun and a violet moon. Over the cross is a Syriac inscription in gold letters : This is the King of the Jews. At the left of the picture Our Lady, with a golden blue-bordered nimbus and clad in a violet robe, stands with St. John. At the other end of the picture are the three ' Marys.' Beneath the cross three men are with brutal indifference dicing for the seamless blue tunic. The bandits, clad only in a loin-cloth, are nailed and apparently also bound around the chest. At Christ's right the ' good thief ' turns towards Him. The crosses are definitely shaped T, and there are no foot-rests.

Our Lord is bearded, with long dark-brown hair falling over His shoulders. There is a gold blue-bordered aureole round His bare head which is slightly inclined to His right. He is living, His eyes are open, there is no expression of suffering. He is clothed in a long sleeveless robe with two gold bands. His arms are horizontal ; and like the two bandits, the nails go through the palms and the insteps. At His right side stands Longinus, in a short red cloak, with a sword at his belt. With both hands he is thrusting the lance into His side. On His left is a man in a long white cloak, a civilian with a Jewish face. With his right hand he is offering the sponge on a stick ; in his left hand he is holding a yellow wooden vessel filled with red liquid.

We here for the first time notice a curious artistic phenomenon which persisted for many centuries. Though Our Lord is alive and is being offered the soaked sponge, He is also represented as having His side being pierced. We might explain this as the inclusion in one picture of two successive incidents. But in the next chapter we shall find a much more satisfactory explanation in the widespread influence of a verse interpolated into St. Matthew's Gospel (see p.312).

Two of the flasks brought by pilgrims from Palestine have been already shown (figs. xii. 3 and 4) as representing a bust of Christ over the empty cross. But there are several others in Monza which depict Him in a long robe.[3] In the encolpium (a thin gold plate

---

[3] See fig. 56 in *The Family at Bethany*: Christ has a halo and is bearded ; His arms are outstretched in the attitude of an *orante* ; there is no trace of a cross ; He appears to be bare to the waist. The two bandits are tied to stakes with their hands behind their backs. Cf. Egyptian amulet, *ibid.* fig. 57.

engraved and enamelled), also now at Monza, shown in fig. xii. 15, all the figures occur except the bandits : Our Lady and St. John, the spear and the sponge, and two figures beneath.[1] The title with the letters ICXC is separate above a T-cross. Our Lord (beardless) is robed, the nails are marked on His feet but not on His hands.

XII. 15.—Medal now at
Monza.   *Garrucci*

Later than these Eastern representations are several Crucifixions which were publicly displayed in Rome. One of them is in S. Maria Antiqua in the Roman Forum, rediscovered in 1900 (fig. xii. 16). This fresco is in the oratory completed under Pope Zachary I (741 /752), whose figure (with square nimbus for a living person) occurs beneath the scene. It is significant that at this time the church was served by Syrian monks.

The cross (✝) carries a title with the Greek inscription : Jesus the Nazarene, the King of the Jews. It is planted among rocks which, like the hill in the background, are split by the earthquake ; its foot is fixed with the help of three pegs. The sun and the moon appear above the arms. On Christ's right stands Our Lady holding a fold of her mantle up to her face (*Sca Maria*). On the opposite side stands St. John holding a book with a jewelled cover, his Gospel (*Scs. Ioannis Evagelista*).

[1] Two sentries, or the dead rising? Note the head under the cross (Adam?). Cf. fig. xii. 34. The Greek inscriptions are : " Father, into Your hands I commit My spirit " above the cross ; and at the sides " Your Mother " and " Your son." On the back is a barbarous transcription of a little Greek poem of St. Gregory of Nazianzus. Garrucci plate 433 (4) ; *Dict. d'arch. chr.* fig. 462.

There are two other figures, made smaller to denote perspective. One, whose name is written *Longinus*, is piercing Christ's right side, from which there gushes out a double stream, white and red, towards his eyes. He is bearded, clad in green with a breastplate ; a sword hangs from his left side ; and he is thrusting the lance with both hands. On the other side a soldier presents the sponge on a stick ; there is a vessel of vinegar at his feet.

The figure of Our Lord (bearded) is nearly life-size. His head, surrounded by a golden crucifer nimbus, is bent slightly to the right. With large open eyes He is looking towards His Mother. He is clad in a long sleeveless robe of dark blue with two vertical golden bands. There is no foot-rest, His feet are close to the ground.

There is an older representation—the first example in Roman art, the only picture of the Crucifixion in all the catacombs—in the cemetery of St. Valentine on the Via Flaminia, Rome (fig. xii. 17). It was made under Pope Theodore, a native of Jerusalem (✝ 649), or under Honorius I (✝ 658). It was seen and studied by Bosio in 1600 and was rediscovered by Marucchi.[5] Unfortunately it is now deteriorated and incomplete. Only the figure of St. John is intact. There were no men with spear and sponge. So this picture is the first example of the scheme M ✝ J (Mary and John with Christ on the cross). We can see the background of a crenellated wall. Our Lord was clad in a long sleeveless robe.

The spear and the sponge reappear in a mosaic of the Oratory of John VII (705/7), which is unfortunately destroyed and can be presented only in a rough drawing[6] by Grimaldi (fig. xii. 18). This is probably the first Crucifixion publicly and officially exhibited in a Roman church. Even in the door of S. Sabina the scene (fig. xii. 8) was so high up that it could hardly be distinguished with the naked eye.

There is another wall painting in the Oratory (the crypt of the present Church) of SS. John and Paul on the Coelian Hill, Rome ; it was discovered by Padre Germano in 1891. A reproduction (omitting the three dicing soldiers) is given in my *Family at Bethany* (fig. 35). Here Our Lord (bearded) is alive, and clad in the long sleeveless tunic. Apparently His feet are nailed to a foot-rest. The sponge is being presented and His side is being pierced, the blood

[5] *El. d'arch. chrét.*, 1903, ii. 391. The reconstruction by Bosio is given in Garrucci, *Storia dell' arte cristiana*, plate 84 (2). But how far can we rely on details—title, footrest, etc.?

[6] E. Müntz, *Rev. arch.* 34 (1877) 208. See also above, p.100.

spurting out.   There are some new features: Four busts (the
evangelists as witnesses) appear above the arms of the cross. Magdalen accompanies Our Lady. Unfortunately we cannot exactly
date the picture: probably 850/950.

XII.   18.—Grimaldi's sketch of the
Mosaic in the Oratory of John VII
(705/707)

To the school of Reichenau we owe many illustrated manuscripts
(about 950/1000 A.D.).   Two illustrations (due to this school)
will be given from the Codex of Abbot Egbert (977/993), now in
Trier.[7] In fig. xii. 19 we see Calvary before Our Lord's death. He
is beardless and is turned towards Our Lady; He is clad in a
sleeved robe. His cross (✝ with title) is golden; there is no foot-
rest, the nails are seen in hands and in feet. His arms are slightly
curved; the hands have the thumbs overlapping. (Several of these
features are common in German art of the eleventh century.) The
two bandits have their arms tied behind their T-crosses; their
names are indicated: Dismas and Gestas. Above we see the red
sun and the white moon. Below are two men dicing for the tunic.
The man holding the sponge on a golden rod is dressed in red with
white hose; his name is given: Stephaton.
    In this manuscript the piercing of Christ's side is definitely shown
as taking place after death (fig. xii. 20). His head is bowed in death,
the gold cross rises from the green earth into a rosy sky. A man, in

[7] F. X. Kraus, *Die Miniaturen in der Stadtbibliothek zu Trier*, 1884, plates 49 and 50.
Figures xi. 10 and 27 are also from the Codex Egberti.

blue and white tunic and red hose, is thrusting with both hands the spear into Christ's right side ; his name is given : Longinus. There is an accompaniment rarely illustrated in art. The legs of the bandits ("Latrones") are being broken by two red-cloaked executioners (" Tortores ") armed with mallets.

(5) The Living Skirted Christ

The Objection to Nudity

The Church of the Holy Apostles at Constantinople was founded by Constantine, completed by his son, entirely rebuilt by Justinian (536/546), and furnished with mosaics by Justin II (565/578). These disappeared a few centuries later. But they are described in a poem of Constantine of Rhodes addressed about 940 to Constantine Porphyrogenitus.[1] Here is the portion concerning the Crucifixion (lines 922-955) :

> Who, however stony-hearted, on beholding the image of the Passion and such an outrage committed on the Master, would not at once in his heart feel wonder at seeing such a strange incident : A cross bearing Christ stretched out naked amid condemned criminals : the Lamb, alas, and the Word of God the Father, who took away the sin of mortal men, pierced with nails in hands and feet, His side marred with the puncture (*nygmē*) of the spear when He had tasted the vinegar and gall, while His body was hanging on the wood of the cross : [Christ] who brought into being this whole creation and removed the ills of the race of mortals, [treated] like a bandit stained with deeds of blood by the people of the hateful and lawless Hebrews. [This happened] too while His holy Virgin-Mother was beholding Him, as also the disciple who was present at the Passion and who was breaking his heart ; while His Mother herself was bewailing, sympathetically pouring forth tears and crying out without restraint : " Alas, alas, my Child for this Your Passion which You have suffered against the laws of justice. Alas, my glory, my beloved offspring, only child of me so lonely and miserable. Where are the promises of Gabriel who spoke to me before Your birth? Where is David's sceptre and the exalted throne which like the light-giving sun was to remain for ever and ever? "

From this we infer that in Byzantine art about 550 the Crucifixion scene included Christ on the cross, Our Lady and St. John,

---

[1] Published by E. Legrand in *Revue des études grecques* 9 (1896) 32-103.

the two bandits, the vinegar being presented and the side being pierced, probably also the sun and the moon. Since Christ is described as "naked," it is unlikely that He was clothed in a long robe.

That there was opposition to representing the Crucified in a skirt or loin-cloth is shown by an incident of about the year 593 narrated by Gregory of Tours.[2] In the Cathedral of Narbonne, which contained the relics of St. Genesius, there was " a picture which showed Our Lord crucified girt with a loin-cloth (*praecinctum lenteo*)." The scandal that ensued can be inferred from a vision reported by a priest called Basil. He asserted that Our Lord appeared to him and said: " All of you are covered with various garments, yet ye look on Me naked. Go at once and cover Me with a garment." He did not understand, so the vision was repeated. Then he told the bishop, " who at once ordered a curtain to be spread over it. And the picture is now seen thus covered. For though sometimes uncovered for viewing (*ad contemplandum*), it is quickly covered by letting down the curtain (*dimisso velo*)." To-day we have grown so familiar with the almost nude Figure on the cross that we fail to do justice to the sense of reverence which for so long insisted on His being clothed.

Christ with Sponge and Spear

We can probably see this influence at work in a miniature (fig. xii. 21) of a manuscript (from Constantinople) of the Homilies of St. Gregory of Nazianus (dated about 880), now in the Bibliothèque Nationale, Paris (ms. grec 510), from which fig. xi. 26 has already been taken. The body of Christ was first drawn with a loin-cloth and afterwards covered with a purple sleeveless robe, which, being partially effaced, allows the surface underneath to be seen. In spite of the deterioration of the miniature we can discern the chief details. Having only a limited space, the artist has omitted the two bandits and the soldiers at the foot of the cross. Above there are two discs : the sun red with rose centre, the moon blue with yellow centre and a black crescent. On the left of the picture stands Our

[2] *Liber in gloria martyrum* 22 : P.L. 71, 724 ; M.G.H., *S. Rer. Merov.* i. 2 (1885) 501. According to Marucchi (*Cath. Enc.* iv. 527), Gregory " speaks of a crucifix robed in a colobium or tunic, which in his day was publicly venerated at Narbonne in the church of St. Genesius and which he considered a profanation—so far was the public cult of the crucifix from having become general up to that time." This is incorrect. The objection was not to the crucifix but to Our Lord being represented in a loin-cloth instead of a robe (colobium).

Lady (in a violet robe) followed by two women. At the other side is John (dressed in blue) with another small-statured person (with green tunic and golden mantle) supported by a soldier. The cross of brown wood seems to bear a title, and has a foot-rest. Christ is living and His head is slightly inclined to His right. On His left is the sponge-bearer, clothed in a green coat, and carrying a bucket. His right side has just been pierced by the soldier, clad in red ; and a stream of blood and water is gushing forth.

More recent in date (10 /11 century), but based on earlier models, is the wall-painting of the church of Kelejlar in Cappadocia, shown in fig. xii. 22. In its present injured state it was rediscovered—with numerous others—by Père de Jerphanion in 1925. Here both the bandits and Our Lord are clothed in a short skirt. The usual features of the scene are discernible, including sun and moon (with their names in Greek). Above Our Lady's head is the general inscription : *Hē Staurōs(is)*, The Crucifixion ; and beneath the arms of the cross Christ's words to His Mother and to St. John. The bandits are tied to their crosses, their arms are bent at an angle. He on the left has his name written, *Gesdas* ; the name of the other is effaced. The sponge-bearer at Christ's left, a bald white-bearded man, holds a vessel of vinegar ; his name is given, *Esopos*. The lance-bearer is denoted *Longinos*. Blood and water, denoted by white and red lines, are gushing from the wound.

Figure xii. 23 shows a fresco in the church of Sant' Urbano alla Caffarella, in the Roman Campagna.[3] Unfortunately it has been painted over, but underneath is an inscription in Latin : " Offered by Bonizzo A.D. 1011." Here we have a four-armed cross with title (INRI) and foot-rest, while the bandits are tied to their crosses. Two angels are over the arms of Christ's cross. A man and a woman at the foot of the cross appear to be holding cloths to receive the blood. The name of the man holding up the sponge (on a peculiar stem) is given as Calpurnius. The man thrusting the lance is called Longinus ; and the blood with water is spurting out apparently towards his eyes. Our Lady is trying to dissuade him from striking the blow.[4]

---

[3] Rohault de Fleury, *L'évangile : études iconographiques*, 1874, ii. 256 (plate 89).
[4] There are many similar representations of the Crucifixion, several of which are given in Dom R. J. Hesbert, *Le problème de la transfixion du Christ*, 1940 : The so-called Gospels of Francis II (Bibl. Nat. latin 257), c.850 ; The Angers Gospels, c.900 ; the Golden Altar (Paliotto) in the Ambrosian Basilica, Milan, prior to 835. Also the Gospels of Iviron, Mount Athos.—Bréhier, *Art chrétien*, p.158 ; and a fresco in St. Mark's, Venice, from which the scene in fig. ix. 6 has already been given.

Irish Crucifixions

The miniatures in Celtic manuscripts seem to us strange and even repulsive. The idea of geometrical pattern predominates ; even the human figure often becomes a decorative symbol as regards form and colour ; there is certainly no attempt at even rough anatomical accuracy. Painting has become absorbed in calligraphy ; the religious idea is expressed not by historical portrayal but in stylised contours. But, apart from these questions of aesthetics and technique, the themes are those found in contemporary and earlier art. This can be seen in the Crucifixion (fig. xii. 24) of the Irish Gospels in Saint-Gall (no. 51), probably of the eighth century, which Dom Leclercq[5] declares to be " worthy of the pencil or the brain of a contemporary cubist or dadaist." Though the miniaturist has deliberately eschewed realism, he has with his pen (not a

XII. 25.—From the Southampton Psalter in St. John's College, Cambridge

brush) put before us the scheme we have been considering : the living Christ being offered the drink and simultaneously having

[5] *Dict. d'arch. chr.* 6 (1924) 139.

His side (the *left* in this case) pierced.[6] Instead of sun and moon above, there are two angels, each holding a book. Christ's feet (utterly out of proportion) emerge from a series of convolutions ; there are nail-marks on the ankles. From His side there is a spurt of blood, represented by a zigzag line, on to the right eye of Longinus.

Figure xii. 25 is a sketch of the similar Crucifixion in the Southampton Psalter of St. John's College, Cambridge : an Irish MS. of uncertain date (9/10 century). The crudely inscribed stone slab of Iniskea (fig. xii. 26) shows the same essentials.

XII.   26.—Inscribed Slab, Iniskea, Co.
Mayo, Ireland

With these we may compare the illustration (fig. xii. 27) from a Syriac Evangelary in the British Museum,[7] which has resemblances to the Irish treatment. Note the ornamented dress, and Longinus at Christ's left side. But both the bandits and Christ are tied, not nailed.

As one of the famous high stone crosses[7a] of Ireland, that erected

---

[6] The interpolated verse in St. Matthew occurs in this Gospel-book.
[7] Add. MS. 7169, fol. 11v : Millet, fig. 447.
[7a] Discussion of the peculiar wheel-structure of these crosses is beyond my scope or competence. Prof. S. P. Ó Riordáin thinks that they were preceded by similarly shaped wooden crosses.—The Genesis of the Celtic Cross, *Féilscríbhinn Torna*, Cork 1947, pp.108-114. It may be worth while to draw attention to Gallic coins : " The most ancient coins of the Gauls were circular, with a cross in the middle ; little wheels, as it were, with four large perforations."—S. Baring-Gould, *Curious Myths of the Middle Ages*, new ed. 1901, p.348 (and illustrations, p.345).

by the Abbot Muiredach (✝ 923) at Monasterboice (17ft. 8 ins.
high) may be selected (figs. xii. 28, 29). There are about seventy
panels altogether with various scenes : Adam and Eve, Cain and
Abel, David and Goliath, Moses striking the rock, the meeting of
Saints Paul and Antony, etc. On one side of the wheel-centre is
Christ in glory presiding over the Last Judgement, and on the other
side (fig. xii. 29) is the Crucifixion. The figure appears nude owing
to the ravages of time ; the contours left suggest a short tunic. There
appear to be nail-marks in the palms, but the feet are tied. Christ is
depicted as alive, and the lance-man is at His left side. Two circular
knobs between the two men and the cross may stand for sun and
moon. Beyond them are two small figures, a woman and a man on
one knee (Mary and John?). Two angels support Christ's head,
and there is a small bird at the foot of the cross. Another example
(fig. xii. 30) from the West Cross of Monasterboice shows Our
Lord's feet tied, and His arms curved down to suit the conformation
of the stone ; neither here nor in the previous figure is there a trace
of the actual cross. Christ seems to be clothed, and there appear to
be ropes round the body.[7b]

XII.   27.—Crucifixion in a Syriac
Gospel-Book in the British Museum

[7b] Dom Louis Gougaud suggested a doubt whether " the sponge was known in
Ireland at the time these crucifixions were depicted."—*Jl. R. Soc. Antiq. of Ireland*
50 (1920) 136. In some of the Irish Passions (e.g. Atkinson, *Passions and Homilies
from the Leabhar Breac*, pp.134, 382) there is a foreign word *machdual* (from *mag-
dalium*?) used for the sponge, though *sponc* is found in Cormac's Glossary. In
Irish art the sponge is always in the form of a cup (in fig. xii. 26 it is two concentric
circles). But the cup-form is also found elsewhere, e.g. in the Perm crucifixion
(fig. xii. 13).

The Living Christ with Mary and John

We have already seen an example (fig. xii. 17) of the more intimate and devotional representation of Calvary, including only the Crucified with Our Lady and St. John. Some other examples will now be given. Figure xii. 31 shows a fresco (injured) in the subterannean church under the Basilica of San Clemente in Rome ; its date is uncertain ; probably it is one of the oldest frescos made under Leo IV (847/855). Christ is alive, Mary is appealing with both hands upraised, John stands with a roll in his left hand and with his right hand raised. There is a title above the cross, and traces of angels above the arms.

Figure xii. 32 shows a crudely carved ivory from the monastery of Rambona, now in the Vatican ; it is dated by an inscription A.D. 898. Reading downwards, we have successively. Two angels supporting a medallion of the glorified Christ blessing. Inscription : *Ego Sum IHS Nazarenus*, continued in the title : *Rex Iudeorum.* The sun and the moon personified are over the cross-beam. Christ is beardless and with long hair ; his arms and hands are in the position shown in Egbert's codex (figs. xii. 19 and 20) ; there is no trace of nails in the feet. Over Our Lady is written *Mulier En* ; over St. John, *Dissipule Ecce.* An original item in the composition is the figure of the she-wolf suckling Romulus and Remus : *Romulus et Remulus a lupa nutriti.*

A fresco (prior to 1100 A.D.) from the nave of the church of Sant' Angelo in Formis, near Capua, is shown in fig. xii. 33. The body of Christ is long and slender and He is standing on a foot-rest. A much superior presentation is in the fresco of Daphni (fig. xii. 34) of about the same date (1100). The scene displays antique calm and dignity. Our Lord (bearded) is alive and looking towards His Mother. His arms are not horizontal ;[8] His feet are nailed to a footrest ; the foot of the cross is fixed with three pegs. He *may* be wearing a narrow crown of thorns. Blood flows vertically from hands and feet ; it flows over Adam's skull at the foot of the cross.[9] Though Longinus is not shown the blood is depicted as spurting from his pierced side. There are traces of angels above the cross.

---

[8] The anatomy is imperfect. The deltoid muscle which should extend towards the arm rises towards the neck. The ventral surface is stylised in a threefold division.

[9] This is our first illustration of this widespread legend that Adam was buried beneath the cross ; this was probably due to identifying ' Calvary ' with the Place of [Adam's] Skull. It was held by Origen, Athanasius, Epiphanius, Basil, Chrysostom, Ambrose. It was rejected by Jerome and Bede. See Sir C. M. Watson, *Golgotha and the Holy Sepulchre*, 1906, app. iii, p.159.

The Dead Christ with Mary and John

There does not appear to have been any objection felt against portraying the Crucified as dead. He is so shown in a finely executed Byzantine triptych in the British Museum (tenth century) the central panel of which is shown in fig. xii. 35. Above the cross are Michael and Gabriel. Our Lord (bearded) has His feet nailed to a foot-rest.

In fig. xii. 36 we see portion of the apsidal mosaic of the Upper Church of San Clemente in Rome. It dates from Paschal II (1099/1118) or from shortly before the dedication (1128). This is the only surviving crucifix in Roman apsidal mosaics. God's hand reaches down, holding a wreath, as it were letting down the cross which takes root in the earth amid luxuriant foliage, where the four streams of Paradise spring and spread right and left. The twelve doves ranged along the cross signify the apostles.

Figure xii. 37 shows the carved ivory cover of the Augsburg Evangelary, now in Munich (perhaps of the 10th century). Notice the personified weeping sun and moon, the title with INRI, the bandits with their hands tied behind their crosses.

(6) The Dead Christ with Church and Synagogue

The Dead Christ was represented when the allegorical figures of Church and Synagogue were introduced to the scene. In the Sacramentary of Drogo bishop of Metz, written 825 /855, now in the Bibliothèque Nationale, the initial O for Palm Sunday contains a

XII. 38.—Sketch in Drogo's Sacramentary (c. 850)   *Cahier*

sketch of Calvary (fig. xii. 38). Here besides Mary and John we see two other figures. The Church, bearing a standard, is receiving in a chalice the blood gushing from the right side of the dead Christ. On the other side is apparently a bearded Jew with hand raised. Note the serpent coiled at the foot of the cross.

In the 9th century Metz ivory[1] shown in fig. xii. 39 there are a number of allegorical figures in addition to the historical. Reading from above down, we have : (1) The sun and moon, the four evangelists seated and writing with angel, eagle, lion and ox respectively. (2) On the beholder's left are Mary and John with Longinus ; on the right, the Synagogue with back to the cross and the Church seated before a city, also the sponge-bearer. (3) Two small circular tombs with the dead emerging. (4) Ocean (personified) on the seashore and Earth holding two children, between them Faith in the form of a woman gazing up at the cross. Christ (bearded) has his eyes closed in death.

XII. 40.—Illustration from the *Hortus Deliciarum* (12th century).   *Cahier*

Allegory is carried very far in fig. xii. 40, an illustration (with the inserted texts omitted) from the twelfth century *Hortus Deliciarum* the original of which was burnt in Strasbourg in 1870. The his-

[1] Bibl. Nat. ms. lat. 9383; *Dict. d'euch. chr.* fig. 8027.

torical personages are present : Our Lady, St. John, the lance-man, the sponge-bearer, the two bandits. Above, in addition to sun and moon, we see the torn veil of the temple. The triumphant Church, receiving the blood in the chalice,[2] rides on the beast of the Apocalypse, and the discomfited Synagogue is shown seated on Balaam's ass. Beneath is Adam's grave, and the dead are rising.

In fig. xii. 41, from a window in Bourges Cathedral (13th century), we again see the Church with the chalice as well as the blindfolded Synagogue. The Psalter of Queen Ingeburga († 1236) contains a miniature of the Crucifixion (fig. xii. 42). On one side are Our Lady and the Church, on the other are St. John and the Synagogue. The arms of Christ are at an angle, and His body is slightly curved to the right.

(7) The Dead Christ with Mary and John

In representations of the Scene on Calvary this allegorism did not win a permanent place in Christian art. So we can now resume our study of the small group M † J. This concentration on the Crucified Christ, with His two devoted adorers, has continued to have a devotional and artistic appeal. The beginnings of the modern treatment can be traced back to the eleventh century. Figure xii. 43 exhibits a miniature from manuscript 376 of St. Gall,[1] a Greek liturgy written in Latin characters between 1022 and 1034. Our Lord's head is turned to the right, His eyes are closed and there is an expression of suffering on His face.

Figure xii. 44 reproduces the Crucifixion in a 12th century window of Chartres Cathedral. Our Lord's eyes are closed, His body is arched, though the arms are horizontal.

Figure xii. 45 is an illustration from the Psalter of Blanche of Castille and of St. Louis (early in the 13th century). (The Church and the Synagogue, in side circles, are omitted.) Notice that the

---

[2] This is connected with the legend of the vase of Joseph of Arimathea, the holy Graal of Perceval and the Knights of the Round Table. Joseph " honoured the body the most he might, rather laid it along in the holy sepulchre, and kept safe the lance whereof He was smitten in the side and the most holy vessel wherein they that believed on Him received with awe the blood that ran down from His wounds when He was upon the rood."—*The High History of the Holy Graal*, trans. from the Old French by Sebastian Evans, (Everyman's Library), p.2. The cup was identified with that used at the Last Supper,

[1] *Revue archéol.*, 1919, plate ii (4) ; *Dict. d'arch. chr.* 6 (1924) 142, fig. 4818.

arms go upward at an angle, and that the body is arched towards the right. The figure thus becomes more supple and suggestive of suffering.

XII. 43.—Crucifixion in a Saint-Gall Manuscript
(c. 1030)

In the thirteenth century, for some reason not explained, artists began to represent the feet as pierced with one nail, while continuing

XII. 44.—From a Window of Chartres Cathedral
(12th century)   *Lassus*

to show the foot-rest.[2] One of the earliest examples is shown in fig. xii. 46, from the Psalter of Hermann of Thuringia (prior to 1217), now in the Staatsbibliothek, Stuttgart.[3] The old symbolic figures are moved out ; the Church is above and the Synagogue underneath. The one nail helps to accentuate the expression of suffering ; there is no longer any suggestion of a rigid figure standing on a platform. Another example is seen in fig. xii. 47, a Crucifixion (about 1250) in St. Alban's Cathedral, England.[4] There is here a considerable advance in drawing and characterisation. Observe that the cross is made of tree-trunks; also there is no foot-rest, and one large spike goes through the crossed feet. In fig. xii. 48 we see a painting of about a century later, by Dietrich of Prague (c. 1365).

It is worth while recording a curious suggestion to account for the transition from four to three nails. There is a widely spread legend—found in Lesbos, Alsace, Lithuania, among the Slavs and even in Scotland—that a gypsy forged the nails for the Crucifixion and thus brought a curse on his race.—Francis Hindes Groome, *Gypsy Folk-Tales*, 1899, p.xxvii. This author quotes a plaint of Our Lady current in Lesbos, from Georgeakis and Pineau, *Le folklore de Lesbos*, 1891, p.273. John in tears came to her with a bloodstained cloth : " These miserable Jews have arrested my Master." On recovering from the shock, she went to see the Jews and found a nailmaker forging the nails : "The Jews have ordered four nails from me, but I am making five . . . They will put two nails in His feet, two others in His hands ; and the other, the sharpest, will pierce His lung." Our Lady swooned, and then predicted a curse for the Tziganes. The gypsies seem to have invented a counter-legend in self-defence. This comes from Alsace : There were two Jews, brothers. One rejoiced at the Crucifixion ; the other tried to save Christ, he did his best by stealing one of the four nails, so that the feet had to be fastened by a single nail. Another version is this : a gypsy woman stole one of the nails. " That is why," said an Alsatian gypsy woman, " Jesus gave the Manousch leave to steal every seven years !" These legends may be ancient. Hence Groome (p.xxx) suggests : " This gypsy counter-legend offers a possible explanation of the hitherto unexplained transition from four nails to three in crucifixes during the twelfth and thirteenth centuries." It is well known that for centuries the gypsies, especially in Eastern

[2] There was opposition. Bishop Lucas of Tuy about 1239 reproached the Albigensians for representing the cross as a T and putting one nail through the feet.—De la Bigne, *Max. bibl. patrum* xxv. 223. See above, p.162.
[3] Haseloff, fig. 15. See note 9, p.4, above.
[4] Borenius and Tristram, *English Medieval Painting*, 1927, plate 14. " The advent of Gothic art is here very definitely proclaimed by the incomparably greater softness and flexibility of line and gentleness of movement and expression " (p.8).

Europe, possessed a monopoly of metal-work. The guess is that the three-nail scheme originated in copper crucifixes made by Byzantine gypsies. Du Cange in his Greek Glossary identifies *komodromoi* (a Greek word literally meaning village-wanderers) with gypsy metal-workers and quotes a phrase from some Greek work on the Passion: "when they arrive at the place, the *komodromos* coming to crucify Him."

The aspect of pain in Christ, and of grief in Mary and John, became greatly emphasised in the fifteenth century. This is shown in the painting by Jan Van Eyck (c.1385-1440), now in the Berlin Gallery (fig. xii. 49). The cross is higher in the next picture by Carlo Crivelli (c.1480) in the Brera, Milan (fig. xii. 50). Both in different ways express the suffering of Christ and the grief of His two faithful ones. In fig. xii. 51, a painting[5] from the school of Champagne (c.1460), the body of Christ is emaciated as well as drenched with blood. (Notice the kneeling figure of the donor.) Figure xii. 52 presents a hideous and gruesome picture of Christ with leprous flesh and expanded thorax. This brutal exaggeration is typical of Grünewald († 1528). This illustration is from his altarpiece at Isenheim.[6]

There is a beautiful picture by Cima da Conigliano (c.1460-c.1517) in the Barber Institute of Fine Arts, Birmingham (fig. xii. 53). He has introduced a spacious background containing the agony in Gethsemani, Peter's denial and the Ecce Homo. Our Lady and St. John show sorrow with dignity. Our Lord is calm and peaceful in death.

To these may be added two later pictures which lack religious feeling. Figure xii. 54, by Simon Vouet (1590-1649), shows a muscular man, as it were standing on a platform and looking down on the bystanders who include His fainting Mother. The modern picture by Franz von Stuck (fig. xii. 55) is better, but too theatrical to be devotional.

(8) The Development of the Crucifix

The artistic evolution of the crucifix[1]—that is the embroidered, the painted or carved image of the Crucified without accompanying figures—was slower than but parallel with the development of

---

[5] Noguier de Malijay, p.42.
[6] Another similar Crucifixion by the same artist is reproduced in my *Family at Bethany*, fig. 40.
[1] The earliest instance of the word *crucifixum* (i.e. the image, not the *Crucifixus*) quoted in Ducange is dated 877—*Glossarium* 2 (1842) 672.

representations of Calvary-groups ; or at least fewer specimens have survived from early times.

The Robed Christ

Figure xii. 56 shows a design on an embroidered vestment from Akhmin-Panoplis in Egypt (6th century).[2] The cross is probably T-shaped and there is a foot-rest ; at the side there are two ornamental plants ; above are the sun and moon. The striped robe has some similarity with Irish representations. Among the objects (now at Monza) presented by St. Gregory to the Lombard Queen Theodelind (✝ 628) is a rock-crystal with gold niello work (fig. xii. 57)[3] Christ, youthful and clad in a long armless robe, has His feet nailed to a foot-rest. Above are sun and moon ; there is a title with ICX ; and under the arms of the cross are written in Greek the words addressed to Our Lady and to St. John, who are represented by two diminutive figures at the ends of the transverse bar.

In fig. xii. 58 we see a similar but more developed crucifix (bronze reliquary) now in the Vatican Museum ;[4] its date is uncertain, perhaps about 750. On the reverse side Our Lady with the Infant on her knees is represented, with the legend *hé Hagia Theotokos* (the Holy Mother of God) ; and at the corners are the medallions of the four evangelists. On the other side we have the usual features : sun and moon, title (with X), sleeveless robe, foot-rest, Mary and John at the ends of the cross-arm. But Christ is bearded and has long hair, His head is inclined slightly to the right, and He is dead.

We now come to the most famous of medieval crucifixes, the Santo Volto of Lucca in carved and painted cedar-wood (fig. xii. 59).[5] Legend says that it was made by Nicodemus ; its date is

---

[2] R. Forrer, *Reallexicon*, 1907, p.427 ; *Dict. d'arch. chr.* fig. 3426. There are many reasons for seeing a connection between Christian Irish and Eastern (particularly Egyptian) art.
[3] *Dict. d'arch. chr.* fig. 3379.
[4] *Ann. archéol.* 26 (1869) 142.
[5] This is a drawing made by Garrucci in 1880 (plate 432), without the superadded clothes, crown or silver slippers. The Latin *vultus*—Italian *volto*; French *vou, voult*—was applied to any image—DuCange, *Glossarium* 6 (1846) 899. William Rufus used, according to Eadmer, to swear by the Holy Image of Lucca. Père Gaffre (p.166f) says that the alleged 14th century painter of the Shroud may have been inspired by this face (which he calls Jewish), which is " among the documents giving us the most exact information on the traditional physiognomy of the Saviour." All this is pure fantasy.
The Volto Santo, as shown to the public, has a long velvet robe, embroidered and jewelled ; a maniple on each sleeve ; an elaborate gold crown on the head ; slippers on the feet ; and there is a chalice placed beneath the right foot.

difficult to estimate, perhaps of the eighth or ninth century. Pilgrims took away figurine-replicas in clay or lead ; there are many crucifixes modelled on it in France, e.g. the Saint-Sauve (12th century) in the Cathedral of Amiens. The head is bowed but the eyes are open ; the hair is long and the beard forked. The loose pleated robe, which has sleeves, is kept together with a cincture.

A curious legend seems to have originated in the Netherlands in the fifteenth century ; it is probably due to a misinterpretation of the Santo Volto or its copies, especially the long robe which in later times seemed incongruous on Our Lord. There are still extant crosses with the crowned and crucified figure of a bearded woman, who was known by various names. The original Dutch designation was Ontkommer, which was turned into Kümmernis in Upper Germany ; other names were Liberata, Hülpe, etc. ; finally Wilgefortis (from *virgo fortis*) became the woman's official name. The legend was that the Christian daughter of a pagan king of Portugal refused to marry the king of Sicily. She asked God to make her ugly, so she grew a beard. Finally her father decided that she should die like Christ. Her feast was inserted in the Roman Martyrology for 20 July, though Papebroch and other Bollandists refuted the legend. See G. Schnürer, (i) Die Kümmernisbilder als Kopien des Volto Santo, *Jahresbericht der Görresgesellschaft*, 1901, pp.43ff ; (2) Die ältesten Legenden der hl. Kümmernis, *Festschrift G. von Hertling*, 1913, pp.96-107.

The Skirted Christ

Figure xii. 60 shows a Byzantine reliquary in cloisonné enamel from Mount Athos (tenth century)[6]. In this Christ (bearded) is portrayed as dead. In fig. xii. 61 is seen a wooden crucifix carved with bold strokes and with considerable anatomical accuracy. This is Gero's Crucifix in the Church of St. George, Cologne. It is generally dated in the tenth century ; but it surely must be of the eleventh or later. The face is beardless ; the hair falls over the shoulders and in front is carved as if it were a close-fitting cap. Whatever date we assign, this crucifix has a very ' modern ' note.

A very different type is the painted crucifix (fig. xii. 62), which is said to have spoken to St. Francis in San Damiano, Assisi. Such crucifixes, of a Byzantine type, were common in Italy in the early thirteenth century. (Note the diminutive Longinus piercing the side of the living Christ.)

[6] In the collection of Sébastianoff : Lacroix, *Les arts au moyen âge*, 1873[4], p.133.

The Later Carved Crucifix

It will be observed already that there was developed a much greater individuality of treatment in the case of the crucifix than for Crucifixion scenes. This will be illustrated in some further selected examples.

Figure xii. 63 shows a graceful carved wooden crucifix in Innsbruck (1150/1200).[7] Quite different from the straight hieratic pose of this crucifix, is the pain-expressing posture of the painted wooden figure (twelfth century French), known as Courajod's crucifix, now in the Louvre, Paris (fig. xii. 64). The fourteenth century Italian crucifix shown in fig. xii. 65 has the figure in an entirely different position. The body hangs from the hands, the head is bent forward, the knees are protruding, and there is one large spike through the feet. Again different is the position of the figure on the ivory crucifix made for the 'Black Penitents of Mercy' in 1659 by Jean Guillermin (fig. xii. 66), now in Avignon Museum. Christ is alive and suffering ; also He is wearing a small crown of thorns made of three interlacing branches chiselled in the ivory.

XII. 66a.—Scheme of Four Crucifixes

The variations in posture of these four crucifix-figures are shown schematically in the subjoined diagram.

Figure xii. 67 shows a crucifix by Montanes (1580-1649) in the Cathedral of Seville. The thorn-crowned head falls forward and to the right ; the two feet are crossed, each being nailed separately.[8]

Four contemporary carved crucifixes will finally be adduced to show variety of treatment.

Figure xii. 68 : a crucifix by Canonica, in the Church of S. Cuore di Maria, Turin.[9]

Figure xii. 69 : a crucifix by the French sculptor Iché.[10]

[7] Geza de Francovich, *Scultura medioevale in legno*, 1943, fig. 56.
[8] As in St. Bridget's *Revelations* (i. 10).
[9] Costantini, p.164.
[10] *Cahiers de l'art sacré* 3 (1945) 45.
[11] Frances Crane Lillie, *Examples of Religious Art*, Chicago 1936.

Figure xii. 70 : the twelfth Station of the Cross by Alfeo Faggi, in the Church of St. Thomas the Apostle in Chicago.[11]

Figure xii. 71 : a wooden crucifix carved in the African style by Peter Vervesi of West Cameroon.[12]

Some Painted Crucifixes

Four specimens of paintings of the Crucified are added. Their variety and their details of treatment will be clear without comment.[13]

Figure xii. 72 : A painting by Guido Reni (1595-1642) in San Lorenzo in Lucina, Rome.

Figure xii. 73 : This is the famous painting by Diego Velazquez (1599-1660), in Madrid.

Figure xii. 74: The painting by Léon Bonnat (1874), in the Petit Palais, Paris.

Figure xii. 75 : A painting by Georges Rouault.[14]

(9) The Panorama of Calvary

The Renascence painters enlarged the presentation of the Crucifixion by re-admitting the figures which appeared in earlier art and by adding more—women, soldiers, Jews—so that the world seems crowded at the foot of the Cross. One of the earliest is Nicola Pisano (c.1206-1278) whose sculptured panel on the pulpit in the Baptistery of Pisa is shown in fig. xii. 76. Though older elements are retained—busts of sun and moon, angels, Adam's skull—the scene is now crowded with friends and foes, massed together in a way reminiscent of late Roman sarcophagi.

The Calvary of Giotto (✝ 1336) in the lower Basilica of St. Francis in Assisi (fig. xii. 77) is a great achievement. To Christ's right is St. John and the group of faithful women ; Our Lady is depicted as having fainted ; while Magdalen is kissing Christ's feet. On His right is a crowd of Jews retiring, while St. Francis and

---

[12] *Illustriete. Zeitung*, 25 March 1937. At first the non-African is perplexed at such carvings. The native style is to divide the human figure into distinct sections usually marked off by a groove or a hollow.—P. Guillaume and T. Munro, *Primitive Negro Sculpture*, 1926, p.35.

[13] The painting by Van Dyck has already been reproduced (fig. x. 20).

[14] A sophisticated attempt to return to primitivism, or perhaps an imitation of stained glass.

his first companions are approaching. Christ's head is bent and his eyes are closed (see fig. vii. 51) in calm dignity ; the arms are no longer horizontal, and His feet are fixed with one nail to the foot-rest. After the rather brutal art of 14th century Germany, we have here a more spiritual conception. The historical scene is suffused with the supernatural ; the angels are seen hovering in grief or collecting the Precious Blood ; the friars break the barriers of time to pay homage to the Crucified.[1]

Figure xii. 78 shows a panel of Duccio's altarpiece in Siena Cathedral (1311). This is a more dramatic but less peacefully devotional rendering. There are two antagonistic crowds, the holy women with St. John and the now friendly soldiers on one side, the fiercely hostile Jews on the other ; humanity is divided by the Crucified. There are three lofty crosses ; Our Lord hangs considerably below the crossbeam ; blood is spurting from His side.

Figure xii. 79 shows the central panel of the altarpiece of Narbonne, now in the Louvre. It is a rectangular piece of white silk, painted in grey tones between 1364 and 1377, perhaps by John of Orleans, painter to Charles V whose kneeling figure is in a panel at the dexter side while his wife is on the opposite. The drawing is angular and awkward, but it is full of religious fervour. In spite of the crowded figures, Christ dominates the scene ; the two bandits are subordinated by being relegated to the second plane. This is one of the first instances of a truly thorn-crowned figure in France. Angels collect the blood in chalices ; there are seraphim in the cusped arches above ; and over the cross is a pelican drawing from her breast sustenance for her young.

Figure xii. 80 is a German Calvary, by Hans Pleydenwurff (c. 1460). The figure of Christ is thickset (as in xii. 48), and the crowd lacks unity or reference to the Crucified. A German town can be seen in the background.

In fig. xii. 81 we see the Calvary painted in 1459 by Andrea Mantegna (1431-1506) for the church of St. Zeno in Verona ; it is now in the Louvre. (The figure of St. John in the left foreground is traditionally regarded as Mantegna himself). There is here a great advance in realistic portraiture, in spite of the fantastic landscape at the back ; the figures stand out with statuesque distinctness. On Our Lord's right are the holy women, with the Blessed Virgin swooning and John desolate. Uninterested soldiers are coming up

[1] There is a larger reproduction in *The Family at Bethany*, fig. 36.

and down the steps at the rear, while others are dicing for His clothes. In spite of the accurate drawing and the effort at historical exactness for the figures, the painting lacks the spirituality of Giotto or Fra Angelico.

Omitting later painters such as Veronese and Tintoretto, we shall end our survey by reproducing two pictures which place the Crucified in a modern setting, and thus bring home to us the eternal significance of Calvary.

In fig. xii. 82 Ignacio Zuloaga brings five present-day Spaniards, sadly thoughtful and reverential, before the Cross which is planted in the Spanish countryside.

Figure xii. 83 shows the painting made by Albert Besnard for the Hospital of Berck. Here the Cross is set up in a factory district and surrounded by working-class people. *O vos omnes qui transitis per viam* !

CHAPTER XIII

CHRIST'S DEATH AND TRANSFIXION

(1) Christ's Voluntary Death

THE Evangelists, though using different expressions, agree that Our Lord's death was accompanied by a loud cry and that it was voluntary. According to St. Mark (15^{39}), " when the centurion saw that it was after so crying out (*kraxas*) that He expired, he said : Truly this man was Son of God." He heard the words of the loud cry, recorded by St. Luke as : " Father, into Your hands I commend My spirit." If he did not understand Aramaic, he must have asked the meaning from a bystander. He had seen the patience of the Crucified, the darkness which now cleared off, the earthquake, the death with a confident appeal to God as Father. The Jews had been saying : If You are the Son of God, come down from the cross. When this pagan saw Him dying, still on the gibbet, he exclaimed : Truly He is the Son of God.

Mark and Luke say : He expired (*exepneusen*). Matthew : He dismissed (*aphēken*) His spirit. John : He gave up (*paredōken*) His spirit, i.e. He entrusted His soul to His Father. None of them says simply : He died (*ethanen*). St. John (10^{18}) had already quoted Our Lord as saying :

> My Father loves Me because I shall lay down My life, that I may take it up again. No one will take it from Me, but of Myself I will lay it down. I have power to lay it down, I also have power to take it up again. This is the command which I have received from My Father.

Accordingly we find in the Fathers and early writers strong emphasis on the voluntary nature of Christ's death.

> Perhaps He hastened His departure from the body so that He might preserve it and so that His legs should not be broken as were those of the bandits who were crucified with Him.—Origen, *Contra Celsum* ii. 16.
>
> After crying with a loud voice, He gave up the ghost, thus forestalling the executioners who break the legs of those crucified in order that their punishment may not be further prolonged.— *Ibid.* iii. 32.
>
> Nailed to the cross, He showed many signs by which His

death was distinguished from that of others. For with a word,
of His own will (*sponte cum verbo*), He dismissed His spirit, thus
forestalling the executioner's task.—Tertullian, *Apol.* 21, 19.

His death was not the common death of all men. For He
was not destroyed by disease nor by the cord nor by fire ; nor
even on the trophy of the cross were His legs cut with steel like
those of the others who were evil-doers. Neither, in a word, did
He reach His end by suffering from any man any of the usual
forms of violence which destroy life. But as if He were only handing His life over willingly to those who plotted against His body,
as soon as He was raised from the earth He gave a cry upon the
tree and commended His spirit to His father, saying these words :
Father into Thy hands I commend My spirit. Thus uncompelled
and of His own free will He departed from the body.—Eusebius,
Dem. Evang. iii. 4 (108c), trans. Ferrar, 1920, i. 125.

He gave up His life not unwillingly, but because He willed,
when He willed, how He willed.—St. Augustine, *De Trinitate*
iv. 16.

Who so sleeps when he wishes, as Jesus died when He willed?
Who so takes off a garment when he wishes, as He frees Himself
from the flesh when He wills? Who so goes away as He when
He willed passed away (*obiit*)? What great power can be hoped
for in Him when He judges, if such great power appeared in Him
when dying?—St. Augustine, *In Ioann.* 119, 6 : PL. 35. 1952.

To expire does not come after bowing the head ; but here on
the contrary it does. For he did not, as happens in our case, bow
His head after expiring ; but He expired after He had bowed His
head. By this the Evangelist has shown that He was Lord of all.—
St. John Chrysostom, *In Ioann.* hom. 85, 3.

In order to clarify these assertions, it will be useful to quote St.
Thomas Aquinas :

Since Christ was true God as well as man, whatever concerned
human nature in Christ was subject to His power. This is not
true for mere men, since natural things are not subject to their
will . . . A violent death occurs because nature yields to the injury
inflicted ; death is delayed so long as nature can resist ; hence
other things being equal, death is delayed longer in the case of
those with a stronger nature. But when nature was to resist
injury inflicted, and when it was to yield, was subject to Christ's
will. Hence, He so willing, nature resisted injury to the end more
than was possible for other men ; so that at the end after much
effusion of blood, He cried out with a loud voice, as if His strength
was unimpaired. And, He so willing, nature immediately
yielded and gave up the ghost, to show that He was Lord of
nature, life and death . . . Accordingly the Jews killed Christ by
inflicting mortal injury on Him, and yet also He Himself laid
down His life and gave up the ghost, because, when He willed,

nature yielded completely to the injury inflicted.—*Quodlibet* 1, art. 3.

Hence we must not so interpret the early writers as to make Our Lord's death self-inflicted or to regard it as without physical cause.[1] In the Gospels His sufferings and His death are constantly described as inflicted by men. The Word having assumed mortal humanity, the injuries done to Him should naturally cause death. Yet by His divine power He could have mastered these death-dealing causes. But He did not choose to do so. Hence His death was both voluntary and natural. He did not inflict it on Himself but He allowed it to be inflicted on Him by others. He even positively offered up His life for our redemption ; He was priest as well as victim.

St. Thomas seems to imply that Christ's death was deferred until He gave leave to natural agencies to act. Our difficulty to-day, like Pilate's surprise, is rather that He succumbed so quickly. We are not thereby entitled to say that He miraculously kept death at bay. We must accept the logical consequences of the Incarnation. Especially owing to the extreme danger of Arianism, many of the Fathers hesitated to admit the fullness of Christ's interior suffering, in particular His shrinking from crucifixion and death. Thus St. Ambrose :

> For me He grieved who for Himself had no cause for grief . . .
> You are grieved, Lord, not for Your wounds but for mine . . . He
> seemed and was really sad, not for His own Passion but for
> our going astray .—*In Lucam* x. 1 : *P.L.* 15. 1817.

And as regards suffering inflicted from outside, the early writers emphasised Our Lord's divine concurrence and His absolute power to suspend nature. This is very true. Blessed Angela of Foligno († 1309), in meditating on the Passion, is amazed that created things—the thorns, the nails, the cross, the lance—were divinely empowered to act against the Son of God.[2] But act they did. *De potentia absoluta* He could have thwarted His enemies and deprived natural agencies of their activity, as He had often done before. But He morally foreclosed this power when at the Last Supper He handed Himself over to death and offered Himself for

---

[1] " Under these circumstances it may not be fitting to speculate on the physical cause of the Lord's death."—Westcott, *Gospel of St. John*, 1908, ii. 317.

[2] " The Creator so humbled Himself for love of us that . . . He gave to irrational and insensible creatures the power to do their task fully against Him . . . To the thorns He gave power to pierce cruelly His divine head."—P. Doncœur, *Le livre de la b. Sœur Angèle de Foligno*, 1926, p.307.

our redemption.[3] And so in Gethsemani He had to drink the chalice of death to which He had vowed Himself. Even here, before the Passion proper, we see the unique paradox of the Christian mystery. The agonising prayer, the blood-sweat, the need of help from an angel. What a pathetic tribute to His humanity, so utterly beyond man's anticipation or invention. Yet it was deliberately and voluntarily undertaken. He went to the garden as usual, " knowing all that was to happen to Him." He could have sought safer refuge for the night. Humanly speaking, at the last moment He could have escaped, His retreat would be covered by His followers. But He advanced to meet the party. He prevented Peter from starting a fight. Then He showed His power by momentarily overthrowing those who had come to arrest Him and by healing the wounded ear of Malchus. He made it plain that His submission was not from want of power. He told Peter that, had He so wished, twelve legions of angels were at His beck. But He who healed the temple-servant's wound accepted His own grievous wounds ; no angelic host, such as appeared to the shepherds near Bethlehem, was seen on Calvary or rescued Him from the cross. He was taunted : He saved others, Himself He cannot save. How true the paradox ! For it was by the self-surrender, not of impotence but of love, that He saved us. " He has loved me and delivered Himself up for me " (Gal. 2[20]).

The pagan, no more than the Jew, could not understand Calvary :

> Why did not Christ utter anything worthy of one who was wise and divine, when brought either before the high priest or before the governor? He might have given instruction to His judge and those who stood by and made them better men. But He endured to be smitten with a reed and spat on and crowned with thorns— unlike Apollonius who, after speaking boldly to the Emperor Domitian, disappeared from the royal court and after not many hours was plainly seen in the city then called Dicaearchia but now Puteoli. But even if Christ had to suffer according to God's commands and was obliged to endure punishment, yet at least He should have endured His Passion with some boldness and uttered words of force and wisdom to Pilate His judge, instead of being mocked like any guttersnipe.—The Pagan Philosopher (Heraclius) in Macarius Magnes, *Apocriticus* (c. 250) iii. 1 : trans. Crafer, 1919, p.52.

But the ultimate creed of paganism is represented, not by the legendary exploits of the post-christian Apollonius of Tyana, but

---

[3] On Christ's obligation to submit to death, see M. de la Taille S.J., *The Mystery of Faith*, Eng. trans., 1 (1941) 123-135.

by Prometheus on his rock. This is the sublimest yet most despondent spectacle imagined in ancient literature : the Titan, chained to the mountainside in age-long torments, too mighty to be crushed by Zeus the Thunderer at whom he hurls defiance. Yet in the last resort both gods above and men below are subject to Fate, grim Ananke, the forerunner of to-day's materialist determinism. Man may rail at fate, but he cannot escape it.

When we turn from the legend of the Caucasus to the reality of Golgotha, we see a new world-view : power coexistent with loving submission in a climax of voluntary dedication. The Figure lifted on the Cross released humanity from its thraldom to sin, to demonic forces, to pitiless fate, even to death itself. Christ died that " He might deliver all those who through fear of death were all their lifetime subject to bondage " (Heb. 2[15]). He who multiplied loaves, subdued storms and ousted disease, submitted to be whipped, nailed and pierced. Wicked men were allowed to wreak their worst on Him while legions of angels stood by unsummoned. And all this for us men and for our salvation, by a sheer gratuitous overplus of love. " Why did He wish to die such a death? . . . To draw us to love of Himself. The worse the death He underwent for us, the more we ought to love Him."[4]

There is a text in St. Paul's Epistle to the Philippians (2[6]) which seems relevant to this issue : " Christ Jesus, though truly God, . . . emptied Himself (ekenōsen, exinanivit), taking the status of a slave, and . . . humiliated Himself by obedience unto death, even to death upon a cross." The ordinary interpretation takes as subject the Word, the Eternal Son of God, and refers the ' emptying ' to the Incarnation.[5] But it seems more in accord with St. Paul's thought to take the Incarnate Word as subject and to refer the ' emptying ' not to the Incarnation but to the humiliations of the incarnate life and to the Redemption.[6] Christ, who was God, did not cling to the rights conferred on His human nature by His personal (hypostatic) union with God. He gave up these privileges to take up the position of a slave, a man like us. And He, who had the right not to die, died for us, He even accepted death by crucifixion. That is why God has bestowed on Him the Name which is above every other name, and

---

[4] Hugo of St. Victor, Summa sententiarum i. 18 : P.L. 176. 780.
[5] There is a Protestant ' kenotic ' interpretation, the theory (against all tradition and theology) that the Word divested Himself of His eternal glory during the period of His mortal life : emptying instead of veiling.
[6] E. Masure, Revue apol. 39 (1924) 328.

every tongue should proclaim that Jesus Christ is Lord.

Thus Christ's death was voluntary in a sense applicable to no other death. Not that it was not due to natural causes, but that He concurred with these causes and voluntarily allowed them to operate.

(2) The Physical Cause of Death

The *fact* of Our Lord's death is in no way dependent on our being able to-day to make an accurate diagnosis. None of the deaths recorded in ancient history was accompanied by a scientific diagnosis or an autopsy. Nor was such necessary for certainty to be had by relatives, soldiers or executioners. So in a sense any present-day investigation into the death of Christ is not only unnecessary for our faith but irrelevant for our devotion. Yet no details of His life or death are without interest and significance. The reverent studies made by medical men help us to appreciate Our Lord's full humanity and the terrible reality of crucifixion. These we will now consider, reserving further details for the next chapter which deals with the piercing of the side after death.

For convenience a brief bibliography is here given :

Dr. P. Barbet, La Passion corporelle de Jésus, *La vie spirituelle,* 1st Feb. 1940, pp.113-133 ; also published as a separate pamphlet, 1940.

Rev. W. Hanna, *The Last Days of Our Lord's Passion,* 1863', pp.290-314, 333-343.

Rev. S. Haughton, M.D., Note in the Speaker's *Bible, N.T.* 4 (1881) 349f, reprinted from the *Church Q.R.,* January, 1880.

R. W. Hynek, M.D., (1) *Science and the Holy Shroud,* Eng. trans., 1936, pp.72-92. (2) *Golgotha, Wissenschaft und Mystik,* 1936, pp.146ff.

Dr. E. Le Bec, The Death of the Cross, *Catholic Medical Guardian* 3 (1925) 126-132.
This is a translation of: Le supplice de la croix, *Revue de philosophie* 30 (1923) 131-143. The translation is also in a separate pamphlet : *The Death of the Cross,* 1926.

Dr. Hermann Mödder, Die Todesursache bei der Kreuzigung—*Stimmen der Zeit* 144 (1949) 50-59.

Sir Alex. Simpson, M.D., The Broken Heart of Jesus, *Expositor* 2 (1911) 310-321.

W. Stroud, M.D., *The Physical Cause of the Death of Christ,* 1847.

J. Ryland Whitaker, S.J., M.B., The Physical Cause of the Death of Our Lord, *Catholic Medical Guardian* 13 (1935) 83-91.

The suspension of the victim on the cross was fraught with serious organic repercussions, apart altogether from wounds or blood-loss. Hanging by the arms was a special punishment sometimes inflicted on Christians, as we know from the testimony of an eye-witness, Phileas of Thmuis:

> Some, with both hands tied behind them, were suspended on the rack (*xylon*), and with the aid of mechanical contrivances they were stretched in every limb . . . Others were attached to the porch by one hand and raised aloft ; and in the tension of their joints and limbs they experienced unequalled agony. Others were bound with their face towards pillars, without their feet touching the ground ; and thus their bonds were drawn tight by the pressure of the body-weight upon them. And this they used to endure not merely while the governor conversed or was engaged with them, but almost throughout the whole day.—Eusebius, *H.E.* viii. 10, 5.

It is amazing that such torture could, without fatal effects, be endured for nearly a day. In later times some Catholic martyrs under Henry VIII were subjected to similar but more prolonged suffering. In 1535 three Carthusian priests were imprisoned for a whole fortnight in the Marshalsea prison, London:

> There they were threatened, tortured and ill-used by men devoid of humanity and utter strangers to all good feeling. Round their necks were chains of iron, their legs were bound by fetters. They were savagely chained to pillars ; and lest a limb left free might help them ever so little, their hands were tightly tied. In this new and cruel form of martyrdom they spent two whole weeks, supporting a heavy weight of iron and stiffened by the strains of their bonds. Night and day without a pause they stood erect and motionless, nor was the slightest relaxation granted for any bodily need.—Dom Maurice Chauncy, *The Passion and Martyrdom of the Holy English Carthusian Fathers* (1570), ed. Curtis, 1935, p.101.

Fathers Middlemore, Exmewe and Newdigate were thus kept for seventeen days, not suspended but standing bolt upright, fastened to pillars by iron collars round their necks and with their legs fastened with great iron bolts. They survived this treatment, and were butchered at Tyburn on 19 June 1535.

Two years later ten other Carthusians—who refused to acknowledge Henry VIII as Peter's successor—were similarly treated in Newgate prison, but this time they were left to their fate. For many days they were helped by Margaret Gigs (Mrs. Clement), St. Thomas More's adopted daughter, who bribed the gaoler ; she put food into their mouths and cleaned them ; but soon she was refused admission. There they stood chained, starved and dirty, all through the summer[1]. The torture started on 26 May 1537, and by 20 September all but one had—as one of Henry's clerics put it—been "despatched by the hand of God." The tenth, a laybrother, recovered ; he continued in prison and was executed at Tyburn on 4 August, 1540.

These examples of martyrdom show that a man can survive a considerable time when fixed in a standing position, provided the feet are supported. But actual suspension by the hands can be borne for only a short time. Dr. Hynek (i. 80 ; ii. 174) refers to the punishment of tying-up (*aufbinden*) practised in the Austrian army. The soldier was roped to a tree so that only the tips of his feet reached the ground ; this ordeal was continued only for five, at the outside ten, minutes. A young man, standing on feet-tips and holding his arms high, can hardly endure the agony longer than five minutes. Even the strongest athlete cannot keep his arms outstretched for more than ten minutes.[1a] P. W. Schmidt[2] describes an experiment on a medical student who for a few minutes hung by his hands from a horizontal bar. The thorax expanded permanently into the position of inspiration, the diaphragm was depressed, breathing became more rapid but much shallower (the difference of chest-circumference at breathing in and at breathing out becoming very small). Finally there was faintness with a tendency to black-out.

___ normal position
..... after hanging for 6 minutes.

XIII. 1.—Changes in Heart and Diaphragm due to Suspension. (*Hynek*)

[1] Chauncy, p.123 (cf. p.23) ; R. W. Chambers, *Thomas More*, 1935, p.331.
[1a] "During the time Theresa visions Christ as being nailed to the cross, she holds her arms straight out in front of her or spread far apart. Now it is known that even a trained athlete cannot endure this for more than eight or ten minutes. Yet this simple country girl does so for several hours."—Hynek i. 98.
[2] *Die Geschichte Jesu*, 1904, ii. 409-414.

Hynek (ii. 174) in 1936 reported some experiments of Dr. Ledeny, an anatomist in Pressburg, which showed the effect on breathing of a position with the arms laterally extended. Such a posture is one of maximum inhelation. The major pectoral muscles expand and lift the chest, enlarging its capacity ; hence the diaphragm is lowered and flattened. Dr. Barbor of Pressburg made observations on the effect of hanging by the arms. Radiographs taken before and after showed that the heart-shadow decreased (owing to a smaller venous return) and the diaphragm was depressed (fig. xiii. 1).

Dr. Mödder of Cologne (p.54f) carried these experiments further A number of young medical students supported themselves by the hands (tied with handkerchiefs to prevent injury) one metre apart on a horizontal rod. A radiograph was taken of the thorax before and after suspension. After a few minutes, with increased exhaustion of the arm, shoulder and chest muscles, the breathing becomes quicker and shallower, the chest-circumference is now the same at breathing in and out (breathing being effected only by the diaphragm) ; the ' vital capacity ' (the litres of air which after intensive inspiration can be breathed out) sinks considerably.[3] After a few minutes the face and upper part of the body become paler owing to lack of blood. Blood collects in the lower part of the body, in the abdominal depots (liver, etc.), and in the veins of the legs. The viscosity of the blood increases, and the capillaries almost cease to function. Less blood reaches the heart, the X-radiograph shows the heart-shadow to be smaller ; to supply blood at the same rate, it must beat faster. There is a rise in the pulse-frequency and a continual fall of blood-pressure. If the subject is allowed to stand on his toes for a short while, the normal circulation is quickly restored. But if he continues suspended, he soon collapses owing to the lack of blood in brain and heart.

Similar observations have been made on animals[3a] :

[3] In six minutes from 5.2 (the value when standing)to 1.5. Many patients with a double pneumothorax live with a capacity of 1.2.

[3a] The first systematic study was made by L. Hill, *Jl. Physiol.* 18 (1895) 15-53. Rabbits, cats and dogs suffered marked impairment of cerebral circulation when held in a vertical position ; monkeys were better able to tolerate passive verticality. H. S. Mayerson studied the hypotension and blood-changes in anaesthetised dogs suspended upright.—Orthostatic Circulatory Failure (Gravity Shock) in the Dog, *Amer. Jl. Physiol.* 141 (1944) 227-234. " Animals kept in the upright position are extremely sensitive to haemorrhage. Irreversible failure is often precipitated by the withdrawal of relatively small quantities of blood (30 to 50 c.c.) " (p.233). This last observation suggests that in crucifixion even a moderate amount of bleeding, superadded to orthostatic circulatory failure, may have considerably hastened death. As regards humans : Taylor, Henschel and Keys— *ibid.* 152 (1948) 141—showed that " any circulatory stress [i.e. from the common cold] in addition to that of verticality might well result in failure of the cerebral circulation and syncope."

Some animals, especially rabbits, when held vertically pass into a state of shock and may quickly die if the vertical suspension is not discontinued. This is more likely to happen in fat animals, and is due to the failure to adapt the vaso-constrictive tonus to the needs of the upright posture so that an adequate blood-supply can be maintained through the central nervous system. The term 'gravity shock' denotes this condition. It is rare in man, but its connexion with syncope is obvious.—H. Rolleston (editor), *British Encyclopaedia of Medical Practice* 11 (1939) 127.

Suspension[4] is not necessary to produce these conditions, which ultimately lead to what is called ' orthostatic collapse.' or ' gravity shock.' It is well known that long-continued standing can cause a man to faint. Soldiers know the severity of the punishment of standing still with full kit in the sun. Usually they fall after half an hour. This fall is a functional remedy of the organism ; for the activity of the leg-muscles is necessary for the return journey of the blood (against gravity) to the heart. In sleep we instinctively seek the horizontal position.

An intensification of this gravity-effect occurs in modern high-speed aviation, particularly in diving and circling, when considerable accelerations occur. Thus in a few seconds there may occur physiological effects which under ordinary gravity could not be reached for many hours.

Strong forces along the long axis of the body, acting from head to seat, result in crowding of the abdominal viscera against the diaphragm and embarrass respiratory movements and heart action . . . The most important problem in this connection is the response of the blood circulatory system . . . The largest columns of blood occur in the great vessels running lengthwise through the body so that forces acting in that direction will produce the most marked effects . . . A direct hydrostatic action on the blood within the large vessels tends to force it into the lower parts of the body. This will result in an accumulation of blood particularly in the abdominal region at the expense of the head, and hinder the venous return to the heart. Thus the

---

[4] According to Mödder (p.53), Dietlen in 1909 saw that Moritz's observation of heart-diminution while standing is nearly always accompanied by an increase of frequency and a decrease of stroke-volume. In 1940 Lauer first registered orthostatic changes in the electrocardiagram.

Motionlessness makes the vertical posture more serious : " Postural sway is a factor of material benefit in combating orthostatic hyperpnoea."—Franseen and Hellebrandt, *Amer. Jl. Physiol.* 138 (1943) 364. The raising (hyperabduction) of the arms (above the head) increases the symptoms, e.g. it results in the obliteration of the arterial pulse (in the wrist), numbness and tingling, even gangrene if prolonged.—I. S. Wright, *Amer. Heart Jl.* 29 (1945) 1.

initial fall of pressure in the vessels of the head region is further augmented by a decreased cardiac output. The net action is a marked fall in intracranial blood-pressure, with a resulting anemia of the brain and sensory organs of the head . . . The visual mechanism, the retinae, optic nerves and cerebral optic centres are particularly sensitive to anoxemia ; and when a marked reduction in blood-pressure in the vessels supplying these areas occurs, disturbances of visual function are a natural consequence. With increased fall in blood-pressure, the cerebral circulation may become so reduced that loss of consciousness results.—H. G. Armstrong, *Principles and Practice of Aviation Medicine*, 1939, p.395f.

Of course these results are due to much greater forces than ordinary gravity. But they display in an aggravated form the effects due to prolonged vertical suspension. As regards crucifixion, the physiological conditions were described with surprising accuracy as far back as 1880 by Rev. Samuel Haughton, M.D. (p.350) :

In this constrained position the operation of breathing, as far as it is performed by means of the intercostal muscles, was seriously interfered with ; because the ribs were fixed by the strain caused by the suspension of the body from the arms . . . The unfortunate sufferer was thus mechanically reduced to the condition of one whose intercostal muscles have been tetanised by the action of strychnia or lock-jaw or other cause capable of producing this result. In consequence of the above-mentioned interference with the free action of the intercostal muscles, the breathing was conducted altogether by means of the diaphragm. [This was] a condition so painful after a short time, that the sufferer involuntarily raised his body by bearing upon the nails that secured his feet, or by swinging himself from the points of suspension of his hands, notwithstanding the agony thus occasioned, which was easily endured in comparison of the greater agony produced by his diaphragmatic breathing. It thus frequently happened that a strong man of resolute will, by raising himself by the hands or lifting himself on his feet, remained alive upon the cross for three or four days.

Thus the respiratory movements of a crucified man are greatly impeded, and accordingly the blood-circulation becomes diminished especially in the upper part of the body. Suppose he is suspended as in Villandre's crucifix (fig. x. 13). The body has sunk with the knees protruding, suspension being almost entirely by the hands. Breathing becomes painful and difficult. With superhuman effort, the victim can for a moment stand on his nailed feet and raise his body, thus relieving the arms and facilitating respiration. See the diagram fig. xiii. 2 (after Legrand, p.46). In this way he escapes partial asphyxiation for a moment by a voluntary movement which costs atrocious suffering. Every time he speaks he has thus to raise himself. Then the body descends once more. What a terrible rhythm !

XIII. 2.—Alternative Positions on the Cross.   (*Legrand*)

Haughton, like most commentators to-day,[5] assumed a seat-peg (*sedile*). If this (or a foot-rest) were employed, it was not for the purpose of alleviation, nor to prevent tearing of the tendons, etc., but solely to cause a deferment of death. Thus the executioners could regulate the length of the agony. This extra support would retard the onset of asphyxia and collapse. Presumably those who lived for a day or so on the cross had some such support. Certainly a foot-rest would produce a considerable alleviation of the deleterious effects due to the erect posture with outstretched arms. A Czech fakir called Zenkl announced that he would have himself nailed to a cross for eighty hours, with his feet on a support. Dr. Hynek (i. 74, ii. 155) challenged him to hang by his hands *from* the cross for ten minutes ; but the challenge was declined.

According to Hynek (i. 81) and Barbet (p.128), the over-tired muscles of the arms and shoulders of a person crucified become tetanised and suffer from cramps ; this tendency is increased by the defect in the circulation and by the injury to the median

[5] Also Dr. Judica Cordiglia ii. 147.

nerves. This also causes an increase of temperature and profuse perspiration. According to Hynek, the cramp of the diaphragm-muscle leads to suffocation. But Mödder (p.58) thinks that this is improbable, since the diaphragm is not so liable to cramp as the muscles of the arms and shoulders ; before the inability to breathe becomes fatal, another effect intervenes : the failure of blood-circulation, especially cerebral anaemia.[6]

In itself orthostatic collapse is not fatal ; recuperation can be quite rapid, provided the patient is placed in a horizontal position. Similarly if an aviator loses vision and consciousness, he quickly recovers when the acceleration is decreased ; there are seldom any after-effects, except a few moments of slight mental confusion. But it seems reasonable to suppose that such physiological disturbances must, if continued long enough, result in death. A number of medical men have come to believe that this occurred in crucifixion.

The views expressed in recent years by such men are worth quoting. In 1923 Dr. Le Bec (p.131) wrote as follows :

> It was to nervous exhaustion that Our Lord succumbed. He was a victim to what old surgeons energetically and significantly called ' the haemorrhage of pain,' comparing thus the exhaustion of the nervous system to a drainage of blood . . . The tortures of crucifixion rapidly exhausted the small measure of vitality that yet remained [after the agony, the scourging, etc.]. The cardiac muscle had been taxed beyond its strength, and Our Lord succumbed to syncope.

This description is vague and unsatisfactory. Writing in 1936, Dr. Hynek was more explicit (i. 82f) :

> Jesus died on the cross in the most agonising manner and in full consciousness. He was seized with painful spasms . . . The spasms first affected the muscles of His chest, thus interfering with their expansion and contraction to inhale and exhale air. Gradually the stronger expansor muscles prevailed over the contractor muscles, particularly when the spasms reached the diaphragm. The thorax then set in a rigid posture, and further aeration of the blood was prevented. The victim turned wan and livid. And when breathing ceased, the action of the heart stopped and death ensued by oedema of the lungs.[7] The direct cause of the death of Christ was suffocation.

---

[6] *Tetanisation* is used by analogy with tetanus, whose bacillus infects the central nervous system, so that the muscles are irritated and protracted spasmodic contractions ensue.
[7] Dr. Moedder rejects this (p.57).

Dr. Hynek (i. 82, 88) holds that his view is corroborated by the evidence of *rigor mortis* shown on the shroud :[8]

The imprints on the Holy Shroud show that the muscles of the crucified Christ, completely exhausted, stiffened immediately after death . . . The best corroboration of my theory—that the direct cause of the death of Christ was spasmodic rigidity of the muscles—can be seen in the imprints of the Holy Shroud, in the clearly outlined major muscles of the chest, which are almost petrified in their mortal rigor and are fairly conspicuous. The thorax is also broadened, indicating the greater strength of the expansor muscles.[8a]

Dr. Hynek's view is accepted by Dr. Barbet :

Death followed the tetanic contraction of all the muscles . . . which eventually reached the respiratory muscles, whence asphyxia and death.—*Les cinq plaies du Christ*, 1948[4], p.52.

Dr. Judica Cordiglia (ii. 148) uses the term ' orthostatic collapse ' due to the vertical position.[9] So does Dr. Moedder :

The factors leading to an orthostatic collapse continue to operate in a case of crucifixion and necessarily lead to death. The heart and the vital centres of the brain must, on account of the defective blood-supply, cease to function.—Moedder, p.59.

My colleague, Dr. P. Kiely, F.R.C.S., Professor of Surgery, to whom I submitted the above, has written to me as follows :

The cause of Our Lord's death would appear to me to be due to a combination of three contributory factors :
(1) The preliminary punishment, scourging, crowning with thorns, and other injuries to which He was subjected before being nailed to the cross, must have seriously broken down His

---

[8] Rigor sets in quickly when the muscles are in a condition of exhaustion, e.g. in the case of hunted animals (deer or fox). There is also a rapid onset of rigidity in cases of sickness involving cramps, e.g. tetanus traumaticus, strychnine-poisoning. Death due to diabetic conditions is followed most quickly by rigor.

[8a] By expansor and contractor muscles apparently inspiratory and expiratory muscles are meant.

[9] This, he says, is not asphyxia but anoxemia. The blood accumulated in the lower viscera and limbs, and consequently decreased in heart and brain. He pertinently observes (p.149) that one about to die of asphyxia could not give a loud cry. But in i. 97 he wrote : " He probably died of asphyxia." I am not clear about this distinction. "The failure of the tissues for any reason to receive an adequate supply of oxygen is called *anoxia* . . . *Anoxemia* is a term which denotes a low tension of oxygen in the arterial blood . . . *Asphyxia* is sometimes used interchangeably with anoxia ; but strictly speaking, this term should be restricted to conditions in which there is anoxia combined with an increased tension of carbon dioxide in the blood and tissues."—Best and Taylor, *The Physiological Basis of Medical Practice* 1945[4], p.358.

physical strength and started a state of shock, as is shown by His inability to carry the cross and perhaps falling under it.

(2)   Orthostatic collapse on the cross, under these circumstances, would be sure to follow from the pain, the suffering, the exhaustion, the loss of blood ; all of which would intensify the shock which had started during His earlier sufferings.

(3)   The position on the cross would cause all the muscles of the chest-wall and shoulder-girdle to tire and tetanise, leaving the diaphragm alone to carry on respiration. Under these circumstances the excursions of the diaphragm would be sure to lessen in amplitude and to increase in speed. Hence after a time the diaphragm would also become exhausted and tetanised. In other words, a condition of asphyxia would ensue, though Our Lord no doubt did not show evidence of asphyxia, nor would we expect Him to do so, because of the other factors involved : exhaustion, loss of blood, shock, accumulation of blood in the lower parts of the body, and consequently greatly diminished cardiac output.

There are some minor variations in the above descriptions, but they agree in assigning as the cause of death the vertical posture accompanied by enforced immobility and extension of the arms. That such a posture could have serious effects we know to-day from the study of gravity-shock and from experiments on suspension. This is confirmed by the evidence of the shroud : expanded thorax and emphasised pectoral muscles, the sunken epigastrium and arched hypogastrium (respectively the upper and lower part of the abdomen), which can best be observed on Villandre's crucifix.

It may well be that disturbance of the circulation, accompanied by toxic effects from the severe scourging as well as by anoxaemia due to the difficulty of diaphragmatic breathing, was the general cause of death on a cross. But we can have no certainty that this applied to the case of Our Lord. One difficulty is that He bowed His head and died after uttering His loud prayer. But orthostatic collapse, like the effect of positive acceleration in aviation, ends in coma, directly due to optic and cerebral anaemia. It may of course be asserted with Hynek (ii. 172) that Christ lost consciousness after the cry ; for the evangelists do not say that He *immediately* expired.[9a]

This discussion will be resumed in the next chapter after the

[9a] Some spiritual writers took the loud cry to be miraculous. " That cry was not natural but miraculous. For a man afflicted with great and prolonged sufferings, and thus from such affliction nigh to death, could not so cry out by natural force." —Ludolph, *Vita I. C.* ii. 64, 2 (ed. Rigollot, 1878, iv. 129).

side-wound has been investigated. Meanwhile some remarks will be made on the suggestion that the drink given to Our Lord caused His death.[10] Usually the case of Kléber's assassin is invoked (see p.185 above). But are the two cases comparable? (1) Our Lord was crucified; this man was impaled and therefore had serious lacerations of his internal organs, including his whole digestive tract. (2) He was given a good drink in a vessel, whereas Our Lord merely had His lips moistened with a wet sponge.[11]

There seems to be no recorded investigation of the fatal effect of a drink in abnormal bodily conditions. An American geologist with experience of desert regions, W. J. McGee, published an article " Desert Thirst as Disease " in the *Interstate Medical Journal* 13 (1906) 279-300. He distinguishes five stages. (1) Normal thirst with a feeling of dryness in mouth and throat and a craving for liquid. (2) A state of functional derangement: saliva scanty and sticky, the tongue may cling to the teeth or to the mouth-roof, there appears to be a lump in the throat, there is a mental concentration on liquids. " Thirst in this phase is best relieved by water, water swallowed in quarts, preferably a gill at a gulp with time for breathing between " (p.295), also by water in the nostrils, on the face, etc. The last three stages are quite pathological. (3) Intensification of the preceding conditions: the lips retract, the eyelids stiffen and the eyeballs set themselves in a winkless stare, breathing is laboured, the heart-beat grows slow and heavy. " In this phase too the throat is relieved only by water, water in gallons applied inside and out, but with caution as to rate lest the dessicated tissues be saturated so suddenly as to set up dangerous disorganisation " (p.296). (4) The stage of structural degeneration. " The eyelids crack and the eyeballs are suffused and fissured well up to the cornea and weep tears of blood . . . In this phase there can be little alleviation ; for water, however judiciously administered, brings hurt rather than healing ; and even if the degenerated tissues are reorganised, the cerebral and neural structures may scarce recover from the shock " (p.298f). (5) The last stage is increased dessication of the organism ; blood and serum ooze from the body-surface ; blow-flies alight and vultures draw near. " In this final phase there is

[10] This appears to be favourably received by Dr. Le Bec (p.131) : " It is well to add that the drinking of water at such a moment would in itself be sufficient to cause death. The ancients had observed that death seemed hastened if the condemned were given drink ; a syncope resulted." Where are these observations of " the ancients " regarding crucifixion recorded? Dr. Le Bec also refers to Kléber's assassin.
[11] How did this ' sponge ' come to be on Calvary? Was it brought by the soldiers to clean their accoutrements? It may not have been a sponge in the literal sense, but a bunch of hyssop or even a flat piece of bread brought by the soldiers to eat with their posca.

no alleviation, no relief save the end " (p.300). There is not a vestige of proof that a crucified man, with internal organs intact, ever reaches even the third stage, except in a tropical climate.

McGee's classification of stages is used and developed in *Physiology of Man in the Desert*, New York 1947, by E. F. Adolph and Associates. It would appear that, at least in the early stages of dehydration, no harm results from drinking. " It seems possible that, at the higher levels of dehydration, the limiting factor to rapid satisfaction of the body's lack of water may be the size of the stomach. Nevertheless, we have seen some men drink 2,000 millilitres [$3\frac{1}{2}$ pints] within ten minutes " (p.266). And in the later stages a person simply could not take a drink. " With the onset of disability to swallow at about 12 per cent. water deficit [McGee's third stage], the individual can no longer recover without assistance " (stomach tube, intravenous drip, etc.) (p.229).

" Stead came to the conclusion that everyone will eventually faint if suspended long enough without support. He remarks that in death by crucifixion the victims were frequently tied to the cross, and the onset of collapse and syncope was hastened by the giving of wine, which caused further relaxation of the vascular system."—Hellebrandt and Franseen, *Physiol. Rev.* 23 (1943) 245. The article by E. A. Stead, *Bull. New Eng. Med. Center*, 1940, ii. 290, is not accessible to me. The remark about the ' relaxation ' caused by the drink of wine is rather vague ; it does not explain how it hastens collapse.

(3) The Jewish Deputation to Pilate

As it was Preparation-Day, in order that the bodies might not remain on the cross during the Sabbath—for this Sabbath was a solemn Festival—the Jews asked Pilate to have their legs broken and [the bodies] removed.—John xix. 31.

The Jews attached great importance to burial. Josephus quotes the Jewish law as follows :

Let him be led forth by their own hands outside the city, followed by the crowd, and then stoned to death. And after remaining exposed to the general view during the whole day, let him be buried at night. This is also to be done with all who for any reason are legally condemned to death. Let burial be given even to your enemies ; and do not let a corpse, paying more than its just penalty, be left without its portion of earth.—*Ant.* xiv. 8, 24 (265).

With us it is ordained that the body of a suicide should be exposed unburied until sunset, though it is considered right to bury even our enemies slain in war.—*B.J.* iii. 8, 5 (377). See also pp.168, 171 above.

This was done even for enemies. Joshua (8[30]) commanded that the corpse of the king of Ai should be taken down from the gibbet at sunset, and it was buried " at the entrance of the city-gate and they raised over it a heap of stones." Similarly the five kings at Makkedah (10[27]) were buried in the cave under a pile of stones. Josephus thus expresses his strongest reproach against the Idumeans and Zealots during the war :

> They actually went so far in their impiety as to throw out corpses without burial (*ataphous*), in spite of the fact that the Jews are so careful about arrangements for burial (*taphas*) that even criminals who have been sentenced to crucifixion (*tous ek katadikēs anestaurōmenous*) are taken down and buried (*thaptein*) before sunset.—*B.J.* iv. 5, 2 (317).
>
> Many starting to desert changed their minds and decided to die inside the walls, since the hope of burial (*taphēs*) made death in their native city seem more tolerable. But the Zealots carried barbarity to the extent of granting interment (*gēs*) to nobody either in the city or on the roads. As if they had resolved to violate the laws of nature as well as those of their country, and to add the pollution of Heaven itself to their outrages against mankind, they left the dead rotting in the sun.—*B.J.* iv. 6, 3 (380).

These quotations show how strong was the normal Jewish feeling that all, even enemies and criminals, should be granted burial. In the Mishnah there is described a custom of double interment for criminals :

> Criminals were not buried in their fathers' burying places ; but two burying places were prepared by the court : one for the stoned and burnt, and one for the decapitated and strangled. When the flesh had been consumed, the bones were gathered and buried in their proper place.—*Sanhedrin*, Mishnah vi. 5-6, p.92 Danby (1919).
>
> When the flesh was consumed, the messengers of the court used to collect the bones and bury them in a coffin ; and even if the criminal were the king of kings, he could not be buried in the burying place of his fathers, but only in that prepared by the court. Two burying places were prepared by the court : one for the stoned and burnt, and one for the decapitated and strangled.—*Sanhedrin*, Tosefta ix. 8-9, p.93 Danby.
>
> To the criminal burial with the other members of his family was first forbidden, only the coffin containing his bones would be admitted there later . . . The criminal is then treated as all other men, for in Jewish thought he has already expiated his crime by execution and by the subsequent decomposition which lasts twelve months.—S. Krauss, *Revue des études juives* 97 (1934) 5.

But even in this scheme there is no question of a common pit, into which corpses were thrown indiscriminately ; for the bones of each individual were identifiable and were subsequently removed to his ancestral vault.   Even if this arrangement ever existed, it is attested only in the Mishnah which at the earliest is of the second century A.D. when the Jewish State had been completely overthrown.   There is no proof that it held in the time of Christ.   Had such been the law, the burial of St. Stephen could hardly have taken place.   It is probable, however, that, like the idealised criminal code with which it is connected, the alleged custom was a piece of belated academic speculation.   Some such arrangement may have prevailed in general so that only ossuaries need be placed in the family vault ; and it seems that bones were brought from abroad for burial in Palestine.   Anyway all this is irrelevant to the case of Our Lord who was executed by the Romans and whose body was outside Jewish jurisdiction.

Whether, in spite of the Jewish law of burial before sunset, the Romans would leave the bodies on the gibbets, is uncertain.   Nor do we know whether on ordinary occasions the Sanhedrists would intervene to have the prescription of Deuteronomy observed by their pagan conquerors.   But this was no ordinary occasion.   The Jewish leaders had handed over to Pilate One who claimed to be the Messiah.   They could not be sure that there would not be a reaction of the crowd in His favour.   It was the Eve of Passover, the festival on which the Jews, crowded in and round the city, commemorated their liberation from Egypt and drank to the rout of the Romans.   So not only were the Sanhedrists desirous of displaying their ritual scrupulosity—just as they had refused to be defiled by going inside the Governor's Residence—but also they were anxious for the removal, at this dangerous festival, of the provocative sight of three Jews on Roman gibbets just outside the walls. Some of the pilgrims, especially the Galileans, might become restive at the insult—a point which Pilate would appreciate.   So whether or not on an ordinary occasion the Jewish leaders would have left to the Romans the onus of derogating from the Jewish law,[1]

---

[1] Dalman says that in J19[31] the deposition of the bodies is " considered from the point of view of the sanctity of the Sabbath. This has no basis either in the Mosaic Law or in Jewish tradition ; nor did it require any such motive. If the reason given is not due to the Evangelist's imperfect knowledge of the actual law, nothing remains but to assume that he considered it legitimate to connect it with the special circumstances of the time."—*Jesus-Jeshua*, 1929, p.186. It is absurd to suggest that the Jewish author of the Fourth Gospel, so accurate as regards ideas

they had a certain amount of responsibility for the burial of One whose condemnation they had actively secured, especially as there would be a special desecration if the bodies were left hanging and unburied on the great national holiday.[2] So they sent to Pilate a deputation with the request that the crucified should be despatched and their bodies taken down before sunset.

Criminals crucified early on Friday morning would not naturally die before sunset on that day ; but they or one of them might very well die at some moment during the ensuing twenty-four hours : in other words, during the Sabbath. On the Sabbath they could not be buried, and the Deuteronomic law would therefore be violated by the corpses remaining on the crosses at sunset. Thus there was a special reason for hastening, if it could be compassed, the death of those hanging on the cross on Friday. But it could only be done, *ex hypothesi*, through the medium of the government and under the authority of the governor ; and it is perhaps hardly probable that on any ordinary occasion the governor would consent . . . On this occasion, however, the Sabbath coincided with the Passover . . . And Passover, with the crowds of Jews that flocked from all quarters to observe it at Jerusalem, was just the time when the danger of an *émeute* was greatest, and when even the most callous of Roman rulers learned to avoid all possible causes of collision with such turbulent subjects.—C. H. Turner, *Church Quarterly Review* 74 (1912) 294.

(4) The Leg-Breaking

After the capture of Jerusalem, Josephus (*Vita* 75) " saw many crucified prisoners and recognised three of his acquaintance." At his request, Titus " immediately ordered that they should be taken down (*kathairethentas*) and receive careful attention. Two of them died in the physicians' hands, the third survived." On the present

customs and topography, did not know the O.T. or the law derived from it. He adduces the imminence of the Festival as the special reason why the Sanhedrin made bold to intervene and why Pilate so readily consented. According to St. John, the primary concern of the Sanhedrists was that there should not be left on the crosses living victims whose presence would profane the Passover and who might die on it. The burial before nightfall seems to have been a secondary consideration.

[2] Preparation-Day : *parasceve*, the eve of sabbath, still used in Greek for Friday. St. John seems to be referring to the festival rather than to the Sabbath. This sabbatic day is called " great " or solemn, not because it happened to fall on a Saturday but because it was the great national festival of the Jews. Later Christians called Holy Saturday " the great sabbath " (e.g. *Ap. Const.* v. 9). To-day Jews call the sabbath before Passover *Shabbath ha-Gadol*. Note that the sabbatic obligation of Passover began at sunset on the eve, i.e. on this occasion on Good Friday about 6 p.m. (I am assuming St. John's chronology.)

occasion there was no such friendly attention. The Jews did not repent of their deed, they had no desire to see their Enemy alive. And Pilate, though he had fought for His acquittal, was in no mood, even if he had the authority, to reverse the decision which had been forced upon him. He revenged himself by derisively placarding their Victim as " The King of the Jews." And now they came to him to get their King buried out of sight. This time it suited his book, for neither he nor they wanted any unnecessary aggravation at Passover, when the garrison in the Antonia had to be alert for trouble.

They suggested that the legs of the crucified should be broken. In spite of the assertion of Lactantius,[1] there is no proof that this was a Roman method for despatching the crucified. " We find no example in secular history ; and the case of the Gospel can hardly be explained except by the Jews' request invoking respect for their legislation."[2] *Crurifragium* may well have been a Jewish custom for securing death before sunset ; at least it may have been adopted by the Romans whenever they decided to observe the Jewish law for executed Jews.

> Leg-breaking (*crura frangere*) is mentioned in Roman authors as a separate punishment quite independent of crucifixion: Cicero, *Phil.* xiii. 12, 17 ; Seneca, *De ira*, iii. 32 ; Suetonius, *Aug.* 67, *Tib.* 44. Ammianus Marcellinus xiv. 9: *fractis cruribus occiduntur.* Firmicus Maternus distinguishes the punishment from crucifixion: *aut tolluntur in crucem aut crura illis publica animadversione franguntur.—Mathesis* viii. 6, 11.

What was the object of the leg-fracture? Says Dr. Ryland Whitaker (p.88) :

> It is difficult to determine what was the precise purpose of this procedure. Unless it was carried out with such brutality as to reduce the whole of the lower limbs to a mass of mangled flesh

---

[1] " Since He had [already] laid down His life while fastened to the cross, His executioners did not think it necessary to break His bones, as was their prevailing custom ; but they merely pierced His side."—*Div. Inst.* iv. 26. But, says Origen, the Jews asked Pilate for the leg-breaking: " Why would it have been necessary to make this request if it would have been done according to custom? "—*In Matt* 140 (928).

[2] Prat, *Jésus-Christ*, 1933⁴, ii. 406. The word *crurifragium* does not occur in Classical Latin, only the word *crurifragius* (one whose legs are broken) in Plautus, *Paen.* iv. 2, 64. Ricciotti says: " The Roman crurifragium consisted in breaking his thigh-bones with a club."—*Life of Christ*, 1947, p.630. But *crus* in Latin seems to mean the shin, not the *femur*. The Greek *skelos* however means any part of the leg from the hip down. Probably the projecting knees were smashed with mallets.

and bone, the mere breaking of the legs would not of itself be sufficient to cause death.

But the answer was given in 1880 by Rev. Dr. Haughton (p.350) :

> The effect of the fracture of the legs and arms was to prevent the sufferer from relieving the agony of diaphragmatic breathing by restoring the action of the intercostal muscles. And he thus perished miserably in a few hours of horrible suffering, instead of prolonging his life for some days by the painful process of relieving the intercostal muscles by lifting himself by the muscles of the arms and legs.

It need not be held that death was instantaneous ; to secure this, other methods (e.g. a spear-thrust) were more obvious. The object apparently was to allow the victim to die on and of the cross, not to alter his mode of execution, but to hasten the end. If the picture of the crucified already given is accepted, we must admit that the deprivation of support from the feet rapidly caused the extinction of life through complete inability to breathe. There may also have been a subsidiary effect of fat-embolism ; fat-drops and cells were liberated from the crushed bone-marrow and invaded the veins, heart and lung-capillaries.[3] The object was therefore to shorten their agony, to kill them so that the bodies could be buried. There was no special cruelty involved in the request or in the procedure.

The Rev. Josef Pickl[4] has a new interpretation which should be rejected as lacking any evidence and as discordant with the historical context. He denies that leg-breaking would cause a speedy death, and in proof he refers (p.272) to his experiences in the 1914/18 war, in which such casualties were not fatal. But these war-wounded were lying on the ground, while the crucified was suspended. He also refers to the punishment of burning alive and to some historically recorded instances of lawless brutality.[5] But how are these relevant to a legal sentence of crucifixion? Usually the Romans left the crucified to die on the gibbet, and their dead bodies to rot or to be devoured.[6] There does not appear to be a single recorded

[3] The so-called *Gospel of Peter* (14) says : " They were angry with him and commanded that his legs should not be broken, so that he might die in torments." This may correctly mean that his agony was prolonged. The reference is to ' the good thief,' not to Christ (as Harnack and Voelter thought).—Vaganay, p.242.

[4] *Messiaskönig Jesus*, 1935. I quote from the American translation : *The Messias*, 1946.

[5] Such as what Sulla is reported to have done to Marius : his legs were broken, his eyes were gouged out, his tongue and his hands were cut off.—Seneca, *De ira* iii, 18, 32,

[6] Says the slave in Plautus : " I know that a cross will be my sepulchre."— *Miles* ii. 4 (19).

instance of a crucified being taken down and buried alive. Yet according to Pickl (p.273) the object of the leg-breaking was merely, in addition to increasing the suffering, to make sure that the victims could not run away while they were being transported to be burnt alive. The Sanhedrists' design was thus to have the excommunicated Nazarene, while still living, thrown into Gehinnom and burnt alive (p.277f). There is not the smallest evidence that the Jewish leaders descended to this depth of malignity. Nor would such a gruesome custom of cremation have been then tolerated for Jews in Jerusalem. Even Joshua did not so treat the King of Ai. And Josephus testifies in the first century to the universal prescription of burial of the dead before sunset. True, the Romans were not bound, except for prudential reasons, to Jewish observances. But in the absence of all textual evidence, it is incredible that in peace-time they used to dump wounded patriots and criminals, while still alive, into the smouldering rubbish-heaps just south of Jerusalem, where sacrifices to Moloch were once performed. Still more incredible would it be for the Sanhedrin to have asked the Romans to deal thus with their compatriots—and at the Passover !

(5) The Spear-Thrust

St. John xix

[32] So the soldiers came and broke the legs of those who had been crucified with Him, first of one man and then of the other.

[33] But when they came to Jesus and saw that He was already dead, they did not break His legs.

[34] But one of the soldiers pierced His side with a lance. And immediately there issued blood and water.

Apparently it was not the sentries on the spot who broke the bandits' legs, probably by blows of a mallet on the protruding knees. Pilate sent a special squad, presumably under a centurion.[1] They seem to have reached the bandits' crosses first ; these may have been further forward, or perhaps two soldiers approached, one from each side. Anyway, they left Jesus till last. A soldier looked and saw that He was dead. What was to be done? The Man on this cross,

[1] Mgr. Poelzl says : " It is more probable that the soldiers guarding the crosses inflicted this further punishment . . . Though St. John says that they *came*, this may very well mean that they had received fresh instructions."—*Passion and Glory of Christ*, 1919, p.245. Or *came* may merely mean that they approached the crosses to perform the task. Note that St. John says " *the* soldiers."

with His inscription and perhaps His crown, was known to have been a prominent leader. Had not the garrison in the Antonia treated Him a few hours ago as a mock king? No chances could be taken in His case. Indeed, if through carelessness or mistake, they allowed any of the crucified to escape alive, they would have answered with their lives. To this Roman posse Calvary had not the significance it has for us; their task was part of their day's work. They were sent to do a job at which they were experts; their own lives depended on their doing it thoroughly. We can be quite certain that when they left the scene, the two bandits were beyond recovery and Jesus was dead.

To fulfil at least the spirit of the command, to ensure that He was really dead in case some spark of life yet remained, one of them gave Him an honourable *coup de grâce*. What were the feelings of this ' unknown soldier ' when, without realising it, he performed the most famous military deed of history? Did he remember the Man's unconquerable patience during the garrison's horse-play? Did the centurion on the spot, and the sentries on guard, tell of His silent suffering and wondrous death? Did this Roman mercenary shrink from inflicting the brutal and dishonouring blow of a mallet? Or was the spear-thrust made by the centurion himself, who may have been the same officer who had been present at the death?

At any rate, it was no mere prick. Since leg-breaking brought quick death, the substitute must also have been a mortal blow, it must have been such a stroke as would deliver Him from His sufferings if perchance He was still alive. This is *a fortiori* true if we suppose brutality in the deed. Indeed one can hardly imagine a strong rough soldier, sent on this hasty errand to kill, gently pricking the body. Besides, he used a lance, with a tapering iron top and a wooden shaft nearly six feet long. St. John himself, an eyewitness, had no doubt of the death and of the subsequent stroke. He immediately applies a Hebrew text containing the term ' transfixed '—*daqar* meaning to pierce with spear or sword—occurring in a context which implies mourning for death. And later (20^{27}) John represents Thomas as being asked to measure the hand-wounds with his finger and the side-wound with his hand.

Origen asserts that it was not unusual for the Romans to administer a fatal stab to one crucified in order to shorten his agony :

Pilate did not give an order—in accordance with the Romans' usual practice as regards those crucified—for Jesus to be stabbed under His armpits. This [abstention from stabbing] is sometimes done by those who condemn men detected in greater crimes. For greater suffering is endured by those who are not stabbed after crucifixion but remain alive in very great torment, sometimes even for the whole night and the following day.—*In Matt.* 140 (928) : PG. 13. 1793B.

There is no support from secular history for such a custom. Origen is probably generalising from the present case. And even if such a practice was known in his time, there is no proof that it existed in the first century. If it had been a regular custom to expedite the death of the crucified by such a stab, the Jews need not have intervened at all. And if it had at least been customary in exceptional cases, the Jews would presumably have asked for it instead of leg-breaking.[1a]

The Greek word for ' pierced ' is *ēnyxen*, the first aorist of the verb *nyssō* which has, according to the context, a wide range of meanings from prod to pierce. It occurs only here in the Gospels. But in the Acts 12[7] we read that the angel " striking (*nyxas*) Peter's side, waked him."

Some other instances of the verb *nyssein* (or *nyttein*) may be given. Pricking the eye : Ecclus 22[19]. Prodding a sleeper to awaken him : III Macc 5[14] (so Homer, *Od.* 14, 485). In the Gospel of Peter (9) : They prodded (or rather struck) Him with a stick ; this refers to the mockery. In the Sibylline Oracles it occurs twice (ii. 373 and viii. 296) of the wounding of Christ's side with a stick (*kalamos*, which need not mean a reed and is probably used for reasons of metre). In the Acts of John (97) both ' sticks and lances ' are specified. In Plutarch (*Cleomenes* 37) we read : " Panteus on pricking (*nyxas*) Cleomenes in the foot, perceived a contortion in his face. So he kissed him and sat down by him till the breath was out of the body. Then embracing the corpse, he slew himself on it." On the other hand, Josephus uses the verb to denote a mortal spear-wound inflicted treacherously by a Jew on a Roman centurion at the capture of Jotapata : " He besought Antonius to extend his hand to him as a pledge of protection and to help him to rise. The centurion incautiously complied, whereupon the Jew from below stabbed him with his spear (*nyttei dorati*) beneath the groin and instantly killed him."— B.J. iii. 7, 35 (334).

[1a] There was a widespread medieval view that the Jews were responsible for the piercing : " One of the soldiers, Longinus by name, opened His right side with a lance . . . O fearful cruelty of the Jews ! . . . This the Jews did out of craft and singular wickedness; for they knew that dishonour shown to the dead would be held to be the same as if done to the living."—Tauler, *Meditations on the Life and Passion of O.L. J.C.*, ch. 53, Eng. trans. 1925, p.323.

As is well known, St. Jerome's Latin version has ' opened ' (*aperuit*) instead of 'pierced.' This reading occurs also in the Peshitta and in the Jerusalem Syriac as well as in two Old Latin codices (*f* and *r*), though the *Vetus Latina* has *perfodit* (with a variant *percussit*). It is doubtful whether St. Jerome read *ēnoixĕn* in his Greek text ;[2] but this would not in later times be pronounced differently from *ĕnyxĕn* and so the Latin may have originated by the translator working from dictated Greek. It is a pity that we have to abandon this reading. Yet, after all, there still remains the beautiful lesson, mystical rather than physical, which St. Augustine has expounded for us :

> The Evangelist used a watchful word ; he said ' opened,' not ' struck ' or ' wounded ' or anything else. That there somehow should be opened the door of life whence have come the Sacraments of the Church without which there is no entry into true life.—*In Ioannem* tr. 120, 2 : PL. 35. 1953.

The usual Greek word for a lance is *dory*, which properly signifies the wood ; another word is *enchos*, the Roman *hasta*. St. John uses the word *lonchē*, which strictly refers to the iron top. The lance consisted of a long shaft terminating in an iron point, shaped like an elongated leaf. It was much lighter than the *pilum*,[3] which had a barbed iron head.

XIII. 3.—The Lance in Rome

A few words may be added about the lance-relic now in Rome.[4] In 570 the Piacenza pilgrim saw it in Jerusalem in the Basilica of Sion (Baldi 741). In 614 the Persians captured Jerusalem. The point of the lance was broken off and sent to Constantinople, while the main piece was carried off by the Persians and eventually restored to the Emperor Heraclius in Jerusalem. It was seen in

---

[2] Two or three minuscule Greek manuscripts have approximations to this reading : *ēnyxe* (56), *ĕnyxe* (58), *ĕnoixe* (68).—Bernard, *Hermathena* 9(1896) 187.
[3] According to Tacitus, the *hasta* was the weapon of the auxiliaries while the legionaries had the *pilum*.—*Ann.* xii. 25, *Hist.* iii. 17. Tertullian says that Christ's side was pierced by a pilum.—*De corona* 11. There is a famous conjecture of Camerarius († 1574) in J19²⁹ : *hyssō* for *hyssōpō*, i.e. a pilum (*hyssos*) instead of hyssop.
[4] F. de Mély, *Exuviae sacrae Constantinopolitanae* 3 (1904) 23-163. The other relics— in Vienna, Cracow, Etchmiatzin—need not be considered. The references to Baldi are to the paragraphs of his *Enchiridion locorum sanctorum*, 1935.

Jerusalem in 670 by Arculf (Baldi 955, 7). It is also mentioned by Bede about 720. Some time later it was removed to Constantinople, on whose capture by the Turks in 1492 it was sent (by Bajazet) to Innocent VIII, since when it has been kept in Rome. A sketch was made in 1898 by Padre Vannutelli and is shown in fig. xiii. 3. On top is the pointless spear-head with a haft of bronze, below this is a modern copper ring above silk and portion of a wooden shaft. The broken-off point also has a history. It was presented by Baldwin to St. Louis, and was in Paris from 1248 until the French Revolution when it disappeared. Meanwhile Benedict XIV secured a measured sketch of the Paris portion and found that it fitted the Roman relic. While this is an ancient lance, there is no proof that it was the actual weapon used on Our Lord.

(6) St: John's Witness

We now come to a famous verse of St. John (19^{35}) :

The eye-witness has been testifying ; and his testimony is authentic.
Also he knows that he is recounting what really happened in order that ye may continue to believe.

Some Notes on the Translation

The eye-witness : *hŏ heōrakōs*, he who has seen or has been seeing. This means one of those present on Calvary ; as the word is masculine, it cannot designate a woman ; hence it refers to the disciple mentioned in verse 26. The Greek word is a perfect participle. In Greek the perfect tense has a fuller meaning than is usually contained in the English perfect ; it connotes not only a past act or event but also the present state resulting therefrom. It is used in cases where English usage prefers the preterite. J6^{25} : When did You come here [and are still here]?. J9^{29} : God spoke to Moses [and this is on record]. The same participle as occurs in our text is found in the plural in J4^{45} : The Galileans having seen (*heōrakotes*) His miracles and being still under the impression produced. In ch. 1 of his First Epistle St. John uses the perfect tense to designate what he once saw and to which he now testified : " What we saw with our own eyes . . . We announce to you what we saw and heard." As the participle occurs in our text absolutely, without an object (e.g. this, the above incident), the best translation seems to be " the eye-witness," the one who not only saw but is still under the impression produced and is now testifying thereto.

Has been testifying: *memartuēke*, also perfect tense. This denotes that he has been testifying and continues to do so, he is a standing witness to the fact. Note that it is followed in the next clause by present tenses: *estin, legei, hina pisteuēte*. His testimony is authentic: the word-order in Greek is emphatic: authentic of him is the testimony. The adjective *alēthinē* (not *alēthe*, true) means real, genuine, first-hand, worthily so called.

What really happened: literally true things (*alēthē*), not ' the truth.'

That ye may continue to believe: *hina kai hymeis pisteuēte* (present tense as at 20³¹ rather than *pisteusēte*). The *kai* is epexegetic and need not be translated ' also ' in English.

For at least eighteen centuries the meaning of this text was regarded as obvious and was disputed by no scholar of any repute. At its face-value, the passage contains the claim that the writer was an eye-witness. This does not suit the theory that the Fourth Gospel was not written by the Apostle John.

The simplest expedient to adopt is to declare the verse an interpolation.

So Renan (*Vie de Jésus*, p.537) and Loisy (*Le quatrième évangile*, p.890). A. E. Garvie in *Expositor* 8 (1914) 377: " Probably it is an editorial gloss, such as may be suspected elsewhere, an attestation of the trustworthiness of the eyewitness whose record the Gospel claims to be . . . Whatever the explanation, we are not compelled to charge the evangelist with an ostentatious display of his own trustworthiness." This last sentence implies that one is actually doing a favour to the Apostle in depriving him of this verse ! Macgregor gets annoyed with the verse and declares: " On the whole the most likely solution is that the verse is a comment interjected by the [hypothetical] Redactor."—*The Gospel of John*, 1936, p.351.

There is this at least to be said for this policy of expunging : its exponents frankly admit that the verse as it stands plainly implies that the author of the Gospel was an eyewitness. This is contrary to their theory of authorship ; so much the worse for the verse ; away with it ! So it is handed over to the executioner—the conveniently excogitated editor whose sole function is to take charge of a few awkward phrases in the Gospel. Anyone, such as the present writer, who comes to New Testament criticism from the study of other subjects is rather astonished at the subjective apriorism of some of the procedures. There is not an iota of textual evidence against the verse ; not even an argument from discrepancy of style. There is nothing but a vicious circle. The verse is first used to invent an otherwise unknown editor ; and then the editor is used to dispose of the verse. The alleged redactor is of course more than an editor ; he is much worse ; he is an impostor ; he is making an *ex hypothesi* fraudulent claim that the writer of the Gospel was an eyewitness. But what an utterly inappropriate place he chose for interpolating his falsification ! One could understand this lying meddler saying ' I was present in Cana,' or ' He who wrote the above saw Lazarus emerging from the tomb.' But why with sudden emphasis declare that he witnessed the dishonour done to the Lord's dead body? How much simpler it would have been to omit the mention of the leg-breaking and of the lance-thrust altogether, especially as they are not contained in the other Gospels? So the hypothetical redactor is not only a liar, he is a very stupid one. It is one thing to assume an editor who occasionally polishes the style or adds a graphic detail, though in the absence of independent proof this is a hazardous assumption. But it is quite another thing to invent gratuitously a ghost-redactor who is not only deliberately mendacious but also a clumsy bungler.

The interest shown in these post-mortem incidents, which are *relatively* trivial as well as dishonouring, is psychologically explicable only if the writer was actually present on Calvary. These were poignant moments for St. John. His grief and his tension did not abate with the Master's death. Would these emissaries smash His legs? Would Joseph get the body for burial? With horror he saw the thrust of the spear which seemed to go through his own heart and—as Simeon predicted long ago—pierced the soul of her who was henceforth his mother also. All this he recorded for us to show us the fullness of Christ's humanity and the completeness of His sacrifice.

Deterred by the lack of any evidence against the authenticity of the verse, others have sought to eviscerate it of its obvious meaning. Hence some desperate attempts to impose a new interpretation.

The difference of interpretation concerns this portion of the text which runs literally thus : " Authentic of him (*autou*) is the witness. And that one (*kakeinos*) knows that he is telling true things." Let us therefore examine some different interpretations.

A. " The witness of the Apostle is authentic. And the Apostle knows that the Evangelist is telling the truth." This assumes that the writer (" Jn ") is different from the Apostle John.

If the writer is the eye-witness, he has already said of himself that his witness is trustworthy ; and he does not strengthen his affirmation by repeating them in so awkward a fashion . . . As we take the words—' and he knows that he says the truth '— they are the words of the Evangelist but not of the witness ; and the repetition is not meaningless : He (the Beloved Disciple himself) knows (for he is yet alive) that he is telling true things . . . Jn. assures his readers that the aged apostle knows exactly what he is saying.—Bernard, *John*, 1928, p.650.

To this it may be replied :

(1) This view rightly admits that *ekeinos* refers to the *autou* of the preceding clause, both pronouns designating the Apostle. Furthermore *ekeinos* is the subject of the verb *oiden* ; but suddenly, without any new pronoun being expressed, a different subject is assumed for the verb *legei*. This is a very artificial assumption on which to found a theory that the writer was *not* the Apostle. It is flying in the face of elementary grammar.

(2) If the writer were really appealing to another authority outside himself, he should at least have given some identification of his guarantor, instead of the vague reference ' that one.' If we assume that the Beloved Disciple is distinct from the Evangelist, we must go back nine verses to discover to whom *ekeinos* is supposed to refer. Surely an appeal to someone else calls for a clear specification of the person to whom the appeal is being made. (The case is different if everyone know that the Apostle himself was the author). Moreover, if the writer were reporting the witness of another, he should have turned the second person (*ye*) of the last clause into the first (*we*), for he was himself one of the believers concerned.

(3) The awkwardness is alleged to occur from the juxtaposition of the two phrases " his witness is trustworthy " and " he knows that he says the truth", when both refer to the same person. But this is due to a punctuation which, though commonly accepted, seems unjustified :

He who has seen has borne witness—and his witness is true and he knows that he is telling the truth—that ye may believe.

The clumsy parenthesis certainly seems to contain two redundantly juxtaposed phrases. But in the translation given at the beginning of this section there is no parenthesis at all : The eye-witness has now given testimony, first-hand testimony. He almost apologises for recording this insult to the body. But he knows that he is recounting these true happenings so that his readers may continue to believe, i.e. in the true humanity and in the real death of the historic Jesus, against the prevalent docetic errors.

(4) In 1897 Harnack[1] tentatively suggested that the author (the alleged John the Presbyter) was not one of the disciples but handed down the traditions of John the Apostle. Bernard (p.lxiv) improves this theory by making the author " a disciple of Jesus, who belonged to the outer circle of disciples although not one of the Twelve." According to him (p.lxix), " the internal evidence of the Gospel indicates that the writer was a distinct person from the witness to whom he appeals . . . The language of 19^{35} is even more conclusive [than 21^{24}] as distinguishing between the evangelist and his authority." We have just seen, however, how precarious is this distinction in the present passage. Certainly, as against those who hold that the Apostle was martyred at an early date, the text seems clearly to imply, by the use of the perfect tense (not the aorist), that the witness was still alive at the time of writing. Compare the Baptist's testimony ($J1^{34}$) : " I have seen and I have borne witness that He is the Son of God."

(5) There is another verse of St. John which clearly asserts the identity of the witness and the author. After referring to himself as " that (ekeinos) disciple," he says (21^{24}) : " This is the disciple who is testifying concerning these things and who wrote them." There is a convenient way, adopted by many opponents of the apostolic authorship, for disposing of this inconvenient text which is opposed to their theory. So much the worse for the text ; it is an interpolation. But Bernard was in the awkward position of being unwilling to adopt this drastic solution. " Prima facie," he admits (p.713), " this indicates that the Beloved Disciple actually wrote the Gospel with his own hand, including the Appendix, and not only that his reminiscences are behind it." He then proceeds irrelevantly to argue against his own phrase " with his own hand." But " who wrote " (grapsas) no more specifies the actual mechanical procedure of writing than the same verb implies it when Pilate

---

[1] Chronologie i. 678. Streeter suggests of the author " that, as a boy of twelve, taken by his father to the Passover, he had been one of the multitude who beheld the Crucifixion."— The Four Gospels, 1927, p.418. He also says that apart from xxi. 24f, which he regards as an interpolation, " there is not a word in the whole Gospel to suggest that it is, or claims to be, by the Apostle John."—ibid. p.431. A gross misstatement made without even a passing notice of $J19^{35}$.

" wrote a title " (19^{19}) ; he merely dictated the wording for incision. A modern author " writes " a book even when he uses a dictaphone or a stenographer and sends copy to the printer. Bernard tries to evade this claim to authorship : " The elders of the Church certified that the Beloved Disciple *caused these things to be written*. They were put into shape by the writer who took them down." This kind of thing is misplaced subtlety. Change " the writer " into the stenographer, omit the gratuitous assumption of " putting into shape "—and we are back at the authorship of St. John ! It is much better to say frankly, with Dom Chapman[2] : " Either the writer was a disciple or he was a liar (with a strong adjective)."

B. " The witness of the Apostle is authentic. And the Evangelist knows that the Apostle is telling the truth." This is the interpretation of Prof. C. C. Torrey :

And he who saw this testified to it, and his testimony is reliable —and I myself know that his word is true—that you also may believe.—*The Four Gospels*, 1947[2], p.229.

There are serious objections to this view.

(1) It contains an unproved parenthesis, a very bad one for it falsifies the grammar. How could anyone have written : His testimony is reliable that you also may believe? Moreover, the ' also ' is unnecessary, and the ' you ' ought to have been ' we.'

(2) Prof. Torrey goes to great trouble to prove that *ekeinos* is a substitute for a pronoun of the first person singular. He takes it as equivalent to the Aramaic *hāhū gabĕrā* (that person) used to designate the speaker or the writer. But all this pedantic labour is quite irrelevant to the point at issue. It can be at once admitted that *ekeinos* refers to the writer, even apart from any Aramaic groundwork. But how does this prove that the next verb *legei* has a different subject, when the obvious construction is that *ekeinos* is the subject of both *oiden* and *legei*? There is a great pother about what can be readily admitted, but not the smallest hint of an argument to dissociate the subjects of the two verbs. In fact the new hypothetical personality is smuggled in without even the justification of a pronoun in the text.

(3) " This is," he says,[3] " perhaps the most important single

[2] *John the Presbyter*, 1911, p.75.
[3] *Our Translated Gospels*, p.52.

verse in the Fourth Gospel''. What a pity then that it has to be so maltreated in order to yield its meaning ! Bernard says it means : The Apostle knows that the Evangelist is telling the truth. Torrey says it means : The Evangelist knows that the Apostle is telling the truth. Of course, they are both right if we identify the Evangelist with the Apostle ! Against Bernard we can object : What is the use of the writer's gratuitous assertion that the Apostle (or rather " that one ") knows (without any written endorsement) that the writer is telling the truth? But Torrey's view is even less plausible. For how could the writer possibly *know* that the Apostle was telling the truth? Unless of course the writer was himself present on Calvary ! But if he was not, does it not sound impertinent for him to vouch for the veracity of the great Apostle? In either case, when and where did the Apostle (assumed to be different from the Evangelist) tell of the incident? It is the writer who is now recounting (*legei*, present tense) what happened—that ye (the readers) may believe. This is confirmed by xx. 31 : " These things have been *written* that ye may believe that Jesus is the Messiah, the Son of God."

C. " The witness of the Apostle is authentic. And Christ knows that the Apostle (who is also the Evangelist) is telling the truth."

This view was suggested by Erasmus and revived by Zahn in 1888. On this interpretation, " the reporter or writer claims to be an eye-witness, he asseverates his words by invoking Christ the Lord (*ekeinos*) as witness to the truth of his statements."[4] It is perfectly orthodox and has been accepted by Catholic commentators such as Tillmann and Lagrange. Nevertheless I propose to argue against it.

(1) There is considerable grammatical difficulty. The natural construction is to take *ekeinos* as referring to the immediately preceding *autou* and as being the subject of the two verbs *oiden* and *legei*. It would require very peremptory arguments to upset this construing.

(2) It is felt that the insertion of *ekeinos* involves emphasis. Even if this were so, it would not dissociate it from the preceding *autou*. Compare J7[22] : " I know Him (*auton*), for I am from Him (*par' autou*) ; and He (*kakeinos*) has sent Me." But in a writer like St. John, liberal in the use of pronouns, we cannot assume that *ekeinos* is emphatic. The references to his First Epistle appear to be fallacious. For if the instances of *ekeinos* there occurring are examined,

[4] Jannaris, *Expos. Times*, July 1903, p.461.

it will be found that John simply uses " he " either because Christ (or God) has been previously mentioned or because the reference is clear from the context.

(3) The use of the third person does not in any way militate against the reference being to the writer. Apart from Aramaic usage, the prevailing Greek fashion of writing history was impersonal ; a similar employment of the third person instead of the first can be found in Thucydides and Xenophon, and also in Caesar. In any case, the present interpretation admits that he who saw and gave testimony was the Evangelist.[5]

(4) It has been urged[6] that if the witness or guarantor were identical with the author, he would be bearing witness to himself (against J5[31] 8[13]). So III J[12] : " We also bear witness [to Demetrius], and you know that our witness is true (alēthēs)." In the text under discussion, nothing would be gained by saying : My witness is true and I know it.

To this it can first be answered that neither would there be any gain in saying : Christ knows it. For nobody, except by a revelation, could be sure that this was so. In the next place, unless we adopt the unproved and already rejected parenthesis, St. John makes no such statement.[7] As the verse is translated by me, the Evangelist is referring to his motive for recounting this unpleasant and dishonouring episode, namely, to convince his readers of the real humanity of Christ. Finally, even if the parenthesis is admitted, the author does not say that he knows his testimony to be true, but : he knows that he is saying true things, i.e. recounting actual physical happenings against those who denied that Jesus Christ came in the flesh (cf. I J4[2]).

(5) This view is also supported by analogy with J21[24] : " This is the disciple who is testifying concerning these things and who wrote them. And we know that his testimony is true (alēthēs)." It is generally held that oidamen (we know) is a true plural, either the author plus others or else a group of Ephesian elders, and

---

[5] Josephus uses ekeinos of himself : " They did not do this, I think, because they grudged him his escape (ekeinou sōtērias), but because they were hoping for their own."—B.J. iii. 7, 16 (202).
[6] Lagrange, Jean, 1925[2], p.500.
[7] Here is Moffatt's translation : " He who saw it has borne witness (his witness is true ; God knows he is telling the truth), that you may believe." It may of course be asserted that it lends emphasis and is almost an oath to add ' Christ knows he is telling the truth.' But would the Evangelist make such an appeal? And if he did, would he not be more explicit in referring to Christ?

therefore conveys external attestation. This view, however, is
subject to serious difficulties.[8] If the author wrote this testimonial
for the elders, they failed to attest it with their signatures. If they
composed the verse, they failed to identify themselves or to give us
the name of the author. Outsiders might declare ' we know the
writer is truthful.' But how could they possibly say ' We know his
witness is true '? In any case, the idea that the author of the Fourth
Gospel was looking for corroboration implies a complete mis-
understanding of his position. It is much simpler to take the first
personal plural—which occurs in the Prologue and in the First
Epistle—as referring to the author himself: a usage common in
later Greek (the *koine*).[9] John says : I know that my testimony is
true. It may well be that the Evangelist is associating himself with
the body of disciples or apostles who were witnesses. But even if we
admit that he is joining himself with his entourage, he is at least
referring to living human persons. There would be no point in
writing ' Christ knows,' unless he felt that doubts would be cast on
his veracity.

This long excursus on a single verse is justified by the claim to be
an eye-witness which the writer makes. This claim is only twice
explicitly asserted, here and at the end of the last chapter (21).
Elsewhere the assumption of being a personal disciple is casual and
incidental, e.g. by his presence at the Last Supper.[10] In the most
doctrinal parts of the Gospel, there is hardly a hint of the author's
presence. Had the Gospel been a literary invention, the claim to
first-hand knowledge would have been more prominent and
frequent. The assertion in 19[35] is highly significant. Impersonation
in literature may in certain cases be justifiable. But there is no excuse
for a writer so disguising himself and then deliberately stating that
he is *not* doing so. " He who has seen has been testifying." " This is

---

[8] Dom J. Chapman, We know that his testimony is true, *Journal of Theol. Studies*
31 (1930) 379-387.
[9] In verse 25—which is often regarded as an addition—the singular *oimai* (I
suppose) occurs. A similar instance occurs in the quotation from Josephus in note 5.
[10] Tertullian assumes the universal consensus of orthodox and heretics that the
Apostle wrote the Gospel : " Was anything concealed from John, the Lord's most
beloved disciple, who used to lean on His breast, to whom alone the Lord desig-
nated Judas as the traitor, whom He commended to Mary as a son in His place?
Of what could He have meant to be ignorant those to whom He showed His glory
with Moses and Elias and the Father's voice from heaven? "—*De praescriptione
haereticorum* 22. John was also the author of chapter 21 : " Even John underwent
death, though there had circulated concerning him an underground expectation
that he would remain until the Lord's coming."—Tertullian, *De anima* 50.

the disciple who is testifying concerning these things and who wrote them."

As to the episode on Calvary, the writer says that he is describing it " that ye may believe," not something about the writer, but the reality of the incident and therefore the real humanity and the true death of Christ. This thrust of a lance, followed by the extra-ordinary exit of blood and water, is not one which would have occurred to anyone to invent. It was not a glorious manifestation of divinity, it involved no exhibition of supernatural power. It was, in fact, a dishonour done to the dead body, only less repugnant than crushing the legs.[11] There is a story told about the first-century Rabbi Johanan ben Zakkai.[12] He was brought, disguised as a corpse, out of besieged Jerusalem. The Roman soldiers wished by a spear-thrust to make sure that he was dead. But his disciples prevented this by pointing out the shame it would be so to dis-honour the body of the renowned teacher. In the case of Our Lord there was no one to stop the outrage, though a beautiful legend tells us that Our Lady tried to dissuade the soldier. St. John tersely and simply records the deed. And then, to reassure his readers that this did not involve any doubt concerning His Messiahship, he quotes two texts of Scripture.

(7) St. John quotes Scripture

For these things happened in fulfilment of this passage of Scripture:
' Not a bone of his will be broken.'
And another passage says:
' They will look upon him whom they have pierced.'

St. John xix. 36f.

It has been incorrectly said[1] that the preceding verse about the witness " rudely interrupts the connection." In an obvious sense,

---

[11] " That is: I did not hear it from others, but I was myself present and saw it ; and the testimony is true. Which may well be supposed ; for he relates an insult which was done, not anything great or admirable."—Chrysostom, *In Ioann.*, hom. 85.
[12] Schlatter, *Jochanan ben Zakkai*, 1896, p.63 ; Schlatter, *Der Ev. Johannes* 1930, p.355. The people should not be able to say : " Our Rabbi died and they pierced him " (*mēth rabbān ve-dĕqārūhū*).—Rabba to Lam1[5].
[1] Macgregor, *Gospel of John*, 1936, p.351. This is in order to hand the verse over to the " redactor." (A redactor is the obliging fellow on whom you foist any text that might spoil your theory.)

of course, the insertion of any new thought is an interruption. But the connection is here made by the phrase "for these things happened," which refers back to the omission of *crurifragium* and to the lance-thrust. This introductory phrase is specially inserted; it does not occur elsewhere in St. John when he alludes to fulfilment of Scripture or prophecy.[2] Notice particularly the particle 'for.' His readers are reassured; these happenings were providential, they were even foreshadowed in Scripture. To his fellow-Jews this was a cogent argument. After much searching, two passages were discovered. They are not such as leap to the eye; they had to be unearthed from hundreds of other more striking statements. It is utterly impossible to think that these prophecies created the story, the incident which *prima facie* involved a dishonour. There is no reason whatever for holding that the Jews of that time feared that the Messiah's bones might be broken or that he was to be transfixed. Obviously the reasoning is *not*: This was prophesied of the Messiah and hence must have been fulfilled in Jesus. The attitude is rather: This happened to the body of Jesus. But we need not be perturbed, for it was adumbrated in Scripture. This appeal of St. John, this otherwise inexplicable prominence given to these phrases, is a further guarantee of the historicity of the lance-thrust which evoked this scriptural apology.

To-day many would be inclined to say: If Jesus were already dead, what did it matter whether or not His legs were broken? But not so for John and his readers. If God had permitted the bone-breaking, contemporary Jews would have seen in the fact a proof that God had rejected Him. Does not Scripture declare that God protects the bones of the good man? "Many are the ills of the righteous. But the Lord delivers him out of them all. He keeps [intact] all his bones; not one of them is broken."[3]

This particular reference is not at all certain. According to most interpreters, St. John is referring to the paschal lamb, whose bones were to be kept unbroken.[4] In this case the passover lamb was for the Evangelist a prophetic type of Christ. Even in a detail of the

---

[2] For example 12³⁸ and 19²⁴. So when he says (18⁹ and 18³²): that the saying of Jesus might be fulfilled. These latter instances show clearly that this means *not* ' in order to fulfil what was said,' but ' in accordance with what was said.'

[3] Ps 34 (33)²⁰. Here in the Greek occurs the same verb *syntribēsetai* as in J19³⁷ (where the Vulgate has *comminuetis*).

[4] Ex 12⁴⁶: Neither are ye to break a bone of it (Greek *syntripsetai*). Num 9¹²: They are not to break a bone of it (*syntripsousin*). Cf. *Pesahim* 7¹¹: "If a man breaks a bone of a clean Passover-offering, he incurs the Forty Stripes."—Danby *Mishnah*, 1933, p.146.

ritual he sees an appropriate reason for His being spared *crurifragium*.[5] " Christ our Passover is sacrificed for us," says St. Paul (I Cor 5[7]).

But St. John wishes to go further and to reconcile his fellow-Jews to the transfixion of Jesus. So he quotes a sentence from the prophet Zachary (12[10]), who foretold the murder of a divinely accredited prophet by the nation and their repentance when their guilt was brought home to them.

> I will pour out on the house of David, and on the inhabitants of Jerusalem, the spirit of grace and of supplication. And they will look upon him whom they have pierced. And they will mourn for him as one mourns for his only son . . . In that day there will be great mourning in Jerusalem, as is the mourning of Hadad-Rimmon in the valley of Megiddon.

He then proceeds to enumerate as mourners all the religious and civil representatives of the nation : the government (David), the prophets (Nathan), the priests (Levi), the temple-ministrants (Shimei). Apparently they as well as the whole people are responsible for the death of the pierced one. But ' on that day,' when God's grace is poured out, there will be immense lamentation, more than for a mere man, even a king.[6]

Many commentators[7] have taken the literal sense of the passage as referring to the Macchabean struggle and triumph. Others have taken it not only typically but literally messianic.[8]

There are some difficulties about the sentence : They will look upon him whom they have pierced.[9]

(1) They will look : John has *opsontai*, the Septuagint *epiblepsontai*.

---

[5] Lactantius says : " All this was done lest His body if injured or broken should be rendered unsuitable for rising again."—*De div. inst.* iv. 26. Cf. Origen cited above, p.266.

[6] Hadad-Rimmon is composed of two names for a west-semitic deity. St. Jerome, thinking a reference to pagan rites improbable, took the name to be geographical (the place near where Josiah died).

[7] St. Ephraem, Theodore of Mopsuestia, Theodoret, Cornelius a Lapide, Calmet, Condamin.

[8] There are several references to Zachary in the account of the Passion. For the triumphal entry 9[9] is quoted. On the way to Gethsemani (Mk 14[27]) Our Lord quoted 13[7]. In connection with the treachery of Judas, St. Matthew (27[9]) cites 11[13].

[9] In addition to commentaries, reference may be made to the following : A. McCaul, *Rabbi David Kimchi's Commentary upon the Prophecies of Zechariah*, 1837, pp.156-163. A. Condamin, S.J., Le sens messianique de Zach. xii. 10, *Recherches de science religieuse* 1 (1910) 52-56. A. Skrinjar, S.J., Aspicient ad me quem confixerunt, *Verbum Domini* 11 (1931) 233-242.

(2) *Upon him*: John has *eis hon*, corresponding to the Hebrew *elaiv*. But the Massoretic text reads *elai* (upon or to me) ; so the Septuagint, Aquila and Symmachus: *pros me*. Père Condamin says that it is not certain that St. John's quotation is literal ; and he prefers *elai* (to me) as the original reading : " The addition of *v* to suppress the difficulty is much more probable than its disappearance in the manuscripts represented by the ancient versions " (p.53).[10] On the other hand, many Hebrew scholars prefer *elaiv* (to him).[10] There is a good deal to be said for this, apart from St. John's quotation. Since the same person is immediately referred to in the third person (they will mourn for *him*), the use of the first person (to *me*) is improbable. Moreover, it is Yahweh who is speaking : how could God be represented as saying that He will be pierced? Taken literally (the real death of God), such a premature explicit revelation would merely have been revolting. Nor can the expression be taken metaphorically ; for he who is pierced is pictured as dead. Some moderns have interpreted ' to me ' as in the person of his representative. But even this would be unacceptable phraseology. There is no parallel with such a saying as ' he who despises you despises Me,' where there is one moral person but two distinct physical persons.

Van Hoonacker[11] has therefore proposed an interpretation, which can be effected by punctuation even without a change in the text : " They will turn towards Him (Yahweh). Him whom they have pierced they will lament."

(3) *Whom*: Hebrew (Massoretic) *eth asher*. Septuagint: *anth'ōn*. Theodotion (as St. John) : *eis hon*. Aquila : *syn hō*. Symmachus: *emprosthen*. The present Hebrew reading is difficult to accept ; it is interpreted by Kimchi as " because they have pierced," but he really wishes to say " because of him whom they have pierced."[12] The phrase *eth asher* may sometimes mean ' because ' (eg. Lev 26[25]), but never ' because of him whom.' If we take it as ' because,' then the transitive verb ' pierced ' is left without an accusative ; in every other passage where the verb *daqar* occurs, the accusative is plainly expressed.

(4) *They have pierced*: This corresponds to the Hebrew (Masso-

---

[10] So Ewald and Dillmann. Also Torrey, who thinks that *v* accidentally dropped out of the Massoretic text and that this necessitated the insertion of *eth* (with).— *Documents of the Primitive Church*, 1941, p.182.

[11] *Les douze petits prophètes*, 1908, p.683. This is accepted by Condamin, p.54.

[12] McCaul, p.156.

retic) *daqārū.* Also Theodotion and Aquila (with St. John) : *exe-kentēsan.* Symmachus : *epexekentēsan.* St. Jerome : *transfixerunt.*
The Septuagint has *katōrchēsanto,* mocked or danced (in triumph over me). This corresponds to a Hebrew *raqādū,* due to the confusion of *r* and *d.* This is easy enough in the square characters used to-day ; it was still easier with Phoenician or ancient Hebrew letters.[13]

Some Jewish interpreters[14] have assumed different subjects for the two verbs ' look ' and ' pierced ' : They (Israelites) will look on him whom they (Gentiles) have pierced. This is a very artificial construction, obviously made to controvert the Christian application. On any natural unforced interpretation, the subject of the two verbs is the same, namely, " the house of David and the inhabitants of Jerusalem " mentioned in the immediately preceding verse.

Moreover, the rabbis felt the difficulty of such excessive grief and fear because of the death of some obscure person during (as they supposed) the times of messianic triumph. To meet this difficulty, and also perhaps that of the Suffering Servant of Isaiah, they invented a secondary or subordinate Messiah, son of Joseph (not of David), who would first appear and after a short career fall fighting before the gates of Jerusalem against the heathen world-power. Messiah ben David was then to appear and secure victory, and (at least in some accounts) he would raise Messiah ben Joseph from the dead. Probably the idea of a Suffering Messiah was at least in some circles accepted at an early date, but not his dying on the cross or his redemptive death.[15] But explicit written admission occurs only later :

> [Zach 12¹²] There are two different ways of explaining this verse. According to one opinion, the prophet is deploring the future death of the Messiah. According to the other, the reference is to the destruction of ' the evil inclination.'—Jerusalem Talmud, *Sukkah* 55a.
>
> [Rab quoted Zach 12¹²]. Thereupon R. Dosa and our teachers disputed about this. One said : It refers to Messiah son of Joseph, who will be slain. Another said : It refers to the ' evil inclination ' which will be slain. The opinion of him who referred it to Messiah

[13] The D and R of the Phoenician alphabet are given in G. Maspero, *The Struggle of the Nations,* 1896, p.75. St. Jerome suggested this confusion of daleth and resh : P.L. 25. 1415.
[14] So the Chizzuk Emunah (McCaul, p.157). The American Jewish version has : " They shall look unto Me because they have thrust him through." The *him* is inserted without warrant. There is a tendentious footnote to the second ' they ' : " That is, the nations. See verse 9."
[15] So the Jewish interlocutor in Justin's *Dialogue* (89), cited above, p.170.

son of Joseph is to be accepted. For it is written : They will look towards me whom they have pierced, and they will mourn over him as one mourns over an only son. Now what mourning can there be for the evil inclination being slain? For this one ought rather make a feast.[16]—Babylonian Talmud, *Sukkah* 52a.

It is curious to observe that, in spite of the Christian application, many Jewish commentators continued to interpret this chapter of Zachary (and in particular the verse about piercing) messianically. Thus Rashi (✝ 1105) says in his commentary on Zachary : " They shall look back to mourn, because the Gentiles had pierced some amongst them and killed some of them." But in his commentary on the Talmud he writes : " Zechariah prophesies of the future, that they shall mourn on account of Messiah the son of Joseph, who shall be slain in the war of Gog and Magog."—McCaul, p.161. Kimchi (✝ 1235) commenting on Zachary 12^{10} says (p.155) : " Our rabbis of blessed memory have interpreted this of Messiah the son of Joseph who shall be killed in the war." So also Ibn Ezra (✝ 1139) and Abarbanel (✝ 1509).—McCaul, p.158. The most interesting comment is that of Moses Alsheik (*floruit* 1550 /1600) :

> They shall look unto me, for they shall lift up their eyes unto me in perfect repentance, when they see him whom they pierced, that is Messiah the son of Joseph. For our rabbis of blessed memory have said that he will take upon himself all the guilt of Israel, and shall then be slain in the war to make an atonement, in such a manner that it shall be accounted as if Irsael had pierced him, for on account of their sin he has died. And therefore in order that it may be reckoned to them as perfect atonement, they will repent and look to the Blessed One, saying that there is none beside Him to forgive those that mourn on account of him who died for their sin. This is the meaning of ' They shall look upon me.'—McCaul, p.163.

This comment rises above the idea of nationalist war. Here we see the concept of atonement brought in and the future repentance of Israel.

It would seem that St. John's reference is eschatological.[17] A day will come, he says, when his fellow-Jews will look to the Pierced One and mourn for their deed. This is clear in the Apo-

[16] But why should the house of David and the people of Jerusalem mourn so bitterly for a son of Joseph, whose death should be a cause of joy since it is to make way for Messiah ben David?
[17] In the Gospel he does not quote the reference to mourning. So the primary reference may really be to Calvary, when the Jews literally looked on the Pierced One.

calypse (i. 7), where he again cites Zachary : " Behold, He comes
with clouds. And every eye will see Him, even those who have
pierced Him. And all the tribes of the earth will mourn over Him."
So also the earliest Christian writers who refer to the text :

> They will say : Is not this He whom we once crucified, rejected,
> pierced and spat upon?—Barnabas vii. 9
> He has two advents : one in which He was pierced by you ;
> a second when you will know Him whom you have pierced and
> your tribes will mourn.—St. Justin, *Dial.* xxxii. 2.

But may we not take this looking to the Pierced One, and this
mourning, as a prophecy that one day Israel will acknowledge her
Messiah?

> Has God cast off His people? Heaven forbid ! . . . Have they
> stumbled to their fall? Heaven forbid ! But by their lapse salva-
> tion has come to the Gentiles . . . If their rejection has been the
> reconciliation of the world, what will their acceptance be but
> life from the dead?—Romans xi. 1, 11, 15.

(8) Piercing Before Death?

We have already studied a number of illustrations of the Crucifixion, in which Our Lord is depicted as both being offered the
soaked sponge and at the same time being pierced in the side. The
time has now come to investigate this artistic phenomenon and to
correlate it with contemporary evidence from literature.

It is easy to dispose of the problem by talking of ' symbolism.'
Thus Mâle refers to Rabula's miniature (fig. xii. 14) : " Contrary
to all probability, it is in the right side that the lance wounds the
Saviour, because the wound is evidently symbolic."[1] Apart from
the fact that—as will be argued in the next chapter—almost
certainly the *right* side was really pierced, there is no proof whatever
of this allegedly evident symbolism. And even if it were admitted,
it must not be forgotten that the ancient idea of symbolism was
based upon and superadded to the historical reality. Everything
points to the fact that Rabula's picture was intended to be a historical presentation of Calvary. So the problem remains : Why did
this artist, as well as so many others down the centuries, depict
Christ as being pierced while alive?

[1] Mâle, *L'art religieux du xii. siècle en France*, 1924², p.80.

In view of the confused terminology prevalent and the loose talk of ' symbolism,' it will be useful to make on Christian art some general remarks which can be verified on the illustrations already given.

(1) The word ' symbolism ' should properly be reserved for those cases where the artist refuses to depict imaginatively the reality which he wishes to suggest mentally. Instead, for reasons of prudence or reverence, he provides a schematic substitute or symbol. Examples are : monogram, fish, lamb, bust, good shepherd. This is strikingly shown in the Bobbio ampulla (fig. xii. 4), where all the realities, including the sponge-offerer and the lance-piercer, are presented—except the Crucified whom the artist deliberately declines to portray as such.

(2) The word ' personification ' may be applied to allegorical figures such as faith, the seasons, earth and ocean, the jaws of hell, etc. In pictures of the Crucifixion the minor elements of sun and moon were first personified. Then the Church and the Synagogue were introduced. But though the Church with her chalice was an allegorical figure, the blood spurting out was regarded as historical. The blood-gush from the living Christ was chronologically prior to the introduction of the Church, and was often represented as having a physical effect on Longinus (the cure of his blindness).[1a]

This allegorism had a considerable vogue in the high Middle Ages, and sometimes ran riot. But in the end it proved to be an episodic divagation from the main stream of Christian art, when depicting scenes from the Gospels.

(3) Historical scenes. The Old Testament seems to have entered art before the New : Isaac, Jonah, Moses, Daniel, Adam and Eve. It is true that the interest of Christian artists was in the typical sense, in what these scenes prefigured. Nevertheless these scenes were

---

[1a] A further reason was invoked by some writers for holding that the stream of blood and water reached not only Longinus but Dismas : " It is credible that the bandit to whom the Lord promised Paradise was sprinkled with water and blood gushing from Christ's side and was saved by such holy baptism, for no one is saved without either baptism or martyrdom."—Ludolph of Saxony, *Vita I.C.* ii. 64, 14 (ed. Rigollot iv. 138).

[2] Ludoph of Saxony († 1378), referring to the Gloss and to Peter Comestor, refers to the devil on Calvary : " As is said in the Gloss on Tobias, when the Lord suffered on the cross, the devil, through whom the Crucifixion was brought about, approached to see if he could find some sin in Him. And in the Histories the Master says that he stood above the arm of the cross until Christ expired ; and then seeing himself defeated he retired. And coming to Tartarus he there found the soul of Christ breaking the gates and locks and leading out the souls of the just."—*Vita Iesu Christi* ii. 64, 3 : ed. Rigollot, 1878, iv. 129.

regarded and treated as historical events. When we come to the Crucifixion, we must beware of applying the narrow modern criterion of reality as purely physical. Some old Irish Crucifixions depicted demons perched on the cross-arm,[2] just as Giotto (fig. xii. 77) painted hovering angels, griefstricken and collecting the Precious Blood ; to the artists these were spiritual realities pictured corporeally, they were real components of the historical scene.

Leaving aside questions of knowledge and technique, we can distinguish three main attitudes towards Christian historical art :

(a) The spiritualist. The chief value is taken to be objective, the action of God towards men, not the attitude of men towards God. By way of overplus there is a subjective value ; thus the Passion awakens our sorrow and our love. But the artist concentrates on Redemption as the intervention of God into the world of time and space, as something once accomplished for us and now portrayed for our prayerful inspection. To accomplish this, the artist is in no way bound to produce the equivalent of a coloured photograph. To prevent dissipation of attention and to concentrate on the essential, he may not only choose the more suitable alternative from what is historically uncertain, but he may omit what he regards as irrelevant features, he may simplify the forms and abstract from their individual characteristics. However various be the execution, the artist's attitude is objective and latreutic.

There is a form of allegorism which is expressed in historical forms. Thus about the twelfth century there was in vogue a credulous natural history, abounding in anecdotal folklore and in fabulous plants and animals. Some of this had no religious reference, e.g. the mandrake, the barnacle goose, the unicorn (subdued only by a virgin). Other supposed facts were invoked to convey religious lessons, e.g. the phoenix rising from its ashes, the pelican feeding its young. Writers and artists were not really interested in natural history ; under the influence of their Neo-Platonist outlook, their minds depreciated all natural values and material truths. But it is hardly accurate to say that they saw " in almost all things symbols of vice or virtue," and " looked upon the world as a symbol."—Pourrat, *Christian Spirituality* 2 (1924) 109. For the material world was held to be more than a symbol or imaginary construction, it was admitted to have its own empirical and inferior reality. We may attribute to these writers and artists the view that " reality is nothing in itself, it is only a veil which must be raised, an envelope which must be broken, in order to attain to that which is spiritual and catch a glimpse of God " (*ibid.* p.116). But this applies only to the order of relative values and must not be twisted into an ontological pronouncement. Vestments and liturgy were equally allegorised in the sense of being explored for higher hidden meanings ; but their reality in their own order was not denied. All this movement gradually lost force with the rise of the Franciscan spirit of sympathy with nature and the growth of modern science. It may be characterised as a one-sided emphasis on transcendental values, just as the modern world is sunk in immanent values. But objectively its expression in art and in literature must be classified as historical in the sense that it portrayed what was conceived to be empirical reality.

(b)   The realist.   In an epoch of cultural heterogeneity, with increasing pride of technique and decreasing religious inspiration, the artist may become more absorbed in the physics of the scene. The anatomy is perfect, the light and shade are accurately balanced, the figures are life-like. But who would kneel before the picture? The soul has vanished from the scene which has become despiritualised. Christ on the cross is degraded to the level of an ordinary criminal, His Mother a fainting woman, Magdalen a voluptuous blonde.

(c)   The naturalist.   Realism sufficiently developed becomes naturalism, the tacit if not deliberate denial of the spiritual. The older Renascence form, imitating antique models, was based on the cult of physical beauty and the repudiation of suffering. Botticelli gives to Our Lady the traits of Venus, Filippo Lippi the features of his mistress.   Christ carrying His cross is smiling impassively (Francia) or simpering (Giorgione).

Later the non-religious outlook was expressed more brutally, sometimes even with a sadistic treatment. The Dead Christ of Mantegna is just a corpse seen in perspective ; that of Holbein Junior is a cadaver ready for dissection. Even the Crucified of Grünewald is a horrible putrefying criminal. There are modern pictures of the Crucifixion which are almost atheistic blasphemies.

(4)   Finally there is the artistic representation of supernatural realities. By this is meant that the subject-matter, while a reality to faith, is not one which comes within the purview of the historian. Examples are : The Descent of Christ to Limbo, the Last Judgement, the Christ of Pity, the Fountain of Life. This vision of the supernatural may also be added as an element in a historical picture. For instance : the presence of St. Francis[3] or of the donor at the

---

[3] In the *Fioretti* (ch. 44) St. John appears to Friar Peter and says : " The Mother of Christ and I sorrowed above all other creatures at the Passion of Christ ; but after us St. Francis felt greater sorrow than any other."—*The Little Flowers of St. Francis*, trans. Okey, 1930, p.130.

Nativity or on Calvary. Both artist and beholder were, in such cases, perfectly aware that these people were not physically present at these scenes. But they also held that in a mystical but real sense we and they can participate in what happened in Bethlehem or on Calvary. The life of the God-Man has abiding ultra-historical significance. It is to convey this deep mystical truth that an artist may depict all of us helping Christ to carry His Cross (fig. xi. 15) or may plant the Crucified among people of to-day (figs. xii. 82 and 83).

In current usage it is, however, difficult to confine the term 'symbol' to the narrower signification given above, namely, the portrayal of a more or less appropriate figure (e.g. a lamb) to symbolise another Figure (e.g. Christ) which, though historical and portrayable, it is not desired to represent literally. Representations such as the Fountain of Life (e.g. *Family at Bethany* fig. 29), the Sacred Heart surrounded by thorns and suchlike are generally called 'symbolical.' It would be preferable to use some other term such as 'mystical,' which is equally applicable, e.g. to suprahistorical elements introduced into historical scenes. For all these features are portrayed, not as a substitute for some other physical reality, but to express a hyperphysical truth of faith.

The foregoing clarification has been necessary, by way of background, in order to dispel a rather widespread exaggeration of the 'symbolic' character of early and medieval Christian art.[4] In Rabula's Crucifixion there is not a trace of allegory, no reason whatever for thinking that what the artist conceived to have been the historical reality has been distorted to provide a dogmatic lesson. The most that might be conceded is that the long robe has been added out of reverence. The anomaly that Christ is depicted as alive when pierced is adequately explained when we find this maintained in Greek Gospel codices more than two centuries older than

---

[4] Reil says that John's account of the dead Christ was "unusable for religious reflection or pictorial representation"; for the West the blood and water were "mere symbols" and *had* to come from a living body.—*Die frühchr. Darstellungen der Kreuzigung Christi*, 1904, p.88. According to Millet, Longinus and Stephaton were "two symbolic personages" representing Gentiles and Jews.—*Recherches sur l'iconographie de l'évangile*, 1916, p.427. "The blood and water which issued from the wound of Jesus Christ are the symbol of the two principal sacraments of the Church" and so the wound was "symbolically located in the right side."—Mâle, *L'art religieux du xiii. siècle en France*, 1925[6], p.190. On p.194 he says: "There cannot be any doubt as to the mysterious signification of the person of Mary at the foot of the cross." She is the Church while John is the Synagogue! Also "the two crucified thieves . . . were themselves considered the symbol of the new Church and the old Synagogue"!

this miniature, in Syriac literature, in Latin manuscripts—especially those of Irish origin and so also in Irish art--and in Passion plays,[5] even down to the fourteenth century. The piercing while Christ was alive was not invented for some mystic reason ; it was believed —erroneously of course—to have really happened.[6]

In a number of Greek manuscripts—six uncials[7] and many cursives—the following verse is interpolated after verse 49 of the 27th chapter of St. Matthew :[8]

But another taking a lance pierced His side, and there issued water and blood.

It occurs also in the Ethiopic version, but especially in a number of Latin manuscripts. It is particularly characteristic of Irish manuscripts—including the Book of Armagh and the Book of Kells ; and thence it penetrated a number of Vulgate codices in North England and the Continent. Apart from minor variants the Latin version, runs:[9] (See Wordsworth and White, *Quattuor Evangelia*, 1889-98, p.16).

Alius autem accepta lancea pupugit latus eius, et exiit aqua et sanguis.

Let us see how this verse fits into the context of M27 :

[46] But at the ninth hour Jesus cried with a loud voice : Eli . . .
[47] But some of the bystanders, hearing this said : This man is calling Elias.
[48] And immediately one of them ran, filled a sponge with vinegar placed it on a stick and gave Him a drink.

---

[5] Passion plays are considered in the next section, p.321.
[6] Vague explanations such as the following are useless : " The Eastern Christians dwelt on the physical sufferings of Jesus. He was to them a living sacrifice ; while yet alive he shed his blood for the redemption of sinners. The belief that Christ was still living when his side was pierced is shown, in all the early representations of the crucifixion, by his open eyes."—Peebles, *The Legend of Longinus*, 1911, p.45. The true explanation has been fully developed by Dom René-Jean Hesbert, *Le problème de la transfixion du Christ*, 1940. The artists and the writers we are considering did not take the lance-thrust as a mortal blow. According to the interpolated Matthew it followed immediately upon the offering of the sponge. In some pictures (e.g. fig. xii. 21) the lance-wound seems to be depicted as having preceded the sponge incident.
[7] Two of these, Aleph (Sinaitic) and B (Vatican) are of the fourth century, and a third C (Ephraemi Rescriptus) is of the fifth century.
[8] In addition to Hesbert, these articles may be consulted : H. J. Vogels, Der Lanzenstich vor dem Tode Jesu, *Biblische Zeitschrift* 10 (1912) 396-405 ; J. van Kasteren, S.J., Der Lanzenstich bei Mt. 27, 49, *ibid.* 12 (1914) 32-34 ; A. Vaccari, S.J., Exivit sanguis et aqua, *Verbum Domini* 17 (1937) 193-198.
[9] Compare this with the Vulgate of John xix. 34 : *Sed unus militum lancea latus eius aperuit, et continuo exivit sanguis et aqua.*

49 But the rest of them said : Let be, let us see if Elias will come to rescue Him.
[But another (*allos dè*) taking a lance pierced His side, and there issued water and blood].
50 But Jesus, again crying with a loud voice, dismissed His spirit.

It is clear that the interpolated verse does not suit the context. After ' one of them ' and ' the rest,' we do not expect to read ' but another.' And, of course, the soldiers—*a fortiori* the bystanders—were not free at their pleasure to stab the Crucified. In St. John's Gospel, the Jews had to go to Pilate for sanction to interfere with the crucified ; and it was Roman soldiers who were sent. In view of its flagrant contradiction with the Fourth Gospel, it is surprising that this interpolated verse received such widespread acceptance for so many centuries. How did it originate? Van Kasteren holds that it is a genuine verse of Matthew, originally indicating a *post mortem* deed but subsequently displaced. Vaccari thinks it was taken from John ; but the wording is different.[10] Vogel says it is from Tatian's Diatessaron, where, however, its occurrence has not been proved. Lagrange thinks it came from Origen ; but there is no evidence that he read it. Whatever be its origin, this insertion in the First Gospel has had great influence on literature, on art and even on liturgy.[11]

In the tenth century Gospel manuscript[12] known as cursive 72, the interpolated verse is placed in the margin with an indication that it is to come before verse 49, which is much more appropriate than after verse 49. There is a marginal note : " According to the Gospel ' according to history ' of Diodorus and of Tatian and of different holy Fathers, this is added." We are not sure about Tatian ; and the commentaries of Diodorus of Tarsus are not extant. More interesting is a quotation from Chrysostom also given in the margin of this manuscript :

When Matthew represents Him as before His death receiving the wound which the soldier with his lance inflicted on His side, and dying only after having been thus pierced, while on the

---

[10] Notice ' water and blood.' This is found as a variant reading in J19³¹ on one uncial, one minuscule, the Coptic-Bohairic, the African-Latin, as well as in Origen, Chrysostom, Eusebius, etc. Was this due to the interpolation in M?
[11] It occurs in some manuscripts of the Acts of Pilate (recension A ch. 10) : *Accipiens autem Longinus miles lanceam, aperuit latus eius ; et (continuo) exiit (exivit) de latere eius sanguis et aqua.*—Hesbert, p.127. This was before death, for Christ proceeds to speak to the bandits ; see Walker's translation, p.136.
[12] B. Mus. Harleian 5647. Hesbert, p.66 ; he gives a facsimile of folio 79a.

contrary John asserts that He was pierced with the lance after death, what they say is not contradictory, both affirm the truth- Matthew, editing his account in his usual manner, anticipates the wound which was inflicted after death ; hence the confusion in the narration. On the other hand, John shows the accuracy of his knowledge when he places after death the wound received by the body.

According to this quotation which does not occur in his printed works, St. John Chrysostom († 407) read the interpolated verse in his copy of Matthew but interpreted it of a postmortal piercing. This is confirmed by his extant commentary :[13]

They thought, he says, that He was calling Elias. And immediately they gave Him vinegar to drink. But another approaching pierced His side with a lance.
What could be more lawless and brutal than these men who carried their madness so far as to offer final insult to a dead body? But observe how He made use of their wickedness for our salvation.   For after the blow (*plēgēn*) the fountains (*pēgai*) of our salvation thence gushed forth.
But Jesus, crying with a loud voice, dismissed His spirit.
—*In Matt.* hom. 88 : P.G. 58. 776.

In Syriac literature as well as art there are also indications that the premortal piercing was accepted :

He was pierced by the Jews, He died and was buried.—Syriac version of the Apology of Aristides, 15 : *Ap. des Arist.*, ed. E. Hennecke, 1893, p.10 ; J. Geffcken, *Zwei griech. Apologeten*, 1907, pp.23, 85. This translation is earlier than the date of the Mt. Sinai manuscript (550 /600) in which it occurs.
When wounded by the lance on the cross, His life did not pass away of necessity, but He bowed His head and gave up the ghost.—Moro Bar Kustant, bishop of Amida (6th cent.), *Tetrevangelion* (in Greek), cited in the *Syriac Chronicle* known as that of Zechariah of Mitylene (c. 570), trans. Hamilton and Brooks, 1899, p.216.
They smote Him with a spear in His side, and He cried out with a loud voice on the cross (My Father, forgive them). And when the preaching of the prophets was accomplished, the sun was darkened from the sixth to the ninth hour.—Syriac *Acts of John* : *Apocryphal Acts of the Apostles*, trans. W. Wright, 1871, ii. 16.
The piercing while alive is also found in Irish literature (as well

---

[13] About 500 there was a discussion of the interpolated text at Constantinople, as recorded by Severus of Antioch († 535), who says that the only old exegetes who accepted it were Chrysostom and Cyril of Alexandria.—Hesbert, p.77. There is no trace of it in Cyril's extant works. The piercing while alive is assumed by Nicephorus († 828) : " He was raised on the cross, His side was pierced, He underwent death, He was buried."—*Antirrheticus* 3 : P.G. 100. 366 ; Hesbert, p.118.

as art). In an Irish version of the Acts of Pilate we read, after the incident of the vinegar :

Then rose up a certain soldier called Longinus and thrust his soldier's lance into Jesus' side, so that there rushed out at once two streams from His side : a stream of blood and a stream of water.—Atkinson, *Passions and Homilies from the Leabhar Breac*, 1887, p.368.

Next the incident of the penitent bandit is described. There follow the darkness and the earthquake. " Then Jesus cried with a loud voice," bowed His head and gave up the ghost. " A mighty man of the Jews (*sic*) named Centurio saw these great miracles ; and he glorified God and said that the man who was crucified and suffered was a righteous man " (p.369).

We find the same assumption in an Irish Passion, which, after giving the cry " Ely, Ely, lama zabatany " proceeds as follows :

Another group of people who heard Him said : It is Ely He is calling to deliver Him. One of the soldiers immediately after-wards ran and put vinegar in a sponge on the top of a rod, and gave it to Jesus to drink. Zefaton was the name of the soldier, as the writings tell. The multitudes in general said : Let Him alone, that we may see whether Ely will come to save Him. But one of the soldiers took a spear, and made a thrust with it into the right side of Jesus, so that blood and water came thereout. After that Jesus spoke to a throng of people whom He saw walking along the road near to Him : O good men, saw ye ever My sickness on any man in the world before? Then Jesus cried again with a loud voice and gave up the ghost.—Atkinson, p.382.

There do not appear to be so many instances of the legend in English literature. But it occurs in Lydgate's poem *Nightingale* :

Longeus with a spear, the hour of none, as Jews him desired, thirled and pierced through His heart and side. He, saying then *Consummatum est*, expired ; and head inclined, the ghost gave up that tide unto the Father.—Lydgate, *Two Nightingale Poems*, ed. O. Glauning, (EETS) 1900, p.14.

Dom Hesbert has shown that the piercing before death also found a place in the liturgy. In particular, he has, with the help of manuscripts with melodies, investigated the response *Tenebrae factae sunt* for Holy Week. There were three original forms (1) The Roman MSS. place the piercing after death. (2) That of Milan : all the Ambrosian MSS. place it before death. (3) The Benevento form : after death. But originally the Roman form had the piercing

before death, as is shown by the most ancient witness, the Anti-
phonary of Compiègne (800/830). It was corrected probably
through the influence of Agobard, Archbishop of Lyons (✝ 840),
who wrote thus in his *De correctione antiphonarii* :

> For all the faithful it is certain that Our Saviour died spontan-
> eously for us without being compelled by any painful violence.
> He did not lose His life through necessity, but with power He laid
> it down, as He Himself said : No one takes My life from Me, but
> of Myself I lay it down that I may again take it up. But this
> [antiphon], against the Gospel order and the truth of faith, says
> that the Lord's side was first pierced with a lance by the soldiers
> and then His spirit was given up. It is an altogether pagan view
> that Christ met His death not by the graciousness of His own will
> but by the force of pain.—P.L. 104. 332 ; Hesbert, p.48.

It is an extraordinary fact that a text, not merely casually read
but solemnly chanted for centuries by monks and clerics in com-
memoration of Christ's death, was thus accepted in contradiction
with the Gospel of St. John. If it was thus permitted in liturgical
chant, we can understand its vogue in art. Early in the fourteenth
century the Church at last intervened officially. Among the errors
of Peter Olivi (✝ 1298) condemned by the Council of Vienne
(1311/12) was this piercing before death. Quoting St. John, the
Council defined that Christ's side was pierced when He was dead.[14]
Olivi's fellow Franciscan, Ubertino of Casale, issued, on behalf of
the Spirituals, a defence which included this point.[15] Olivi, according to Ubertino, in his *Postilla super Joannem*, " without any assertion
and from a certain devotion on the occasion of some saying or
revelation, investigates whether the text of John's Gospel could be
satisfied if one held that Christ was then living." In support of the
tenability of this view, Ubertino quotes several authorities. First
a work attributed [incorrectly] to St. Bernard :

> Christ with side bared shows to the Father His side and His
> wounds . . . It is indeed a great thing that pardon is granted to
> the bandit. But this is really wonderful : that, after completing
> the dispensation of the Incarnation, Jesus, about to expire,
> honours His Mother with such affection, . . . when, with His
> wounded side and nailed hands and feet, He was already at the
> point of death (*in ultimis*).—Bernard [really his friend Ernald of
> Bonneval], *De laudibus B.V.M.* cap. 7 : P.L. 189. 1726 ; Ehrle,
> p.403.

---

[14] Denzinger-Bannwart, *Enchiridion Symbolorum*, 1908[10], n.480, p.209.
[15] Printed by (Cardinal) Franz Ehrle in *Archiv für Litteratur und Kirchen-Geschichte
des Mittelalters*, 2 (1886) 402.

Next he quotes the Gospel of St. Matthew, " as corrected through Jerome." He " made an extract from a very old book " of the Gospel and the reading " is also found in very many other copies." In other words, Ubertino accepted the interpolated verse as a genuine part of the Gospel. Finally he cites the Gospel of Nicodemus (Acts of Pilate) with the sentence already given above (p.312), but with *fixit in latus* for *aperuit latus.*

After this date the piercing before death gradually disappeared from art and literature.

(9) The Legend of Longinus[1]

It is generally held that the name Longinus is derived from *tonchê*, the Greek word for lance. This, however, is extremely doubtful.[2] There is reference to St. Longinus a martyr in Cappadocia before there is any mention of the lance-relic.[3] And the name (in Greek) is found applied to the soldier on Calvary in the Syrian miniature of Rabula (586). There are many saints called Longinus.[4] It was in fact a prechristian Roman name. The man who stabbed Julius Caesar was called Caius Cassius Longinus. His name may have been thought appropriate for him who pierced Christ. There is in fact a legend that before his conversion our Longinus was called Cassius.[5]

The soldier of St. John was generally identified with the centurion of the Synoptic Gospels.[6] But apparently this was not the original

[1] Much information has been collected by Rose Jeffries Peebles in her Bryn Mawr thesis : *The Legend of Longinus in Ecclesiastical Tradition and in English Literature and its Connection with the Grail*, Baltimore, 1911.
[2] There are also various names assigned to the sponge-bearer. The most widespread is *Stephaton*. This is found in a 9th century Gospel-book at Angers (Hesbert, p.100), in the Codex Egberti (fig. xii. 19), in a 10th century ivory in Berlin Museum etc. It is given in an Irish Homily (see p.315). Another name is Esopos (see fig. xii. 22). Still another is Calpurnius, given in the 11th century painting in Sant' Urbano (fig. xii. 23). There is no satisfactory explanation of these names, only suggestions of derivation from *spongos, hyssopos.*
[3] *Martyrologium Hieronymianum* (probably c.500) : P.L. 30. 462.
[4] F. G. Holweck, *Biog. Dict. of the Saints,* 1924, p.614 ; Peebles, p.32.
[5] Peebles, p.28. In the Passion of St. Paul by Pseudo-Linus, one of the three soldiers conducting Paul to execution was called Longinus. But in the Greek Acts the name is Longus—James, *Apocr. N.T.,* 1924, p.296.
[6] In the A-text of the *Acta Pilati* xvi. 7, we read " Longinus the soldier pierced His side with a spear."—Tischendorf, *Ev. apocr.* p.283 ; Walker, p.147 ; James, *Apocr. N.T.,* p.113. In the B-text (which contains no reference to the piercing) we read in ch. xi of " Longinus the centurion."—Tisch. p.309, Walker, p.160. The Letter of Pilate to Herod (James, p.155) refers to " Longinus the believing centurion " who was in charge of the guard at the tomb. According to the Gospel of Peter (31), Pilate gave the Jews " Petronius the centurion with soldiers to watch the sepulchre." There is a curious Latin annotation to the *Martyrology of Oengus,* ed. Whitley Stokes, 1905, p.226 : " Longinus and Egitianus are the names of the soldiers who stood beside Christ's cross." Egyptian (gipsy) ?

version. The entry in the Roman Martyrology for 15th March is : " At Caesarea in Cappadocia, the passion of St. Longinus, the soldier who is said to have pierced the Lord's side with a lance." The version of Hrabanus Maurus (a pupil of Alcuin, † 856) as follows :

> March 15th, in Cappadocia the passion of St. Longinus martyr. The following is related in the account of his martyrdom. When serving under a Roman centurion at the Lord's Passion, with a lance he opened His side on the cross. Seeing the earthquake and the miracles, he believed in Christ and repented of his previous deeds. He became a monk and served Christ for 34 years, converting many to the faith. Finally he was martyred in Cappadocia under Octavius the governor, who by divine judgement was owing to his infidelity struck with bodily blindness but whom [Longinus] illuminated after his martyrdom.—P.L. 110. 1135 ; Peebles p.15. Similarly in Bede : P.L. 94. 859.

The documents (apparently of the tenth century) given in the *Acta Sanctorum* (15 March) distinguish between the soldier and the centurion.[7] The life of Longinus the soldier is a developed form of that just quoted. That of the centurion (also called Longinus) is different. After acting on Calvary, he is sent to watch the sepulchre. He is converted, resigns and retires to Cappadocia. There he is beheaded by emissaries of Pilate. His head is brought to Jerusalem. A woman called Christina has her health restored after recovering and restoring the head of Longinus. In the Eastern Church there was a special feast of the ' invention ' of the head.[8]

But the identification of the soldier and the centurion became accepted, especially in the West. Thus in an Irish Passion of St. Longinus we read :

> When Christ was being crucified by the Jews, one of the soldiers who was at His crucifixion, called Centurus and also Longinus, came and brought a long spear in his hand, with which He wounded Christ in His side and split His heart in twain, so that blood and wine [*sic*] came out. Then great darkness covered all the face of the earth. The sun was darkened; the rocks were rent; and the graves were wide open. When therefore Longinus saw that great miracle, he forthwith believed in the one God, Jesus Christ. And he cried with a loud voice, saying: In truth this is Christ the Son of God.—trans. Atkinson, *Passions and Homilies from the Leabhar Breac*, 1887, p. 300. But in the Irish version of the Acts of Pilate (cited on p. 315 above) the soldier and the centurion are distinguished.

[7] Summarised in Peebles, pp.16ff.
[8] Mantua also claimed to have the head of Longinus (identified with the soldier) and some drops of Christ's blood brought by him. His position as patron saint of Mantua led Mantegna to make him the subject of several paintings.—Peebles, p.52.

So far there has been no reference to the blindness of Longinus. The first literary allusions seem tentative :[9]

> One of the soldiers pierced His right side with a lance, and at once there issued blood and water. And, as some relate, as his eyes were almost darkened, when the man who lanced Him had touched his eyes with His blood, he saw clearly.—Petrus Comestor (12th century), *Hist. Schol.* : P.L. 198. 1633.

> Longinus was a certain centurion who, standing by the Lord's cross with other soldiers, by Pilate's order pierced the Lord's side with a lance. Seeing the miracles—the darkened sun and the earthquake—he believed in Christ. This, as certain people say, was especially due to the fact that, as his eyes were darkened by infirmity or age, he by chance touched his eyes with the blood of Christ which ran down the lance, and at once he saw clearly.— Jacobus de Voragine († 1298) *Legenda aurea*, cap. 47 : ed. Graesse 1890, iii. 202 ; T. de Wyzewa, *La légende dorée*, 1929, p.208.

In art, however, there appear to be much earlier indications of the legend that Longinus' blindness was cured by Christ's blood. This may be indicated in S. Maria Antiqua (fig. xii. 16), it is certainly contained in the Saint-Gall Crucifixion (fig. xii. 24) and in that of Sant' Urbano (fig. xii. 23).

The story of the cure became generally adopted about the thirteenth century. It was a beautiful legend, perhaps originating in a corporeal rendering of the illumination of faith, perhaps an adaptation of the words *Qui vidit testimonium perhibuit*. It is not found in the Meditations[10] of ' Bonaventure,' but later spiritual writers—such as St. Vincent Ferrer and Ludolph of Saxony—have it. It is found especially in popular vernacular literature.[11]

> Beside the rood stood a knight, that long had foregone his sight. Longeus was that knight's name, he was both blind and lame. They made him under Jesus stand, and put a spear in his hand. They led the spear to Jesus' side ; Put up, they said, what so betide. Longeus put the spear him fro, to Jesu heart it gan go. The blood gan anon out spring, and the water anon out wring. Fro sin we were with the blood bought, and fro hell thar we were brought. Longeus stood well still than, by his fingers the blood ran. With that blood he wiped his face, then of his sight he had grace. On his knees he gan down fall, and of Jesu mercy call. He say, I wist not what I did, but as others had me bid.—

[9] " He draws water with his hands from a fountain and he anointed his eyes, as it seems, that he might have cleansing."—Gregory of Nazianzus, *Christus patiens*, 1093 : P.G. 38. 223. But this is a pseudonymous work of the 11 /12 century.
[10] It is added in a 15th century English translation of Bonaventure.—Peebles, p.109.
[11] Even yet in Irish the soldier is called *An Dall* (The Blind Man).

The ' Northern Passion,' from Ashmole MS. 61 : Peebles, p.98. I have modernised the spelling.

Along with them was a soldier named Longis ; blind was he, he saw not a drop ; he was a man of worth. Into his hands a spear was put by the Jews, and a sharp point for him to pierce to mild Jesus' heart. Longis, sure, was on the right side of Jesus' cross. To the soldier by his name they bade that he should pierce. Into the body of lovable Jesus the sharp spear he darted right under the ribs, so that it was through the heart. From the heart there came a great spring, water and blood mixed, and ran down by the spear to the hands of him that struck him. He bathed his eyes with his one hand that was bloodied. Through the blood's grace he saw how Jesus was dighted. Great sorrow seized him for the work he had done. On his knees he fell. ' Lord, forgiveness,' he said. ' Blind was I, I saw not well, that I was living so vilely.' Jesus forgave him when He saw his sorrow.—*Pascon agan Arluth*, a Mid-Cornish poem (15th century), trans. W. Stokes, *Trans. Phil. Soc.*, 1860, stanzas 217-219 ; Peebles, p.101f.

The blindness is contained in the English versions of the Gospel of Nicodemus (Acts of Pilate).[12] For example, in the black letter edition by Wynken de Worde (1509) :

This knight Longeus was blind, and so the princes of the Law made him for to pierce Our Lord's side. And so there came out of it both blood and water, and so the blood came running down by the spear-shaft unto Longeus' hand. And he by adventure wiped his eyes with his hand, and anon he did see.—Peebles, p.89.

The story is also found in the *Vision of Piers Plowman*.[13] The blind knight Longeus was persuaded to make a thrust with his spear ; the blood running down his weapon cured his sight. He cried : " Against my will it was, Lord, to wound You so sore . . . Have on me ruth, rightful Jesu ! " But the author will not accept the excuse : " Cursed caitiff, knighthood was it never to misdo a dead body."

It was the religious drama which, from the thirteenth century, brought Longinus into prominence and popularised the cure of his blindness.[14] In the Chester Passion Play,[15] Cayphas and the Jews bid

---

[12] W. H. Hulme, *The Middle-English Harrowing of Hell and Gospel of Nicodemus*, EETS, 1907, p.62f.

[13] Ed. Skeat, B-text xviii. 78ff. ; Peebles, p.122.

[14] A. Jeanroy, *Le théatre religieux en France du xi. au xiii. siècle*, 1937, p.66. See the illustration of Longinus wiping his eye in G. Cohen, *Le théatre en France au moyen âge* 1 (1928) plate 32.

[15] T. Wright, *The Chester Plays* 2 (1847) 66 (play xvii) ; Peebles, p.132. So in a York play (where Longinus is sent by Pilate) : L. Toulmin Smith, *York Plays*, 1885, no. 36 p.368 ; Peebles, p.134. And in a 15th century Cornish Passion Play : E. Norris, *The Ancient Cornish Drama* i. 460 ; Peebles, p.137f. Similarly in a Coventry Play : J. O. Halliwell, *Ludus Coventriae*, 1841, p.334. In all these cases the piercing was after death.

Longeus to take his spear. "I will do as ye bid me, but on your peril it shall be. What I do I may not see, whether it be good or evil." He strikes and is cured : " Of mercy, Lord I thee pray, for I wist not what I did."

Longinus, in several of the Passion Plays, pierces Our Lord while He is alive. In the Palatinus Passion (c.1300), Marques orders Longin to pierce Christ. He asks for pardon, receives his sight, and is told by Christ to strike.[16] In the Biard Passion Longinus complains that owing to his bad sight he is unable to earn his living. A Jew asks him to use his lance, which he did " without any evil intent." His lance was bloodied, and suddenly he recovered his sight. Christ says : " Longinus, My side is pierced. I pardon you your sin. You are not to be blamed for this misdeed. Ask for mercy and you will obtain it." Our Lady laments and Christ says to her : " My friend and cousin John will guard you henceforth." Then follow the Eli cry, the incident of the bandits, the offering of the vinegar (which He refuses), *Consummatum est* and death.[17]

While usually[18] Longinus is pictured as an innocent blind man misled by the soldiers or the Jews, there are several instances in which he is represented as brutal and hard-hearted, deaf to the entreaties of Our Lady and the holy women.[19] Thus ' Bonaventure.'

> Longinus—at that time impious and proud but afterwards a penitent, a martyr and a saint—stretching forth his spear at a distance, notwithstanding the cries and entreaties of the holy women, plunged it into the right side of our Lord Jesus.—*Life of Christ*, ch. 80, Eng. trans 1881, p.273.

But, even when devotion to Our Lady of Dolours grew, she is not depicted as laying blame on the soldier. In a Lamentation of Saint Mary (14th century), after describing how the knight was induced to thrust the spear " to my Son's side," she merely says : " Then waxed my heart heavy as lead when that I saw that rueful sight . . . Then fell I down as I were dead."[20]

---

[16] *La Passion du Palatinus*, ed. Frank, 1922, p.42.
[17] *La Passion d'Autun*, ed. Mrs. Grace Frank, 1934, pp.111ff. Similarly in the *Passion de Roman.—ibid.* pp.203ff.
[18] Here are contradictory entries in two Irish martyrologies : " Oct. 23 : The departure of Longinus to the kingdom that is highest. He wounded—deed that is noblest—Jesus' splendid delightful side."—*Martyrology of Oengus* (c.800), tr. Whitley Stokes, 1905, p.218. " March 15 : Longinus by whose cruel spear Christ was wounded on the cross ; it was a sin without any defence thereof."—*Martyrology of Gorman* (1150/1200), tr. W. Stokes, Bradshaw Society, 1895, p.55.
[19] He is also pictured as wicked and venomous in some Passion Plays.—Peebles, p.139. In the *Donaueschinger Passion*, Longinus says : " I will revenge myself on You who on earth would not help me and let me remain blind."—Mone, *Schauspiele des Mittelalters*, 1846, ii. 326. He is also wicked in Gréban's *Mistère de la Passion*, ed. Gaston Paris, 1878, p.346.
[20] W. Fröhlich, *De lamentacione sancte Marie*, 1902, p.63 : MS. Rawlinson Poet. 175 (c. 1350) : Peebles, p.113.

(10) Joseph secures the Body

M 27	Mk 15	L 23	J 19

Joseph of Arimathea

[57] When it was late in the day, a rich man from Arimathea, called Joseph, who had himself become a disciple of Jesus,	[42] Though it was now late in the day, yet since it was the Preparation Day—that is, the eve of the Sabbath — [43] Joseph from Arimathea, a distinguished member of the Council, who was himself expecting the Kingdom of God,	[50] Now there was a man named Joseph, a member of the Council, [51] a good and upright man, who had not agreed to the decision and action of the Council. He was from Arimathea, a town of Judea, and was expecting the Kingdom of God	[38] After this, Joseph from Arimathea, who was a disciple of Jesus—but he had been secretly so owing to fear of the Jews—

He asks for the Body

[58] went to see Pilate. And he asked him for the body of Jesus.	had the courage to go in to Pilate and to ask him for the body of Jesus.	[52] He went to Pilate and asked for the body of Jesus.	asked Pilate to let him remove the body of Jesus.

Pilate's Inquiry

		[44] Now Pilate wondered whether He was yet dead. So he sent for the Centurion and asked whether He was yet dead.	

The Body is granted

And Pilate ordered it to be given to him.	[45] Having learnt from the Centurion that He was [dead], he granted the corpse to Joseph.		And Pilate gave him permission.

Notes on the Text

Late in the day (*opsia*) : This means the early evening or late afternoon, which lasted from 3 to 6 p.m., when on this occasion the sabbatic obligation came into operation. "The Lord remained on the gibbet almost until evening ; and towards evening (i.e. sunset, *pros hesperan*) they buried Him."—Justin, *Dial.* 97, 1. Mark here, like John (see p.284), does not refer to the prescription of Deuteronomy which applied to *any* day, but to the special character of *this* day, namely, that in a few hours (at about 6 p.m.) the festival began. Apparently it was this special consideration which led to the successful appeal to Pilate.

Preparation-Day : See p.285., above. There may be a particular reference to the period from 3 to 6 p.m. Augustus decreed that Jews " should not be obliged to appear in court either on the Sabbath or on the preceding Preparation-Day after the ninth hour."—Josephus, *Ant.* xvi. 6, 2. Mark's remark is relevant only if this Friday was not a festival.

Arimathea : This is probably the modern village of Rentis north-east of Lydda. *From* is *apo*, not *ex* ; this *may* mean he was resident there, not a native of the place. See my *Family at Bethany*, p.186.

Joseph : He had been secretly a disciple (pluperfect), but now he came out into the open. If Joseph and Nicodemus became Christians, it is curious what little influence these wealthy and learned men had. He had not agreed with the Sanhedrin's decision. It is uncertain whether this means inward disagreement (perhaps plus physical absence) or else a dissentient vote. While Matthew calls him wealthy (*plousios*), Mark says he was distinguished (*euschēmōn*) ; according to the grammarian Phrynichus this last term was in popular parlance equivalent to ' wealthy.'

Joseph's request : that he might remove (*arē, tolleret*) the body of Jesus. This obviously means here : to take down and to bury. So also in the Sanhedrin's request J19[31]: *arthōsen, tollerentur*.

Pilate's inquiry : There are two evenly balanced readings— *ēdē* (Vulgate *iam*), already ; *palai*, long since. According to Sepp there is condensation or intermixture here as elsewhere in Mark : " Pilate asked : Is He already dead? The officer answered : Yes, long since. The evangelist, joining question and answer, simply says that Pilate asked if he were long dead."—*Vie de J.C.*, 1861, iii. 65.

The Gospel of Pseudo-Peter gives a very inferior account. Even before the trial Joseph asked the Lord's body from Pilate (3), and the latter asked Herod (4) ! Herod told Brother Pilate that he had intended himself to bury Him and quotes Deuteronomy (5). When the sun shone out again at the ninth hour, the Jews were glad (23), apparently because it was not yet really evening. So the Jews gave the body to Joseph.

There is some difficulty in deciding which came first : the Sanhedrists' deputation or Joseph's interview with Pilate. This is due to the laconic accounts in the Gospels. Only John tells of the Jewish deputation, the leg-breaking and the piercing ; only Mark tells us of Pilate's surprise and verification. At first sight it looks as if " Pilate would not have sent to verify the death of Jesus had he already given orders for the victims to be killed. Such a command left no doubt about their death."[1] Hence Père Lagrange considered that Joseph's interview with Pilate preceded that of the Jews :

> Joseph of Arimathea lost no time. As he left Pilate's house, he may have met the Jews coming to ask permission to have the executed killed so that they might be buried anywhere. He had to reach the cross before the soldiers started to carry out their orders, which Pilate had doubtless issued without thought of modifying them so far as Jesus was concerned. Joseph did not want merely to receive the body from the soldiers ; he meant to take it away himself.—p.277.

This arrangement is not quite satisfactory. The Jews must have gone to Pilate shortly—say, a quarter or half an hour—before Christ's death. They certainly meant to include Him in their request. And Pilate's order seems to have been general ; the legs of all three were to be broken. Does John imply that if Our Lord had not been already dead, His legs would have been broken? Yet, according to Lagrange, Joseph had already seen Pilate who, after verifying the death of Jesus, had granted the body to Joseph. Moreover, it is not easy to whittle down so drastically St. John's chronological note : after these things (*meta tauta*). Even if Joseph's démarche did not take place after the piercing, it can hardly have occurred *before* the Jewish deputation. These objections are not decisive ; for, with our very incomplete information, there are difficulties in forming any complete account.

Assuming John's order, let us first suppose that Joseph's intervention took place after the piercing of Christ and the shin-breaking of the bandits but before their actual death. We really do not know how long they would have survived ; there must have been at least a short interval. But we need not even assume that they were alive if we slightly modify the usual interpretation of Pilate's inquiry. Joseph may have seen the soldiers preparing to take down the bodies and to bury them. He, let us assume, made his intention known to the Centurion who had himself been deeply moved by the death of Jesus. Pending the result of Joseph's mission, the Centurion delayed action in the case of Christ. Joseph hurried to the Procurator and informed him that Jesus had been already (or for some time) dead

---

[1] Lagrange, *The Gospel*, 1938, ii. 277.

and that it had not been necessary to break His legs. Pilate, surprised at this information, sent for the Centurion and received an assurance on the point.[2] He at least wanted an official certificate of death which he had not yet received. Only then did he grant the body to Joseph. There is nothing strained in this interpretation of the exceedingly condensed account given by St. Mark, who omits all mention of the leg-breaking mission.

Alternatively, " we can suppose that Pilate's messenger, bearing the command to break the legs of the executed men, had but just departed when Joseph presented himself with his request for the corpse. Pilate knew therefore that his command was not yet fulfilled."[3] He was surprised to be told by Joseph that Jesus had already died and that in His case the operation of leg-breaking was unnecessary. He insisted, however, on obtaining verification of this from his officer. On this otherwise tenable view we must deny full chronological value to St. John's phrase " after these things," and interpret it as an expression introducing a new section (the burial).

The late C. H. Turner went further ; he suggested that Joseph's petition to Pilate was made at the same time as the Sanhedrin's request for leg-breaking.[4] It is certainly more plausible to assume that Joseph (with Nicodemus) formed part of, or accompanied, the Sanhedrist deputation, rather than that the Governor gave two separate audiences on the matter. Apart, however, from the difficulty contained in the phrase " after these things," there is another objection. According to John, the Sanhedrin makes its request on the assumption that the sufferers are still alive, while Mark's account assumes that Joseph was cognisant of Christ's death before he approached Pilate. " It is," says Turner, " one of the discrepancies which not unnaturally arise when what is at

[2] Pickl objects : " If breaking the shinbones could cause speedy death, Pilate could not have in wonder asked Joseph whether Christ was already dead."— *Messias*, 1946, p.272. We can answer : (1) Pilate did not want to be rushed into granting a living body, there must have been some short interval before death. (2) But we are entitled to assume that Pilate was surprised to learn that Christ was already dead when the soldiers arrived to perform the *crurifragium* which was omitted as unnecessary in His case. (The lance-thrust by a soldier was unofficial).

[3] Le Camus, *Life of Christ* 3 (1923) 392. According to Dr. T. E. Bird—*Study of the Gospels*, 1945, p.239f—after receiving the Jewish deputation, Pilate " sent soldiers to dispatch the victims." The bandits' legs were broken ; and " to guard against any mistake, one of the soldiers pierced the side of Christ with a lance." Joseph then interviewed Pilate. " To make sure that he was really dead, Pilate sent a centurion to Calvary ; and on being assured on the point, he gave Joseph permission to take down the body."

[4] *Church Quarterly Review* 74 (1912) 297f. This view was accepted by Bernard, *John*, 1928, p.653 ; also by Père Braun—Pirot, *La sainte Bible* 10 (1935) 473.

bottom the same story filters down through independent channels."
But there is really no need to see a discrepancy here at all. We are
supposing that Joseph, himself a Sanhedrist, accompanied the
deputation. When the members requested *crurifragium*, Joseph
courageously dissociated himself from the request as regards Jesus
whom he asserted to be already dead. Pilate, on verifying this,
exempted the body of Jesus from the operation. Perhaps he once
more ordered the soldiers to make doubly sure that Jesus was dead
before handing over the body ; a zealous soldier, interpreting this
literally but having no authority to break His legs, inflicted a spear-
thrust. The only difficulty then is that St. John has deferred narrat-
ing Joseph's intervention until he comes to tell us of Joseph's part in
the deposition and the burial.

The foregoing problem is not really of any importance. None of
the evangelists had any intention of giving us a complete account.
St. Luke does not even trouble to tell us explicitly that Pilate granted
Joseph's request. As has been just shown, there are several possible
ways in which the intervention of the Sanhedrin and that of Joseph
can be arranged. Both events—the Jewish leaders' anxiety to have
the victims despatched and buried before nightfall, the granting
of the body to a man called Joseph— are in themselves intrinsically
probable. No one would dream of disputing them were it not for
the inconvenient story of what happened on Easter Sunday.

Normally, if the body of one executed were given up at all, it
would be taken and buried by relatives or close disciples on whom
the duty primarily devolved. John the Baptist was buried by his
faithful followers ($M14^{12}$ $Mk6^{29}$ $L 9^{29}$), Stephen by his colleagues
($A8^{2}$). But the Apostles or disciples of Christ could not be recorded
as having paid Him this last service. The absence of the Apostles
has always seemed strange to popular Christian sentiment. The so-
called Gospel of Peter (26) finds it necessary to excuse the Apostles
on the ground that they were in hiding from the Jews who were
looking for them " as malefactors and as men wishing to burn the
Temple." The piety of the faithful, as well as the imagination of
artists, has insisted on including at least Our Lady and St. John
as assisting at the burial. But the initiative, the courageous intervention, the holding of the official license, had to be assigned to an
unknown stranger who acted without help or co-operation from the
Apostles. Clearly they do not show up well in this account, which
was not very creditable to them and so could not possibly have been

invented at a time when apostolic authority was high in Jerusalem and in Rome.

The chief participant is mentioned only here, never before or after. Unlike even Simon from Cyrene, he did not give prominent sons to the Church. His name is enshrined for ever in the Gospel simply because he did for the dead Christ what the Baptist's disciples did for their beheaded master. His courage infected a colleague ; and the last rites were rendered to Christ by two men who had never dared to avow themselves His disciples. What a picture of utter failure and abandonment of the Crucified !

Joseph, a native of or a resident in Arimathea, was a man of standing, a member of the Sanhedrin. He was influential enough to secure an interview with the Governor. Why then did it require courage on his part to intervene? Surely not as regards Pilate, who had wished to spare this unusual, politically innocent Prisoner, but whose hand had been forced. The courage Joseph displayed was against his colleagues and coreligionists. He wished to honour this condemned excommunicate and to bury Him as an Israelite.[5] He had disagreed with the recent action of the Sanhedrin ; his further action was tantamount to a public protest. The call of truth had hitherto been insufficient to make him take the drastic step of open adherence ; he failed to break the bonds of class-loyalty. But at this crisis he refused to stand aside or to take refuge in neutrality. He would be no party to war against the Dead. So he flouted the public opinion of his religious party. He foiled the Sanhedrin's decision by appealing over their heads to Pilate. In spite of his colleagues' scruples, he probably entered the pagan Governor's Residence.[6] And, by contact with the dead, he made himself ritually unable to join in the Passover celebration. No wonder that he aroused resentment ; the apocryphal documents are surely right when they tell us of the hierarchs' anger against Joseph.

There is an illogical modernist view which accepts as historical one half of the story (Joseph's name and deed) but rejects the other half (his secret discipleship) which alone explains the incident.

---

[5] " The community, whether it possessed a cemetery or not, could prevent its officers or even any other Jew, under pain of excommunication, from performing Jewish funeral rites for Jews whom it had excluded from its midst. Thus it possessed a terrible weapon."—J. Juster, Les juifs dans l'empire romain, 1914, i. 485.

[6] Courageously he went in (tolmēsas eisēlthen).—Mark 15⁴³. But his colleagues would not go inside.—J18²⁸. There was no binding law of the Torah against such entry on this day. The prohibition was one of the minhag chasiduth (counsels of perfection) imposed by the Pharisees who professed to be chasidim.

Joseph seems to have behaved simply as a pious member of the Sanhedrin, who was anxious to obey the law of Deuteronomy . . . Nor is it possible to say whether, in asking Pilate for Jesus' body and burying it, he was moved by pious scruples of his own or was acting on behalf of the Sanhedrin.—J. Midleton Murry, *The Life of Jesus*, 1926, p.312f.

The suggestion that Joseph was acting on behalf of the Sanhedrin, in this *post mortem* rehabilitation of this excommunicated messianic claimant, is simply absurd. Nor could his motive have been to comply with the Jewish burial-law, which was in any case being attended to. There were three bodies to be disposed of before sunset. Joseph interested himself only in one ; and for this he allowed the use of his own private tomb. It is quite clear that his sole motive was to pay respect to the remains of Christ.

St. Mark gives us a valuable detail concerning Pilate's attitude. Having once passed sentence, the Procurator was determined to have it carried out to the end ; he was not going to connive at any rescue. He refused to accept Joseph's word ; he insisted on an official verification of the death. Only then did he grant the request of this influential Jew. Once he was sure that Jesus was really dead, he was not interested in the disposal of the body. He did not ask Joseph where he meant to bury it, nor did he provide Roman soldiers to assist him. With the termination of the interview, Pilate thought that the matter was ended. He did not anticipate a further Jewish request for guarding the tomb, nor could he foresee the events of the following Sunday. That the followers of this mild or mock King might found a rival sect of Judaism, this was to him a matter of indifference, if not of malicious pleasure. Little could he, or anyone else, foresee that the obscure Galilean followers of the Crucified were going to found a religion which would ultimately vanquish the Empire he represented.

The ordinary procedure, at least for slaves in Rome, was to allow the cross to stand with the body until it fell to pieces or was the prey of vultures and dogs.[7] It is very improbable that this was the Roman peace-time custom in Judea. At the request of the Jewish authorities, Pilate made no difficulty in conceding that the bodies should be taken down and buried before sunset. So it was not such a great concession for him to allow Joseph to give private burial to Jesus.

[7] There is evidence (for the first century) that the bodies of the crucified were guarded to prevent burial by friends or relatives.—Petronius, *Satyricon* 111, 5f: Phaedrus, app. xiii. 8 ; Romulus 59.

We learn from Philo of a similar custom in Egypt on the eve of the Emperor's birthday :

> I have known cases when, on the eve of a holiday of this kind, people who had been crucified (*anĕskolopismĕnōn*) had been taken down and their bodies delivered to their relatives, because it was thought proper to give them burial and to allow the ordinary rites. For it was right that even the dead should have kind treatment upon the birthday of an Emperor and also that the sanctity of the festival should be upheld. But Flaccus gave orders not to take down those who had died on the cross, but to crucify those who were alive, to whom the season should have afforded not the remission but the deferment of punishment.[8]—Philo, *In Flaccum* 10, 83.

The eve of the great Jewish national festival of Passover was therefore, apart from any individual circumstances, an appropriate occasion for granting the body to Joseph, who most probably had authority to represent the Mother of Jesus. Even on an ordinary occasion Pilate was entitled, except in cases of notorious treason, to grant a body to relatives, under the milder régime introduced by Augustus.[9] And apparently he did so without the pecuniary considerations which weighed with some of his colleagues.[10] Let us gratefully record Pilate's one good deed.

---

[8] I notice that H. Box, in his edition and translation (1939), renders *anaskolpizò* by ' impale.' It seems certain that crucifixion is meant here.

[9] "The bodies of those condemned to death are not to be refused to their relatives. Augustus writes that he observed this . . . But sometimes it is not allowed, especially in the case of those condemned for treason."—Ulpian in the *Digest* 48, 24. Paulus is there cited as even more liberal : " The bodies of those executed are to be given for burial to whoever ask for them." " The crosses are cut down, the executioner does not forbid the executed to be buried."—Quintilian vi. 9. Towards the end of his reign, Tiberius was blamed for his cruelty in refusing.— Suetonius, *Tib.* 61 ; Tacitus, *Ann.* vi. 19 and 29.

[10] Governors exacted payment from relatives for the bodies of the crucified : Cicero, *Verr.* ii. 45, v. 45 ; Plutarch, *Galba* 28. There is a record of buying the body of the martyr Bonifacius († 290 in Tarsus) from the *officialis.*—Ruinart *Acta Martyrum*, 1859, p.331.

CHAPTER XIV

THE PIERCED SIDE

(1) On the Shroud

WE come to the most interesting mark on the shroud, that of the wound on the right side (see fig. ii. 5). This will now be examined in detail. A separate illustration of the wound is given in fig. xiv. 1. This will be better understood by comparing the smaller fig. xiv. 2 with the diagram fig. xiv. 3. The part of the cloth recording the outer edge of the flow was destroyed in the fire of 1532, and we can now see the linen patch[1] put on by the nuns in 1534. At the top of the stain we can clearly distinguish the wound itself (except as regards its lower lip) with its upper edge elliptical. The long axis of the ellipse is inclined slightly downwards towards the centre of the body. Its length is about 48 mm. (2 inches), its greatest breadth 15 mm. (three-fifths of an inch). Below the actual wound there is an irregular flow, about 15 cm. (6 inches) long and 6 cm. (2½ inches) broad. In the flow there are a number of clear interstices.

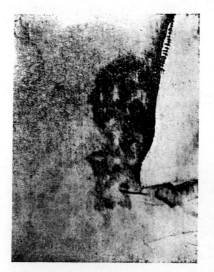

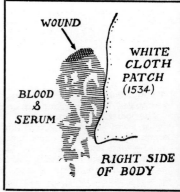

XIV. 2—The Side-Wound on the Shroud. XIV. 3—Explanatory Diagram

[1] Underneath the patch we can see portion of the blood-flow. It seems clear that most of the flow was sideways down the slope of the right side.

The flow has definite contours adapted to the inequalities of the surface over which its course lay. This result could not have been obtained by allowing blood to trickle over the cloth. If we were to ignore the evidence contained in the rest of the shroud, we could regard this marking as due to some sort of stain applied with enormous skill. But it carries its own intrinsic marks of self-authentication. Much of the blood must have fallen on the ground, but some coagulated slowly on the skin, leaving a broken irregular train. It flowed more rapidly on the slopes of ribs and muscles (serratus anterior). Here we have not a quick-flowing stream, still less a spurting jet, pumped out by a living heart. We see an issue of thick blood which slowly oozed out, solely under the influence of gravity, from a heart no longer beating.

In the annals of painting there is nothing whatever resembling this thick flow with undulating edges. We have already seen several artists' representations of the flow. See for example Francke (fig. vii. 45), the pupil of Van der Weyden (fig. vii. 46), Fra Angelico (fig. vii. 52). To facilitate comparison four further art-representations of the side-wound are given. Figure xiv. 4, from a 14th century painting in Padua, shows the wound as a horizontal slit with isolated drops underneath. Figure xiv. 5, from Holbein's Crucifixion, shows a continuous vertical flow, divided into separate jets of blood and water. Figure xiv. 6, from Perugino's Crucifixion, exhibits a thick clot with vertical outflows. Figure xiv. 7, from the Crucifixion of Velazquez (reproduced in xii. 66), shows a series of thin isolated streams from an oblique wound. None of these is comparable with the representation on the shroud (fig. xiv. 1).

The irregular contour of the shroud-stain is also partly explained by the mode in which the impression on the cloth has probably been obtained.[2] Since the outer edge of the wound is about seven inches from the axis of the body, it would not normally have left any mark on the cloth which, resting on arm and chest, would not be in contact with the wound. It has already been suggested (see fig. ii. 6) that some pious hand must have gently applied the cloth against the wound.

Thus the whole configuration of this wound plus flow is unique in pictorial record. Its most striking feature lies in the lighter portions—blood and water! The probability—even the very

[2] " Its inner margin is strangely cut up into rounded indentations which can hardly be explained in a blood-flow from a motionless cadaver. Did some hand apply the shroud against this part of the thorax? "—Barbet ii. 42.

possibility—that this is an authentic record of what St. John saw
should fill us with awe. Have we here a record from Calvary? Does
he who saw bear witness even to-day?

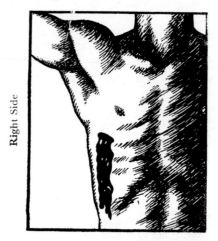

Right Side

XIV. 8—Location of the Side-Wound

Let us now examine the situation of the wound. Its location is
roughly sketched in fig. xiv. 8. Dr. Barbet (ii. 43) was able to locate
the wound externally by measurements on shroud-photographs of
natural size, on which the pectoral muscles, the nipples and the
umbilicus can be discerned. The wound is about 9 cm. (3½ inches)
below and slightly to the outside of the right nipple. Below the
root of the neck (see fig. ii. 5) there is a series of stains ; the
lower border of the middle stain seems certainly to correspond to the
hollow just above the sternum. In the epigastric hollow there is a
roughly rectangular stain whose upper margin is the lower end of
the sternum. The sternum thus delimited measures 18 cm. (7.2 in.)
in height. The lower medial extremity of the wound is half a
centimetre (one-fifth of an inch) below the end of the sternum and
16 cm. (6.4 in.) from the median line. The wound is thus located
relatively to the skeleton (lower end of breast-bone).

The next problem Dr. Barbet faced was the location of the wound
with reference to the remainder of the skeleton and to the internal
organs. Living pupils about 6 feet high were chosen, a metal plate
of the same size as the wound was fixed in its place, and X-rays
were employed. The radiograph showed that the wound was in the

fifth intercostal space (just over the sixth rib). This is shown[3] diagramatically in fig. xiv. 9. From fig. xiv. 10 we see that the wound is distant 4.8 inches from the median plane of the body, and that in an oblique upward stroke the lance would reach the right convexity of the heart after travelling 3.2 inches. This is a natural direction for the blow. A more vertical direction is unlikely, not only because it would be very difficult thus to penetrate between the ribs but also because it would mean transfixing only the lung and consequently causing at most the exudation of a few drops of blood. It is most probable that the cross was low, so that Our Lord's mouth and side could easily be reached by a man standing on the ground and holding a stick or spear. A horizontal blow is possible but a slightly upward thrust is more likely. In either case the lance would after a few inches of penetration reach the heart on its right side. (See the horizontal section[4] of the thorax shown in fig. xiv. 11). Indeed such a stroke may be assumed to have been practised as a *coup de grâce* by Roman soldiers in training, since the opponent would be more easily able to protect his *left* side with his shield.

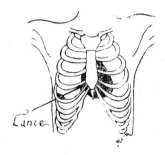

XIV. 9—Side-Wound, Ribs and Heart
Anterior aspect of the thorax, showing
the lance and the outline of the heart as
seen in *living* subjects

There is a curious parallel to this discussion of Our Lord's wound. In four passages of II Samuel (ii. 23, iii. 27, iv. 6, xx. 10) there is reference to striking a man, with a spear or a sword, in the *homesh*. The Septuagint has *psoas* (loin), the Vulgate *inguen* (groin). The Douay version has *groin*, so has the latest Jewish

[3] It has been shown by radiographic methods that in the living the heart is about two inches lower in the thorax than in dead subjects (on which anatomical text books are based).—Mainland and Gordon, *Amer. Jl. Anatomy* 66 (1941) 457.
[4] This (fig. xiv. 11) shows the position of the structures in a dead body approximately at the level of the 8th thoracic vertebra.

American translation ; the Authorised Version is more accurate :
" the fifth rib." See an article by D. Macht, A Biblical Adventure
in Anatomy, *Bull. Hist. Med.* 16 (1944) 169-174. " The Talmudic
and later rabbinical authorities agree that in these four passages
the word *homesh* refers to the fifth intercostal space " (p.173),
where the heart-apex comes close to the chest-wall. There was
a dispute as to whether the reference was to the right or to the
left side. R. Yochanan held that the wounds referred to in these
passages were on the right side and that death resulted from
piercing the liver (*Sanhedrin* 49a).

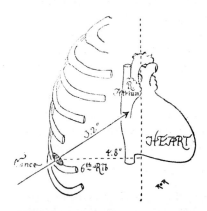

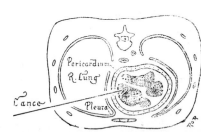

XIV. 10—The Lance-Thrust and the   XIV. 11—Horizontal Section through
Heart   the Thorax

(2) Dr. Barbet's Experiments

Dr. Barbet (ii. 46) next proceeded to experiment with upright
cadavers :

> I first used a long needle mounted on a large syringe. Marking
> the position of the wound, I rapidly plunged the needle in the
> fifth intercostal space of the right side, aiming inwards in a
> direction slightly upwards and backwards. After 9 to 10 centi-
> metres I entered the right auricle (atrium) of the heart ; and on
> aspirating, I filled the syringe with liquid blood. As long as I was
> traversing the lung, continual aspiration drew no liquid, neither
> blood nor water.
> Next, under the same conditions, I plunged a large amputation-
> knife. At the same depth, it opens the right auricle and blood
> flows along the blade through the tunnel bored in the lung . . .
> All my experiments, followed by dissection, were made on
> corpses more than twenty-four hours old.

Leaving the problem of the ' water ' for subsequent discussion, let us consider this blood-flow from a pierced cadaver, and in particular from a transfixed heart. During life the pressure in the pleural cavity is sub-atmospheric ; this partial vacuum allows the lung to move and expand. When air is admitted to the pleural cavity of a living person, the lung partially collapses and what is called a pneumothorax is formed. If the spear-thrust had been made on a living man, the lung would have shrunk and formed a considerable cavity which would have first to be filled before any could overflow. It is well known that, in the case of such wounds, very little blood flows from a living person. Dr. Hynek (i. 66 and ii. 141) describes a case of attempted suicide which he witnessed as a student. A man had stuck a penknife into his heart. There were only slight traces of blood on his clothes, but in the pleural cavity there were $1\frac{1}{2}$ litres (more than $2\frac{1}{2}$ pints) of blood. After removal of this blood, the heart began again to beat. The surgeon succeeded in stitching the wounded heart ; and the man went home after a fortnight.[1]

Reference may be made to some cases of heart-wounds in the living.

T. Schrire, *Lancet*, 1941, ii. 638, describes four cases of stab wounds of the heart, three on left and one on right side. In this last case, that of a man aged 21 years, the wound was one inch from the right border of the sternum in the fifth intercostal space. He did not bleed much. Tamponade was diagnosed ; he was operated on. There was some blood in the pleural cavity, but the lung owing to old adhesions had not retracted. About half a pint of blood escaped with a rush when the pericardium was opened. No bleeding point was found in the heart or on the pericardial walls. The patient subsequently developed pericarditis, but survived.

R. A. Griswold and C. H. Maguire, Penetrating Wounds of the Heart and Pericardium, *Surg. Gynec. Obst.* 74 (1942) 406-418. In most cases " the wound of entry is between the second and seventh left costal cartilage anteriorly, usually traversing the left pleura." The right ventricle, being anterior, is most frequently injured. Bleeding from the coronary vessels and heart-muscles, in cases where the heart-cavity is not penetrated, is " surprisingly brisk and may be rapidly fatal." As little as 200 c.c. of blood may cause a fatal tamponade (heart stoppage) if the bleeding occurs rapidly. If the opening into the pericardium is large, the blood

[1] The Empress Elizabeth of Austria was assassinated with a file through her heart. The bleeding was internal, only two or three blood-drops appeared externally.

flows to the exterior or into the pleura. The authors describe
several cases of such wounds with extrapericardial haemorrhage ;
there may be as much as 3,000 c.c. of blood in the pleural cavities.

A dead lung, however, does not collapse when the pleura or the
lung is pierced ; the tissue has lost its elasticity. Hence when Dr.
Barbet's needle or knife penetrated the lung of a cadaver, a sloping
tunnel was formed through and down which the blood from the
heart (right atrium) flowed. It must be pointed out, however, that
the bodies experimented upon were dead for more than two days.
There does not appear to be any information available as to how
soon after death this non-contractility is established. But if before
death the lower lobes of the lungs were engorged and oedematous,
they would hardly collapse even if transfixed during life.

Next, let us see why the blood-flow occurs only when the *right*
side of the dead man is pierced.[2]

> The part of the heart to the right of the sternum is the right
> auricle [atrium]. And in the cadaver this auricle, prolonged
> upwards by the vena cava superior and downwards by the vena
> cava inferior, is *always filled with liquid blood* . . . If the lance-
> thrust had been delivered on the left side, it would have pierced
> the ventricles which in the cadaver are empty of blood.—Barbet,
> i.30 and ii. 45.
>
> A few words concerning blood-circulation may not be irrele-
> vant. Returning from all parts of the body except the lungs, the
> blood is poured through the two principal veins (*venae cavae*)
> into the right atrium. (See fig. xiv. 12). Thence it is transferred
> to the right ventricle, back-flow being prevented by a valve. By
> powerful contraction the right ventricle pumps the blood through
> the pulmonary arteries to the lungs where the blood is aerated. (It
> discharges carbon dioxide, and takes on a load of oxygen, thereby
> becoming bright crimson in colour). Returning from the lungs
> by the four pulmonary veins, the renovated blood passes into
> the left atrium. Thence it enters the left ventricle by whose

---

[2] In the literature I find slightly discrepant accounts of the blood-filling of the
various cavities of the post-mortem heart. " At the onset of rigor mortis—which
begins at the earliest within a half-hour after death and as a rule disappears after
twenty-four hours—the left ventricle contracts and forces most of its blood into
the empty arteries ; whereas the right ventricle, whose muscle is not so strong, is
not able to expel a considerable amount of blood into the pulmonary vessels
which became engorged during agony. Hence the right ventricle remaining filled
with blood during the period of rigor mortis, while the volume of the left ventricle
is greatly diminished. When rigor mortis ceases, the latter relaxes, yet it contains
little or no blood, for the contents of the aorta and the left atrium have coagulated
[?] in the meantime and cannot flow into the left ventricle. The right ventricle,
on the contrary, retains its engorgement almost unchanged."—W. Dressler,
Amer. Heart Jl. 19 (1940) 141ff.

contraction it is pumped through the aorta into the arteries and
capillaries of the body.

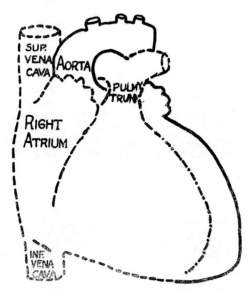

XIV. 12—Diagram of the Heart

Harvey[3] noted long ago that in dissected bodies the veins and
right side of the heart were filled with blood, while there was little
in the arteries and in the left chamber. Dr. Barbet's statement is
probably too absolute, for there is some diversity.[4] In the case of
death from asphyxia (reduced oxygen supply to blood and tissues),
the veins are gorged with blood, the blood itself coagulates much

[3] This is how he explained why, in the dissection of dead bodies, so much blood
is found in the veins and right atrium and so little in the arteries and the left
chamber: " The true cause is that there is no passage to the arteries save through
lungs and heart. When an animal ceases to breathe and the lungs to move, the
blood in the arterial vein [pulmonary artery] no longer passes therefrom into the
venal artery [pulmonary vein] and thence to the left ventricle [auricle]. But the
heart not ceasing to act as soon as the lungs but surviving them and continuing
to pulsate for a while, the left ventricle and the arteries continue to distribute
their blood to the body at large and to send it into the veins."—Cited by C.
Singer, *Evolution of Anatomy*, 1925, p.181.
[4] " If death has occurred slowly, the lungs are found intensely engorged ; if
death has occurred very rapidly, the lungs may be quite anaemic, their condition
varying inversely with that of the right side of the heart, which in the first case
[slow death] is only moderately distended with blood, but in the latter is so
distended as to seem almost on the point of bursting."—Taylor's *Principles and
Practice of Medical Jurisprudence*, ed. Smith and Cook, 1934[9], i. 588f.

more slowly. There is more or less distention of veins and heart in different cases. But as a general rule, the blood in a corpse is collected in the veins and in the venous cavities of the heart (i.e. the atria or auricles).

After death the arteries contract and by their contraction empty the blood into the capillaries and veins, provided that it has not coagulated too soon ; the heart having ceased to beat and the veins being much weaker than the arteries, the blood remains in the veins in a stagnant condition and probably still uncoagulated. In these circumstances, if a vein has been wounded before death, or even if it be opened after death, it may bleed *post mortem* and give rise to a suspicion that the wound was produced before death.—Taylor's *Principles and Practice of Medical Jurisprudence*, ed. Smith and Cook, 1934[9], i. 209.

Hence in general the only accessible blood-filled portion of the heart is the right atrium which extends to the right of the median plane. At the left there are only the ventricles which are empty in a corpse ; a blow at this side would not cause bleeding. The left atrium is at the *back* of the heart. Moreover this blood remains liquid until the body becomes dried or putrescent. It even remains living for some hours ; the transfusion of blood from a corpse has been successfully practised in Russia. The blood does not coagulate in the veins, but only after exit, e.g. when extravasated interiorly[5] or on the skin.

Exegetes often make the incorrect statement that the blood-flow recorded in J19[34] could not *naturally* come from a dead body. Dr. Barbet's experiments are a disproof. " A post-mortem lacerated wound occurring as the result of accident may be attended with such an effusion of blood as to deceive a medical man, unless all the facts of the case are known."—Taylor i. 351. This bleeding followed by clotting may occur many hours after death. Dr. Taylor says : " If the wound be not made until twelve or fourteen hours have elapsed from the time of death, it cannot be mistaken for one produced during life. Either no blood is effused, or it is of a venous character, i.e. it may have proceeded from some divided vein. The blood is in small quantity, commonly liquid, and it does not coagulate as it falls on surrounding bodies, like that poured out of a wound in the living." To this Dr. Taylor's editors append a note (i. 351) : " This statement of Dr. Taylor is too absolute in regard to time and clotting, as the blood remains liquid and capable of clotting for many hours after death. Clots frequently form on the post-mortem table when

---

[5] See further on, p.351.

an autopsy is performed twelve or fourteen hours after death."[6]

Accordingly it is important to realise that the bloodstain recorded on the right side in the shroud is the result of a flow of liquid blood which *subsequently* became clotted and dried on the skin. That this was a postmortal flow is shown by three considerations. (1) The appearance of the stain shows that the blood slowly oozed out first along the gently sloping lung-tunnel and then over the skin. (2) It did not spurt out from a living heart. Indeed it could not ; for if the man were living, the lung would collapse and form a large internal cavity for the reception of the blood.[7] (3) According to Dr. Hynek (i. 110, ii. 144) and other medical authorities, the blood which comes from a dead body on to a cloth behaves quite differently from the blood which issues from a living body. " When bleeding occurs during life, blood and lymph come out in one mass, pale-rose to red and dark-brown in colour. In postmortal bleeding, however, the saturation of the cloth separates the serum from the congealed blood, absorbing it to a considerable distance " (i. 110). That is, blood from a living person soaks into the material (e.g. a bandage) and has one colour (rose to carmine), later becoming brown. But post-mortem blood coagulates at once on the cloth, forming a typical configuration : a central dark clot surrounded by serum, with serrated edges (as in the lozenges made by the water on the shroud).

(3) Right or Left Side?

St. John does not tell us which side was pierced. The earliest specifications, of doubtful historical value, specify the right side. Thus the *Acts of Pilate*[1] say : " A soldier lanced (*eloncheusen*) Him in the right side." In the Arabic Gospel of the Infancy (n. 35), there is a curious story that a possessed boy " struck Jesus on the right side." The youthful Christ wept, and the demon flew out :

> This boy who struck Jesus, and from whom the demon went out in the form of a dog, was Judas the Iscariot who gave Him up to

[6] This was noted long ago : " In the majority of cases the blood does not coagulate in the body for the first four hours after its rest has commenced, and in many it remains fluid for six, eight or more hours, and yet coagulates within a few minutes of its being let out of the vessels."—Dr. James Paget, *London Med. Gazette* 1 (1840) 613 ; cited by Stroud, pp.155, 404.
[7] Of course the stain might indicate the overflow. But, in Our Lord's case, St. John says that blood-cum-water *immediately* came out.
[1] Recension B, xi 2 : Tischendorf, *Ev. apocr.*, 1876[2] p.311. The right side is also specified in the Ethiopian version (6th century) of the Gospels.

the Jews ; and the side on which Judas struck Him is the side which the Jews pierced with a lance.—P. Peeters, *Evangiles apocr.* 2 (1914) 43.

The value of such a story lies merely in the fact that the piercing of the right side is taken for granted. It is unlikely that there was any real tradition involved. It may be dependent on some Old Testament text.[2] By the time of St. Bernard[3] the right side was accepted without discussion. It occurs in the allegorical interpretation of the breaking of the Host at Mass. Thus we read in an Irish tract on the Mass (10th century?) found in the Stowe Missal :

> The particle that is cut off from bottom of the half which is on the [priest's] left hand is the figure of the wounding with the lance in the armpit of the right side. For westwards was Christ's face on the cross, to wit, *contra civitatem*, and eastwards was the face of Longinus ; what to him was the left to Christ was the right.— Whitley Stokes and John Strachan, *Thesaurus Palaeohibernicus,* 1903, ii. 254.

In Eastern liturgies the Host was pierced with a small lance. In that of St. Chrysostom[4], preceding the recitation of J19[34] is the rubric " piercing it in the right side with the lance."

Though the literary attestations of the piercing on the right side are comparatively few, the artistic representations are very numerous. Almost invariably Longinus is on Christ's right side ; so are Our Lady, Dismas, and (when represented) the Church with a chalice. There are exceptions, however, e.g. the Syrian plate found in Perm (fig. xii. 13). In particular, in early Irish art (though not in the few literary references) the piercing is usually on the left side.[5]

There is a peculiar view in Prudentius (✝ c. 413)[6]. He says that

---

[2] Thus St. Bede accepts the piercing of the right side, referring to the door of the temple being on the right according to I (III) Kings 6[8].—P.L. 91. 722. Similarly Rupert of Deutz : P.L. 167. 1151. There may also have been a reference to Ezekiel 47[2] : *Ecce aquae redundantes a latere dextro.* This text is echoed in the antiphon at Paschal time : *Vidi aquam egredientem de templo a latere dextro.*

[3] *Sermo* 7 *in Ps. Qui habitat* : P.L. 183. 208.

[4] Brightman, *Eastern Liturgies,* p.357. On the liturgical lance see *Dict. d'arch. chr.* 8 (1928) 1234.

[5] Thus figs. xii. 24, 25, 26, 29, 30. Also the Syriac xii. 27, but probably not the British Museum casket (fig. xii. 8). But the Irish Passion of Longinus has the right side : " It was I that wounded Christ with a soldier's spear in His right side so that His heart burst. But I repented of that deed, and God pardoned me my sins." —Atkinson, *Passions and Homilies from the Leabhar Breac,* p.301.

[6] *Dittochaeon* 42 : P.L. 60. 108. Also *Cathemerinon* 9 and *Peristephanon* 8. St. Bridget says : " One of them coming up plunged the lance so strongly into His side that it almost penetrated to the other side."—*Revelationes* i. 10, ed. 1680, p.18. She then speaks of *cor perforatum* ; and elsewhere (iv. 70, p.290) she speaks of *cor transfixum.* But it is incorrect (with Stroud, p.397) to think that St. Bridget is referring to heart-rupture (before death) ; she is referring to the lance-pierced heart.

the thrust pierced both sides, from one of which blood issued, from the other water. Cornelius a Lapide[7] interprets this to mean that the lance pierced the heart from the right side and emerged on the left. This view, however, is exceptional and unnecessary. So fixed had the theory of the right side become by the thirteenth century that the Spanish bishop Lucas of Tuy († 1249)[8] reproached the Albigensians with holding that the left side had been pierced, and he quoted the case of St. Francis. It has however been already indicated that the wounds of stigmatics cannot be quoted as deciding historical questions concerning the Crucifixion. While St. Francis, and apparently most stigmatics, had the wound on the right side, there were a number of cases in which the wound (if it existed at all) was on the left side.[9]

Several modern commentators, without much thought, favour the left side.

It was naturally at the heart that the soldier aimed, as the last resort of life. Besides, standing in front of the Crucified to watch attentively if He were still breathing, and holding the lance in his right hand, he had to strike to the left side.—Le Camus, *Life of Christ* 3 (1923) 388.

The lance held in the right hand must have struck the left side and reached the heart.—Prat, *Jésus-Christ*, 1933[4], ii. 407.

The left side in order that the test might be the more certain.— Lagrange, *The Gospel*, 1938, ii. 276

We may take this as watery blood, i.e. the serous part of the blood which had already decomposed so that the part called cruor had coagulated : a sure sign that death had occurred and that the body had begun to cool. Or else, if we use the expression to mean that blood and pericardial water flowed, this implies that the thrust pierced the heart. Hence the blow could not have been on the right side.[10]—Sepp. *Vie de JC*, 1861, iii. 62.

---

[7] " He seems to mean that through the larger wound [on the right side] so much blood burst forth that the water could not be seen, but through the left wound smaller and nearer the pericardium, water burst forth."—*Commentaria* 16 (1866) 620.

[8] *Adversus Albigensium errores* i. 2 : *Max. Bibl. Patrum* xxv. 224.

[9] On St. Francis : Thomas of Celano, *Vita Prima* (1228) nn. 95, 113. On the left side : S. Catherine of Siena, Anne C. Emmerich, Louise Lateau, Therese Neumann. When the last-named was asked why it was on the left side, she answered : " It is an idle question. The Saviour does all things well."—F. von Lama, *Further Chronicles of Therese Neumann*, 1932, p.155.

[10] Alleged physiological reasons for choosing the left side were adduced by C. F. Grüner, *Commentatio antiq. med. de Jesu Christi morte*, 1805, p.40 ; also by Stroud, *op. cit.* p.144. Misled by Stroud, Bernard also says that the wound was on the left side.—*John*, p.646. Most cases of heart-rupture are in the left ventricle ; see p.354.

There is of course not a vestige of proof that the soldier was not at the side, or did not move to it, when delivering the blow. As to the physiological arguments alleged in favour of the left side, they are completely out of date, as well as being in contradiction with Dr. Barbet's experiments.[11]

(4) The Dorsal Stain

A statement has already (p.38) been quoted from the nuns in 1534, that they noticed " vestiges of the iron chain which had bound Him." This was an unsuccessful attempt to explain a mysterious transverse stain on the dorsal image of the shroud (fig. viii. 1). In the small of the back there is a meandering stain, with intersections and irregular clots, broader at the right, and seeming as if it had flowed towards the left.

This stain is unexpected and hard to explain. It is certainly a further mark of authenticity. What artist could have thought of it? It bears all the signs of being a post-mortem flow.[1] Also it is connected with the frontal stain of the side-wound, of which it indeed appears to be the continuation. But how explain its peculiar situation in the lumbar region? The medical men who have examined the shroud —Barbet, Hynek, Judica-Cordiglia—agree that it is due to the body being moved from a vertical to a horizontal position. In the vertical position there is a great mass of blood below the heart, none of which can be discharged (like that from the upper *vena cava*) through the pleural tunnel made by the lance. But when the body is laid flat, blood from the long and broad lower *vena cava* (see fig. xiv. 8) can flow along the tunnel. But why did the blood flow not towards the hip but towards the elbow and from right to left along the small of the back?

This is what Dr. Hynek says (i. 89, 110) :

> The arching of the muscles of the back and the loins, forming a great arch frontally, is characteristic of traumatic tetanus. This arching of the front (lordosis) is clearly illustrated in the imprints of the Holy Shroud. The corpse of Christ was placed in a horizontal position after being taken down from the cross. Because of the arching of the chest the blood from the wound on

---

[11] Somebody has suggested to me that Longinus might have been left-handed !
[1] " This stain is a flow of blood, for I have observed its special red-tinted colour on the shroud seen in daylight."—Barbet ii. 47.

the right side could not flow downwards towards the flanks but found an easier path to the left side and elbow . . . It gathered below the right elbow and then passed in two streams over to the left elbow, but not quite so low as on the right side. There we can clearly see the dark-coloured congealed blood and around it the serum—commonly called ' water '—where it saturated the Holy Shroud in a wide margin around the blood-stains.[2]

But even if we accept this plausible explanation, there now arises a difficulty: *When* did this blood-flow impregnate the shroud? According to Dr. Hynek, the body was placed in the cloth (shroud) immediately after it was taken down from the cross (i. 111) :

> The congealed blood in the region of the loins came out very soon after Christ's death, say, immediately after His removal from the cross. But it was not until [it was] in the sepulchre that the impressions were developed, tinted and fixated on the Holy Shroud by the action of the aloes. If the body had been wrapped in the winding-sheet only after it had been brought to the sepulchre, or later, we should not have the imprints of the blood and water so emphatically mentioned by the beloved disciple.

But, according to Dr. Barbet (ii. 51), the body was placed in the shroud only when the tomb was reached :

> Otherwise the dorsal part of the shroud would have been *flooded* with the blood from the *vena cava inferior* during the journey. On the contrary, the duration of the transport must have been sufficient for this vein to empty itself through the heart-wound. Most of the blood was lost (or was collected without touching the body). There remained only the portion which coagulated on the skin during the flow. After the body was thus transported naked and then deposited on the shroud, this received only the imprint of the blood-clots formed on the skin during the journey.

Moreover, Dr. Barbet (ii. 53) thinks, it is difficult to imagine the dorsal flow *ascending* from the posterior median line to the left side. He therefore makes the ingenious suggestion that, during transport to the tomb, the body was supported by a twisted cloth, forming a kind of cincture, passing under the small of the back. This cloth would have become impregnated with blood, portion of which

---

[2] Dr. Gedda (p.8) does not admit this arching (lordosis) for he thinks that the spinal column has in the lumbar region left a clear imprint on the shroud (see fig. viii. 1). But, apart from this, we might ask how, if this region were so arched, the dorsal stain has become impressed on the shroud. There may have been a mattress or cloth underneath. Gedda thinks that the stain is due to blood which flowed on the flexor surface of the forearms and arms on the cross ; after deposition this flowed from the elbows on to the cloth underneath. This is not a satisfactory explanation.

would irregularly clot on the skin and thus leave the transverse dorsal marking.

Thus this lumbar stain, which is certainly not an unmeaning artistic product, is not easy to understand. The plausible explanations offered show us how many details are lacking from the concise Gospel accounts. There is at least considerable probability that the stain is due to a second post-mortem flow from the side-wound.

(5) **Was the Flow miraculous?**

St. John is emphatic that he saw the immediate flow of blood and water from the wound ; he saw it, he bore witness, his testimony is first-hand. He gives no explanation or interpretation, he makes no comment. He simply records the stark fact. There is not the smallest indication that he considered the phenomenon to be miraculous. On the contrary, the context seems to imply that the evangelist regarded the happening as a sure proof of Christ's full humanity.[1]

According to Mgr. Poelzl,[2] St. John " looked upon the occurrence as miraculous." But the proofs adduced are not convincing. (1) There was not only real blood but real water. The popular term ' water ' does not prove this. It is difficult to see the purpose of the alleged production of chemically pure water. (2) There was a separate flow of blood and of water. The text need not imply this ; nor has a natural explanation of a separate flow been shown to be impossible. (3) St. John lays emphasis on his witness. But this is to the fact, not necessarily to its miraculous nature. (4) He appeals to messianic prophecy and he " never writes thus of any natural event however important." This is incorrect. Was the soldiers' refraining from breaking His legs a miracle? Was it miraculous that the Jews looked at the Pierced One? St. John in fact does not quote any scriptural text concerning the blood and water. Nor can the general rule be admitted. St. John quotes the Old Testament concerning the cleansing of the temple, the reception of the parables, the betrayal by Judas, and so on, not one of which can be called miraculous.

One of the earliest extant commentaries on J19[34] is that of St. Irenaeus (✝ c. 200), who does not assume a miracle. He lays stress

---

[1] In a second-century docetic work (*Acts of John* 101), Christ is represented as saying that there was no real flow of blood from His body.
[2] *The Passion and Glory of Christ*, Eng. trans., 1919, p.249.

on Christ's real humanity: He was hungry and tired, He shed tears, He sweated blood. Then he adds: " If He had taken nothing from Mary . . . there would never have issued blood and water from His stabbed side. For all these are signs of the flesh which was taken from the earth."[3]

Origen († 254/5) was the first to hold that the flow was miraculous. Celsus mockingly asked: " What is the nature of the *ichor*[4] in the body of the crucified Jesus? Is it such as flows in the bodies of the immortal gods? " Origen replied :

> In other dead bodies the blood coagulates, and pure water does not flow forth. But in the case of the dead body of Jesus the miraculous feature was that around the dead body blood and water flowed forth from the side.—*Contra Celsum* ii. 36.
> He was unlike other dead men ; even in death He manifested signs of life in the water and the blood.—*Ibid.* ii. 69.

Apart from mystic interpretations (to be treated elsewhere), there appears to have been little discussion concerning the physical aspect of the phenomenon.[5] So we can pass to a letter of Innocent III (1209) which was included in the Decretals :

> As there was true spirit and true blood, so without doubt there was true water, since Christ is truth and all deceit is quite alien from truth. For if it were not water but phlegm which issued from the Saviour's side, he who saw and bore witness to the truth would certainly have said phlegm, not water . . . It follows then that of whatever kind was that water—natural or miraculous, created afresh by divine power or resulting from component [humours]—it was without doubt true water.—Decretals of Gregory IX, iii. 41, 8: Friedberg, *Corpus Iuris Canonici* 2 (1881) 641. Cf. Denzinger, n. 417.

In this passage emphasis is laid on the issuing of ' true water,' not on its miraculous origin. St. Thomas comments :

> The water flowing from the side of Christ hanging on the cross was not phlegmatic humor, as some have said. For baptism could not be performed with such humour . . . It was pure water miraculously issuing from a dead body, just as was the blood, . . .

---

[3] *Contra haereses* iii. 22, 2.
[4] The divine liquid serving as blood for the gods.—Homer, *Iliad* v. 340.
[5] Poelzl (p.249) refers to St. Cyril of Jerusalem as asserting that the flow was miraculous. He says indeed: " Moses changed the river into blood, Jesus gave out water with blood from His side."—*Cat.* xiii. 21. But the saint is interested merely in the mystical interpretation. In any case a Catholic is quite free to propose a natural explanation of the red Nile, e.g., Canon Arendzen in *Religion and Science* (Cambridge Summer School, 1949, p.216.

to show that Christ's body was truly composed of the four elements of which water is one, and to show through the blood that it was composed of the four humours.—*Summa theol.* iii. 66, 4 (ad 3).

The four elements which concur to form the body were: earth, water, air and fire. The four compound humors were: blood, choler, phlegm and melancholy. Thus an ephemeral chemical theory was assumed by these exegetes. This demoded view is still defended by Cornelius a Lapide (✝ 1637):

> Calvin is wrong when he says that water is contained in the pericardium [heart-sac], from which, in the case of Christ pierced with a lance, water naturally flowed out. For doctors teach that this is false; they assert that this pericardial liquid is not water but bilious humor.—*Commentaria* 16 (1866) 621.

Let a modern Jesuit answer his confrère:

> A declaration of Innocent III seems to oppose this view [water=serum]; he rejects the opinion that not water but only phlegm or a watery substance had flowed from the sacred heart. But we must observe in the first place that serum is not phlegm, but holds 90 per cent. of water. Again, in the days of Innocent III phlegm was reckoned as one of the four humors that were distinguished from the four elements; consequently it was supposed not to contain any water.—A. J. Maas S.J., *The Life of Jesus Christ*, 1927[8], p.546.

To-day, with a rehabilitated historical sense, we can realise that St. John was not thinking of the subsequent (and now discarded) theory of elements and humors; nor was he thinking of the chemical substance whose formula is HOH. There was blood, he said, and there was ' water.' i.e. a fluid of a lighter colour.[6] What this fluid was—serum or hydro-pericardium or something else—is a matter for discussion.

There are subsequent commentators who regard the phenomenon

---

[6] It would be easy to show that any light-coloured liquid was called water by the ancients. It is more interesting to observe that medical writers long continued to use the word. Thus Bonet, speaking of an autopsy on a young girl, says: " I found the heart twice the usual size, the auricles large, the veins and arteries distended with water and dark thick blood."—*Sepulchretum*, 1700, i. 585; cited by Stroud, p.399. At an inquest held in Manchester in Nov. 1834, the medical witness testified: " The pericardium contained about a quart of blood and water." —Stroud, p.401. It is therefore pedantic and unhistorical to argue with Poelzl (p.248): " The gospel narrative is decidedly in favour of the theory that real true blood and real true water flowed from the wound in Christ's side." Can we really imagine St. John investigating whether the clear fluid was HOH, or being interested in the question? Even to-day we speak of water on the brain, watering eyes, passing water, bag of waters, etc., to designate various body-fluids.

as miraculous,[7] not because of any purist interpretation of ' water,' but because they do not think that such a flow could naturally come from a dead body. No longer is any *a priori* reason adduced. It is presumably admitted that it is our duty to seek for a natural explanation (cf. p.56) and not to desist prematurely. It may be asserted[8] that " naturalistic explanations of the sign are not only inadequate but also inconsistent with the facts." But this interim verdict must be received with caution. So-called scientific theories of the moment must not hinder the quest, especially since the circumstances are not fully reproducible. But already experiments on cadavers have shown that the blood-flow can be reproduced, and, as we shall see, a plausible explanation of the ' water ' has been found. Hence the problem must not be foreclosed by appeal to miracle.[9]

Following Baur, modern sceptics have with rash facility accepted the impossibility of a natural explanation. And, as they refuse to admit a miracle, they seek to discredit St. John's statement :

That the statement of the eye-witness has come down to us in its original form, cannot be safely asserted because of the impossibility of explaining the issuing of ' blood and water ' from an internal source physiologically.—Rev. T. K. Cheyne, *Enc. Biblica* i. 960.

In support of this dogmatic assertion, the writer appeals to the following verdict of a certain Dr. Charles Creighton :

May it not have been a thoughtless rather than a brutal act, the point of the lance being directed at something on the surface of the body—perhaps a coloured wheal, bleb or exudation such as the scourging might have left or the pressure of the (assumed)

---

[7] The medievals wrongly regarded blood-flow from a wounded corpse as necessarily miraculous. " In others, when they give up their souls, the blood congealeth : but from Christ's side, not without miracle, as from a living well, there flowed forth true blood and water."—John Tauler († 1361), *Meditations*, Eng. tr. 1925, p.325. " This was done miraculously. For neither blood nor pure water flows from a dead body, in which the blood immediately coagulates through the coldness of death and is converted into clot (*tabes*)."—Ludolph († 1378), *Vita I.C.*, ii. 64, 3 (ed. Rigollot 1870, iv. 137). I see that St. Ambrose took the same view (P.L. 15. 1842) : Christ's body was dissimilar to ours by grace, since from His dead but incorrupt body the blood flowed and was not congealed.

[8] Westcott, *Gospel of St. John*, 1908, ii. 319.

[9] There is a temptation to rid oneself of medical discussion in this way. Thus Mgr. Poelzl (p.250), after citing Belser, whose language is theologically objectionable (see p.350 later on), writes : " This interpretation removes all the difficulties which medical science might raise if the occurrence were purely natural." But other contemporary commentators favour a miracle, e.g. Lagrange, *Jean*, 1925[2], p.499.

ligature supporting the weight of the body might have produced?
Water not unmixed with blood from some such superficial
source is conceivable ; but blood and water from an internal
source are a mystery.

The unspeakable vulgarity of this pimple-theory is equalled only
by the author's medical incompetence, which will be presently
exposed. Just imagine St. John, at this solemn moment, recording
for us the playful pricking of this thoughtless soldier !

(6) **Blood and Water**

The physical cause of Our Lord's death has already been discussed.[1] The investigation will now be resumed in order to see how
far the phenomenon of the blood and water throws light on the
death. A preliminary observation is in order. The medical men
who have discussed the matter have generally been entirely too
dogmatic in their respective verdicts, which incidentally are
mutually destructive. Even at the present day it may be quite
evident even to laypeople that a man is dead. There are of course
some exceptional cases of apparent death, e.g. by drowning, where
restoration is still possible. But in general, especially after a time-
lapse or in the case of violent death, ordinary people are capable of
forming a practical judgement without expert assistance. To
assign the actual cause of death is, however, quite a different
matter, not only as regards historical personages but in the case of
a contemporary demise. Here, in many instances, even a medical
expert cannot give a reliable opinion without an autopsy. We can
be quite certain about Christ's death without being in a position to
specify the exact cause—a remark which applies to thousands of
other cases of crucifixion and impalement. The belated diagnosis
of men of to-day must accordingly be regarded as having at most a
certain degree of probability. We must discount all overconfident
assertions.

Heart-Rupture

In 1847 Dr. William Stroud published his view that Our Lord died
from rupture of the heart :

> The effusion of blood and water from the side of Christ, whereof
> no satisfactory solution can otherwise be given, is fully explained

---

[1] See p.271 above, especially for the brief relevant bibliography.

by the rupture of His heart . . . Rupture of the heart is the result of its own violent action, and generally occurs in the left or principal ventricle. Of such action the mental agony endured by Christ during the last three hours of His crucifixion, and which not long before forced from Him a bloody sweat, was a real and adequate cause. And the rapid manner of His death implies that the rent was large and sudden. Rapid as it was, the space of a minute or two would naturally however intervene ; and this would afford a sufficient time for uttering . . . Father, into Thy hands I commit My spirit.—Stroud, p.142f.

This verdict is based upon the issue of blood and water when His side was pierced. The blood is interpreted as clot and the water as serum, both being contained in the pericardial cavity owing to the bursting of the heart :[2]

As the object of the soldier in wounding the body of Christ must have been either to ascertain or to insure His death, he would purposely aim at the heart, and therefore transfix the lower part of the left side . . . In so doing he would open the pericardium obliquely from below. And, supposing that capsule to be distended with crassamentum and serum and consequently pressed against the side, its contents would by the force of gravity be instantly and completely discharged through the wound, in a full stream of clear watery liquid intermixed with clotted blood . . . Whilst such an effusion would necessarily have followed rupture of the heart, it could not have occurred under any other conceivable circumstances.—Stroud, p.144.

This explanation has been accepted by many medical men, a few of whom may be quoted :

I do not believe that anything could possibly account for this appearance as described by that Apostle except a collection of blood effused into the distended sac of the pericardium in consequence of the rupture of the heart and afterwards separated—as is usual with extravasated blood—into these two parts, viz. (1) crassamentum or red clot and (2) watery serum.—Sir James Y. Simpson, M.D. (†1870), in Hanna, p.338.
I do not think that any intelligent medical man will read Dr. Stroud's treatise without being satisfied with the explanation.

---

[2] The heart is a hollow muscular organ about the size of the closed fist. The heart and the roots of the great vessels (such as the aorta) are enclosed in two intimately connected sacs. The outer (fibrous pericardium) is attached to the diaphragm and the chest-wall. The inner (serous pericardium) is a two-layered sac invaginated by the heart from above and behind. The outer and the inner layers of the serous pericardium are called the parietal (adherent to the fibrous pericardium) and visceral (adherent to the heart) layers respectively. The potential space between these two continuous layers is termed the pericardial cavity.

No other hypothesis will satisfactorily explain the separate escape of blood and water from that region.—Sir John Struthers (anatomist), in Hanna p.341.

Any intelligent jury of medical men would certify that the cause of [Christ's] death was internal haemorrhage, the origin of which was a ruptured or broken heart.—Dr. Lewis D. Mason of Brooklyn, in Sir A. R. Simpson, p.314.

It is interesting to note that this theory has been allowed or adopted by a number of Catholic exegetes and medical men :

Rupture of the heart is followed by an effusion of blood into the pericardium, where it quickly separates into its solid and liquid constituents called crassamentum and serum or in ordinary language, blood and water.—A. J. Maas, S.J., *Life of Jesus Christ*, 1927[8], p.543.

Learned English physiologists have tried to explain the water and blood by presupposing that Jesus' heart was literally broken before being pierced by the lance . . . Whatever the merits of such an explanation, the Evangelist who witnessed the incident sees much deeper and more mysterious meanings in it.—Ricciotti, *Life of Christ*, 1947, p.643.

As a matter of fact, medicine has encountered no case analogous to this. But it cannot without temerity assert that Jesus, with His perfectly delicate nature and with the superhuman weight of suffering which He had borne, did not constitute an exception. The lively pangs which He had experienced might have formed aqueous deposits around the heart. The rupture of an important blood-vessel, after the great cry that preceded His last breath, had also perhaps gathered in His chest a quantity of still fluid blood, which was beginning to be transformed into serum and blackish blood.[3]—Bishop Le Camus, *Life of Christ* 3 (1923) 388f.

Belser accepted heart-rupture, but accounted for it by something dangerously akin to suicide :

The heart of Jesus had been ruptured, not however in consequence of excessive mental agony, but by an act of His almighty power . . . The Evangelist views this gushing forth of blood as a

---

[3] The language of this quotation is obviously loose and inaccurate. So also is the Bishop's remark (p.486) : " From the wound came forth a mixture of water and blood, which revealed a rapid decomposition of the vital elements." Coagulation is merely the disaggregation of the blood into clot and serum. Decomposition is due to the action of microbial agents on fluids or tissues which have lost their vitality and resistance. Hence this objection of Poelzl must be rejected : " Any such resolution of His body into its constituent parts would be the beginning of decomposition."—*Passion and Glory of Christ*, 1919, p.248. Resolution into clot and serum (subsequently absorbed) may occur in internal haemorrhage of a living person.

miraculous event, because he saw in it evidence that the heart of Jesus had been ruptured . . . The immediate gushing forth of blood and water made it manifest that Jesus, by an act of His omnipotence and love, had rent His heart asunder.—J. E. Belser, *History of the Passion, Death and Glorification of our Saviour Jesus Christ*, 1929, pp.551, 553.

Two Catholic medical men will now be quoted. Dr. J. Ryland Whitaker, S.J. (p.90) thinks that Stroud's hypothesis is the " only one [which] satisfactorily explains the facts " :

Grief and pain, partial asphyxia and continuous physical strain are factors which can soon overtax the most sturdy heart ; and all these elements were operative in Our Lord's last hours in the most exceptional degree.

Dr. F. Oliver Walker writes as follows :

Rupture of the heart-muscle itself is the most likely cause of Our Lord's death . . . The heart does not cease beating at the time of rupture, but goes on pumping the blood with some force into the pericardial cavity until its own blood-supply is cut off. The blood would remain under tension in the pericardium and would separate into its constituent layers, the solid portion sinking to the bottom. When the soldier, with an overarm throwing movement as was the Roman way of using the javelin, thrust it through the intercostal space and penetrated the pericardium, blood and serum (described as water) would issue immediately . . . From this evidence we can deduce that Jesus died of rupture of the heart.—*The Catholic Nurse* (Birmingham), June, 1945 : *Catholic Digest*, March 1946, p.16.

Extravasation—the escape of blood into the surrounding tissues— leads to coagulation, just as if the blood had emerged on to the skin or a foreign body. Hence haemopericardium, the escape of blood from the ruptured heart (or included aorta) into the heart-sac, at or before death, is followed by separation into serum and clot. In spite of denials (see p.338), this assumption of Stroud's theory is certainly correct. It may be advisable to quote some medical authorities on the point.[4]

The rapidity of the resulting death is regulated by the size and shape of the ruptured opening. But usually death very speedily ensues in consequence of the blood escaping from the interior of the heart into the cavity of the large surrounding heart-sac or pericardium ; which sac has, in cases of rupture of the

[4] Several older writers are quoted by Stroud, pp.93, 99f.

heart, been found on dissection to contain sometimes two, three, four or more pounds of blood accumulated within it and separated into red clot and limpid serum, or 'blood and water.'—Sir James Y. Simpson, in Hanna, p.347.

[Description of an autopsy]. When the thorax was opened, the pericardium was seen to be greatly distended, so that an incision into it let out a large quantity of clear serum, and the heart lay high up at the back of the sac embedded in a mass of firm coagulum. A small aneurism behind one of the aortic valves had burst, and the blood distending the pericardium had stopped the action of the heart. After death the effused blood had undergone the invariable change to be seen on any occasion when blood passes from a living blood-vessel into a cup outside the body or into another cavity in the interior. The fibrin had coagulated carrying with it the red corpuscles to the most dependent part, whilst the serum had risen to the surface. We remarked that if the body of that patient had been placed at death in the upright position, and a free opening afterwards made into the pericardium from below, the red clot would have been seen escaping first, followed by the water-like serum.—Sir Alexander R. Simpson († 1916), p.315f.

That which most commends itself is the explanation given by Dr. Stroud, which has been energetically supported by Sir Alexander R. Simpson: that in the agony the heart or one of its great arteries ruptured into the bag enveloping the heart, into which the blood escaped. I have examined several cases of rupture, both of the heart and of the great artery, in which the pericardial bag was greatly distended and the blood had separated into clot and watery serum. The statement which has been made by some writers, that this separation does not take place when the blood flows into the pericardium, is therefore incorrect; for the clot in such a case forms a cake surrounding the whole or the greater part of the heart and remains for days without undergoing decomposition. If the pericardium were to be pierced shortly after the rupture by a short weapon such as a spear, both blood-clot and watery serum would escape from the wound.— Sir William Turner (anatomist, 1822-1916), *Expositor* 11 (1916) 336.

Such a condition [haemopericardium] is always produced with great suddenness and results generally from the rupture of an aneurism affecting the intra-pericardial portion of the aorta. But it may, of course, result from rupture of the heart, whether as the result of disease or of injury. Soon after the blood has been poured out, it coagulates. But the coagulation is not the cause of the fatal event which supervenes, for death occurs almost immediately, and in any case before the effused blood has had time to clot.—Lazarus-Barlow, *Pathological Anatomy and Histology*, 1903, p.260.

Criticism of the Theory of Heart-Rupture

Some of the assertions of Stroud and of other advocates of the foregoing theory are entirely too absolute and positive ; it cannot possibly be more than a plausible hypothesis. We must also eliminate from consideration any irrelevant sentimental associations clinging to the idea of a " broken heart." So far as the argument goes, there is nothing which would eliminate rupture of the aorta.[6]

The fact that Our Lord prayed loudly before dying is not a decisive argument. Yet it would seem to show that the rupture, if it occurred, was not a violent sudden rent but allowed an interval of survival.

> [Haemopericardium] may be due to rupture of the heart itself or to rupture of an aneurism,[5] or again it may result from rupture of the aorta without the presence of an aneurism. It may be produced also by a stabbing wound involving the heart or a large vessel. When the bleeding takes place rapidly, the pressure of the accumulated blood acts on the ventricles and interferes with their diastolic filling. The output of blood from the left ventricle is thus greatly diminished, the blood-pressure rapidly falls, and death from heart-failure results. When the bleeding is more gradual, a considerable accumulation of blood with passive distension of the sac may follow, and there may be little interference with the cardiac action for a considerable time.—Muir, *Textbook of Pathology*, 1936[4], p.376.

According to Stroud (p.73), " agony of mind " can of itself produce heart-rupture without any organic weakness. In fact (p.97) " rupture of the left ventricle may take place without any previous alteration of tissue and whilst the walls of the heart are perfectly sound." This, however, has never been proved.

> It must be borne in mind that rupture of the heart is comparatively a rare affection, and that the cases of it on record are (so far as I know) limited to those advanced in life or to such as have been labouring under some degeneration of the structure of the organ."—Dr. James Begbie (a supporter of Stroud), in Hanna, p.334.

The natural causes of rupture of the heart are violent mental emotions such as anger, fright, terror, paroxysms of passion, sudden or excessive muscular efforts, or violent physical exertions

---

[5] An aneurism is an abnormal dilatation of a blood-vessel, e.g. from weakening of the wall ; it is liable to rupture.

[6] In such a case the rupture of certain portions of the aorta might fill not the pericardium but the lungs with blood which would then coagulate. Stroud (p.407f) quotes some old cases demonstrating this.

in constrained positions . . . Rupture of the healthy heart from
any of these natural causes is however a rare occurrence, if it has
ever been seen.—Taylor, *Principles and Practice of Medical Jurisprudence*, 1 (1934[9]) 432.

Rupture of the heart is an explanation which I reject outright
for many reasons. Rupture of a healthy heart never occurs,
apart from wounds ; grief, sorrow and suffering never cause
rupture of the heart, especially when there is diminished cardiac
output. Even rupture of a diseased heart is rare, quite rare, though
rupture of the aorta at the seat of an aneurism is not uncommon.
But aneurism of the aorta is itself not very common ; it occurs
in elderly people and is most often due to a certain disease which
need not be specified. The observer whom you quote as having
seen several cases of rupture of the heart was probably referring
to intrapericardial rupture of an aortic aneurism.—Prof. P.
Kiely, F.R.C.S., in a letter to the author.

Since the foregoing was printed, I have looked up some recent
literature. From this it is clear that heart-rupture is comparatively
rare as a cause of death. It occurs mostly in elderly people and
appears to be always due to some organic defect. Blood in the
pericardial cavity is nearly always due to rupture and causes death
by compressing or plugging the heart into immobility. All these
indications render the occurrence of heart-rupture extremely
unlikely in Our Lord's case.

E. B. Krumbhaar and C. Crowell, Spontaneous Rupture of
the Heart, *Amer. Jl. Med. Science* 170 (1925) 828-856. The
authors quote Harvey's description (1647, the first) of a rupture
and thus comment : " It seems then that a person dies from a
broken heart, not in young adult life from a great grief or emotion,
but usually in old age " from a diseased heart. Admiral Villeneuve " after his defeat by the English was said to have committed suicide by lacerating the right auricle with a needle
introduced between the ribs," as in Barbet's experiments. The
authors found 632 cases of ventricular-wall rupture in the
literature of the preceding 50 years and added 22 unpublished
cases. This cause of death, in thousands of autopsies, occurred
only in 0.06 per cent. of the cases. It is somewhat commoner in
the male, and mostly occurs between the ages of 50 and 70 years.
Rupture is found in any of the four heart-cavities, but in the
great majority of cases it occurs in the left ventricle.

A. B. Davenport — *ibid.* 176 (1928) 62-65 — describes 92 further
cases of heart-rupture.

H. A. Edmonson and H. J. Hoxie, Hypertension and Cardiac
Rupture, *Amer. Heart Jl.* 24 (1942) 719-733. They found 72 cases
of heart-rupture of all types in 25,000 consecutive autopsies ;

this is a somewhat higher percentage (0.29) than that given by other writers. They also say that it is commoner in women, and usually occurs in the seventh and eighth decades of life. Before 1861 authors failed to observe that heart-disease was the underlying cause of rupture. " From an institution which cares predominantly for elderly patients with mental disturbances, Beresford and Earl (1930/31) reported an incidence of 31 ruptures among 2,374 autopsies " (1.3 per cent.). Rupture of the left ventricle is commonest ; next the right ventricle. " By far the most common cause of haemopericardium is myocardial rupture." The amount of blood varied from 150 to 700 c.c., in most cases being between 200 and 250 c.c. " Because of the inelastic nature of the parietal pericardium, this volume is probably sufficient to cause tamponade," i.e. compression or plugging of the heart due to the blood in the pericardial cavity. But in cases of chronic pericarditis the pericardium has had time to distend and may contain a litre or more of fluid.

H. N. Segall, Rupture of Ventricular Myocardium, *Amer. Heart Jl.* 30 (1945) 39-54. The author describes four cases of elderly patients with diseased hearts. The pericardial cavity contained fluid blood and clot. In one case " the right pleural cavity contained 300 c.c., and the left 200 c.c., of straw-coloured fluid."

The next difficulty concerns the clotting of the extravasated blood. How soon after death is the process completed? Information does not appear to be readily available. Stroud himself says (p.411) :

> How soon the blood thus extravasated coagulates, has not been precisely ascertained. But as in such cases death is usually sudden, and the separation of the blood into serum and crassamentum exactly resembles that which occurs out of the body, there is every reason to believe that it takes place with similar rapidity, especially when the quantity is large, and certainly far within the allotted period of two hours.

There is, however, no proof that in case of internal haemorrhage coagulation takes places so rapidly.[7] In the accounts of post-

---

[7] According to Dr. Hynek (i. 69, ii. 142) the blood would not coagulate for at least 24 hours, much later in cases of asphyxiation ; but he does not seem to be referring to extravasated blood. " We must accept the fact that when retained in its original vessels it coagulates very much more slowly than when it has been removed to a receptacle of any sort, or has come in contact with what for it is foreign tissue, i.e. blood effused into the tissues or cavities of the body clots fairly rapidly." —Taylor i. 209. But how soon does this happen in a cadaver?
My colleague Dr. W. J. O'Donovan will not accept the ruptured-heart theory ; for he considers that the short time-interval of an hour or so would be insufficient to allow for gross clot and retraction, and hence the ' water ' is not accounted for. He thinks that there is no case for intra-vascular or extra-vascular clotting as an explanation of the water. Clotting would take place so slowly that an appreciable amount of clear serum would not have been formed at the time of piercing.

mortems after heart-rupture quoted by Stroud (e.g. pp.127,150), the clot is described as quite solid and as adhering to the lower portion of the pericardium, while the serum floats above. This condition is also quoted in books on forensic medicine as a criterion of post-mortem origin :

> In the heart and great vessels we frequently find large masses of clot. If these be of post-mortem origin, they will show (a) that the red corpuscles, being of a greater specific gravity than the serum or the white corpuscles, have sunk to the lowest part, and (b) that the clot as a whole is in consequence divided into a lower coloured and an upper colourless or white-coloured part with a buff-coloured layer between.—Taylor i. 271.

But it remains to be proved that the blood *ex hypothesi* extravasated into the pericardium would be clotted less than an hour after death. Yet such clotting is essential to Stroud's theory in order to provide the ' water ' as well as the blood. But even if this is conceded, the theory has still to explain the *flow*. For if the blood were coagulated, it would seem that only the serum could come out. The elastic half-solid clot could not flow, it would remain adherent to the lowest portion of the pericardium.

So serious is this last difficulty that Dr. Haughton, as long ago as 1880, expressed the view (p.350) that " mere rupture of the heart without crucifixion " cannot " account for the flow of blood as well as water." According to him, the ruptured heart would, on the pericardium being pierced, explain only the flow of liquid serum, the clot remaining *in situ*. He therefore held that the liquid blood originated elsewhere, namely in the lung : " From the lung was poured out the dark fluid blood characteristic of crucifixion."

> His blood, in consequence of imperfect oxidation, became more and more venous and fluid, and was lodged in a larger proportion than was natural in the substance of his lungs ; so that if pierced after death, these organs would have given forth a copious flow of fluid black blood, like that observed to flow from the lungs of an animal killed by strychnia or suffocated in water after much struggling . . . Death was ultimately produced by deficient oxidation of the blood ; and a post-mortem wound of the lung would be followed by a copious flow of dark and fluid blood.—Haughton, p.350.

" It is well known," says Taylor (i. 209), " that in rapid death from certain vegetable and animal poisons, and in asphyxia, the blood remains fluid and of a darker colour than normal." But where is the evidence that in death through crucifixion (orthostatic collapse) the lungs are suffused with liquid blood? And if the blood quickly coagulates in the pericardium (as Haughton assumes in order to account for the ' water '), why should it completely fail to coagulate in the lungs (as he assumes to explain the ' blood ')?

Moreover, Haughton assumes two different and independent causes of death. First, orthostatic collapse ; see the quotation on p.276, above. Secondly, heart-rupture ; for he says that the issue of copious blood followed by copious water would occur only from the after-death piercing of " a crucified person who had died upon the cross from rupture of the heart." From one cause he assumes the complete suffusion of the lungs with liquid blood, which he supposes to exist in persons who died of crucifixion, drowning or strychnine-poisoning. From the other cause, he assumes coagulated blood in the pericardium and the issue of serum therefrom when it is pierced after death.

These difficulties are so serious that Haughton is quite unjustified in declaring that " there remains no supposition possible to explain the recorded phenomenon except the combination of the crucifixion and rupture of the heart."

Pleural Effusion

The ' water ' has also been explained as pleural effusion. Thus Dr. Le Bec:

> It was a pathological liquid which had accumulated as a result of exudation into the thorax. As the Gospel does not say on which side He was pierced, many people have thought that the lance entered the pericardium or envelope of the heart. We have no reason to suppose so. We may just as well conclude that the pleura, the covering of the lung, was perforated and that it contained a certain quantity of the fluid described in medicine as ' pleural effusion.' Such an effusion might well be produced during the last hours of Our Lord's life by extreme exhaustion coupled with the circulation troubles that inevitably accompany crucifixion.—Le Bec, p.131 (p.22 of pamphlet).

This is unsatisfactory. If Dr. Le Bec had assumed rupture of the aorta, he could have assumed the escape of blood into the pleural cavity. He could then account for the blood by assuming that it had not yet coagulated. But apparently he makes no attempt to explain the blood which followed the lance-thrust, for he holds that

the pericardium or the heart was not pierced. His theory of a
'pleural effusion' or hydrothorax might explain the 'water,'
if he could show (1) that such pleural liquid could be of purely
agonic origin, and (2) how it could come out through the wound
since it would be accumulated behind and below the level of the
wound-orifice.

Nevertheless, owing to the difficulty of assuming pericardial
serum in sufficient quantity to form observable 'water,' there
remains the possibility that the water is pleural effusion provided
that the blood is assumed to come from the pierced heart.

> We could, I suppose, assume that St. John may have merely
> meant blood and more watery blood, or perhaps blood-clot
> followed by a paler liquid, perhaps serum. But the origin of the
> serum would be rather difficult to explain, if it is to be taken as
> having escaped in any quantity. Blood and pleural effusion would,
> in my opinion, meet the case. For if Our Lord was beaten on the
> chest with sufficient force to contuse the pleura and lung, an
> effusion of moderate dimensions could form in six to twelve
> hours.—Note by Prof. P. Kiely.

My colleague Prof. W. J. O'Donovan is also inclined to favour this
view. Pleural or pericardial effusion (or both) seems to him a
reasonable explanation of the 'water' (serous fluid) in an exhausted,
traumatised and anoxic subject. This effusion hypothesis would
result in the water issuing in advance of the blood and so being
noticed.

Cognate with the above explanation is the suggestion made by
Prof. F. Hayek to Dr. Hynek (ii. 170), that there was post-mortem
hypostasis[7a], i.e. a collection of fluid in pericardium and lung.

A Distended Stomach

In all reverence, a Catholic doctor, John Lyle Cameron,[8] has
recently propounded a new theory to account for the 'water':

> The soldier . . . would know which part of the body to pierce
> in order that he might obtain a speedily fatal result or ensure
> that the victim was undeniably dead. He would thrust through
> the left side of the chest a little below the centre. Here he would

[7a] The post-mortem condition in which the blood and lymph vessels become
permeable, and owing to gravity the fluids sink. Hence the explanation of 'corpse-
stains.'
[8] How Our Lord Died, a paper read at the Third International Congress of
Catholic Doctors at Lisbon, June 1947 ; printed in the *Universe*, 25 July 1947.

penetrate the heart and the great blood vessels at their origin, and also the lung on the side.

The soldier, standing below our crucified Lord as He hung on the cross, would thrust upwards under the left ribs. The broad clean-cutting two-edged spearhead would enter the left side of the upper abdomen, would open the greatly distended stomach, would pierce the diaphragm, would cut wide open the heart and great blood-vessels, arteries and veins . . . Blood from the greatly engorged veins, pulmonary vessels and dilated right side of the heart, together with water from the acutely dilated stomach, would flow forth in abundance.

Apparently it is known that acute dilatation of the stomach may follow from surgical shock, especially after abdominal injuries or operations. But what is the statistical frequency of such a complication? So far as I can ascertain, it is comparatively rare. Next, in what proportion of cases is the result fatal? As to its causation, nothing appears to be known: " The reasons why it happens in some cases of shock, and not in others, are quite unknown." What then is the evidence that this occurred in the case of Christ?

There is good evidence that our divine Lord died unexpectedly soon. This is a clear indication that a fatal complication had suddenly developed. That fatal complication could only have been acute dilation of the stomach. The post-mortem dealing with the Sacred Body of our divine Lord completely substantiates this conclusion.

There is really no excuse for such decisive language.[9] The fact that Christ died unusually soon does *not* prove the occurrence of a sudden fatal complication. And even if it did, there are numerous possibilities between which, at this distance of time and without recorded symptoms, it would be impossible to choose with any certainty: orthostatic collapse, heart-rupture, and so on. It

[9] " Acute dilatation of the stomach could not be sustained. Had Our Lord suffered from this, He would have vomited incessantly. In any case, the time incidence was too early for this complication, which is seldom if ever seen until at least twenty-four hours after a severe injury or operation."—Note by Prof. P. Kiely, F.R.C.S.

Acute dilatation of the stomach was first described by Kundradt in 1871.— Lee and Somerville, *Brit. Med. Jl.*, 1941, i. 751. It is a rare condition ; fatal cases have been recorded. It is usually a post-operative or a post-anaesthetic complication. But it has been known to occur after the overloading of the stomach with food.—Markowski, *ibid.*, 1947, ii. 128. There are various theories concerning its cause, e.g. it may be due to " a manifestation of a tendency to a sympatheticotonic state or to incoordinated overaction of the sympathetic."—MacRae, *ibid.*, 1943, ii. 579. If it originates viâ the autonomic nervous system, it is presumably connected with shock.

is ridiculous to say that the fatal complication, even if there were such " could *only* have been acute dilatation of the stomach." No medical man would be justified in making this summary diagnosis even of a contemporary case which he had never seen. A comparatively rare syndrome is assumed, it is supposed to have a very sudden onset and to have been immediately fatal. The soldier is then assumed to have stood at the left side and to have pierced both stomach and heart, and thus he " completely substantiates " this surgical guess. It is very doubtful if anyone will take this latest theory seriously. Its only value lies in its *ad hominem* relevance, against those who deny that there could be any natural explanation of the ' water.'

Pericardial Fluid

The preceding explanations are unsatisfactory. The ' water ' is not blood-serum, since without internal haemorrhage the blood remains liquid and is not divided into clot and serum. And *if* rupture is assumed, and *if* the extravasated blood has already clotted, the semi-solid clot would not flow out. Nor is the water likely to have been pleural liquid, for, even if it could be accounted for, a great quantity would be required to reach the level of the wound.

We revert therefore to the theory that the blood came from the heart and the water from the pericardium. This is not an explanation of Christ's death, which is assumed to have occurred, though with unusual speed, from whatever cause operated fatally in the case of other crucifixions (e.g. orthostatic collapse). It is an attempt to account for the blood and water from the side pierced after death. In spite of occasionally expressed doubts, there is no difficulty in accounting for the post-mortem bleeding, which has been reproduced in Dr. Barbet's experiments (see p.334). The problem is to find a natural explanation of the ' water.'

Stroud (p.135) mentions that this was the view of Hieronymus Bardus in his *Epistula ad Thomam Bartholinum*, Leyden 1646, though he thought that the separate issue of the two fluids was miraculous. His correspondent Bartholinus thought that in this hypothesis the contents would not have flowed out but would have filled the lowest part of the chest, i.e. the dead lung would have collapsed. He held that the lungs were full of bloody serum. The Grüners, father and son, agreed with Bardus, but they thought that the outflow would not have occurred unless Christ still had a feeble spark of life : " Blood and water flowed from the wound together and, as it appears, with force, which is the act not of a dead but of a living body. Therefore when Christ on the cross was stabbed by the soldier, He still retained a degree of life, although extremely feeble and ready to expire. But on receiving the wound in His breast, He must be regarded as having truly and suddenly died."—Cited by Stroud, p.141.

Against the view that the ' water ' was pericardial fluid there is the strong argument that the quantity would be quite insufficient. In health the pericardial cavity contains a thin layer of fluid, which after death is found to be only about 200 c.c. ; though if gradually effused during life, it may stretch to hold three litres.[10] Hence the quantity is variable. Apparently little is known of the factors which influence the quantity.[11] Hence the following objections are not decisive, as they do not cover abnormal cases which have not been investigated :

> If you open a living animal as a dog, or if you open suddenly the body of suicides, or if you have brought to the dissecting room the body of a criminal who has just been hanged, there is not in the pericardium one single particle of water to be found. When such fluid is to be found, it is of the same nature with the dropsical fluids of other cavities.—John and Charles Bell, *Anatomy*, 1797, ii. 55 ; cited in Stroud, p.138.
>
> In the ordinary state of things the quantity of water found in the pericardium after death is so minute that in a case like that under consideration it would have been absolutely imperceptible . . . For the statement of the Grüners that, after death accompanied by anxiety, the pericardium is full of water, there is no evidence . . . It is not in every case of violent death, but chiefly in cases where there has been much struggle for breath—as in strangling, drowning, etc.—that serum is found in the pericardium, and even then the quantity is but small.—Stroud, pp.138f, 416.

Nevertheless, Dr. Barbet's experiments have gone a long way to

[10] Mainland, *Anatomy*, 1945, p.346. " The pericardial cavity is the space between the two layers of the [serous] pericardium. The space normally is virtual, that is, the layers are in contact and moistened with a small amount of viscid fluid ; but after death some free fluid is usually to be found in it. The capacity of the pericardial cavity, as measured by the amount of fluid which can be injected into it, is about 400 to 600 c.c. But greater amounts of fluid than this may collect in conditions of chronic pericarditis."—T. Walmsley, " The Heart," Quain's *Elements of Anatomy*, 1929.[11] vol. iv. part 3, p.134.
[11] The composition of healthy human pericardial fluid is unknown ; its amount is scanty and the autopsy samples may have undergone post-mortem changes. Animal observations suggest that, like lymph, it is extracellular tissue fluid derived from blood.—Maurer, *Amer. Jl. Physiology* 129 (1940) 635.

rehabilitate the theory. They are best described in his own words
(ii. 47) :

> In my first autopsies I had observed that the pericardium always
> contained a quantity of serosity—hydropericardium, probably
> agonic and not the serosity of pericarditis—sufficient to be seen
> flowing on incision of the parietal layer. In certain cases it was
> even very abundant.
>
> So I again took up my syringe, pushing the needle very slowly,
> and continuously aspirating. Thus I was able to feel the resis-
> tance of the fibrous pericardium ; and as soon as I had per-
> forated it, I pumped out a notable quantity of serosity. Then,
> pushing the needle further, I aspirated blood from the right
> auricle.
>
> Next I took up the knife again ; and plunging it with the same
> precautions, I observed the serosity to flow, and with further
> penetration, the blood.
>
> Finally, if the knife is brutally thrust in, a large blood-flow is
> seen to issue from the wound. But at its edges there can be
> distinguished a less important quantity of pericardial serosity.
>
> Hence the ' water ' was pericardial liquid. We can suppose
> that after an exceptional agony, as was that of the Saviour, this
> hydropericardium was particularly abundant, sufficient for the
> eye-witness St. John to have distinctly seen both blood and water
> flowing. For him the serosity could only have been ' water,' of
> which it had the appearance. As in the body the only water is
> serous fluids, there can be no question of pure water. We
> ourselves speak of hydropericardium, i.e. water contained in the
> pericardium.

This view is the most plausible of those considered, and it is
partly supported by experiment. There remains, however, a
quantitative gap. And in the present case it is precisely the amount
of water, sufficient to be observed and noted, that constitutes the
difficulty. Hence various modifications of Barbet's theory have
been proposed. For example, Dr. Judica Cordiglia (i. 97, ii. 93f)
thinks that the water was not ordinary pericardial fluid but a larger
amount of fluid of inflammatory origin (due to scourging, etc.).
According to him, traumatic pericarditis with abundant exsudate
can occur in a short time and has been observed by physicians.
With some such proviso for an abnormal amount of ' water ' from
pleura and /or pericardium, the picture given by Dr. Barbet is the
most satisfactory hypothesis. But, as was said at the beginning of
this section, it is impossible at this date to arrive at any apodictic
conclusion, and all medical dogmatising is to be deprecated.

(7) **Doubts about Our Lord's Death**

The earliest of the liberal critics[1] had an astuter insight than many of their successors. They maintained that Christ's death was only apparent ; He recovered and was nursed back to health by the disciples. They saw that the evidence for the empty tomb could not be gainsaid. So they adopted the only reasonable natural explanation of that fact: Our Lord's body left the tomb *alive*. Hence they had to adopt weird expedients to show that He did not die on the cross. According to Paulus (1828), the lance-thrust merely served the purpose of blood-letting and assisted His subsequent recovery in the tomb ! In any other case the historical evidence for death, especially in the case of an official Roman execution, would be accepted as a matter of course. The excogitation of this bizarre hypothesis is thus a striking tribute to the strength of the evidence for the Resurrection ; its advocates betray their conviction that the Appearances of the Risen Christ can be naturally accounted for only by denying His death.

This denial involves the wholesale rejection of documentary evidence, which provides an unusually multifarious and detailed account. Furthermore it presupposes gross carelessness on the part of the Roman Governor and his officials. This point was long ago considered by the Unitarian Priestley :

> The death of Jesus was so evident to the soldiers who attended the execution—and who no doubt (being used to the business) were sufficient judges of the signs of death—that, concluding him to be actually dead, they did not break his bones, as they did those of the other persons who were executed along with him. One of them, however, did what was fully equivalent to it, for he thrust a spear into his side, so that blood and water evidently flowed out of the wound. Now, though we may be at a loss to account for the water, it was certainly impossible to pierce the body as that blood should visibly and instantly flow from the wound, without piercing either the heart itself or some large blood-vessel, the rupture of which would have been mortal.— Joseph Priestley, *Discourse on the Evidence of the Resurrection of Jesus*, 1791, p.12f: cited by Stroud, p.133.

The fate of Jesus of Nazareth was not a matter of indifference. Not only is there not a single recorded instance of escape from a Roman capital sentence, carried out and not revoked. But there

[1] Christ did not die on the cross : Bahrdt (1782), Venturini (1800), Paulus (1828), even Schleiermacher (1832).

were watchful and powerful enemies determined to see the end of this messianic claimant. Caiaphas was an even better surety of death than Pilate. " The best guarantee which the historian has on such a point," admits Renan,[2] " is the suspicious hate of the enemies of Jesus." " You want to make us responsible for the death of this Man," said the Sanhedrin to Peter (Acts 5[28]). The Jews were quite sure ; they have never denied the death of Jesus on Calvary.

But there is a further consideration which shows the moral impossibility of any survival of Christ. It was urged long ago by Origen :

> In addition to other causes for the crucifixion of Jesus, this may also have contributed to His dying a conspicuous death on the cross, that no one would be able to assert that He deliberately retired from men's sight and only seemed to die without really doing so, and on reappearing played the trick of rising from the dead. I find a still clearer proof of the resurrection in the conduct of His followers who devoted themselves to teaching a doctrine at the risk of their lives ; had they invented the resurrection of Jesus from the dead, they would not have been such courageous teachers.—*Contra Celsum* ii. 56.

How could the unanimous lifelong belief of His disciples have been founded on the appearance of a Man just recovering from wounds and coma, requiring care and nursing, having to be helped and concealed? Did the Apostles—including the ex-Pharisee Paul —sacrifice their lives for a feeble convalescent? And if such were the case, how can we acquit not only the Apostles but Christ Himself from conniving at a gigantic fraud? By itself, isolated from the historical context, the recovery of Our Lord in the tomb, and His rescue therefrom, may appear tenable to a hard-pressed rationalist. But the real absurdity emerges when we think of the rise of Christianity. This was seen long ago even by Strauss :

> It is impossible that a being who had stolen half-dead out of the sepulchre, who crept about weak and ill, wanting medical treatment, who required bandaging, strengthening and indulgence, and who still at last yielded to his sufferings, could have given to the disciples the impression that he was a conqueror over death and the grave, the Prince of Life: an impression which lay at the bottom of their future ministry. Such a resuscitation could only have weakened the impression which he had made upon them in life and in death, at the most could only have given it an elegiac voice, but could by no possibility have

[2] *Vie de Jésus*, 1891[20], p.444.

changed their sorrow into enthusiasm [or] have elevated their reverence into worship.—*New Life of Jesus*, Eng. trans. 1869, i. 412.

After this devastating criticism, one could expect only an occasional irresponsible amateur[3] to deny Christ's death *pour épater le bourgeois*. A few 19th century biologists, however, engaged in the sorry business. The *enfant terrible* of the Darwinists, Samuel Butler, declared : " I can nowhere find any detailed account of the reasons which led him [Strauss] to feel so positively about Our Lord's death."[4] It is hard to know whether he was serious or merely mischievous. But he fooled Charles Darwin who wrote to Butler :

> I have been surprised at the strength of the case which you make for Jesus not having died upon the cross ; but I do not know whether to be convinced . . . Your book must have cost you much labour and I heartily hope it will be widely distributed.— H. F. Jones, *Samuel Butler* 1 (1920) 187.

Not content with destroying the basis of rationality and ethics, Thomas Henry Huxley[5] " argued that there was no valid evidence of actual death having taken place." Apparently nothing short of a personally performed autopsy would have convinced him ! He was well answered by another biologist who urged the moral (as distinguished from the physical) impossibility :

> He adopted the unusual position of questioning whether Christ had really died, and suggested that He had been removed on His supposed death by some of His followers and had been subsequently revived. How these followers derived from this conscious deception the enthusiasm to spread abroad the news of Christ's resurrection and conquest of death over the whole Roman Empire, and to face persecution and death in the campaign, Huxley did not explain.—E. W. MacBride, F.R.S., *Huxley*, 1934, p.85.

Another medical man has recently come on the scene to rehabilitate this discredited theory. The liberal-unitarian *Hibbert Journal* in its issue for July 1949 included an article which was hailed by shallow agnostics as " the best and biggest scoop for a long time."[6] This attitude towards an irresponsible and ignorant attack on the faith of millions resembles that of a gamin throwing stones at a cathedral window. A Glasgow anaesthetist, Dr. W. B.

[3] Such as George Moore in *The Brook Kerith*.
[4] *The Fair Haven*, 1873[2], p.227.
[5] *Life and Letters*, 1900, i. 319.
[6] *News Review*, 21 July 1949.

Primrose, called his article " A Surgeon looks at the Crucifixion."
—*Hib. Jl.* 47 (1949) 382-388. It may be worth while to comment
on the article, as the author claims to have been enabled by
" modern medicine . . . to view these matters from a new and
objective angle." Unfortunately he is completely ignorant of all
preceding historical or medical investigations on the subject, such
as have been discussed in this book. It will be sufficient to catalogue
the author's errors which, implicitly or explicitly, have already
been refuted in the preceding pages.

(1) *Scourging.* The victim " was secured " to the whipping-post
" *facing* the multitude," i.e. so that most or all of the wounds were
in front. There were " two kinds of implement, the official
flagrum and the birch or staves." Unlike other non-Roman
provincials, Our Lord was scourged with staves. Apparently
the Jews used the flagrum, for " in the case of the flagrum,
thirteen strokes would be allowed." Or perhaps the Jews imposed their Deuteronomic code on the Romans?

(2) *Affixing to the cross.* " Accounts [unspecified] mention the
use of ropes to hold the victims up on the crosses, the use of little
seats, and much more commonly the use of a central arm projecting from the middle of the upright of the cross (rhinosceros
[*sic*] horn, Cicero [!]) upon which the victim was straddled.
These were all means of relieving the hands of the weight of the
body. The foot-rests were to allow of the nails being driven
through the feet. The Roman convention eliminated all these
difficulties and proved most efficient." Apparently the foot-rest
and the other items were the pre-Christian, if not pre-Roman,
" original method of fixation to the cross." And what was the
Roman innovation? " The nails were no longer driven through
hands and feet, but between the bones of the forearm above the
wrists, and similarly above the ankles in the case of the legs."
In fact, " it is the use of this convention that permitted the
fulfilling of the prophecy that in the case of the Messiah there
would be no bones broken at his crucifixion." That is, the text
quoted by St. John does *not* refer to Christ's exemption from leg-
breaking !

Presumably this hitherto undiscovered Roman " technically
satisfactory convention for the infliction of this barbarous punishment " is in need of no historical proof. It is merely necessary to
invent two reasons for this alleged change in the old method.
(*a*) " The change was adopted because the tissues of the hands
often could not support the weight of a heavy body for any
length of time without being torn through the nails." Apparently
it never occurred to the Romans to nail the wrists, they nailed
the forearms. (*b*) " It is extraordinarily difficult to drive a nail
through the foot unless it is supported below by some rigid body

such as a block or sandbag." Dr. Barbet found no difficulty ; but then he wasn't a Roman !⁷

(3) *The Shroud.* It is unexpected to find that Dr. Primrose accepts the authenticity of the shroud ; he has glanced at Vignon's first book (1901). The figure on the shroud is " very much as Western art has pictured Christ since the eleventh or twelfth century." " The nail-wounds were not through the hands and feet, but where we have already shown them on medical grounds [or by Roman custom?] to be," i.e. on forearms and above ankles⁸ ! It is worth while quoting Dr. Primrose verbatim on the sidewound : " The wound on the right side of the chest is considered by Vignon *not* to be the spear-thrust. In this we have concurred, but upon more anatomical and surgical fact than he was in a position to use. As already mentioned, there would be very little blood or exudate from the actual spear-wound at the enshrouding, and so no visible impression would be made by it upon the cloth." Comment is unnecessary⁹ ! The writer also accepts Vignon's superseded vaporagraphic theory and categorically rejects " any impression produced by direct contact."

The intrinsic value of this article hardly merited the foregoing exposure. But it was published in a review claiming to be scholarly, it was exploited in the popular press, and it has not yet been publicly refuted. It is well to have demonstrated the writer's flippant incompetence before examining his alleged proof from " modern medicine " that Our Lord did not die on the cross. This is his account of the blood and water from the lance-thrust :

The use of staves or birches in scourging produced quite

---

⁷ " On a freshly amputated foot I tried to nail the anterior tarsus, the least thick portion of the ankle. For one foot alone, it required twenty hammer-blows to pierce this bony mass while crushing it."—Barbet ii. 39. But Dr. Primrose, in spite of the shroud whose evidence he professes to accept, thinks that the foot-nail was *above* the ankle, between tibia and fibula, i.e. the nail was through the leg, not the foot. It would be difficult to drive a nail of any size between these two leg-bones except high up in the region below the knee. Near the ankle one would be almost certain to fracture the fibula. Also the nail might tear upwards through the soft tissues of the leg and could hardly support any of the body-weight. There would in this case be no need for crurifragium. Finally, Dr. Primrose is the only author known to me who propounded this position for the nails i.e. through the legs above the ankles. Why he has done so is a puzzle.
⁸ The positions of the wound-marks on the shroud has already been investigated (wrist and sole). By careful measurements Dr. Barbet (ii. 21) has shown that the hand-wound is in the wrist, not in the forearm. In order to fit a nail 8 mm. broad between the two bones (radius and ulna) of the forearm, a position 5 cm. (2 ins.) above the flexion-fold of the wrist would have to be chosen.
⁹ Yet a protest must be made against this complete reversal of Vignon's view. In his book—*The Shroud of Christ*, Eng. trans. 1902, p.26—Vignon definitely and clearly identifies the side-mark with the post-mortem wound from the piercing. The casual reference to unspecified " anatomical and surgical fact "—not known to Vignon in 1901—is just a piece of bluff to justify contradicting the eye-witness St. John.

different effects [from the severe effects of the flagrum]. Here the immediate effect was the production of intense pain with remarkably little damage to tissues or organs, even where the abdomen was the part principally thrashed . . . There is as a rule no damage to abdominal viscera ; otherwise, in the case under consideration, there would have been internal bleeding of such a nature that the writer of the Fourth Gospel could not have reported that ' water ' was seen issuing from the spear-wound . . .

The ' water ' mentioned by John is the result of the nervous upset of the blood-vessels locally due to the overstimulating effect of the scourging by staves. Certain individuals are very sensitive to such stimulation, and the capillary vessels supplying the underlying tissues and membranes become paralysed and allow the blood fluids which they convey to escape . . . Where a membrane lies in a cavity, the seepage of fluid from the vessels takes place into that cavity, gravitating to its lowest part. The fluid exuded in this way is clear and of pale straw colour, the red cellular part of the blood being retained in the undamaged vascular system . . . According to the Gospel account, Christ collapsed about three o'clock in the afternoon, more than six hours after the scourging, within which time about two pints of fluid appear [!!] to have been exuded into the abdominal cavity . . .

The spear-thrust was made somewhere on the lower and more protuberant part of the abdomen, probably on the left side. There would be an initial rush of ' water ' which, for anatomical reasons, would quickly stop and it would be tinged with blood issuing from a small vessel opened by the spear . . . Surgically, this penetrating wound of the abdomen is unimportant . . . There were no sequelae from the spear-wound.[10]

So this is the ridiculous mouse emerging from the parturient medical mountain ! In spite of the jargon adopted, there is nothing new whatever in his description of a severe beating, except the inaccurate statement that " as a rule " a man beaten up with sticks suffers " no damage to abdominal viscera." Against the brunt of evidence, he adroitly assumes that Christ was beaten (a) with rods (b) only or chiefly in front. His object is to secure in the abdominal cavity an accumulation of water, which (like an eye-witness or rather an autoptist !) he estimates at " about two pints."

Having thus prepared the stage, he brings Longinus on the scene. This is a very stupid fellow who does not know how to deliver a mortal blow. For no assignable reason, he pricks the abdomen, and out comes the fluid. There is also a little blood, for he could not

---

[10] A medical practitioner who would thus lightheartedly pronounce on the location and on the unimportance of a patient's spear-wound which he had never seen would be guilty of unprofessional conduct.

help opening some ' small vessel'. The whole business was just a trifle, a playful pricking.

Christ, it is assumed, was alive but " under complete anaesthesia," with which Dr. Primrose is familiar. The experienced centurion was wrong in his report to Pilate. The donation of the body to Joseph was premature. The precaution of the lance-thrust as a substitution for leg-breaking was a farce. " With everyone satisfied that Christ had died when he collapsed, little further interest was shown by his enemies." The Sanhedrists were evidently an easy-going lot ! So Christ's friends went off with the body and placed it in a tomb :

> With the change of decubitus from the vertical to the horizontal, some recovery would be expected to take place, and an early sign of this would be a rigor or shivering fit as the initial muscular effort to produce more bodily heat . . . Medical knowledge would lead us to suppose that Christ could not have spent any length of time in the tomb, certainly not much more than one hour ; it would have been impossible for anyone in his condition to survive even a night in such a place covered only by a linen sheet.

One does not expect fairy-tales from Glasgow ; but here is one. After about an hour, the Crucified got a shivering fit. He got up— and seemingly went out. But how? The tomb could not be opened from the inside ; only with considerable force could the stone be rolled away from the outside. Dr. Primrose who accepts (but garbles) St. John can hardly reject St. Matthew's account of the guarding of the tomb. Can we believe that it was sealed up without verifying that the corpse was inside? After giving this " nonmiraculous explanation of the Resurrection," the writer is discreetly silent concerning the difficulties which even Strauss found insuperable. We are not told how Christ recovered without medical care, how He made His exit, where He went, how He fooled—*sit venia verbo*—the Apostles into believing that He had risen, not only healthy but glorious, from the dead, how the Appearances were contrived and the Ascension faked.[11] The psychological miracle of

---

[11] Dr. Primrose is amusingly ingenious in trying to evade St. John's account (which he accepts) of the Appearance to Thomas : " This wound lay over the sixth rib approximately and was due to the splitting of the skin and tissues over it by the flagrum " [stave?]. In fact, St. Thomas was invited to put his hand—into a skin-graze ! " There appear to be surgical [!] reasons for stating that this obvious wound could not be that produced by the spear, for a penetrating wound in this vicinity would certainly pierce the lung . . . with every chance of a fatal outcome." In other words, Dr. Primrose's theory of abdomen-pricking would be exploded. *Quod est inconveniens* !

the first disciples devoting their lives to, and dying as martyrs for, a conscious lie, is not referred to, much less explained.

By way of summary the following points may be urged.

(1) It is a delusion to think that our certitude regarding the death of a person of the past is in any way dependent on our being able to-day—sometimes thousands of years later—to make an accurate diagnosis or to construct on paper an imaginary autopsy. Think of such cases as those of Alexander, Socrates, Julius Caesar, Tiberius. After this lapse of time various medical possibilities are in most cases open ; we must not be misled by the learned vocabulary of those who wish to foreclose the issue. Uncertainty about the exact causation does not affect our certainty about the death.

(2) In some cases, if we accept the historical accounts, the cause of death is physically obvious without any medical advice. No one needs a tailor to tell him that his coat is torn ! This holds when we are told of fatal wounds, of the condition of the body, of burial or cremation. In particular, in the case of official Roman executions there is an overwhelming *a priori* probability that the result was fatal. History does not record a single instance of escape, barring an occasional instance of a sentence being revoked before being fully carried out (like the three crucified mentioned by Josephus, p.285).

(3) But, in the case of world-figures, the really decisive argument is moral, not physical, namely, the impossibility of explaining the course of history otherwise. The behaviour of men after the recorded death is incompatible with the person's continued survival, especially if connived at.

(4) This is especially true in the unique case of Our Lord. Apart altogether from the death on the cross—certified by the centurion and accepted (at the risk of his post) by Pilate—and independently of St. John's evidence about the transfixing, Christ's death is assured by the conduct of His foes and that of His followers and confirmed by the burial and the guarded tomb.

(5) Moreover, there is the moral impossibility of attributing fraud to a surviving Christ and to His disciples. In the early days before Christianity was recognised to be more than superstitious fanaticism it was possible to assign fraud as its origin. Such a statement was also credible to many minds in the shallow unhistorical eighteenth century. But to-day such a thesis would be propounded by no serious scholar. In the beginning the Jews spread the rumour

that the disciples had stolen the body. But even they did not query death ; nor did they believe their own rumour which had a temporary plausibility before the figures of Peter and the Apostles emerged into history. The medieval *Toledoth Yeshu* may have found credence in the ignorant circles of the ghettos. But Jewish scholarship of to-day is voiced by Joseph Klausner when he writes :

> It is impossible to suppose that there was any conscious deception ; the nineteen hundred years' faith of millions is not founded on deception. There can be no question but that some of the ardent Galileans saw their lord and Messiah in a vision.— *Jesus of Nazareth*, 1925, p.359.

It is therefore not only an insult to millions but also an outrage on scholarship when half-educated rationalists, as well as biologists and medical men, try to rob us of our faith with irresponsible and irrelevant medical chatter.

I. 2—Angel showing the marked Shroud to the Women at the Sepulchre : from St. Elizabeth's Psalter (prior to 1217)

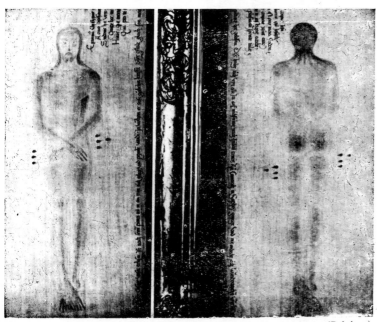

II. 4—Copy of the Shroud made by Dürer in 1516, now in Lierre (Belgium). (For convenience the frontal and the dorsal reproductions have been cut out and juxtaposed)

See pages 4 and 32

Left   Right

A

Dorsal Image

C

D

Frontal Image

B

Left   Right

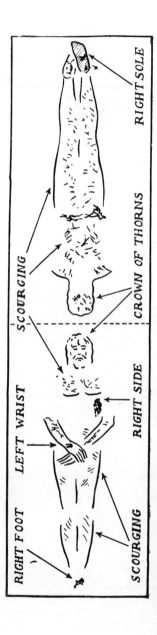

RIGHT SOLE

CROWN OF THORNS

SCOURGING

LEFT WRIST

RIGHT SIDE

RIGHT FOOT

SCOURGING

II. 5—Enrie's Photograph of the Shroud, with Diagram

See page 33

7—Figure on a Cloth in
Chambéry (16th century)

II. 8—Frontal Image of
the Shroud reproduced by
Chifflet (1624)

See page 41

II. 9—Painting in Turin Gallery (16th century)

II. 11 and 12—Copies of the Figure on the Besançon Cloth

See pages 41 and 43

III. 1—Photo of Pius X

III. 2—Negative of fig. III. 1

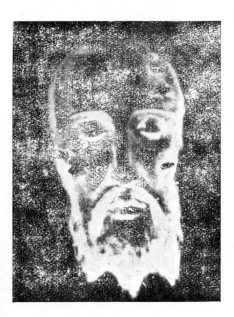

III. 3—Negative of fig. VII. 67

III. 4—Negative of fig. VII. 46

See pages 47 and 49

Right   **Left**

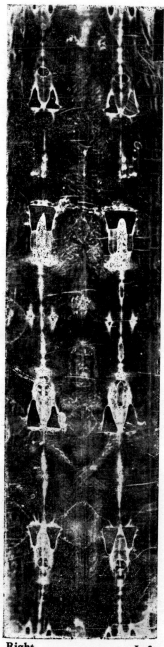

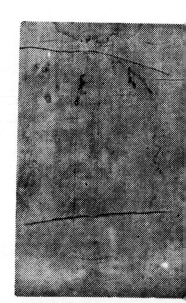

III. 6—The Face on the Shroud

III. 7—Photographic Negative of the
Face

Right   **Left**

III. 5—Photographic Negative of
the Shroud   (*Enrie*)

See page 47

IV. 1—Cloth-Impression alleged to have been obtained from a statue-head by Clément

IV. 2—Photographic Negative of IV. 1

IV. 3—Image obtained by direct contact with a corpse, then softened by water vapour. (*Judica Cordiglia*)

IV. 4—Negative of fig. IV. 3

See pages 63 and 66

IV. 5—On a fine interposed veil

IV. 6—Negative of fig. IV. 5

IV. 7—On the outer cloth (after exposure to water vapour)

IV. 8—Negative of fig. IV. 7

See page 67

VII. 2, 3
4, 5

VII. 2—Catacomb of Domitilla
(before A.D. 100)

VII. 3—Catacomb of Domitilla
(A.D. 300 /350)

VIII. 4—From a Lateran
Sarcophagus (about A.D.
350)

VII. 5—From a Mosaic in the Mausoleum
of Galla Placidia, Ravenna (about 440)

See pages 88 and 89

VII. 6—Catacomb of Domitilla (about 300)

VII. 7—Bust from a Statuette (about 30·

VII. 9—Fragment of a Sarcophagus (about 300/350) now in Berlin

VII. 8—Panel from the Sarcophagus Junius Bassus († 359)

See page 89

VII. 11—Fresco in the Catacomb
of Domitilla (about 250)

VII. 13—Mosaic in the Apse of
the Lateran Basilica (c. 330)

VII. 14—Catacomb of SS, Peter and
Marcellinus (about 400)

See page 90

VII.   16—From the Catacomb of St.
Pontianus (about 800?)

VII.   15—Detail from the Apse-
Mosaic of St. Pudentiana (about 395)

VII. 18—Manuscript of St. Gregory of
Nazianzus (about 880) in the Bibliothèque
Nationale

VII.   17—Catacomb of St. Callistus
(7th century)

See pages 91 and 93

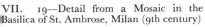

VII.   20—From a recently uncovered
Mosaic in St. Sophia, Constantinople

VII.   19—Detail from a Mosaic in the
Basilica of St. Ambrose, Milan (9th century)

VII. 21—Mosaic in the Church of Daphni,
Greece (about 1100)

VII.   22—Head of a Statue in Amiens
Cathedral (1200/50)

See page 93

VII. 23—From the Last Judgement by Pietro Cavallini (about 1293) in the Church of St. Cecilia, Rome

VII. 24—Painting by Jan Van Eyck (dated 1438), now in Berlin

VII. 25—Study by Leonardo da Vinci († 1519), Brera Gallery, Milan

VII. 26—Fresco by Sodoma († 1554), Convent of St. Anne, Camprena

See page 94

VII. 27—Detail from "The Tribute Money" by Titian († 1576). Dresden Gallery

VII. 28—Picture in Toledo Cathedral by El Greco (1604/09)

VII. 29—Detail from "The Tribute Money" by Anthony Van Dyck († 1641) in the Palazzo Beanci, Genoa

VII. 30—Picture by Rembrandt († 1669) in Berlin

See page 95

VII. 31—Munkacsy

VII. 32—Vasnetsof

VII. 33—Charlier

VII. 34—Rouault

See page 95

VII. 35—Oak Statue in Fischbeck Monastery, Saxony (12/13 century)

VII. 36—Bermejo (c. 1480), in Vich, Spain

VII. 37—Cima da Conegliano (c.1500), in the National Gallery, London

VII. 38—Fra Bartolommeo († 1517), in the Pinacoteca, Florence

See page 95

VII. 39—Murillo († 1682), in Madrid   VII. 40—Carlo Dolci († 1686)

CHRIST CARRYING HIS CROSS

VII. 41—Perugino († 1524), in Perugia   VII. 42—El Greco († 1614), in the Prado, Madrid

See page 95

VII. 43—From the Painting by Guido
Reni († 1642)

VII. 44—From the Crucifix of Limpias
probably by Pedro de Mena († 1688)
See page 95

THE CHRIST OF PITY

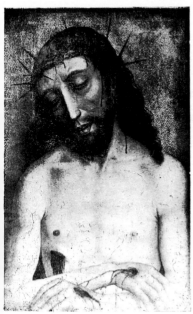

VII. 45—By Meister Francke, in
Leipzig

VII. 46—From the School of Roger
van der Weyden, in Strasbourg

See page 96

VII.   47—Bronze Crucifix at
Werden (1050/1100)

VII.   48—Fragment from the
Crucifix by Claus Sluter (c.1398),
in Dijon Museum

VII.   49—Fragment in Beauvais
Museum (15th century)

VII. 50—Carved Wooden Crucifix by Wit
Stwosz in Cracow (15th century)

See page 96

VII. 51—Fresco by Giotto († 1336) in Padua

VII. 52—From the Crucifixion by Fra Angelico († 1455) in San Marco, Florence

VII. 53—Detail from El Santo Cristo in Burgos Cathedral (c. 1475)

VII. 54—From a painting by Corregio († 1534) in Palermo Museum

See page 96

VII. 55—From the Altarpiece by Grünewald
(† 1528) at Colmar

VII. 57—Pietà by Luis Mora
(† 1586) in Madrid

VII. 56—Detail from the Diptych of
Quentin Matsys († 1530) in Antwerp

VII. 58—Detail from the Descent from
the Cross by Rubens († 1640) in Lill
Museum

See page 97

VII. 59—Image in Rome, formerly in San
Silvestro, now in the Vatican
(Copy by Heaphy)

VII. 61—German Woodcut of about 1476

VII. 62—Woodcut by Durer († 1528)

VII. 63—Painting by Matsys († 1530)

See page 98

VII. 64—Engraving by Schongauer
(† 1488)

VII. 67—Heaphy's Copy of the
Veronica in St. Peter's, Rome

VII. 68—Image propagated by Dupont
(1797-1876)

VII. 69—Copy of the Face on the Shroud
made by Sister Céline, 1898

See pages 99 and 103

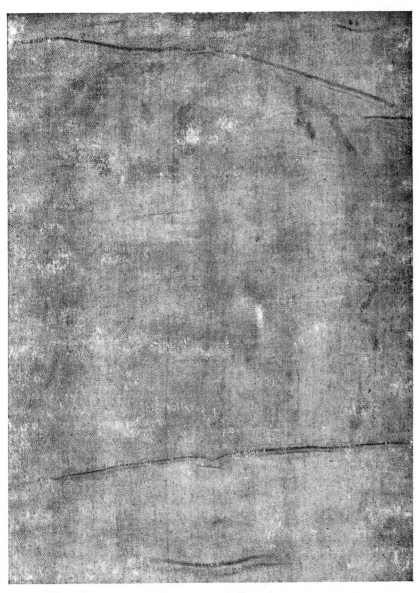

Left **Right**

VII. 70—The Face as seen on the Shroud (Enrie's Photograph)

See page 104

Right   **Left**

VII. 71—Chemograph of the Face (Negative of Enrie's Photograph)
See page 104

Wounds at
the back of
the head

Left
Shoulder

Marks
of the
Scourging

Marks on
the loins
(Lumbar
Stain)

Right Shoulder

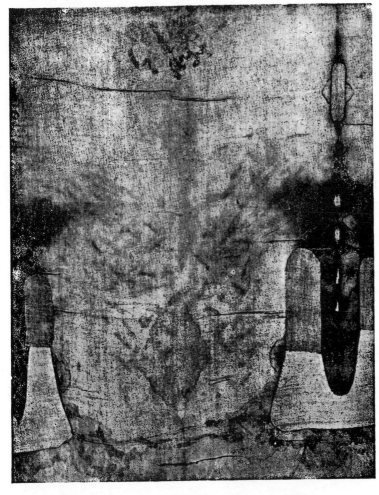

VIII. 1—The Back : Enrie's Photograph of the Shroud

See page 111

THE SCOURGING

VIII. 4—S. Urbano alla Caffarella, Rome (11th century).
Sketch by Rohault de Fleury

VIII. 5—From an English Psalter (12th century) in the British Museum

VIII. 6—Duccio († 1320) (detail)

VIII. 7—The Master of the Passion (of Lyversberg), Cologne Art Gallery (15th century) (detail)

EGO IN FLAGELLA PARATVS SVM, ET DOLOR MEVS IN CONSPECTV TVO SEMPER PS.

VIII. 8—Fra Angelico († 1455), St. Mark's, Florence See page 114

VIII. 9—Fresco in St. Praxedis, Rome (sketch by Rohault de Fleury)

VIII. 11—Sodoma († 1554), Siena Art
Gallery

See page 114

VIII. 12—Pedro de Mena
(1679), Cistercian Convent,
Malaga

VIII. 14—Georges Desvallières (1910)
(Collection Maurice Denis)

VIII. 13—Hernandez († 1636),
Carmelite Convent, Avila

See page 115

VIII. 15—Velazquez († 1660), National Gallery, London

VIII. 16—Murillo († 1682)

See page 115

IX. 4—Dürer († 1528)

IX. 5—Titian († 1576)

VIA CRUCIS

IX. 6—St. Mark's, Venice (11th century). Sketch by Rohault de Fleury

IX· 7— Painting in the Church of Elmale Kilisse, Cappadocia (12th century)

See page 125

IX. 9—Crucifix in the Church of St.
Peter, Bologna (1160 /80)

IX. 8—Crucifix in the Vatican (12th
century)

IX. 10—Stone Crucifix of Tuam
(Ireland)

See page 126

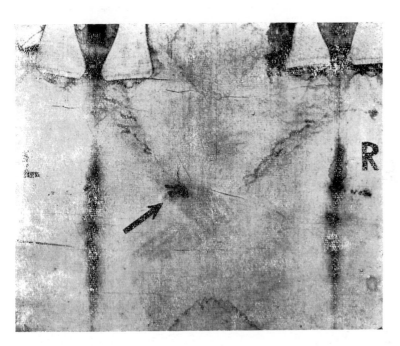

X. 1—Portion of the Shroud showing the Forearms and Hands. L denotes the left side, R the right. The arrow points to the Wrist-wound. (Enrie's photograph)

See page 128

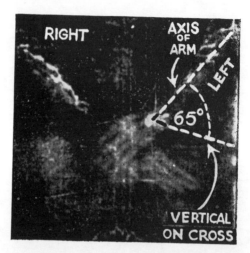

X. 5—Negative of the Arms on the Shroud, with Angle marked between the Arm-Axis and the Flow from the Wrist-wound

X. 6—Body on the Cross with Angle of Arm marked

See page 132

X. 9—The Sole of the Right
Foot (Enrie's Photograph)

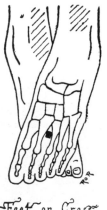

X. 10—Left Foot
nailed over Right

CORPSE CRUCIFIED BY DR. BARBET

X. 11—Front View

X. 12—Side View

See pages 134 and 136

X. 13—Front View
See page 136

X. 14—Side-Veiw

See page 136

CRUCIFIXES

WITH SITTING-BLOCK   WITH FOOT-BLOCK

X. 17—Crucifix by Costantini   X. 18—Living Man representing a Crucified (*Costantini*)

WITH NAILS THROUGH WRISTS

X. 21—Duquesnoy
(† 1646)

X. 20—Van Dyck († 1641)

See pages 153 and 143

XI. 7—British Museum Ivory (400/425) *Garrucci*

XI. 8—Ravenna Mosaic (6th century) *Garrucci*

See page 202

XI.   9—S. Maria Antiqua (705/707)

XI. 11—Fresco in Norwich Cathedral

XI. 10—Codex Egberti, Trier (977/993)

See page 202

XI. 13—Station of the Cross by Eric Gill,
Westminster Cathedral

XI. 12—Sculpture in the Louvre, Paris
(16th century)

XI. 14—Station of the Cross by Seán Keating, Clongowes Wood College

See page 203

XI. 15—From St. Elizabeth's Prayer-
Book (prior to 1217)

XI. 16—Group in Carved Wood, now in
Cluny Museum (15th century)

XI. 17—Fresco in Notre-Dame de Chauvigny (Vienne)

See page 204

XI. 20—Fra Angelico († 1455), San
Marco, Florence

XI. 22—Alabaster Carving at Afferden,
Holland

XI. 21—Passion-Play at Valenciennes, 1547

See page 216

XI. 24—Philippe de Champagne († 1674), Toulouse Museum

XI. 25—Rubens († 1640),
Antwerp Cathedral

See page 217

XI.   26—Greek Manuscript in Paris (c.880)
Rohault   de   Fleury

XI. 27—Codex Egberti, Trier (c. 980)   XI.   28—Greek MS. in Florence
                                                    (10th century)

See page 111

XI. 31—Living Man tied to X-Cross
Costantini

XI. 32—Y-Cross: Marzolini
Triptych, Perugia

XI. 33—Psi-Cross in the Church
of Puenta la Reina, Navarre

XI. 34—Cross of Herculaneum

See page 223

XII. 1—A Sarcophagus in the Lateran Museum (500/550)

XII. 4—Flask from Palestine, now in
Bobbio (c.600)

XII. 5—S. Stefano Rotondo, Rome
(c. 645)

See page 232

XII. 7—British Museum Ivory Panel (c. 400/450)

XII. 8—Wooden Panel in Santa Sabina, Rome (c. 430)

See page 238

XII. 13—Detail from a
Silver Plate found in Perm,
Russia (450/550)

XII. 14—Rabula's Syriac Gospels,
Florence (586)

XII. 16—Fresco in Santa Maria Antiqua,
Rome (c. 750)

XII 17—Fresco in the Cemetery of St.
Valentine, Rome (c. 650)

See page 242

XII.   19—The Offering of the Sponge and the Dicing for the Tunic

XII.   20—The Piercing of the Side and the Breaking of the Bandits' Legs

See page 246

XII. 21—Greek MS. in the Bibliothèque Nationale, Paris (c. 880)

XII. 22—Wall-Painting in the Church of Kelejlar, Cappadocia (c. 1000)
Jerphanion

See page 248

XII. 23—Fresco in the Church of S. Urbano, Rome (A.D. 1011

XII. 24—From an Irish Gospel Book in Saint-Gall (8th century)

See page 249

XII. 29—Central Portion of Muiredach's Cross. (*Courtesy of National Museum, Dublin*)

XII. 28—Muiredach's Cross, Monasterboice, Ireland (prior to 923)

XII. 30—Central Portion of the West Cross, Monasterboice. (*Courtesy of Nat. Mus., Dublin*)

See page 252

XII. 31—Fresco in the Underground
Church of San Clemente, Rome (c. 850)
Parker

XII. 32—The Rambona Ivory (A.D. 898)

XII. 33—Fresco in S.
Angelo in Formis,
Capua (before 1100)

XII. 34—Fresco in Daphni (c. 1100)

See page 253

XII. 35—Byzantine Ivory in the British Museum (10th century)

XII. 36—Mosaic in the Upper Church of San Clemente, Rome (c. 1112)

XII. 37—Ivory Cover of the Augsburg Gospel-Book, now in Munich

See page 254

XII. 41—From a Window in Bourges
Cathedral (13th century)
Martin and Cahier

XII. 39—Ivory Book Cover from Metz,
now in Paris (9th century)

XII. 42—From the Psalter of Queen
Ingeburga († 1236), now in the Musée
Condé, Chantilly

See page 255

XII. 45—From the Psalter of Blanche of Castille (1230), in the Bibliothèque de l'Arsenal, Paris

XII. 46—From the Psalter of Hermann of Thuringia (prior to 1217), now in Stuttgart. *Haseloff*

XII. 47—Fresco in St. Alban's Cathedral, England (c. 1250)
Tristram

XII. 48—Painting by Dietrich of Prague (c. 1365), in the Kunsthistorisches Hofmuseum, Vienna

See page 256

XII. 49—By Jan Van Eyck († 1440),
in the Nationalgalerie, Berlin
Hanfstaengel

XII. 50—By Carlo
Crivelli (c. 1480), in
the Brera, Milan

XII. 51—A painting of the School of
Champagne (c. 1460)

XII. 52—Altarpiece of the Church at
Isenheim by Grünewald († 1528)

See page 254

XII. 53—By Cima da Conegliano († *c.* 1517), in the Barber Institute of Fine Arts, Birmingham

XII. 54—By Simon Vouet († 1649), in Lyons Museum

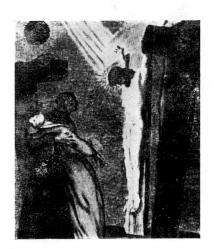

XII. 55—By Franz von Stuck

Hanfstaengel

See page 259

XII. 56—Design on a Vestment from Akhmin, Egypt (c. 550)
Forrer

XII. 57—Crucifix at Monza (c. 600)

XII. 58.--Bronze Crucifix in the Vatican Museum (about 750)

XII. 59—The Santo Volto of Lucca
Garrucci

See page 260

XII. 60—Byzantine Reliquary from
Mount Athos (10th century)

XII. 61—Gero's Crucifix in St.
George's Church, Cologne
(c. 980)

XII. 62—Painted Crucifix from San
Damiano, now in the Poor Clares' Convent
Assisi (c. 1150)

XII. 63—Carved Wooden Crucifix,
Ferdinandeum, Innsbruck (1150/1200)

See page 261

XII. 64—Courajod's Crucifix in the
Louvre, Paris (12th century)

XII. 65—Crucifix in S. Maria Novella,
Florence (14th century)

XII. 66—Ivory Crucifix by Jean
Guillermin (1659), in Avignon
Museum

XII. 67—Crucifix by Montanes († 1649),
in Seville Cathedral

See page 262

XII. 68—Crucifix by Canonica, Church of S. Cuore di Maria, Turin

XII. 69—Crucifix by Iché

XII. 70—The Twelfth Station, by Alfeo Faggi, in the Church of St. Thomas the Apostle, Chicago

XII. 71—Crucifix carved by Peter Vervesi, West Cameroon, Africa

See page 262

XII. 72—By Guido Reni († 1642), in
San Lorenzo in Lucina, Rome

XII. 73—By Velazquez († 1660), in
Madrid

XII. 74—By Léon Bonnat (1874),
now in the Petit Palais, Paris

XII. 75—By Georges Rouault

See page 263

I. 76—Nicola Pisano († 1278), in the
Baptistery of Pisa

XII. 77—Giotto († 1336), in the lower
Church of St. Francis, Assisi

XII. 78—Duccio († 1320), in the Cathedral of Siena

See page 263

XII. 80—Hans Pleydenwurff (c. 1460), in the
Alte Pinakothek, Munich

XII.   79—Narbonne Painting on Silk
(c. 1370), now in the Louvre

XII. 81—Andrea Mantegna (1459), for the altarpiece of St. Zeno in Verona, now
in the Louvre   See page 264

XII. 82—By Ignacio Zuloaga

XII. 83—By Albert Besnard

See page 265

XIV. 1—The Side-Wound on the Shroud.   *Enrie's Photograph*

See page 330

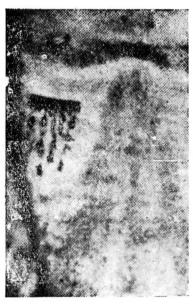

XIV. 4—From a Painting of the Son and the Father in the Capitular Basilica, Padua

XIV. 5—From the Crucifixion by Hans Holbein the Elder (1460-1516) in Augsburg Museum

XIV. 6—From the Crucifixion by Perugino (1446-1524)

XIV. 7—From the Crucifixion by Velazquez (1599-1660) in the Prado, Madrid

Sources

All the books and other sources which have been cited are included here. No attempt is made to set down a bibliography of the Shroud of Turin. A survey of the material on this subject is to be found in E. Dervieux, *Bibliografia della SS. Sindone di N.S.G.C. venerata a Torino, dedicata a S. Altezza Reale Umberto di Savoia, Principe di Piedmonte, compilata con note critiche* (Chieri 1929-36) and L. Fossati, *Breve saggio critico di bibliografia e di informazione sulla Sacra Sindone. Dal primo Congresso nazionale di studi (1939) al Secondo Congressi internazionale (1978)* (Torino 1978). This can be complemented and brought up to date by reading the various issues of *Sindon* (Journal of the International Centre of Sindonology in Turin) from 1959 onwards.

A

MANUSCRIPTS AND PUBLISHED WORKS

a Lapide, C. A., *Commentaria in Scripturam Sacram* XV-XVI (Parisiis 1866).

Acta Sanctorum (Antverpiae 1643-1867).

Acts of John: Apocryphal Acts of the Apostles (trans. by W. Wright, London 1871).

Adolph, E. F., *Physiology of man in the desert* (New York 1947).

Analecta Bollandiana 19 (1900) 215, 350.

Annales archéologiques 26 (1869) 142; 27 (1870) 12.

Antoninus, Martyr, *Of the Holy Places visited by Antoninus, Martyr, circa 560-570 A.D.* (trans. by A. Stewart, London 1887).

Apostolical Constitutions, The (ed. J. Donaldson, London 1870).

Apuleius, L. *Metamorphoseon libri XI* (ed. J. van de Vliet, Lipsiae 1897).

Aquinas, St Thomas, *Summa Theologica I-V* (Parisiis 1887-9).

——— *Quaestiones quodlibetales* (ed. R. P. Mandonnet, Parisiis 1926).

Aristides, *Die Apologie des Aristides* (ed. E. Hennecke, Leipzig 1893).

Aristophanes, *Aristophanis comoediae et perditarum fragmenta* I-II (ed. E. P. M. Longueville, Parisiis 1838).

Armstrong, H. G., *Principles and practice of aviation medicine* (London 1939).

Arnobius, A., *Arnobii disputationum adversus gentes libri septem* (ed. J. C. Ortellius, Lipsiae 1816).

Arrianus, F., *Flavii Arriani quae exstant omnia* I-II (ed. A. G. Roos, Lipsiae 1907).

Artemidorus, D., *Artemidori Oneirocritica* I-II (eds. N. Rigalti and J. J. Reisk, Lipsiae 1805).

Atkinson, R., *The passions and homilies from the Leabhar Breac* (Dublin 1887).

Aubert, J. M., *Ensevelissement de N.S.J.C. d'après les saintes écritures à l'occasion du S. Suaire de Turin* (Paris 1947).

Aulus Gellius, *Auli Gellii Noctium Atticarum libri xx* (ed. C. Hosius, Lipsiae 1903).

Aurelius, V. S., *Sexti Aurelii Victoris liber De Caesaribus. Praecedunt Origo gentis Romanae et liber De viribus illustris urbis Romae. Subsequitur Epitome de Caesaribus* (ed. F. Pichlmayr, Lipsiae 1911).

Babylonian Talmud, The (ed. I. Epstein, London 1935-52).

Bahrdt, K. F., *Briefe über die Bibel im Volkston* (Halle 1782).

Baldi, D., *Enchiridion locorum sanctorum* (Jerusalem 1935).

Balfour, R., *The seraphic keepsake* (London 1905).

Barbet, P., 'La passion corporelle de Jésus', *La vie spirituelle* 1 February 1940.

———— *Les cinq plaies du Christ* (Paris 1937, 1948).

———— *A doctor at Calvary* (New York 1953).

———— *The Passion of Our Lord Jesus Christ* (Dublin 1954).

Bardus, H., *Epistolae ad Thomam Bartholinum* (Leyden 1646).

Baring-Gould, S., *Curious myths of the middle ages* (London 1901).

Barnes, A. S., *The Holy Shroud of Turin* (London 1934).

Bartholinus, T., *De cruce Christi* (1651).

Basle Nomina Anatomica [of Wilhelm Hiss] (1895 — rev. ed., Birmingham 1933).

Baudot, J. L., *Dictionnaire practique des connaissances religieuses* 6 (1928) 474-5.

Beecher, P. A., *The Holy Shroud. A reply to the Rev. Herbert Thurston, S.J.* (Dublin 1928).

Bell, C., *The hand: its mechanism and vital endowments as evincing design* (London 1837).

Bell, G. K. A., and Deissman, G. A. (eds.), *Mysterium Christi. Christological Studies* (London 1930).

Bell, J. and C., *The anatomy of the human body* II (London 1797).

Bellarmine, R., *The seven words spoken by Christ on the cross* (trans. from Latin, London 1933).

Belser, J. E., *History of the Passion, Death and Glorification of Our Saviour Jesus Christ* (ed. A. Preuss, London 1929).

Benson, R. H., *A book of the love of Jesus* (London 1923).

Bernard, J. H., 'The Vulgate of St John', *Hermathena* 9 (1896).

————— *A critical and exegetical commentary on the gospel according to St John* I-II (Edinburgh 1928).

Berthelot, P. E. M., *Science et morale* (Paris 1897).

Best, C. H., and Taylor, N. B., *The physiological basis of medical practice* (London 1945).

Bezold, C. (ed.), *Die Schatzhöhle [Cave of Treasures] Syrisch und Deutsch* I-II (Leipzig 1883-8).

Bible, The Holy (trans. from the Latin Vulgate, ed. James A. Casey, New York 1938).

Bibliothèque Nationale, Paris: Ms grec 510.
                                 latin 257.
                                 9383.

Biot, J. B., *Mélanges scientifiques et littéraires* I (Paris 1858).

Bird, T. E., *A study of the gospels* (London 1945).

Black, M., *An Aramaic approach to the Gospels and Acts* (Oxford 1946).

Bonaventura, St, *Meditations on the life of Christ* (ed. W. H. Hutchings, London 1881).

————— *Opera omnia* (eds. P. P. Collegii a S. Bonaventura, Ad Claras Aquas, 1882-1902).

————— *The Mirrour of the Blessed Lyf of Jesu Christ* (ed. L. F. Powell, Oxford 1908).

————— *The life of St Francis of Assisi* (trans. by E. G. Salter, San Francisco 1931).

Bonet, T., *Sepulchretum sive anatomia practica, ex cadaveribus morbo denatis* I (Genevae 1700).

Bonner, R. J., and Smith, G., *The administration of justice from Homer to Aristotle* II (Chicago 1938).

Book of the Popes, The — Liber Pontificalis (trans. by L. R. Loomis, New York 1916-   ).

Borenius, C. T., and Tristram, E. W., *English medieval painting* (Paris 1927).

Bosio, G., *Crux triumphans et gloriosa a J. Bosio descripta libris sex* (Antverpiae 1617).

Bouchage, L., *Le sainte-suaire de Chambéry, à Sainte-Claire en Ville (Avril-Mai 1534)* (Chambéry 1891).

Bouvier, P., 'Le suaire de Turin et l'évangile', *Quinzaine* 47 (1902).

Boylan, P., *The Psalms* I (Dublin 1920).

Braun, C., *Ueber Kosmogonie vom Standpunkt Christlicher Wissenschaft, mit einer Theorie der Sonne einigen darauf bezüchlichen philosophischen Betrachtungen* (Münster 1895).

Braun, F. M., 'Le linceul de Turin: note complémentaire', *Nouvelle revue théologique* 67 (1940).

—————— *Le lincuel de Turin et l'évangile de S. Jean* (Paris 1940).

—————— *Jésus, histoire et critique* (Paris 1947).

—————— *Évangile selon S. Jean — traduit et commenté par François Marie Braun* [*La sainte Bible* 10] (Jerusalem 1950).

Bréhier, L., *L'art chrétien, son développement iconographique des origines à nos jours* (Paris 1928).

Bridget of Sweden, St, *Revelationes . . . S. Birgittae Suecae* (ed. F. S. Hörmann, Moguntiae 1680).

Brightman, F. E. (ed.), *Eastern liturgies* (Oxford 1896).

British Museum: Additional Ms 7169, fol. iv.
　　　　　　　　Harleian MS 5647.

Broussolle, J. C., *Le Christ de la Légende Dorée* (Paris 1904).

Brucker, J., 'Le Saint Suaire et l'exégèse', *Études* 92 (1902).

Bryce, T. H., 'Certain points in the anatomy and mechanism of the wrist-joint reviewed in the light of a series of Röntgen Ray photographs of the living hand', *Journal of anatomy and physiology* 31 (1896).

Burkitt, F. C., 'On "Lifting Up" and "Exalting"', *Journal of Theological Studies* 20 (1919).

Burnet, G., *The history of the reformation of the Church of England* (London 1685).

Butler, S., *The fair haven* (London 1873).

Caesar, C. J., *C. Julii Caesaris commentariorum pars prior qua continentur libri vii de bello Gallico, pars posterior qua continentur libri iii do bello civili cum libris de bello Alexandrino Africo Hispaniensi* I-II (ed. R. Du Pontet, Oxonii 1900).

Cahier, C., *Nouveaux mélanges d'archéologie, d'histoire et de littérature sur le moyen age* I-IV (Paris 1874-7).

——————, and Martin, A. M., *Mélanges d'archéologie, d'histoire et de littérature* I-IV (Paris 1847-56).

Cahiers de l'art sacré 3 (1945) 45.

Calmet, A., *Antiquities sacred and profane, or a collection of critical dissertations on the Old and New Testament* (ed. N. Tindal, London 1727).

Camerarius, J., *Notatio figurarum sermonis in libris quattuor Evangeliorum, et indicata verborum significatio* (Lipsiae 1572).

Cameron, J. L., 'How Our Lord died', *Universe* 25 July 1947.

Camuzat, N., *Promptuarium sacrarum antiquitatum tricassinae diocesis* (Augustae Trecarum 1610).

Cardwell, E., *Synodalia* I (London 1842).

Cato, M. P., *De re rustica* (ed. H. Iordan, Lipsiae 1860).

Catullus (Caius Valerius), *Catulli carmina* (ed. C. Stuttaford, London 1909).

Celi, G., 'Commemorazione del xiii centenario di s. Colombano, Bobbio, 1-3 Settembre 1923', *La Civiltà Cattolica* (1923).

Chambers, R. W., *Thomas More* (London 1935).

Chapman, J., *John the presbyterian* (Oxford 1911).

——— '"We know that his testimony is true"', *Journal of Theological Studies* 31 (1930).

Chariton, A., *De Chaerea et Callirhoe* IV (ed. W. E. Blake, Oxford 1926).

Chauncy, M., *The passion and martyrdom of the holy English Carthusian fathers* (ed. G. W. S. Curtis, London 1935).

Chevalier, C. U. J., *Étude critique sur l'origine du S. Suaire de Lirey-Chambéry-Turin* (Paris 1900).

——— *L'art et l'autel*, June 1902, p. 238.

——— 'Le saint suaire de Turin et le Nouveau Testament', *Revue biblique* 11 (1902).

Cheyne, T. K., and Black, J. S. (eds.), *Encyclopaedia Biblica* I (London 1899) 960.

Chifflet, G. G., *De linteis sepulchralibus Christi Servatoris* (Antverpiae 1629).

Chopin, H., *Le Saint suaire de Turin photographié à l'envers* (Paris 1902).

Cicero, M. T., *M. Tullii Ciceronis opera omnia* I-XI (eds. J. G. Baiter and C. L. Kayser, Lipsiae 1860-9).

Clement of Alexandria, St, *Clementis Alexandrini opera quae extant* I-II (ed. J. Potter, Oxonii 1715).

Clermont-Ganneau, C., *Archaeological researches in Palestine during the years 1873-1874* I (trans. by A. Stewart, London 1899).

Clos, E. M., *Kreuz und Grab Jesu* (Kempten 1898).

Cohen, G., *Le théâtre en France au Moyen Age:* I *Le théâtre religieux* (Paris 1928).

Colson, R., *Le Saint Suaire de Turin en 1914. Le portrait du Christ* (Poitiers 1914).

Condamin, A., 'Le sens messianique de Zach. XII, 10', *Recherches de science religieuse* I (1910).

Constitution of the Church of Ireland, 1934, The (ed. J. Fitzgibbon, Dublin 1934).

Conybeare, F. C. (ed.), *The Armenian Apology and Acts of Appolonius* (New York 1896).

Coppier, A. C., *Mercure de France* 1 January, 1 June 1938.

Cordonnier, G., *La Passion et la Crucifiement* (Paris 1934).

Cormac's Glossary (ed. W. Stokes, Dublin 1868).

Cornutus Lucius Annaeus, *Cornuti theologiae grecae compendium* (ed. C. Lang, Lipsiae 1881).

Costantini, C., *Il crocifisso nell' arte* (Firenze 1911).

Curtius Rufus, Q., *Q. Curtii Rufi De gestis Alexandri Magni* (ed. H. E. Foss, Lipsiae 1862).

Cyril, St, Patriarch of Jerusalem, *The Catechetical Lectures of S. Cyril* (ed. E. H. Gifford, Oxford 1894).

d'Alès, A., 'La condition du corps du Christ dans la mort', *Recherches de science religieuse* 21 (1931).

——— *Études* 228 (1936) 135.

Dalman, G. H., *Jesus and Jeshua. Studies in the gospels* (trans. by P. P. Levertoff, London 1929).

——— *Sacred sites and ways* (trans. P. P. Levertoff, London 1935).

Dalman, G. H., and Laible, H., *Jesus Christ in the Talmud* (trans. by A. W. Streane, London 1893).

Danby, H. (ed.), *The Mishnah* (Oxford 1933); see also under Talmud.

Daniel-Rops, H., *Jésus en son temps* (Paris 1946).

Daremberg, C. V., and Saglio, E., *Dictionnaire des antiquités grecques et romaines* I (Paris 1877).

Davenport, A. B., 'Spontaneous heart rupture — statistical summary', *American Journal of Medical Sciences* 176 (1928).

de Barenton, H., *La dévotion au Sacré Coeur* (Paris 1914).

de Combes, L., *The finding of the cross* (trans. by L. Cappadelta, London 1907).

de Corrieris, L., *De Sessorianis praecipuis Passionis reliquiis commentarius* (Romae 1831).

de Feis, L., *Bessarione* 7 (1900) 473.

de Francovich, G., *Scultura mediaevale in legnano* I-II (Milano 1943).

de Hovre, E., *The riddle of Konnersreuth* (Chicago 1933).

de Iriarte, M., *Razon y Fe* (1945), aprile, 517-41.

——— *Arbor* 10 (1948), giugno, 201-24.

de Jerphanion, G., *La voix des monuments* (Paris 1930).

―――― 'Bulletin d'archéologie chrétienne et Byzantine ― Questions connexes. Le Saint-Suaire de Turin', *Orientalia Christiana Periodica* 4 (1938).

―――― 'La Croix d'Herculanum?', *Orientalia Christiana Periodica* 7 (1941).

―――― 'L'image de Jésus-Christ dans l'art chrétienne', *Nouvelle revue théologique* 65 (1938).

de La Bigne, M., *Maxima Bibliotheca Veterum Patrum et Antiquorum Scriptorum Ecclesiasticorum* 1-28 (Lugduni, Genuae 1677-1707).

de la Taille, M., *The mystery of faith* (trans. by J. Carroll, London 1941).

Della Rovere, G. Cardinal, *De sanguine Christi* (1474).

de Mély, F. D., *Exuviae sacrae Constantinopolitanae* 3 (Paris 1904).

de Meurville, M., *Correspondant* 10 May 1902, p. 560.

de Wyzewa, T., *La légende dorée* (Paris 1929).

Delage, Y., *Revue scientifique* 31 May 1902, 683-7.

―――― *L'hérédité et les grands problèmes de la biologie générale* (Paris 1903).

Demosthenes, *Demosthenis orationes* I-III (eds. S. H. Butcher and others, Oxonii 1903-31).

Denzinger, H. J. D.,-Bannwart, C., *Enchiridion Symbolorum* (Freiburg im Breisgau 1908).

Destot, E. A. J., *Injuries of the wrist, a radiological study* (London 1925).

Devarius, M., *Index Eustathii commentarios in Homeri Iliadem et Odysseam* (ed. J. G. Stallbaum, Lipsiae 1828).

Dictionnaire d'archéologie chrétienne et de liturgie, see Leclercq, H.

Dictionnaire d'euchariste chrétienne, fig. 8027.

Didron, A. N., *Christian Iconography or, the history of Christian art in the middle ages* 2 (trans. by E. J. Millington, London 1851).

Didry, M., and Wallemacq, A., *Louise Lateu of Bois d'Haine, 1850-1883* (trans. by Dom Izard, Paris 1930).

Diodorus, Siculus, *Diodori Siculi Bibliothecae historicae quae supersunt* (ed. L. Dindirfii, Parisiis 1842).

Dion Cassius, *Dio's Roman History* I-IX (trans. by E. Cary, London 1914-27).

Dionysius, of Halicarnassus, *Dionysii Halicarnasensis antiquitatum Romanarum quae supersunt* IV (trans. by E. Cary, London 1943).

Dives et Pauper [attributed to H. Parker] (Westmonstre 1496).

Dobson, C. C., *The face of Christ, earliest likenesses from the catacombs* (London 1933).

Doerr, F., *Der Prozess Jesu in Rechtsgeschichtlicher Beleuchtung* (Berlin 1920).

Dölger, F. X. J., *Ichthys: Das Fischsymbol in frühchristlicher Zeit* (Rome 1910).

Doncoeur, P. (ed.), *Le livre de la B. Soeur Angèle de Foligno* (Paris 1925).

——— *Le Christ dans l'art français* I (Paris 1939).

Donnadieu, M. L. A., *Le saint suaire de Turin devant la science* (Paris 1903).

Dossiers du Saint-Suaire de Turin, No. 1, May 1939.

Dressler, W., 'Cardiac topography. Pathological studies of the anterior aspect of the heart and its relationship to the anterior wall of the chest in common heart diseases', *American Heart Journal* 19 (1940).

Ducange Anglicus, *Glossarium* 2 (London 1842), 6 (London 1846).

Duchesne, L. (ed.), *Le Liber Pontificalis* I (Paris 1886).

Durand, L. (joint-ed.), *La Sainte Bible* (Paris 1872).

Durandus, G., *Rationale divinorum officiorum* VI (Antverpiae 1570).

Edmonson, H. A., and Hoxie, H. J., 'Hypertension and cardiac rupture', *American Heart Journal* 24 (1942).

Ehrle, F., Archiv für Literatur und Kirchengeschichte des *Mittelalters* 2 (Berlin 1886).

Ellis, W., *History of Madagascar* I (London 1838).

Emmerich, A. C., *The Dolorous Passion* (trans. by Abbé de Cazalès, London 1926).

Enrie, G., *La Santa Sindone Rivelata dalla Fotografia* (Torino 1938).

Ephraim, St, *Sancti Ephraem Syri Hymni et Sermones* (ed. T. J. Lamy, Mechliniae 1882).

Eskenazy, M., *Le saint suaire de Turin devant l'histoire, la science et la médicine* (Paris 1938).

Etheria, *The Pilgrimage of Etheria* (trans. by M. L. McClure and C. L. Feltoe, London 1919).

Euripides, *Iphigeneia at Aulis* (ed. C. E. S. Headlam, Cambridge 1939).

——— *Iphigenia in Tauris* (ed. M. Platnauer, Oxford 1938).

Eusebius, Pamphili, *The life of the Blessed Emperor Constantine* (London 1845).

———— *Historiae Ecclesiasticae libri decem* (ed. E. Burton, Oxonii 1856).

———— *The proof of the gospel, being the Demonstratio Evangelica of Eusebius of Caesarea* (trans. by W. J. Ferrar, London 1920).

Eustathius, archbishop of Thessalonica, see Devarius, M.

Fabri, F., *Book of the wanderings* I (trans. by A. Stewart, London 1892).

Facchinetti, V., *Le stimmate di s. Francesco d'Assisi* (Milano 1924).

Farrar, F. W., *The life of Christ as represented in art* (London 1894).

Favre, R., 'Credo in Filium Dei mortuum et sepultum', *Revue d'histoire ecclésiastique* 33 (1927) 587-624.

———— 33 (1937) 722.

Festus, S. P., *De verborum significatu* (ed. C. Mueller, Lipsiae 1839).

Fifteenth century guide-book to the principal churches of Rome, A (trans. by C. E. Woodruff, London 1871).

Fillion, L. C., *The life of Christ* III (London 1929).

Firmicus Maternus, Julius, *Julii Firmici Materni Matheseos libri VIII* I-II (eds. W. Kroll and F. Skutsch, Lipsiae 1897, 1913).

Fletcher, L., *Introduction to the study of meteorites* (London 1908).

Forrer, R., *Reallexikon der prähistorischen, klassischen und frühchristlichen Altertümer* (Berlin 1907).

Fortunatus, V. H. C., *Opera omnia* I-II (ed. M. A. Luchi, Romae 1786).

Francez, J., *Un pseudo-linceul du Christ* (Paris 1935).

Frank, G. (ed.), *La Passion du Palatinus, mystère du XIVᵉ siècle* (Paris 1922).

———— *La Passion d'Autun* (Paris 1934).

Franseen, E. B., and Hellebrandt, F. A., 'Postural changes in respiration', *American Journal of Physiology* 138 (1943).

———— 'Physiological study of the vertical stance of man', *Physiological Reviews* 23 (1943).

Friedberg, E., *Corpus Juris Canonici* 2 (Leipzig 1881).

Freidlieb, J. H., *Archéologie de la Passion de Notre-Seigneur Jésus* (adapté en français par F. Martin, Paris 1897).

Froehlich, W. (ed.), *'De lamentacione sancte Marie'; eine englische Dichtung* (Gotha 1902).

Fuerst, J., *A Hebrew and Chaldee Lexicon to the Old Testament* (trans. by S. Davidson, Leipzig 1871).

Gaffre, L. A., *Les Portraits du Christ. Étude d'iconographie religieuse* (Paris 1903).

Gardner, H., *Art through the ages* (London 1936).

Garrucci, R., *Storia dell' Arte Cristiana nei primi otto secoli della Chiesa* I (Prato 1872).

Garvie, A. E., 'Notes on the fourth gospel, xvii', *The Expositor* 8 (1914).

Gazier, A., 'Les Christs prétendus jansénistes', *Revue de l'art chrétienne* 60 (1910).

Gedda, L., *Tabor*, January 1947, p. 8.

Geffcken, J., *Zwei griechische Apologeten* (Leipzig 1907).

Georgeakis, G., et Pineau, L., *Le folklore de Lesbos* (Paris 1891).

Germanus, Father, *The life of the servant of God, Gemma Galgani* (London 1914).

Gillett, H. M., *The story of the relics of the Passion* (London 1935).

Gougaud, L., 'The earliest Irish representations of the crucifixion', *Journal of the Royal Society of Antiquaries of Ireland* 50 (1920).

——— *Devotional and ascetic practices in the middle ages* (trans. by G. C. Bateman, London 1927).

Graffin, R. L. M., *Patrologia Syriaca* I (Parisiis 1894).

Graham, S., *The quest of the face* (London 1918).

Greban, A., *Le mystère de la Passion* (ed. Gaston, Paris 1878).

Gretser, J., *De cruce Christi* (Ingolstadii 1600-5).

Grisar, H., *History of Rome and the popes in the middle ages* 3 (London 1912).

Griswold, R. A., and Maguire, C.H., 'Penetrating wounds of the heart and pericardiam', *Surgery, Gynaecology and Obstetrics* 74 (1942).

Groome, F. H., *Gypsy folk-tales* (London 1899).

Grüner, C. G., *Commentatio antiqualis medievalis de Jesu Christi morte* (Jennae 1805).

Guillaume, P., and Munro, T., *Primitive Negro sculpture* (London 1926).

Ha-Reubeni, E., 'L'épine de la couronne de Jésus', *Revue biblique* 42 (1933).

Halliwell, J. O., *Ludus Coventriae* (London 1841).

Hanfstaengel, E., *Meisterwerke der Alteren Pinakothek in München* (München 1922).

Hanna, W., *The last days of Our Lord's Passion* (Edinburgh 1863).

Haseloff, A. E. G., *Eine Thüringisch-sächsische Malerschule des 13. Jahrhunderts* (Strasburg 1897).

Haughton, S., 'Note in the speaker's Bible', *New Testament* 4 (1881).

Heaphy, T., *The likeness of Christ* (ed. W. Bayliss, London 1886).

Heisenberg, A. (ed.), *Die Palastrevolution des Johannes Komnenos* (Würzburg 1907).

Hereford, R. T., *Christianity in Talmud and Midrash* (London 1903).

Herodotus, *Histories* I-III (ed. G. W. Harris, London 1906-7).

Hesbert, R. J., *Le problème de la transfixion du Christ* (Paris 1940).

Hesiod, *Theognis* (ed. J. Davies, London 1873).

Hesychius, A., *Lexicon* (Jena 1867).

Hewitt, J. W., 'The use of nails in the crucifixion', *Harvard Theological Review* 25 (1932).

High history of the holy grail, The (trans. by S. Evans, London 1910).

Hildburgh, W. L., 'English Alabaster Carvings as Records of the Medieval Religious Drama', *Archaeologia* 93 (1949).

Hill, G. F., *Catalogue of the Greek coins of Palestine* (London 1914).

Hill, L., 'The influence of the force of gravity on the circulation of the blood', *Journal of Physiology* 18 (1895).

Hippocrates, *Works* I-IV (trans. by W. H. S. Jones, London 1923-31).

Hippolytus, St, of Rome, *The treatise on the Apostolic Tradition* (ed. G. G. E. A. Dix, London 1937).

Hoepfl, H., *Die Stationen des heiligen Kreuzwegs* (Paderborn 1913).

Holweck, F. G., *A biographical dictionary of the saints* (St Louis 1924).

Holzmeister, U., *Crux Domini atque crucifixio* (Romae 1934).

——— 'De Christi crucifixione quid e *Deut.* 21^{22} et *Gal.* 3^{13} consequatur', *Biblica* 27 (1946).

——— 'Innitzer Theodor Kard., "*Kommentar zur Leidens-und Verklärungs-geschichte Jesu Christi*" ', *Biblica* 29 (1948).

Homer, *Iliad* (ed. D. B. Monro, Oxford 1899).

——— *Odyssey* (eds. W. W. Merry and others, Oxford 1899).

Horatius, Q. F., *Opera omnia* (ed. E. C. Wickham, Oxford 1897).

Huby, J., *L'Évangile et les Évangiles* (Paris 1940).

Hucher, E. F. F., *Le Saint Grael* II (Paris 1877).

Hulme, W. H., *The Middle-English harrowing of hell and gospel of Nicodemus* (London 1907).

Huxley, L., *Life and letters of Thomas Henry Huxley* I-II (London 1900).

Hynek, R. W., *Konnersreuth: a medical and psychological study of the case of Teresa Neumann* I-II (London 1932).

——— *La Passion du Christ* (Prague 1935).

——— *Science and the Holy Shroud* (trans. by A. Studeny, Chicago 1936).

———— *Golgotha, Wissenschaft und Mystik* (Karlsruhe 1936).

Illustrierte Zeitung 25 March 1937.

Innitzer, T., *Kommentar zur Leidens-und Verklärungs-geschichte Jesu Christi* (Wien 1948).

Isidore, St, *Isidori Hispalensis Episcopi Etymologiarum sive Originum libri xx* I-II (ed. W. M. Lindsay, Oxford 1911).

James, M. R., *The Apocryphal New Testament* (Oxford 1924).

Jameson, A., and Eastlake, E., *The history of Our Lord as exemplified in works of art* II (London 1864).

Jannaris, A. N., 'Who wrote the fourth gospel?', *The Expository Times,* July 1903.

Janssens, J. H., *Herméneutique sacrée, ou Introduction à l'Écriture sainte en général, et en particulier à chacun des livres de l'Ancien et du Nouveau testament* (ed. A. Sionnet, Paris 1845).

Je Sais Tout, November 1934.

Jeanroy, A., *Le théâtre religieux en France du xie au xiiie siècle* (Toulouse 1937).

Jellett, J. H., and Haughton, S. (eds.), *The collected works of J. MacCullagh* (Dublin 1880).

Jewish Encyclopedia, The VII (eds. I. Singer and others, New York 1904), p. 166.

Johnston, H. M., 'Varying positions of the carpal bones in the different movements at the wrist, Parts I and II', *Journal of Anatomy and Physiology* 41 (1907).

Jones, F. W., *The principles of anatomy as seen in the hand* (London 1941).

Jones, H. F., *Samuel Butler, author of Erewhon, 1835-1902,* I (London 1920).

Jörgensen, J., *An autobiography* 2 (trans. by I. Lund, London 1929).

Josephus, F., *Flavii Josephi opera* I-II (ed. G. Dindorfius, Parisiis 1845-7).

Joüon, P., *L'évangile* (Rome 1930).

Judica-Cordiglia, G., *Gesù, uomo fra gli uomini; la persona di Cristo studiata da un medico del nostro secolo* I-II (Torino 1952).

Julian the Apostate, *The works of the Emperor Julian* III (trans. by W. C. Wright, London 1923).

Julius Firmicus Maternus, see Firmicus Maternus, Julius.

Juster, J., *Les Juifs dans l'empire romain* I (Paris 1914).

Keramopoullos, A. D., *Ho apotympanismos. Symbole archaiologike eis ten historian tou poinikou dikaiou kai ten laographian* (Athens 1923).

Kirch, C., *Enchiridion fontium historiae ecclesiasticae antiquae* (Freiburg im Breisgau 1910).

Klausener, J. G., *Jesus of Nazareth, his life, times and teaching* (trans. by H. Danby, London 1925).

Kneller, K. A., *Geschichte der Kreuzandacht* (Freiburg im Breisgau 1908).

Konnersreuth Chronik 1928, p. 176.

Konnersreuth Jahrbuch 1929, p. 145.

[Koran] *Alcoranus. The Koran commonly called the Alcoran of Mohammed* (trans. by G. Sale, London 1795).

Kosegarten, J. G. L., *Chrestomathia Arabica* (Leipzig 1842).

Kraus, F. X., *Die Miniaturen in der Stadtbibliothek zu Trier* (Freiburg im Breisgau 1884).

——— *Geschichte des christlichen Kunst* 2 (Freiburg im Breisgau 1897).

Krauss, S., 'La double inhumation chez les Juifs', *Revue des études juives* 97 (1934).

Krumbhaar, E. B., and Crowell, C., 'Spontaneous rupture of the heart', *American Journal of Medical Sciences* 170 (1925).

Künstle, C., *Ikonographie der christlichen Kunst* 2 (Freiburg im Breisgau 1928).

Lacroix, P., *Les arts au moyen âge* (Paris 1873).

Lactantius [Lucius Coelius, seu Coecilius], F., *Opera omnia* (eds. S. Brandt and G. Laubman, Leipzig 1890).

Lagrange, M. J., *Évangile selon St Jean* (Paris 1925).

——— *Évangile selon St Marc* (Paris 1929).

——— *The gospel of Jesus Christ* I-II (ed. R. Ginns, London 1938).

Lalaing, A., *Collection des voyages des souverains des Pays-Bas* I (ed. L. P. Gachard, Bruxelles 1876).

Lancet, The 26 April 1902, p. 1216.

Lassus, J. B. A., *Monographie de la Cathédrale de Chartres. Architecture, sculpture d'ornement et peinture sur verre* 1-9 (Paris 1842-65).

Lattey, C., 'The Semitisms of the Fourth Gospel', *Journal of Theological Studies* 20 (1919).

——— '"Lifting Up" in the Fourth Gospel', *Journal of Theological Studies* 21 (1920).

—— (ed.), *Religion and science* (London 1940).

Lauer, P. (ed.), *La conquête de Constantinople* (Paris 1924).

Layard, A. H. *Discoveries in the ruins of Nineveh and Babylon* (London 1853).

—— *Nineveh* II (London 1854).

Lazarus-Barlow, W. S., *The elements of pathological anatomy and histology* (London 1903).

Le Bec, E. L., 'The death of the cross', *Catholic Medical Guardian* 3 (1925).

Le Camus, E., *The life of Christ* III (trans. by W. A. Hickey, London 1923).

Le Figaro 22 June 1902.

Lebon, J., 'Une ancienne opinion sur la condition du corps du Christ dans la mort', *Revue d'histoire ecclésiastique* 23 (1927).

Lebreton, J., *The life and teaching of Jesus Christ* II (London 1935).

Leclercq, H., 'Croix, signe de la', *Dictionnaire d'archéologie chrétienne et de liturgie* 3 (1914).

—— 'The original Title is preserved in Rome', *Dictionnaire d'archéologie chrétienne et de liturgie* 7 (1926).

—— *Dictionnaire d'archéologie chrétienne et de liturgie* 2 (1905), fig. 1537; 3 (1914) 3048; 6 (1924) 139, 142, 177-80, 427-8, 455; 7 (1926) 1154, 2458; 8 (1928) 927, 1234.

Lee, M., and Somerville, E., 'Acute dilatation of the stomach', *British Medical Journal* 1941, I.

Legenda Aurea: Jacobus, de Voragine, *Jacobi a Voragine Legenda Aurea vulgo historia lombordica dicta* III (ed. T. Graesse, Vratislaviae 1890).

Legrand, A., *Dossiers du Saint Suaire* (Paris 1939).

Legrand, E., 'Description des oeuvres d'art et de l'église des saints apôtres de Constantinople. Poème en vers iambiques par Constantin Le Rhodien', *Revue des études grecques* 9 (1896).

Lépicier, A. H. M., *Diatessaron: seu Concordia quatuor evengeliorum in unum redactorum, cum notis ac delucidationibus exegeticis, dogmaticis, asceticis, historicis, etc.* I-IV (Romae 1924-7).

Les dossiers du S.S. de Turin, May 1939, p. 6.

Lesêtre, H., *Dictionnaire de la Bible* 5 (1922) 2255.

Lévesque, E., 'Le suaire de Turin et l'évangile', *Nouvelle Revue Apologétique* I (1939).

Lewis, C. T., and Short, C., *A Latin dictionary* (Oxford 1933).

Liddell, H. G., and Scott, R., *A Greek-English lexicon* (Oxford 1925-40).

Lillie, F. C., *Examples of religious art* (Chicago 1936).

Lippmann, G., *Leçons d'acoustique et d'optique* (ed. A. Cadot, Paris 1899).

Lipsius, J., *J.L. opuscula, quae antiquitates Romanas spectant, selectissima* I-II (Lugduni Batavorum 1693).

Little flowers of St Francis, The (trans. by T. Okey, London 1930).

Livius, T., *Livy* I-III (trans. by B. O. Foster, London 1919).

Loisy, A. F., *Le Quatrième Évangile* (Paris 1903).

——— *L'Épître aux Galates* (Paris 1916).

Longer commentary of R. David Kimchi on the first book of Psalms, The (trans. by R. G. Finch, London 1919).

L'Ostensione della S. Sindone (Torino 1931).

Loth, A., *Le portrait de N.S. Jésus Christ d'après le Saint-Suaire de Turin* (Paris 1900).

Louis, E., *La Semaine Sainte à Konnersreuth* (Mulhouse 1931).

Love, N., *The mirrour of the Blessed Lyfe of Jesu Christ* (ed. L. F. Powell, London 1926).

Lowrie, W., *Art in the Early Church* (London 1947).

Luard, H. R. (ed.), *Matthaei Parisiensis Chronica Majora* 3 (London 1876).

Lucanus, M. A., *The Pharsalia of Lucan* I-II (trans. by E. Ridley, London 1919).

Lucas of Tuy, 'Adversus Albigensium errores I', *Maxima Bibliotheca Veterum Patrum* XXV (ed. M. de la Bigne et alii, Lugduni, Genuae 1677-1707).

Lucian [Lucianus Samosatensis], *Works* (trans. by H. W. Fowler and F. G. Fowler, Oxford 1905).

——— *Works* (trans. by A. M. Harmon, New York 1915).

Ludolph of Saxony, *Vita Jesu Christi* II (ed. L. M. Rigollot, Paris 1878).

Luther, M., *Enarrationes in Genesim: Opera 6* (Witenburg 1556).

Lydgate, J., *Minor poems: the two Nightingale poems* (ed. O. Glauning, London 1900).

Lysias, *Lysias* (with English trans. by W. R. M. Lamb, London 1930).

Maas, A. J., *The life of Jesus Christ according to the gospel history* (London 1921).

Mabillon, J., and Germain, M., *Museum italicum, seu collectio veterum scriptorum ex bibliothecis Italicis* II (Lutetiae Parisiorum 1687).

Macalister, R. A. S., *A century of excavation in Palestine* (London 1925).

Macarius, M., *Apocriticus* (trans. by T. W. Crafer, London 1919).

MacBride, E. W., *Huxley* (London 1934).

McCaul, A., *Rabbi David Kimchi's commentary upon the prophecies of Zechariah* (London 1887).

McGee, W. J., 'Desert thirst as disease', *Interstate Medical Journal* 13 (1906).

Macgregor, G. H. C., *The gospel of John* (London 1936).

Macht, D., 'A Biblical adventure in anatomy', *Bulletin of the History of Medicine* 16 (1944).

Mack, J. E., and Martin, M. J., *The photographic process* (New York 1939).

McNaspy, C. J., 'The shroud of Turin', *Catholic Biblical Quarterly*, April 1945.

MacRae, R. D., 'Acute dilatation of the stomach', *British Medical Journal* 1943, II.

Macrobius, A. A. T., *Saturnalia. Commentaria in Somnium Scipionis* (ed. F. Eyssenhardt, Leipzig 1868).

Madden, F. W., *History of Jewish coinage and of money in the Old and New Testament* (London 1864).

Mainland, D., *Anatomy as a basis for medical and dental practice* (London 1945).

—— and Gordon, E. J., 'The position of organs determined from thoracic radiographs of young adult males, with a study of the cardiac apex beat', *American Journal of Anatomy* 66 (1941).

Mâle, E., *L'art religieux de la fin du moyen age en France* (Paris 1922).

—— *L'art religieux du xiie siècle en France* (Paris 1924).

—— *L'art religieux du xiiie siècle en France* (Paris 1925).

Malou, J. B., *De culte du Saint Sang et de la relique de se Sang conservé à Bruges* (Louvain 1851).

Mansi, G. D., *Sanctorum Conciliorum ... collectio nova* (ed. P. Labbeo et G. Cossertio, Venetiis 1748).

Marcellinus, A., *Ammiani Marcellini Rerum Gestarum libri qui supersunt* (eds. C. U. Clarke, L. Traube, G. Heraeo, Berolini 1910-15).

Markowski, B., 'Acute dilatation of the stomach', *British Medical Journal* 1947, II.

Martyrology of Gorman (ed. W. Stokes, London 1895).

Martyrology of Oengus (ed. W. Stokes, London 1905).

Marucchi, O., *Éléments d'archéologie chrétienne* II (Paris 1903).

———— 'The cross and crucifix', *The Catholic Encyclopedia* IV (eds. C. G. Herbermann and others, New York 1908).

Maspero, G., *The struggle of the nations, Egypt, Syria and Assyria* (ed. A. H. Sayce, trans. by M. L. McClure, London 1896).

———— *The passing of the empires [of the east] 850 B.C. to 330 B.C.* (ed A. H. Sayce, trans. by M. L. McClure, London 1900).

Masure, E., 'Aux origines du dogme Chrétien: Le mystère de l'Incarnation', *Revue Apologétique* 39 (1924).

Maurer, F. W., 'Warren, M. F., and Drinker, C. K., "The composition of mammalian pericardial and peritoneal fluids"', *American Journal of Physiology* 129 (1940).

Mayerson, H. S., 'Orthostatic circulatory failure in the dog', *American Journal of Physiology* 141 (1944).

Meir, ben Baruch, of Rothenburg, *His life and his works as sources for the religious, legal and social history of the Jews of Germany in the thirteenth century* I-II (ed. I. A. Agus, Philadelphia 1947).

Meistermann, B., *New guide to the Holy Land* (London 1923).

Meldola, R., 'The Holy Shroud of Turin', *Nature Magazine* 67 (1903).

Migne, J. P. (ed.), *Patrologiae cursus completus. Series Latina* (Parisiis 1844-64).

———— *Patrologiae cursus completus. Series Graeca* (Lutetiae Parisiorum 1857-1912).

Millet, P., *Recherches sur l'iconographie de l'évangile au XIVe, XVe, et XVIe siècles* (Paris 1916).

Minucius Felix, *Octavius* (trans. by G. H. Rendall, London 1931).

Mirabilia Urbis Romae (Romae 1515).

Misson, F. M., *A new voyage to Italy with a description of the chief towns, churches, palaces and antiquities of that country* I-II (trans. by T. Godwin, London 1714).

Mödder, H., 'Die Todesursache bei der Kreuzigung', *Stimmen der Zeit* 144 (1949).

Moffatt, J., *The New Testament. A new translation* (London 1926).

Mone, F. J., *Schauspiele des Mittelalters* II (Leipzig 1846).

Monumenta Germaniae Historica: *Scriptores Rerum Merovingicarum* I (eds. G. H. Pertz et alii, Hannoverae 1885) 491, 501, 860-3.

Moore, G., *The brook Kerith* (London 1937).

Morin, G., *La Cité Chrétienne* 5 May 1940, p. 349.

Morris, R., *Legends of the holy rood* (London 1871).

Muir, R., *Textbook of pathology* (London 1936).

Müntz, E., 'Notes sur les mosaïques chrétiennes de l'Italie. IV.
L'Oratoire du pape Jean VII', *Revue archéologique* 34 (1877).

——— *Dictionnaire d'archéologie chrétienne et de liturgie* 7 (1927)
2214, fig. 6167.

Murray, J. M., *The life of Jesus* (London 1926).

Nature Magazine 66 (1902), p. 13.

News Review 21 July 1949.

Nicephorus, St, *Nicephori Archiepiscopi Constantinopolitani opuscula
historica* (ed. C. de Boor, Leipzig 1880).

Nicquet, H., *Titulus Sanctae Crucis; seu historia et mysterium tituli
Sancti Crucis Domini Nostri Jesu Christi* (Antverpiae 1670).

Noguier de Malijay, N., *Le Saint-Suaire de Turin* (Paris 1929).

Nonius Marcellus, *De compendiosa doctrina* I (ed. L. Mueller, Leipzig
1888).

Norfolk Archaeology 13 (1898) 303.

O'Gorman, P. W., 'The holy shroud of Jesus Christ. New discovery
of the cause of the imprint', *American Ecclesiastical Review* 102
(1940).

Oldfather, W. A., 'Livy I, 26 and the Supplicium de More Maiorum',
Transactions of the American Philological Association 39 (1908).

Ollivier, M. J. H., *The Passion* (trans. by E. Leahy, Boston 1901).

O'Rahilly, A., 'The stigmata of St Francis', *Studies*, June 1938.

——— *The burial of Christ* (Cork 1942).

——— 'The title of the cross', *Irish Ecclesiastical Record*, May
1945.

——— *The family at Bethany* (Cork 1949).

Origen, *Origenis Hexaplorum quae supersunt* I-II (ed. F. Field,
Oxonii 1875).

Ó Ríordáin, S. P., 'The genesis of the Celtic Cross', *Féilscríbhinn
Torna* (Cork 1947).

Osservatore Romano 14 June 1898; 7-8 September 1936; 5 May, 16
June 1939.

Oxford English Dictionary, The (eds. J. A. H. Murray and others,
Oxford 1933).

Paget, J., 'On white spots on the surface of the heart and on the
frequency of pericarditis', *London Medical Gazette* I (1840).

Paleotti, G., *Description of the Holy Shroud* (Bologna 1598).

Parcot, L., *La sainte tunique d'Argenteuil* (Versailles 1934).

Parker, J. H. *Historical photographs illustrative of the archaeology of Rome* I-VII (Oxford 1872-5).

Pastor, L., *History of the popes from the close of the middle ages* I (London 1906).

Pearson, K., *Die Fronica* (Strasburg 1887).

Peebles, R. J., *The legend of Longinus in ecclesiastical tradition and in English literature and its connection with the Grail* (Baltimore 1911).

Peeters, P., *Évangiles apocryphes* 2 (Bruxelles 1914).

Pègues, T., *Jésus Christ dans l'Évangile* I-II (Paris 1898).

Peter, H., *Historicorum Romanorum fragmenta collegit, disposuit, recensuit Hermannus Peter* (Leipzig 1883).

Petronius [Titus] Arbiter, Massiliensis, *The Satyricon of Petronius* (trans. by P. Dinnage, London 1953).

Phaedrus, *Phaedri Fabulae Aesopiae cum Nicolai Perotti prologo et decem novis fabulis* (J. P. Postgate, Oxonii 1920).

Philippe, A., and Marot, P., 'Le sépulcre de l'église des Cordeliers: De Neufchâteau en Lorraine', *Revue d'histoire franciscaine* I (1924).

Philo, Judaeus, *In Flaccum* (ed. H. Box, Oxford 1939).

Pia, S., *Memoria sulla riproduzione fotografia della santissima Sindone* (included in R. Colson, *Le Saint Suaire de Turin en 1914. Le portrait du Christ* (Poitiers 1914)).

Piaget, A., 'Le livre messire Geoffroy de Charny', *Romania* 26 (1897).

Pickl, J., *The Messias* (trans. by A. Green, London 1946).

Pijoán, J., *Art in the middle ages* (Chicago 1938).

Pirot, L., *La sainte Bible* 9-10 (Jerusalem 1935).

Plato, *Gorgias* (ed. W. H. Thompson, London 1894).

Plautus, T. M., *Opera* (trans. by P. Nixon, London 1916-38).

Plinius Secundus, senior, *Natural history* (trans. by H. Rackham and W. H. S. Jones, London 1938-).

Plutarchus, Chaeronensis, *Coriolanus* (ed. R. H. Carr, Oxford 1906).
——— *Roman questions* (ed. H. J. Rose, Oxford 1924).

Poelzl, F. X., *The Passion and Glory of Christ* (trans. by A. M. Buchanan, New York 1919).

Pohle, J., and Preuss, A., *Christology* (London 1916).

Polybius, *Polybius. The Histories* I-VI (with English trans. by W. R. Paton, London 1922-7).

Pourrat, P., *Christian Spirituality* 2 (trans. by W. H. Mitchell and

S. P. Jacques, Paris 1924).

Power, E., 'Colonnes de la Flagellation', *Dictionnaire Biblique, Suppl.* 2 (1934).

Prat, F., *Jésus Christ* I-II (Paris 1933).

Priestly, J., *Discourse on the evidence of the resurrection of Jesus* (Birmingham 1791).

Primrose, W. B., 'A surgeon looks at the crucifixion', *Hibbert Journal* 47 (1949).

Pratten, B. P. (ed.), *Syriac documents of the Ante-Nicene Period* (Edinburgh 1871).

Proceedings of the Paris Academy of Sciences: *Comptes Rendus* 134 (1902) 902-4.

Quaresmius, F., *Historica, theologica et moralis Terrae Sanctae elucidatio* (Antverpiae 1639).

Quennell, M., *Everyday things in Homeric; Archaic; Classical Greece* I-III (London 1929-32).

Quicherat, J. E. J., *Aperçus nouveaux sur l'histoire de Jeanne d'Arc* (Paris 1850).

Quintilianus, M. F., *Quintiliani quae feruntur Declamationes XIX majores* (ed. G. Lehnert, Leipzig, 1905).

Rabelais, F., *Oeuvres complètes* (ed. J. Boulenger, Paris 1934).

Ramsay, W., *The Mostellaria of Plautus* (London 1869).

Rawlinson, G., *The five great monarchies* II (London 1854).

Recueil des historiens des croisades: 'William of Tyre', *Histoire Occidentale* I (Paris 1844) 985.

Reil, J., *Die frühchristlichen Darstellungen der Kreuzigung Christi mit Tafeln* (Leipzig 1904).

Reinach, A., *Revue archéologique* 24 (1914) 32-53; 25 (1915) 1-36.

Renan, J. E., *Souvenirs d'enfance et de jeunesse* (Paris 1883).

―――― *Vie de Jésus* (Paris 1891).

―――― *Correspondence* (Paris 1898).

Renié, J., *Manuel d'Écriture Sainte* II (Paris 1930).

Riant, P. E. D., *Exuviae sacrae Constantinopolitanae* 2 (Genevae 1878).

Ricciotti, G., *The life of Christ* (trans. by A. I. Zizzamia, Milwaukee 1949).

Rickaby, J., *Waters that go softly* (London 1919).

Robert, de Borron, *The history of the Holy Grail . . . from the French prose of Sires Robert de Borron* (London 1874).

Robinson, P., *The writings of St Francis of Assisi* (London 1906).

Rogers, B. B., *The comedies of Aristophanes* (London 1907).

Rohault de Fleury, C., *Mémoire sur les instruments de la Passion de N.S.J.C.* (Paris 1870).

———— *L'évangile: études iconographiques et archéologiques* I-II (Tours 1874).

Rolleston, H. (ed.), *British Encyclopedia of Medical Practice* II (1939) 127.

Roman Law: *Corpus Iuris Civilis:* I *Institutiones* (ed. P. Krueger), II *Digesta* (ed. T. Mommsen) (Berolini 1899).

———— *Codex Theodosianus* (ed. C. Baudi a Vesme, Augustae Taurinorum 1838).

Romulus, *Aesopus: Der lateinische Äsop des Romulus und die prosa -fassungen des Phädrus: kritischer text mit kommentar von Georg Thiele* (Heidelberg 1910).

Roy, C. E., and Joyce, W. A., *Theresa Neumann of Konnersreuth* (London 1940).

Ruinart, T. (ed.), *Acta Martyrum* (Ratisbon 1859).

Sabatier, P., *Life of St Francis of Assisi* (trans. by L. S. Haughton, London 1904).

Sailly, B., *Catholic Digest*, September 1945, p. 65.

Salembier, L., *The great schism of the west* (trans. by M.D., London 1907).

Sallustius (Caius Crispus), *Catilina* (ed. W. C. Summers, Cambridge 1900).

Sanhedrin: *Tractate Sanhedrin, Mishnah and Tosefta* (trans. by H. Danby, Oxford 1919).

Schenkel, D., *Bibel-Lexikon . . . mit Dr Bruch, Dr Diestel und Dr Dillmann* (Leipzig 1869-75).

Schlatter, A., *Jochanan ben Zakkai* (Leipzig 1896).

———— *Das Evangelium des Johannes* (Leipzig 1930).

Schleiermacher, F. E. D., *Der christliche glaube nach den grundsätzen der evangelischen kirche im zusammenhange dargestellt* (Berlin 1830-1).

Schmidt, P. W., *Die Geschichte Jesu* II (Berlin 1904).

Schnürer, G., 'Die Kümmernisbilder als Kopien des Volto Santo', *Jahresbericht der Görresgesellschaft* 1901.

———— 'Die ältesten Legenden der hl. Kümmernis', *Festschrift Georg von Hartling* (Kempten 1913).

Schrire, T., 'Stab wounds of the heart and pericardium', *The Lancet* 1941, II.

Segall, H. N., 'Rupture of ventricular myocardium', *American Heart Journal* 30 (1945).

Seneca, L. A., *Ad Lucilium epistolae morales* I-III (trans. by R. M. Gummere, London 1917-25).

Sepp, J. N., *La Vie de N.S. Jésus Christ* III (trans. by C. Sainte-Foi, Paris 1861).

Servius seu Sergius Honoratus, *Servianorum in Vergilii carmina commentariorum editio Harvardiana* (ed. E. K. Rand and others, Vol II: in Aeneidos libros I et II explanationes, Lancaster, Pennsylvania 1946-).

Sibylline Oracles: *Die Oracula Sibyllina* (ed. J. Geffcken, Leipzig 1902).

Sickenberger, J. *Leben Jesu nach den vier Evangelien; kurzgefasste Erklärung* I-IV (Münster 1914-26).

Simpson, A. R., 'The broken heart of Jesus', *The Expositor* 2 (1911).
——— *Contributions to Obstetrics and Gynecology* (Edinburgh 1880).

Singer, C., *The evolution of anatomy; a history to Harvey: with figures* (London 1925).

Skrinjar, A., 'Aspicient ad me quem confixerunt', *Verbum Domini* II (1931).

Smith, L. T., *York plays; the plays performed by the crafts or mysteries of York on the day of Corpus Christi in the fourteenth-sixteenth centuries* (Oxford 1885).

Sonnenschein, E. A. (ed.), *Mostellaria* (Oxford 1907).

Speculum Humanae Salvationis. Being a reproduction of an Italian manuscript of the fourteenth century. (Described and prefaced by M. R. James, Oxford 1926.)

Stead, E. A., 'Changes in the circulation produced by poor postural adaptation', *Bulletin of the New England medical centre* 1940, II.

Stokes, W., and Strachan, J. (eds.), *Thesaurus Palaeohibernicus* (Cambridge 1903).

Strack, H. L., and Billerbeck, P., *Kommentar zum Neuen Testament aus Talmud und Midrasch* I-III (München 1922).

Strauss, D. F., *A new life of Jesus* I-II (authorised trans., London 1869).

Streeter, B. H., *The four gospels; a study of origins, treating of the Ms tradition, sources, authorship and dates* (London 1927).

Stroud, W., *A treatise on the physical cause of the death of Christ and its relation to the principles and practice of Christianity* (London 1847).

Strutt, R. J., *John William Strutt, Third Baron Rayleigh* (London 1924).

Strzygowski, J., *Orient oder Rom; beiträge zur geschichte der spätantiken und frühchristlichen kunst* (Leipzig 1901).

Suetonius (Caius) Tranquillus, *De vita Caesarum libri VII-VIII* (ed. G. W. Mooney, London 1930).

Sulzberger, M., 'Le symbole de la croix et les monogrammes de Jésus chez les premiers Chrétiens', *Byzantion* 2 (1925).

Syriac Chronicle, known as that of Zachariah of Mitylene (trans. by F. J. Hamilton and E. W. Brooks, London 1898).

Tacitus, P. C., *P. Cornelii Taciti Annalium Libri* I (ed. H. Furneaux, Oxford 1896).

―――― *The Histories* (trans. by C. H. Moore) and *The Annals* (trans. by J. Jackson) I-II (London 1925-37).

Talmud: *Tractate Shabbath, Mishnah* (trans. by W. O. E. Oesterley, London 1927).

―――― *The Talmud of Jerusalem* (trans. by M. Schwab, London 1886).

Tauber, J., *Meditations on the life and passion of Our Lord Jesus Christ* (trans. by A. P. J. Cruikshank, London 1925).

Taylor, A. S., *Principles and practice of medical jurisprudence* I-II (eds. S. Smith and W. G. H. Cook, London 1934).

Taylor, H. L., Henschel, A., and Keys, A., 'Cardiovascular response to posture and the problem of faintness and syncope in the semi-starved individual', *American Journal of Physiology* 152 (1948).

Teodorowicz, J., *Mystical phenomena in the life of Theresa Neumann* (London 1940).

Terentius (Publius) Afer, *P. Terentii Andria* (eds. C. E. Freeman and A. Sloman, Oxford 1936).

Terquem, H., *Le Linceul de Turin serait-il le véritable Linceul du Christ?* (Paris 1936).

Theodoret, bishop of Cyrus, *Theodoreti . . . Ecclesiasticae Historiae libri quinque* (ed. T. Gaisford, Oxonii 1854).

Thomas, de Celano, *Vita Prima S. Francisci Assisiensis et eiusdem legenda ad usum chori* (eds. P.P. Collegii S. Bonaventurae, Ad Claras Aquas (Quaracchi) 1926).

―――― *Tractatus de miraculis S. Francisci Assisiensis 1247-57* (eds. P.P. Collegii S. Bonaventurae, Ad Claras Aquas 1928).

Thucydides, *History of the Peloponnesian war* (trans. by C. F. Smith, London 1919-23).

Thureau-Dangin, P., *St Bernardine of Siena* (London 1906).

Thurston, H., 'St Mary Magdalen and the early saints of Provence', *Month* 93 (1899).

———— 'The Praetorium of Pilate and the pillar of the scourging', *Dublin Review*, January 1906.

———— 'Crown of thorns', *The Catholic Encyclopedia* IV (eds. C. G. Habermann and others, New York 1908).

———— 'The sign of the cross', *Month* 118 (1911).

———— 'The Holy Shroud', *The Catholic Encyclopedia* XIII (eds. C. G. Habermann and others, New York 1912).

———— 'Some physical phenomena of mysticism: Stigmatization II', *Month* 134 (1918).

———— 'The problem of Anne Catherine Emmerich', *Month* 138 (1921).

———— 'Relics, authentic and spurious', *Month* 155 (1930).

Timossi, V., *La Santa Sindone nella costituzione tessile* (Torino 1933).

Tissot, J. J. J., *The life of Jesus Christ; 365 compositions from the four gospels, with notes and explanatory drawings* II (London 1897).

Tixeront, L. J., *Les origines de l'église d'Édesse et de la légende d'Abgar; étude critique, suivie de deux textes orientaux inédits* (Paris 1888).

[Toledoth Jeshu] *Toldot Yeshu. The Jewish life of Christ, being the Sepher Toldoth Jeshu, or book of the generation of Jesus* (trans. by G. W. Foote and J. M. Wheeler, London 1919).

Tonelli, A., *La Santa Sindone* (Torino 1931).

Torrey, C. C., *The four gospels; a new translation by Charles Cutler Torrey* (London 1934).

———— *Our translated gospels, some of the evidence* (London 1937).

———— *Documents of the Primitive Church* (London 1941).

Tristram, E. W., *English medieval wall painting* (London 1944).

Trossarelli, F., 'Convegno nazionale di studi sulla S. Sindone', *La Civilità Cattolica* 1939, II.

Turner, C. H., 'The gospel narrative of Our Lord's burial', *Church Quarterly Review* 74 (1912).

———— W., 'The physical cause of the death of Christ', *The Expositor* 11 (1916).

Ugolinus, B., *Thesaurus Antiquitatum Sacrarum, complectens selectissima . . . opuscula, in quibus veterum Hebraeorum mores, leges, instituta, ritus sacri et civiles illustrantur* 1-34 (Venetiis 1744-69).

Vaccari, A., 'Exivit sanguis et aqua', *Verbum Domini* 17 (1937).

Vaganay, L. (ed.), *Évangile de Pierre* (Paris 1930).

Valerius Maximus, *Valerii Maximi factorum et dictorum memorabilium libri novem* (ed. C. Kempf, Lipsiae 1888).

van Bebber, J., *Zur Chronologie des Lebens Jesu. Eine exegetische Studie* (Münster 1898).

Van Hoonacker, A., *Les douze petits prophètes* (London 1908).

Van Kasteren, J., 'Der Lanzenstich bei Mt. 27, 49', *Biblische Zeitschrift* 12 (1914).

Velleius Paterculus, M., *Compendium of Roman History. Res Gestae Divi Augusti* (trans. by F. W. Shipley, New York 1924).

Venturi, A., *A short history of Italian art* (trans. by E. Hutton, London 1926).

Venturini, C. H. G., *Natürliche geschichte des grossen Propheten von Nazareth* (Bethlehem, Copenhagen 1800).

Vervaeck, L., 'La découverte du tombeau de S. Albert de Louvain', *Analecta Bollandiana* 40 (1922).

Victoires, conquêtes . . . des Français de 1792 à 1815, 12 (Paris 1819).

Vignon, P., *The Shroud of Christ* (trans. from the French, Westminster 1902).

——— *Le Saint Suaire de Turin devant la science, l'archéologie, l'histoire, l'iconographie, la logique* (Paris 1938).

Vincent, L. H., and Abel, F. M., *Jérusalem. Recherches de topographie, d'archéologie et d'histoire* I-II (Paris 1912-26).

Vincent Ferrer, St, *Oeuvres de Saint Vincent Ferrier* (ed. H. Fages, Paris 1909).

Virgilius, P. M., *Virgil* (trans. by H. R. Fairclough, London 1935).

Vogels, H. J., 'Der Lanzenstich vor dem Tode Jesu', *Biblische Zeitschrift* 10 (1912).

Volckringer, J., *Le Saint Suaire de Turin — Le problème des empreintes devant la science* (Paris 1942).

von Dobschütz, E., *Christusbilder: Untersuchungen zur christlichen Legende* (Leipzig 1899).

von Ewald, G. H. A., *The life of Jesus Christ* (trans. by O. Glover, Cambridge 1865).

von Grimm, F. M., and Diderot, D., *Correspondence littéraire, philosophique, et critique de Grimm et de Diderot* 3 (eds. Chéron et Thory, Paris 1829).

von Harnack, A., *Chronologie* I (Leipzig 1897).

von Lama, F. R., *Further chronicles of Therese Neumann* (trans. by A. P. Schimberg, New York 1932).

von Mansberg, R., *Zeitschrift für Kulturgeschichte* 7 (1900) 61, 65.

von Tischendorf, L. F. C., *Evangelia apocrypha* (Leipzig 1876).

Vosté, J. M., *Studia Joannea* (Romae 1930).

Walker, A., *Apocryphal gospels, acts and revelations* (London 1873).

——— F. O., *The Catholic Nurse* (Birmingham), June 1945.

——— *The Catholic Digest*, March 1946.

Walmsley, T., 'The heart', *Quain's elements of anatomy* IV (1929).

Ward, J., *History and methods of ancient and modern painting* 2 (London 1917).

Watkin, E. I., *Catholic art and culture; an essay* (London 1944).

Watson, C. M. (ed.), *Golgotha and the holy sepulchre* (London 1906).

Westcott, A., (ed.), *The gospel according to St John* II (London 1908).

Whitaker, J. R., 'The physical cause of the death of Our Lord', *Catholic Medical Guardian* 13 (1935) 83-91; 120.

Willibald, St, *The Hodoeporicon of St Willibald [circa 754 A.D.]* (trans. by W. R. B. Brownlow, London 1891).

Wilpert, J., *Die Malerein der Katacomben Roms: herausgeg. von J. Wilpert; mit Tafeln und Abbildungen* (Freiburg im Breisgau 1903).

Wiseman, N. P. S., *The connexion between science and revealed religion* (London 1842).

Woltmann, A., and Woermann, K., *History of painting* I (ed. S. Colvin, London 1880).

Wordsworth, J., and White, H. J. (eds.), *Quattuor Evangelia* (Oxford 1889-98).

Worringer, W., Reiners, H., and Seligman, L. (eds.), *Festschrift zum sechzigsten Geburtstag von Paul Clemen 31 Oktober 1926* (Bonn 1926).

Wright, I. S., 'The neurovascular syndrome produced by hyper-abduction of the arms', *American Heart Journal* 29 (1945).

Wright, R. D., 'A detailed study of movement of the wrist joint', *Journal of Anatomy* 70 (1935).

Wright, T. (ed.), *The Chester Plays* 2 (London 1847).

——— *Early travels in Palestine* (London 1848).

Wuenschel, E. A., 'The Shroud of Turin and the burial of Christ', Part 1, *The Catholic Biblical Quarterly* 7 (1945); Part 2, 8 (1946).

Xenophon, Atheniensis, *Opera omnia* I-V (ed. E. C. Marchant, Oxford 1900-19).
——— Ephesius, *Corpus scriptorum eroticorum Graecorum* (ed. Franciscus-Passow, Leipzig 1833).
——— *Ephesiacorum de amoribus Anthiae et Abrocomae libri V* (Paris 1885).

Zerwick, M., 'De Cruce Herculanensi', *Verbum Domini* 20 (1940).
Zoeckler, O., *The cross of Christ; studies in the history of religion and the inner life of the Church* (trans. by M. J. Evans, London 1877).

B

PERSONS

Bieler, Professor Ludwig, Faculty of Arts, University College, Dublin.
Kiely, Professor Patrick, Faculty of Medicine, University College, Cork.
Kissane, Monsignor Edward J., President of St Patrick's College, Maynooth, County Kildare.
O'Donovan, Professor William J., Faculty of Medicine, University College, Cork.
O'Rahilly, Associate Professor Ronan, Faculty of Medicine, Wayne State University, Detroit, Michigan, U.S.A.
Smyth, S.J., Father Kevin, Institute of Theology and Philosophy, Milltown Park, Dublin 6.
Twohig, John P., President of the Association of the Woollen and Worsted Manufacturers of Ireland, Parkview, Abbeyleix, County Laois.

Index